THIS DATE IN
NEW YORK *Yankees* HISTORY

THIS DATE IN NEW YORK

HISTORY

A day by day listing of events in the
history of the New York American League
Baseball Team

NATHAN SALANT
with
Carl Wolfson, Research Assistant

5B
A SCARBOROUGH BOOK
STEIN AND DAY/Publishers/New York

"Dedicated to Dennis E., Bill S., Doug L.,
Marshall R., Dave C., Dr. Bob F., "Doc" S., Bob O.,
Lenny G., Dick S. . . . and the dozens of others who
made Albany State the best 4 years of my life."

A Scarborough Book

First published in 1979

Copyright © 1979 by Nathan Salant
Designed by Palisade Printing Co. and Art Ballant
Printed in the United States of America
Stein and Day/*Publishers*/ Scarborough House,
Briarcliff Manor, N.Y. 10510

Library of Congress Cataloging in Publication Data

Salant, Nathan.
    This date in New York Yankees History.

    1. New York (City). Baseball club (American League) —
History. I. Title.
GV 875 .N4S24   396.375'64'097471   78-24105
ISBN 0-8128-6020-9

TABLE OF CONTENTS

Date Section 1
  January 1
  February 6
  March 12
  April 17
  May 28
  June 44
  July 60
  August 74
  September 88
  October 105
  November 117
  December 122
Nicknames 131
The All-Time Yankee Roster 138
Building A New Franchise: 1903 169
Trades 170
The Playoffs 219
The Yankees and The World Series 222
The Parks They Played In 267
Managers and Their Records 276
Yankee Team Owners 276
Yankees Who Lost Years In World War II 277
Batting Records 277
Pitching Records 291
Miscellaneous Awards, Records, and Seasonal Leaders 304
Yankees and All-Star Games 321
Roger Maris' 61 Home Runs — 1961 322
Babe Ruth's 60 Home Runs — 1927 324
Joe DiMaggio's 56-Consecutive Game Hitting Streak — 1941 .. 325
Yankees For A Day 326
The Longest Days 328
Yankees In The Hall of Fame 330
The Yankees and The Mets 340
1978 — The Miracle Year 341
Why The Yankees Won The Pennant 361
The 1978 World Series 363
Remarkable Ron Guidry 369
How Can I Get Good Seats 372
Andy Carey Remembers 379
The Language Called Stengelese 381
Career Highlights 382
A Chat With George M. Steinbrenner III 391
A Rookie (?) In The Front Office 393
Cheers and Rhymes 398
An Autograph For Every Fan 401

ACKNOWLEDGEMENT

Without the encouragement and cooperation of many wonderful people, this book would never have been possible. This is an attempt to say thanks to . . .

. . . Mike Rendine (Yankee Ticket Manager), Betty Rosenblum (his secretary) and the rest of the Yankee ticket department (Marty Rothe, Irving Mehlman and Luis Morales) who have helped personalize the New York Yankees in their dealings with me since 1972. Their interest and cooperation dates back to the days when the author was a teenager who could not get enough Yankee baseball, an era in which loyalty to the pinstripes was not fashionable.

. . . Mickey Morabito (Director of Public Relations), Larry Wahl (Assistant), and their staff (Dale Weeks, Joe D'Ambrosio, and Jim Rosen) who extended their fullest cooperation, answered countless questions, opened the doors of the archive room, introduced me to everyone from Al Rosen to Pete Sheehy, and made me feel welcome in the Yankees executive offices. Special thanks to their wonderful secretaries, Ann Mileo, and Debbie Nicolosi who went out of their way to help me and make me feel at home.

. . . George Steinbrenner, for rebuilding the Yankees and helping to re-create a city of Yankee fans for whom this book is written.

. . . Al Rosen, for graciously spending more time with me than with any other writer or media person.

. . . Pat Kelly (stadium manager), for agreeing to sit down and discuss the operation of Yankee Stadium in all its complexities.

. . . Marsh Samuels (Vice-President of Promotions) for his encouragement, interest, and introduction to the director of the Yankee Alumni Association, Jim Ogle.

. . . Jim Ogle, for his informative chats about the old timers I would be contacting.

. . . the former Yankees who took the time and interest to answer my questions.

. . . special thanks to those former Yankees who agreed to permit their current addresses to be published herein so fans can write to them for autographs.

. . . Extra special thanks to Vic Raschi, a man I never met before July 29th, 1978, but who took the time to introduce me to every one of his teammates present that day; and to Johnny Mize, for his tremendous cooperation.

. . . Reggie Jackson, Roy White, Bucky Dent, Lou Piniella, Cliff Johnson and Chris Chambliss, all of whom took the time to answer my questions.

. . . Stan Fischler, my mentor in the literary world.

. . . Bill Chanin, Steve Hesse, Jim Walsh, Art Gunther, Myra Dembrow, Serge Duss, and Dick Yerg, all of whom made important contributions to my development as a writer.

. . . To Senorita Rodriguez, Dick Arnold, Faith Schuster and Morris Licker, teachers par excellence.

. . . The members of the Elias Bureau for statistical tidbits to fill in the gaps in the Yankees records.

. . . John Redding, the Head Librarian at the Baseball Hall of Fame in Cooperstown, NY, for his cooperation and guidance.

. . . Ralph Ray and The Sporting News for permission to use information from their Official Baseball Guide, Official Baseball Register, and Official Baseball Record Book.

. . . Al Whayland of United Press International, for taking the time to unearth a picture of Ty Cobb and Babe Ruth, posed together at the Polo Grounds.

. . . Raymond Gonzalez and Ken Witkowski for historical and statistical information about the early Yankee teams.

. . . Bill Darden and Abe Schuster, the men who gave me my first job as an assistant baseball coach and thereby fostered my interest in this great game.

. . . Cos Tocci, who helped guide me through some difficult summers while coaching the Spring Valley Yankees.

. . . The members of the Salant Family, especially my parents and Uncle Sam, who supported me in this endeavor.

. . . My editors at Stein and Day, Art Ballant and Karen Boghosian, who helped create this opportunity and manuscript, and my special proof-reader John DeMartini.

. . . The loyal Yankee fans of the world, who deserve only the best.

. . . AND, last but far from least, my research assistant, Carl Wolfson, who spent countless hours uncovering bits and pieces of invaluable information, and helped compile the statistics and information contained in these pages. Without his help, this book would never have been completed on time, if at all.

JANUARY

1

1874 — Virgil "Ned" Garvin B (P 1904)

1881 — Rudolph Bell (OF 1907)

1910 — Charles Devens B (P 1932-34)

1924 — Clifford "The Earl of Snohomish" Torgeson B (1B 1961)

2

1973 — Rumors of the imminent sale of the Yankees to a group from Cleveland appear on sports pages across the continent.

3

1891 — John O'Dowd B (SS 1912)

1912 — Stanley "Frenchy" Bordagaray B (OF 1941)

1920 — The Yankees formally announce their purchase of Babe Ruth from the Boston Red Sox for $125,000 immediate cash, and a $350,000 loan against a mortgage on Fenway Park. It was a trade Yankee fans have relished for decades, and proved to be the forerunner of several one-sided deals between those same two teams.

By way of background, Red Sox owner Harry Frazee was more interested in his theatrical investments than his Red Sox baseball team. Frazee had made several bad investments in the theater industry, backing several consecutive losers, and needed money to stage the opening performance of new shows. He subsequently came up with the hit show "No, No Nanette," but was never forgiven for selling Ruth to the hated Yankees.

1923 — Three years to the day after the announcement of the purchase of Babe Ruth, the Yankees reveal another trade with Boston, this time obtaining pitcher George Pipgras in return for catcher Al DeVormer. Pipgras starred on the Yankee teams of the late 20s. DeVormer did nothing in a Red Sox uniform.

1923 — In a separate transaction, the Yankees purchased infielder Harvey Hendrick from the Red Sox. Hendrick proved to be a valuable pinch hitter, with six hits in 24 at-bats, and an overall .273 batting average that year.

1973 — A syndicate headed by George M. Steinbrenner III purchases the Yankees from CBS for approximately $12 million. Among the limited partners were Gabe Paul and Mike Burke. Paul soon succeeded Burke as President of the Yankees, and it was under Paul's guidance that the Yankees re-established themselves as the force to be reckoned with in the American League.

1906 — John "Blondy" Ryan B (INF 1935)

1908 — George "Twinkletoes" Selkirk B (OF 1934-42)

1925 — Thomas (Tom) Gorman B (P 1952-54)

1928 — Yankees purchase infielders Lyn Lary and (Jimmy) Reese from the Oakland franchise of the Pacific Coast League for $150,000.

1940 — Yankees obtain pitcher Leonard "Lee" Grissom from the Reds for pitcher Joseph (Joe) Beggs.

1966 — Yankees obtain outfielder Lucien "Lu" Clinton from the Indians for catcher Howard "Doc" Edwards.

1890 — Benjamin (Benny) Kauff B (OF 1912)

1915 — John (Jack) Kramer B (P 1951)

1934 — Yankees release pitcher Herb Pennock and third baseman Joe Sewell.

1951 — Donald (Don) Gullett B (P 1977-current)

1951 — Edward Ricks B (P 1977)

1915 — Thomas (Tom) Ferrick B (P 1950-51)

1926 — Ralph Branca B (P 1954)

1931 — Yankees sign third baseman Joe Sewell after he was released by the Cleveland Indians.

1936 — Ruben Amaro B (SS, 3B, 1B 1966-68)

1967 — Former Yankee manager Johnny Keane dies of a heart attack at 55. He never really recovered from the trauma of managing the sixth place team of '65 and the awful start the '66 team had under his reign.

1970 — Yankees purchase outfielder Rick Bladt from the Chicago Cubs for an undisclosed amount of cash.

1876 — William (Billy) Wolfe B (P 1903-04)

1900 — John "Nig" Grabowski B (C 1927-29)

1913 — John "The Big Cat" Mize B (1B 1949-53)

1924 — Yankees purchase outfielder Earle Combs from Louisville

1935 — Richard "Ducky" Schofield B (SS 1966)

1913 — Yankees sign first baseman Frank "Husk" Chance after he was released by the Cubs. He did double duty as the club's second player-manager.

1897 — Roy French B (SS 1920)

1900 — Frank "Lefty" Barnes B (P 1930)

1903 — Frank Farrell and Bill Devery purchase the Baltimore franchise of the fledgling American League and announce their intention to move the team to New York City. The purchase price: $18,000.

1916 — Charles Stanceu B (P 1941, 46)

1925 — Yankees release pitcher Al Mamaux.

1936 — Ralph Terry B (P 1956-57, 59-64)

1888 — Derrill "Del" Pratt B (2B 1918-20)

1924 — Yankees release Hall of Fame third baseman Frank "Homerun" Baker.

1915 — Colonels Jacob Ruppert and Tillinghast L'Hommedieu Huston purchase the Yankees for $460,000.

1928 — Loren "Bee-Bee" Babe B (3B 1952-53)

1934 — Yankees release infielder Edward "Doc" Farrell.

1953 — Terry Whitfield B (OF 1974-76)

1915 — Michael "Mollie" Milosevich B (SS, 2B 1944-45)

1927 — Yankees obtain catcher Johnny Grabowski and infielder Ray Morehart from the White Sox for shortstop Aaron Ward.

1978 — Former Yankee manager Joseph McCarthy dies at 90.

1908 — John "Grandma" Murphy B (P 1932, 34-43, 46)

1916 — Yankees purchase outfielder Lee Magee from the Brooklyn franchise of the Federal League for an undisclosed amount of cash.

1896 — Michael Cantwell B (P 1916)

1947 — Tolia "Tony" Solaita B (OF, 1B 1968)

Nothing of note happened on this date.

1936 — Yankees obtain pitcher Irving "Bump" Hadley and outfielder Roy Johnson from the Senators for pitcher James "Jimmy" DeShong and outfielder Jesse Hill.

1972 — Yankees purchase outfielder John Callison from the Cubs for an undisclosed amount of cash.

1903 — Clifford "Nolan" Richardson B (SS 1935)

1954 — Scott MacGregor B (P 1976-77)

1888 — Patrick "Patsy" Maloney B (OF 1912)

1972 — Yankees purchase pitcher Fred Beene from the Baltimore Orioles.

1907 — Jesse Hill B (OF 1935)

1912 — Frank Makosky B (P 1937)

1921 — Yankees obtain outfielder Bob Roth from the Senators for outfielder Duffy Lewis and pitcher George Mogridge.

1926 — Yankees purchase first baseman Spencer Adams from the Senators for an undisclosed amount of cash.

1936 — Jesse Gonder B (C 1960-61)

1977 — Yankees obtain outfielder Paul Blair from the Orioles for outfielder Elliott Maddox and minor league outfielder Rick Bladt.

1916 — Yankees purchase pitcher Nick Cullop, infielder Elmer Gedeon, and outfielder Harold "Germany" Schaeffer from Newark of the Federal League.

1941 — Richard Beck B (P 1965)

1881 — Ira Thomas B (C, 1B 1906-07)

1918 — Yankees obtain infielder Del Pratt and pitcher Eddie Plank from the St. Louis Browns for pitchers Urban Shocker and Nick Cullop, infielder Fritz Maisel, and catcher Les Nunamaker. It was a trade the Yankees came to regret for two reasons: Plank refused to report to NY, and Shocker was a big hit in St. Louis (his absence undoubtedly cost NY the pennant in 1920 and 1924).

1927 — Yankees release catcher Hank Severeid.

1943 — Yankees obtain first baseman Nick Etten from the Philadelphia Phillies for catcher Tom Padden, pitcher Al Gerheauser and $10,000.

23

1890 — Edward (Ed) Barney B (OF 1915)

1905 — Otto "Jack" Saltzgaver B (3B, 2B, 1B 1932, 34-37)

1916 — John Sturm B (1B 1941)

1918 — Randy Gumpert B (P 1946-48)

1936 — Donald (Don) Nottebart B (P 1960)

1951 — Leslie "Charlie" Spikes B (OF 1972)

24

1885 — Earl Gardner B (2B 1908-12)

25

1876 — Frederick (Fred) Glade B (P 1908)

1908 — Roydan "Roy" Sherid B (P 1939-41)

1918 — Emerson "Steve" Roser B (P 1944-46)

1943 — Yankees sell pitcher Vernon "Lefty" Gomez to the Boston Braves for an undisclosed amount of cash.

26

Nothing of significance happened on this date.

27

1888 — Alan Wickland B (OF 1919)

1896 — Nathaniel "Milt" Gaston B (P 1924)

1901 — Fred "Lefty" Heimach B (P 1928-29)

1921 — Yankees obtain shortstop John Mitchell from the Vernon minor league team for pitchers Ernie Shore and Bob McGraw, and catcher James "Truck" Hannah.

28

1884 — Thomas (Tom) L. Hughes B (P 1906-07, 09-10). (Not to be confused with Thomas J. Hughes also a pitcher with the 1904 Highlanders.)

1903 — Guy "Rebel" Cooper B (P 1914)

1906 — Lyn Lary B (INF, OF, 1B 1929-34)

1916 — Robert "Bobby" Muncreif B (P 1951)

29

1885 — George "Hack" Simmons B (INF 1912)

1943 — Yankees obtain pitcher Bill Zuber from the Senators for infielder Gerry Priddy and pitcher Milo Candini.

1955 — John Williams Cox buys Yankee Stadium from the Topping-Webb partnership, and immediately sells the grounds to the Knights of Columbus. He subsequently left the Stadium itself to Rice University in 1962.

30

1923 — Yankees raid the Red Sox again, this time obtaining pitcher Herb Pennock from Boston for outfielder Camp Skinner, infielder Norm McMillan, pitcher George Murray, and an undisclosed amount of cash. Pennock starred on the "Murderers Row" clubs of the late '20s, while the three players exiled to Boston did little.

1948 — Twenty-five years to the day after what Herb Pennock called "the birth of my major league career, that trade to New York," the 54-year-old Pennock dies of a stroke.

31

1891 — Timothy (Tim) Hendryx B (OF 1915-17)

1893 — George Burns B (1B 1928-29)

1900 — John "Honey" Barnes B (C1926)

1931 — Duane "Duke" Maas B (P 1958-61)

FEBRUARY

1

1921 — David "The Squeakin, Deacon" Madison B (P 1950)

1924 — Yankees purchase outfielder Nick Cullop from the Omaha minor league team for an undisclosed amount.

1943 — Ronald '(Ron) Woods B (OF 1967-71)

1944 — Paul Blair B (OF, 2B, SS, 3B 1977-current)

2

1884 — Charles "Ray" Demmitt B (OF 1909)

1908 — Wesley (Wes) Ferrell B (P 1939)

1916 — Michael (Mike) Garbark B (C 1944-45)

1930 — Yankees waive infielder Leo "The Lip" Durocher to the Reds.

1933 — Jack Reed B (OF 1961-63)

1972 — Yankees purchase utility infielder Harold (Hal) Lanier from the San Francisco Giants.

3

1896 — Nelson "Chicken" Hawks B (OF 1921)

1925 — Harold (Harry) Byrd B (P 1954)

1944 — Celerino Sanchez B (3B, SS, OF, DH 1972-73)

1951 — Michael (Mike) Wallace B (P 1974-75)

4

1875 — Alfonzo "Lefty" Davis B (OF 1903)

1878 — Herman "Germany" Schaeffer B (OF 1916)

1916 — Yankees release outfielder William "Birdie" Cree.

1928 — Yankees release infielder Julian "Julie" Wera.

5

1891 — Roger Peckinpaugh B (SS, MGR 1913-21)

1921 — Yankees purchase a 20-acre plot of land in the Bronx which will be the site of a new Yankee Stadium. It still is!

1936 — James "Lee" Thomas B (OF, 1B 1961)

1942 — Yankees obtain first baseman John "Buddy" Hassett, outfielder Gene Moore, and an undisclosed amount of cash from the Boston Braves for outfielder Thomas "Tommy" Holmes.

1955 — Michael "Mike" Heath B (C 1978)

6

1880 — Frank "Pot" LaPorte B (INF, 1B, OF 1905-08, 09-10)

1895 — George "Babe" Ruth B (OF, P, 1B 1920-34)

1926 — Dale Long B (1B 1960, 62-63)

1926 — Yankees obtain pitcher George Mogridge and an undisclosed amount of cash from the Browns for catcher Walter (Wally) Schang.

7

1936 — Frank Leja B (1B 1954-55)

1957 — Damaso Garcia B (2B 1978-current)

1967 — Yankees obtain pitcher Joe Verbanic from the Phillies for pitcher Pedro Ramos.

8

1911 — Donald "Jeep" Heffner B (INF 1934-37)

1927 — Yankees obtain outfielder Cedric Durst and pitcher Joseph Giard from the Browns for pitcher "Sad" Sam Jones.

1937 — Cletis "Clete" Boyer B (INF, OF 1959-66)

1942 — Frederick "Fritz" Peterson B (P 1966-74)

1956 — Yankees obtain pitcher Maury McDermott and shortstop Bob Kline from the Senators for pitcher Bob Wiesler, second baseman Herb Plews, outfielders Dick Tettelbach and Whitey Herzog, and pitcher Lou Berberet. Herzog was not actually transferred to the Senators' roster until April 2, 1956.

9

1902 — Julian "Julie" Wera B (3B 1927, 29)

10

1894 — Herbert "The Knight of Kennett Square" Pennock B (P 1923-33)

1915 — Allie "Superchief" Reynolds B (P 1947-54)

1975 — Yankees sign free agent minor leaguer Damaso Garcia. Garcia saw action with the 1978 team as a second baseman, filling in for the injured Willie Randolph.

11

Nothing of note happened on this date.

1895 — Thomas "Shotgun" Rogers B (P 1921)

1902 — George "Kiddo" Davis B (OF 1926)

1912 — Walter "Monk" Dubiel B (P 1944-45)

1921 — Donald Bollweg B (1B 1953)

1942 — Patrick (Pat) Dobson B (P 1973-75)

13

1883 — Harold "Prince Hal" Cha.. B (1B, INF, OF 1905-13)

1887 — Guy Zinn B (ᴜF 1911-12)

1888 — Edward "Kid" Foster B (SS 1910)

1890 — Daniel "Big Dan" Tipple B (P 1915)

1927 — James (Jim) Brideweser B (INF 1951-53)

1941 — James (Jim) Brenneman B (P 1965)

14

1879 — Timothy "Tim" Jordan B (1B 1903)

15

1915 — Cyril "Roy" Weatherly B (OF 1943-46)

1916 — Yankees purchase Hall of Fame third baseman Frank "Homerun" Baker from the Philadelphia Athletics for $35,000. Baker had several good years in New York, and helped anchor the hot corner for the pennant winners of the early '20s.

1938 — Yankees obtain infielder Billy "Knick" Knickerbocker from the Browns for infielder Donald Heffner and an undisclosed amount of cash.

1945 — Ross "Mickey Mantle's Legs" Moschitto B (OF 1965,67)

16

1897 — James Alesandes (Alex) Ferguson B (P 1918-21)

1948 — Yankees release pitcher Louis "Bobo" Newsom.

1953 — Yankees purchase pitcher Johnny Schmitz from the Reds for an undisclosed amount of cash.

17

1893 — Walter "Wally" Pipp B (1B 1915-25)

1901 — Edward "Eddie" Phillips B (C 1932)

1936 — Yankees purchase first baseman Ellsworth "Babe" Dahlgren from the Red Sox. Dahlgren is famous for replacing Lou Gehrig on the day Gehrig removed himself from the Yankee lineup after playing 2,130 consecutive games.

18

1879 — Louis Leroy B (P 1905-06)

1887 — Curtis (Curt) Coleman B (3B 1912)

1889 — George Mogridge B (P 1915-20)

1915 — Joseph "Flash" Gordon B (2B, 1B 1938-43, 46)

1927 — Luis Arroyo B (P 1960-63)

19

1957 — Yankees obtain pitchers Art Ditmar and Bobby Shantz, and infielders Clete Boyer, Jack McMahon, and Wayne Belardi from Kansas City for pitchers Rip Coleman, Tom Morgan and Maury McDermott, shortstop Billy Hunter, and outfielders Irv Noren and Milt Graff. Baseball Commissioner Ford Frick ruled that Boyer, a Kansas City "bonus baby," had to remain with the Athletics until his bonus term expired, so he was not transferred to New York until June 4, 1957.

The key to the trade was Boyer, a badly needed infielder of outstanding defensive ability. The bait was Noren, a .300 hitter in the past, but never to be repeated in the Athletics' uniform.

20

1887 — Carroll "Boardwalk" Brown B (P 1914-15)

1888 — Edward "Stubby" Magner B (SS, 2B 1911)

1896 — Herold "Muddy" Ruel B (C 1917-20)

1913 — Thomas "Old Reliable" Henrich B (OF, 1B 1937-42, 46-50)

1947 — Thomas "Tom" Buskey B (P 1973-74)

21

1919 — Yankees obtain pitcher John Quinn from the Vernon minor league franchis for pitcher Joe Finneran, first baseman Zinn Beck and other considerations.

1945 — Thomas "Tom" Shopay B (OF 1967,69)

1947 — Terrence "Terry" Ley B (P 1971)

1903 — Edward "Peck" Monroe B (P 1917-18)

1919 — John Lucadello B (2B 1947)

1920 — Karl Drews B (P 1946-48)

1929 — Ryne Duren B (P 1958-61)

1939 — Steve Barber B (P 1967-68)

1903 — Roy Johnson B (OF 1936-37)

1918 — Edward "Truck" Kearse B (OF 1936-37)

1929 — Elston "Ellie" Howard B (C, OF, 1B 1955-67; coach 1968-current)

1954 — Yankees sell pitcher Vic Raschi to the St. Louis Cardinals for $85,000. A member of the Yankee organization told the author that Raschi was traded because of a contract dispute following a holdout in 1953.

1875 — Henry "Monte" Beville B (C, 1B 1903-04)

1877 — James "Champ" Osteen B (3B, SS, 1B 1904)

1927 — Robert "Suitcase Bob" Seeds B (OF, 3B 1936)

1948 — Yankees obtain pitcher "Steady" Eddie Lopat from the Cleveland Indians for catcher Aaron Robinson and pitchers Fred Bradley and Bill Wight. The Indians later traded Robinson to the White Sox, along with Wight. Neither amounted to much, although Wight did lead the league in walks allowed in 1948!

As for Lopat, he spent several invaluable seasons with New York, and played on the five consecutive world championship teams of 1949-53. He won 21 games in 1952, and led the league in percentage with a 16-4 mark in 1954.

1941 — Yankees sell first baseman Ellsworth "Babe" Dahlgren to the Braves for an undisclosed amount of cash.

1940 — Daniel (Danny) Cater B (3B, 1B, OF 1970-71)

1942 — Yankees sign free agent outfielder George "Tuck" Stainback after his release by the Detroit Tigers. Stainback lasted four seasons with New York as a substitute outfielder during the "war years."

1872 — Louis Criger B (C 1910)

1896 — Harold "Rip" Collins B (P 1920-21)

1932 — John Blanchard B (C, OF, 1B 1955, 59-65)

1896 — Ralph "Cy" Perkins B (C 1931)

1912 — Yankees announce that they will begin wearing the famous pinstripped uniforms.

1943 — Robert (Bob) Oliver B (DH, 1B 1975)

1948 — Martin (Marty) Perez B (3B 1977)

1970 — Yankees obtain infielder Ron Hansen from the Chicago White Sox for an undisclosed amount of cash believed to have been less than the waivers price.

It only happens once every four years, and nothing has happened in Yankee history so infrequently!

MARCH

1

1944 — Ronald (Ron) Klimkowski B (P 1969-70, 72)

1953 — Larry Murray B (OF 1974-76)

1969 — Mickey Mantle makes his rumored retirement official at a spring training press conference in Ft. Lauderdale. He was the last real link to the great Yankee teams of the '50s and early '60s (Mel Stottlemyre also played for the '64 team). Many fans hated to see Mantle retire, but, in all honesty, Mantle's badly injured knees simply could not take any more punishment. In fact, Mantle probably should have retired after the 1964 or '65 season, while he still had a .300 batting average, but his loyalty to the franchise, and the hopes of hitting more than 500 homeruns, kept him in the pinstripes.

2

1917 — James "Jim" Konstanty B (P 1955-56)

1918 — Frank Coleman B (OF 1946-47)

1921 — Richard (Dick) Starr B (P 1947-48)

3

1867 — Jack "Peach Pie" O'Connor B (C, 1B 1903)

1872 — William "Wee Willie" Keeler B (OF, 2B, 3B 1903-09)

1918 — Yankees purchase first baseman George Burns from the Detroit Tigers for an undisclosed amount and immediately trade him to the Philadelphia Athletics for outfielder Ping Bodie.

4

1891 — Clarence "Dazzy" Vance B (P 1915-18). That's right, the Yankees had him but let him go. It could have meant the pennant in 1920 and 1924.

1897 — Neal Brady B (P 1915, 18)

1897 — Francis "Lefty" O'Doul B (P 1919-20, 22)

1918 — Melvin (Mel) Queen B (P 1942, 44, 46-47)

5

1891 — Walter (Walt) Alexander B (C 1915-17)

1903 — Martin Autry B (C 1924)

1912 — James (Jimmy) Gleeson B (coach)

1919 — Donald "Don" Savage B (3B, OF 1944-45)

1921 — Elmer Valo B (OF 1960)

6

1919 — Yankees sell pitcher Ray Keating to the Braves for an undisclosed amount of cash.

7

1914 — Joseph "Muscles" Gallagher B (OF 1939)

8

1893 — Raymond (Ray) Francis B (P 1925)

1930 — Robert (Bob) Grim B (P 1954-58)

1939 — James "Jim" Bouton B (P 1962-68)

9

1875 — Elmer Bliss B (OF 1903-04)

1908 — Myril Hoag B (OF 1931-32, 34-38)

1927 — (Jackie) Jensen B (OF 1950-52)

10

1880 — Daniel (Danny) Hoffman B (OF 1906-07)

11

1870 — Herman (Herm) McFarland B (OF 1903)

1945 — Dock Ellis B (P 1976-77)

12

1903 — The New York Highlanders (later known as the Yankees) are officially approved as members of the American League.

1936 — Ray "Buddy" Barker B (1B 1965-67)

1939 — John (Johnny) Callison B (OF, DH 1972-73)

1943 — Jim "The Toy Cannon" Wynn B (OF, DH 1977)

13

1886 — Frank "Homerun" Baker B (3B 1916-19, 21-22)

1922 — Clifford "Tiger" Mapes B (OF 1948-51)

14

1944 — John Miller B (OF, 1B 1966)

1969 — Yankees purchase outfielder Jimmy Hall from the Cleveland Indians for an undisclosed amount.

15

1889 — Charles (Charley) Mullen B (1B, 2B, OF 1914-16)

1898 — Wilfred "Rosy" Ryan B (P 1928)

1919 — Yankees sell pitcher Ray Fisher to the Reds for an undisclosed amount of cash.

1944 — Wayne Granger B (P 1973)

1946 — Robert (Bobby) Bonds B (OF, DH 1975)

16

1927 — Clinton "Scrap Iron" Courtney B (C 1951)

1888 — Edward "Big Ed" Klepfer B (P 1911, 13)

1938 — James (Jimmy) Hall B (OF 1969)

18

1901 — John Cooney B (OF 1944)

19

1884 — Clyde "Hack" Engel B (OF 1909-10)

1935 — Fritz "Fritzie" Brickell B (2B, SS 1958-59)

20

1875 — Patrick "Willie" Greene B (INF 1903)

21

1892 — William (Bill) Stumpf B (INF, OF, 1B 1912-13)

1897 — William "Good Time Bill" Lamar B (OF 1917-19)

22

1903 — Advance tickets for the Highlanders' home opener go on sale on the same day the team announces that it will build a new ballpark at 168th Street and Broadway in Manhattan. Their new home, Hilltop Park, was an all-wood structure with a small covered stand in the infield, and open bleachers down the line. It sat approximately 15,000, including on-the-field, "bring your own seat" tickets. Hilltop Park was finished in time for the 1903 opener, and was the home of the Highlanders (Yankees) through the 1912 season.

1915 — Norman "Red" Branch B (P 1941-42)

1972 — In one of their all-time greatest trades, the Yankees obtain left-handed relief pitcher Walter "Sparky" Lyle from the Red Sox in return for first baseman Danny Cater and shortstop Mario Guerrero. Cater had one good year in Boston, batting .313 in 1973 as a part-time player, and was subsequently dumped on the St. Louis Cardinals. Guerrero never amounted to much, and was eventually banished to Oakland.

Lyle became the greatest relief pitcher in Yankee history. His 35 saves in 1972 led the American League, and helped the Yankees contend for the Eastern Division Championship until the last week of the season. His heroics during the 1977 Playoffs and World Series will never be forgotten by Yankee fans, and came after Lyle notched 26 saves and a 13-5 won-loss record during the regular season. Holds the career mark for saves (210), and has never started a major league game.

1974 — Yankees purchase outfielder Elliott Maddox from the Texas Rangers for an amount reported to be in the neighborhood of $100,000. Maddox had always been a fine defensive outfielder, but came alive with his bat as well during the '74 season in New York.

For a while, Maddox was the center of a great controversy surrounding himself and Bobby Murcer. Murcer had been the Yankee centerfielder for three solid seasons, and was billed as the heir apparent to Mickey Mantle. In early May, 1974, Yankee manager Bill Virdon replaced Murcer with Maddox, and moved Murcer to right field. Murcer proved to be the best right fielder in the league after resigning himself to the switch. Maddox batted .303, Murcer dropped to .274, and the Yankees were eliminated from the pennant race on the next-to-last day of the season.

Unfortunately, the Maddox story did not end on a happy note. Maddox's manager in Texas was Billy Martin, and when Martin took over the Yankee helm in 1975, the pair re-newed their old feelings of dislike which culminated in Maddox's trade to Baltimore in 1977.

Maddox might have stayed in a Yankee uniform longer, but he seriously injured his knee on the rain-soaked field at Shea Stadium and required two operations. The second surgery was performed without the Yankees' consent, and his exile to Baltimore was a foregone conclusion.

One final note: Maddox filed a one million dollar suit against the city of New York, charging that its negligence in maintaining Shea Stadium had caused the injury which ruined his career. The suit is still on the docket of the New York Court, awaiting trial.

24

1891 — Ernest (Ernie) Shore B (P 1919-20)

1925 — Richard (Dick) Kryhoski B (1B 1949)

1930 — John "Bob" Tillman B (C 1967)

25

1920 — Yankees release outfielder Ping Bodie.

1929 — Yankees release pitcher Fred Heimach.

1932 — Woodson "Woodie" Held B (SS, 3B, OF 1954)

26

1913 — William (Bill) Zuber B (P 1943-46)

1949 — Roger Hambright B (P 1971)

1952 — Yankees waive infielder Gene Mauch to the Cardinals.

1910 — Steve "Smokey" Sundra B (P 1936, 38-40)

1946 — William (Bill) Sudakis B (C, 3B, 1B, DH 1974)

28

1919 — Victor "The Springfield Rifle" Raschi B (P 1946-53)

1923 — Robert (Bob) Kuzava B (P 1951-54)

29

1948 — Yankees and Red Sox clash for 17 innings and end in a 2-2 tie during one of the longest spring training exhibition games ever played. The game lasted four hours, two minutes.
30

1945 — Richard (Dick) Woodson B (P 1974)

1955 — Yankees sell pitchers Ewell Blackwell and Tom Gorman, and first baseman Dick Kryhoski to the Kansas City Athletics for $50,000.

1965 — Yankees sell pitcher Stan Williams to the Cleveland Indians for an amount greater than the standard waivers price.

31

1894 — Thomas Sheehan B (P 1921)

1971 — Yankees release infielder Pete Ward.

1972 — Yankees re-purchase outfielder Frank Tepedino from the Milwaukee Brewers for an amount reported to be in the neighborhood of $40,000.

APRIL

1

1912 — Jacob "Whistlin' Jake" Wade B (P 1946)

2

1931 — Jackie Mitchell strikes out Babe Ruth and Lou Gehrig on six straight pitches and thereby becomes the only WOMAN in baseball history to kayo the heart of "Murderers Row." Needless to say, the scene was an exhibition game in Chattanooga, Tennessee, and the strikeouts were part of the act.

1945 — Michael (Mike) Kekich B (P 1969-73)

3

1879 — John Frill B (P 1910)

1929 — Arthur (Art) Ditmar B (P 1957-61)

1952 — Richard (Rick) Earle B (P 1976)

1961 — Yankees re-acquire pitcher "Duke" Maas from the Los Angeles Angels for shortstop "Fritz" Brickell.

1967 — Yankees obtain infielder John Kennedy from the Dodgers for outfielder John Miller, pitcher Jack Cullen, and the temporary transfer of outfielder Roy White to the Dodgers' Spokane minor league team.

1972 — Yankees release pitchers Jim Hardin and Gary Waslewski.

4

1883 — John "Silent John" Hummel B (OF, INF 1918)

1971 — Former Yankee pitching ace Carl Mays dies at 79.

1972 — Yankees release shortstop Ron Hansen.

5

1877 — William "Wid" Conroy B (INF, OF 1903-08)

1921 — Robert (Bobby) Hogue B (P 1951-52)

1938 — Ronald (Ron) Hansen B (INF 1970-71)

1973 — Yankees obtain infielder Tom Matchick from the Orioles for shortstop Frank "No Homerun" Baker.

1977 — Yankees obtain shortstop Russell "Bucky" Dent from the White Sox for outfielder-designated hitter Oscar Gamble and minor league pitchers Bob Polinsky and Dewey Hoyt.

6

1954 — Kenneth (Kenny) Clay B (P 1977-current)

1973 — Yankee Ron Blomberg becomes the first designated hitter in the history of the major leagues when he walks in the first inning of the Yankees road opener at Fenway Park. He went 1-for-three, drove in a run and scored a run in the Yankees 15-5 loss.

1974 — The Yankees play their first home game outside the friendly confines of Yankee Stadium since 1922 when they host the Indians at Shea Stadium. The Yankees were tenants of the New York Mets for the 1974-75 seasons while New York City renovated Yankee Stadium. By the way, the Yanks beat Cleveland, 6-1, behind Mel Stottlemyre's pitching and a two-run homerun by Graig Nettles.

7

1875 — John Ganzel B (1B, INF 1903-04)

1907 — Oral "Hildy" Hildebrand B (P 1939-40)

1933 — Robert (Bobby) Del Greco B (OF 1957-58)

1948 — Richard (Rick) Sawyer B (P 1974-75)

1952 — Yankees waive pitcher Dave "The Squeakin Deacon" Madison to the Browns.

1977 — The Yankees open the defense of their A.L. championship by defeating the Milwaukee Brewers, 3-0, at the Stadium. Sparky Lyle recorded the first of his 26 saves (in relief of Catfish Hunter, who had hurled seven innings of three-hit baseball before being kayoed by a line drive off the bat of Von Joshua which struck the Cat's left instep).Designated hitter Jim Wynn homered in his first at bat.

8

1899 — Theodore (Ted) Kleinhans B (P 1936)

1946 — James "Catfish" Hunter B (P 1975-current)

9

1888 — James "Hippo" Vaughn B (P 1908, 10-12)

1925 — In the so-called "Year of the Great Stomach Ache," Yankee outfielder Babe Ruth is rushed to the hospital after collapsing during spring training.Newspapers around the world bore headlines of his imminent, or alleged, death.

To this day, fans around the globe have been left to speculate as to what ailment troubled the Babe for so long that he missed the first 66 games of the season. Different "confidential" sources have told reporters and authors that the problem ranged from simple food poisoning to serious venereal disease. This author makes no attempt at sorting out the malady. The only established facts are that Ruth had eaten a huge meal, as was his common habit, prior to collapsing, and that he was gravely ill for a few weeks. More than that will never be known for certain.

1965 — The Yankees play the Houston Astros in the first major league baseball game (albeit exhibition) ever held in the Houston Astrodome. Mickey Mantle responded with the first Astrodome homerun, but the Yankees lost, 2-1, in 12 innings.

1971 — Yankees obtain first baseman-outfielder Felipe Alou from the Oakland A's for pitchers, Rob Gardner and Ron Klimkowski.

10

1895 — Robert (Bob) McGraw B (P 1917-19)

1976 — When is a game-winning grand slam homerun not a game-winning grand slam homerun? When Sparky Lyle is the pitcher, Milwaukee's Don

19

Money the hitter, and first base umpire Jim McKean calls time out before the pitch is delivered.

Here are the facts behind this incredible event: The Yankees led, 9-6, at Milwaukee, when the Brewers loaded the bases with no outs in the bottom of the ninth inning. Reliever Lyle threw to Money, and Money slammed the ball deep into the seats in left field, for what appeared to be a stunning come-from-behind win . . .

BUT, McKean had called time out at Yankee first baseman Chris Chambliss' request just prior to the pitch. Chambliss had requested time because he heard Yankee manager Billy Martin yelling instructions out to Lyle, instructions which Chambliss knew Lyle could not hear over the crowd noise. Lyle also failed to hear the time out call, as did most of the players, so he served up the pitch.

After a lengthy debate, play resumed, Money struck out, and the Yankees eventually came home 9-7 winners.

11

1872 — Frank Kitson B (P 1907)

1954 — Yankees obtain outfielder Enos "Country" Slaughter from the Cardinals for pitcher Mel Wright, outfielders Emil Tellinger and Bill Virdon, and catcher Hal Smith. Slaughter cried for more than 20 minutes after learning of the trade, and originally decided to retire a Cardinal rather than go to NY. Fortunately for Yankee fans, he reconsidered, went to NY, and helped the Yankees win four pennants in four years.

12

1895 — Samuel (Sammy) Vick B (OF 1917-20)

1927 — Yankees defeat Philadelphia, 8-3, before the largest confirmed paid opening day attendance in baseball history to that time (73,206), as Waite Hoyt out-dueled Lefty Grove.

1948 — Yankees release pitcher Spurgeon "Spud" Chandler.

1959 — Yankees obtain outfielder Bob Martyn and infielder Mike Baxes from the Athletics for outfielder Russ Snyder and shortstop Tommy Carroll.

13

1866 — Herman "Germany" Long B (SS, 2B 1903)

1879 — Garland "Jake" Stahl B (1B, OF 1908)

1915 — Oscar Grimes B (INF 1943-46)

1919 — Yankees release outfielders Ham Hyatt and Hugh High, and pitcher Ed Monroe.

1926 — Yankees edge Boston, 12-11, at Fenway Park, in one of the wildest opening day games in the history of both clubs.

14

1910 — Yankees and Red Sox play a 14-inning, 4-4 tie at Yankee Stadium. Yankee pitcher Hippo Vaughn went the distance, allowing 11 hits.

1931 — Kal Segrist B (2B 3B 1952)

1967 — Rookie Red Sox hurler Bill Rohr hurls 8-and-two-thirds innings of no-hit baseball before Elston Howard's ninth inning single saves the Yankees the embarassemnt of a no-hit loss. Final score: Boston 3, NY 0.

1969 — Yankees purchase outfielder Jimmie Hall from Cleveland.

15

1886 — Leonard "King" Cole B (P 1914-15)

1913 — Yankees purchase infielder Bill McKechnie from the Braves for an undisclosed amount of cash.

1933 — Yankees release pitcher Charles Devens.

1976 — Yankee Stadium re-opens after a two-year renovation period, and the Yankees celebrate their return home in fine fashion with an 11-4, come-from-behind win against the Twins. Yankee starter Rudi May was chased early, after spotting the Twins a 4-0 lead, and surrendering a tremendous homerun over the centerfield wall to Dan Ford (the first ever in the new Stadium). Dick Tidrow came on in relief and held the Twins off, while the Yankees rallied for a run in the third, 4 in the fourth, and 6 in the eighth to win going away. The crowd: 52,613.

16

1929 — The Yankees become the first team in major league history to permanently add uniform numbers to their game-clothes. The numbers were done according to the players' regular spots in the batting order (thus, Ruth 3, Gehrig 4). Substitutes were numbered according to seniority, as were pitchers.

1937 — Yankee Stadium opens its 15th season with a new enlarged right field stand. Prior to the '37 season, the triple-decked seating areas ended at the foul poles, and the bleachers extended across the outfield from pole to pole. The extended decks included new box and reserved seats, and thereby reduced the Stadium's seating capacity below the 72,000 it once allegedly held. (Bleacher seats were wood benches in those days.)

1939 — Bernard "Bernie" Allen B (INF 1972-73)

1943 — Frank Fernandez B (C 1967-69)

1959 — The Yankees unveil the first message scoreboard in Stadium history. It listed the lineups, out of town scores, and a wide expanse for paragraph-type messages, posted via electronic devices.

1967 — Yankees edge Boston, 7-6, in 18 innings. The five-hour 50-minute marathon ended when Jake Gibbs walked, stole second base, and scored on a single by Joe Pepitone. Carl Yastrzemski and Tony Conigliaro each had five hits for the Sox. (For more details, see the "Longest Days" section).

1973 — Yankees purchase designated hitter Jim Ray Hart from the Giants for an undisclosed amount of cash believed to exceed $50,000.

1903 — Paul "Big Poison" Waner B (OF 1944-45)

17

1888 — Thomas "Rebel" McMillan B (SS 1912)

1951 — Hall-of-Famer Mickey Mantle makes his first appearance in a regular-season game. He went 1-for-4, the hit (a single) coming in the sixth inning off pitcher Bill Wight, and driving in a run during New York's 5-0 win against Boston at the Stadium.

1953 — Mantle celebrates his "anniversary" with a 565-foot homerun in Washington.

1973 — Yankees release pitcher Casey Cox.

18

1888 — George "Duffy" Lewis B (OF 1919-20)

1923 — Yankee Stadium opens its doors for the first time, and an estimated crowd of 74,000 is on hand as the Yankees defeated the Red Sox, 4-1. Babe Ruth, who had told friends that he'd give up a year of his life to hit the first homerun in the new ballpark, drove a three-run homerun into the right field stands to accomplish his heart's desire. Yankee starting pitcher Bob Shawkey scored the first run in the Stadium, and also homered later on. Unfortunately, not all the first game accolades were reserved for the Yankees, since the visitors got the first hit.

(NOTE: According to the official Yankee records, the real paid attendance was 62,281.)

1929 — Steve "Lefty" Kraly B (P 1953)

1950 — New York overcomes a 9-run deficit to come-from-behind and defeat the Red Sox, 15-10. The Yankees trailed, 9-0, in the sixth inning, when they rallied with four runs, as an omen of things to come. Then, after giving the Sox a one-inning respite, the Yankees exploded for 9 runs in the eighth inning.

(The eighth inning play-by-play: Yogi Berra led off with a single off Yankee nemesis Mel Parnell. Billy Johnson walked, Johnny Lindell flied out, Billy Martin doubled home Berra, and Johnny Mize followed with a two-run double to knock Parnell out of the box.

Reliever Walt Masterson came in and induced Phil Rizzuto to ground out, but Tommy Henrich tripled to center field, driving in Mize, and came around to score on a wild pitch. Gene Woodling walked, and Masterson was replaced by Earl Johnson.

Johnson was greeted by singles by Joe DiMaggio and Berra, which loaded the bases, and was replaced by Al Papai. Billy Johnson greeted him with a two-run single. Papai walked Lindell, and was replaced by Charley Schanz, who gave up a single to Martin before retiring Mize on a fly ball to end the inning.

19

1887 — John (Jack) Martin B (INF 1912)

1935 — John Wyatt B (P 1968)

1946 — Yankees move to the first base dugout as their new clubhouse opens for the first time.

1973 — In a major shake up of his newly-purchased team's front office, owner George Steinbrenner fires President Mike Burke and replaces him with Gabe Paul. It was the first step in a three-year battle to make the Yankees champions again, and it worked.

In fairness to Burke, he never had the money that Steinbrenner brought to the Yankees, so his record of weak teams cannot be laid on his shoulders. In fact, an in depth study of the decline of the Yankees in the mid '60s shows that the real destruction began in the late 50s, when the owners kept trading away young players to patch together short-run winners. By the time 1965 rolled around, the farm system had been traded dry, and no money was being spent to rebuild it.

1974 — Yankees obtain outfielder Walter "No Neck" Williams and pitcher Ed Farmer from the Indians as part of a three-way deal in which New York sent catcher Gerry Moses to the Tigers, and Detroit in turn sent pitcher Jim Perry to the Indians.

20

1876 — Charles "Eagle Eye" Hamphill B (OF 1908-11)

1912 — The Yankees are the visiting team when the Red Sox open Fenway Park's doors for the first time. To the great thrill of the home crowd, the Sox did what they usually do to the Yankees in Boston. Final score: Boston 7, New York 6 (11 innings).

1939 — Red Ruffing surrenders Ted Williams' first major league hit, a double off the 407 sign in right center field in the pre-renovation Stadium. Ruffing struck Williams out in the "Splendid Splinter's" first two at-bats. Interestingly enough, this game set the pattern for Williams' confrontations with the Yankees. He would always get his hits, but rarely came through with a game-winner or clutch hit, especially in New York. Fans often debated a Joe DiMaggio for Ted Williams exchange, based on the advantage each hitter would have enjoyed in the other team's ballpark. (DiMaggio batted righty, and the wall in left field in Fenway is a mere 315-feet. Williams hit lefty, and the wall in right field in Yankee Stadium during his playing days was 296-feet.) However, the Yankees were wise to turn down any alleged offers of a swap, because as great a hitter as Williams was, he was never the outfielder DiMaggio was, and led the Sox to only one pennant in his 19-year career. DiMaggio only played about 13 seasons, but the Yankees won the pennant in 11 of them.

1944 — Steve Blateric B (P 1972)

1957 — Talk about prodigious clouts, then you've got to include the shot Bill Skowron hit on this date in Yankee history, in Fenway Park, of all places. Skowron laid into a fastball and drove it completely out of Fenway to the right of the flag pole in centerfield. He was only the third player in history to accomplish this feat.

21

1901 — Phillip "Lefty" Weinert B (P 1931)

1912 — Yankees drop an 11-2 decision to the Giants in a special benefit game for the survivors of the Titanic.

1963 — Yankees obtain pitcher Steve Hamilton from the Senators for pitcher Jim Coates.

1963 — Yankees obtain infielder Harry Bright from the Reds for an undisclosed amount of cash.

1977 — With the Yankees in the throes of a 2-8 slump, manager Billy Martin draws the starting lineup out of a hat, and the Yankees respond with an 8-6 win against Toronto. Chris Chambliss, normally the cleanup hitter, was dropped to eighth, and drove in five runs with a homerun and two doubles. Graig Nettles also homered, and pitcher Ken Holtzman won the game, with relief help from Lyle.

22

1881 — Neal Ball B (SS, 2B 1907-08)

1903 — The New York Highlanders (forerunners of the Yankees) open their first major league season in a 3-1 loss to the Senators in Washington. New York's Jack Chesbro was the starter and loser. The Highlanders scored in the bottom of the first inning (that's right, the Senators elected to bat first under the rule which gave the home team its choice of batting first or last). Willie Keeler walked, Dave Fultz singled to right field, and Jimmy Williams grounded out.

The game lasted 1:45, and a record crowd of 11,950 was kept well entertained, according to contemporary accounts.

1904 — After surrendering a lead-off single to Kip Selbach, Yankee hurler Jack Chesbro pitches no-hit ball the rest of the game and beats the Senators, 2-0.

1915 — The Yankees don the famed pinstripes for the first time. The pinstripes became the symbol of the great Yankee teams, along with the NY emblem and Hat-in-the-Ring insignia.

1920 — Babe Ruth plays his first regular-season game as a Yankee. He went hitless, and his error in right field proved to be the game-losing miscue in a 6-5 defeat in Philadelphia.

1928 — Yankee Stadium opens its doors for the sixth consecutive season, and sports an extended left field stand for the first time. Prior to the 1928 season, the bleachers extended from foul pole to foul pole, across the outfield. During the off-season, the Yankees extended the famous triple-decked stands beyond the pole in left. (see photos)

1933 — Robert "Bob" Schmidt B (C 1965)

1959 — Yankee ace Whitey Ford strikes out 15 Senators en route to a 14-inning, 1-0 win in Washington. The lone Yankee run came on a Moose Skowron homerun in the 14th inning, and set a record for the longest game in baseball history which ended 1-0 on a homerun.

1970 — The Yankees drop an 18-inning, 2-1, decision to the Senators in Robert F. Kennedy Stadium when Mike Epstein's sacrifice fly scores Ed Stroud. Bobby Murcer's ninth inning homerun tied the game 1-1. (For more details, (see the "Longest Days" section.)

23

1903 — The Highlanders notch their first major league victory, a 7-2 decision at Washington. Harry Howell was the winning pitcher, and helped his own cause by stroking the first triple in Highlander history. Lefty Davis scored what proved to be the winning run when Washington outfielder Jimmy Ryan dropped a fly ball hit by Willie Keeler.

1937 — Leon "Duke" Carmel B (1B 1965)

1947 — Yankees release pitcher Johnny Murphy.

24

1895 — Harry Harper B (P 1921)

1905 — The Yankees suffer a triple play during Washington's 4-3 victory.

1917 — Pitcher George Mogridge becomes the only lefthanded pitcher in Yankee history to hurl a no-hitter (and at Fenway Park, no less!) in a 2-1 win.

1943 — Joseph (Joe) Verbanic B (P 1967-68, 70)

1883 — Russell (Russ) Ford B (P 1909-13)

1904 — Pitcher Jack Chesbro notches his first win of the season. He would go
on to win 41 games that year, the American League record for wins in
one season.

1924 — Arthur (Art) Schallock B (P 1951-55)

1933 — Rookie Russ Van Atta makes four singles in his first major league game
and thereby ties the modern major league record for singles in a first
game. (For the bonus, name the player he shares the record with?
legnetS yesaC.)

1873 — James (Jim) Cockman B (3B 1905)

1888 — Ray "Slim" Caldwell B (OF 1910-18)

1913 — Yankees purchase catcher John Gossett from Columbus.

1919 — Virgil "Fire" Trucks B (P 1958)

1917 — Salvatore (Sal), "The Barber" Maglie B (P 1957-58)

1929 — Yankees turn a triple play during a loss to the Athletics.

1936 — After surrendering six runs to the Red Sox in the first inning, the
Yankees rebound with seven of their own runs in the top of the second
inning, en route to a 12-9 win at Fenway Park.

1953 — Yankees sell third baseman Loren Babe to the Athletics for $30,000.

1961 — Roger Maris hits his first homerun of the season. 60 more follow, and
he ends the year with a record 61 homeruns, the most in a single season
in baseball history.

1974 — Yankees obtain first baseman Chris Chambliss, and pitchers Dick
Tidrow and Cecil Upshaw from the Indians for pitchers Fred Beene,
Fritz Peterson, Steve Kline, and Tom Buskey.

1894 — Robert (Bob) Williams B (C, 1B 1911-14)

1903 — The Highlanders suffer the first shutout in their history, a 6-0 loss at
Philadelphia.

1916 — Enos "Country" Slaughter B (OF 1954-55, 56-59)

1935 — The Yankees turn a first inning triple play during a 9-8 win against
Philadelphia. The Athletics had runners on first and second with no
outs when Jimmy Foxx lined out to Tony Lazzeri, who fired across the
diamond to first baseman Lou Gehrig, who threw on to shortstop

Frank Crosetti, completing the play. The Yankees also turned a game-ending double play in the ninth inning when the Athletics had the bases loaded.

1977 — Yankees obtain pitcher Mike Torrez from the As for pitcher Dock Ellis, infielder Marty Perez and outfielder Larry Murray.

28

1925 — Clarence "Cuddles" Marshall B (P 1946, 48-49)

1930 — Thomas "Snake" Sturdivant B (P 1955-59)

1935 — Pedro "Pete" Ramos B (P 1964-66)

1950 — Yankees sell outfielder Dick Wakefield to the White Sox as part of a deal which brought pitcher John Ostrowski to the Yankees' minor league club in Kansas City. This touched off the great Wakefield controversy, because Wakefield refused to report to the White Sox unless they gave him a $5,000 bonus in lieu of the world series share he expected in NY.

Wakefield claimed that the Yankees had convinced him to sign for the 1950 season for $17,500, $5,000 less than he had been receiving with his 1949 club, the Tigers, by "guarantying him a world series share." The White Sox, relying on a guarantee of their own (that the Yankees would force him to report by April 30 or the trade would be off), cancelled the deal. NY refused to return Ostrowski; nor would NY pay Wakefield's salary.

The teams appealed to baseball commissioner Albert "Happy" Chandler, who ruled in favor of Chicago and cancelled the deal.

1953 — A terrific brawl erupts at Busch Stadium in the 10th inning of a Yankees-Browns game. Six players are fined a total of $850, an American League record up to that date. Here's the background and play-by-play:

The Yankees and former Yankee catcher Clint Courtney had been carrying a personal war of their own over the two seasons. (Courtney had been traded away from New York.) In the top of the 10th inning, the Yankees took the lead (7-6) when baserunner Gil McDougald bowled over Courtney as he scored the go-ahead run.

In retaliation, Courtney slid into Yankee shortstop Phil Rizzuto, "spikes up," in what the Yankees viewed as a deliberate attempt to injure, especially because Courtney was trying to stretch a single into a double and was a dead out.

Both benches cleared, and umpire John Stevens suffered a dislocated collarbone while attempting to separate the combatants. When peace was restored, the fans littered the field with garbage, causing a 17-minute delay, and near forfeit.

Courtney was fined $250, and teammate Billy Hunter was nailed for $150. The Yankees fined were:

Billy Martin $150, Gil McDougald $100, Joe Collins $100, and Allie Reynolds $100.

1972 — Yankees purchase pitcher Jim Roland from the A's on waivers.

29

1879 — Frank "Noodles" Hahn B (P 1906)

1883 — Walter "Rube" Manning B (P 1907-10)

1888 — Ernest (Ernie) Johnson B (INF 1924-25)

1899 — Herbert (Herb) McQuaid B (P 1926)

1914 — Marvin (Marv) Breuer B (P 1939-43)

1938 — Yankees stage their first Ladies Day promotion.

1975 — Yankee first baseman Bob Oliver sets an American League record by participating in six doubleplays in a nine inning game.

1977 — Southpaw Ron Guidry gets his first starting assignment of the season and blanks the Mariners, 3-0, with late-inning relief help from Sparky Lyle. Thurman Munson hits a two-run homerun. The win pulled NY into second place.

30

1903 — Highlanders play their first home opener and defeat the Senators, 6-2, before 16,293 fans at Hilltop Park. Jack Chesbro was the winning pitcher.

Wee Willie Keeler made the first Highlanders home hit, a single in the first inning. He went to second base on an error and scored the first Highlander home-field run on a double by Jimmy Williams.

1907 — Walter "Jumbo" Brown B (P 1932-37)

1939 — Gehrig makes the fateful decision to remove himself from the lineup after 2,130 games, but keeps the move to himself for another two days. (The Yankees had an off day on May 1.)

1946 — Indians' flame-thrower Bob Feller no-hits the Yankees at the Stadium, 1-0. The only run scored on a ninth-inning homerun by Frank Hayes.

MAY

1

1913 — Yankees release pitcher Chester Hoff.

1920 — Babe Ruth hits his first Yankee homerun. It was the 50th of his career, and the blast cleared the roof in right field in the Polo Grounds, a feat matched only by Joe Jackson of the White Sox up to that time.

1896 — William "Wild Bill" Piercy B (P 1917, 21)

1923 — Yankee shortstop Everett Scott plays his 1,000th consecutive major league game while Senators' pitching immortal Walter Johnson hurles his 100th career shutout to beat the Yankees, 3-0. Scott's streak extended for another 307 games, giving him the major league record of 1,307 until a fellow named Lou Gehrig came around.

1939 — Lou Gehrig makes it official by sitting out the Yankees' game against the Tigers, thereby ending his consecutive game streak at 2,130. Gehrig's replacement Babe Dahlgren led the Yankees' attack with a homerun and a double as New York trounced Detroit, 22-2.

1948 — Lawrence (Larry) Gowell B (P 1972)

3

1894 — Clifford (Cliff) Markle B (P 1915-16, 24)

1904 — Charles "Red" Ruffing B (P 1930-42, 45-46)

1916 — Kenneth "Hawk" Silvestri B (C 1941, 46-47)

1922 — New York City mayor John Hylan approves the Yankees' petition which asked the city to close the local streets on and around the building site of the proposed Yankee Stadium.

1945 — Yankees release outfielder Paul "Big Poison" Waner.

1949 — Yankees obtain pitcher Edward "Babe" Kleiman on waivers from the Senators.

1950 — Yankee pitcher Vic Raschi commits four balks in his 4-3 victory against the White Sox, thereby tying the major league record for balks in a game. He finished the season with a record-tying six balks.

1951 — Gil McDougald ties the modern major league record by driving in six runs in one inning by tripling home two runs and adding a grand slam homerun later. The Yankees scored 11 runs in that ninth inning, a major league record for runs scored in the final inning of regulation play, chased three St. Louis pitchers, and won the game, 17-3, in St. Louis.

Mickey Mantle led off the inning with a double. Phil Rizzuto bunted for a hit and Gil McDougald tripled home two runs to chase starter Irv Medlinger. Jackie Jensen greeted reliever Sid Schact with a run-scoring triple. Joe Collins hit a homerun to score two runs. Billy Johnson doubled, Gene Woodling walked, and pitcher Allie Reynolds singled in a run to chase Schact.

Reliever Tito Herrera walked Mantle. Billy Martin pinch hit for Rizzuto and struck out, but McDougald followed with a grand slam homerun. On the next pitch thereafter, Jensen homered. The inning ended when Yogi Berra flied out to right field for the second time that inning.

29

1952 — Yankees obtain outfielder Irv Noren and infielder Tom Upton from the Senators for outfielders Jackie Jensen and Archie Wilson, pitcher Spec Shea, and infielder Jerry Snyder.

1965 — Yankees obtain catcher Doc Edwards from the Athletics for catcher John Blanchard and pitcher Rollie Sheldon.

4

1918 — The Yankees set a major league record by recording eight sacrifices in one game (six bunts and two sacrifice flies) during their 5-4 win at Boston. New York took advantage of the less-than-nimble, and far-from-sure-handed, Boston pitcher — a fellow named Babe Ruth!

Those recording sacrifices were: Roger Peckinpaugh 2, Elmer Miller 2, Wally Pipp, Ping Bodie, Del Pratt, and Truck Hannah.

1929 — Lou Gehrig hits three consecutive homeruns against the Tigers during New York's 11-9 victory at Yankee Stadium. Furthermore, in the sixth inning, Gehrig's second homerun of the game was sandwiched between homeruns by Babe Ruth and Bob Meusel.

1933 — Lefty Gomez' no-hit bid is spoiled in the ninth inning when Tiger second baseman Charlie Gehringer leads off the inning with a homerun. Gerald Walker followed with a double, advanced to third on a wild pitch, and scored on an infield out before Gomez settled down and retired the side. Final score: Yankees 5, Tigers 2.

1935 — Hall-of-Famer Joe DiMaggio plays his first game as a Yankee and gets three hits in New York's 14-5 win against the Browns at the Stadium. DiMaggio hit a triple and two singles, drove in a run, and scored three runs.

1936 — Yankees waive outfielder Dixie Walker to the White Sox.

5

1903 — The Yankees turn the first triple play in their history during an 11-3 win against the Athletics.

1914 — Yankees turn a triple play, but lose to the Senators, 6-0.

1922 — Construction begins at 161st Street and River Avenue in the Bronx in hopes of creating a three- tiered stadium which would be ready for the opening of the 1923 season. Eleven months later, Yankee Stadium opened its doors for the first time.

1925 — Yankees obtain outfielder Bobby Veach and pitcher Alex Ferguson from the Red Sox for pitcher Ray Francis and $8,000.

1926 — Robert (Bob) Cerv B (OF 1951-56, 60-62)

6

1890 — Luke "Danny" Boone B (INF 1913-16)

1907 — Ivy "Poison" Andrews B (1931-32, 37-38)

1911 — Yankees turn a triple play during their 6-3 win against the Red Sox.

1914 — Yankees win a scheduled 7-inning game versus the Senators, 4-0. During the pre-flight era, games were occasionally shortened to seven innings by mutual agreement so as to enable the visiting team to catch the train on "getaway day."

1915 — Babe Ruth makes his major league debut pitching for the Red Sox against the Yankees at the Polo Grounds. New York edged Ruth, 4-3, in 13 innings. However, Ruth also hit his first major league homerun, a bases empty shot off Yankee pitcher Jack Warhop.

1921 — Richard "Dick" Wakefield B (PH 1950)

1925 — Yankee shortstop Everett Scott's 1,307- consecutive-games-played-in streak comes to an end. He held the record until Gehrig came along.

1930 — Yankees obtain pitcher Red Ruffing from the Red Sox for outfielder Cedric Durst and $50,000.

7

1896 — Jonathan "Tom" Zachary B (P 1928-30)

1903 — The Highlanders lose to the Red Sox, 6-2, in the first game ever played between the New York and Boston franchises of the American League. It was the start of the greatest rivalry in the history of sports. Bill Dineen was the winner. Snake Wiltse lost for NY. Boston's Hobe Ferris hit a homerun.

1913 — Yankee pitcher Ray Keating yields a second-inning single to Chas Deal and pitches no-hit ball the rest of the way in a 6-0 win against Detroit. Keating managed to strike out Hall-of-Famer Ty Cobb in his first two at-bats, after which Cobb quit for the day!

1943 — Steven (Steve) Whitaker B (OF 1966-68)

1957 — Indians pitcher Herb Score is struck in the face by a line drive hit by Yankee Gil McDougald in the first inning of a night game in Cleveland. The shot broke three bones in Score's face, permanently impaired the great pitcher's eyesight, and prematurely ended his career. McDougald did not escape unscathed, according to the late Casey Stengel, because he never really recovered from the emotional upset of causing the injury and never became the great player Stengel believed McDougald could have been. New York won the game, 2-1.

1959 — The largest crowd in baseball history (93, 103) jams the Los Angeles Coliseum to watch the world champion New York Yankees play the Dodgers in an exhibition game held for the benefit of crippled former Dodger catching star Roy Campanella. The Yankees defeated the Dodgers, and future world series nemesis Sandy Koufax, 6-2.

1966 — Yankees fire manager Johnny Keane. The managerial duties are assumed by general manager Ralph Houk.

31

1891 — Chester "Red" Hoff B (P 1911-13)

1903 — The Highlanders turn the tables on the Red Sox, 6-1, to even their rivalry at one game apiece. Jack Chesbro hurled a six-hitter, but Sox second baseman Hobe Ferris stole the headlines by hitting his second homerun in as many days, a real rarity in the days of the so called "dead ball." Ferris went on to hit 9 homeruns that year.

1919 — Yankee ace Bob Shawkey retires the first 14 men he faces before surrendering a single to future Yankee Braggo Roth. It was the Athletics' only hit in New York's 2-0 win.

1937 — Arturo Lopez B (OF 1965)

1959 — Yankees obtain pitcher Mark Freeman from the Athletics for pitcher Murray Dickson.

1934 — Yankees obtain infielder Fred Mullen and $20,000 from the Red Sox for infielder Lyn Lary.

1959 — Yankees sell pitcher Murry Dickson back to the Athletics.

1900 — Garland Braxton B (P 1925-26)

1913 — The Yankees commit 8 errors, but edge Detroit, 10-9, in 10 innings. The errant players: Claud Derrick (shortstop 3), Hal Chase (first baseman 2), Roy Hartzell (second baseman), Birdie Cree (left fielder), and Ray Fisher (pitcher).

1933 — Yankee pitcher Monte Pearson allows a first inning single by Larry Rosenthal and pitches no-hit ball for the rest of the game in a 7-0 win against Chicago.

1946 — Joe DiMaggio hits a grand slam, but the Yankees fall to Boston, 5-4. It was the Red Sox' 15th straight victory in a streak which pushed the Yankees out of contention for the rest of the season. (In fact, the streak put everyone else out of contention.)

1947 — John Cumberland B (P 1968-70)

1961 — Yankees obtain outfielder Bob Cerv and pitcher Truman Clevenger from the Angels for pitchers Ryne Duren and Johnny James, outfielder Leroy Thomas, and a player to be named later.

1965 — Yankees obtain first baseman Buddy Barker from the Indians for infielder Pedro Gonzalez.

1903 — John Ganzel belts the first Highlander homerun in the franchise's history to lead New York to an 8-2 win at Detroit. Wid Conroy also homered for N.Y.

1919 — New York and Washington battle to a 12-inning, 0-0 tie, called because of darkness. Yankee pitcher Jack Quinn matched immortal Senator hurler Walter Johnson zero for zero, but Johnson yielded only two hits to Quinn's 10.

1928 — Mel Wright B (coach 1974-75)

1946 — Yankee pitcher Tiny Bonham puts a brake on the Red Sox 15-game winning streak by defeating Boston, 2-0, at the Stadium.

1954 — Yankees sell infielder Jim Brideweser to the Orioles for an undisclosed amount of cash.

1955 — Yankees obtain pitcher Sonny Dixon from the Athletics for outfielder Enos "Country" Slaughter and pitcher Johnny Sain.

In an unrelated transaction, the Yankees sold pitcher Art Schallock to the Orioles for an undisclosed amount of cash.

1966 — Yankees purchase shortstop Dick Schofield from the Giants.

1889 — Al "Lefty" Schulz B (P 1912-14)

1897 — Joseph "Jumpin Joe" Dugan B (3B 1922-28)

1915 — The Yankees edge Cleveland, 4-2, despite hitting into a triple play.

1916 — Henry (Hank) Borowy B (P 1942-45)

1919 — For the second consecutive day, the Yankees and Senators battle into extra innings with no result. This time the score was 4-4 when darkness halted the affair after 15 innings.

1925 — Lawrence "Yogi" Berra B (C, OF 1946-63; manager 1964; coach 1976-current)

1930 — Yankees waive pitcher Tom Zachary to the Braves.

1932 — Infielder Otto Saltzgaver draws a record four walks in his first major league game.

1933 — Yankees sell infielder Billy Werber and pitcher George Pipgras to the Red Sox for $100,000.

1935 — Felipe Alou B (1B, OF, DH 1971-73)

1914 — Yankees purchase catcher Les Nunamaker from the Red Sox for an undisclosed amount.

1946 — The Yankees use air transport as a team for the first time.

1947 — Charlie Keller, Joe DiMaggio and John Lindell hit consecutive homeruns in the sixth inning off Browns starter Fred Sanford to lead New York to a 9-1 win.

1948 — Yankees obtain outfielder Leon Culberson and $15,000 from the Senators for outfielder Ed Stewart.

1952 — Yankees waive pitcher Stubby Overmire to the Browns.

1953 — Yankees waive pitcher Johnny Schmitz to the Senators.

1955 — Mickey Mantle slams three consecutive homeruns into the centerfield bleachers in Yankee Stadium during a game against the Tigers. He hit two left-handed and one right-handed, and thereby became the sixth player in major league history to hit a homerun from both sides of the plate in the same game. Each shot traveled more than 463 feet (the distance to the wall).

1967 — Mickey Mantle hits the 500th homerun of his career, a seventh-inning game-winning homerun off Oriole pitcher Stu Miller, on a 3-2 pitch at Yankee Stadium.

1977 — Ed Figueroa wins his fourth straight complete game, beating the Angels, 3-0. Thurman Munson hit his seventh homerun of the season in Figueroa's support.

14

1899 — Earle "The Kentucky Colonel" Combs B (OF 1924-35)

1937 — Richard "Dick" Howser B (INF 1967-68, coach 1968-1978)

1947 — Richard (Dick) "Mr. Dirt" Tidrow B (P 1974-current)

1951 — Yankees obtain first baseman Don Bollweg and $15,000 from the Cardinals for infielder Billy Johnson.

1958 — Yankees waive pitcher Al Cicotte to the Senators.

1977 — Yankee pitcher Don Gullett hurls a four-hitter and outduels Angels' flame-thrower Nolan Ryan, 4-1, before 41,000 fans at California.

15

1908 — Yankees purchase pitcher Hippo Vaughn from Macon of the Georgia State League for an undisclosed amount of cash.

1912 — Tiger Hall-of-Famer Ty Cobb enters the Polo Grounds stands in pursuit of a particularly vocal fan. Cobb proceeded to pummel his verbal tormentor, and American League President Ban Johnson proceeded to "pummel" Cobb with a $100 fine and a 10-day suspension. The Tigers rallied around their star and threatened to strike. Johnson refused to give in, and warned the Tiger management that if the Tigers failed to play their game the next day, the team would be fined $5,000. The management rounded up a collection of college and sandlot youths, played the Athletics, and lost 24-1. The next day, the players relented, at Cobb's request.

1934 — Yankees obtain infielder Fred Muller and $20,000 from the Red Sox for infielder Lyn Lary.

1935 — Yankees sell pitcher Dan MacFayden to the Braves for an undisclosed amount.

1940 — Yankees release pitcher Leo Grissom.

1941 — Joe DiMaggio begins his record 56-consecutive-games hitting streak of the Yankees 13-1 loss to Chicago. It was also "Jimmy Dykes Day" at Yankee Stadium, held in honor of the ChiSox manager who had just announced his retirement as a player.

1949 — Yankees sell pitcher Ed Kleiman to the White Sox for an undisclosed amount.

1950 — Yankees waive outfielder John Lindell to the Cardinals. In a separate transaction, the Yankees sell pitcher Clarence Marshall to the Browns.

1970 — Yankees obtain pitcher Gary Waslewski from the Expos for first baseman Dave McDonald.

16

1919 — Frank "Stubby" Overmire B (P 1951)

1928 — Alfred "Billy" Martin B (INF, OF 1950-53, 55-57; manager 1975-78, and signed as manager in 1980)

1946 — Yankees release pitcher Bud Metheny.

1957 — The infamous "Copacabana Incident" in which Hank Bauer allegedly struck a non-player, Edward Jones, in the Copacabana Club. Bauer swears that he never hit Jones, but the newspapers had a field day with the whole thing, and the scapegoat was Billy Martin, who was somehow blamed for the whole thing and exiled to Kansas City.

Now, for the details, as they can best be pieced together. The Yankee players present included Hank Bauer, Mickey Mantle, Whitey Ford, Yogi Berra, Billy Martin and Johnny Kucks. The occasion was Martin's 29th birthday, and after stops at two other night spots, the group headed for the Copacabana Club, along with their wives (Martin was a bachelor) to watch Sammy Davis, Jr.

35

During the show, Jones, allegedly drunk at the time, made several racial remarks about Davis. This infuriated Bauer, a friend of Yankee catcher Elston Howard. Bauer told Jones to shut up, and Jones told Bauer to make him shut up. Another of Jones' friends (he was with a group of fellow bowlers) allegedly told Bauer not to try his luck or he'd be sorry.

The bowlers continued to annoy the Yankee party, and Martin eventually became disgusted with the way his birthday celebration was being disrupted. He allegedly told the bowlers that if they'd like to, the two groups could step outside and settle the whole thing, and thereby cease disturbing the rest of the audience.

Mantle, Martin and Bauer got up to go "outside"(which happened to be another way of referring to the men's room). A group of audience members and club personnel rose with them, in an attempt to head off any confrontation. Martin and one of the bowlers supposedly realized the foolishness of the whole thing, and agreed to keep Bauer and Jones apart. Just when it looked like the storm would blow over, Martin and the un-named friend found Bauer being restrained by Ford and Berra, and Jones laid out unconscious on the floor of the men's room.

The situation clearly implied that Bauer had struck Jones, but Bauer swears that he never did. Bauer said that two bouncers had given the drunk a severe beating.

In any event, the Yankees quickly fled the Club, but were spotted by an entertainment columnist from a New York daily newspaper, who interviewed only Jones and the bowlers, thereby getting only one side for his story.

The case exploded onto the front page of at least one major New York paper the next day, and resulted in the convening of a grand jury to discuss the matter. After the players testified, the charges were dropped.

Unfortunately, the Yankee management was not satisfied. General manager George Weiss, supposedly never a fan of Billy Martin, blamed Martin for the whole incident, according to most of those involved. Owner Dan Topping added to the fire by fining Ford, Berra, Bauer, Mantle, and Martin $1,000 each. He also fined Kucks $500. The matter ended Martin's Yankee career for all intents and purposes because it gave Weiss the excuse he sought to trade Martin.

1976 — Yankees obtain catcher Fran Healy from the Royals for pitcher Larry Gura.

17

1920 — James "Hot Rod" McDonald B (P 1952-54)

1948 — Carlos May B (OF, DH 1976-77)

1977 — After the Yankees dropped two straight games to the Oakland A's, pitcher Ron Guidry comes through again by hurling nine solid innings, and is relieved by Sparky Lyle, who hurls six scoreless frames in a 15-inning win against Oakland, 5-2.

1885 — Eros "Cy" Barger B (P 1906-07)

1905 — Arthur (Art) Jorgens B (C 1929-39)

1935 — Earl Averill personally ruins Lefty Gomez's no-hit bid by making two singles, the only Cleveland hits in a 3-0 Yankee win.

1946 — Reginald "Reggie" Jackson B (OF, DH 1977-current)

1968 — Yankees purchase pitcher John Wyatt from the Red Sox for an undisclosed amount of cash.

1976 — Yankees obtain outfielder Carlos May from the White Sox for pitcher Ken Brett and outfielder Rich Coggins.

19

1891 — George Clark B (P 1913)

1928 — Gilbert (Gil) McDougald B (INF, 1B 1951-60)

1960 — Yankees re-obtain outfielder Bob Cerv from the Athletics for infielder Andy Carey.

1969 — Yankees obtain outfielder Jose Vidal from the Seattle Pilots for outfielder Dick Simpson.

20

1890 — Jesse "Jim" Buckles B (P 1916)

1893 — Walter Bernhardt B (P 1918)

1897 — Wilcy (Cy) Moore B (P 1927-29, 32-33)

1904 — Peter Appleton (also known as Peter Jablonski) B (P 1933)

1913 — Yankees obtain shortstop Roger Peckinpaugh from the Indians for shortstop Bill Stumpf and outfielder Jack Lelivelt.

1930 — Thomas "Plowboy" Morgan B (P 1951-52, 54-56)

1943 — David McDonald B (1B 1969)

1946 — Robert (Bobby) Murcer B (OF, SS, 3B, DH 1965-66, 69-74)
James (Jim) Lyttle B (OF 1969-71)

1959 — Plagued by injuries to virtually every starting player, the decimated Yankees sink into last place for the first time since May, 1940.

1969 — Yankees acquire pitcher Jack Aker from the Pilots for pitcher Fred Talbot.

1976 — Another Yankee-Red Sox brawl, this time at Yankee Stadium, and this time the pile-on produced a serious injury. Red Sox pitcher Bill Lee wound up on the bottom of the pile and seriously injured his pitching arm, an injury from which he never recovered.

The "festivities" began when Yankee outfielder Lou Piniella crashed into Red Sox catcher Carlton Fisk while trying to score from second base on a single Graig Nettles. Right fielder Dwight Evans' throw had Piniella dead out, so Piniella barreled into the catcher.

If you ask Piniella, he'll tell you that Fisk punched him first, after complaining about the collision. Fisk says Piniella kicked him and punched him first. In any event, both benches emptied, and Bill Lee claims that he was held by one Yankee while another, supposedly, Mickey Rivers, sucker-punched him. Eventually, Lee also wound up on the bottom of a pile of players, and he suffered damage of some sort to his shoulder. He has never been the same pitcher since.

Lee originally held Yankee third baseman Graig Nettles responsible for the injury, but after viewing the replay and allegedly discussing it with Nettles, made a public retraction of any accusations against Nettles. He has never forgiven Rivers, and still holds Yankee manager Billy Martin indirectly responsible, because Martin represented the "fighting" manager Lee despised.

21

1906 — Henry (Hank) Johnson B (P 1925-26, 28-32)

1912 — Lawrence (Larry) Rosenthal B (OF 1944)

1922 — Yankee owner Jacob Ruppert buys out co-owner Tillinghast Huston for $1,500,000. Huston had been unhappy since the day Ruppert had hired Miller Huggins to manage the team over Huston's objections. (Huston would have prefered Wilbert Robinson.)

1923 — Babe Ruth's 15th-inning two-run homerun gives pitcher Herb Pennock and the Yankees a 3-1 win against the White Sox. Pennock pitched all 15 innings, and allowed just 4 hits!

1941 — Robert (Bobby) Cox B (3B, 2B 1968-69, coach 1969-76)

1948 — Joe DiMaggio's two homeruns, triple, double, and single pace the Yankees' 22-hit attack in a 13-2 victory against the White Sox.

22

1930 — Babe Ruth hits three consecutive homeruns in one game for the first time in his career, but foolishly bats righthanded in his fourth at-bat against right-hander Jack Quinn and strikes out, thereby costing himself an opportunity to become the first player to hit four consecutive homeruns in one game. Ruth's final at-bat came in the ninth inning. After the first two called strikes, Ruth switched back to his normal left-handed stance, but he swung at the next pitch and struck out.

1946 — The Yankees turn a triple play during a 5-3 win in Detroit. The Tigers had runners on first and third when Dick Wakefield hit a ground ball to Yankee first baseman Nick Etten. Etten threw home to get the lead runner. Catcher Bill Dickey chased that lead runner back towards third, and then threw to third baseman Snuffy Stirnweiss, who made the tag. Meanwhile, the runner on first base had foolishly strayed beyond second base, apparently undecided whether or not to attempt to advance to third during the rundown. A throw to shortstop Phil Rizzuto trapped this runner between second and third, and Rizzuto eventually tagged him out. During this rundown, Wakefield attempted to reach second base, and Rizzuto's quick flip to second baseman Joe Gordon completed the triple play.

1947 — Richard "Rich" Hinton B (P 1972)

1953 — Irv Noren gains the dubious distinction of becoming the most recent Yankee to hit into a triple play when he lines back to pitcher Bob Porterfield during New York's 12-4 loss to the Senators. Noren actually hit the ball as hard as he could — the force of the blow knocked Porterfield down when he caught the ball. The runners on first and second were off with the pitch, so Porterfield had time to regain his feet, fire to first base for the second out, and still allow time for the first baseman (Mickey Vernon) to throw to second baseman Pete Runnels in time to nail the runner sliding back to the bag.

1962 — Four Yankee pitchers (Whitey Ford, Jim Coates, Bud Daley, and Bob Turley) combine for a 12-inning one-hitter as the Yankees defeat the Angels, 2-1. Coates yielded the only safety, a ninth inning single by Bob Rogers with one out. Ford was the starter, but had to leave after the seventh inning because of back pains.

Yankee outfielder Roger Maris set a record by drawing four intentional walks, and tied a record by drawing five walks in nine innings.

1963 — Mickey Mantle unloads another "space shot" homerun off the facade in right field in Yankee Stadium. The victim was Kansas City hurler Bill Fischer. Experts estimated that the ball would have traveled 620 feet if left unobstructed. It struck the facade less than six feet below the roof.

No major league player has ever hit a fair ball out of Yankee Stadium. In fact, the only player to come close has been Mantle, on at least two occasions. Mantle later called this shot the hardest ball he ever hit.

There are unconfirmed reports that Negro League star Josh Gibson once drove a ball over the rear retaining wall behind the bleachers in left center field. That shot would have cleared the Stadium, but to reach that distance it would have had to travel some 800 feet — little wonder why this report is unconfirmed at best.

1970 — Yankee pitcher Mel Stottlemyre hurls eight-and-one-third innings of scoreless baseball, and sets a major league record by walking 11 batters. Stott also threw two wild pitches, and needed flawless relief help from Steve Hamilton, who came on with the bases loaded and one out in the ninth inning. Final score: New York 2, Washington 0.

1977 — After three straight losses to the Orioles, the Yankees turn the starting assignment in the second game of a doubleheader over to Ron Guidry, and Guidry responded with an 8-2, 4-hit victory.

23

1921 — William "Dutch" Drescher B (C 1944-46)

1946 — Joe DiMaggio, Nick Etten and Joe Gordon hit consecutive homeruns during New York's eight-run fifth inning against the Tigers. Virgil Trucks surrendered the first two shots. Reliever Hale White gave up Gordon's blow. New York won, 12-6.

1948 — Joe DiMaggio hits three consecutive homeruns during New York's 6-5 victory against the Indians in the first game of a doubleheader at Cleveland. The first two shots came at the expense of Hall-of-Famer Bob Feller. The final blow came off reliever Bob Muncreif, and proved the game-winner.

The Indians rebounded with a 5-1 win in the nightcap.

1960 — Yankees release outfielder Elmer Valo.

1962 — Rookie Joe Pepitone hits two homeruns in the Yankees' nine-run 8th inning against the Athletics, and thereby becomes the only Yankee other than Joe DiMaggio to hit two homeruns in one inning. Pepitone led off the inning with a homerun off starter Dan Pfister, and later hit a three-run homerun off reliever John Wyatt. Rookie Phil Linz also homered — his first major league hit — as the Yankees beat KC, 13-7.

24

1876 — Frederick (Fred) Jacklitsch B (C 1905)

1900 — Allan Shealy B (P 1928)

1918 — Pitcher Joe Wood's 19th-inning homerun leads the Indians to a 3-2 win over New York, and spoils a heroic pitching performance by Stan Coveleski, who had hurled all 19 innings and yielded just 12 hits.

1926 — Guillermo "Willie" Miranda B (INF 1954)

1936 — Tony Lazzeri drives in 11 runs in one game, and Ben Chapman sets the modern major league record by reaching first base safely 7 times in a nine inning game, during New York's 25-2 win over the Athletics. Lazzeri hit two grand slam homeruns, a solo homerun, and a two-run triple. Chapman hit two doubles and drew five walks.

Frank Crosetti hit two homeruns, and Joe DiMaggio also homered in this wild affair.

1937 — Tiger Hall-of-Famer Mickey Cochran's career is brought to a jarring premature end when he is struck in the side of the head by a Bump Hadley fastball at Yankee Stadium. Cochrane suffered a bad concussion and probable fracture, and never really came back.

40

1946 — Eliseo "Ellie" Rodriguez B (C 1968)

1946 — Yankee manager Joe McCarthy suddenly resigns for reasons he took with him to his grave. There were persistent rumors that he and new owner Larry MacPhail never got along, but these were never confirmed. McCarthy told the press the resignation was for health and personal reasons, and because he needed a rest. No one will ever know for sure.

Bill Dickey was named the interim replacement.

1977 — Graig Nettles and Carlos May slam back-to-back homeruns in the seventh inning during New York's 6-5, come-from-behind win at Boston.

25

1974 — Yankees obtain pitcher Larry Gura from the Rangers for catcher Duke Sims.

26

1928 — The Athletics kick in with 7 errors to lift the Yankees to a 7-4 win.

1952 — Yankees release outfielder Johnny Hopp.

1959 — Yankees obtain pitcher Ralph Terry and infielder- outfielder Hector Lopez from the Athletics for pitchers Johnny Kucks and Tom Sturdivant, and infielder Jerry Lumpe.

1971 — Yankees obtain pitcher Rob Gardner from the A's for first baseman Curt Blefary.

27

1914 — Yankees sell pitcher Guy Cooper to the Red Sox for an undisclosed amount of cash.

1933 — The Yankees score 12 runs in the eighth inning to down the White Sox, 15-11. The Yankees entered the inning trailing 11-3, and had been unable to do much with White Sox hurler Ted Lyons. Ben Chapman led off with a single. Tony Lazzeri and Bill Dickey walked. Frank Crosetti singled in one run. Red Ruffing, in a pinch-hitting role, singled in another run, and Earle Combs walked to force in a run and knock Lyons out of the game.

Reliever Jake Miller yielded a run-scoring single to Joe Sewell, a two-run single to Babe Ruth, and a run-scoring double to Lou Gehrig, before leaving in favor of Ed Durham.

Durham walked Chapman intentionally, loading the bases in hopes of getting a double play, but Lazzeri singled in the tying run, and Dickey followed with a game-winning grand slam homerun.

1946 — The Senators edge the Yankees, 2-1, in the first night game ever played at Yankee Stadium. Some 49,917 fans were attracted to the nocturnal outing, making quite clear the value of night games over day affairs, especially on weeknights.

1956 — Yankees waive pitcher Gerry Staley to the White Sox.

1960 — Yankee manager Casey Stengel is hospitalized with a virus, forcing Ralph Houk to take over the helm for 13 games. Houk made several changes which were retained when Stengel returned, including the insertion of Clete Boyer at third base, which clearly helped New York rally from third place to win the pennant.

The other changes: moving third baseman Hector Lopez from third base to left field, and letting Johnny Blanchard do some of the catching.

By the way, the team went 7-6 under Houk.

1971 — Yankees obtain pitcher Jim Hardin from the Orioles for pitcher Bill Burbach.

1977 — Ron Guidry has a rare bad outing, dropping a 9-4, 16-hit loss to the White Sox before a Jacket Day crowd of 54,881 at Yankee Stadium.

1875 — David (Dave) Fultz B (OF, 3B 1903-05)

1941 — John Kennedy B (INF 1967)

1977 — Pitcher Ed Figueroa wins his seventh consecutive complete game, beating Chicago, 5-2. First baseman Chris Chambliss supplied most of the support with a two-run homerun and a rare steal of home plate in the eighth inning.

1884 — Rueben (Rube) Oldring B (SS 1905)

1894 — Albert (Al) Mamaux B (P 1924)

1902 — Louis McEvoy B (P 1931)

1912 — After a minor fire at Hilltop Park, the Yankees play a separate admission, day-night doubleheader versus the Athletics at the Polo Grounds. New York lost the morning game, 7-1. The second game was rained out.

1913 — Yankees purchase second baseman Bill McKechnie from the Braves for an undisclosed amount.

1930 — Yankees obtain pitcher Owen Carroll, shortstop George Weustling and outfielder Harry Rice from the Tigers for pitcher Waite Hoyt and shortstop Mark Koenig.

1938 — 81,841 fans jam Yankee Stadium for a doubleheader with the Red Sox, and watch New York sweep the Sox, 10-0 and 5-4. This date also featured the infamous battle between Yankee outfielder Jake Powell and Boston player-manager Joe Cronin.

First, a word about the crowd. Contemporary reports listed the crowd at 83,533, with some 511 additional fans receiving refunds because they could not find a standing room location from which they could see the game. Another 6,000 fans were reported to be outside, clamoring for tickets which simply did not exist.

As for the fight, the festivities began when Powell charged the pitcher's mound after reliever Archie McKain had thrown two pitches at his body, the latter of which hit Powell in the stomach. Cronin, playing shortstop at the time, came charging in to protect his pitcher, intercepted Powell short of the mound, and landed a right to Powell's face. The two engaged in a wild punch-a-thon for two or three minutes before the umpires were able to separate the combatants.

Cronin and Powell were both ejected from the game. In those days, the only approach to the visitors' clubhouse was through the Yankee dugout. When Cronin passed through the dugout, Powell and several Yankees followed. When the Red Sox players saw what was happening, they followed their manager off the field, with most of the remaining Yankees going with them. The umpires were right behind the players.

When all parties reached the area under the stands, Powell and Cronin were discovered wailing away at each other. Cronin came out on the short end of the fight, largely thanks to the numerous scratches he received while the Yankees "separated" the combatants.

Both players were fined and suspended for 10 days for their actions.

1977 — Graig Nettles and Reggie Jackson hit back-to-back homeruns in the second inning to lead New York to a 5-4 win against the Red Sox.

31

1913 — Yankees obtain infielder Rollie Zeider and first baseman Bill Borton from the White Sox for first baseman Hal Chase.

1932 — Yankees obtain pitcher Dan MacFayden from the Red Sox for an undisclosed amount of cash and other considerations.

1933 — Yankees sign free agent pitcher John Broaca.

1938 — Yankee pitcher Joe Beggs surrenders the first of three grand slam homeruns Hall-of-Famer Jimmy Foxx would hit him off in the 1938 season.

1950 — Felix "Tippy" Martinez B (P 1974-76)

1956 — Mickey Mantle unleashes the first of several "space shots" in an "attempt" to clear the roof in right field at Yankee Stadium. This shot, a three-run homerun off a Pedro Ramos change-up palm ball, struck the facade in right field, less than 18 inches from the top. (See the note on

May 22, 1963 for further information about alleged homeruns which cleared the Stadium roof.)

JUNE

1

1891 — Henry (Hank) Severeid B (C 1926)

1914 — Yankees purchase outfielder Fritz Meara from Reading for an undisclosed amount of cash.

1915 — Arthur (Art) Metheny B (OF 1943-46)

1918 — With the score 5-4 in favor of the Yankees, and the bases loaded with Tigers, the Yankees turn a game-saving triple play when Detroit's Chick Gandil lines a shot down the left field line which is speared by Frank Baker. The third baseman regained his feet, threw to Del Pratt at second for an out, and the play was completed when Pratt threw on to Wally Pipp at first base.

1925 — First baseman Wally Pipp picks the wrong time and place to come down with a headache. His replacement, Lou Gehrig, never relinquished the spot until illness forced his retirement in 1939. Gehrig's streak was 2,130 games, a record.

1931 — Marshall "Sheriff" Bridges B (P 1962-63)

1932 — Louis "The Nervous Greek" Skizas B (OF 1956)

1933 — Gerald "Jerry" Lumpe B (INF 1956-59)

1934 — Yankees release pitcher George Uhle.

1935 — In a rare display of homeruns with the bases empty, the Yankees hit six solo shots during a 7-2 win against the Red Sox, at Yankee Stadium, and thereby set the record for most homeruns with no one on base in one game. The homeruns hitters were: Bill Dickey 2, Frank Crosetti, Ben Chapman, George Selkirk, and Red Rolfe. To add to the Red Sox' misery, Tony Lazzeri just missed a homerun in the seventh inning when outfielder Roy Johnson robbed Lazzeri with a circus catch in front of the right field bullpen. New York's seventh run scored on a single by Chapman, an errant throw back to the infield, and a single by Gehrig.

By the way, the Sox' two runs came on a two-run homerun by Mel Almeda in the eighth inning.

1936 — The Yankees score seven runs in the bottom of the first inning, but wind up on the short end of an 11-9 score, during a game against the White Sox at Yankee Stadium.

1938 — Eugene (Gene) "Stick" Michael B (INF 1968-73, coach 1975-78)

1940 — Horace "Hoss" Clarke B (INF 1965-73)

44

1941 — Lou Gehrig succumbs to a rare form of polio known as amyotrophic lateral sclerosis. He was 37-years-old.

3

1929 — Yankees release first baseman George "Tioga" Burns.

1932 — Lou Gehrig slams four consecutive homeruns during New York's 20-13 victory versus the Athletics, and thereby set the major league record for homeruns by one player in one game, and homeruns in consecutive at-bats.

1933 — After yielding 11 runs to the Athletics in the second inning, the Yankees rebound with 10 runs of their own in the fifth inning and go on to outslug Philadelphia, 17-11.

The Yankees entered the fifth trailing 11-4. Tony Lazzeri led off with a homerun off starter Gowell Claset. Art Jorgens, Frank Crosetti, and Earle Combs each singled. The mildly shaken infield responded with a pair of errors, allowing two runs to score, and kayoing Claset.

Reliever Jim Peterson came on, and walked Babe Ruth to load the bases. Lou Gehrig singled in two runs, and Ben Chapman followed with a three-run homerun.

Connie Mack summoned a third reliever, Tony Freitas, and he gave up hits to Lazzeri, Jorgens, and Crosetti, good for two more runs, before finally ending the inning.

Also of note: the Yankees' third relief pitcher, Walter Brown, came on in the second inning with two outs, and finished the final six-and-one-third innings, striking out 12 Athletics.

With all that Yankee run production, it seemed only proper when Ruth added a three-run homerun in the eighth inning to complete New York's scoring.

1968 — The Yankees turn the 21st triple play in their history, but lose to the Twins, 4-3. With the bases loaded, and the go-ahead run already across the plate, Dooley Womack faced veteran Twins' catcher John Roseboro. The hitter lined a shot right back at Womack, who made the catch, threw to Bobby Cox at third base, and then watched in awe when Cox's throw to Mantle at first base was in time to complete the triple play.

1972 — The Yankees score 8 runs in the 13th inning, six of which scored on three-run homeruns by Thurman Munson and Bobby Murcer, to down the ChiSox, 18-10. Murcer had 4 hits on the day, scored five runs, and had three runs batted in.

There was one other unusual happening: Yankee relief pitcher Sparky Lyle actually hit a double.

4

1885 — Robert (Bobby) Vaughn B (2B, SS 1909)

45

1889 — Leo "Lee" Magee B (OF, 2B, 1B 1916-17)

1928 — Gordon (Billy) Hunter B (SS, 3B 1955-56)

1933 — Yankee pitcher Johnny Allen's no-hit bid is spoiled in the first inning on Ed Coleman's single. Allen did not allow another hit in pitching the Yankees to a 6-0 win against the Athletics.

1939 — Phillip (Phil) "Supersub" Linz B (INF, OF 1962-65)

1977 — Reggie Jackson hits a pair of run-scoring doubles to highlight a seven-run second inning in New York's 8-6 victory against Chicago. Don Gullett was the winner. Sparky Lyle notched his 10th save.

5

1874 — John "Happy Jack" Chesbro B (P 1903-09)

1878 — Frederick (Fred) Mitchell B (C 1910)

1891 — James "Truck" Hannah B (C, 1B 1918-20)

1926 — The Cleveland Indians add insult to injury by turning a triple play against the Yankees during Cleveland's 15-3 win.

1932 — Yankees obtain pitcher Dan MacFayden from the Red Sox for pitchers Ivy Andrews and Henry Johnson, and $50,000.

1941 — Duane "Duke" Sims B (C, OF 1973-74)

1977 — Carlos May, Bucky Dent, Thurman Munson, Reggie Jackson, Graig Nettles and rookie George Zeber each hit a homerun during New York's 8-6 win against the White Sox. The six homeruns were the most the Yankees hit in one game in three years. Zeber's shot was his first in the big leagues, and proved to be the gamewinner.

6

1887 — Delmar (Del) Paddock B (3B, 2B, OF 1912)

1907 — William (Bill) Dickey B (C 1928-46)

1931 — The Yankees turn a triple play, but lose to the Indians, 7-5.

1934 — Yankee outfielder Myril Hoag strokes six singles in six at-bats (a major league record for a nine-inning game) during New York's 15-3 win against Boston. Hoag scored three runs and drove in one.

All that hitting moved Hoag up from the seventh slot in the batting order in Game I to the third spot in Game II. Hoag responded by going 1-for-5 in a 7-4 loss . . . but at least that one hit was a single, too!

1937 — Red Ruffing's pinch-hit homerun leads the Yankees to a 6-5 win against the Tigers. Ruffing, the ace pitcher on the Yankee staff, was also a dangerous hitter, and frequently got the call when the Yankees needed an extra bat off the bench. He hit .269 lifetime, including .254 as a pinch hitter (58 pinch hits in 228 pinch at-bats). Ruffing also hit 36 career homeruns.

1949 — James (Jim) Deidel B (C 1974)

1953 — David (Dave) Bergman B (OF, 1B 1975, 77)

1965 — Tom Tresh hits three consecutive homeruns in the second game of a doubleheader with the White Sox, to lead New York to a 12-0 win. Tresh's first shot came with the bases empty in the first inning, off starter Juan Pizzaro. He added a two-run shot in the third inning, off reliever Bruce Howard, and hit another solo shot off Howard in the fifth. New York also won the opener, 6-1.

1965 — Yankees claim shortstop Bill Bethea on waivers from the Twins.

1972 — Yankees obtain pitcher Wade Blasingame from the Astros for a player to be named later.

1977 — Catfish Hunter comes off the disabled list and pitches a six-hit complete game victory against the Rangers, 9-2. Reggie Jackson hit his 10th and 11th homeruns.

7

1900 — Edwin (Ed) Wells B (P 1929-32)

1911 — Ralph "Buck" Buxton B (P 1949)

1913 — The Yankees end a 13-game winless streak (12 losses, one tie) by edging Chicago, 3-2. It was the club's longest winless streak ever.

1936 — The Yankees and Indians combine to set a major league record by playing 16 innings of baseball with no player on either team striking out. The game lasted close to four hours, and ended when George Selkirk hit a homerun off Cleveland starter Oral Hildebrand to give New York a 5-4 win. Red Ruffing pitched all 16 innings for New York, scattering 10 hits.

1947 — Thurman Munson B (C, OF, DH 1969-current)

1971 — Yankees obtain outfielder Danny Walton from the Brewers for infielder-outfielder Mike Tepedino and outfielder Bobby Mitchell.

1973 — In separate transactions, the Yankees purchase pitcher Sam McDowell from the Giants for $100,000; and obtain pitcher Pat Dobson from Atlanta for first baseman Wayne Nordhagen, outfielder Frank Tepedino, and two players to be named later.

8

1927 — Tony Lazzeri hits three homeruns during New York's come-from-behind win against Chicago, 12-11, in 11 innings. Lazzeri hit two homeruns off starter Red Faber, and hit a game-tying two-run homerun in the ninth inning off reliever George Connally.

The Yankees trailed, 11-6, entering the bottom of the ninth inning. They scored three runs before Lazzeri came to bat, and Lazzeri's game-tier was a line drive that landed less than two feet to the fair side of the foul pole in right field.

New York won the game in the 11th when Cedric Durst led off with a triple, Lazzeri was intentionally walked, and Ray Morehart singled.

1941 — Yankee catcher Bill Dickey makes an unassisted double play in the first game of a doubleheader with the Browns, and thereby ties the major league record for unassisted doubleplays in one game by a catcher.

With the runner on first (John Beradino) running on the pitch, Browns batter Bob Swift lifted a pop foul up the first base line. Dickey made the catch, and upon noticing that Bernadino had not headed back to first base, continued on to the bag to make the second putout. New York swept the doubleheader, 9-3, 8-3.

1942 — Yankees obtain pitcher Bill Trotter and outfielder Roy Cullenbine from the Browns for pitcher Steve Sundra and outfielder Mike Chartak.

1969 — Mickey Mantle Day at Yankee Stadium. The Yankees officially retire Mantle's uniform number 7, and the "Greatest Living Player in Baseball History," Joe DiMaggio, is on hand to present a plaque to Mantle, which now hangs on the center field wall.

When Mantle finally got to the microphone, his "final task" was to present a similar plaque to DiMaggio, who knew nothing about it. All the Yankee Clipper could say was "I'm out there in great company."

Mantle followed with a short, heart-warming speech, which reflected on the late Lou Gehrig's statement that he (Gehrig) was "the luckiest man on the face of the earth." Mantle said "I've often wondered how a man who knew he was going to die could stand here and say he was the luckiest man on the face of the earth, but now I guess I know how Lou Gehrig felt." It left the fans silent for about 30 seconds, and then the 60,096 voices let loose with a thundering ovation.

With all that emotion in the air, the Yankees came through with a 3-1, 11-2 sweep of the visiting White Sox.

1977 — Mike Torrez's five-hit, 9-2 victory against the Brewers vaults the Yankees into first place for the first time since May 20.

9

1931 — William (Bill) Virdon (Mgr. 1974-75)

1946 — The Yankees draw 66,545 fans for their doubleheader with the Cleveland Indians in New York, and thereby break the 1,000,000-mark in home attendance on the earliest date in major league history. The teams split, with New York dropping the opener, 9-5, but winning the nightcap, 7-4.

1969 — Yankees purchase pitcher Ken Johnson from Atlanta for an undisclosed amount of cash.

1977 — Bucky Dent's three hits highlight New York's 10-1 win at Milwaukee, as Don Gullett wins his fifth.

10

1870 — Patrick (Pat) McCauley B (C 1903)

1892 — Frank "Flash" Gilhooley B (OF 1913-18)

1894 — Frederick (Fred) "Bootnose" Hofman B (OF 1916)

1903 — Yankees obtain shortstop Kid Elberfeld from the Tigers for shortstops Herm Long and Ernie Courtney.

1905 — Daniel "Deacon Danny" MacFayden B (P 1932-34)

1921 — Babe Ruth hits the 120th homerun of his career off Indians' pitcher Jim Bagby in the third inning during New York's 8-6 loss. The homerun broke the recognized career mark held by Gavvy Cravath, who hit 119 with the Red Sox, White Sox, and Phillies during his 11-year career.

1966 — Yankees obtain pitcher Fred Talbot from the Athletics for outfielder Roger Repoz and pitchers Gil Blanco and Bill Stafford.

1977 — Pitcher Ron Guidry does it again, stopping the Twins, 4-1, with ninth inning relief help courtesy of Sparky Lyle. The key hit: a two-run double by Willie Randolph.

11

1886 — Claud "Deek" Derrick B (INF 1913)

1927 — After Babe Ruth hits two consecutive homeruns, Indians' catcher Luke Sewell demands that the umpires inspect Ruth's bat. The bat was ruled legal, but the commotion created gave the Cleveland crowd a thrill, exceeded only by Ruth striking out in his third at-bat.

1961 — Roger Maris hits his 20th homerun of the season in route to the magic 61.

12

1907 — Yankees commit 11 errors in their 14-6 loss to the Tigers. The errant Highlanders were: Elberfeld (ss) 4, Chase (1b), LaPorte (3b), Williams (2b), Moriarty (2b), Conroy (lf), Orth (p) and Hogg (p).

After the game, Highlanders' Manager Clark Griffith assaulted a spectator, a merchant named Mr. Frank, and was charged with assault. Griffith argued self defense and was merely fined.

1938 — Yankees score seven runs in the sixth inning to come-from-behind and defeat the Indians, 7-6.

1945 — Gary Jones B (P 1970-71)

1953 — Yankees obtain infielder Willie Miranda from the Browns for an amount greater than the waiver price.

1962 — Yankees obtain outfielder Tom Umphlett and an undisclosed amount of cash from the Red Sox for infielder Billy Gardner.

1969 — Yankees obtain pitcher Rob Gardner from the A's for John Orsino.

1973 — Yankees obtain pitcher Lowell Palmer from the Indians for pitcher Mike Kekich. Kekich's days were numbered after he and Fritz Peterson announced their wife swap prior to the 1973 season.

13

1913 — The Yankees notch their 13th win of the season at this incredibly late date. They had already lost 36.

1921 — Babe Ruth is the Yankee pitcher for the first five innings, allows four runs, strikes out Ty Cobb, and hits two homeruns to lead the Yankees to an 11-8 win. New York held the lead all game long, so Ruth was the winning pitcher.

Ruth's second homerun traveled more than 460-feet and landed in the right center field bleachers in the Polo Grounds. The homerun was acclaimed as the longest homerun in baseball history up to that date.

1924 — A riot by a frenzied crowd of 18,000 Detroit fans forces the forfeiture of a game to the visiting Yankees. The histrionics began after Yankee outfielder Bob Meusel was hit by a pitch thrown by Bert Cole. Meusel charged the mound, swung at Cole, missed, but precipitated a bench-clearing brawl. During the "festivities," Babe Ruth and Ty Cobb got into a little tilt of their own, including the "exchange of numerous vile epithets."

Meusel and Ruth were both ejected. When the pair went out to get their gloves, the fans poured onto the field. Meusel and Cole received 10-day suspensions. Ruth and Meusel were fined $1,000 each. Cobb received a formal reprimand.

By the way, the Yankees led, 10-6, prior to the brawl, subsequent entry on to the field by the fans, and resultant forfeiture when order could not be restored.

1937 — Joe DiMaggio hits three consecutive homeruns in the nightcap of a doubleheader with the Browns. The game ended in an 8-8 tie, called because of darkness, but pursuant to the rules of the game, all records in the tie game count.

In the opener, New York scored seven runs in the top of the ninth inning to break a 9-9 tie and win, 16-9.

1939 — Yankees obtain infielder Roy Hughes from the St. Louis Browns for outfielder Joe Gallagher.

1948 — Babe Ruth's uniform is retired prior to the Yankees 5-3 win against the Indians. It proved to be his final appearance at Yankee Stadium.

1975 — Yankees purchase shortstop Ed Brinkman from the Tigers for an undisclosed amount of cash.

1978 — Roy White hits a homerun from each side of the plate during New York's 5-3 win against the A's. It was the fifth time in the switch hitter's career that he had accomplished this.

14

1925 — Fenton "Muscles" Mole B (1B, 1949)

1932 — The Yankees pull a rare triple steal, led by Ben Chapman on third base, during the Yankees' 7-6 win against the Indians. The Yankees had the bases loaded when Chapman broke for the plate, and the other runners also moved up.

1934 — John Broaca allows just one hit, a third inning single by Browns outfielder Sammy West, during the Yankees' 7-0 win at St. Louis.

1936 — Yankees obtain outfielder Al "Jake" Powell from the Senators for outfielder Ben Chapman.

1946 — Yankees sell third baseman Hank Majeski to the Athletics for an undisclosed amount of cash.

1953 — The Yankees sweep the Indians, 6-2, 3-0, before 74,708 fans to extend their winning streak to 18 games.

1956 — Yankees obtain pitcher Ed Burtschy, outfielder Bill Renna, and an undisclosed amount of cash from the Athletics for outfielder Lou Skizas and first baseman Eddie Robinson.

1961 — Yankees obtain pitcher Bud Daley from the Athletics for pitcher Art Ditmar and outfielder Deron Johnson.

In a separate transaction, the Yankees obtain infielder Billy Gardner from the Twins for pitcher Dan McDevitt.

1977 — Don Gullett wins his fifth straight start as the Yankees come-from-behind to down the Twins, 6-5.

1978 — The Yankees repeatedly rally to defeat the Mariners, 10-9, in 10 innings. New York trailed into the eighth inning, when Cliff Johnson pinch hit a homerun to tie the game. The Yankees then spotted the Mariners an extra-inning lead before Paul Blair hit a two-out, three-run homerun in the tenth inning to give New York a desperately needed win.

15

1912 — Ellsworth "Babe" Dahlgren B (1B 1937-40)

1916 — Edward "Bud" Stewart B (OF 1948)

1923 — Alfred "Allie" Clark B (OF 1947)

1926 — Yankees obtain outfielder Roy Carlyle on waivers from the Red Sox.

1935 — The Reds return pitcher Dan MacFayden to the Yankees upon the expiration of the "try-out" period allowed for in the deal which sent

51

him to Cincinnati in 1934. The Yankees immediately sold him to the Browns for an undisclosed amount of cash.

1943 — Allan (Al) Closter B (P 1971-72)

1950 — Yankees obtain pitchers Joe Ostrowski, Tom Ferrick, and Sid Schact, and third baseman Leo Thomas, from the Browns for infielder Snuffy Stirnweiss, outfielder Jim Delsing, pitchers Don Johnson and Duane Pillette, and $50,000.

1951 — Yankees obtain pitchers Bob Kuzava and Bob Ross from the Senators for pitchers Fred Sanford, Bob Porterfield, and Tom Ferrick.

In a separate transaction, the Yankees also obtain pitcher Stubby Overmire from the Browns for pitcher Tommy Byrne and $25,000.

1957 — Yankees obtain pitcher Ryne Duren and outfielders Jim Pisoni and Harry Simpson from the Athletics for pitcher Ralph Terry, infielders Billy Martin and Woodie Held, and outfielder Bob Martyn. This trade broke Casey Stengel's heart because the late, great manager of the Yankees loved Martin as if "Billy the Brat" were his own son.

1958 — Yankees obtain pitchers Virgil Trucks and Duke Maas from the Athletics for pitcher Bob Grim and outfielder Harry Simpson.

1966 — Yankees sell pitcher Bob Friend to the Mets for an undisclosed amount of cash.

1968 — Yankees sign outfielder Rocky Colavito after his release by the Dodgers, and sell pitcher John Wyatt to the Tigers for approximately $30,000.

1974 — Yankees purchase pitcher Rudy May from the Angels for an amount believed to be between $75,000 — $100,000.

1976 — Yankees obtain pitchers Ken Holtzman, Doyle Alexander, and Grant Jackson, catcher Elrod Hendricks, and minor leaguer Jim Freeman from the Orioles for pitchers Rudy May, Tippy Martinez, Dave Pagan, and Scott MacGregor, and catcher Rick Dempsey.

1977 — Yankees obtain catcher-first baseman-designated hitter Cliff Johnson from the Astros for minor leaguers Randy Neimann, Mike Fischlin and Dave Bergman.

16

1882 — Robert (Bob) Keefe B (P 1907)

1903 — The Yankees register their first shutout victory ever, 1-0 against Chicago, with Clark Griffith the winning pitcher. (Of course, it was actually the Highlanders' first shutout win.)

1925 — Yankees sign first baseman Fred Merkle after his release by the Cubs.

1933 — Kenneth (Ken) Johnson B (P 1969)

1950 — Yankees waive catcher Gus Niarhos to the White Sox.

1953 — Johnny Mize notches the 2000 hit of his career, a fifth inning run-scoring single off Browns pitcher Duane Pillette. It was the only run New York scored during a 3-1 loss which ended the Yankees' 18-game winning streak.

1977 — Remarkable Ron Guidry hurls his first complete game (a shutout, no less) and defeats the Royals, 7-0.

17

1903 — Benjamin "Big Ben" Shields B (P 1924-25)

1918 — Yankees play an eight inning 5-5 tie with the Tigers, called because New York had to catch a train to Cleveland.

1936 — Red Ruffing hits two singles and two homeruns in the first game of a doubleheader with the Indians. He also pitched the complete game, a 15-4 win, and allowed 13 hits. The Yankees won the nightcap, 12-2.

1977 — The Yankees open a three game series in Boston, and do it in a disastrous manner, as starter Catfish Hunter is raked for first inning homeruns by Rick Burleson, Fred Lynn, Carlton Fisk and George Scott in route to an 11-1 loss.

1978 — Ron Guidry sets a new Yankee strikout record by "K"-ing 18 Angels in nine innings, one short of the major league record held by Tom Seaver and Nolan Ryan. Guidry had a solid shot at the record — he had 15 strikeouts after six innings, but missed. (See the 1978 section.)

18

1916 — The Yankees score in every inning, except the eighth, and trounce the Indians, 19-3.

1946 — Yankees waive pitcher Bill Zuber to the Red Sox.

1977 — The infamous "Billy Martin — Reggie Jackson Incident" in Boston proves to be the low point in the Yankees '77 season. With the Yankees trailing 7-4 in the bottom of the sixth inning, Yankee rightfielder Jackson appeared to "loaf" after a bloop hit by Jim Rice, and, in the opinion of Martin, allowed Rice to turn a single into a double. Martin left the Yankee dugout, made a stop at the pitcher's mound to remove starter Mike Torrez from the game, and then headed out to right field to remove Jackson as well.

After a brief argument on the field, the pair returned to the dugout, where seconds later Martin had to be physically restrained from attacking Jackson. The Yankees eventually lost the game, 10-4, and appeared ready to explode into a civil war. Fortunately for Yankee fans, cooler heads prevailed, and the team turned it all around less than a week later.

1903 — Henry "Lou" Gehrig B (1B, SS 1925-39)

1904 — Yankees obtain outfielder Pat Dougherty from the Red Sox for infielder Bob Unglaub.

1913 — Yankees waive pitcher Ed Klepfer to the Giants.

1918 — Yankees purchase outfielder Ham Hyatt from the Braves for an undisclosed amount.

1949 — Eugene (Gene) Locklear B (OF 1976-77)

1950 — Jose "Fernando" Gonzalez B (INF 1974)

1975 — Rich Coggins purchased from the Expos for an undisclosed amount.

1977 — The Yankee pitching staff unwittingly aids the Red Sox in establishing a major league record by surrendering five more homeruns to Boston in an 11-1 loss at Fenway Park. When combined with the six homeruns Boston hit on the 17th, and the five on the 18th (both against New York), the Sox hit 16 homeruns in three games, a record. Worst of all, the Yankees went homerun-less for the series.

20

1908 — William (Billy) Werber B (INF 1930-33)

1913 — Three of the first four Yankee batters are hit by pitches thrown by Washington's Bert Gallia in the first inning of the second game of a doubleheader. A total of six Yankees were similarly "brutalized" during the game, the major league record. Relievers Joe Engel (2) and Tom Hughes (1) supplied the other blows. New York swept the games, 9-3, 9-3.

In a side note, Yankee outfielder Bert Daniels set an American League record by getting hit by pitches three times that day. He was hit in the first game of the doubleheader, and twice more in the second affair.

1918 — Yankees purchase pitcher John Robinson from the Browns for an undisclosed amount of cash.

1928 — Arthur (Art) "Dutch" Schult B (PR 1953)

1934 — Red Ruffing yields one hit, a fifth inning single by Hal Trosky, en route to a 3-0 victory against the Indians.

1939 — Yankees re-obtain pitcher Jim DeShong on waivers from the Senators.

1940 — The Yankees-White Sox game, won by the Sox in 11 innings, 1-0, is successfully protested by the Yankees and replayed on September 18.

The controversial call involved a "catch" (?) which the Yankees claimed White Sox left fielder Moose Solters had dropped. Manager McCarthy protested the game, and subsequent testimony apparently indicated that the umpire (Mr. George Quinn) had goofed.

The teams split a doubleheader on Sept. 18, and since neither game was officially designated as the replay, there is really no way of knowing what happened in the makeup.

1946 — Yankees purchase outfielder Hal Peck from the Athletics for an undisclosed amount of cash.

1950 — Joe DiMaggio gets his 2,000th career hit, an eighth inning run-scoring single off Marino Pieretti, during New York's 8-2 victory against Cleveland.

1963 — In the first Annual Mayor's Trophy Game between the Yankees and Mets, the Mets down the Yanks, 6-2, before 52,430 fans at Yankee Stadium. The profits of the game are annually turned over to the sandlot baseball programs of the City of New York.

21

1897 — Spencer Adams B (INF 1926)

1906 — Russell (Russ) "Sheriff" Van Atta B (P 1933-35)

1916 — George Foster no-hits the Yankees, 2-0, at Boston.

1918 — Edward "Steady Eddie" Lopat B (P 1948-55)

1930 — Babe Ruth hits three homeruns in one game for the first time in his regular-season career, but the Yankees lose to Philadelphia, 15-7. Ruth homered in the first inning off starter George Earnshaw, touched Earnshaw again in the third inning, and hit third homerun off Lefty Grove in the eighth inning, as the Yankees built a 6-0 lead. Unfortunately, the Athletics scored nine runs in the seventh inning.

To make matters worse, Philadelphia won the nightcap, 4-1. Ruth took no solace in the fact that his third homerun of the day was acclaimed as the longest homerun ever hit in Shibe Park. The ball landed in a back yard more than one block beyond the right field wall.

1939 — Doctors at the Mayor Clinic reveal that Lou Gehrig has amyotrophic lateral sclerosis, a rare form of polio.

1967 — A weird doubleheader split between New York and Boston up in Fenway Park. In the opener, the Yankees took a 5-2 lead in the eleventh inning, only to lose the game, 6-5. In the nightcap, New York entered the ninth inning, trailing 3-2, and came up with four runs to win, 6-3.

22

1890 — Michael "Mickey" Fitzgerald B (OF 1911)

1930 — Lou Gehrig hits three homeruns in the second game of a doubleheader with the Athletics, and Babe Ruth, who had hit two homeruns in the opener, adds another homerun, as the Yankees sweep the Athletics,

10-1, 20-13. The three homeruns in two games gave Ruth a share of the record for most homeruns in two games at that time. The three blows also gave him six homeruns in three games with Philadelphia, also a share of the record.

1936 — James (Jim) Bronstad B (P 1959)

1977 — Graig Nettles' three-run homerun, and Reggie Jackson's two-run triple, snap the Yankees' five game losing streak and create a come-from-behind victory, 12-11, at Detroit.

23

1907 — Allen "Dusty" Cooke B (OF 1930-32)

1911 — Yankee first baseman Hal Chase sets a major league record by making 21 putouts during New York's 3-2 win against the Senators.

1915 — Aaron Robinson B (C 1943, 45-47)

— The Yankees draw a major league record 16 walks in one nine inning game against Philadelphia pitcher Bruno P. Haas. It was Haas' first major league game, and he added three wild pitches to the fire he created, all of which led to a 15-0 burning of the Athletics.

1917 — Yankees purchase shortstop Aaron Ward and outfielder Howie Camp from Louisville. (There is a great deal of uncertainty concerning the terms of this trade.)

1924 — Harry "Lefty" Schaeffer B (P 1952)

1927 — Lou Gehrig hits three homeruns in the Yankees 11-4 victory against the Red Sox at Boston.

1950 — The Yankees and Tigers combine for 11 homeruns during Detroit's 10-9 win at Brigg's Stadium. A major league record five homeruns were hit in the fourth inning. (For Detroit, the 4th inning homeruns were hit by Hoot Evers; Dizzy Trout, a grand slam, to boot; Gerry Priddy; and, Vic Wertz. The Yankee shot came off the bat of Hank Bauer.)

The other homeruns were hit by Hank Bauer (his second of the game), Yogi Berra, Jerry Coleman, Joe DiMaggio, Tommy Henrich (a pinch-hit, two-run off Trout which gave New York a short-lived, 9-8 lead), and Detroit's Evers (his second of the game, a two-run, inside-the-park shot off Joe Page in the ninth inning).

24

1889 — Luther "Doc" Cooke B (OF 1913-16)

1907 — Ralston "Rollie" Hemsley B (C 1942-44)

1908 — After a 6-6 tie with Philadelphia, the Highlanders fire manager Clark Griffith and name shortstop Kid Elberfeld the interim manager.

1930 — The Yankees sweep their second consecutive doubleheader from the Athletics, 10-6, and 11-1, as Babe Ruth hits two more homeruns and thereby sets a major league record with eight homeruns in six games.

1933 — Yankees sign pitcher George Uhle after his release by the Giants.

1936 — Joe DiMaggio hits two homeruns in the fifth inning of the Yankees 18-11 victory against the White Sox, and thereby became the fifth player in baseball history to do so. DiMaggio's first shot came off starter Babe Phelps and was good for two runs. Reliever Russ Evans surrendered the latter blow, a three-run homerun. Sandwiched in between was a grand slam by Jake Powell, as the Yankees scored nine of their 10 runs that inning on homeruns.

1970 — Bobby Murcer ties Lou Gehrig's record of four consecutive homeruns during a doubleheader with the Indians at Yankee Stadium. Murcer's first four-bagger came in the ninth inning of a 7-2 loss to Sam McDowell. He hit a solo shot in the first inning of the second game (off starter Mike Paul), walked in the fourth inning, hit a two-run shot in the fifth (also off Paul), and then hit a game-tying homerun in the eighth inning off reliever Fred Lasher. New York salvaged the nightcap, 5-4, with a run in the bottom of the ninth inning.

1977 — Roy White's two-out, two-run homerun in the bottom of the ninth inning at Yankee Stadium turns what appeared to be a disastrous 5-3 loss to the Red Sox into an extra-inning affair, won by the Yankees, 6-5, in ten innings. This was the MOST important Yankee hit of the season, and was certainly the turning point of the year.

One need only consider the setting to come to such a strong conclusion. The previous weekend had been a disaster in Fenway Park, where the Yankees were blown out by the rampaging Sox. Now, the Sox, in first place by 4 games, were invading the Stadium for a MUST three-game series. The Yankees entered the ninth inning, trailing 5-3, and faced Boston's ace reliever Bill Campbell. Campbell retired the first two Yankees he faced. Willie Randolph was the Yankees' last hope, and he responded by driving a triple off the glove of Carl Yastrzemski and up the left centerfield alley.

So, all the pressure, the whole season, rested on the shoulders of the Yankees' time-honored veteran, and the popular White came through with a line drive into the seats in right field. The crowd of 54,940 went into hysteria — give or take a few thousand Sox fans.

Boston went down easily against Sparky Lyle in the top of the tenth inning, and Reggie Jackson's bases loaded single to right field gave New York a 6-5 win in the bottom of the inning.

25

1878 — John Deering B (P 1903)

1897 — Elisha "Camp" Skinner B (OF 1922)

1903 — The Yankees and White Sox battle to an 18-inning, 6-6, tie in Chicago.

1934 — Yankee pitcher John Broaca ties a major league record for futility by striking out five consecutive times in one nine inning game. Fortunately, he was able to scatter 10 Chicago hits and pitch the Yankees to a 11-2 win.

1947 — Yankees purchase infielder Lonnie Frey from the Cubs.

1962 — Jack Reed's 22nd-inning homerun gives the Yankees a 9-7 victory in the longest game in Yankee history. It proved to be Reed's only career homerun. The game lasted seven hours.

1971 — Yankees obtain outfielder Ron Swoboda from the Expos for outfielder Ron Woods.

1977 — Mike Torrez hurls a seven hitter, and Graig Nettles hits a three-run homerun off Yankee nemesis Luis Tiant, as the Yankees make it two straight over the Red Sox, 5-1, at the Stadium. The win brought the Yankees back within three games of the first place Sox.

26

1912 — Yankees sell pitcher James "Hippo" Vaughn to the Senators for an undisclosed amount of cash.

1929 — Richard (Dick) "Tut" Tettlebach B (OF 1955)

1941 — Yankee southpaw ace Marius Russo throws no-hit ball for six-and-one-third-innings before future Yankee George McQuinn spoils the no-hit bid with a homerun. It was the Browns' only hit in a 4-1 Yankee win.

1943 — William (Bill) Robinson B (OF, 1B 1967-69)

1977 — With 55,039 crazed fans on hand, the Yankees complete a three-game sweep of the Red Sox and avenge the previous week's three straight losses in Fenway. New York led, 4-1, into the top of the ninth inning, when the Red Sox tied the score, but in the bottom of the inning, the Yankees loaded the bases and Paul Blair made a loser out of Bill Campbell by bouncing a single over the head of third baseman Butch Hobson for the game-winner.

27

Nothing happened on this date.

28

1915 — Yankees purchase pitcher Bob Shawkey from the Athletics for $85,000.

1919 — Future Yankee pitching ace Carl Mays hurls complete games in both ends of a doubleheader and comes out with a split against the Yankees. Mays gave Boston a 2-0 win in the opener, but dropped the nightcap, 4-1.

1939 — The Yankees hit 13 homeruns during a doubleheader sweep in Philadelphia.

First game: Joe DiMaggio 2, Babe Dahlgren 2, Joe Gordon, Billy Dickey, George Selkirk, and Tommy Henrich. Final score: 23-2.

Second game: Gordon 2, DiMaggio, Dahlgren, and Crosetti. Final score: 10-0.

1941 — Alfonso (Al) Downing B (P 1961-69)

1941 — Frederick (Fred) Talbot B (P 1966-69)

— Leonard (Len) Boehmer B (OF 1969, 71)

— Joe DiMaggio steps out of bed in his hotel room in Boston and miraculously discovers no further pain in the ankle spur which had sidelined him since spring training. He went out to Fenway Park to rejoin the Yankees, and celebrated his return to the lineup with a homerun, as the Yankees edged the Sox, 5-4, before a record Fenway night game crowd: 36,350.

Joe Page also put on a special performance. The fine reliever enticed Sox star Ted Williams to pop out with the tying run on base in the bottom of the ninth inning.

29

1888 — Andrew "Skeeter" Shelton B (OF 1915)

— Robert (Bobby) Veach B (OF 1925)

1932 — Yankees sign pitcher Charles Devens straight out of Harvard University.

1941 — Joe DiMaggio ties and then breaks George Sisler's modern major league consecutive game hitting streak during a doubleheader with the Senators. DiMaggio doubled in the sixth inning of the first game, to extend the streak to 41, and thereby tied Sisler. Then, after going 0-for-three in Game II, he singled in the seventh inning. New York swept: 9-4, 7-5.

1947 — The Yankees begin a 19-game winning streak by defeating the Senators, 3-1.

1966 — Bobby Richardson, Mickey Mantle and Joe Pepitone hit homeruns in the third inning of a 6-5 win at Boston. Former Yankee Rollie Sheldon served up the first two homers, while reliever Lee Stange was greeted by the third four-bagger.

30

1890 — Charles "Casey" Stengel B (Mgr. 1949-60)

1908 — Red Sox Hall-of-Famer Cy Young hurls a no-hitter against the Yankees during Boston's 8-0 win.

1937 — Lefty Gomez has another no-hit bid foiled, this time on a fifth-inning homerun by Philadelphia's Ron Johnson. It was the only hit Gomez allowed in the 5-1 win.

1944 — Ronald (Ron) "Rocky" Swoboda B (OF, 1B, DH 1971-73)

1945 — Gerald "Jerry" Kenney B (INF 1967, 69-72)

1954 — Yankee pitcher Tom Morgan ties the major league record by hitting three batters with pitches in one inning, during a 5-1 loss to Boston. The third inning started innocently enough, as Morgan retired the first two Red Sox he faced easily. The next batter was Billy Goodman, and Morgan hit him on the foot with a pitch in the dirt. After an error by the shortstop, Morgan hit Ted Lepcio on the hand, and then hit Milt Bolling in the back to force in a run. The Red Sox wound up scoring three runs that inning.

For the record, New York's lone run came on a homerun by Mickey Mantle.

This game was also the final game Bobby Brown played as a Yankee. He went two-for-four, and then retired to practice medicine.

1977 — Designated hitter Cliff Johnson hits three consecutive homeruns to lead the Yankees to a crucial 11-5 win at Toronto. The win raised the Yankees' record to 42-33, and moved New York within one-half game of the first place Red Sox.

Johnson has made a career out of devastating the Blue Jays. In 1977, he hit .381 against Toronto, with six of his 12 Yankee homeruns coming at the expense of the Blue Jays' staff.

JULY

1

1915 — Yankeess purchase pitcher Dan Tipple from Indianapolis for an undisclosed amount of cash.

1938 — Yankee catcher Bill Dickey drives in seven runs during New York's 8-0 win against the Senators. Dickey hit a three-run homerun in the fourth inning off starter Harry Kelley, and added a grand slam homerun in the fifth (also off Kelley). The Yankees eighth run came on a homerun by Frank Crosetti . . . but at least the Senators had the sense to remove Kelley in favor of Elon Hogsett.

1941 — Joe DiMaggio ties Willie Keeler's all-time major league record 44 consecutive game hitting streak when he singles in the fourth inning off Red Sox hurler Jack Wilson in the second game of a doubleheader in New York. The Yankees swept, 7-2, 9-2.

1952 — Kerry Dineen B (OF 1975-76)

2

1938 — Harold (Hal) Reniff B (P 1961-67)

1941 — Joe DiMaggio shatters Willie Keeler's major league record 44 consecutive game hitting streak. DiMaggio's historic hit came in the fifth inning, and was a big one, a homerun off Boston's Heber Newsome. New York won, 8-4.

1943 — After three scoreless innings, the Indians explode for 12 runs in the fourth, and future Yankee ace Allie Reynolds coasts to a three-hit, 12-0 win.

1946 — The Yankees edge the Red Sox, 2-1, behind Spud Chandler, with 69,107 fans on hand. Chandler had a no-hitter going until Bobby Doerr singled with one out in the ninth inning (although the Yankee ace had kept the fans on the edges of their seats by walking nine Red Sox during the first four innings of the game).

1961 — Roger Maris hits his 30th homerun, a solo shot off Senators' pitcher John Klippstein, to lead New York to a 13-4 win. Maris had hit his 29th homerun in the third inning.

1978 — Ron Guidry wins his 13th consecutive game, raising his record to 13-0, and thereby records the best start for any Yankee pitcher in history. The Yankees edged the Tigers, 3-2. (See the 1978 section.)

3

1896 — William "Curt" Walker B (PH 1919)

1914 — Warren "Buddy" Rosar B (C 1939-42)

1922 — Arthur (Art) Fowler B (Coach 1975-78)

1923 — For the second time in the 1923 season, Babe Ruth hits a 15th-inning, game-winning homerun. This time the beneficiary was Yankee hurler Joe Bush, who pitched all 15 innings and allowed a mere eight hits. Bush also hit a homerun of his own, a late-inning shot which tied the score at 1-1. The losers, 2-1, were the Washington Senators and pitcher George Mogridge, a former Yankee.

1925 — Yankees release outfielder Whitey Witt.

1932 — Earle Combs and Lyn Lary each hit a pair of doubles in one innings (the sixth), thereby tying the American League record for most players hitting more than one double in the same inning. George Pipgras was the Yankee pitcher that day, and he hit two singles in that same inning. The victims: the Athletics, 13-2 losers, largely thanks to a nine-run sixth inning.

1939 — Lou Gehrig Day at Yankee Stadium. A crowd of 61,808 attend to honor the Hall of Fame Yankee first baseman. During the between-game ceremonies, Gehrig makes his immortal "luckiest man on the face of the earth," speech. The Yankees split the doubleheader, 2-3, 11-1, versus the Senators.

1941 — Joseph "Casey" Cox B (P 1972-73)

1950 — Casey Stengel makes a rare managerial error when he asks Yankee owner Dan Topping to ask Joe DiMaggio to play first base. Members of the Yankee team of 1950 say that DiMaggio was clearly uncomfortable at the unfamiliar position. In fact, the sweat poured down DiMaggio's face for six innings, according to contemporary reports, before Hank Bauer pulled up lame in the outfield and enabled DiMaggio to return to more familiar pastures. Members of the team also believed that DiMaggio lost a lot of respect for Stengel because Stengel did not come to DiMaggio and make the request himself.

(Note: DiMaggio himself would never comment on this, or any other, managerial decision.)

As a further note, it is important to understand why the request was made in the first place. The Yankees faced a serious problem at first base. Their highly touted rookie, Joe Collins, simply was not hitting. Experiments with other players had proven failures, so Stengel apparently hoped DiMaggio could solve the problem. After all, according to those close to Stengel, DiMaggio was the greatest player on the team in Casey's eyes, and the manager hoped the move to first would help the team and extend DiMaggio's career.

Eventually, the Yankees solved the problem when Tommy Henrich moved to first base and played admirably.

1977 — Ron Guidry pitches his second consecutive shutout of the season, a six-hit, 2-0 win versus Detroit. Roy White broke up the scoreless duel with a run-scoring double in the eighth inning.

4

1884 — John (Jack) Warhop B (P 1908-15)

1927 — The Yankees sweep the Senators, 12-1, 12-1.

1942 — Harold (Hal) Lanier B (INF 1972-73)

1954 — Yankees purchase pitcher Marlin Stuart from the Orioles on waivers.

— James (Jim) Beattie B (P 1978-current)

1967 — Yankees obtain pitcher Steve Barber from the Orioles for first baseman Ray Barker, outfielders Chet Trail and Joe Brody, and an undisclosed amount of cash.

1977 — Chris Chambliss, Graig Nettles, Roy White and Lou Piniella each hit homeruns during the Yankees 7-5 win against the Indians. The win solidified New York's hold on first place, one game ahead of Boston.

5

1884 — John (Jack) Quinn B (P 1909-12, 19-21)

1896 — Herbert "Lefty" Thormahlen B (P 1917-20)

1904 — Irving "Bump" Hadley B (P 1936-40)

1906 — The Yankees exploit nine Red Sox errors to dump the Sox, 8-3, at Boston.

1937 — Joe DiMaggio hits his first career grand slam, a sixth inning shot off Red Sox hurler Rube Walberg, to lead New York to an 8-4 win in the second game of a doubleheader. The Yankees took the opener, 15-0.

1943 — Curtis (Curt) Blefary B (OF, 1B, C 3B, 2B 1970-71)

1951 — Richard "Goose" Gossage B (P 1978-current)

6

1881 — Roy Hartzell B (INF, OF 1911-16)

1891 — Steven O'Neill B (C 1925)

1917 — Kenneth "Ziggy" Sears B (C 1943)

1928 — Yankee release pitcher Urban Shocker.

1932 — Yankee catcher Bill Dickey is suspended for 30 days and fined $1,000 for assaulting Senators outfielder Carl Reynolds and breaking Reynolds' jaw. Reynolds had bowled Dickey over on a successful squeeze play to score the tying run in the second game of a doubleheader. Dickey got up and attacked Reynolds, breaking the outfielder's jaw with one punch. Technically, the suspension was until Reynolds recovered.

New York lost both games, 5-3 and 12-6.

1944 — Yankees sell outfielder Larry Rosenthal to the Athletics for an undisclosed amount of cash.

1954 — William (Willie) Randolph B (2B 1976-current)

1962 — Mickey Mantle hits homeruns in his first two at-bats. When combined with the two consecutive homeruns he registered in his last two at-bats in the last game New York played, he tied the major league record of four consecutive homeruns.

7

1884 — George Moriarty B (INF, OF, 1B 1906-08)

1913 — Yankees obtain first baseman Jack Knight from the Senators on waivers.

1936 — William (Bill) Kunkel B (P 1963)

1977 — Catfish Hunter hurls a four-hit, complete game victory against the Indians as the Yankees register an 8-2 win and complete a three-game sweep of the Tribe.

8

1931 — Zachary (Zach) Monroe B (P 1958-59)

1932 — Hector Lopez B (OF, 3B, 2B, 1B 1959-66)

1974 — Yankee shortstop Jim Mason ties the major league record by hitting four doubles in one nine inning game during the Yankees 12-5 win at Texas. Mason scored one run and drove in two.

— Yankees purchase infielder Sandy Alomar from the California Angels for an undisclosed amount of cash believed to exceed $50,000.

1977 — Thurman Munson and Graig Nettles each hit a homerun during New York's 7-5 win against the Orioles. Don Gullett was the winner, his seventh win of the season.

9

1874 — John (Jack) Powell B (P 1904-05)

1899 — Walter Beall B (P 1924-27)

1932 — Truman "Tex" Clevenger B (P 1961-62)

— Yankee outfielder Ben Chapman hits two inside-the-park homeruns in the second game of a doubleheader at Yankee Stadium, and thereby ties the record for the most inside-the-park homeruns in one game. He also slammed a line drive into the right field seats, giving him three in one game, and six runs batted in. The Yankees won that game, 14-9, and also downed the Tigers, 7-6 in the opener, behind homeruns by Babe Ruth, Lou Gehrig and Joe Sewell.

10

1916 — Yankees sign free agent shortstop Rube Oldring, again.

1917 — Yankee pitcher Ray Caldwell hurls 9-and-two-thirds innings of no-hit relief, and comes out a winner, 7-5, when New York scores a pair of runs in the 17th inning to down the Browns in St. Louis.

1947 — Yankees sell first baseman Mel Queen to the Pirates for an undisclosed amount.

— Relief ace Joe Page hits his second major league game-winning homerun, this time a ninth inning drive, to edge the Browns, 4-3, in St. Louis.

1977 — A 5-0 loss to the Orioles drops the Yankees into second place, one-half game behind the Red Sox. The Yankees would not re-enter first place until August 23, and would soon fall five games behind the Red Sox.

11

1884 — Harold (Harry) Wolter B (P 1907)

1911 — Vitautis "Vito" Tamulis B (P 1934-35)

1939 — The Yankees are the hosts for the Seventh Annual Major League All Star Game (the first ever held at Yankee Stadium). Yankee Hall-of-Famer Joe DiMaggio thrills the home-town fans by hitting a homerun which leads the American League to a 3-1 win.

DiMaggio's hitting helped bail out manager Joe McCarthy, the Yankee skipper who came under heavy criticism for starting six Yankees: Red Rolfe, Joe Gordon, Red Ruffing, Bill Dickey, George Selkirk, and DiMaggio.

1949 — Stanley (Stan) Thomas B (P 1977)

12

1943 — A team of Armed Forces All-Stars managed by Babe Ruth, and featuring such stars as Joe DiMaggio and Ted Williams, plays the Braves at Boston to raise money for war bonds. Ruth, inactive as a player since May, 1935, actually pinch hit in the eighth inning, and the 48-year-old Hall of Famer drove a Dave Odom offering deep to right field . . . where it was caught. The Ruth All-Stars edged the Braves, 9-8, on a homerun by Williams.

1951 — Yankee pitching mainstay Allie Reynolds no-hits the Indians, 1-0, with Gene Woodling's seventh inning homerun off Indians starter Bob Feller the difference.

In an interesting side note, the night before this game Yankee manager Casey Stengel was asked why he refused to allow Yankee relief pitchers to ride in the golf carts on their way in from the bullpen. Stengel replied that Yankees only ride in Cadillacs, whereupon Indians general manager Hank Greenberg had a Cadillac placed in the Yankee bullpen for the next game. Obviously, it went unused.

1968 — Yankees obtain pitcher Lindy McDaniel from the Giants for pitcher Bill Monbouquette.

1977 — Southpaw Don Gullett comes through with another crucial victory, a 5-2 win against the Brewers, which ends a three-game losing streak. Second baseman Willie Randolph hit a game-winning homerun.

13

1889 — Stanley (Stan) "The Silent Pole" Coveleski B (P 1928)

1920 — Frank "Dutch" Hiller B (P 1946, 48-49)

1923 — Pitcher Bob Shawkey hits a triple and a double in the third inning, and thereby ties the American League record for most extra-base hits by a pitcher in one inning. The Yankees downed the Athletics, 10-6.

1934 — Kenneth (Ken) Hunt B (OF 1959-60)

— Babe Ruth hits his 700th career homerun to lead the Yankees to a 4-2 win at Detroit.

1940 — Jack Aker B (P 1969-72)

1940 — Joe DiMaggio drives in 7 runs during the Yankees 10-4 win against the Browns in the first game of a doubleheader. DiMaggio had four hits in that game: two homeruns and two singles.

In the second game, DiMaggio added a two-run homerun, to finish the day with nine runs batted in, and help New York complete a sweep, 12-6.

1960 — The 29th Annual Major League All-Star Game is held at Yankee Stadium, with the National League coming out on top, 6-0. The N.L. had also won the first game (they played two All-Star Games in 1959-62), 5-3, and thereby became the only league to sweep a pair in one year.

In the game at Yankee Stadium, Eddie Matthews, Willie Mays, Stan Musial, and Ken Boyer each hit homeruns before a crowd of 38,362.

1973 — Bobby Murcer hits three homeruns, all off Royals starter Gene Garber, to lead the Yankees to a 5-0 win. Murcer slammed a three-run shot in the first inning, and added solo shots in the sixth and eighth, to account for all the Yankee runs. Mel Stottlemyre was the beneficiary, and deservedly so — he hurled a six-hit shutout, the 39th shutout of his career.

14

1874 — Jesse Tannehill B (P, OF 1903)

1888 — William "Babe" Borton B (1B 1913)

1947 — Daniel "Mickey" Walton B (OF, 3B 1971)

15

1892 — Eugene "Bubbles" Hargrave B (C 1930)

1908 — Alvin "Jake" Powell B (OF, 2B 1936-40)

1913 — Yankees obtain infielder Rollie Zeider and first baseman Bill Borton from the White Sox for first baseman Hal Chase.

1917 — Yankees obtain outfielder Armando Marsans from the Browns for outfielder Lee Magee.

1920 — Babe Ruth ties his old record of 29 homeruns in one season during New York's 13-10 win against the Browns.

16

1920 — Babe Ruth breaks his old record of 29 homeruns in one season during New York's 5-2 win against the Browns. He went on to hit 54 that year, more than all but two teams in baseball hit that year.

1940 — Thomas Metcalf B (1963)

1942 — Yankees obtain pitcher Jim "Colonel" Turner from the Reds as a partial payment for outfielder Fran Kelleher.

1947 — Two days after donning the pinstripes, pitcher Bobo Newsom notches; his 200th career win, and his first as a Yankee, during a 3-1 victory at Cleveland. It was the Yankees' 18th straight win.

The streak advanced to 19 when Vic Raschi stopped the Indians, 7-2, in the second game of the doubleheader.

17

1919 — The Yankees (21) and Browns (17) combine for 38 hits during St. Louis' 7-6, 17-inning win. Strangely enough, the winning run scored on a squeeze play, without the benefit of a base hit!

1923 — An unsympathetic Miller Huggins refuses to remove Yankee starting pitcher Carl Mays, and allows the Indians to batter Mays for 20 hits and 13 runs during Cleveland's 13-0 win. Huggins and Mays never got along well, and Mays was subsequently sold to the Reds after the season.

1938 — Deron Johnson B (3B, OF, 1B 1960-61)

1941 — Joe DiMaggio's 56-game hitting streak ends in Cleveland when the Yankee Clipper grounds into a double play in his final at-bat. The Cleveland combo of Al Smith and Jim Bagby stopped DiMaggio on three ground balls and a walk, but the Yankees defeated the Indians, 4-3, before 67,468 fans.

1961 — Roger Maris, destined to break Babe Ruth's single season record of 60 homeruns, has a first inning homerun against the Orioles rained out when play is called in the top of the fifth inning. Interestingly enough, when Ruth hit his 60 homeruns in 1927, none of the Bambino's shots were lost to rain or darkness.

(Note: Much ado was made about the Ford Frick asterisk because Maris accomplished his 61 homeruns in a 162-game schedule, while Ruth hit his 60 in 154 games. Had the July 17 game not been rained out, Maris still would have come up short of the 154-game limit ... BUT who cares. The record is for homeruns in a season, not in a particular number of games, and for my part, they can eat the stupid asterisk. It's about time Maris got the acclaim he deserves as the greatest single-season homerun hitter of our time.)

1977 — The Yankees drop their third straight game to the Royals during a seven losses in nine games sour streak. The 8-4 loss dropped New York three games behind the first place Orioles.

1978 — Controversial slugger Reggie Jackson is suspended indefinitely, without pay, for disregarding a hit sign in the bottom of the tenth inning of a game the Yankees eventually lost to the Royals, 9-7. The loss dropped the Yankees 14 games behind the first place Red Sox. The suspension was later reduced to five games. This date was clearly the nadir of the 1978 season. (For further details, see the 1978 section herein.)

18

1916 — John "Hippity" Hopp B (1B, OF 1950-52)

1918 — Albert (Al) Lyons B (P 1944, 46-47)

1937 — Joe DiMaggio hits a tie-breaking grand slam in the ninth inning to give New York a 5-1 victory versus the Indians.

1944 — Rudy May B (P 1974-76)

1947 — The Yankees' 19 game winning streak comes to an end in Detroit when Tiger hurler Fred Hutchinson shuts New York out, 2-0.

19

1887 — Charles "Butch" Schmidt B (P 1909)

1888 — Edward (Eddie) Sweeny B (C, 1B, OF 1908-15)

1896 — Robert (Bob) Meusel B (OF, 3B, 1B 1920-29)

1902 — Mark Koenig B (SS 1925-30)

1914 — Marius "Lefty" Russo B (P 1939-43, 46)

1927 — William (Billy) Gardner B (INF 1961-62)

1942 — Yankees sign free agent catcher Rollie Hemsley.

1949 — Eugene (Gene) Locklear B (OF, 1B 1976-77)

1977 — The 48th Annual Major League All-Star Game is held at Yankee Stadium. Some 56,683 fans jammed the New Stadium, only to watch the National League emerge on top, 7-5.

1978 — Ed Figueroa six-hits the Twins as the Yankees open a five-game winning streak, 2-0. This date and game are important because from this day on, the Yankees embarked upon their legendary drive back to the top of the American League's Eastern Division, in one of the greatest comebacks in baseball history.

20

1923 — The Yankees hit into a triple play, but defeat the Athletics, 9-2 behind Carl Mays' four-hitter.

1941 — The Yankees end a 17-inning affair at Detroit by scoring six runs in the last inning, to win, 12-6.

1956 — Whitey Ford ties the American League record for consecutive strikeouts by fanning six straight Athletics: Joe Ginsberg (last out the second inning), Joe DeMaestri, Clete Boyer, Jack McMahon, Hector Lopez, and Al Pilarcik. Enos Slaughter broke the string by flying out to right field.

Strangely enough, Ford finished the game with eight K's on the day, a 6-3 winner.

1970 — Yankees obtain pitcher Mike McCormick from the Giants for pitcher John Cumberland.

1890 — Howard "Hank" Shanks B (3B, OF, 2B 1925)

1891 — Raymond (Ray) Keating B (P 1912-16, 18)

1910 — The Yankees take advantage of eight St. Louis errors to down the Browns, 19-2.

1921 — The Yankees hit 7 doubles, the Indians add nine of their own, and the teams combine for a record 16 in one nine-inning game. The final score showed the Indians on top, 17-8, and the loss ended a nine-game Yankee winning streak.

1941 — Gary Waslewski B (P 1970-71)

1942 — Michael (Mike) Hegan B (1B, DH 1964, 66-67, 73-74)

1947 — The Boston Braves edge the Yankees, 4-3, in the Annual Hall of Fame Game in Cooperstown, New York.

1977 — Catfish Hunter comes through with an important 7-0 win against the Brewers, ending a three-game Yankee losing streak, in the first game of a doubleheader. Milwaukee took the nightcap, 5-4, in ten innings.

22

1918 — Yankees and Browns battle to a 15-inning, 4-4 tie.

1925 — Yankees purchase infielder Leo Durocher from Hartford for an undisclosed amount of cash.

1926 — The Yankees obtain catcher Hank Severeid from the Senators on waivers.

1944 — Walter "Sparky" Lyle B (P 1972-78)

1947 — Clifford "Heathcliff" Johnson B (C, 1B, DH 1977-current)

23

1880 — Lewis (Lew) Brockett B (P 1907, 09, 11)

1901 — Malcolm "Mack" Hills B (2B 1924)

1904 — Yankees obtain pitcher Al Orth from the Senators for pitcher Tom Hughes.

1917 — Raymond (Ray) Scarborough B (P 1952-53)

1922 — Yankees obtain third baseman Joe Dugan and outfielder Elmer Smith from the Red Sox for outfielders Chick Fewster and Elmer Miller, pitcher Frank O'Doul, and shortstop John Mitchell. This trade was heavily criticized by the other contending teams in the American League because it handed the Yankees the third baseman they needed to solidify their infield and replace the aging Frank Baker.

This trade is also cited as the reason for the introduction of the June 15 trading deadline brought in by former baseball commissioner Judge Kennesaw Mountain Landis.

1933 — John (Johnny) James B (P 1958, 60-61)

1977 — Ron Guidry downs the Brewers, 3-1, on Paul Blair's ninth inning, three-run homerun.

24

1922 — Duane "Dee" Pillette B (P 1949-50)

1923 — Carl Mays wins his 23rd consecutive game against the Athletics. The streak ended on October 4.

1933 — Yankees sign free agent pitcher George Uhle.

1934 — Yankee outfielder Earle Combs suffers a fractured skull and other injuries when he crashes into the center field wall in St. Louis while attempting a desperation catch. The injuries caused a premature end to this great outfielder's career. The Yankees lost the game, too, 4-2.

1978 — Yankee manager Billy Martin resigns after three turbulent years (less than three seasons) behind the helm. The straw that broke the camel's back was some comments Martin made regarding Yankee owner George Steinbrenner (something to the effect that Steinbrenner and Reggie Jackson were made for each other because one is a liar and the other is a convict). Dick Howser assumed the managerial duties for one day, lost to the Royals 5-4, and was replaced by Bob Lemon at his own request. Martin was later re-hired for the 1980 season. (See the 1978 section.)

25

1920 — The Red Sox turn a triple play against the Yankees, but New York rides Babe Ruth's 35th homerun of the season to an 8-2 win.

1959 — The final straw falls to break the Yankees' backs in this disastrous year when Moose Skowron breaks his arm in two places while diving for a bad throw by third baseman Hector Lopez. As Skowron dove, Tiger batter-baserunner Cot Veal ran into Skowron, and the collision combined with the fall to do the damage. The Yankees wound up in third place that year, just four games over .500.

1961 — Roger Maris hits his 40th homerun of the year, and his fourth of the afternoon (two in each game), as the Yankees sweep the White Sox, 5-1 and 12-0. With 40 homeruns on this date, Maris is 24 games ahead of Babe Ruth's 1927 pace.

1966 — Yankee manager Casey Stengel is elected to the Baseball Hall of Fame by a special vote of the Major League Baseball Writers' Association and the Old Timers' Committee. The purpose of the premature election* was clear: Stengel had been in a serious accident, and the press, which had always idolized Stengel, wanted to be certain that his election would not be one of those posthumous affairs. It was a great idea, and will hopefully be extended to some of the other greats of the game.

*(Normally, the player or other electee must have been out of baseball for five years prior to his election.)

1978 — Yankees name Hall-of-Famer Bob Lemon as manager. His debut is a 4-0 win versus the Royals.

26

1892 — Samuel "Sad Sam" Jones B (P 1922-26)

1920 — Edward (Eddie) Bockman B (3B 1946)

1926 — William (Bill) Miller B (P 1952-54)

1928 — Yankees score 11 runs in the top of the 12th inning to dump the Tigers, 12-1, in the first game of a doubleheader. The inning's play-by-play: Lou Gehrig led off with a walk, but was forced out at second on Tony Lazzeri's ground ball. Mark Koenig singled. Gene Robertson doubled in a run. John Grabowski walked. Waite Hoyt singled in a run, as did Earle Combs. Bob Meusel tripled in a pair, Babe Ruth doubled home Meusel, and then Gehrig singled in Ruth. Lazzeri tripled to score Gehrig, Robertson singled in Lazzeri, and Grabowski doubled in Robertson.

The Yankees lost the nightcap, 13-10.

1933 — Norman (Norm) Siebern B (OF, 1B 1956, 58-59)

1939 — Peter (Pete) Ward B (1B 1970)

— Yankee catcher Bill Dickey hits three consecutive homeruns during the Yankees' 14-1 win against the Browns. The deserving beneficiary of the Yankees' 20-hit attack was Red Ruffing, who pitched a three-hitter. The Yankees tied the major league record by scoring in every inning.

1948 — Yankees waive pitcher Randy Gumpert to the White Sox.

1952 — Mickey Mantle hits his first grand slam, but the Yankees lose to Detroit, 10-6.

1967 — The Twins edge the Yankees, 3-2, in 18 innings at Yankee Stadium when Rich Rollins singled home Rod Carew. (See the Longest Days section)

1969 — Yankees sell outfielder Billy Cowan to the Angels for an undisclosed amount of cash.

1977 — In the opening game of the Yankees' final series with the Orioles, Cliff Johnson's ninth inning, two-run pinch hit homerun ties the score, 4-4, and then Reggie Jackson leads off the 10th inning with a homerun to win the game.

Red Sox fans in particular bitterly denounced the schedule-maker for matching New York and Baltimore for their final series at this early date. Of course, the schedule-maker has no way of knowing which teams will draw which numbered spots when he produces the schedule. (The schedule is made using team numbers. The teams subsequently draw the numbers out of a hat.)

27

1898 — James "Zach" Taylor B (C 1934)

   — Benjamin (Benny) Bengough B (C 1923-30)

1905 — Leon "Leo the Lip" Durocher B (INF 1925-29)

1933 — John (Johnny) Kucks B (P 1955-59)

1945 — Yankees sell pitcher Hank Borowy to the Cubs for $97,000.

1947 — Yogi Berra starts an incredible 148-game errorless streak, a record for catchers.

28

1890 — Elmer Miller B (OF 1915-18, 21-22)

1906 — The Yankees turn a triple play during a 6-4 win at Cleveland.

1924 — After scoring 10 runs in the first inning, the Yankees barely hang on to edge the White Sox, 12-10.

1934 — Earle Combs retires. He had never been the same since running into the wall in St. Louis on July 24.

1940 — Right fielder Charlie Keller slams three homeruns to pace a 13-hit Yankee attack as the New Yorkers outslug Chicago, 10-9, in the first game of a doubleheader. The Sox rebounded with an 8-4 win in the nightcap.

   Keller's third shot, a solo job, came on the heels of Joe DiMaggio's second homerun of the game, and proved to be the gamewinner.

1943 — Richard (Dick) Simpson B (OF 1969)

1972 — Yankees re-purchase pitcher Ron Klimkowski from the A's for an undisclosed amount of cash.

1977 — A Thursday afternoon crowd of 40,918 is on hand for New York's 14-2 destruction of the Orioles. The 15-hit New York attack featured homeruns by Graig Nettles, Thurman Munson, and Roy White.

29

1878 — Earle "Crossfire" Moore B (P 1907)

1951 — Gary Thomasson B (OF, DH 1978-current)

1977 — Ron Guidry and relief ace Sparky Lyle combine for a 4-0 win as the Yankees streak to their fifth win in six games. Cliff Johnson and Graig Nettles each hit a homerun.

1978 — It's Old Timers' Day at Yankee Stadium, and "former" Yankee manager Billy Martin steals the show when his introduction to the fans includes the announcement that he has been re-hired as Yankee manager, commencing in 1980. (See the 1978 section)

30

1914 — Steven (Steve) Peek B (P 1941)

1919 — Yankees obtain pitcher Carl Mays from the Red Sox in return for pitchers Hubert McGraw and Alan Russell, a minor leaguer to be named later, and $25,000.

1940 — Cesar "Pepi" Tovar B (OF, 3B 1976)

1947 — James (Jim) Spencer B (DH, 1B 1978-current)

1977 — Don Gullett wins his 10th game of the season, 9-3, against the A's. Unfortunately, this proved to be his final win until September because he injured his shoulder in the seventh inning.

31

1881 — Robert (Bob) Unglaub B (INF 1904)

1893 — Allan (Al) Russell B (P 1915-19)

1922 — Henry (Hank) Bauer B (OF, C 1948-59)

1925 — Yankees release catcher Steve O'Neill.

1927 — Wilmer "Billy" Shantz B (C 1960)

1931 — Walter "Rip" Coleman B (P 1955-56)

1938 — Spud Chandler scatters eight hits and pitches all 15 innings during the Yankees' 7-3 win against the White Sox.

— After the game with the Sox, Yankee outfielder Jake Powell is suspended for 10 days for telling a Chicago radio audience that "he'd hit every colored person in Chicago over the head with a club" if he had the chance. Contemporaries of Powell's confirmed that he was one of the most virulent racists in the game. One sportswriter told the author this past winter that Powell once said his off-season job was "riding shotgun over niggers" as a sheriff.

1951 — Yankees obtain pitchers Bob Hogue and Lou Sleater, third baseman Kermit Wahl and shortstop Tom Upton from the Browns for outfielder Cliff Mapes.

73

1977 — The Yankees close out the month of July with their eighth win in nine games. Cliff Johnson and Graig Nettles each had a big hand in New York's 9-2 win versus the A's. Johnson hit a big homerun, and Nettles scored three runs, as New York pulled within one game of first place.

1978 — The Yankees finish the month of July with a 6-1 win versus Texas, to close the gap to 7-and-one-half games behind the first place Red Sox.

AUGUST

1

1893 — Elmer "Slim" Love B (P 1916-18)

1903 — Highlander shortstop Kid Elberfeld ties the major league record by making all four of New York's hits during a 3-2 win against the Athletics.

1922 — Yankees purchase catcher Benny Bengough from Buffalo.

1932 — The Tigers successfully protest New York's 6-3 victory, but gain nothing when the rematch is ended by darkness with the score tied 8-8.

1937 — Lou Gehrig hits for the cycle (single, double, triple, homerun) during the Yankees' 14-5 win against the Browns.

1941 — Lefty Gomez ties a major league record by walking 11 Browns during his 9-0 shutout win at Yankee Stadium. Gomez also allowed five hits.

1952 — Yankees purchase pitcher Johnny Schmitz from the Dodgers for an undisclosed amount.

1973 — The famous "Thurman Munson — Carlton Fisk" brawl at Fenway Park. With the score tied, 2-2 in the top of the ninth inning, and Munson on third base with one out, Yankee shortstop Gene Michael misses a suicide squeeze bunt attempt. Munson and Fisk crashed together at home plate, and came up swinging. Both benches emptied, and the enmity between the Yankee and Red Sox catchers remains through this day.

The Yankees lost the game, 3-2, in the bottom of the ninth, when former Yankee Mario Guerrero singled home Bob Montgomery. The loser: Sparky Lyle (who came to New York for Danny Cater and . . . Mario Guerrero!).

2

1893 — Angel Aragon B (OF 1914, 16-17)

1931 — Former Yankee relief ace Wilcy Moore notches a 1-0 win against his former teammates. The next day, New York began a 308-game skein during which the Yankees were not shutout.

1975 — Yankees fire manager Bill Virdon and hire Billy Martin. Virdon was the unfortunate victim of an injury-plagued season, which included the loss of star centerfielder Elliott Maddox, and a virtually crippled Bobby Bonds. The Yankees were 53-51 when Virdon was axed. They improved for a 30-26 mark under Martin . . . but the change worked out in 1976-77, when Martin led New York to two pennants and a world championship.

1978 — The Yankees and Red Sox play a 14-inning 5-5 tie which is suspended by league curfew. New York led, 5-0, after five innings, but three key wild pitches, two bases loaded walks, and some unique bloop hits enabled the Sox to come back and tie the score in the eighth. The Yankees' big bats were repeatedly frustrated by Sox relievers Bob Stanley and Tom Burgmeier — the curfew went into effect after Reggie Jackson struck out for the third time with the go-ahead run on base. (See the 1978 section.)

3

1914 — Yankee catcher Les Nunamaker throws out three consecutive Tiger baserunners in the first inning of New York's 4-1 loss to Detroit. The first three batters in the Tiger lineup each singled, and each was gunned down trying to steal second base.

1920 — James (Jim) Hegan B (coach 1966-73)

1933 — The Yankees' 308-game scoring streak comes to an end when Athletics Hall-of-Famer Lefty Grove hangs a five-hit, 7-0 win on the New Yorkers. The Yankees responded by scoring at least one run in every game they played for the rest of the season.

1940 — Roger Repoz B (OF, 1B 1964-66)

1967 — Yankees obtain pitchers Ron Klimkowski and Peter Magrini from the Red Sox for catcher Elston Howard.

1978 — In the continuation of the previous evening's suspended game, the Red Sox score twice in the 17th inning and down the Yankees, 7-5. Former Yankee Mike Torrez then added to the New Yorkers' woes by stopping the Yankees, 8-1, in a rain-shortened regularly scheduled game. The double dip dropped the Yankees 8-and-one-half games behind the Sox.

4

1910 — George "Tuck" Stainback B (OF 1942-45)

1928 — Yankee purchase pitcher Fred Heimach from St. Paul for an undisclosed amount of cash and other considerations.

1932 — James (Jim) Coates B (P 1956, 59-62)

1939 — Robert (Bob) Meyer B (P 1964)

1952 — Yankees sell pitcher Bob Hogue to the Browns for an undisclosed amount of cash.

1953 — Yankee pitcher Vic Raschi sets a major league record by driving in 7 runs in New York's 15-0 win versus the Tigers, still the record for runs batted in by a pitcher in one game.

Raschi singled in two runs in the second inning, doubled home three more in the third, and capped it off with a two-run single in the eighth. His Yankee teammates responded by filling his locker to the roof with bats after the game.

1973 — Yankee relief ace Lindy McDaniel hurls 13 innings of near perfect relief, and comes out a winner when Horace Clarke's 13th inning homerun gives New York a 3-2 win versus Detroit. Fritz Peterson was the starter, but he departed in the first inning with a muscle pull.

5

1872 — Merle "Doc" Adkins B (P 1903)

1899 — Samuel (Sam) Gibson B (P 1930)

6

1903 — James (Jim) Turner B (P 1942-45, coach 1966-73)

1937 — The Yankees' 7-6 win against Cleveland is erased when Indians manager Steve O'Neill successfully protests the game. The controversial call came in the bottom of the tenth inning, with the Indians ahead, 6-5. The Yankees placed runners on second and third with one out, and Joe DiMaggio stepped up to bat. DiMaggio smashed a line drive down the third base line which third baseman Odell Hale dove for and deflected into foul territory. Plate umpire Charlie Johnston ruled that Hale had touched the ball while the ball was in foul territory, and thereby touched off a tremendous argument.

(Both Yankee runners had already scored, and the Yankees believed they had a 7-6 win.)

Johnston eventually eluded the debators and consulted with third base umpire George Moriarty(the crew chief), and a former Yankee.Moriarty said the ball was in fair territory when touched, was therefore a fair ball, and told Johnston that both runners should be allowed to score. Based on that testimony, Johnston reversed his call and allowed the runners to score on what was now a double.

O'Neill came storming out of his dugout, and rightly protested that the plate umpire had jurisdiction over the call because the ball was touched before it passed third base, and that Moriarty should not have been consulted. O'Neill also believed that Moriarty had "over-ruled" Johnston, which would have been completely improper.

(Note: baseball and softball fans of the world wake up — NO UMPIRE CAN EVER OVER-RULE ANOTHER! Calls may be changed by the umpire who originally made the controversial call, but an umpire is never over-ruled.)

76

The game was replayed on Sept. 15, and on that date the teams split a doubleheader, with New York winning the nightcap, 3-1, after dropping the opener, 5-4.

1945 — John   (Andy) Messersmith B (P 1978-current)

1949 — Yankees sell first baseman Jack Phillips to the Pirates for an undisclosed amount of cash.

7

1886 — James (Bill) McKechnie B (INF, 1B 1913)

1918 — Marlin Stuart B (P 1954)

1929 — Donald (Don) Larsen B (P 1955-59)

1938 — Red Ruffing's no-hit bid ends in the ninth inning when Cleveland outfielder Roy Weatherly doubles with one out. The Yankees won, 7-0.

1954 — Yankees waive pitcher Bob Kuzava to the Orioles.

1956 — Red Sox star Ted Williams spits at the crowd during the Yankees 2-1 loss to the Sox at Fenway, and is hit with a $5,000 fine. His rather poor behavior came before a gathering of some 36,350 fans, the largest single-game crowd in modern Fenway history.

1973 — Yankees obtain pitcher Wayne Granger from the Cardinals for future considerations (pitcher Ken Crosby) and an undisclosed amount of cash.

1977 — Mike Torrez wins his third straight game to snap a three-game Yankee losing streak, and start the Yankees on a destructive march through the American League Western Division during which the Yankees won 21 of 24 games.

8

1897 — Kenneth (Ken) Holloway B (P 1930)

1913 — Yankees obtain third baseman Fritz Maisel from Baltimore of the International League for third baseman Ezra Midkiff and outfielder Bert Daniels.

1920 — The Yankees lose the shortest game in A.L. history, 1-0, in just one hour and 13 minutes. The masters were the Detroit Tigers and one Howard Ehmke, a pitcher whose future world series feats are well-known to baseball fans.

Yankee centerfielder Ping Bodie added to the embarassment by falling for the hidden ball trick when New York had runners on first and second with no outs in the fifth inning.

1967 — Yankees purchase catcher Bob Tillman from the Red Sox for an undisclosed amount of cash.

1972 — The Yankees sign a 30-year lease to play in a remodeled, New York City-owned, Yankee Stadium, to commence in 1976. The plans called for a 24-million-dollar renovation over two years. The actual cost approached at least $55 million, and may well have topped the $100 million mark, but it was all worth it in the long run because of the added revenues the Yankees bring into New York City each year, and because the Yankees are really the South Bronx's only thriving business.

9

1894 — John Mitchell B (SS, 2B 1921-22)

1919 — John (Fred) Sanford B (P 1949-51)

— Ralph "The Major" Houk B (C 1947-54, manager 1961-63, 66-73)

1925 — Outfielder Bobby Veach pinch hits for Babe Ruth. This was the only time in Ruth's career that a Yankee batted in his place. For the record, Veach flied out, and the Yankees lost, 4-3, in 12 innings.

1934 — Eli Grba B (P 1959-60)

1941 — Paul Lindblad B (P 1978)

1946 — Gerry Moses B (C, DH 1973)

1948 — Yankees waive pitcher Karl Drews to the Browns.

1978 — The Yankees rally for five runs in the bottom of the ninth inning to come-from-behind and defeat the Brewers, 8-7, at Yankee Stadium. New York scored five runs on a single by Bucky Dent, a two-run homerun by Mickey Rivers, an error on Willie Randolph's grounder to shortstop, a walk to Thurman Munson, Chris Chambliss' run-scoring double, an intentional walk to Graig Nettles, Reggie Jackson forcing in a run by getting hit with a pitch, and Lou Piniella pulling off a successful suicide squeeze bunt.

10

1923 — Erwin (Bob) Porterfield B (P 1948-51)

1926 — Yankees drop a scheduled seven inning game, 5-3, at Washington. The shortened affair was necessitated by travel requirements.

1933 — Rocco "Rocky" Colavito B (OF, P 1968)

1969 — Bobby Murcer, Thurman Munson and Gene Michael hit consecutive homeruns in the sixth inning off Royals' starter Lew Krause during New York's 5-1 win.

1977 — Manager Billy Martin inserts slugger Reggie Jackson into the fourth position in the Yankee batting order, and the Yankees down Oakland, 6-3. Remarkable Ron Guidry outpitched Vida Blue, and Graig Nettles hit his 26th homerun.

Jackson would bat fourth for the rest of the season, and the Yankees stretch drive coincide with the batting order change.

11

1907 — Norman "Bobo" Newsom B (P 1947)

— John "Dusty" Rhodes B (P 1929-32)

1929 — Babe Ruth hits the 500th homerun of his career when he drives Cleveland's Willis Hudlin's first pitch in the second inning deep into the right field bleachers. The Yankees lost the game, 6-5.

1936 — William (Bill) "Monbo" Monboquette B (P 1967)

1946 — Eduardo (Eddie) Leon B (SS 1975)

1967 — Yankee pitcher Al Downing throws exactly nine pitches to the three batters he faces in the third inning, and strikes out the side. As trivial as this feat may seem, only 12 other major league pitchers have ever used exactly three pitches for each of three batters and struck them out in one inning. The Yankees won, 5-3, versus the Indians.

1969 — Yankees sell pitcher Ken Johnson to the Cubs for an undisclosed amount of cash.

12

1934 — Some 41,766 fans mob Fenway Park to say goodbye to Babe Ruth. The Sox fans had correctly guessed that this date would be his final American League appearance in Boston. (For more details, see the career highlights section under George Selkirk.)

1964 — Mickey Mantle hits another homerun over the black screen in dead centerfield of the old Stadium, to lead the Yankees to a 7-3 victory against the White Sox, and help make pitcher Mel Stottlemyre's debut a success. This 502-foot blast is considered his longest shot in Yankee Stadium, and came at the expense of pitcher Ray Herbert.

1977 — Catfish Hunter and Ed Figueroa combine for a sweep of the California Angels, 10-1 and 9-3, as the Yankees bang out 25 hits. Chris Chambliss hit a pair of homeruns in the opener, and Reggie Jackson launched two into outer space in the nightcap. Both Yankee pitchers hurled six-hitters.

13

1875 — Norman "Kid" Elberfeld B (SS 1903-1909, Mgr. 1909)

1906 — Kemp Wicker B (P 1936-38)

1930 — William (Bill) Wiesler B (P 1951, 54-55)

1932 — Yankee pitcher Red Ruffing hits a 10th inning homerun to win his own game, 1-0. Only one other major league pitcher ever accomplished this extra-inning, game-winning homerun in a 1-0 game, feat. (Tom Hughes, 1906, the Senators)

1938 — William (Bill) Stafford B (P 1960-65)

1939 — Yankees pound the Athletics, 21-0, and thereby set the A.L. record for the largest margin of victory in a shutout win. Babe Dahlgren and Joe DiMaggio each hit two homeruns, as the Yankees routed starter Cotten Pippen and his lone reliever, Bill Potter.

(By the way, the Yankees dropped the opening game of the doubleheader that day, 12-9!)

1947 — Frederick (Fred) "Chicken" Stanley B (INF 1973-current)

1973 — Yankees sell infielder Bernie Allen to the Expos for approximately $25,000.

14

1919 — Yankee catcher Muddy Ruel hits into a triple play durinng the Yankees' 5-4, 15-inning win against the Tigers.

1919 — The Yankees get a court injunction barring further interference by league owners who sought to prevent Carl Mays from playing for New York. (Mays had virtually forced the Red Sox to trade him to the Yankees by refusing to pitch for them and demanding to be traded to New York. The other club owners, seeing the potential problems of honoring such a demand, repeatedly attempted to block the trade through the office of the A.L. President. When a previous court injunction stayed the league from formally barring Mays, individual club owners tried to take matters into their own hands by barring the pitcher from their ballparks.)

1924 — Yankees purchase outfielder Ben Paschal and pitcher Ray Francis from Atlanta of the Southern League for an undisclosed amount of cash.

1937 — Yankees obtain pitcher Ivy Andrews from the Indians for $7,500.

1944 — Michael (Mike) Ferraro B (INF 1966, 68)

1950 — James (Jim) Mason B (SS 1974-76)

1960 — An injury-plagued Mickey Mantle fails to run out an infield ground ball, and thereby allows the opposition to turn a tough double play into an easy twin-killing. Yankee manager Casey Stengel, usually the last to criticize Mantle, removed the Hall-of-Famer in favor of Bob Cerv, and castigated Mantle before the sportswriters after the game.

In fairness to Mantle, who suffered an incredible number of injuries, and played with most of them, the ligament damage to his right knee was such that the team physician himself wondered how Mantle could stand the pain and play at all.

1977 — Dick Tidrow makes the first of several key late-season starts and yields just two hits in six innings, as the Yankees bomb the Angels, 15-3. New York's 15-hit attack was highlighted by homeruns by Mickey Rivers and Graig Nettles.

15

1912 — Yankee outfielder Guy Zinn sets a major league record by stealing home twice in one game. Zinn singled with two outs in the first inning of New York's 5-4 win versus the Tigers, stole second and third . . . and home! In the sixth inning, he walked, was sacrificed to second, took third on a passed ball, and then stole home to bring in the game-winning run!

1944 — Wayne Granger B (P 1973)

1977 — Mike Torrez wins his fifth consecutive complete game, a 6-2, six-hit victory against the White Sox, as the Yankees keep pace with the division leading Red Sox, 4½ games out of first place.

16

1889 — Henry "Rube" Robinson B (P 1918)

1903 — In a game played at Toledo, Ohio, Detroit outslugs New York, 12-8. No one seems certain as to why this game was played in Toledo. One newspaper report said that the Tigers ballpark was undergoing repairs. Another mentioned a fire, while other sources cite a special exhibition game and alleged plans to shift the Tiger franchise to Toledo.

1913 — Ernest "Tiny" Bonham B (1940-46)

1920 — Carl Mays' fastball strikes Indians' shortstop Ray Chapman square on the head, resulting in Chapman's death the next day. This remains baseball's only major league fatality.

1922 — Eugene (Gene) Woodling B (OF 1949-54)

1948 — Babe Ruth succumbs to cancer of the throat at 53.

1976 — Mickey Rivers becomes the most recent Yankee to hit an inside-the-park homerun. The victim was Texas' Gaylord Perry, and the blow helped the Yankees to a 5-1 win. Fred Stanley also homered for New York . . . it was Stanley's 4th career homerun in 762 major league at-bats!

1977 — In the wildest game of the season, the Yankees blow a 9-4 lead in the top of the ninth inning, but rebound with a two-run homerun by Chris Chambliss in the bottom of the inning to defeat the White Sox, 11-10.

17

1915 — The Yankees are idled by the first of four consecutive rainouts versus the Browns.

1919 — Ernest (Ernie) Nevel B (P 1950-51)

1924 — Yankees release outfielder Bobby Veach and pitcher Alex Ferguson to the Senators for future considerations and the waiver price.

1944 — Johnny Lindell ties the major league record by hitting four doubles in one game during the Yankees 10-3 win against the Indians. Lindell drove in two runs, scored two runs, and joined 19 other major leaguers in accomplishing the 4-doubles trick in one game.

18

1893 — Burleigh "Ol Stubblebeard" Grimes B (P 1934)

1926 — Yankees purchase pitcher Wilcy Moore from Greenville of the South Atlantic League.

1946 — James (Jim) Magnuson B (P 1973)

1950 — After sitting out a week to relax from some personal emotional problems, Joe DiMaggio returns to the Yankee lineup and hits a game-winning homerun in the ninth inning of New York's 3-2 win in Philadelphia.

1973 — Yankees purchase first baseman Mike Hegan from the A's for an undisclosed amount of cash, and release outfielder John Callison.

19

1891 — Albert (Al) DeVormer B (C, 1B 1920-21)

1910 — Atley Donald B (P 1938-45)

1935 — Robert (Bobby) Richardson B (INF 1955-66)

1977 — Mike Torrez hurles his sixth straight complete game victory, a four-hit 8-1 win versus Texas. Reggie Jackson and Roy White each hit homeruns, and the win moved the Yankees to within two-and-one-half games of the first place Red Sox.

20

1895 — Peter (Pete) Schneider B (P 1919)

1923 — Yankee pitcher Waite Hoyt is suspended for 10 days after attacking an umpire. Hoyt's "victim" was plate umpire Marv Owens during the previous day's 4-3 loss to the White Sox.

The controversial call involved a play at the plate in which Hoyt believed he had tagged the runner out, but Owens saw otherwise. Fortunately, the infuriated Hoyt never actually laid hands on Owens . . . thanks to five teammates who restrained Hoyt!

1944 — Graig Nettles B (INF, DH 1973-current)

1977 — Dick Tidrow, with relief help from Sparky Lyle, turns in another winning performance as the Yankees down Texas, 6-2, and pull to within 1½ games of the first place Red Sox. Bucky Dent's three-run homerun proved to be the key blow.

21

1891 — John (Dick) Gossett B (C 1913-14)

1914 — The Browns commit eight errors and enable New York to pull out a 4-3 win.

1916 — Murry Dickson B (P 1958)

1917 — Yankees purchase catcher Muddy Ruel from the Browns for an undisclosed amount.

1920 — Gerry Staley B (P 1955-56)

1933 — In the first major league All-Star Game ever played, Babe Ruth's two-run homerun in the third inning proves to be the game-winner, as the A.L. downs the N.L., 4-2, at Comiskey Park.

1948 — John "Thunder" Ellis B (C, 1B, 3B 1969-72)

1958 — Yankees obtain pitcher Murry Dickson from the Athletics for a player to be named later (John Bella).

1977 — Graig Nettles' homerun and double account for both Yankee runs as Ron Guidry notches his 10th win, a 2-1 edging of the Rangers. The victory pushed the Yankees to within ½ game of the first place Sox.

1889 — Walter (Wally) Schang B (C 1921-25)

1890 — Urban Shocker B (P 1916-17, 25-28)

1933 — Yankees purchase first baseman Don Heffner from Baltimore of the International League for an undisclosed amount.

1936 — Yankees purchase outfielder Bob Seeds from the Indians for an undisclosed amount.

1947 — William (Bill) Burbach B (P 1969-71)

1949 — Yankees purchase first baseman Johnny Mize from the Giants for $40,000.

1952 — Yankeess purchase pitcher Ray Scarborough from the Red Sox on waivers.

1954 — Yankees purchase pitcher Jim Konstanty from the Phillies on waivers.

1960 — Yankees obtain first baseman Dale Long on waivers from the Giants.

1977 — The Yankees' eight game winning streak ends in a 5-3 loss to Chicago. Fortunately, Boston also lost, so New York remained ½ game behind the Sox.

1896 — Cedric Durst B (OF, 1B 1927-30)

1910 — Linus (Lonnie) Frey B (2B 1947-48)

1918 — Kenneth (Ken) Holcombe B (P 1945)

1924 — John (Sherm) Lollar B (C 1947-48)

1928 — Yankees purchase pitcher Tom Zachary on waivers from the Senators.

1930 — John "Zeke" Bella B (OF 1957)

1942 — Babe Ruth and Walter Johnson square off in a pitching-homerun-hitting contest prior to the regularly scheduled game in a special War Bonds benefit which attracted some 69,000 fans. Ruth drilled Johnson's first pitch about ten rows deep into the lower stands in right field, and then drove the 21st pitch high into the upper deck in right . . . foul by less than 10 feet . . . but the Babe realized that his strength was fading fast, so he circled the bases in the familiar homerun trot, and retired for the afternoon.

1948 — Ronald (Boomer) Blomberg B (DH, OF, 1B 1969-77)

1968 — The Yankees and Tigers play a 19-inning, 3-3 tie in the second game of a doubleheader at Yankee Stadium.

1977 — Mike Torrez wins his seventh straight complete game, 8-3 versus the White Sox, to enable the Yankees to leap over Boston and into first place (to stay!) by ½ game. Mickey Rivers went 5-for-5, and Graig Nettles hit his 30th homerun.

24

1964 — The Yankees notch their first victory in the new Mayor's Trophy Game series versus the Mets, 6-4, at Shea Stadium, before 60,167 fans.

1977 — In what proved to be his final victory of the season, Catfish Hunter hurls a four-hit, 11-1 win against the Twins. Roy White, Mickey Rivers, Chris Chambliss and Bucky Dent each homered.

25

1889 — Leslie (Les) Nunamaker B (C, 1B 1914-17)

1913 — Yankees obtain outfielder Frank Gilhooley from the Cardinals for an undisclosed amount of cash.

1921 — Yankee hurler Harry Harper ties a major league record by hitting three batters with pitches in one inning. The righthander nicked Indians' outfielder Charles Jamieson in the ribs with one out in the eighth inning, hit third baseman Larry Gardner in the arm, and then nailed catcher Steve O'Neill in the back. O'Neill picked up the pitched ball and hurled it back at Harper, precipitating a bench-clearing brawl. Fortunately, cooler heads soon prevailed, and the Indians took advantage of Harper's wildness and four errors by Bob Meusel to take a 15-1 decision.

1928 — Darrell Johnson B (C 1957-58)

1939 — Horace "Dooley" Womack B (P 1966-68)

1956 — Yankees purchase outfielder Enos Slaughter from the Athletics for more than $50,000.

1976 — The Yankees edge the Twins, 5-4, in 19 innings, when Mickey Rivers singles home Oscar Gamble. The five hour, 36 minute marathon featured stellar relief pitching by Grant Jackson.

1977 — Trailing the Twins, 4-2, in the seventh inning, the Yankees tie the score on a two-run single by Mickey Rivers, and go on to victory on a run-scoring single by Reggie Jackson in the eighth.

1978 — Ron Guidry posts his 18th win, and Reggie Jackson hits his 331st career homerun and drives in his 1,001 run, as the Yankees belt the A's, 7-1.

The game was officiated by four amateur umpires because of the major league umpires' short-lived strike. The win kept the Yankees 7½ games behind the first place Red Sox.

26,

1916 — The Yankees turn a big triple play during a 10-6 win versus the Browns. With New York leading by three runs, the Browns filled the bases with no outs in the seventh inning, only to watch a line drive to third clear the bases in a most unorthodox way.

1918 — The Yankees are awarded pitcher John Quinn after a year-long battle with the White Sox over the rights to the veteran pitcher. Quinn had jumped to the ill-fated Federal League in 1914, after finishing the 1913 season as property of the Yankees. He attempted to return to the American League as a White Sox, but the Yankees successfully filed a grievance with the National Commission (the predecessors of the Baseball Commissioner) which ordered his return to New York.

1977 — The Yankees streak to their 12th win in 13 games when Graig Nettles triples home two runs in the ninth inning, to give New York a come-from-behind 6-5 win versus Texas. The win, coupled with a Red Sox loss, moved the Yankees two full games ahead of the Sox.

27

1880 — Edward (Ed) Hahn B (OF 1905-06)

1885 — William "Baldy" Louden B (3B 1907)

1909 — Jack Chesbro makes his final appearance in a Yankee uniform and is ineffective in relief of starter Pete Wilson, during New York's 17-6 loss to Detroit.

1926 — Yankees obtain pitcher Dutch Ruether on waivers from the Senators.

1938 — Yankee hurler Monte Pearson no-hits the Indians, 13-0, in the second game of a doubleheader. Joe DiMaggio hit three triples to pace the Yankee attack. New York took the opener, 8-7.

1946 — Edward (Ed) Hermann B (C, DH 1975)

1947 — James (Jim) York B (P 1976)

1977 — Tobby Harrah and Bump Wills hit back-to-back inside-the-park homeruns off Yankee reliever Ken Clay during Texas' 8-2 win at the Stadium.

1978 — The "Miracle of Catfish Hunter" continues, as the veteran Yankee pitcher continues his amazing comeback by downing the A's, 6-2, and thereby finishing the month of August with a 6-0 record and 1.64 ERA. The win, although of great psychological value, merely enabled the Yankees to keep pace with the first place Red Sox, 7½ games out.

28

1875 — Joseph "Little Joe" Yeager B (INF 1905-06)

1892 — Robert "Braggo" Roth B (OF 1921)

1896 — Aaron Ward B (INF, OF 1917-26)

1916 — Michael "Shotgun" Chartak B (OF 1940)

1924 — Yankees purchase pitcher Walter Beall from Rochester for $50,000.

1938 — William (Billy) Cowan B (OF, 1B 1969)

1943 — Louis "Sweet Lou" Piniella B (OF, DH, 1B 1974-current)

1946 — Michael (Mike) Torrez B (P 1977)

1950 — Ronald "Louisiana Lightning" Guidry B (1976-current)

1952 — Yankees purchase pitcher Ewell Blackwell from the Reds for $35,000. The deal also included a player swap, with the Yankees sending pitchers Johnny Schmitz and Ernie Nevel, and outfielders Bob Marquis and Jim Greengrass to the Reds for other considerations.

1977 — In his finest performance of the season, Ron Guidry faces just 28 Rangers in pitching a two-hit, complete game, 1-0 win. The Yankees scored when Reggie Jackson's sacrifice fly scored Graig Nettles from third base, after Nettles had tripled. It was Guidry's third shutout of the year.

29

1888 — Ensign Cottrell B (P 1915)

1911 — The Highlanders overcome seven errors and down the Browns, 7-4. The errant New Yorkers were: Roy Hartzell (3B) 2, Charlie Hemphil (cf), Otis Johnson (ss), Mike Fitzgerald (lf), Jim Williams (c) and Hippo Vaughn (p).

1925 — Babe Ruth is suspended indefinitely by Yankees manager Miller Huggins, and fined $5,000, for insubordination and laxity on and off the playing field. Ruth had never gotten along too well with Huggins, and had often engaged in conduct which infuriated the manager. On more than one occasion, Ruth and Bob Meusel had held the "Mighty Mite" manager out of the window of trains and buses in which the team traveled.

The events leading up to the suspension can be summed up by pointing out that the Yankees were having a weak year, partially because of Babe Ruth's infamous "stomach ache." In the days preceding the action, Ruth and others had become increasingly vocal in their criticisms of Huggins, and blatantly violated the manager's rules for on and off the field conduct. When Ruth arrived late for the pre-game warmups that day, Huggins informed him that he was suspended. (Of course Huggins had previously discussed the Ruthian problem with Yankee general manager Ed Borrow, and owner Jake Ruppert, both of whom assured the manager of their support.)

Ruth reacted by throwing a mild tantrum, and then left the club to head for New York and a meeting with Ruppert. He also told several reporters that he was through with the Yankees for as long as Huggins was the manager.

1928 — Maurice (Mickey) McDermott B (P 1956)

1937 — Harold (Hal) Stowe B (P 1960)

1950 — George Zeber B (2B 1977-78)

1951 — Yankees purchase pitcher Johnny Sain from the Braves for $50,000 and the transfer of pitcher Lew Burdette to the Braves' franchise.

1967 — The "longest day" in Yankee history comes to an end when New York edges Boston, 4-3, in the 20-inning second game of a doubleheader. The two teams played 29 innings that day: 2:10 in Game I (a Sox 2-1 win) and 6:09 in Game II.

1977 — Chris Chambliss' three-run, pinch-hit homerun in the eighth inning gives the Yankees a come-from-behind 5-3 win against the Royals.

30

1906 — Hal Chase becomes the first Yankee (Highlander) to hit three triples in one game during a 9-8 win against the Senators.

1910 — Yankee righthander Tom Hughes hurls nine no-hit innings against the Indians, but surrenders a hit in the tenth inning, and then yields five runs in the eleventh, to go down to a 5-0 defeat. No other Yankee has ever pitched so hard, for so little!

1916 — John "Lindy" Lindell B (OF, 1B, P 1941-50)

1917 — Charles "Red" Embree B (P 1948)

1918 — William (Billy) Johnson B (3B, 1B, 2B 1943, 46-51)

1925 — George (Teddy) Wilson B (OF 1956)

1925 — Babe Ruth holds a press conference upon his arrival in New York and assails manager Miller Huggins. Ruth also makes known his intentions of seeing owner Jake Ruppert to settle the matter of Ruth's suspension to his satisfaction. (Ironically, the "his" proved to be Huggins!)

1941 — Archibald (Archie) Moore B (OF, 1B 1964-65)

1973 — Yankees obtain pitcher Casey Cox from the Rangers for pitcher Jim Roland.

1977 — After allowing the pesky Mariners to tie the score at 5-5 in the eighth inning, the Yankees finally beat Seattle, 6-5, when Mickey Rivers leads off the 11th inning with a homerun.

31

1916 — Raymond (Ray) Mack B (2B 1947)

1925 — Babe Ruth meets with Yankee owner Jake Ruppert and learns that Ruppert is 100% behind manager Miller Huggins' suspension and fining of Ruth. Ruppert also announces that Ruth will remain suspended until such time as he apologizes to Huggins, and until such time as Huggins decides to lift the suspension. The $5,000 fine, the largest ever levied by a club on one of its own players, would also stick. (It was later refunded after Huggins' death in 1929.)

1942 — Yankees obtain outfielder Roy Cullenbine from the Senators on waivers.

1977 — Sparky Lyle is the reliever on the mound again, as the Yankees come-from-behind to beat the pesky Mariners, 5-4, when Graig Nettles hits his second homerun of the game. It was the third straight game New York won on late-inning homerun heroics, and was also the third straight game won by Lyle in relief, in as many days.

The win enabled the Yankees to finish the month of August in first place, four games ahead of the Red Sox.

SEPTEMBER

1

1903 — Foster (Eddie) Edwards B (P 1930)

1905 — Yankees sell pitcher Jack Powell to the Browns for an undisclosed amount of cash.

1957 — Yankees obtain pitcher Sal Maglie from the Dodgers for $25,000 and two minor leaguers.

2

1884 — Joseph (Joe) Ward B (2B, SS, 1B, OF 1909)

1909 — Monte Pearson B (P 1936-40)

1927 — Trade rumors fill the New York papers alleging that Lou Gehrig would be dealt to the Tigers, or that Bob Meusel would be exiled to Chicago. While no specifics were mentioned in the Gehrig deal, the Meusel trade had New York sending Meusel, infielder Mike Gazella, catcher Pat Collins and an unnamed pitcher to the White Sox for third baseman Willie Kamm (a lifetime .281 hitter), catcher Harry McCurdy (a .282 hitter), and outfielder Bibb Falk (a .314 hitter over 14 seasons).

1933 — Marvin "Marvelous Marv" Throneberry B (1B 1955, 58-59)

1978 — Ed Figueroa wins his 14th game of the season, and Reggie Jackson and Chris Chambliss each hit a homerun, as the Yankees dump the Mariners, 6-2, and move within 5½ games of the first place Red Sox. Jackson's homerun (No. 20 of the year) makes him the 19th player in baseball history to hit 20 or more homeruns for 11 straight seasons.

3

1906 — The Yankees (Highlanders) are awarded the second game of a doubleheader with the Athletics on FORFEIT! This was one of the wildest days in the history of the A.L. franchise in New York. A huge crowd (in excess of 20,000) had filled Hilltop Park (capacity approximately 16,000) because a sweep of the schedule twin-bill would catapult New York into first place.

The Highlanders won the opener, 4-3, but the behavior of New York's shortstop Kid Elberfeld sickened the crowd. The "Kid" objected to umpire Mike O'Loughlin's safe call on a steal of third by the visitor's Danny Murphy. O'Loughlin waved the "Kid" away, and thereby infuriated the volatile shortstop. Elberfeld went after the umpire and on no less than six occasions attempted to kick the man in blue, forcing the police to enter the playing field to protect the umpire and remove Elberfeld from the game. The fans booed Elberfeld soundly.

That set the stage for an even wilder second game. The Highlanders staged a three-run rally in the ninth inning, with two of the runs scoring on a controversial ruling of no interference by New York's Willie Keeler on what could have been an infield out. Two runs scored on the play after Keeler had precipitated a collision with the Athletics shortstop, and a tremendous argument followed.

When the umpires refused to yield to the Athletics' objections, the Philadelphians marched off the field. After repeatedly ordering the resumption of play, the umpires ruled the game forfeited to New York. The score had been 3-3, but is officially listed as a 9-0 win.

89

1939 — Thirty-three years to the day after the great forfeit of 1906, the Yankees are again declared winners on forfeit when hostile Red Sox fans litter the field repeatedly with garbage, and render it unplayable.

The setting was the second game of a doubleheader at Fenway Park. Boston won the opener, 12-11.

In the second game, with the score tied 5-5 and New York batting in the eighth inning, a quick glance at the clock showed that less than 15 minutes remained before curfew (6:30 p.m. on Sundays). The Yankees quickly scored two runs, to take a 7-5 lead, and realized that Boston had to bat in the bottom of the inning in order to make it an official game. Similarly, the Red Sox realized that if the Yankees could be kept at bat long enough, the game would end before the Sox batted.

What followed was a nice cat and mouse game between the rival managers. First, the Sox attempted to walk Babe Dahlgren, in hopes of prolonging the inning. The Yankees responded by having their runner on third base, George Selkirk, "attempt" to steal home, whereupon he was easily tagged out. The Sox continued their attempt at walking Dahlgren, but the uncooperative batter swung at what would have been balls three and four. On the fifth pitch, the succeeding Yankee runner on third base (Joe Gordon) attempted to steal home, and was put out.

A tremendous argument ensued, with Boston manager Joe Cronin claiming it was illegal for the Yankees to "deliberately" make outs. Umpire Cal Hubbard infuriated the Sox and their fans by ruling that deliberately making an out was not against the rules. When it became clear that Boston had lost the argument, the fans littered the field with debris. Attempts at cleaning the playing area were repeatedly frustrated by the fans, who continued to pour out their wrath (and garbage) onto the field.

Eventually, the umpires had no choice but to order the game forfeited to the Yankees.

1947 — The Yankees bang out 18 hits, all of them singles, during an 11-2 win at Fenway Park. The "sluggers" were: Tommy Henrich (4), Joe DiMaggio (4), John Lindell (2), George McQuinn (2), Billy Johnson (2), Aaron Robinson (2), Phil Rizzuto and George Stirnweiss.

In the nightcap of the doubleheader, the Yankees made 16 hits and outslugged Boston, 9-6.

1954 — Yankees purchase pitcher Tommy Byrne from Seattle of the Pacific Coast League for an undisclosed amount of cash and other considerations.

1978 — In the greatest relief performance of the year, flame-thrower Rich Gossage enters the game in the top of the ninth inning with Mariners on second and third, no outs, and the Yankees clinging to a 4-3 lead. Gossage proceeds to throw 11 pitches, and strikes out the side. The win enabled the Yankees to keep pace with the first place Red Sox, 5½ games out of first place.

4

1923 — Yankee ace Sam Jones no-hits the Athletics, 2-0.

1941 — The Yankees clinch their 12th pennant by beating Boston, 6-3, behind Atley Donald's five-hitter.

1946 — Kenneth (Ken) Wright B (P 1974)

1977 — Southpaw Don Gullett comes off the disabled list and hurls his first American League shutout, a 4-0 win versus the Twins. Cliff Johnson's first inning grand slam homerun accounted for all of the scoring. The win enabled New York to open up a 4½ game lead over the Red Sox.

1978 — Ron Guidry wins his 20th game of the season, and Chris Chambliss' bases loaded triple highlights an 8-run seventh inning, as New York beats Detroit, 9-1, in the first game of a doubleheader. The Tigers rebounded with a 5-4 win in the nightcap. The split pulled New York to within five games of the first place Red Sox.

1911 — John "Buddy" Hassett B (1B 1942)

1922 — Babe Ruth closes out the Yankees seven-year tenure as tenants of the Giants in the Polo Grounds by hitting a tremendous homerun off Red Sox pitcher Herb Pennock. The Yankees lost, 4-3.

(Note: Pennock also surrendered Ruth's first Yankee homerun.)

1927 — Boston edges New York, 12-11, in an 18-inning battle during the first game of a doubleheader at Fenway Park. Red Ruffing, a future Yankee, pitched 15 innings for Boston, and got no decision, but he made a permanent impression upon the Yankee management.

New York won the nightcap, 5-0.

1936 — In a day the Yankees would just as soon forget, New York drops a 3-2 decision to Boston in the first game of a scheduled doubleheader, and then throws away the second game by allowing the Sox to come-from-behind and tie the score in time for darkness to end it at 7-7. Adding to the second game woes were two errors apiece for Joe DiMaggio and Bill Dickey, and a triple play against New York.

Then again, with all that going against them, perhaps the Yankees should gladly settle for the tie.

1950 — Yankees purchase infielder Johnny Hopp from the Pirates on waivers.

1952 — The Yankees re-sign former Yankee outfielder Charlie Keller after his release by the Tigers.

1952 — Manager Casey Stengel makes his famous "bus ride speech" to his "loafing Yankees." New York had just dropped two out of three games to the hapless Athletics (normally easy prey), while the Indians were on a hot streak, and the result was the possibility that the first place

Clevelanders might break the race open. Fortunately, the speech had its effect, because New York went on a 15/18 streak.

1955 — Gilbert (Gil) Patterson B (P 1977)

1964 — Yankees purchase pitcher Pedro Ramos from the Indians for an undisclosed amount of cash.

1977 — The Cleveland Indians stage the first "Hate the Yankees Hanky Night", and the Tribe responds by ending an 18-game losing streak against New York and sweeping the Yankees, 4-3 and 5-4. The soon to be imitated promotion swelled the crowd to 28,184 fans, more than triple the Indians' average attendance.

6

1921 — Jack "Stretch" Phillips B (1B, 3B 1947-49)

1946 — Francis (Fran) Healy B (C 1976-78)

1950 — Doyle Alexander B (P 1976)

1954 — The Yankees use a record 10 pinch hitters during a doubleheader versus the Red Sox. The Yankees came from behind to capture the opener, 6-5, thanks to a pinch hit homerun by Joe Collins, but dropped the nightcap, 7-6, after blowing a 6-0 lead.

1973 — Yankees sell outfielder-first baseman Matty Alou to the Cardinals, and send his brother, Felipe Alou, to the Expos, for undisclosed amounts of cash and future considerations.

1977 — The Yankees rebound from a doubleheader loss the night before and clobber Cleveland, 8-3. The big blow is a Reggie Jackson three-run space shot. The win kept the Yankees 2½ games ahead of the Sox.

7

1889 — William (Bill) Holden B (OF 1913-14)

1894 — Joseph "Shags" Horan B (OF 1924)

1952 — Johnny Mize's pinch hit grand slam homerun off Washington's Walt Masterson leads the Yankees to a come-from-behind 5-1 win. The sixth inning shot gave Mize the distinction of hitting a homerun in every major league ballpark he ever played in.

1955 — Whitey Ford becomes the fifth pitcher in major league history to hurl consecutive one hitters by beating the Athletics, 2-1, and allowing only a double to Jim Finnigan in the seventh inning.

Ford had one-hit the Senators, 4-2, in his last previous start, with Washington's Carlos Paula spoiling the no-hit bid with a single in the seventh inning.

Ford was improving — the hit against Washington came with one out; the hit against the Athletics with two!

1978 — The 1978 version of the Boston Massacre begins with a 15-3 Yankee victory in Fenway Park. The win pulls New York within three games of the first place Red Sox. Sixteen of New York's 21 hits were singles!

8

1928 — The Yankees sweep the Athletics, 3-0 and 7-3, to move back into first place to stay. The Athletics had engineered an August surge which carried them past New York, but they ran out of gas in September.

1937 — Trailing the Red Sox 6-1 in the ninth inning, the Yankees rally for 8 runs with two outs, and down Boston, 9-6, in the second game of a doubleheader. The rally started when Don Heffner tripled home two runs. Pinch hitter Bill Dickey doubled Heffner home, and Jack Saltzgaver (pinch running for Dickey) came home when Red Sox shortstop Joe Cronin bobbled Frank Crosetti's ground ball. Red Rolfe walked, and Joe DiMaggio singled home Crosetti to kayo pitcher Jack Wilson.

Reliever Al Thomas threw one pitch to Lou Gehrig, and watched it sail over the wall for a game-winning homerun.

In the first game of the doubleheader, Myril Hoag's ninth inning single scored the winning run in a 3-2 victory.

1939 — In another wild adventure with Boston, the Yankees take a 4-1 lead into the seventh inning, and are declared the winners when a. terrible thunderstorm causes the umpires to declare the field unsafe. Contemporary sources said the lightning show was the best they'd ever seen.

1952 — Lawrence (Larry) McCall B (P 1977-current)

1973 — Light-hitting Fred Stanley hits the final grand slam in the Old Yankee Stadium, a left field foul pole shot off Brewers' hurler Kevin Kobel during New York's 15-1 win.

1977 — Chris Chambliss' fifth inning sacrifice fly provides the margin of victory as the Yankees edge Cleveland, 4-3, behind Ed Figueroa. The win opened a 3½ game lead over Boston.

1978 — In the second part of the 1978 Boston Massacre, the Yankees bang out 17 hits, including homeruns by Reggie Jackson and Lou Piniella, to trounce the Sox, 13-2.

9

1877 — Frank "Peerless Leader" Chance B (1B 1913-14)

1880 — Ambrose Puttman B (P 1903-05)

1895 — Daniel "Dashing Dan" Costello B (PH 1913)

1899 — Waite "Schoolboy" Hoyt B (P 1921-30)

1916 — Yankees release shortstop Rube Oldring.

1927 — Tony Lazzeri Day at Yankee Stadium.

1928 — Urban Shocker dies of heart failure in Denver at 38. The veteran pitcher had suffered from a swollen heart for more than two years, a malady which prevented him from sleeping in a prone position. As the facts of his serious health problem came to light, his teammates came to realize that he was as tragic a hero as any man who ever wore the pinstripes.

1932 — Truman "Tex" Clevenger B (P 1961-62)

1932 — Frank Crosetti equals the major league record by striking out twice in one inning. His teammates ignored his example and scored four runs that inning. As if it were not enough to strike out at the start and end of an inning, Crosetti also struck out his first four out of five times at bat in that game.

By the way, the Yankees lost, 14-13.

1936 — The Yankees clinch their eighth pennant while sweeping the Indians, 11-3 and 12-9. New York went on to record a 102-51 mark, and finished 19½ games ahead of the Tigers, the largest margin in Yankee history.

1970 — Yankees sell pitcher Steve Hamilton to the Cubs for an undisclosed amount of cash.

1977 — Mike Torrez notches a three-hit, 2-0 win against Toronto, and Cliff Johnson continues his one-man assault on the Blue Jays pitching staff with a homerun, as the Yankees maintain a three game lead over the Red Sox, who swept a doubleheader.

1978 — In the third event of the 1978 Boston Massacre, Lou Piniella's wind-blown double opens the flood-gates for a seven-run fourth inning, and the Yankees dump the Red Sox, 7-0.

10

1880 — Harry Niles B (2B, OF, SS 1908)

1919 — Cleveland's Ray Caldwell no-hits the Yankees, 3-0, in the first game of a doubleheader. New York also dropped the nightcap, 3-2.

1921 — Wally Schang's five hits pace a 21-hit attack as the Yankees down the Athletics, 19-3, behind Carl Mays' 13-hitter!

1922 — The largest crowd in the history of the Polo Grounds (up to that time) is on hand as the Yankees sweep the Athletics, 10-3 and 2-1, behind Joe Bush and Waite Hoyt.

1925 — Bob Meusel, Babe Ruth, and Lou Gehrig hit consecutive homeruns in the fourth inning of the first game of a doubleheader with the Athletics to lead New York to a 7-3 win.

In the second game, Ruth and Ben Paschal hit back-to-back homeruns in the fourth inning, but the Athletics edged New York, 5-4, in 12 innings.

1934 — Roger Maris B (OF 1960-66)

1950 — Joe DiMaggio hits three homeruns to highlight the Yankees' 8-1 win at Washington. The three homeruns combined with a double to give DiMaggio 4 RBI's on the day.

1957 — Yankees purchase Bobby "The Greek" Del Greco from the Cubs for the waiver price.

1966 — Yankees obtain pitcher Thad Tillotson and an undisclosed amount of cash for shortstop Dick Schofield.

1974 — Yankees purchase designated hitter Alex Johnson from the Rangers for an undisclosed amount of cash believed to be in the neighborhood of $50,000. Johnson arrived in Boston, where the Yankees and Red Sox were locked in an extra inning duel, suited up, and hit a game-winning homerun in the 12th inning to give his new team a 2-1 win!

1977 — The Blue Jays shock the Yankees with a 20-hit attack en route to a 19-3 win. Catfish Hunter was the Yankee starter and loser. Roy Howell had five hits and nine runs batted in for Toronto.

(Note: Hunter did not pitch again until the world series.)

1978 — The Yankees complete a four game sweep in the 1978 Boston Massacre, behind Ed Figueroa's 16th win. The 7-4 win added up to a 42-9 Yankee advantage over the four games. New York outhit Boston, 67-21.

11

1923 — After surrendering a controversial leadoff single by Whitey Witt, Red Sox pitcher Howard Ehmke retires 27 consecutive Yankees and wins, 3-0. The Sox crowd vehemently called for a reversal of the one hit, which was awarded on a hard shot to third base which third baseman Howard Shanks booted.

1926 — Bob Meusel ties the major league record for sacrifice flies in one game when he hits three during a 6-4 win at Cleveland. In the same game, shortstop Mark Koenig handles 16 chances without an error, one short of the record set by the Browns' Bob Wallace in 1902.

1940 — After winning the first game of a doubleheader in Cleveland, the Yankees spend a few brief hours in first place. Those three or so hours were the sum total of time New York found itself in the top spot that year. A second game loss dropped the Yankees back to the second spot.

1966 — Johnny Miller becomes the only Yankee to hit a homerun in his first major league at-bat.

1969 — Yankees obtain Terry Bongiovanni and an undisclosed amount of cash for outfielder Jimmie Hall.

12

1907 — Spurgeon "Spud" Chandler B (P 1937-47)

1916 — Charles "King Kong" Keller B (OF 1939-49, 52)

1954 — The largest crowd in American League history, some 86,563 fans (84,587 paid), is on hand to watch their Indians sweep the Yankees, 4-1 and 3-2, at Cleveland. The sweep erased New York's pennant hopes for 1954.

1977 — With their lead cut to 1½ games over the second place Red Sox, the Yankees have a badly needed day off to prepare for their upcoming three game series against Boston at Yankee Stadium.

13

1893 — Walter "Dutch" Ruether B (P 1926-27)

1893 — Michael (Mike) McNally B (INF 1921-24)

1896 — Patrick (Pat) Collins B (C 1926-28)

1927 — Waite Hoyt becomes the only 20-game winner on the 1927 Yankees when he scatters 10 Indians' hits during New York's 5-3 win. He finished the season 22-7.

1932 — The Yankees clinch their seventh pennant by defeating the Indians, 9-3, behind George Pipgras.

1949 — Richard (Rick) Dempsey B (C, DH 1973-76)

1977 — Mickey Rivers' two-run homerun in the fifth inning proves the gamewinner, and Ron Guidry spins a neat five-hitter, as the Yankees take the first game of a crucial three-game series with Boston, 4-2, at Yankee Stadium. The largest regular season crowd in the New Stadium, 55,269, attended.

1978 — The Yankees down Detroit, 7-3, and move into first place, ½ game ahead of Boston.

14

1884 — Andrew (Andy) O'Connor B (P 1908)

1924 — Gerald (Jerry) Coleman B (INF 1949-57)

1936 — Stanley (Stan) Williams B (P 1963-64)

1942 — The Yankees clinch their 13th pennant behind the hitting of Joe DiMaggio and the pitching of Tiny Bonham. DiMaggio hit a homerun and three singles to lead the Yankees to an 8-3 win, while Bonham was notching his 20th victory of the season.

1952 — The Yankees win a crucial showdown with the Indians, 7-1, as Eddie Lopat outpitches Yankee nemesis Mike Garcia. Garcia entered the game with a 4-0 mark against New York that year, and the Indians had closed the gap to ½ game behind the front-running Yankees. When the season ended, New York finished just two games ahead of the Indians.

1953 — The Yankees clinch their 20th pennant during an 8-5 win against the Indians. Billy Martin led the attack with four RBIs on two doubles and a single.

1977 — Reggie Jackson's two-run homerun in the bottom of the ninth inning off Boston starter Reggie Cleveland gives New York a 2-0 win, and puts the Yankees 3½ games ahead of the Sox in the hot battle for first place. Ed Figueroa went the distance for New York, and scattered seven hits while picking up his 15th win. The Red Sox found the long stretches of open space in left center and center fields with great regularity, but the Yankee outfielders proved up to the task of running down several long drives. In Fenway Park, this would have come out a lot differently.

1978 — The Yankees defeat the Tigers, 4-2, to take a 1½ game lead into their weekend series with Boston at Yankee Stadium.

15

1881 — Judd "Slow Joe" Doyle B (P 1906-10)

1925 — Yankees obtain pitcher Herb McQuaid from St. Paul of the American Association for an undisclosed amount of cash.

1937 — Charles (Charlie) Smith B (3B 1967-68)

1947 — The Yankees clinch their 15th pennant when the White Sox beat the Red Sox, 6-3, while New York is idled by rain.

1949 — David (Dave) Pagan B (P 1973-77)

1950 — Johnny Mize hits three homeruns in one game for the sixth time in his career, but the Yankees go down to defeat, 9-7, at Detroit.

1977 — The Red Sox salvage the final game of the three game series, 7-3, behind Luis Tiant and Bill Campbell.

The loss left the Yankees in first place by 2½ games, and all eyes pointed north to Boston, where the teams would meet in seven days for another crucial two-game series.

1978 — Ron Guidry wins his 22nd game, and Graig Nettles and Chris Chambliss hit homeruns, as the Yankees bop the Sox, 4-0, at Yankee Stadium to open a 2½ game lead.

16

1877 — George McConnell B (P 1909, 12-13)

1905 — Joseph "Sandy" Vance B (P 1937-38)

1908 — Colonel "Buster" Mills B (OF 1940)

1939 — The Yankees clinch their 11th pennant in an 8-5 victory against the Tigers behind pitcher Marius Russo.

1955 — The Yankees open a key series with the Red Sox. On this day, the Yankees trail first place Cleveland by ½ game with 11 games remaining in the schedule of both teams. Cleveland supposedly had the easier schedule because they did not face the tough Sox.

In game I of the series, the Yankees opened an early 3-0 lead, only to fall behind, 4-3, in the eighth inning. Adding to the Yankee woes were Moose Skowron's violent reaction to an out (he kicked the water cooler and broke his toe) and Mickey Mantle's apparent muscle tear (he pulled up lame after beating out a bunt).

The Yankees came to bat in the bottom of the ninth. With one out, Hank Bauer hit a homerun off reliever Ellis Kinder to tie the score. One out later, Yogi Berra hit a game-winning homerun.

The Indians lost to Detroit, and the Yankees were in first place to stay.

1972 — Yankees purchase pitcher Steve Blateric from the Reds for the waivers price.

1977 — The Yankees rally for four runs in the eighth inning to come-from-behind and defeat Detroit, 5-4. Paul Blair's two-run homerun provided the margin of victory, and Don Gullett went the distance to record his 12th win of the season.

1978 — The Yankees stretch their lead over the second place Red Sox to 3½ games by edging Boston, 3-2, at the Stadium. Catfish Hunter was the winner, and the game-winning run scored on Thurman Munson's sacrifice fly after Mickey Rivers had led off the ninth inning with a triple.

17

1917 — Allen Gettel B (P 1945-46)

1917 — Fritz Maisel's seventh inning single breaks up Indians' pitcher Stan Coveleski's no-hit bid during a 2-0 loss to Cleveland.

1936 — Thomas (Tom) Carroll B (SS, 3B 1955-56)

1950 — Johnny Hopp pinch hits grand slam homerun off Browns pitcher Al Widmar during a five-run, ninth inning rally which carried the Yankees to a 6-1 win.

1951 — With the bases loaded and one out in the bottom of the ninth inning, Phil Rizzuto's suicide squeeze bunt scores Joe DiMaggio from third base with the winning run in a crucial 2-1 win against the Indians. The win gave New York a sweep of the two game series with Cleveland, and nudged the Yankees into first place to stay.

1956 — The Yankees clinch their 22nd pennant when Mickey Mantle hits his 50th homerun of the season to end an 11-inning battle with the ChiSox, 3-2.

1977 — The Yankees slam five homeruns (two by Reggie Jackson and one by the newly-acquired Dave Kingman) and make 17 hits in route to a 9-4 win against the Tigers.

1978 — The Red Sox salvage the final game of their three game series with the Yankees, 7-3, to creep back to 2½ games behind New York. The three game series drew a combined attendance of more than 165,000 fans, the largest attendance for a three game series since 1958.

18

1898 — George "The Bull" Uhle B (P 1933-34)

1909 — Robert (Bob) Collins B (C 1944)

1927 — Luis "Yo-yo" Arroyo B (P 1960-63)

1938 — The Yankees "back into" their 10th pennant when the Red Sox are rained out a doubleheader with Chicago. This was all the more unique because the New Yorkers were in the process of losing a twin-bill to the Browns. In those days, rain outs were not made up.

1948 — Kenneth (Ken) Brett B (P 1976)

1967 — Yankees purchase outfielder Len Boehmer from the Reds for an undisclosed amount, and return the "favor" by selling pitcher Bill Henry to the Reds for the same undisclosed amount.

1977 — The Yankees survive a five-run Tiger ninth inning to edge the Tigers, 6-5. Detroit proved to be a stubborn opponent down the stretch, perhaps egged on by former Yankee skipper Ralph Houk, who never really forgave the Yankees for what most observers called a "forced" resignation.

19

1890 — Ralph Young B (SS 1913)

1909 — Hersh Martin B (OF 1944-45)

1913 — Nicholas (Nick) Etten B (1B 1943-46)

1921 — Yankees obtain pitcher Oscar Roettger from Joplin of the Western League in return for an extension of the agreement whereby the Yankees loaned Joplin Jack Doyle and Larry Christianson.

1930 — Robert "Bullet Bob" Turley B (P 1955-62)

1966 — Mike Burke is named president of the Yankees.

1977 — The Yankee-Red Sox showdown moves to Fenway Park, where the Sox down the Yankees, 6-3, to cut the Yankee lead to three games.

20

1911 — The Yankees commit seven errors in the first game of a doubleheader with the Indians (a 12-9 loss), and then commit five more in the nightcap (a 5-4 win). The 12 errors in one day is still the Yankee record for the dropsies.

1938 — Thomas (Tom) Tresh B (OF, SS, 3B 1961-69)

1954 — Eugene "Mickey" Klutts B (SS, 3B 1976-78)

1961 — Roger Maris' 59th homerun of the season comes in the third inning of the 154th game of the year. The pitcher was Milt Pappas. The significance is for those antiquarians who still subscribe to the Ford Frick asterisk deal, which required Maris to hit his homeruns within the same 154-game schedule Babe Ruth had in 1927, or suffer an asterisk designate the difference in games played.

For the record, Maris almost hit his 60th in the seventh inning, when his drive down the right field line hooked less than 10 feet foul. More importantly, the homerun led New York to a 4-2 win, and helped clinch the Yankees' 26th pennant.

1977 — Rain postpones Game II of the showdown in Boston.

21

1875 — Frank McManus B (C 1903)

1892 — Elmer Smith B (OF 1922-23)

1906 — Yankee first baseman Hal Chase ties the major league record by handling 22 put outs in a nine inning game during New York's 6-3 win in the first game of a doubleheader with the White Sox.

1942 — Samuel "Sudden Sam" McDowell B (P 1973)

1956 — The Yankees strand a record 20 baserunners during a 13-9 loss at Fenway Park. This game was also highlighted by a Mickey Mantle space shot which traveled more than 500 feet into the bleachers. The ball struck the rear retaining wall 10 inches below the top, after passing the playing field wall more than 40 feet to the right of the flagpole.

1958 — Thirty-five-year-old knuckleballer Hoyt Wilhelm no hits the Yankees during Baltimore's 1-0 win. Gus Triandos' seventh inning homerun accounted for the only run.

1977 — George Scott's sixth inning homerun, and diving stab of a ninth inning line drive, lead the Red Sox to a 3-2 win and bring Boston to within 2 games of the Yankees.

22

1870 — Michael (Mike) Powers B (C, 1B 1905)

1885 — James (Jimmy) Walsh B (OF, INF 1914)

1920 — Robert (Bob Lemon B (coach 1976, manager 1978-current)

1925 — Outfielder Ben Paschal hits two inside-the-park homeruns during the Yankees' 11-6 win against the White Sox in the first game of a doubleheader at Yankee Stadium. The Yankees lost the nightcap, 4-2.

1927 — Earle Combs connects for three triples during the Yankees' 8-7 win against the Tigers.

1929 — Harry Bright B (1B, 3B 1963-64)

1952 — Wendell (Del) Alston B (OF 1977-78)

23

1898 — George "Smiler" Murray B (P 1922)

1910 — After a 7-2 loss to the Indians, Highlander manager George Stallings resigns. The Highlanders were having their most successful season since 1904 (79-61, good for second place) but trailed the Athletics by 15 games.

1933 — The Yankees commit seven errors (Frank Crosetti 3, Doc Farrell 2, Bill Rensa, and Lyn Lary) but outslug Boston, 16-12.

1950 — Leading the Red Sox by two games, and sharing first place with the Indians, the Yankees open a crucial series with Boston at Yankee Stadium. In the first game of that series, Joe DiMaggio's first inning, two-run, homerun off Yankee nemesis Mel Parnell gets the Yankees off and running to an 8-0 win.

1977 — Graig Nettles' ninth inning, two-run, homerun puts Yankee fans' fears to rest as the New Yorkers rebound from the two-game sweep in Boston by downing season-long nemesis Toronto, 5-3, behind Don Gullett's five-hitter.

1978 — A 10-1 loss to Cleveland drops the Yankee lead to one game over the Red Sox.

24

1910 — Frederick "Dixie" Walker (OF 1931, 33-36)

1910 — Hal Chase is named manager of the Highlanders.

1919 — Babe Ruth hits his 28th homerun of the season and thereby breaks the old record for homeruns in one season, held by Ed Williamson of the 1884 Chicago Cubs. The victims: his future teammates, the Yankees, and future buddy, Bob Shawkey.

1934 — Babe Ruth makes his final appearance as a Yankee in Yankee Stadium. He walked in the first inning, and left the game for a pinch runner. Less than 2,500 fans attended.

1950 — In the second game of a key series with Boston, the Yankees outslug the Sox, 9-5, before 66,924 fans. Phil Rizzuto (single, double, and a rare homerun) and Yogi Berra (three singles and a rare triple) keyed the New York attack.

1954 — The Yankees tie a major league record when three consecutive Yankee pinch hitters strike out in one inning. The ninth inning victims of Athletics' pitcher Arnold Portocarrero were Lou Berberet, Gus Triandos and Frank Leja. A total of 11 Yankees "K'd" that day, and New York lost, 5-1.

1973 — Yankees purchase catcher Duke Sims from the Tigers on waivers.

1978 — Ron Guidry raises his record to 23-3, lowers his ERA to 1.74, and pitches his third two-hitter in a row during New York's 4-0 win against Cleveland. The shutout, his ninth of the season, broke the Yankee record for shutouts in one season, and left Guidry one short of the A.L. record set by Babe Ruth in 1916.

25

1902 — Pierce (Pat) Malone B (P 1935-37)

1918 — John Sain B (P 1951-55)

1918 — Phillip "Scooter" Rizzuto B (SS, 2B 1941-42, 46-56)

1926 — The Yankees sweep the Browns, 10-2 and 10-4, to nail down their fourth A.L. pennant.

1929 — Yankee manager Miller Huggins dies of exhaustion and blood poisoning at 50 years of age.

1934 — Lou Gehrig plays his 1,500th consecutive game during New York's 5-0 win against Philadelphia.

1942 — Yankees purchase third baseman Hank Majeski from the Braves on waivers.

1966 — The smallest crowd in Yankee Stadium history, 413 fans, see the Yankees lose to Chicago, 4-1.

1977 — Cliff Johnson continues his personal assault on the Toronto Blue Jays by slamming two homeruns in the second game of a doubleheader to lead New York to a 2-0 win. Ron Guidry won the opener, 15-0, as the Yankees boosted their lead over the Sox to three games. The double-shutout was the Yankees first since July 21, 1972.

(Note: Johnson hit six of his 12 Yankee homeruns off the Blue Jays, and batted .381 against Toronto, compared to .296 against the rest of the league.)

26

1921 — The Yankees edge the Indians 4-2 in the first game of a crucial doubleheader at the Polo Grounds. The Yankees entered the four-game series leading Cleveland by ½-game in the battle for first place. Waite Hoyt got New York off and running in the opener, but the Indians evened matters in the second game by dumping New York, 9-0.

1925 — Robert (Bobby) Shantz B (P 1957-60)

1926 — The Yankees and Browns play the shortest doubleheader in major league history: 2 hours and 7 minutes, or so the contemporary reports claimed. The Yankees had already clinched the pennant, so dropping the opener, 6-1, in one hour and twelve minutes did not faze them; nor did losing the nightcap, 6-2 in 55 minutes.

1952 — The Yankees clinch their 19th pennant in an 11-inning 5-2 win at Philadelphia behind Eddie Lopat and Johnny Sain.

1961 — Roger Maris hits his 60th homerun of the season as the Yankees come-from-behind to down Baltimore, 3-2. Orioles' hurler Jack Fisher surrendered the historic blow in the third inning. Interestingly enough, Fisher also surrendered Ted Williams' final homerun.

1964 — Yankee pitcher Mel Stottlemyre hits four singles and one double in a nine inning game to tie the major league record for hits by a pitcher in one game. The Yankees rode Stottlemyre's bat (2 RBI's) and two-hit pitching to their 11th straight win, 7-0 versus the Senators.

27,

1919 — Pitcher Bob Shawkey records 15 strikeouts in a nine inning, 9-2, win versus his former teammates from Philadelphia. This remained the Yankee strikeout record until 1978, when Ron Guidry fanned 18 Angels.

1921 — The largest crowd to ever see the Yankees play in the Polo Grounds (estimated to exceed 40,000 people) jammed the 30,000-seat stadium and the Yankees responded with a 21-7 shellacking of the Indians in Game III of their big series to determine the 1921 pennant winner. The victory moved New York 1½ games ahead of Cleveland.

1923 — Lou Gehrig hits his first major league homerun. The victim: Boston's Bill Piercy. The location: Fenway Park. The final score: New York 8, Boston 3.

28

1885 — Wilbur "Lefty" Good B (P 1905)

1892 — Jack Fournier B (2B 1917-18)

1895 — Lawton "Whitey" Witt B (OF 1922-25)

1923 — The Yankees overwhelm the Red Sox, 24-4. Among the battered Red Sox pitchers was Howard Ehmke, who staggered through six innings, allowing 17 runs and 21 hits. Sixteen Yankees batted in the 11-run sixth inning, but only Babe Ruth and Aaron Ward hit homeruns in Fenway Park that day.

1928 — The Yankees clinch their sixth A.L. pennant by defeating the Tigers, 11-6, behind George Pipgras.

1930 — Lou Gehrig's 885 consecutive game errorless streak at first base ends during the Yankees' 9-3 win versus Boston. This game also featured a rare Yankee pitching performance by Babe Ruth, who hurled an 11-hit complete game win.

1942 — Grant "Buck" Jackson (P 1976)

1951 — David (Dave) Rajsich (P 1978)

1951 — Allie Reynolds pitches his second no-hitter of the season, an 8-0 win against the Red Sox, and thus becomes the first A.L. pitcher to pitch two no hitters in one season. The game is best remembered for Yogi Berra's muff of a pop foul by Ted Williams, always a tough out, and the last batter in the ninth inning. Fortunately, Reynolds induced Williams to hit virtually the same pop foul, and this time Berra caught the ball.

In the second game of the doubleheader, Vic Raschi pitched the Yankees to an 11-3 pennant clinching win, the 18th pennant in Yankee history.

29

1886 — Edwin "Cy" Pieh B (P 1913-15)

1901 — Anthony "Pug" Rensa B (C 1933)

1911 — The Yankees draw 13 walks and steal 15 bases in a wild 16-12 win against the Browns. The game also featured a major league record six stolen bases in one inning, the second.

1914 — John "Swede" Johnson B (P 1944)

1921 — It's the fourth game of the crucial series with the Indians. New York is in first place by 1½ games. Manager Miller Huggins asks his players to select their starting pitcher, and the team elects to go with veteran Jack Quinn . . . but Quinn is battered in the first inning, and is replaced by Waite Hoyt after yielding three runs. Babe Ruth got the Yankees going with a first inning homerun, and then doubled home a run and scored in the third inning. Ruth put New York ahead to stay by hitting a two-run homerun in the fifth inning. Reliever Carl Mays (New York's third pitcher) held the Tribe in check until the ninth inning, when the Indians put runners on second and third with two outs. Faced with the most important task of his career (getting that final out without letting the runners score) Mays settled down and struck out Steve O'Neill to win the game, and thereby enable the Yankees to virtually clinch the pennant.

1927 — Babe Ruth hits his second grand slam homerun in as many consecutive games, thereby tying the major league record. He would repeat the performance on 8/6/29 and 8/7/29.

1928 — The Yankees and Tigers combine to set the American League record for most hits by both teams in a nine inning game (45), when Detroit records 28 hits and New York adds 17. The Tigers won the game, 19-10.

1938 — Michael (Mike) McCormick B (P 1970)

1978 — The Yankees maintain a one game lead over the Red Sox when Rich Gossage earns his league-leading 26th save of the season in a 3-1 win against Cleveland.

1882 — Charles "Gabby" Street B (C 1912)

1885 — Zinn Beck B (1B 1919)

1922 — The Yankees clinch their second pennant by defeating the Red Sox, 3-1, behind Waite Hoyt and Joe Bush.

1927 — Babe Ruth hits the 60th homerun of his season to lead the Yankees to a 4-2 win at Yankee Stadium. The victim was Washington's Tom Zachary.

1934 — Babe Ruth plays his final game in a Yankee uniform. He went 0-for-three with a walk and a run scored. The Yankees lost to Washington, 5-3.

1937 — Augustus (Gus) Triandos B (1B, C 1953-54)

1947 — The Yankees explode for five runs in the fifth inning to defeat the Dodgers, 5-3, before the largest crowd in world series history up to this year, 73,365 fans, at Yankee Stadium.

1948 — Rosendo "Rusty" Torres B (OF 1971-72)

1968 — Yankees purchase pitcher Jim Rooker from the Tigers in a waiver transaction.

1973 — The Yankees close out the 50th year of the Old Yankee Stadium by losing to the Tigers, 8-5. Duke Sims hit the last Yankee homerun in the old ballpark. Tigers relief ace John Hiller was the winner, while Yankee reliever Lindy McDaniel lost the finale.

OCTOBER

1

1889 — Charles "Dutch" Sterrett B (OF, 1B, C, 2B 1912-13)

1904 — James (Jimmy) Reese B (2B, 3B 1930-31)

1908 — Jack Chesbro notches his final victory in a (Highlander) Yankee uniform, a five-hit win against Walter Johnson and the Senators, 2-1.

1912 — The Yankees lose their 100th game of the season, 4-3, at Philadelphia. New York finished the year 50-102, some 55 games behind the first place Red Sox, the worst finish in the franchise's history.

1921 — After clinching their first pennant by defeating the Athletics, 5-3, in the first game of a doubleheader, Babe Ruth comes in to pitch in the eighth inning of the nightcap and comes out a winner. Ruth took the mound in the top of the eighth inning, and promptly allowed the Athletics to score six runs to tie the score (6-6), but then settled down and held them scoreless until the Yankees won the game with a run in the 11th.

1931 — Frederick (Fred) Kipp B (P 1960)

1932 — Babe Ruth's famous "called" homerun off Chicago Cubs' hurler Charlie Root during the third game of the world series.

The score was tied, 4-4, in the top of the fifth inning at Wrigley Field, when Ruth came to bat. He took the first pitch for a called strike one, raised his finger to indicate the strike, and then yelled something out to Root. The second pitch also split the strike zone, and Ruth raised two fingers and again called out to Root. After two waste pitches, Ruth made a gesture out towards the pitcher or the bleachers (depending upon whom one asks), and then drove a tremendous shot into the seats. Did Ruth really predict the homerun? No one will ever know for sure, but see the World Series section herein for contemporary opinions.

1933 — With the Yankees already eliminated from the pennant race, Babe Ruth is named the starting pitcher of today's game, and responds by beating the Red Sox, 6-5. Ruth allowed 11 hits, did not walk a man, struck out three, and in the immortal Ruthian way, hit the game-winning homerun.

1944 — The Yankees drop their fourth straight game to the Browns in St. Louis, 5-2, giving the Browns the only pennant their franchise ever won in St. Louis.

1949 — Some 69,551 fans jam Yankee Stadium to watch the Yankees and Red Sox battle to a 5-4, come-from-behind New York win. The Yankees entered the game trailing Boston by one game, with two games remaining (both against the Sox).

The pitching matchups pitted Yankee ace Allie Reynolds against Boston's Mel Parnell but neither of them lasted long.

The game opened with the Sox scoring a run in the first inning, on two singles and a sacrifice fly. In the third inning, Reynolds walked the first three men he faced, and then allowed a single which made it 2-0. Into the game came ace reliever Joe Page, who horrified the fans by walking the first two batters he faced, thereby upping the Boston lead to 4-0.

Fortunately, Page settled down and did not allow a run for the rest of the game, and the Yankee bats came alive in the fourth inning.

Joe DiMaggio led off the inning with a ground rule double. After Billy Johnson struck out, Hank Bauer singled home DiMaggio, advanced to third on John Lindell's hit, and scored on a Jerry Coleman sacrifice fly.

The Yankees tied the score in the fifth. Phil Rizzuto led off with a single, and moved around the bases on hits by Tommy Henrich and Yogi Berra. Joe Dobson replaced Parnell, and gave up an infield hit to DiMaggio which loaded the bases. The tying run scored when Dobson induced Johnson to hit into a doubleplay. The score remained knotted until the bottom of the eighth inning, when John Lindell drove a waist-high fastball into the seats in left field, about 10 feet to the fair side of the foul pole. It proved to be the gamewinner.

1961 — Roger Maris hits the 61st homerun of HIS season. The historic blow came in the fourth inning, and accounted for the only run in a 1-0 win. The pitcher was Tracy Stallard, the opposition the Red Sox, and the pitch itself was a fastball.

106

1977 — While the Yankees and Tigers sit out a 2:42 rain delay, the Orioles defeat the Red Sox, 8-7, at Boston, and thereby hand the Yankees their second consecutive Eastern Division Championship. The Yankees added insult to injury by losing the game, 10-7, after the rain delay ended, but New York won the final game of the year the next day, so no one can say the Yankees "backed into it."

1978 — The Indians belt the Yankees, 9-2, at Yankee Stadium, and drop the Yankees into a first place tie with the Red Sox. This resulted in the first Divisional Championship Playoff Game in baseball history, won by the Yankees, 5-4, at Boston, on October 2.

2

1905 — Yankees sign shortstop Rube Oldring and immediately sell him to the Athletics.

1919 — Joseph (Joe) Buzas B (SS 1945)

1920 — Frank "Spec" Shea B (P 1947-49, 51)

1930 — John "Gabe" Gabler B (P 1959-60)

1936 — Tony Lazzeri becomes the first Yankee (and the second player in major league history) to hit a grand slam homerun in a world series game. His drive capped a seven-run third inning during the Yankees 18-4 shellacking of the Giants.

1947 — Yogi Berra becomes the first player in major league history to hit a pinch hit homerun in a world series game. The historic blow came in the seventh inning off pitcher Ralph Branca, and pulled the Yankees to within one run of the Dodgers . . . but the Yankees failed to score off reliever Hugh Casey, and lost, 9-8.

1949 — With the two teams in a dead tie for first place on this last day of the regular season, the Yankees and Red Sox square off at Yankee Stadium, with the winner to get the A.L. Championship. New York scored first, when Phil Rizzuto tripled leading off the first inning, and scored on Tommy Henrich's ground out, and that's the way things stood until the bottom of the eighth inning, when the Yankees reached Ellis Kinder for four runs (three scored on a bases loaded hit by Jerry Coleman).

Yankee ace Vic Raschi took that five run lead into the top of the ninth inning, and quickly gave up three runs in exchange for two outs. The Red Sox had the tying run at the plate in the person of Birdie Tebbets, but Raschi settled down and got him to pop out to end the game and clinch the Yankees 16th pennant.

1965 — Mel Stottlemyre wins his 20th game of the season, 6-1, at Boston.

1977 — The Yankees win their final game of the season, 8-7, versus Detroit, ending all complaints that they had backed into the Eastern Division Championship because of the previous day's Oriole victory over Boston.

1978 — The Yankees win their third straight Eastern Division Championship when they come-from-behind to edge Boston, 5-4, at Fenway Park, in the first Divisional Playoff Game in major league baseball history. (See the 1978 section)

3

1887 — Armando Marsans B (OF, 3B, 2B 1917-18)

1909 — John Broaca B (P 1934-37)

1947 — Yankee pitcher Floyd Bevens flirts with immortality when he pitches no-hit baseball for the first 8-and-two-thirds innings of a world series game against the Dodgers, only to lose the no-hitter and the game when pinch hitter Cookie Lavagetto doubles off the right field wall to score the tying and winning runs. (See the world series section.)

1960 — The Yankees end their season with an 8-7 win against Boston and ride a 15-game winning streak into the world series.

1965 — Whitey Ford becomes the winningest pitcher in Yankee history when he notches career win number 232 against Boston, 8-7, in Fenway.

4

1884 — Harry Ables B (P 1911)

1887 — Raymond (Ray) Fisher B (P 1910-17)

1910 — Frank Crosetti B (INF 1932-48, coach 1949-70)

1929 — Yankees sign free agent first baseman George Burns.

1947 — Joe DiMaggio's fifth inning homerun is the gamewinner in New York's 2-1 world series win at Ebbet's Field. The Yankees may well have thought lightning was about to strike twice when Cookie Lavagetto came to bat with the tying run on third base in the ninth inning, but Spec Shea struck him out to end the game.

1953 — Mickey Mantle's third inning grand slam off Dodger ace Johnny Podres leads the Yankees to an 11-7 win, and a three-games-to-two lead in the world series.

1955 — "Next Year" finally comes to Brooklyn when the Dodgers defeat the Yankees and win their first world championship. (For more details, see the world series section.)

5

1895 — Norman "Bub" McMillan B (OF, 3B 1922)

1912 — The Yankees win their final game at Hilltop Park, 8-6, when Hal Chase hits a three-run homerun to defeat the Senators.

1921 — The Yankees play their first world series game ever, and down the Giants, 3-0. (For details, see the world series section.)

1922 — The Yankees and Giants play their infamous 3-3 tie in the world series. (See the world series section)

1939 — Monte Pearson two-hits the Reds, 4-0, in the world series.

1941 — Mickey Owens earns eternal goat's horns by dropping the third strike thrown to the Yankees' Tommy Henrich in the ninth inning, and thereby opens the floodgates for a Yankee win. (See the world series section.)

1941 — Andrew (Andy) Kosco B (OF, 1B 1968)

1949 — The Yankees edge Brooklyn, 1-0, on Tommy Henrich's lead off homerun in the bottom of the ninth inning.

1953 — Billy Martin makes a record 12th hit in the world series as the Yankees win their fifth consecutive championship.

1956 — Yogi Berra becomes the fourth Yankee to hit a grand slam homerun in the world series, but it goes to waste when the Dodgers rally from a 6-0 deficit and down the Yankees, 13-8.

1977 — The Royals shell Don Gullett for three homeruns and notch a 7-2 win the opening game of the 1977 A.L. Playoffs. (See the Playoffs section.)

6

1885 — John "Schoolboy" Knight B (INF, 1B 1909-11, 13)

1908 — The Yankees lose their 100th game of the year, 11-3, at Boston. When the season ended, the Yankees showed a 51-103 record, some 38½ games behind the Tigers.

1914 — George Wasburn B (P 1941)

1926 — Babe Ruth awakens from a three-game slumber and explodes for three homeruns in Game IV of the world series, to lead the Yankees to a 10-5 win.

1939 — John (Jack) Cullen B (P 1962, 65-66)

1938 — The famous heart-breaking performance by veteran pitcher Dizzy Dean during the world series with the Yankees. The sore-armed pitcher, no longer the flame-thrower of his youth, used a mixture of curves and off-speed pitches to carry a 2-1 lead into the late innings, only to watch it disappear on tough luck. (See the world series section.)

1960 — Mickey Mantle hits two homeruns in the second game of the world series to lead the Yankees to a 16-3 win at Pittsburgh. It was the second time Mantle had paired up homeruns in a world series game.

1977 — The Yankees turn to remarkable Ron Guidry to even their Playoff series with the Royals. Guidry turns in a three-hit, 6-2 win, highlighted by Cliff Johnson's fifth inning homerun and sixth inning run-scoring double.

1978 — The Yankees overcome three homeruns by George Brett and edge the Royals, 6-5 in a thrilling Game III at Yankee Stadium. The winning run scored on Thurman Munson's two-run homerun in the bottom of the eighth inning, after the Yankees had fallen behind, 5-4, in the top of the inning. (For details, see the playoff section)

7

1898 — Joseph "Peco" Giard B (P 1927)

1916 — Alva (Russ) Derry B (OF 1944-45)

1927 — Herb Pennock is the first of several Yankee pitchers to flirt with immortality when he retires the first 22 consecutive Pirates he faces, only to lose the perfect game and no-hitter when Pie Traynor singles in the eighth inning. Pennock won, 8-1.

1933 — Leavitt "Bud" Daley B (P 1962-64)

1950 — Whitey Ford wins his first world series game, 5-2, thereby clinching New York's 13th championship.

1968 — Yankees release outfielder-pitcher Rocky Colavito.

1977 — The Royals push the Yankees to the brink of elimination with a 6-2 victory at Kansas City.

8

1887 — Frank "Ping" Bodie B (OF 1918-21)

1948 — Richard (Rick) Stelmaszek B (C 1976)

1956 — Yankee pitcher Don Larsen hurls the only no-hitter (and a perfect game, to boot!) in world series history, a 2-0 win versus the Dodgers.

1960 — Bobby Richardson's grand slam homerun backs some stellar pitching by Whitey Ford as the Yankees down the Pirates, 10-0.

1977 — The Yankees rip Royals starter Larry Gura for six hits and four runs in two innings, and continue on to a 6-4 win to even their series with Kansas City at 2-2. Sparky Lyle turns in 5-and-one-third innings of sparkling relief to gain the win.

1978 — The Yankees clinch their third straight A.L. Championship, by defeating the Royals, 2-1, at Yankee Stadium, behind the pitching of Guidry and Gossage, and the homerun power of Graig Nettles and Roy White.

9

1898 — Joseph (Joe) Sewell B (3B, 2B 1931-33)

1921 — Babe Ruth hits his first world series homerun to lead the Yankees to their first world series game victory, 3-0. In an interesting sidelight, this proved to be the only Sunday game Yankee pitcher Carl Mays ever hurled in his 15-year career!

1940 — Joseph (Joe) Pepitone B (1B, OF 1962-69)

1951 — Gil McDougald's grand slam homerun highlights the Yankees' 13-1 win against the Giants.

1961 — Whitey Ford breaks Babe Ruth's old record of 29-and-two-thirds consecutive scoreless world series innings during New York's 7-0 win against the Reds.

1976 — The Yankees open their first post-season play since 1964 (and their first American League Playoff Series appearance ever) by dousing the Royals, 4-1, in Kansas City. Catfish Hunter tossed a five-hitter.

1977 — The Yankees come-from-behind to defeat the Royals, 5-3, and win their 31st pennant. New York entered the ninth inning trailing the Royals, 3-2, but rallied for three big runs to win. (See playoff section.)

10

1904 — With the Highlanders trailing Boston by two games in the battle for first place, the teams square off in a season-ending doubleheader at Hilltop Park. In the opener, Highlanders' Hall of Fame pitcher Jack Chesbro (a 41-game-winner that year) uncorks a wild pitch in the top of the ninth inning which allows Boston's Lou Criger to score from third base, and gives the Sox the game (3-2) and the pennant. It was the closest Chesbro ever came to playing for a pennant-winner in New York, and the closest the New York franchise would come to a pennant until 1921.

(Boston's Bill Dineen was the winner, and pitched his 37th consecutive complete game.

The Highlanders won the nightcap, 1-0.)

1926 — Cardinals Hall-of-Famer Grover Cleveland Alexander relieves starter Jess Haines with the bases loaded and two outs in the seventh inning, and helps create baseball history by striking out Tony Lazzeri. (For the exciting details, see the world series section.)

1929 — Robert (Bob) Tiefenauer B (P 1965)

1956 — Bill Skowron's seventh inning grand slam is the final nail in the Dodgers' coffin as the Yankees win the final subway series, four games to three, by downing Brooklyn, 9-0.

1958 — Bob Turley's briliant relief stint (six-and-two-thirds scoreless innings) completes the Yankees' miraculous world series comeback against the Braves. New York trailed, three games to one, but swept the final three games of the series.

1976 — The Royals even their playoff series with New York by coming from behind to beat the Yankees, 7-3.

1978 — The Yankees and Dodgers open the 75th Annual World Series. L.A. takes advantage of its home turf, and Ed Figueroa, to beat the Yankees, 11-5.

11

1931 — Gary Blaylock B (P 1959)

1977 — The Yankees defeat the Dodgers, 4-3, in Game I of the 74th World Series. L.A. led, 2-1, in the sixth inning, but New York tied matters in the eighth on a Willie Randolph homerun. Thurman Munson doubled home the go-ahead run that same inning, but the Dodgers tied matters in the ninth to send the game into extra innings. In the 12th inning, with Randolph on second (via a lead off double) and Munson intentionally passed, Paul Blair singles home the winning run.

1978 — The Dodgers edge the Yankees, 4-3, in Game II of the 75th world series.

12

1922 — Yankees transfer pitcher Lefty O'Doul to the Red Sox to complete the Dugan deal of 7-24-22.

1936 — Anthony (Tony) Kubek B (INF, OF 1957-65)

1948 — Casey Stengel is named manager of the Yankees.

1977 — In what many baseball fans still refer to as "the throwaway game," Yankee manager Billy Martin starts Catfish Hunter against the Dodgers. "The Cat" had not pitched for more than a month, but the Yankees badly needed an extra day of rest for their pitching staff. Unfortunately, the "Cat" was not up to the task, and L.A. won, 6-1. The "resting" part of the strategy worked — when New York left for L.A., the Yankees had Mike Torrez and Ron Guidry fresh for duty in Games III and IV.

13

1876 — William "Wild Bill" Donovan B (P 1915-16)

1883 — Walter "Heavy" Blair B (C, OF, 1B 1907-11)

1895 — Benjamin (Ben) Paschal B (OF 1924-29)

1896 — Michael (Mike) Gazella B (INF 1923, 26-28)

1924 — Charles (Charlie) Silvera B (C, 3B 1948-56)

1937 — Luciean (Lu) Clinton B (OF 1966-67)

1960 — Bill Mazeroski's lead off homerun off Ralph Terry in the bottom of the ninth inning gives the Pirates a wild 10-9 win, and the world championship. (This was the strangest game in Yankees' world series history — see the world series section.)

1971 — Yankees obtain pitcher Rich Hinton from the Indians for outfielder Jim Lyttle.

1978 — Trailing the Dodgers two games to none, the Yankees turn to remarkable Ron Guidry to get them back into the world series, and Guidry (with five great fielding gems by Graig Nettles) gets the 5-1 win. (See the 1978 World Series.)

14

1913 — Hugh Casey B (P 1949)

1924 — William "Big Bill" Renna B (OF 1953)

1948 — Eduardo (Ed) Figueroa B (P 1976-current)

1964 — Joe Pepitone's eighth inning grand slam homerun is the gamewinning blow in New York's 8-3 win against the Cardinals in Game VI of the series. This proved to be the Yankees' final world series game victory until 1977!

1976 — Talk about GREAT moments in baseball and Yankee history, and you've got to select Yankee first baseman Chris Chambliss' ninth inning, lead off homerun off Royals reliever Mark Littell which clinched New York's 30th pennant, and first since 1964.

1977 — Mike Torrez scatters seven hits and goes the distance in New York's 5-3 win in Game II at Los Angeles.

15

1906 — Samuel (Sammy) "Babe Ruth's Legs" Byrd B (OF 1929-34)

1923 — Yankees clinch their first world championship by defeating the Giants, 6-4, at Yankee Stadium.

1977 — Ron Guidry turns in a masterful performance as he four-hits the Dodgers in Game IV. Reggie Jackson's second inning double triggers a three-run inning to build the 4-2 win.

1978 — The Yankees make it three straight wins against the Dodgers in a 12-2 crusher at the Stadium.

16

1895 — William (Bill) Skiff B (C 1926)

1900 — Henry "Tomato Face" Cullop B (PH 1926)

1929 — Yankees sell outfielder Bob Meusel to the Reds.

1956 — Yankees sell outfielder Bob Cerv to the Athletics for an undisclosed amount of cash.

1961 — Yankees purchase veteran pitcher Robin Roberts from the Phillies for an undisclosed amount. The Yankees made a major mistake when they wrote him off as washed up in spring training in 1962.

1977 — Don Sutton keeps the Dodgers alive by beating the Yankees, 10-4.

17

1908 — Robert "Red" Rolfe B (3B, SS 1931, 34-42)

1962 — The Yankees win their 20th world championship when Giants' power hitter Willie McCovey lines a bullet right to Yankee second baseman Bobby Richardson for the final out in the ninth inning. Yankee pitcher Ralph Terry had nursed a 1-0 lead into the ninth, but had allowed the tying run to reach third base, and the potential winning run to reach second, before getting McCovey.

1964 — Yankees fire manager Yogi Berra.

1978 — The Yankees clinch their 22nd world championship via a 7-2 win in L.A. behind Catfish Hunter.

18

1889 — Charles "Dutch" Sterrett B (OF, 1B, C, 2B 1912-13)

1903 — George "Yats" Wuestling B (SS, 3B 1930)

1914 — Roy Cullenbine B (OF, INF 1942)

1931 — Andrew (Andy) Carey B (INF 1952-60)

1977 — Reggie Jackson slams three consecutive homeruns during the Yankees 8-4 win against the Dodgers. The homeruns tied Ruth's record of three in one series game, and the win gave the Yankees their first championship since 1962 (their 21st overall). Reggie also set numerous records for homeruns and RBIs — see the world series section.

19

1891 — George Batten B (2B 1912)

1943 — Conde "Sandy" Alomar B (INF 1974-76)

1946 — Yankees obtain pitcher Allie Reynolds from the Indians for second baseman Joe Gordon and infielder Eddie Bockman.

1966 — Yankees release pitcher Whitey Ford and outfielder Hector Lopez.

20

1903 — Archer (Archie) Campbell B (P 1928)

1931 — Mickey Mantle B (OF, 1B, INF 1951-68)

1940 — Thaddeus (Thad) Tillotson B (P 1967-68)

1960 — Yankees name Ralph Houk as the managerial replacement for Casey Stengel, and name Roy Hamey as the successor to general manager George Weiss.

1978 — Just days after the Yankees' world series victory against the Dodgers, rumors circulate that the Yankees plan to trade reliever Sparky Lyle and others to the Texas Rangers for outfielder Juan Beniquez and pitcher Paul Mirrabella.

Yankee owner George Steinbrenner reiterates that another rumor (Lyle and Thurman Munson for Pirates slugger Dave Parker) is hogwash, and is quoted for the record as saying that Munson and Reggie Jackson will both be Yankees in 1979.

21

1885 — Augustus (Gus) Fisher B (C 1912)

1916 — Floyd (Bill) Bevens B (P 1944-47)

1928 — Edward "Whitey" Ford B (P 1950, 53-67)

1946 — Yankees obtain pitcher Art Cuccurullo from the Pirates for pitcher Ernie Bonham.

22

1882 — William "Birdie" Cree B (OF, INF 1908-15)

1897 — Myles Thomas B (P 1926-29)

1942 — Cecil Upshaw B (P 1974)

1943 — Robert (Bobby) Mitchell B (OF 1970)

1974 — Yankees obtain outfielder Bobby Bonds from the Giants for outfielder Bobby Murcer.

23

1907 — Lee "Lefty" Grissom B (P 1940)

1922 — Ewell "The Whip" Blackwell B (P 1952-53)

24

1887 — Hugh "Lefty" High B (OF 1915-18)

1904 — William (Harry) Smythe B (P 1934)

1930 — Yankees release catcher Bubbles Hargrave.

1946 — Frank "No Homerun" Baker B (SS 1970-71)

1950 — Rawlins (Rawley) Eastwick B (P 1978)

1972 — Yankees obtain infielder Fred Stanley from the Padres for pitcher George Pena.

25

1869 — Jack "Dirty Jack" Doyle B (1B 1905)

1924 — Robert (Dr. Bobby) Brown B (SS, 3B, OF 1946-54)

1939 — Peter (Pete) Mikkelsen B (P 1964-65)

26

1877 — Eustace "Doc" Newton B (P 1905-09)

1918 — George "Snuffy" Stirnweiss B (INF 1943-50)

1938 — Yankees obtain pitcher Oral Hildebrand and outfielder Colonel Mills from the Browns for catcher Joe Glenn and outfielder Myril Hoag.

27

1876 — Patrick (Patsy) Dougherty B (OF 1904-06)

1972 — Yankees obtain catcher Rick Dempsey from the Twins for outfielder Danny Walton.

28

1904 — Elias (Liz) Funk B (OF 1929)

1916 — Edward (Ed) Levy B (OF, 1B 1942, 44)

1917 — Joseph "Fireman" Page B (P 1944-50)

1920 — The Yankees raid the Red Sox again, this time signing away Ed Barrow to become the new Yankee general manager. Barrow engineered the deals that created the great Yankee teams of the 20s and 30s.

29

1882 — Arthur "Circus Solly" Hofman B (OF 1916)

1891 — Joseph "Happy Joe" Finneran B (P 1918)

1968 — Yankees release infielder Dick Howser as a player, and then sign him as a coach.

30

1888 — Martin (Marty) McHale B (P 1913-15)

1941 — James (Jim) Ray Hart B (DH, 3B 1973-74)

1948 — John "Mickey" Rivers B (OF, DH 1976-current)

1882 — Bernard (Bert) Daniels B (OF 1910-13)

NOVEMBER

1

1884 — Robert "Ham" Hyatt B (OF, 1B 1918)

1893 — Alexander (Alex) Burr B (OF 1914)

2

1960 — The Yankees make it official by announcing that general manager Al Weiss will retire after 29 years of service to the Yankee organization.

1964 — CBS purchases 80% of the Yankees ownership for an estimated $11,200,000. The network later purchased the remaining 20%.

3

1878 — Walter Clarkson B (P 1904-07)

1911 — John Keane B (Mgr. 1965-66)

1945 — Kenneth (Ken) Holtzman B (P 1976-78)

4

1910 — Joseph (Joe) Beggs B (P 1930)

1947 — Lloyd Colson B (P 1970)

5

1883 — Otis Johnson B (INF 1911)

1892 — Alfred "Roxy" Walters B (C, OF 1915-18)

1924 — John "Sonny" Dixon B (P 1956)

6

1942 — The Yankees are notified that infielder Frank Crosetti will be suspended for 30 days, commencing with opening day of the 1943 season, for pushing umpire William Summers in Game III of the 1942 world series. Crosetti was fined $250, as was second baseman Joe Gordon.

7

1911 — Herbert "Workhorse" Crompton B (C 1945)

1933 — Robert Hale B (1B 1961)

1938 — Jerry (Jake) Gibbs B (C 1962-71)

8

Nothing of significance happened on this date.

9

1889 — Thomas (Tommy) Thompson B (P 1912)

1897 — Harvey "Gink" Hendrick B (OF 1923-24)

1908 — Ray Schalk B (C 1921-25)

1919 — Jerald (Gerry) Priddy B (INF, 1B 1941-42)

1923 — Theodore (Ted) Sepkowski B (OF 1947)

1953 — The United States Supreme Court upholds the special status of baseball as a "sport" exempt from anti-trust actions. The suit was brought by several players who claimed they were unfairly buried in the minor leagues because they were the property of the better teams. Among the complainants was Yankee farmhand George Toolson, who joined the others in arguing that they could have played for other major league teams, and thereby made a great deal more money, if there were no reserve clause.

The Court upheld the reserve clause, and re-affirmed baseball's immunity from the anti-trust charge.

10

1895 — Wilson "Chick" Fewster B (INF, OF 1917-22)

1948 — The Yankees draft Ken Silvestri out of the Phillies organization.

1978 — Yankees obtain outfielders Juan Beniquez and Greg Jemison, and pitchers Dave Righetti, Paul Mirabell and Mike Griffin from the Rangers for pitchers Sparky Lyle, Dave Rajsich and Larry McCall, catcher Mike Heath and infielder Domingo Ramos.

(Beniquez is considered among the top five defensive centerfielders in the game. Righetti will be another Guidry, according to Yankee President and General Manager Al Rosen — an opinion shared by many baseball experts. Mirabella is considered ready to pitch in the majors, and Griffin is a highly-touted 21-year old prospect.

Lyle was the Cy Young award winner in 1977, but was unhappy with the Yankees' acquisition of Rich Gossage in the free agent market prior to the 1978 season. He went 9-3 with a 3.47 ERA and 9 saves, but was ineffective for most of the second half of the season.

Heath is a top catching prospect who batted .228 with New York this year. McCall and Rajsich are top pitching prospects who saw limited action with the Yankees, while Ramos is considered a good bet to play shortstop for a major league team some day.)

11

1902 — Owen (Ownie) Carroll B (P 1930)

12

1926 — Donald (Don) Johnson B (P 1947, 50)

1965 — Yankees obtain infielder Ruben Amaro from the Phillies for infielder Phil Linz.

13

1882 — Ezra "Salt Rock" Midkiff B (INF 1912-13)

1884 — Thomas (Pete) Daley B (OF 1914-15)

1925 — James (Jim) Delsing B (OF 1949-50)

1934 — Yankees sell pitcher Dan MacFayden to the Reds on a conditional basis.

1941 — Melvin (Mel) Stottlemyre B (P 1964-74)

1968 — Yankees sell infielder John Kennedy to the Pilots for an undisclosed amount of cash.

1978 — Yankees sign 37-year-old free agent pitcher Luis Tiant. (Tiant was 13-8 with the Sox in 1978. The new contract calls for $235,000/year for two years, with an option to play a third year at the same rate. He will also receive a post-playing career job as director of Latin American Affairs with a salary of roughly $35,000/year for up to 10 years.)

14

1876 — Harry "Handsome Harry" Howell B (INF, P 1903)

1885 — Jack LeLivelt B (OF 1912-13)
15

1916 — Joseph "Professor" Ostrowski B (P 1950-52)

16

1883 — Rollie "Bunions" Zeider B (INF, 1B 1913)

1950 — Yankees draft pitcher Bob Muncrief from the Cubs organization.

17

1913 — Lee Stine B (P 1938)

1932 — Daniel "Deacon Danny" McDevitt B (P 1961)

1954 — Yankees obtain pitchers Bob Turley and Don Larsen, and shortstop Billy Hunter, from the Orioles for outfielder Gene Woodling, pitchers Harry Byrd and Jim McDonald, catchers Hal Smith and Gus Triandos, and shortstop Willie Miranda, as the first half of an 18-player trade. Upon its completion on December 1, this became the largest trade in major league history.

1976 — Yankees sign free agent pitcher Don Gullett for an estimated $1.5 million. He is the first player the Yankees sign in the 1976 re-entry draft.

19

1881 — William (Bill) Bailey B (OF 1911)

1892 — Everett "Deacon" Scott B (SS 1922-25)

1908 — Joseph (Joe) Glenn B (C 1932-33, 35-38)

20

1869 — Clark "The Old Gray Fox" Griffith B (P 1903-07, MGR 1903-08)

1882 — Andrew (Andy) Coakley B (P 1911)

1919 — Rugger Ardizoia B (PH 1947)

1929 — Louis (Lou) Berberet B (C 1954-55)

1945 — John (Jay) Johnstone B (OF, DH 1978-current)

1966 — Yankees obtain outfielder Bill Robinson from the Braves for infielder Clete Boyer.

1967 — Yankees obtain infielder and future coach Bobby Cox from the Braves for Dale Roberts and Bob Tillman.

1978 — Yankees reach agreement with free agent pitcher Tommy John for a five-year $1.2 million contract. (John was the southpaw ace of the Dodgers' staff in recent years, following miraculous surgery on his throwing arm in 1974. John's bread and butter pitch is a sinkerball.)

21

1885 — Harold (Harry) Billiard B (P 1908)

1891 — Carl "Sub" Mays B (P 1919-23)

1934 — Yankees purchase outfielder Joe DiMaggio from San Francisco of the Pacific Coast League.

22

1901 — Harold (Harry) Rice B (OF 3B 1930)

1926 — Selva (Lew) Burdette B (P 1950)

1943 — Wade Blasingame B (P 1972)

1946 — Richard (Rich) McKinney B (3B 1972)

1957 — In the closest election in the history of the award, Mickey Mantle edges out Ted Williams by one vote for the Most Valuable Player.

1947 — Frank Tepedino B (1B, OF 1967, 69-71, 71-72)

1951 — Yankees obtain pitcher Jim McDonald from the Browns for catcher Clint Courtney.

1930 — Robert "Warrior" Friend B (P 1966)

1942 — Frederick (Fred) Beene B (P 1972-74)

1903 — James "Big Jim" Weaver B (P 1931)

1914 — Joseph (Joe) DiMaggio B (OF 1B 1936-51)

1923 — Archibald (Archie) Wilson B (OF 1951-52)

1951 — Russell "Bucky" Dent B (SS 1977-current)

1972 — Yankees obtain outfielder-designated hitter Matty Alou from the A's for pitcher Rob Gardner and infielder Rich McKinney.

1878 — Thomas "Long Tom" Hughes B (P 1904)

1909 — Vernon "Lefty" Gomez B (P 1930-42)

1947 — Lawrence (Larry) Gura B (P 1974-76)

1962 — Yankees obtain pitcher Stan Williams from the Dodgers for first baseman Bill Skowron.

1892 — Leslie "Bullet Joe" Bush B (P 1922-24)

1920 — John "Bear Tracks" Schmitz B (P 1960)

1947 — Joe DiMaggio wins his third Most Valuable Player Award when he edges out Ted Williams by one vote.

1972 — Yankees obtain third baseman Graig Nettles and catcher Gerry Moses from the Indians for first baseman-outfielder John Ellis, outfielders Rusty Torres and Charlie Spikes, and infielder Jerry Kenney. (Technically, Moses came via the Tigers, who were also involved in what was really a three-way deal.)

28

1884 — Wilbur "Roxy" Roche B (SS, OF, 2B 1910-11)

1927 — Yankees release pitchers Bob Shawkey and Dutch Reuther.

1974 — Yankee principal owner George M. Steinbrenner III is suspended from all team operations by baseball commissioner Bowie Kuhn as a penalty for alleged illegal political campaign contributions. The sentence was originally of two years duration, but was subsequently reduced to one year.

29

1924 — Irving (Irv) Noren B (OF, 1B 1952-56)

1950 — Otoniel (Otto) Velez B (OF, 1B, DH, 3B 1973-76)

1976 — Yankees sign free agent outfielder Reggie Jackson to an estimated $3.5 million, five-year, contract.

30

1909 — James (Jimmy) DeShong B (P 1934-35)

1936 — Steven (Steve) Hamilton B (P 1964-70)

1967 — Yankees purchase shortstop Gene Michael from the Dodgers for an undisclosed amount of cash.

1975 — Yankees purchase outfielder Jim Wynn from the Braves for an estimated $100,000.

DECEMBER

1

1940 — Cecil Perkins B (P 1967)

1951 — Yankees release Tommy Henrich as a coach.

1954 — Yankees complete their 18 player deal with the Orioles by obtaining first baseman Dick Kryhoski, pitcher Mike Blayzka, catcher Darrell Johnson, and outfielders Jim Fridley and Ted Del Guercio from the Orioles for pitcher Bill Miller, third baseman Kal Segrist, second baseman Don Leppert, and two minor leaguers to be named later.

1971 — Yankees obtain second baseman Bernie Allen from the Rangers for pitchers Terry Ley and Gary Jones.

1978 — Yankees assign the contract of lefthanded reliever Paul Lindblad to the Seattle Mariners for future considerations. (The 37-year-old Lindblad was 0-0 with New York in 1978, 1-1 overall; with a 4.42 ERA in New York, 3.88 overall.)

2

1899 — Raymond (Ray) Morehart B (INF 1927)

1903 — Donald (Don) Brennan B (P 1933)

1950 — Robert (Bob) Kammeyer B (P 1978-current)

1967 — Yankees obtain catcher John Boccabella from the Cubs for an undisclosed amount of cash.

1972 — Yankees obtain infielder Rich McKinney from the White Sox for pitcher Stan Bahnsen.

1974 — Yankees purchase outfielder-first baseman Bob Oliver from the Orioles for an undisclosed amount of cash.

3

1915 — Charles "Butch" Wensloff B (P 1943, 47)

1922 — Joseph (Joe) Collins B (1B, OF 1948-57)

1925 — Harry "Suitcase" Simpson B (OF, 1B 1957-58)

1974 — Yankees obtain pitcher Skip Lockwood from the Angels for catcher-infielder Bill Sudakis.

4

1881 — Luther (Luke) Nelson B (P 1919)

1890 — Robert "Sailor Bob" Shawkey B (P 1916-27)

1938 — William (Bill) Bryan B (C, 1B 1966-67)

1968 — Yankees obtain outfielder Dick Simpson from the Astros for pitcher Dooley Womack.

1968 — Yankees obtain pitcher Mike Kekich from the Dodgers for outfielder Andy Kosco.

1969 — Yankees obtain first baseman-outfielder Curt Blefary from the Astros for first baseman-outfielder Joe Pepitone.

5

1871 — Lewis "Snake" Wiltse B (P 1903)

1969 — Yankees obtain first baseman-third baseman Danny Cater from the A's for pitcher Al Downing and catcher Frank Fernandez.

1974 — Yankees obtain infielder Eddie Leon from the White Sox for pitcher Cecil Upshaw.

6

1873 — Harry Wolverton B (3B, mgr 1912)

1881 — Joseph (Joe) Lake B (P 1908-09)

1882 — Alvin "Cozy" Dolan B (3B 1911-12)

1894 — Joseph (Joe) Gedeon B (2B 1916-17)

1903 — Anthony (Tony) Lazzeri B (INF 1926-37)

1920 — Constantine (Gus) Niarhos B (C 1946, 48-50)

1946 — Yankees obtain catcher Sherm Lollar and second baseman Ray Mack from the Indians for pitchers Al Gettel and Gene Bearden, and outfielder Hal Peck.

1968 — Yankees obtain second baseman Nate Oliver from the Giants for infielder Charlie Smith.

1973 — Yankees purchase shortstop Jim Mason from the Rangers for approximately $100,000.

7

1930 — Mark Freeman B (P 1959)

1933 — Yankees release pitcher Wilcy Moore and second baseman Ray Schalk.

1942 — Alex "The Bull" Johnson B (OF, DH 1974-75)

1949 — Yankees release outfielder Charlie Keller.

1950 — Richard (Rich) Coggins B (OF 1975-76)

1973 — Yankees obtain outfielder-designated hitter-first baseman Lou Piniella and pitcher Ken Wright from the Royals for pitcher Lindy McDaniel.

1973 — Yankees purchase catcher Bill Sudakis from the Rangers for $40,000.

8

1874 — Joseph Connor B (C, 1B 1905)

1879 — James (Jim) Austin B (3B 1909-10)

1880 — Jack "Bullet Jack" Thoney B (OF, 3B 1904)

1941 — Edward (Ed) Brinkman B (INF 1975)

1966 — Yankees obtain third baseman Charlie Smith from the Cardinals for outfielder Roger Maris.

9

1946 — Richard (Rick) Bladt B (OF 1975)

1948 — George "Doc" Medich B (P 1972-75)

1977 — Yankees sign free agent pitcher Rawly Eastwick for an estimated $1.2 million.

10

1900 — Roy "Dizzy" Carlyle B (OF 1926)

1924 — Yankees obtain infielder-outfielder Howard Shanks from the Red Sox for infielder Mike McNally.

1930 — Yankees purchase catcher Ralph Perkins from the Athletics.

1946 — Yankees sign free agent first baseman George McQuinn after his release by the Athletics.

1947 — Yankees obtain pitcher Red Embree from the Indians for outfielder Allie Clark.

1965 — Yankees obtain pitcher Bob Friend from the Pirates for pitcher Pete Mikkelsen.

1973 — Yankees release shortstop Hal Lanier.

11

1923 — Yankees sell pitcher Carl Mays to the Reds.

1924 — Hector (Hal) Brown B (P 1962)

1935 — Yankees obtain pitchers Monte Pearson and Steve Sundra from the Indians for pitcher John Allen.

1956 — Yankees obtain catcher Harry Chiti and two minor leaguers from the Cubs for catcher Charlie Silvera.

1959 — Yankees obtain outfielder Roger Maris, and infielders Kent Hadley and Joe DeMaestri from the Athletics for pitcher Don Larsen, first baseman Marv Throneberry, and outfielders Hank Bauer and Norm Siebern.

1973 — Yankees release outfielder Ron Swoboda.

1975 — Yankees obtain outfielder Mickey Rivers and pitcher Ed Figueroa from the Angels for outfielder Bobby Bonds.

1975 — Yankees obtain pitchers Dock Ellis and Ken Brett, and second baseman Willie Randolph, from the Pirates for pitcher George Medich.

12

1885 — Frank Truesdale B (2B, 3B 1914)

1902 — Paul "Pee Wee" Wanninger B (INF 1925)

1907 — Highlanders sell catcher Ira Thomas to the Tigers.

1924 — Yankees obtain catcher Steve O'Neill from the Red Sox for the waiver price.

1938 — Pedro Gonzalez B (INF 1963-65)

1977 — Yankees obtain first baseman-designated hitter Jim Spencer, and pitchers Bob Polinsky and Tom Cruz from the White Sox for pitchers Stan Thomas and Ed Ricks, and an undisclosed amount of cash.

1977 — Yankees purchase pitcher Andy Messersmith from the Braves for $100,000.

1916 — Henry (Hank) Majeski B (3B 1946)

1935 — Lyndall (Lindy) McDaniel B (P 1968-73)

1940 — Nathaniel (Nate) Oliver B (2B 1969)

1948 — Yankees obtain pitcher Fred Sanford and catcher Roy Partee from the Browns for pitcher Rich Starr, catcher Sherm Lollar, and $100,000.

1873 — John Anderson B (OF 1904-05)

1942 — James (Jim) Roland B (P 1972)

1948 — Yankees obtain outfielder Jim Delsing from the White Sox for outfielder Steve Souchock.

1960 — Yankees obtain pitcher Marshall Bridges from the Reds for catcher Jesse Gonder.

1960 — Yankees lose outfielders Bob Cerv and Ken Hunt, and pitcher Elia Grba to the Angels in the expansion draft. The Yankees also lost first baseman Dale Long and pitcher John Gabler to the "new" Senators.

15

1918 — Yankees obtain pitchers Ernie Shore and Hubert Leonard, and outfielder Duffy Lewis from the Red Sox for outfielder Frank Gilhooley, pitchers Ray Caldwell and Slim Love, and a catcher Al Walters.

1920 — William (Eddie) Robinson B (1B 1954-56)

1920 — Yankees obtain pitchers Waite Hoyt and Harry Harper, catcher Wally Schang, and infielder Mike McNally from the Red Sox for pitcher Herb Thormahlen, catcher Muddy Ruel, third baseman Del Pratt, and outfielder Sam Vick.

1944 — Stanley (Stan) Bahnsen B (P 1966, 68-71)

1945 — Gilbert (Gil) Blanco B (P 1965)

1953 — Former Yankee general manager, and franchise mastermind, Ed Barrow, dies at 85.

1959 — Yankees sign free agent outfielder Elmer Valo.

16

1909 — Yankees sell shortstop Kid Elberfeld to the Senators for $5,000.

1953 — Yankees obtain pitcher Harry Byrd, first baseman Eddie Robinson, outfielders Carmen Mauro and Tom Hamilton, and third baseman Loren Babe from the Athletics for first basemen Vic Power and Don Bollweg, outfielder Bill Renna, catcher Jim Robertson, third baseman Jim Finigan, and pitcher John Gray.

1960 — Yankees obtain infielder Harry Bright, pitcher Ben Daniels, and first baseman R.C. Stevens from the Pirates for pitcher Bobby Shantz.

1960 — The Yankees also purchase pitcher Dan McDevitt from the Dodgers in a separate transaction.

17

1924 — Yankees reobtain pitcher Urban Shocker from the Browns for pitchers Bullet Joe Bush, Milt Gaston and Joe Giard.

1934 — Kent Hadley B (1B 1960)

1936 — Roland (Rollie) Sheldon B (P 1961-62, 64-65)

1942 — Yankees obtain outfielder Roy Weatherly and infielder Oscar Grimes from the Indians for catcher Buddy Rosar and outfielder Roy Cullenbine.

1947 — Charles (Charlie) Sands B (PH 1967)

1949 — Yankees obtain first baseman Dick Wakefield from the Tigers for first baseman Dick Kryhoski.

1953 — The Yankees obtain the required American League approval of their sale of Yankee Stadium and Blue's Stadium (in Kansas City) to the Arnold Johnson Corp. The price was $6,500,000. The Johnson Corp. immediately leased both stadia back to the Yankees for 70 years, at an annual rate of $240,000.

In another financial move, Yankee owners Dan Topping and Del Webb dissolved the New York Yankees, Inc., and replaced the corporation with a simple two-man partnership, thereby enabling themselves to collect capital gains.

18

1930 — William (Bill) "Moose" Skowron B (1B, 3B, 2B 1954-62)

1950 — Yankees release Tommy Henrich as a player and sign him as a coach.

1969 — Yankees obtain infielder Pete Ward from the White Sox for pitcher Mickey Scott and an undisclosed amount of cash.

19

1915 — Nicholas "Mickey" Witek B (PH 1949)

1933 — Gordon Windhorn B (OF 1959)

1943 — Walter "No Neck" Williams B (OF, DH 1974-75)

1944 — Richard (Rob) Gardner B (P 1970-72)

20

1876 — James "Buttons" Williams B (2B 1903-07)

1881 — Wesley (Branch) Rickey B (OF, C, 1B 1907)

1885 — Charles "Paddy" Baumann B (2B, 3B 1915-17)

1888 — Frederick (Fred) "Bonehead" Merkle B (1B 1925-26)

1899 — George Pipgras B (P 1923-24, 27-33)

1921 — Yankees obtain pitchers Joe Bush and Sam Jones, and shortstop Everett Scott from the Red Sox for pitchers Jack Quinn, Harry Collins and Bill Piercy, and shortstop Roger Reckinpaugh.

1928 — Yankees release infielder Mike Gazella.

1966 — Yankees obtain shortstop Dick Howser from the Indians for pitcher Gil Downs and an undisclosed amount of cash.

21

1927 — Yankees sign veteran pitcher Stan Coveleski after his release by the Senators.

1934 — Yankees sell outfielder Sammy Byrd to the Reds.

1948 — Elliott Maddox B (OF, 3B, DH 1974-76)

1948 — David (Dave) Kingman B (OF, DH 1977)

1973 — American League President Joe Cronin rules that former Yankee Manager Ralph Houk is free from all contractural obligations to the New York Club, and is free to sign with the team of his choice. The A.L. Pres. also rules that former Oakland A's manager Dick Williams is still bound to the A's, and repudiates the contract Williams signed with the Yankees earlier this autumn.

22

1938 — Matteo (Matty) Alou B (1B, OF, DH 1973)

1940 — Elrod (Ellie) Hendricks B (C, DH 1975-76)

23

1882 — George Whiteman B (OF 1913)

1889 — Frederick "Fritz" Maisel B (3B, OF, 2B 1913-17)

1898 — Henry "Hinky" Haines B (OF 1923)

1923 — The Yankees announce the sale of pitcher Carl Mays to the Reds for $85,000.

1929 — Al "Bozo" Cicotte B (P 1957)

24

Nothing of significance happened on this date.

25

1881 — Joseph McCarthy B (1905 C)

1899 — Eugene (Gene) Robertson B (SS, 3B 1928-29)

1908 — William (Ben) Chapman B (OF, INF 1930-36)

26

1889 — James "Queenie" O'Rourke B (INF, OF 1908)

1901 — Edward "Doc" Farrell B (INF, P 1932-33)

1919 — Yankees and Red Sox reach a formal, written agreement for the transfer of Babe Ruth to the Yankees. The deal was not announced until after the turn of the new year.

1948 — Carroll (Chris) Chambliss B (1B, DH 1974-current)

27

1890 — Ernest (Ernie) Krueger B (C 1915)

1943 — Roy White B (OF, DH, 2B, 1B 1965-current)

28

Nothing of significance happened on this date.

29

1885 — Franklin "Pudgie" Delahanty B (OF 1905-06, 08)

1893 — Salvatore "Joe" Smith B (C 1913)

1911 — William "Billy" Knickerbocker B (2B, SS 1938-40)

1928 — Yankees waive third baseman Joe Dugan to the Braves.

30

1927 — Yankees release infielder Ray Morehart and pitcher Joe Giard.

1940 — Yankees obtain infielder Don Lang and $20,000 from the Reds for pitcher Monte Pearson.

31

1919 — Thomas (Tommy) Byrne B (P, PH 1943, 46-51, 54-57)

1924 — Theodore (Ted) Gray B (P 1955)

1940 — Yankees obtain catcher Ken Silvestri from the White Sox for infielder Billy Knickerbocker.

1974 — Yankees sign free agent super-pitcher Catfish Hunter to a record $3 million contract.

REMEMBER THESE OLD TIMERS? Above is a picture of the 1908 New York Highlanders (now the Yankees). The top row, left to right, are Jake Stahl, Bill Hogg, George Moriarity, Tax Neuer, H. Blake, Manning and Al Orth. Second row: Neal Ball, Jack Kleinow, Hal Chase, Wid Conroy, Wee Willie Keeler, Joe Doyle, Rube Zellers, Tom Hughes. Bottom row: Jack Chesbro, C. Hempil, Rudy Baerwold, Mgr. Clark Griffith, Harry Niles, Blair, Ed Sweeney and Dr. Tom Martin, trainer. Baerwold, now a resident of Albuquerque and ardent fan, was a catcher for the Highlanders and presented this picture to The Journal. He called Keeler "the greatest hitter of all time" and Hal Chase "the greatest first baseman."

This is the oldest known Yankee (Highlander) team picture, the 1908 Highlanders. Despite the presence of Hall-of-Famers Willie Keeler, Jack Chesbro, Clark Griffith, and All-Star candidates Hal Chase and Wid Conroy, the team finished in last place with a 51-103 record.

The greatest of all baseball teams, the 1927 Yankees.

One of the great Yankee teams which is often ignored was the 1936 squad, which featured Lou Gehrig at his prime and an exciting rookie named Joe DiMaggio. Other Hall of Fame members pictured included: Bill Dickey, Lefty Gomez, and Red Ruffing. Six of the team's 8 regulars batted more than .300.

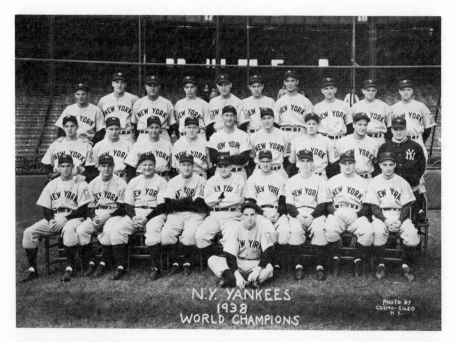

Managers Joe McCarthy often called the 1938 Yankees his favorite team. It featured Gehrig, DiMaggio, Bill Dickey, Tommy Henrich . . .

The 1947 Yankees were manager Bucky Harris' only championship team. They finished with a 97-57 record, 12 games ahead of the second place Tigers, and edged out the Brooklyn Dodgers in an exciting 7-game world series.

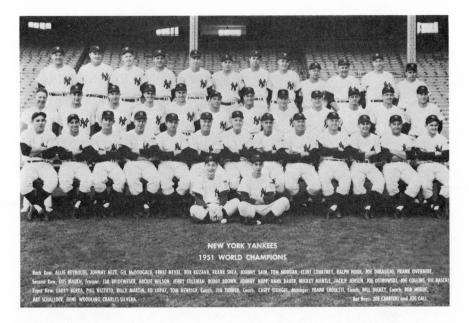

NEW YORK YANKEES
1951 WORLD CHAMPIONS

Back Row: ALLIE REYNOLDS, JOHNNY MIZE, GIL McDOUGALD, ERNIE NEVEL, BOB KUZAVA, FRANK SHEA, JOHNNY SAIN, TOM MORGAN, CLINT COURTNEY, RALPH HOUK, JOE DiMAGGIO, FRANK OVERMIRE.
Second Row: GUS MAUCH, Trainer; JIM BRIDEWESER, ARCHIE WILSON, JERRY COLEMAN, BOBBY BROWN, JOHNNY HOPP, HANK BAUER, MICKEY MANTLE, JACKIE JENSEN, JOE OSTROWSKI, JOE COLLINS, VIC RASCHI.
Front Row: LARRY BERRA, PHIL RIZZUTO, BILLY MARTIN, ED LOPAT, TOM HENRICH, Coach; JIM TURNER, Coach; CASEY STENGEL, Manager; FRANK CROSETTI, Coach; BILL DICKEY, Coach; BOB HOGUE, ART SCHALLOCK, GENE WOODLING, CHARLES SILVERA.
Bat Boys: JOE CARRIERI and JOE CALI.

The 1951 Yankees were the only team on which Joe DiMaggio and Mickey Mantle played together. It represented a "changing of the guard", as the Yankee stars of the 1950's began to take over.

The 1961 New York Yankees were among the finest teams in major league history. They posted a 109-53 record, won the pennant by 8 games, and featured a record six players who hit 20 or more homeruns that year.

First Row, Left to Right: Whitey Ford, Bill Skowron, Hal Reniff, Jim Hegan, Frank Crosetti, Ralph Houk, John Sain, Wally Moses, Earl Torgeson, Cletis Boyer, Yogi Berra, Mickey Mantle.

Second Row, Left to Right: Gus Mauch (Trainer), Billy Gardner, Bob Hale, Joe De Maestri, Tony Kubek, Tex Clevenger, Ralph Terry, Hector Lopez, Bob Cerv, Elston Howard, Roger Maris, Bob Turley, Joe Soares (Trainer).

Third Row, Left to Right: Bobby Richardson, Al Downing, Luis Arroyo, John Blanchard, Bill Stafford, Roland Sheldon, Jim Coates, Spud Murray (batting Practice Pitcher), and Bud Daley.

Seated on Ground in Front: Batboys Frank Prudenti, Fred Bengis.

1978 NEW YORK YANKEES

First Row Seated — THURMAN MUNSON, ELSTON HOWARD, DICK HOWSER, BOB LEMON, YOGI BERRA, ART FOWLER, CLYDE KING, GENE MICHAEL, GARY THOMASSON, ROY WHITE, ED FIGUEROA.

Second Row — GENE MONAHAN (TRAINER), DOM SCALA (BULLPEN CATCHER), BRIAN DOYLE, BUCKY DENT, RON GUIDRY, KEN CLAY, LARRY McCALL, JIM BEATTIE, RICH GOSSAGE, DICK TIDROW, LOU PINIELLA, FRED STANLEY, HERMAN SCHNEIDER (TRAINER), PETE SHEEHY (EQUIPMENT MANAGER).

Back Row — REGGIE JACKSON, CLIFF JOHNSON, JAY JOHNSTONE, WILLIE RANDOLPH, CATFISH HUNTER, CHRIS CHAMBLISS, PAUL LINDBLAD, PAUL BLAIR.

Seated on Ground — (BATBOYS), GREGG PINDER, JIM PLATTNER, SANDY SALLANDREA.

Official Photo—New York Yankees

The 1978 New York Yankees, a team which will someday be recognized as one of the greatest of Yankee teams. Trailing the first place Red Sox by 14 games in mid-July, the team rallied to overtake Boston, defeated the Sox in a playoff game, took the Royals in four games for the A.L. Pennant, and then overcame a 2-games-to-0 deficit to win the world series.

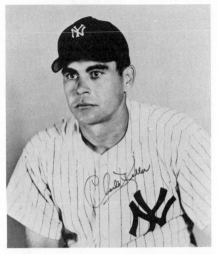

When Babe Ruth was released to the Boston Braves in 1935, the heir to his rightfield spot was George "Twinkletoes" Selkirk. Selkirk patroled the outfield from the latter part of the '34 season through 1942, finishing with a .290 career batting average, and a reputation as one of the finest gentlemen to ever don the pinstripes. He later enjoyed a successful managerial career in the minor leagues. His best Yankee years were 1936 (.308, 107 RBI's, SA — .511) 1937 (.328, SA — .629), and 1939 (.306, 101 RBI's, 103 runs scored, SA — .517).

Charlie "King Kong" Keller joined DiMaggio and Henrich as part of the great Yankee outfield from 1939-49. A lifetime .286 hitter, Keller also had a knack for drawing the base on balls. (He drew more than 100 walks in five of his 10 full seasons in New York).

His best year was probably 1941, when he batted .298, drove in 122 runs, scored 102, walked 102 times, and showed a .580 SA. He also drove in more than 100 runs in '42 and '46, and scored 102 or more runs in '40 and '42.

Too many Yankee fans have forgotten that Hall-of-Famer Joe Sewell graced the pinstripes in the final three years of his career. He joined the Yankees in 1931, and proceeded to bat .302 while scoring 102 runs as the Yankees third baseman. He also batted .272 for the 1932 world champions, scoring 95 runs and a .392 SA. His overall career spanned 14 seasons, 11 of them in Cleveland, and his most notable career stats are a .312 batting average and a .413 SA.

Tommy Henrich was appropriately nicknamed "Old Reliable." From 1937-50, he combined with Joe DiMaggio as two-thirds of one of baseball's finest outfields. Few fans realize that Henrich spent 11 years in a Yankee uniform and never recorded a SA less than .411. In fact, he topped the .500 mark in that category six times.

Whitey Ford, inducted into the Hall-of-Fame in 1974, had the best winning percentage for a 20-game winner until Ron Guidry shattered his record in 1978.

(Photo Courtesy of N.Y. Yankees and Michael Grossbardt)

Catfish Hunter joined the Yankees as the first million dollar free agent in 1975. He compiled a 23-14 record that year, before arm trouble reduced his effectiveness in 1976-77. After some unique treatment in 1978, he rebounded by winning 7 straight games down the stretch, to lead the Yankees to the world series.

Ron Guidry set many American League and Yankee records during his 25-3, 1.74 E.R.A., 248 strikeout season in 1978. For the breakdown, see the special section on the remarkable southpaw from Louisiana.

Many eyebrows were raised when the Yankees obtained Ed Figueroa (and Mickey Rivers) from the Angels for Bobby Bonds . . . But "Figgy" has proved his worth with a 19-win season in 1976, and a 20-9 mark in '78.   (Photo Courtesy of N.Y. Yankees and Michael Grossbardt)

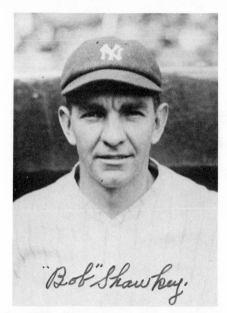

"Bob" Shawkey.

In 1916, Hall-of-Famer Bob Shawkey compiled a 23-14 record with a Yankee team that won only 80 games. He reached the 20-victory plateau again in 1919 (20-11), 1920 (20-13) and 1922 (20-12) while compiling a 158-131 mark during his 12 seasons in the pinstripes.

Good Luck
Waite C Hoyt

Hall-of-Famer Waite Hoyt was the ace of the Yankee staff in the 1920's. He was the only 20-game-winner on the '27 squad, but had his winningest season in 1928 (23-7).

(From the author's private collection)

Hall-of-Famer Lefty Gomez combined with Red Ruffing to give the Yankees the deadliest pitching duo of the 1930's. Gomez compiled a 189-101 mark in 13 seasons with New York, including a league-leading 26-5 (2.33 ERA) in 1934.

(From the author's private collection)

"From rags to riches," as the saying goes, was the pleasant fate of Hall-of-Famer hurler Red Ruffing. After leading the league in losses for 2 straight years (1928: 10-25; 1929: 9-22), he was traded from Boston to New York, where he paired with Lefty Gomez for 15 winning seasons, including 4 straight 20-victory campaigns (1936-39).

"Superchief" Allie Reynolds joined Raschi and Lopat as one of the "Big Three" from 1949-53. Actually, Reynolds came to the Yankees in 1947 and proceeded to post a 19-8 mark (good for a league-leading .704 pct.) His 7-2 world series record equals that of Red Ruffing, and places him tied for 2d in world series wins. Reynolds went 131-60 in his eight Yankee years, including 20-8 with a league-leading 2.06 E.R.A. in 1952.

Vic Raschi

"Steady Eddie" Lopat was the lefthanded member of the Yankees "Big Three" of the late 40's and early 50's. In 1953, Lopat posted a 16-4 record, good for an incredible .800 winning pct. and a league-leading 2.42 E.R.A. He is best known for his collection of off-speed curves and slip pitches which helped him post a 166-112 lifetime mark (113-69 as a Yankee).

A rare action shot of southpaw Herb Pennock, the left-handed ace of the Murderers Row teams of the 1920's. Pennock posted a 5-0 mark in world series action, second only to Lefty Gomez (6-0) in percentage. He also won 19 or more games 4 times, including a 23-11 mark in 1926.

The name may be familiar, but can you match it to this Hall-of-Famer's face and form? He's Jack Chesbro, in a rare close-up shot showing the righthander at his prime. Chesbro notched a 41-12 mark in 1904, still the modern day record for wins in one season.

Fireballer Al Downing struck out a league-leading 217 batters in 1964. Unfortunately, that was the highlight of his 9-year Yankee career, as arm-trouble and weak Yankee teams combined to limit his effectiveness. He later won 20 games for the Dodgers in 1971, but slipped to 9-9 the following 2 years.

Downing was the first black to fill a starting pitcher's role in Yankee history.

Few Yankee hurlers have endured the agony of Mel Stottlemyre. A rookie with the 1964 American League pennant-winners, Stottlemyre spent the rest of his 11-year career hoping to play for another contender. Ironically, his career was cut short by a torn rotator cuff in his pitching arm in 1974, and he was released in April, 1975. One year later, the Yankees began the first of three straight pennant-winning seasons.

Stott posted a 164-139 mark, all the more impressive because the Yankees played sub-.500 ball in four of his 11 seasons, and were successful from a contender's pint of view only in 1964, 70, 74. Threw the hard sinker in an era known for the Yankee infield's inconsistency. One can only wonder what he'd have done with the Yankees of the 1950's.

Hall-of-Famer Waite Hoyt was the only 20-game winner on the 1927 Yankees. Hoyt spent 21 years in the big leagues (9-plus seasons as a Yankee) and compiled a 237-182 record (157-98 as a Yankee), including a league-leading 22-7 (.759 Pct., 2.63 E.R.A.) in 1927. The autograph was "added" in 1977, 50 years to the date of his 20th win that year.

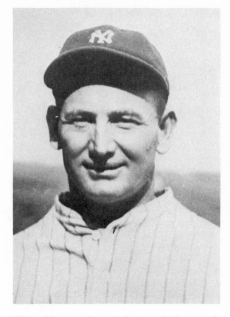

Wilcy Moore: the relief ace of Murderer's Row posted a 19-7 mark with 13 saves for the 1927 Yankees.

Jim Turner: While Murphy was lost to the World War II, the Yankees relied on "Milkman Jim" from 1943-45. He led the A.L. with 10 saves in 1945.

Joe Page: From 1947-49, Page was the stopper. Time and again, the "Fireman" came out of the bullpen to put down late-inning uprisings by the opposition. His best year was 1949, when he showed a 13-8 record with a league-leading 27 saves. An arm injury in 1950 cut short his career.

Most Yankee fans have never even heard of Tom Ferrick. But in 1950, he posted an 8-4 record with 9 saves to lead the Yankee bullpen. It was the only effective season in his nine-year career.

Bob Kuzava: 1951 was not much of a year for Yankee relief pitchers, especially with Lopat, Raschi, and Reynolds starting three out of every four games. Kuzava posted an 8-4 record for N.Y. (5 wins in relief) with 5 saves that year.

John Sain: 1954 was the year all of the A.L. prayed for rain instead of Sain. The veteran hurler chalked up six wins and a league-leading 22 saves.

Bob Grim: In 1954, Grim posted a 20-6 record, including 6 wins as a reliever. In 1957, Grim posted a 12-8 mark (all in relief) with a league-leading 19 saves, and was the defacto Fireman of the Year. (Rolaids awards are a thing of the recent past).

Luis Arroyo: 1961 was the year that put Arroyo's name in the record books. The southpaw posted a 15-5 record (all in relief) with 29 saves, hands down the fireman of the year. He faded to 1-3, 7 saves in 1962 and disappeared from the m.l. after 1963.

Three keys to the success of the mid 1950s: Jim Konstanty (1955: 7-2, 11 saves), Tom Morgan (1955: 7-3, 10 saves; and 1956: 6-7, 11 saves) and Tom Sturdivant (1956: 16-8, 6-2 in relief, 5 saves).

Ryne Duren: Another flame-thrower the opposition preferred to do without. Duren's trademarks were his thick eye-glasses and wildness during warmups. (He frequently tossed his warmup pitchers into the seats, completely over the backstop.)
In 1958, he posted a 6-4 record with a league-leading 20 saves. The 1959 (3-6, 14 saves) and 1960 (3-4, 9 saves) seasons were less successful, and he was traded in 1961.

Johnny Murphy 1929

Lindy McDaniel: McDaniel handled the Yankees relief chores from 1968-73. His out pitch was the forkball (he is shown demonstrating the grip). In 1970, McDaniel compiled a 9-5 record with 29 saves.

In 1924, Gehrig was farmed out to the Yankees' friendly Hartford franchise in the old Eastern League. Gehrig never cared much for Hartford. He missed the closeness to his family that playing in New York provided. (Photo courtesy of the Baseball Hall of Fame).

Lou Gehrig in a Columbia University Baseball uniform. Gehrig attended Columbia for almost 2 years before the need for money for medical expenses "encouraged" him to sign with the Yankees.

The "classic" Lou Gehrig swing and follow-through as captured in 1936. Gehrig hit .354 that year, and drove in an American League record 167 RBI's. He also hit 49 homeruns, scored 152 runs, and showed a .696 slugging percentage.

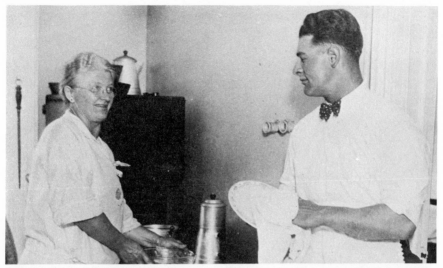

Gehrig caught wiping the dishes at home in 1934, while his beaming mother looks on. For those who know the Gehrig story, Momma Gehrig played an important, and dominating role in the Hall-of-Famer's life. At first, she virulently opposed a baseball career for her son, Louie, but she later grew to accept it. One thing she had even more trouble accepting was Lou's marriage to Eleanor Twitchell, the surviving "First Lady of the New York Yankees." It was a most unfortunate situation, because they both survived Gehrig by many years, and could have at least had each other, but teammates and friends agreed that the mother and wife never really got along.   (Photo courtesy of the Baseball Hall of Fame.)

Hall-of-Famers (l to r) Lefty Grove, Lou Gehrig, Al Simmons, and Mickey Cochran graced the cover of the Japanese Baseball Souvenir Program issued during the Connie Mack All-Star team's trip to Japan in 1933.

You'd never know it by the look on Gehrig's face, but the youngster he's congratulating is Babe Dahlgren . . .

The photo is dated May 2, 1939, the date Dahlgren replaced Gehrig at first base and ended the Hall-of-Famer's 2,130-consecutive games played in streak.

The truth of the matter is that Gehrig was never one to be jealous, and even though his streak had ended less than three hours earlier that day he is still the pleasant, smiling man Yankee fans knew and loved.

. . . And here is the award-winning closeup of an emotionally overwhelmed Gehrig, wiping the tears away while telling the multitude that he considered himself "the luckiest man on the face of the earth."

(Photo courtesy of the Baseball Hall of Fame.)

July 4, 1939 . . . Lou Gehrig Day at Yankee Stadium. Here, Gehrig is shown accepting the congratulations of master of ceremonies Dan Daniel, while his teammates of the 20's (left) and 30's (right) look on in admiration . . .

A rare photo of Ruth as the player-assistant manager of the Boston Braves in 1935. The Babe does not appear to be too thrilled . . . and his employment with Boston lasted less than a month of the season.

Ruth and Braves manager Bill McKechnie posed for reporters on Opening Day 1935 at Braves Field.

(Courtesy of Baseball Hall of Fame)

Babe Ruth and Bill Dickey awaiting a pitch during an Old Timer's game at a packed Yankee Stadium.

These two rare photographs shows Babe Ruth batting against Hall-of-Famer Walter Johnson at a Yankee Stadium benefit for War Bonds during 1942. More than 60,000 fans came out to watch Ruth in what proved to be his final at-bats at Yankee Stadium.
Here, the Babe gets ready to receive Johnson's 21st pitch . . .

(Courtesy of the Baseball Hall of Fame)

. . . and Ruth swings . . . and drives the ball deep into the upper deck in right field. Although the ball hooked a few feet foul, the exhausted Ruth knew it would be his best shot, so he circled the bases for the final time in Yankee Stadium . . .

Babe Ruth buys tickets for Red Cross charity game between Yanks and Dodgers from owner Larry MacPhail and Mrs. Julius Ochs Adler.
Apr. 6, 1945

1948 Old Timers Day: Babe Ruth addresses the Multitudes for the final time in what proved to be his last appearance at Yankee Stadium. This is the front view, . . . showing the Babe's cancer-wracked body and drawn face. No wonder this photo is rarely used.

Few things in Yankee-land are tougher to come by than an authentic autographed picture of Joe DiMaggio.

Lou Gehrig gives a few well-received words of encouragement to rookie Joe DiMaggio in 1936.

'Hold still, Joe! Nick Altrock, funny man of the Washington Senators, couldn't resist having a frolic with Joe DiMaggio, Yankee star, who reported for duty May 1 after spending the night in a Washington Hospital following a collision with a fellow player in the previous day's game. Here's Nick patting Joe's sore head with one hand and preparing to bounce a ball off it with the other.

Old Timers' Day 1957. You wouldn't know that Joe DiMaggio had been out of baseball for six years, as the centerfielder drives a homerun into the left-field stands.

Two of the greatest players in Yankee (and baseball) history, Hall-of-Famers Lou Gehrig and Joe DiMaggio, in 1937.

Joe DiMaggio presents the 1948 Sporting News Trophy to Babe Ruth for meritorious service to American youth.

A young Roger Maris is all smiles after hitting his first Yankee homerun.

Maris, (signed) and posed for action.

Quick . . . what's "wrong" with this picture? Answer: Maris batted left-handed! The fellow on the right should also be familiar to followers of the Pinstripes.

Maris launches his 60th homerun into orbit. The pitcher was Jack Fisher . . .

October 1, 1961. Roger Maris approaches home plate welcome from Yogi Berra and batboy after hitting his 61st home run off Red Sox pitcher Tracy Stallard in final game of season. Yanks won game, 1-0.

Fans always remember Roger Maris for his homeruns, but few recall the ones he prevented. In fact, Maris was one of the finest right fielders in Yankee history.

Here, Maris is shown robbing the Angels' Bobby Knoop of a game-tying homerun during the Yankees 3-2 win in April, 1965.

Propelled by a shove from Hector Lopez, Roger Maris steps from the Yankee dugout to wave his cap in response to cheering crowd. Roger had just done what no baseball player ever before had been able to accomplish — connected for his 61st home run in a single season.

Another great catch by Maris, this time robbing Washington's Ken Retzer of a homerun to save the Yankees 4-2 win in May, 1962.

Mantle and Maris join hands to raise the 1977 World Championship banner to the flagpole in left center field.   (N.Y. Yankees)

Mantle launches his 50th homerun of the 1961 season.

Mickey Mantle is the batter, Denny McLain the pitcher, and homerun No. 535 is just seconds away from being launched into the right field seats. McLain allegedly asked Mantle where he wanted the pitch thrown, and served it up to his boyhood hero. (The Tigers were leading 8-0 at the time.) Mantle hit another homerun later that season to finish with a career total of 536.

Mickey Mantle and Whitey Ford pose with their favorite manager, Casey Stengel, during their induction to the Baseball Hall of Fame in 1974.

An authentic autographed photo of Mickey Mantle.

Hank Bauer was one of several fine outfielders who graced the pinstripes during the Dynasty of 1949-58. During those years, his slugging percentage never fell below the .423 mark. From 1950-54, Bauer topped the .293 batting average, including a .320 average in '50.

Enos "Country" Slaughter cried for 20 minutes when he learned that his beloved Cardinals had traded him to the Yankees after the 1953 season. The Yankees dealt him to Kansas City in '55. They re-acquired the lifetime .300 hitter from the Athletics, and Slaughter turned in three fine seasons. In 1958, Slaughter batted .304, his best year in N.Y. (Photo courtesy of N.Y. Yankees)

From 1949-53, the "Big Cat" terrorized American League pitching as a part-time first baseman and pinch hitter. He led the league in pinch hits three straight years (1951-53) and his lowest slugging percentage was .394.

No book on the Yankees could be complete without a picture of the World Championship Trophy the franchise has "owned" 22 times.

(Photo courtesy of the N.Y. Yankees)

A real rarity: an autographed picture of Grover Cleveland Alexander (the 2d winningest pitcher in major league history) and the Yankees Bob Shawkey (at the tail-end of his 15-year-career) taken prior to the sixth game of the 1926 World Series. Alexandes outpitched Shawkey, 10-2.

Babe Ruth crosses the plate after hitting his "called" homerun in Wrigley Field during the 1932 World Series.

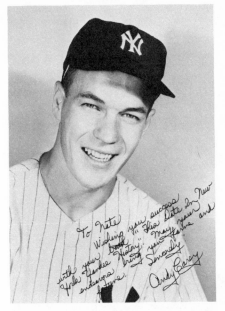

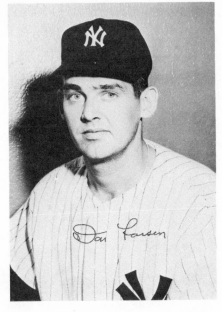

Andy Carey anchored the "hot corner for the great teams of the '50s, overcoming many injuries which eventually caused the premature end of his career. His best season was the 1954 campaign, when he batted .302 in 122 games. He was largely responsible for preserving Don Larsen's perfect game in 1956, thanks to a pair of outstanding plays at third base.

An autographed picture of Yankee righthander Don Larsen.

". . . One ball, two strikes, two outs, bottom of the ninth inning. Larsen takes the sign and delivers to pinch hitter Dale Mitchell. Strike three! A no-hitter, a perfect game . . .." For Don Larsen, a perfect game in the world series, and instant immortality.

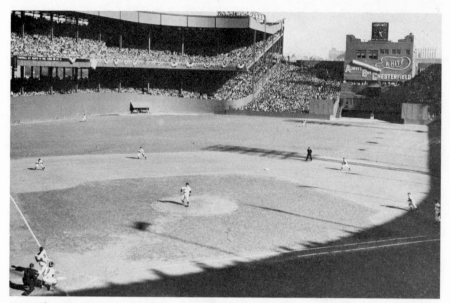

New York: Joltin' Joe DiMaggio, the Yankee Clipper, is shown the instant after he slammed a two-run homer into the upper deck of the left-field stands at the Polo Grounds, in the top half of the fifth inning, fourth World Series game, Oct. 8. Yogi Berra, who scored ahead of DiMaggio, is shown just moving off first. The ball can be seen headed for the stands just to the left of Giant left-fielder Monte Irvin. Other players are: Giant catcher Wes Westrum (9); first-baseman Whitey Lockan; second-baseman Eddie Stanky; center-fielder Willie Mays; shortstop Alvin Dark; third-baseman Bobby Thomson, Home plate ump is Al Barlick; second base ump, Lee Ballanfant; third base ump, Joe Paparella. Ump on left field foul line is John Stevens. The four-sacker was Joe's second hit in the current series, and the Bombers evened up the series with a 6-2 win. Sal Maglie pitching.
It was DiMaggio's final major league homerun.

1977 was the Year of the Reggie . . . Jackson, that is. Here is the classic Jackson swing, and the excited look out towards the bleachers in right center field, where Jackson is depositing his third homerun of the Sixth Game of the world series.
(Photo Courtesy of N.Y. Yankees and Michael Grossbardt)

CLARKE GRIFFITH
PITCHER OF THE NEW YORK (A. L.) CLUB

The first manager of the New York Highlanders was Hall-of-Famer Clarke Griffith, who guided the club from 1903 until he "retired" one-third of the way through the 1908 season. His most successful season was the 1904 campaign, when the team finished in second place. His New York totals: 419-370.

"The Mighty Mite", Miller Huggins, guided the Yankees from 1918-1929, and compiled a career pinstripes record of 1067-719. He came to the Yankees at the suggestion of American League President Ban Johnson, after several years at the Cardinals' helm. Huggins, a lawyer by way of the University of Cincinnati, led the Yankees to their first world series (1921) and world championship (1923). He died of exhaustion towards the end of the 1929 season.

The fellow on the right is "Marse Joe" McCarthy, a man generally recognized as the greatest manager of his era. McCarthy piloted the Yankees from 1931-46, good for 8 pennants and 7 world championships. His Yankee totals were 1460-867, and he also managed the Cubs and Red Sox with great success.

When Joe McCarthy stunned the baseball world by resigning as Yankee manager during the 1946 season, Bill Dickey was named to guide the team for the rest of the season. The team went 57-48 under his helm, and finished in 3rd place.

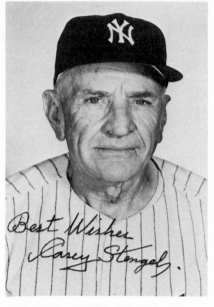

Bucky Harris' two year stint as the manager of the Yankees produced a world championship in 1947. He also managed the Seantors (1924-28, 1935-42, 1950-54), Tigers (1929-33, 1955-56), Red Sox (1934), Phillies (1943) during his 29-year career. He is third in total career victories as a manager (2159), and second in games (4410) and losses (2219). His Yankee stats: 191-117.

The many faces of Casey Stengel.

Yogi Berra led the 1964 Yankees to the A.L. Pennant, and just missed winning the world series against the Cardinals. Unfortunately, the decision to fire Berra was made during mid-season, while the Yankees were slipping and sliding. It was a terrible public relation move.
(Photo Courtesy of N.Y. Yankees and Michael Grosbardt)

In July 1922, the Yankees acquired third baseman Joe Dugan from the Red Sox, re-kindling cries of outrage from the rest of the league which swore the Sox and Yankees were in a league with the Devil.
Dugan solidified the infield, and stayed in N.Y. through the 1928 season. His best year was 1924, when he batted .302 and scored 105 runs.

Spring training in 1908 at Little Rock, Arkansas. Notice the strenuous activities: mule-back riding through the hills; and a chaperoned horse-and-buggy ride down the main thoroughfare.

On a serious vain, these photos are so rare that the Baseball Hall of Fame did not know they existed, and they have never been printed before, as far as anyone knows.

There are three Hall of Famers in the picture, all of who were members of the Highlanders of that era. Can you pick them out?

(left to right: unidentified reporter, Jack Chesbro (H of F), Red Kleinow, Kid Elberfeld, Larry Stahl, Al Orth, Bill Hogg, Willie Keeler (H of F), Clark Griffith, and reporter Sam Crane.

Out for a leisurely stroll in spring training, 1908.

(These two photos are the oldest known shots of a Highlander team, and are among the oldest still preserved of any spring training.) (Courtest of the Baseball Hall of Fame)

HISTORIC DAYS AT YANKEE STADIUM
MONUMENT AND PLAQUE DEDICATIONS

MILLER HUGGINS
May 30, 1932

JACOB RUPERT
April 23, 1940

LOU GEHRIG
July 4, 1941

BABE RUTH
April 19, 1949

EDWARD BARROW
April 15, 1954

MICKEY MANTLE — JOE DIMAGGIO
April 12, 1970

Unfortunately, the fans are no longer able to get a close-up view of the plaques and monuments which grace the Stadium's hallowed walls and ground in left-center field. The small memorial park is inaccessible.

In the pre-renovation Stadium, fans were frequently invited into the field after home games, and the highlight was always a visit out to the plaques and monuments in centerfield.

Occasionally, a long drive to center would be lost, momentarily, behind the three monuments erected to Miller Huggins, Lou Gehrig, and Babe Ruth.   (Photo courtesy of the Baseball Hall of Fame)

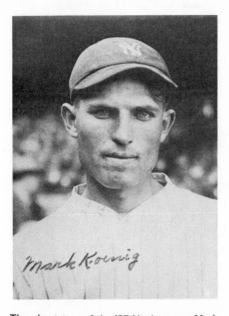
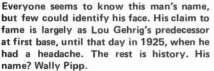

The shortstop of the '27 Yankees was Mark Koenig. As a rookie in 1926, Koenig suffered through a tough world series, and was blamed by many people for the Yankees defeat at the hands of the Cardinals. In 1927, he starred in the series against the Pirates, leading both teams with a .400 batting average.

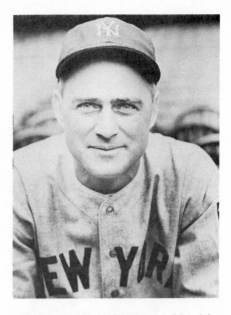

Hall-of-Famer Earle Combs, considered by many to have been the greatest leadoff hitter in Yankee history.

Everyone seems to know this man's name, but few could identify his face. His claim to fame is largely as Lou Gehrig's predecessor at first base, until that day in 1925, when he had a headache. The rest is history. His name? Wally Pipp.

One of the stars of the Yankees of the 30's was Ben Chapman, a fine baserunner who also played for the Boston Red Sox.

A rare photograph of Willie Keeler bunting during the 1904 season. Notice the old wool uniform and the absence of shin guards on the catcher.

NICKNAMES

Al — Alphonso Downing
Alex — Alexander Johnson
And I'll See Ya Later — Danny Cater
Andy — John Messersmith, Andrew O'Connor

Babe — George Ruth
Babe Ruth's Legs — Sammy Byrd
Baldy — William Louden
The Bambino — George Ruth
The Barber — Sal Maglie
Bear Tracks — Johnny Schmitz
Bee Bee — Loren Babe
Bert — Bernard Daniels
Big Ben — Ben Shields
Big Bill — Bill Renna
The Big Cat — John Mize
Big Dan — Dan Tipple
Big Ed — Ed Klepfer
Big Jawn — John Mize
Big Jim — James Weaver
Big Poison — Paul Waner
Bill — Floyd Bevens
Billy — Alfred Martin, Wilmer Shantz
Birdie — William Cree
Biscuit Pants — Henry Gehrig
Blondy — John Ryan
Boardwalk — Carroll Brown
Bob — John Tillman, Erwin Porterfield
Bobo — Norman Newsom
Bonehead — Fred Merkle
Boomer — Ron Blomberg
Bootnose — Fred Hoffman
Bozo — Al Cicotte
Braggo — Robert Roth
Branch — Wesley Rickey
The Brat — Alfred Martin
Brownie — Robert Brown
Bub — Norman McMillan
Bubbles — Eugene Hargrave
Bubby — Fred Talbot
Buck — Ralph Buxton, Grant Jackson, Norman Newsom
Bucky — Russell Dent
Bud — Leavitt Daley, Art Metheny, Edward Stewart
Buddy — Ray Barker, John Hassett, Warren Rosar
Buffalo Bill — Bill Hogg
The Bull — Billy Johnson, George Uhle
Bullet Bob — Bob Turley
Bullet Jack — Jack Thoney
Bullet Joe — Leslie Bush
Bulldog — Jim Bouton
Bump — Irving Hadley
Bunions — Rollie Zeider

131

Bunny — Hugh High, Thomas Madden
Buster — Colonel Mills, Henry Gehrig
Butch — Charles Schmidt, Charles Wensloff
Buttons — James Williams

Camp — Elisha Skinner
Casey — Joseph Cox, Charles Stengel
Catfish — James Hunter
The Chairman of the Board — Edward Ford
Champ — James Osteen
Charlie — Leslie Spikes
Chick — Wilson Fewster
Chicken — Nelson Hawks, Fred Stanley
Chief — John Warhop
Chris — Carroll Chamblis
Circus Solly — Art Hofman
Clem — Clement Llewellyn
Clete — Cletis Boyer
Columbia Lou — Henry Gehrig
The Commerce Comet — Mickey Mantle
The Count — Walter Lyle
Country — Enos Slaughter
Cozy — Alvin Dolan
Crab — John Warhop
Crossfire — Earl Moore
The Crow — Frank Crosetti
Cuddles — Clarence Marshall
Curt — William Walker
The Curveless Wonder — Al Orth
Cy — Wilcy Moore, Ralph Perkins, Edwin Pieh

The Danish Viking — George Pipgras
Danny — Luke Boone
Dashing Dan — Dan Costello
Dazzy — Clarence Vance
Deacon — James McKechnie, Everett Scott
Deacon Danny — Dan Mac Fayden
Dee — Duane Pillette
Deek — Claud Derrick
Del — Wendell Alston
Dick — John Gossett
Dirty Jack — Jack Doyle
Dixie — Fred Walker
Dizzy — Roy Carlyle
Dobber — Pat Dobson
Doc — Merle Adkins, Bobby Brown, Luther Cook, Howard Edwards,
    Edward Farrell, George Medich
Dooley — Horace Womack
Ducky — Dick Schofield
Duffy — George Lewis
Duke — Leon Carmel, Duane Maas
Dusty — Allen Cooke, John Rhodes
Dutch — Bill Drescher, Art Schult, Charles Sterrett

Eagle Eye — Charlie Hemphill

Earl — Clifford Torgeson
The Earl of Snohomish — Clifford Torgeson
Ed — Eduardo Figueroa, Edwin Wells
Eddie — Foster Edwards, William Robinson
Ellie — Elrod Hendricks, Elston Howard, Eliseo Rodriguez

Fernando — Jose Gonzalez
Fire — Virgil Trucks
Fireman — Johnny Murphy, Joe Page
Flash — Frank Gilhooley, Joe Gordon, Frederick Maisel
Fordham Johnny — Johnny Murphy
Fred — John Sanford
Frenchy — Stanley Bordagaray
Fritz — Fred Peterson, Frederick Maisel
Fritzie — Fritz Brickell

Gabber — Joe Glenn
Gabby — Charles Street
Gabe — John Gabler
Gator — Ron Guidry
The Gay Castillon — Vernon Gomez
The Gay Reliever — Joe Page
Germany — Herman Long, Harold Schaeffer
Gink — Harvey Hendrick
Go Away — Ken Clay
Golden Boy — Robert Brown
Goober — Bill Zuber
Good Time Bill — Bill Lamar
Goofy — Lefty Gomez
Goose — Rich Gossage
Gordon — John Rhodes
Grandma — Johnny Murphy
The Great Debater — Thomas Henrich
Gus — Augustus Fischer, Constantine Niarhos, Augustus Triandos

Hack — Clyde Engle, George Simmons
Hal — Hector Brown
Ham — Robert Hyatt
Handsome Harry — Harry Howell
Hank — Henry Bauer, William Karlon, Howard Shanks, Herbert Thormalen
Happy Jack — Jack Chesbro
Happy Joe — Joe Finneran
Harry — William Smythe
Hawk — Ken Silvestri
Heavy — Walter Blair
Heeney — Hank Majeski
Helpless Hal — Hal Lanier
Hinky — Henry Haines
Hippity — John Hopp
Hippo — James Vaughn
Homer — Thomas Thompson
Homerun — Frank Baker
Honey — John Barnes
Hooks — Bill Miller
Hopeless Hal — Hal Lanier

Hoss — Horace Clarke
Hot Rod — Jim McDonald
Husk — Frank Chance

The Iron Horse — Henry Gehrig

Jack — Otto Saltzgaver, John Warhop
Jake — Jerry Gibbs, Alvin Powell, Garland Stahl, Jacob Wade.
Jay — John Johnstone
Jeep — Don Heffner
Jim — Jess Buckles
Jimmy — James Walsh, James Williams
Joe — Salvatore Smith
Joltin' Joe — Joe DiMaggio
Julie — Julian Wera
Jumbo — Walt Brown
Jumpin' Joe — Joe Dugan
Junior — Linus Frey

The Kentucky Colonel — Earle Combs
Kid — Norman Elberfeld, Eddie Foster
Kiddo — George Davis
King — Leonard Cole
King Kong — Charlie Keller
Klondike — Frederick Smith
Kong — Dave Kingman
The Knight of Kennett Square — Herb Pennock

Languid Bob — Robert Meusel
The Lawyer — Miller Huggins
Lee — James Thomas
Lefty — Alfonzo Davis, Vernon Gomez, Wilbur Good, Lee Grissom,
    Fred Heimach, Hugh High, Herbert Karpel, Steve Kraly, Francis O'Doul,
    Harry Schaeffer, Al Schulz, Ben Shields, Herbert Thormalen,
    Phillip Weinert, Billy Wight
Lew — Clement Llewellyn
Lindy — Lyndell McDaniel
The Lip — Leo Durocher
Little Joe — Joe Yeager
Little Mr. Everywhere — Miller Huggins
Liz — Elias Funk
Lobo — Jerry Kenney
Long Bob — Robert Meusel
Long Tom — Tom Hughes
Lonny — Linus Frey
Lou — Henry Gehrig
Louisiana Lightning — Ron Guidry
Lu — Luciean Clinton
Luke — Luther Nelson

Mack — Malcolm Hills
The Mahatma — Wesley Rickey
The Major — Ralph Houk
Marse Joe — Joseph McCarthy
Marvelous Marv — Marv Throneberry

134

Matty — Mateo Alou
Mick The Quick — John Rivers
Mickey — Gene Klutts, Maurice McDermott, John Rivers, Danny
    Walton, Nicholas Witek
Mickey Mantle's Legs — Ross Moschitto
Milkman — Jim Turner
Milt — Nathaniel Gaston
The Mite Manager — Miller Huggins
Mollie — Mike Milosevich
Monbo — Bill Monbouquette
Monk — Walt Dubiel
Monte — Henry Beville
Moose — Bill Drescher, Bill Skowron
Mr. Dirt — Dick Tidrow
Muddy — Harold Ruel
Muscles — Joe Gallagher, Fenton Mole, Mickey Mantle

The Naugatuck Nugget — Frank Shea
Ned — Virgil Garvin
The Nervous Greek — Lou Skizas
The New London Strongboy — John Ellis
Nick — Henry Cullop
Nig — John Grabowski
No Homerun — Frank Baker
No Neck — Walter Williams
Nolan — Clifford Richardson
Noodles — Frank Hahn

Oats — Joe DeMaestri
Ol' Stubblebeard — Burleigh Grimes
The Old Gray Fox — Clark Griffith
Old Redneck — Gil McDougald
Old Reliable — Tommy Henrich
Old Sarge — Charles Street
Otto — Otoniel Velez
Ownie — Owen Carroll

Paddy — Charles Baumann
Pat — Pierce Malone, Tharon Collins
Patsy — Patrick Dougherty
Peach Pie — Jack O'Connor
Peck — Ed Monroe
Peco — Joe Giard
Pee Wee — Nate Oliver, Paul Wanninger
Peerless Leader — Frank Chance
The People's Cherce — Fred Walker
Pepi — Joe Pepitone, Cesar Tovar
Pepito — Cesar Tovar
Pete — Tom Daley, Pedro Ramos
Pipp The Pickler — Wally Pipp
Plowboy — Tom Morgan
Poison — Ivy Andrews
Poosh 'Em Up — Tony Lazzeri
Porky — Hal Reniff, Gene Woodling

Pot — Frank LaPorte
Prince Hal — Harold Chase
Professor — Joe Ostrowski, Charles Stengel
Pudgie — Frank Delahanty
Pug — Tony Rensa

Queenie — James O'Rourke

Rawley — Rawlins Eastwick
Ray — Charles Demmitt
Rebel — Guy Cooper, Tommy McMillan
Red — Norm Branch, Charles Embree, Chester Hoff, Robert Rolfe,
   Charles Ruffing, Marius Russo
Reggie — Reginald Jackson
Rip — Harry Collins, Walter Coleman
Rocky — Rocco Colavito, Ron Swoboda
Roll Out the Barrel — Ken Wright
Rollie — Ralston Hemsley, Roland Sheldon
Rosy — Wilfred Ryan
Roxy — Wilbur Roach, Alfred Walters
Roy — Royden Sherid, Cyril Weatherly
Rube — Walter Manning, Reuben Oldring, Hank Robinson
Russ — Alva Derry
Rusty — Dan Tipple, Rosendo Torres

Sad Sam — Sam Jones
Sailor Bob — Robert Shawkey
Salt Rock — Ezra Midkiff
Sandy — Conde Alomar, Joe Vance
Sarge — Bob Kuzava
Schoolboy — Waite Hoyt, John Knight
Scooter — Phil Rizzuto
Scrap Iron — Clint Courtney
Shags — Joseph Horan
Sheriff — Russ Van Atta, Marshall Bridges
Sherm — John Lollar
Shotgun — Mike Chartak, Billy Gardner, Tom Rogers
Silent John — John Hummel
The Silent Pole — Stan Coveleski
Silvio — Felix Jimenez
Simon — Roy Sanders
Single, Double, Triple, Homerun — Ron Klimkowski
Skeeter — Andrew Shelton
Slim — Ray Caldwell, Elmer Love
Slow Joe — Judd Doyle
Smash — Gil McDougald
Smiler — George Murray
Smokey — Steve Sundra
Snake — Tom Sturdivant, Lewis Wiltse
Snuffy — George Stirnweiss
The Southern Gentleman — Earle Combs
Sparky — Walter Lyle
Spec — Frank Shea
The Springfield Rifle — Vic Raschi
Spud — Spurgeon Chandler

Steady — Eddie Lopat
Steve — Emerson Roser
The Stick — Gene Michael
Stormy — Cyril Weatherly
Stretch — Jack Phillips
Stubby — Frank Overmire, Ed Magner
Sub — Carl Mays
Sudden Sam — Sam McDowell
Suds — Bill Sudakis
Sugar — Francis Kane
Suitcase — Harry Simpson
Suitcase Bob — Bob Seeds
The Sultan of Swat — George Ruth
The Super Chief — Allie Reynolds
Supersub — Phil Linz
Swede — Johnny Johnson, Charlie Silvera
Sweet Lou — Lou Piniella

Tabasco Kid — Norman Elberfeld
Tacks — Johnny Neuer
Teddy — George Wilson
Terry — Terrence Ley
Tex — Truman Clevenger
Thunder — John Ellis
Tiger — Cliff Mapes
Tom — Jonathan Zachary
Tomato Face — Henry Cullop
Tony — Tolia Solaita
The Toy Cannon — James Wynn
Truck — James Hannah, Eddie Kearse
Tuck — George Stainback
Tut — Dick Tettelbach
Twinkletoes — George Selkirk

Vito — Vitautis Tamulis

Wally — Walter Schang
Warrior — Bob Friend
Wee Willie — William Keeler
Weser — Jim Brideweser
The Whip — Ewell Blackwell
Whistlin' Jake — Jacob Wade
Whitey — Edward Ford, Lawton Whitt
Wid — William Conroy
Wild Bill — William Donovan, Bill Piercy
Willie — Patrick Green
Woodie — Woodson Held
Workhorse — Herb Crompton

The Yankee Clipper — Joe DiMaggio
Yats — George Wuestling

Zach — James Taylor
Zeke — Johhn Bella
Ziggy — Ken Sears

THE ALL-TIME YANKEE ROSTER

Fans are frequently curious as to whether a given player ever played for a particular team. The purpose of this section is to list the name of every player who ever wore the Yankee uniform for at least one fraction of an inning and made an appearance on the playing field in some capacity during a regular-season game.

The players are listed in alphabetical order under their real last names. Nicknames are shown in quotation marks. Shortened versions of names are in parenthesis. The year(s) in which the player was on the Yankee roster, and his position(s) are shown immediately to the right of the name. The player's date of birth and date of death (if deceased, and if available) are also shown.

Code:

INF — indicates the player played third base (3B), shortstop (SS), and second base (2B) with roughly equal frequency during his Yankee career.

OF — indicates the player played one or more outfield positions

C — indicates the player played as a catcher

1B — first baseman

P — Pitcher

PH — Indicates that the player's only major league appearance(s) in a Yankee uniform was (were) as a pinch hitter.

PR — Indicates that the player's only Yankee appearance(s) was (were) as a pinch runner.

DH — Designated hitter.

Note: pitchers are listed separately after all of the other positions. Also, for a complete list of every nickname for every player, see the separate nicknames section. (Space prevents a complete nicknames listing in the roster section.)

————————→

THE ALL–TIME YANKEE ROSTER (Continued)

NON–PITCHERS

Name	Years	Pos.	Born	Died
Spencer Adams	1926	INF	6/21/97	11/25/70
Walter (Walt) Alexander	15-17	C	3/5/91	
Bernard "Bernie" Allen	72-73	INF	4/16/39	
Conde "Sandy" Alomar	74-76	INF	10/19/43	
Felipe Alou	71-73	1B, OF, DH	5/12/35	
Matteo "Matty" Alou	73	1B, OF, DH	12/22/38	
Wendell (Del) Alston	77-78	OF, DH	9/22/52	
Ruben Amaro	66-68	SS, 3B, 1B	1/6/36	
John Anderson	04-05	OF	12/14/73	7/23/49
Angel Aragon	14, 16-17	OF	8/2/93	1/24/52
Rugger Ardizoia	47	PH	11/20/19	
James (Jimmy) Austin	09-10	3B	12/8/79	4/6/65
Martin (Marty) Autry	24	C	3/5/03	1/26/50
Loren "Bee-Bee" Babe	52-53	3B	1/11/28	
William (Bill) Bailey	11	OF	11/19/81	10/27/67
Franklin "Homerun" Baker	16-19, 21-22	3B	3/13/86	6/28/63
Frank "No Homerun" Baker	70-71	SS	10/24/46	
Neal Ball	07-08	SS, 2B	4/22/81	10/15/57
Ray "Buddy" Barker	65-67	1B	3/12/36	
John "Honey" Barnes	26	C	1/31/00	
Edward (Ed) Barney	15	OF	1/23/90	10/4/67
George Batten	12	2B	10/19/91	
Henry (Hank) Bauer	48-49	OF, C	7/31/22	
Charles "Paddy" Baumann	15-17	2B, 3B	12/20/85	11/20/69
Zinn Beck	18	1B	9/30/85	unknown
Rudy Bell	07	OF	1/1/81	7/28/55
John "Zeke" Bella	57	OF	8/23/30	
Benjamin (Benny) Bengough	23-30	C	7/27/98	12/22/68

THE ALL–TIME YANKEE ROSTER (Continued)

NON–PITCHERS

Name	Years	Pos.	Born	Died
Louis (Lou) Berberet	54-55	C	11/10/29	
David (Dave) Bergman	75, 77	OF, 1B	6/6/53	
Henry "Monte" Beville	03-04	C, 1B	2/24/75	1/24/55
Juan Bernhardt	76	1B, OF		
Richard (Rick) Bladt	75	OF	12/9/46	
Paul Blair	77-current	OF, INF, DH	2/1/44	
Walter "Heavy" Blair	07-11	C, OF, 1B	10/13/83	8/20/48
John (Johnny) Blanchard	55, 59-65	C, OF, 1B	2/26/33	
Curtis (Curt) Blefary	70-71	OF, 1B, C, 3B, 2B	7/5/43	
Elmer Bliss	03-04	OF	3/9/75	3/18/62
Ronald (Ron) Blomberg	69, 71-77	OF, 1B, DH	8/23/48	
Edward (Eddie) Bockman	46	3B	7/26/20	
Frank "Ping" Bodie	18-21	OF	10/8/87	12/17/61
Leonard (Len) Boehmer	69, 71	INF, 1B	6/28/41	
Donald (Don) Bollweg	53	1B	2/12/21	
Luke "Danny" Boone	13-16	INF	5/6/90	
Robert (Bobby) Bonds	75	OF, DH	3/15/46	
Stanley "Frenchy" Bordagaray	41	OF	1/3/12	
William "Babe" Borton	13	1B	7/14/88	7/29/54
Cletis (Clete) Boyer	59-66	INF, OF	2/8/37	
Fritz (Fritzie) Brickell	58-59	2B, SS	3/19/35	10/15/65
James "Weser" Brideweser	51-53	INF	2/13/27	
Harry Bright	63-64	1B, 3B	9/22/29	
Robert (Bobby) Brown	46-54	SS, 3B, OF	10/25/24	
Edward (Eddie) Brinkman	75	INF	12/8/41	
William (Bill) Bryan	66-67	C, 1B	12/4/38	
George "Tioga" Burns	28-29	1B	1/31/93	8/15/66
Alexander (Alex) Burr	14	OF	11/1/93	11/1/18

140

Name	Years	Pos.	Born	Died
Joseph (Joe) Buzas	45	SS	10/2/19	
Samuel (Sammy) Byrd	29-34	OF	10/15/06	
Thomas Byrne	43-51, 54-57	PH (P)	12/31/19	
John (Johnny) Callison	72-73	OF, DH	3/12/39	
Raymond "Slim" Caldwell	10-18	OF	4/26/88	8/16/67
Howard "Red" Camp	17	OF	7/1/93	5/8/60
Andrew (Andy) Carey	52-60	INF	10/18/31	
Leon "Duke" Carmel	65	1B	4/23/37	
Roy "Dizzy" Carlyle	26	OF	12/10/00	11/22/56
Thomas (Tommy) Carroll	55-56	SS, 3B	9/17/36	
Daniel (Danny) Cater	70-71	1B, 3B, OF	2/25/40	
Robert (Bob) Cerv	51-56, 60-62	OF	5/5/26	
Frank "Husk" Chance	13-14	1B	9/9/77	9/14/24
Carroll "Chris" Chambliss	74-current	1B, DH	12/26/48	
Lester "Dude" Channell	10, 14	OF	4/3/86	5/7/54
William (Ben) Chapman	30-36	OF, INF	12/25/08	
Michael "Shotgun" Chartak	40	OF	8/28/16	7/25/67
Harold "Prince Hal" Chase	05-13	1B, INF, OF	2/13/83	5/18/47
Alfred (Allie) Clark	47	OF	6/15/23	
Horace "Hoss" Clarke	65-73	2B, SS, 3B	6/2/40	
Lucican (Lu) Clinton	66-67	OF	10/13/37	
James (Jim) Cockman	05	3B	4/26/73	9/28/47
Richard (Rich) Coggins	75-76	OF, DH	12/7/50	
Rocco "Rocky" Colavito	68	OF, P	8/10/33	
Curtis (Curt) Coleman	12	3B	2/18/87	
Gerald (Jerry) Coleman	49-57	INF	9/14/24	
Robert (Bob) Collins	44	C	9/18/09	
Joseph (Joe) Collins	48-57	1B, OF	12/3/22	
Orth "Buck" Collins	04	OF	4/27/80	12/13/49
Patrick (Pat) Collins	26-28	C	9/13/96	5/20/60

THE ALL—TIME YANKEE ROSTER (Continued)

NON—PITCHERS

Name	Years	Pos.	Born	Died
Frank Colman	46-47	OF	3/2/18	
Earle "Kentucky Colonel" Combs	24-35	OF	5/14/99	7/21/76
Thomas (Tom) Connelly	1920-21	OF	10/20/98	
Joseph (Joe) Connor	05	C, 1B	12/8/74	11/8/57
William "Wid" Conroy	03-08	INF, OF	4/5/77	12/6/59
Luther "Doc" Cook	13-16	OF	6/24/89	6/30/73
Allen "Dusty" Cooke	30-32	OF	6/23/07	
John Cooney	44	OF	3/18/01	
Phillip (Phil) Cooney	05	3B	9/14/86	unknown
Daniel "Dashing Dan" Costello	13	PH	9/9/95	3/26/36
Clinton (Clint) Courtney	51	C	3/16/27	
Ernest (Ernie) Courtney	03	INF	1879	unknown
William (Billy) Cowan	69	OF, 1B	8/28/38	
Robert (Bobby) Cox	68-69	3B, 2B	5/21/41	
William "Birdie" Cree	08-15	OF, INF	10/22/82	11/8/42
Louis (Lou) Criger	10	C	2/6/72	5/14/34
Herbert "Workhorse" Crompton	45	C	11/7/11	
Frank "The Crow" Crosetti	32-48	SS, 2B, 3B	10/4/10	
Roy Cullenbine	42	OF, INF	10/18/14	
Henry (Nick) Cullop	26	PH	10/16/00	
James (Jim) Curry	11	2B	1889	8/1/38
Frederick (Fred) Curtis	05	1B	unknown	unknown
Ellsworth "Babe" Dahlgren	37-40	1B	6/15/12	
Thomas (Pete) Daley	14-15	OF	11/13/84	12/2/34
Bernard (Bert) Daniels	10-13	OF	10/31/82	6/6/58
George "Kiddo" Davis	26	OF	2/12/02	
Alfonzo "Lefty" Davis	03	OF	2/4/75	2/7/19
John Deidel	74	C	6/6/49	
Frank "Pudgie" Delahanty	05-06, 08	OF	12/29/85	7/22/66

Name	Years	Pos.	Born	Died
Robert (Bobby) Del Greco	57-58	OF	4/7/33	
James (Jim) Delsing	49-50	OF	11/13/25	
Joseph (Joe) DeMaestri	60-61	INF	12/9/28	
Charles "Ray" Demmitt	09	OF	2/2/84	2/19/56
Richard (Rick) Dempsey	73-76	C, DH, OF	9/13/40	
Russell "Bucky" Dent	77-current	SS	11/25/51	
Claud "Deek" Derrick	13	INF	6/11/86	7/15/74
Alva "Russ" Derry	44-45	OF	10/7/16	
Albert (Al) DeVormer	21-22	C	8/19/91	8/29/66
William (Bill) Dickey	28-46	C	6/6/07	
Joseph (Joe) DiMaggio	36-51	OF	11/25/14	
Kerry Dineen	75-76	OF	7/1/52	
Alvin "Cozy" Dolan	11-12	3B	12/6/82	12/10/58
Michael (Mike) Donovan	08-3B	SS	10/13/83	2/3/38
Patrick (Patsy) Dougherty	04-06	OF	10/27/76	4/30/40
Brian Doyle	78-current	2B	1/25/57	
John "Dirty Jack" Doyle	05	1B	10/25/69	12/31/58
William (Bill) Drescher	44-46	C	5/23/21	5/15/68
Joseph "Jumpin' Joe" Dugan	22-28	3B	5/12/97	
Leo "The Lip" Durocher	25-29	INF	7/27/05	
Cedric Durst	27-30	OF, 1B	8/23/96	
Howard "Doc" Edwards	65	C	1/29/19	
Norman "Kid" Elberfeld	03-09	SS	8/13/75	1/13/44
Eugene (Gene) Elliott	11	OF, 3B	2/8/88	
John "Thunder" Ellis	69-72	C, 1B, 3B	8/21/48	
Clyde "Hack" Engle	09-10	OF	3/19/84	12/26/39
Nicholas (Nick) Etten	43-46	1B	9/19/13	
Edward "Doc" Farrell	32-33	INF	12/26/01	12/20/66
Frank Fernandez	67-69	C	4/16/43	
Michael (Mike) Ferraro	66,68	INF	8/14/44	
Wilson "Chick" Fewster	17-22	INF, OF	11/10/95	4/16/45

THE ALL—TIME YANKEE ROSTER (Continued)
NON—PITCHERS

Name	Years	Pos.	Born	Died
Augustus (Gus) Fisher	12	C	10/21/85	4/9/70
Justin "Mike" Fitzgerald	11	OF	6/22/90	1/17/45
Edward "Kid" Foster	10	SS	2/13/88	1/15/37
John (Jack) Fournier	18	1B	9/28/92	9/5/73
Raymond (Ray) French	20	SS	1/9/97	
Linus "Lonny" Frey	47-48	2B	8/23/10	
David (Dave) Fultz	03-05	OF, 3B	5/29/75	10/29/59
Elias (Liz) Funk	29	OF	10/28/04	1/16/68
Joseph (Joe) Gallahger	39	OF	3/7/14	
Oscar Gamble	76	OF, DH	12/20/49	
John Ganzel	03-04	IB, INF	4/7/75	1/14/59
Michael (Mike) Garbark	44-45	C	2/2/16	
Damaso Garcia	78-current	2B	2/7/57	
William (Billy) Gardner	61-62	INF	7/19/27	
Earl Gardner	08-12	2B	1/24/85	3/2/43
Michael (Mike) Gazella	23, 26-28	INF	10/13/96	9/11/78
Joseph (Joe) Gedeon	16-17	2B	12/6/94	5/19/41
Henry (Lou) Gehrig	23-39	IB, OF, SS	6/19/03	6/2/41
Jerry "Jake" Gibbs	62-71	C	11/7/38	
Frank "Flash" Gilhooley	13-18	OF	6/10/92	7/11/59
Frank "Inch" Gleich	19-20	OF	3/7/94	3/27/49
Joseph "Gabber" Glenn	32-33, 35-38	C	11/19/08	
Jesse Gonder	60-61	C	1/20/36	
Jose (Fernando) Gonzalez	74	INF	6/19/50	
Pedro Gonzalez	63-65	INF	12/12/38	
Joseph (Joe) Gordon	38-43, 46	2B, 1B	2/18/15	
John "Dick" Gossett	13-14	C	8/21/91	10/6/62
John "Nig" Grabowski	27-29	C	1/7/00	5/23/46
Patrick "Willie" Greene	03	INF	3/20/75	10/20/34

144

Name	Years	Pos.	Born	Died
Oscar Grimes	43-46	INF	4/13/15	
Kent Hadley	60	1B	12/17/34	
Edgar (Ed) Hahn	05-06	OF	8/27/80	11/29/41
Henry "Hinky" Haines	23	OF	12/23/98	1/9/79
George Halas	19	OF	2/2/95	
Robert (Bob) Hale	61	1B	11/7/33	
Jimmie Hall	69	OF	3/17/38	
James "Truck" Hannah	18-20	C, 1B	6/5/91	
Aloysius "Coalyard Mike" Handiboe	11	OF	7/21/87	1/31/53
Ronald (Ron) Hansen	70-71	INF	4/5/38	
Joseph (Joe) Hanson	13	C	unknown	unknown
Eugene "Bubbles" Hargrave	30	C	7/15/92	2/23/69
Joseph "Moon" Harris	14	OF, 1B	5/20/91	12/10/59
James (Jim Ray) Hart	73-74	3B, DH	10/30/41	
Roy Hartzell	11-16	INF, OF	7/6/81	11/6/61
John "Buddy" Hassett	42	1B	9/5/11	
Nelson "Chicken" Hawks	21	OF	2/3/96	
Francis (Fran) Healy	76-78	C	9/6/46	
Michael (Mike) Heath	78	C	2/5/55	
Donald "Jeep" Heffner	34-37	INF	2/8/11	
Michael (Mike) Hegan	64, 66-67, 73-74	1B, DH	7/21/42	
Woodson (Woodie) Held	54	SS, 3B, OF	3/25/32	
Charlie "Eagle Eye" Hemphill	08-11	OF	4/20/76	6/22/53
Ralston "Rollie" Hemsley	42-44	C	6/24/07	7/31/72
Harvey "Gink" Hendrick	23-24	OF	11/9/97	10/29/41
Elrod (Ellie) Hendricks	76-77	C, DH	12/22/40	
Timothy (Tim) Hendryx	15-17	OF	1/31/91	
Thomas "Old Reliable" Henrich	37-42, 46-50	OF, 1B	2/20/13	8/14/57
Edward (Ed) Herrmann	75	C, DH	8/27/46	

THE ALL–TIME YANKEE ROSTER (Continued)
NON–PITCHERS

Name	Years	Pos.	Born	Died
Hugh "Bunny" High	15-18	OF	10/24/87	11/16/62
Jesse Hill	35	OF	1/20/07	
Malcolm "Mack" Hills	24	2B	7/23/01	6/16/61
Myril Hoag	31-32, 34-38	OF	3/9/08	7/28/71
Daniel (Danny) Hoffman	06-07	OF	3/10/80	3/14/22
Arthur "Circus Solly" Hofman	16	OF	10/29/82	3/10/56
Fred "Bootnose" Hofman	19-25	C	6/10/94	11/19/64
William (Bill) Holden	13-14	OF	9/7/89	9/14/71
Frederick (Fred) Holmes	03	1B	unknown	unknown
John "Hippity" Hopp	50-52	1B, OF	7/18/16	
Joseph "Shags" Horan	24	OF	9/7/94	2/13/68
Ralph "The Major" Houk	47-54	C	8/9/19	
Elston (Ellie) Howard	55-67	C, OF, 1B	2/23/29	
Harry "Handsome Harry, Harry Howell	03	INF, P	11/14/76	5/22/56
Richard (Dick) Howser	67-68	INF	5/14/37	
John "Silent John" Hummel	18	OF, INF	4/4/83	5/18/59
Kenneth (Ken) Hunt	59-60	OF	7/13/34	
Gordon (Billy) Hunter	55-56	SS, 3B	6/4/28	
Robert "Ham" Hyatt	18	OF, 1B	11/1/84	9/?/63
Frederick (Fred) Jacklitsch	05	C	5/24/76	7/18/37
Reginald (Reggie) Jackson	77-current	OF, DH	5/18/46	
Jack (Jackie) Jensen	50-52	OF	3/9/27	
Felix "Elvio" Jimenez	64	OF	1/6/40	
Alexander (Alex) Johnson	74-75	OF, DH	12/7/42	
William (Billy) Johnson	43, 46-51	3B, 1B, 2B	8/30/18	
Clifford (Cliff) Johnson	77-current	C, DH, 1B, OF	7/22/47	
Darrell Johnson	57-58	C	8/25/28	
Deron Johnson	60-61	3B, OF, 1B	7/17/38	

146

Name	Years	Pos.	Born	Died
Ernest (Ernie) Johnson	24-25	INF	4/29/88	5/1/52
Otis Johnson	11	INF	11/5/83	11/9/15
Roy Johnson	36-37	OF	2/23/03	9/11/73
John "Jay" Johnstone	78-current	OF, DH	11/20/45	
Timothy (Tim) Johnson	03	1B	2/14/79	9/13/49
Arthur (Art) Jorgens	29-39	C	5/18/05	
Francis "Sugar" Kane	19	OF	3/9/95	12/2/62
William "Hank" Karlon	30	OF	6/21/09	12/7/64
Herbert "Lefty" Karpel	46	PH (P)	12/27/17	
Benjamin (Benny) Kauff	12	OF	1/5/90	11/17/61
Edward "Truck" Kearse	42	C	2/23/18	7/15/68
William "Wee Willie" Keeler	03-09	OF, 2B, 3B	3/3/72	1/1/23
Charles "King Kong" Keller	39-49, 52	OF	9/12/16	
John Kennedy	67	INF	5/29/41	
Jerry "Lobo" Kenney	67, 69-72	INF	6/30/45	
David (Dave) Kingman	77	DH, OF	12/21/48	
Harry Kingman	14	1B	4/3/92	
Eugene "Mickey" Klutts	76-78	SS, 3B	9/20/54	
William (Bill) Knickerbocker	38-40	2B, SS	12/29/11	
John "Schoolboy" Knight	09-11, 13	INF, 1B	10/6/85	12/19/65
Mark Koenig	25-30	SS	7/19/02	
Andrew (Andy) Kosco	68	OF, 1B	10/5/41	
Ernest (Ernie) Krueger	15	C	12/27/90	4/22/76
Richard (Dick) Kryhoski	49	1B	3/24/25	
Anthony (Tony) Kubek	57-65	SS, 3B, 2B, OF	10/12/36	
William (Bill) Lamar	17-19	OF	3/21/97	7/19/70
Harold (Hal) Lanier	72-73	INF	7/4/42	
Frank "Pot" LaPorte	05-08, 09-10	INF, 1B, OF	2/6/80	9/25/39
Lynford (Lyn) Lary	29-34	INF, OF, 1B	1/28/06	1/9/73

147

THE ALL—TIME YANKEE ROSTER (Continued)

NON—PITCHERS

Name	Years	Pos.	Born	Died
Eugene (Gene) Layden	15	OF	3/14/94	unknown
Anthony (Tony) Lazzeri	26-37	INF	12/6/03	8/6/46
John (Jack) Lelivelt	12-13	OF	11/14/85	1/20/41
Eduardo (Eddie) Leon	75	INF	8/11/46	
Edward (Ed) Levy	42, 44	OF, 1B	10/28/16	
George "Duffy" Lewis	19-20	OF	4/18/88	
John (Johnny) Lindell	41-50	OF, 1B, P	8/30/16	
Phillip (Phil) Linz	62-65	INF, OF	6/4/39	
William "Jack" Little	12	OF	3/12/91	7/27/61
Eugene (Gene) Locklear	76-77	OF, 1B	7/19/49	
John (Sherm) Lollar	47-48	C	8/23/24	
Richard (Dale) Long	60, 62-63	1B	2/6/26	
Herman "Germany" Long	03	SS, 2B	4/13/66	9/17/09
Arturo Lopez	65	OF	5/8/37	
Hector Lopez	59-66	OF, 3B, 2B, 1B	7/8/32	
William "Baldy" Louden	07	3B	8/27/85	12/8/35
John (Johnny) Lucadello	47	2B	2/22/19	
Roy Luebbe	25	C	9/17/01	
Jerry Lumpe	56-59	INF	6/2/33	
James (Jimmy) Lyttle	69-71	OF	5/20/46	
Raymond (Ray) Mack	47	2B	8/31/16	5/7/69
Thomas "Bunny" Madden	10	PH	1884	unknown
Elliott Maddox	74-76	OF	12/21/48	
Leo (Lee) Magee	16-17	OF, 2B, 1B	6/4/89	3/14/66
Edmund (Stubby) Magner	11	SS, 2B	2/20/88	9/6/56
Frederick (Fritz) Maisel	13-17	3B, OF, 2B	12/23/89	4/22/67
Henry (Hank) Majeski	46	3B	12/13/16	
Patrick (Pat) Maloney	12	OF	1/19/88	
Mickey Mantle	51-68	OF, 1B, 3B, SS, 2B	10/20/31	unknown

148

Name	Years	Pos.	Born	Died
Clifford "Tiger" Mapes	48-51	OF	3/13/22	
Roger Maris	60-66	OF	9/10/34	
Armando Marsans	17-18	OF, 3B, 2B	10/3/87	unknown
Alfred (Billy) Martin	50, 52, 55-57	2B, SS, 3B, OF	5/16/28	
Herschel (Hersh) Martin	44-45	OF	9/19/08	
John (Jack) Martin	12	INF	4/19/87	
James (Jim) Mason	74-76	SS	8/14/50	
Carlos May	76-77	OF, DH	5/17/48	
Joseph (Joe) McCarthy (Not mgr.)	05	C	12/25/81	1/12/37
Patrick (Pat) McCauley	03	C	6/10/70	1/23/17
Lawrence (Larry) McClure	10	OF	10/3/85	8/31/49
David (Dave) McDonald	69	1B	5/20/43	
Gilbert (Gil) McDougald	51-60	INF, 1B	5/19/28	
Hermus (Herm) McFarland	03	OF	3/11/70	9/21/35
Henry "Irish" McIlveen	08-09	OF	7/27/80	7/18/60
William (Bill) McKechnie	13	INF, 1B	8/7/86	10/29/65
Charles (Rich) McKinney	72	3B	11/22/46	
Frank McManus	04	C	9/21/75	9/1/23
Norman "Bub" McMillan	22	OF, 3B	10/5/95	9/28/69
Thomas "Rebel" McMillan	12	SS	4/17/88	7/15/66
Michael (Mike) McNally	21-24	INF, 1B	9/13/93	5/29/65
George McQuinn	47-48	1B	5/29/09	12/24/78
Charles "Goggy" Meara	14	OF	4/16/91	2/8/62
Frederick (Fred) Merkle	25-26	1B	12/20/88	3/2/56
Arthur "Bud" Metheny	43-46	OF	6/1/15	
Robert "Long Bob" Meusel	20-29	OF, 3B, 1B	7/19/96	11/28/77
Eugene "Stick" Michael	68-73	INF, P	6/2/38	
Ezra "Salt Rock" Midkiff	12-13	INF	11/13/83	3/21/57
Elmer Miller	15-18, 21-22	OF, 1B	7/28/82	3/21/57
John Miller	66	OF, 1B	3/14/44	
Colonel "Buster" Mills	40	OF	9/16/08	
Michael "Mollie" Milosevich	44-45	SS, 2B	1/13/15	2/3/66

149

THE ALL–TIME YANKEE ROSTER (Continued)

NON–PITCHERS

Name	Years	Pos.	Born	Died
Guillermo (Willie) Miranda	54	INF	5/24/26	
Robert (Bobby) Mitchell	70	OF	10/22/43	
Frederick (Fred) Mitchell	10	C	6/5/78	10/13/70
John (Johnny) Mitchell	21-22	SS, 2B	8/9/94	11/4/65
John (Johnny) Mize	49-53	1B	1/7/13	
Fenton "Muscles" Mole	49	1B	6/14/25	
Archie Moore	64-65	OF, 1B	8/30/41	
Raymond (Ray) Morehart	27	2B	12/2/99	
George Moriarty	06-08	INF, OF, 1B	7/7/84	8/8/64
Ross "Mickey Mantle's Legs" Moschitto	65, 67	OF	2/15/45	
Gerald (Gerry) Moses	73	C, DH	8/9/46	
Charles Mullen	14-16	1B, 2B, OF	3/15/89	6/6/63
Thurman Munson	69-current	C, OF, DH	6/7/47	
Robert (Bobby) Murcer	65-66, 69-74	OF, SS, 3B, DH	5/20/46	
Larry Murray	74-76	OF	3/1/53	
Graig Nettles	73-current	INF, DH	8/20/44	
Constantine (Gus) Niarhos	46, 48-50	C	12/6/20	
Harry Niles	08	2B, OF, SS	9/10/80	4/18/53
Irving (Irv) Noren	52-56	OF, 1B	11/29/24	
Leslie (Les) Nunamaker	14-17	C, 1B	8/25/89	11/14/38
John (Jack) O'Connor	03	C, 1B	3/3/67	11/14/37
Francis "Lefty" O'Doul	19-20, 22	OF, P	3/14/97	12/7/69
John O'Dowd	12	SS	1/3/91	
Reuben (Rube) Oldring	05	SS	5/30/84	9/9/61
Nathaniel (Nate) Oliver	69	2B	12/13/40	
Robert (Bob) Oliver	75	DH,1B	2/28/43	
Stephen (Steve) O'Neill	25	C	7/9/91	1/26/62
James "Queenie" O'Rourke	08	OF, INF	12/26/89	12/22/55
Albert (Al) Orth	04-09	OF, 1B, 2B, P	9/5/72	10/8/48

Name	Years	Pos.	Born	Died
James "Champ" Osteen	04	3B, SS, 1B	2/24/77	12/14/62
Paul "Bill" Otis	12	OF	12/24/89	unknown
Delmar (Del) Paddock	12	3B, 2B, OF	6/6/87	2/6/52
Benjamin (Ben) Paschal	24-29	OF	10/13/95	11/10/74
Roger Peckinpaugh	13-21	SS, MGR	2/5/91	11/17/77
Joseph (Joe) Pepitone	62-69	1B, OF	10/9/40	
Martin (Marty) Perez	77	3B	2/28/48	
Ralph "Cy" Perkins	31	C	2/27/96	10/2/63
Edward (Eddie) Phillips	32	C	2/17/01	1/26/68
Jack "Stretch" Phillips	47-49	1B, 3B	9/6/21	
Louis (Lou) Piniella	74-current	OF, DH, 1B	8/28/43	
Walter (Wally) Pipp	15-25	1B	2/17/93	1/11/65
James (Jim) Pisoni	59-60	OF	8/14/29	
Alvin (Jake) Powell	36-40	OF, 2B	7/15/08	11/4/48
Michael (Mike) Powers	05	C, 1B	9/22/70	4/26/09
Derrill (Del) Pratt	18-20	2B	1/10/88	9/30/77
Gerald (Jerry) Priddy	41-42	INF, 1B	11/9/19	
John Priest	11-12	2B, 3B	6/23/91	
Domingo Ramos	78	SS	3/29/58	
William (Willie) Randolph	76-current	2B	7/6/54	
John (Jack) Reed	61-63	OF	2/2/33	
James (Jimmy) Reese	30-31	2B, 3B	10/1/04	
William "Big Bill" Renna	53	OF	10/14/24	
Anthony "Pug" Rensa	33	C	9/29/01	
Roger Repoz	64-66	OF, 1B	8/3/40	
William (Bill) Reynolds	13-14	C	1888	unknown
Harry Rice	30	OF, 3B	11/22/01	1/1/71
Robert (Bobby) Richardson	55-66	INF	8/19/35	
Clifford (Nolan) Richardson	35	SS	1/18/03	9/25/51
Wesley (Branch) Rickey	07	OF, C, 1B	12/20/81	12/9/65
John (Mickey) Rivers	76-current	OF	10/30/48	
Phillip (Phil) Rizzuto	41-42, 46-56	SS, 2B	9/25/18	

151

THE ALL–TIME YANKEE ROSTER (Continued)
NON–PITCHERS

Name	Years	Pos.	Born	Died
Wilbur "Roxy" Roach	10-11	SS, OF, 2B	11/28/84	12/25/47
Eugene (Gene) Robertson	28-29	3B, SS	12/25/99	
Aaron Robinson	43, 45-47	C	6/23/15	3/9/66
William (Bill) Robinson	67-69	OF, 1B	6/26/43	
William (Eddie) Robinson	54-56	1B	12/15/20	
Eliseo (Ellie) Rodriguez	68	C	5/24/46	
Jay Rogers	14	C	8/3/88	7/1/64
Robert "Red" Rolfe	31, 34-42	3B, SS	10/17/08	7/8/69
Warren "Buddy" Rosar	39-42	C	7/3/14	
Lawrence (Larry) Rosenthal	44	OF	5/21/12	
Robert "Braggo" Roth	21	OF	8/28/92	9/11/36
Herold "Muddy" Ruel	17-20	C	2/20/96	11/13/63
George "Babe" Ruth	20-34	OF, 1B, P	2/6/95	8/16/48
John "Blondy" Ryan	35	INF	1/4/06	11/28/59
Otto "Jack" Saltzgaver	32, 34-37	3B, 2B, 1B	1/23/05	2/1/78
Celerino Sanchez	72-73	3B, OF, SS, DH	2/3/44	
Charles (Charlie) Sands	67	PH	12/17/47	
Donald (Don) Savage	44-55	3B, OF	3/5/19	12/25/61
Herman "Germany" Schaeffer	16	OF	2/4/78	3/16/19
Roy Schalk	32	2B	11/09/08	
Walter (Wally) Schang	21-25	C	8/22/89	3/6/65
Robert (Bob) Schmidt	65	C	4/22/33	
John "Ducky" Schofield	66	SS	1/7/35	
Arthur "Dutch" Schult	53	PR	6/20/28	
William (Bill) Schwartz	14	C	1/30/91	6/24/49
Everett "Deacon" Scott	22-25	SS, 3B	11/19/92	11/2/60
Pius Schwert	14-15	C	11/22/92	3/11/41
Kenneth "Ziggy" Sears	43	C	7/6/17	
Robert "Suitcase Bob" Seeds	36	OF, 3B	2/24/07	
Kal Segrist	52	2B, 3B	4/14/31	

152

Name	Years	Pos.	Born	Died
George "Twinkletoes" Selkirk	34-42	OF	1/4/08	
Theodore (Ted) Sepkowski	47	OF	11/9/23	
Henry (Hank) Severeid	26	C	6/1/91	12/17/68
Joseph (Joe) Sewell	31-33	3B, 2B	10/9/98	
Howard "Hank" Shanks	25	3B, 2B, OF	7/21/90	7/30/41
Wilmer (Billy) Shantz	60	C	7/31/27	
Andrew "Skeeter" Shelton	15	OF	6/29/88	1/9/54
Thomas (Tom) Shopay	67, 69	OF	2/21/45	
Norman (Norm) Siebern	56, 58-59	OF, 1B	7/26/33	
Charles "Swede" Silvera	48-56	C, 3B	10/13/24	
Kenneth "Hawk" Silvestri	41, 46-47	C	5/3/16	
George "Hack" Simmons	12	2B, 1B, SS	1/29/85	4/26/42
Richard (Dick) Simpson	69	OF	7/28/43	
Harry "Suitcase" Simpson	57-58	OF, 1B	12/3/25	
William (Bill) Skiff	26	C	10/16/95	12/25/78
Elisha "Camp" Skinner	22	OF	6/25/97	4/4/44
Louis (Lou) Skizas	56	OF	6/2/32	
William "Moose" Skowron	54-62	1B, 3B, 2B	12/18/30	
Enos "Country" Slaughter	54-55, 56-59	OF	4/27/16	
Charles (Charlie) Smith	67-68	3B	9/15/37	
Elmer Smith	22-23	OF	9/21/92	
Salvatore "Joe" Smith	13	C	12/29/93	
Frederick "Klondike" Smith	12	OF	1889	unknown
Tolaita (Tony) Solaita	68	OF, 1B	1/15/47	
Stephen "Bud" Souchock	46, 48	1B	3/3/19	
James (Jim) Spencer	78	1B, DH	7/30/47	
Leslie (Charlie) Spikes	72	OF	1/23/51	
Garland (Jake) Stahl	08	1B, OF	4/13/79	9/18/22
George "Tuck" Stainback	42-45	OF	8/4/10	
Frederick (Fred) Stanley	73-current	INF	8/13/47	
Richard (Rick) Stelmaszek	76	C	10/8/48	
Charles "Dutch" Sterrett	12-13	OF, 1B, C, 2B	10/1/89	12/9/65

153

THE ALL—TIME YANKEE ROSTER (Continued)
NON—PITCHERS

Name	Years	Pos.	Born	Died
Edward "Bud" Stewart	48	OF	6/15/16	9/15/58
George "Snuffy" Stirnweiss	43-50	INF	10/26/18	2/6/51
Charles "Old Sarge" Street	12	C	9/30/82	2/14/66
William (Bill) Stumpf	12-13	INF, OF, 1B	3/21/92	
John (Johnny) Sturm	41	1B	1/23/16	
William (Bill) Sudakis	74	C, 3B, 1B, DH	3/27/46	
Edward (Ed) Sweeney	08-15	C, 1B, OF	7/19/88	7/4/47
Ronald "Rocky" Swoboda	71-73	OF, 1B, DH	6/30/44	
Jesse Tannehill	03	OF, P	7/14/74	9/22/56
James "Zach" Taylor	03	C	7/27/98	7/6/74
Frank Tepedino	67, 69-71, 71-			
	72	1B, OF	11/23/47	
Richard "Tut" Tettelbach	55	OF	6/26/29	
Ira Thomas	06-07	C, 1B	1/22/81	10/11/58
James (Lee) Thomas	61	OF, 1B	2/5/36	
Gary Thomasson	78-current	OF, DH	7/29/51	
Thomas "Homer" Thompson	12	C	6/1/92	9/12/57
John "Bullet Jack" Thoney	04	OF, 3B	12/8/80	10/24/48
Marvin "Marvelous Marv" Throneberry	55, 58-59	1B, OF	9/2/33	
Edward (Eddie) Tiemeyer	09	1B	5/9/85	9/27/46
John (Bob) Tillman	67	C	3/24/37	
Clifford "The Earl of Snohomish" Torgeson	61	1B	1/1/24	
Rosendo "Rusty" Torres	71-72	OF	9/30/48	
Cesar "Pepito" Tovar	76	3B, OF	7/30/40	
Thomas (Tom) Tresh	61-69	OF, SS, 3B	9/20/37	
Augustus (Gus) Triandos	53-54	1B, C	9/30/37	
Frank Truesdale	14	2B, 3B	12/12/85	
Robert (Bob) Unglaub	04	INF	7/31/81	11/19/16

154

Name	Years	Pos.	Born	Died
Elmer Valo	60	OF	3/5/21	
Robert (Bobby) Vaughn	2B, SS	6/4/85	4/11/65	
Robert (Bobby) Veach	OF	6/29/88	8/7/45	
Otoniel (Otto) Velez	73-76	1B, 3B, OF, DH	11/29/50	
Frank Verdi	53	SS	6/2/26	
Samuel (Sammy) Vick	17-20	OF	4/12/95	
Richard (Dick) Wakefield	50	PH	5/6/21	
William (Curt) Walker	19	PH	7/3/96	12/9/55
Fred "Dixie" Walker	31, 33-36	OF	9/24/10	7/3/62
James (Jimmy) Walsh	14	OF, INF	9/22/85	1/6/67
Joseph (Joe) Walsh	10-11	C	10/14/87	6/3/56
Alfred "Roxy" Walters	15-18	C, OF	11/5/92	
Daniel "Mickey" Walton	71	OF, 3B	7/14/47	
Paul "Big Poison" Waner	44-45	OF	4/16/03	8/29/65
Clarence "Jack" Wanner	09	SS	5/14/84	4/8/62
Paul "PeeWee" Wanninger	25	INF	12/12/02	
Aaron Ward	17-26	INF, OF	8/28/96	1/30/61
Joseph (Joe) Ward	09	2B, SS, 1B, OF	9/2/84	8/11/34
Peter (Pete) Ward	70	1B	7/26/39	
Cyril (Roy) Weatherly	43, 46	OF	2/15/15	12/12/75
Julian (Julie) Wera	27, 29	3B	2/9/02	
William (Billy) Werber	30, 33	INF	6/20/08	
Steven (Steve) Whitaker	66-68	OF	5/7/43	
Roy White	65-current	OF, 2B, DH, 1B	12/27/43	
George Whiteman	13	OF	12/23/82	2/10/47
Terry Whitfield	74-76	OF	1/12/53	
Allan Wickland	19	OF	1/27/88	
Edward (Ed) Wilkinson	11	OF, 2B	1890	unknown
Robert (Bob) Williams	11-14	C, 1B	4/27/94	8/6/62
Harry Williams	13	1B	1891	unknown
James (Jimmy) Williams	03-07	2B	12/20/76	1/16/65
Walter "No Neck" Williams	74-75	OF, DH	12/19/43	

THE ALL—TIME YANKEE ROSTER (Continued)
NON—PITCHERS

Name	Years	Pos.	Born	Died
Archie Wilson	51-52	OF	11/25/23	
George (Teddy) Wilson	56	OF	8/30/25	
Gordon (Gordie) Windhorn	59	OF	12/19/33	
Nicholas "Mickey" Witek	49	PH	12/19/15	
Lawton "Whitey" Witt	22-25	OF	9/28/95	
Harry Wolter	10-13	OF, 1B	7/11/84	7/7/70
Harry Wolverton	12	3B, MGR	12/6/73	2/4/37
Eugene (Gene) Woodling	49-54	OF	8/16/22	
Ronald (Ron) Woods	69-71	OF	2/1/43	
Henry (Hank) Workman	50	1B	2/5/26	
George "Yats" Wuestling	30	SS, 3B	10/18/03	4/26/70
James (Jimmy) Wynn	77	OF, DH	3/12/42	
Joseph "Little Joe" Yeager	05-06	INF	8/28/75	7/2/37
Ralph Young	13	SS	9/19/90	1/24/65
John "Zach" Zalusky	03	C, 1B	6/22/79	8/11/35
George Zeber	77-78	INF	8/29/50	
Rollie "Bunions" Zeider	13	INF, 1B	11/16/83	9/12/67
Guy Zinn	11-12	OF	2/13/87	10/6/49

(Note: For additional nicknames of players, see the complete Nicknames section.)

THE ALL—TIME YANKEE ROSTER
PITCHERS

Name	Years	Born	Died
Name (L) — indicates lefty			
Harry (Hal) Ables (L)	1911	10/4/84	2/8/51
Jack "Chief" Aker	69-72	7/13/40	
Merle "Doc" Adkins	03	8/5/72	2/21/34
John (Johnny) Allen	32-35	9/30/04	3/29/59
Doyle Alexander	74	9/04/50	
Ivy "Poison" Andrews	31-32, 37-38	5/6/07	
Peter (Pete) Appleton	33	5/20/04	1/18/74
Luis "Yo-Yo" Arroyo (L)	60-63	9/18/27	
Stanley (Stan) Bahnsen	66, 68-71	12/15/44	
Stephen (Steve) Barber (L)	67-68	2/22/39	
Eros "Cy" Barger	06-07	5/18/85	9/23/64
Frank "Lefty" Barnes (L)	30	1/9/00	9/27/67
Walter Beall	24-27	7/9/99	1/28/59
James (Jim) Beattie	78-current	7/4/54	
Richard (Rich) Beck	65	1/21/41	
Fred Beene	72-74	11/24/42	
Joseph (Joe) Beggs	38	11/4/10	
Walter (Walt) Bernhardt	18	5/20/93	7/26/58
Floyd "Bill" Bevens	44-47	10/21/16	
Harry Billiard	08	11/21/85	6/3/23
Ewell "The Whip" Blackwell	52-53	10/23/22	
Gilbert (Gil) Blanco (L)	65	12/15/45	
Wade Blasingame (L)	71	11/22/43	
Stephen (Steve) Blateric	72	4/20/44	
Gary Blaylock	59	10/11/31	
Ernest "Tiny" Bonham	40-46	8/16/13	9/15/49
Henry (Hank) Borowy	42-45	5/12/16	
James (Jim) Bouton	62-68	3/8/39	

157

THE ALL—TIME YANKEE ROSTER (Continued)

PITCHERS

Name	Years	Born	Died
Cornelius (Neal) Brady	15, 17	3/4/97	6/19/47
Ralph Branca	54	1/6/26	
Norman "Red" Branch (L)	41-42	3/22/15	
Edgar (Garland) Braxton (L)	25-26	5/10/00	2/15/66
James (Don) Brennan	33	12/2/03	4/26/53
James (Jim) Brenneman	65	2/13/41	
Kenneth (Ken) Brett (L)	76	9/18/48	
Marvin "Baby Face" Breuer	39-43	4/29/14	
Marshall "Sheriff" Bridges (L)	62-63	6/2/31	
John (Johnny) Broaca	34-37	10/3/09	
Lewis "King" Brockett	07, 09, 11	7/23/80	9/19/60
James (Jim) Bronstad	59	6/22/36	
Carroll "Boardwalk" Brown	14-15	2/20/87	2/8/77
Hector (Hal) Brown	62	12/11/24	
Walter "Jumbo" Brown	32-37	4/30/07	10/2/66
Jess (Jim) Buckles (L)	16	5/20/90	8/2/75
William (Bill) Burbach	69-71	8/22/47	
Selva (Lew) Burdette	50	11/22/26	
Leslie "Bullet Joe" Bush	22-24	11/27/92	11/1/74
Thomas (Tom) Buskey	73-74	2/20/47	
Ralph "Buck" Buxton	49	6/7/11	
Harry Byrd	54	2/3/25	
Charles (Charlie) Caldwell	25	8/2/01	11/1/57
Raymond "Slim" Caldwell	10-18	4/26/88	8/17/67
Archer (Archie) Campbell	28	10/20/03	
Michael (Mike) Cantwell (L)	16	1/15/96	1/5/53
Owen "Ownie" Carroll	30	11/11/02	6/18/75
Richard (Dick) Carroll	09	7/21/84	11/22/45
Hugh Casey	49	10/14/13	7/3/51
Roy Castleton (L)	07	1886	unknown

Name	Years	Born	Died
Spurgeon "Spud" Chandler	37-47	9/12/07	
John "Happy Jack" Chesbro	03-09	6/5/74	11/6/31
Alva "Bozo" Cicotte	57	12/23/29	
George Clark (L)	13	5/19/91	11/14/40
Walter Clarkson	04-07	11/3/78	10/10/46
Kenneth (Kenny) Clay	77-current	4/6/54	
Truman "Tex" Clevenger	61-62	7/9/32	
Alan (Al) Closter (L)	71-72	6/15/43	
Andrew (Andy) Coakley	11	11/20/82	9/27/63
James (Jim) Coates	56, 59-62	8/4/32	
Leonard "King" Cole	14-15	4/15/86	1/6/16
Walter "Rip" Coleman (L)	55-56	7/31/31	
Harry "Rip" Collins	20-21	2/26/96	5/27/68
Lloyd Colson	70	11/4/47	
Guy "Rebel" Cooper	14	1/28/93	8/2/51
Ensign Cottrell (L)	15	8/29/88	2/27/47
Stanley (Stan) Coveleski	28	7/13/89	
Joseph (Casey) Cox	72-73	7/3/41	
John (Jack) Cullen	62, 65-66	10/6/39	
John Cumberland (L)	68-70	5/10/47	
Leavitt "Bud" Daley	62-64	10/7/32	
George "Iron" Davis	12	3/9/90	6/4/61
John Deering	03	6/25/78	2/15/43
James (Jimmie) DeShong	34-35	11/30/09	
Charles (Charlie) Devens	32-34	1/1/10	
Murry Dickson	58	8/21/16	
Arthur (Art) Ditmar	57-61	4/3/29	
John "Sonny" Dixon	56	11/5/24	
Patrick (Pat) Dobson	73-75	2/12/42	
Atley "Swampy" Donald	38-45	8/19/10	
William "Wild Bill" Donovan	15-16	10/13/76	12/9/23

159

THE ALL-TIME YANKEE ROSTER (Continued)

PITCHERS

Name	Years	Born	Died
Alphonso (Al) Downing (L)	61-69	6/28/41	
Judd "Slow Joe" Doyle	06-10	9/15/81	11/21/47
Karl Drews	46-48	2/22/20	8/13/63
Walter "Monk" Dubiel	44-45	2/12/19	10/25/69
Rinold (Ryne) Duren	58-61	2/22/29	
Rawlins (Rawley) Eastwick	78	10/24/50	
Foster "Eddie" Edwards	30	9/1/03	
Charles "Red" Embree	48	8/30/17	
Dock Ellis	76-77	3/11/45	
John Enright	17	1896	unknown
James (Alex) Ferguson	18-21	2/16/97	4/28/76
Wesley (Wes) Ferrell	39	2/2/08	12/9/76
Thomas (Tom) Ferrick	50-51	1/6/15	
Joseph "Happy Joe" Finneran	18	10/29/91	2/3/42
Eduardo (Ed) Figueroa	76-current	10/14/48	
Raymond (Ray) Fisher	10-17	10/4/87	
Russell (Russ) Ford	09-13	4/25/83	1/24/60
Edward "Whitey" Ford (L)	50, 53-67	10/21/28	
Ray Francis (L)	25	3/8/93	7/6/34
Robert (Bob) Friend	66	11/24/30	
John Frill (L)	10	4/3/79	9/29/18
John (Gabe) Gabler	59-60	10/2/30	
Richard (Rob) Gardner (L)	70-72	12/19/44	
Virgil "Ned" Garvin	04	1/1/74	6/16/08
Nathaniel (Milt) Gaston	24	1/27/96	
Allen (Al) Gettel	45-46	9/17/17	
Joseph "Peco" Giard (L)	27	10/7/98	7/10/56
Samuel (Sam) Gibson	30	8/5/99	
Frederick (Fred) Glade	08	1/25/76	11/21/34
Vernon "Lefty" Gomez (L)	30-42	11/26/09	

160

Name	Years	Born	Died
Wilbur "Lefty" Good (L)	05	9/28/85	12/30/63
Arthur (Art) Goodwin	05	2/27/76	6/19/43
Thomas (Tom) Gorman	52-54	1/4/25	
Richard "Goose" Gossage	78-current	7/1/51	
Lawrence (Larry) Gowell	72	5/2/48	
Wayne Granger	73	8/15/44	
Ted Gray (L)	55	12/31/24	
Eli Grba	59-60	8/9/34	
Clark "The Old Gray Fox" Griffith	03-07	11/20/69	10/27/55
Robert (Bob) Grim	54-58	3/8/20	
Burleigh "Ol Stubblebeard" Grimes	34	8/18/93	
Lee "Lefty" Grissom (L)	40	10/23/07	
Ronald "Louisiana Lightning" Guidry (L)	77-current	8/28/50	
Donald (Don) Gullett (L)	77-current	1/5/51	
Randall (Randy) Gumpert	46-48	1/23/18	
Lawrence (Larry) Gura (L)	74-76	11/26/47	
Irving "Bump" Hadley	36-40	7/5/04	2/15/63
Frank "Noodles" Hahn (L)	06	4/29/79	2/6/60
Roger Hambright	71	3/26/49	
Steve Hamilton (L)	64-70	11/30/35	
James (Jim) Hanley	13	unknown	unknown
James (Jim) Hardin	71	8/6/43	
Harry Harper	21	4/24/95	4/23/63
Fred "Lefty" Heimach (L)	28-29	1/27/01	6/1/73
William (Bill) Henderson	30	11/4/01	10/6/66
William (Bill) Henry (L)	66	2/15/42	
Oral (Hildy) Hildebrand	39-40	4/4/07	9/8/77
Frank "Dutch" Hiller	46, 48-49	7/13/20	
Richard (Rich) Hinton (L)	72	5/22/47	
Chester "Red" Hoff (L)	11-13	5/8/91	unknown
William "Buffalo Bill" Hogg	05-08	1880	12/8/09

THE ALL—TIME YANKEE ROSTER (Continued)

PITCHERS

Name	Years	Born	Died
Robert (Bobby) Hogue	51-52	8/23/18	
Kenneth (Ken) Holcombe	45	4/5/21	
Kenneth (Ken) Holtzman (L)	76-78	11/3/45	
Wallace (Wally) Hood	49	9/24/25	
Waite "Schoolboy" Hoyt	21-30	9/9/99	
Thomas "Long Tom" Hughes	04	11/26/78	2/8/56
Thomas (Tom) Hughes	06-07, 09-10	1/28/84	11/1/61
James "Catfish" Hunter	75-current	4/8/46	
Grant "Buck" Jackson (L)	76	9/28/42	
John (Johnny) James	58, 60-61	7/23/33	
Donald (Don) Johnson	47, 50	11/12/26	
Henry (Hank) Johnson	25-26, 28-32	5/21/06	
John (Johnny) Johnson (L)	44	9/29/14	
Kenneth (Ken) Johnson	69	6/16/33	
Gary Jones (L)	70-71	6/12/45	
Samuel "Sad Sam" Jones	22-26	7/26/92	7/6/66
Michael (Mike) Jurewicz (L)	65	9/20/45	
Robert (Bob) Kammeyer	78-current	12/2/50	
Raymond (Ray) Keating	12-16, 18	7/21/91	12/29/63
Robert (Bob) Keefe	07	6/16/82	12/7/64
Michael (Mike) Kekich (L)	69-73	4/2/45	
Fred Kipp (L)	60	10/1/31	
Frank Kitson	07	4/11/72	4/14/30
Theodore (Ted) Kleinhans (L)	36	4/8/99	
Edward "Big Ed" Klepfer	11, 13	3/17/88	8/9/50
Ronald (Ron) Klimkowski	69-70, 72	3/1/45	
Steven (Steve) Kline	70-74	10/6/47	
Casimir (Jim) Konstanty	55-56	3/2/17	
Steve "Lefty" Kraly (L)	53	4/18/29	6/11/76

Name	Years	Born	Died
John (Jack) Kramer	51	1/5/18	
John (Johnny) Kucks	55-59	7/27/33	
William (Bill) Kunkel	63	7/7/36	
Robert (Bob) Kuzava (L)	51-54	3/28/23	6/30/50
Joseph (Joe) Lake	08-09	12/6/81	
Donald (Don) Larsen	55-59	8/7/29	
Louis LeRoy	05-06	2/18/79	10/10/44
Terrence (Terry) Ley (L)	71	2/21/47	
Clement (Lew) Llewellyn	22	8/1/95	
Paul Lindblad (L)	78-current	8/9/41	
Johnny Lindell (as a pitcher only)	42	8/30/16	
Edmund "Steady Eddie" Lopat (L)	48-55	6/21/18	11/30/42
Elmer "Slim" Love (L)	16-18	8/1/93	
Joseph "Scootch" Lucey	20	3/27/97	
Walter "Sparky" Lyle (L)	72-78	7/22/44	
Albert (Al) Lyons	44, 46-47	7/18/18	12/20/65
Duane "Duke" Maas	58-61	1/31/31	11/7/76
Daniel "Deacon Danny" MacFayden	32-34	6/10/05	8/26/72
David (Dave) Madison	50	2/1/21	
Salvatore "Sal the Barber" Maglie	57-58	4/26/17	
James (Jim) Magnuson (L)	73	8/18/46	
Frank Makosky	37	1/20/12	
Pierce "Patty" Malone	35-37	9/25/02	5/13/43
Albert (Al) Mamaux	24	5/30/94	1/2/63
Walter "Rube" Manning	07-10	4/29/83	4/23/30
James (Jim) Marquis	25	11/18/00	
Clifford (Cliff) Markle	15-16, 24	5/3/94	
Felix "Tippy" Martinez (L)	74-76	5/31/50	
Rudy May (L)	74-76	7/18/44	
Carl "Sub" Mays	19-23	11/21/91	4/4/71
Larry McCall	77-78	9/8/52	
George McConnell	09, 12-13	9/16/77	5/10/64

163

THE ALL—TIME YANKEE ROSTER (Continued)
PITCHERS

Name	Years	Born	Died
Michael (Mike) McCormick (L)	70	9/29/38	
Lyndall "Lindy" McDaniel	68-73	12/13/35	
Maurice "Mickey" McDermott (L)	56	8/29/28	
Daniel (Danny) McDevitt (L)	61	11/18/32	
James (Jim) McDonald	52-54	5/17/27	
Samuel "Sudden Sam" McDowell (L)	73	9/21/42	
Louis (Lou) McEvoy	30-31	5/30/02	12/6/53
Robert (Bob) McGraw	17-19	4/10/95	
Scott McGregor (L)	76-77	1/18/54	
Martin (Marty) McHale	13-15	10/30/88	
Herbert (Herb) McQuaid	26	4/29/99	4/4/66
George "Doc" Medich	72-75	12/9/48	
John "Andy" Messersmith	78	8/4/45	
Thomas (Tom) Metcalf	63	7/16/40	
Robert (Bob) Meyer (L)	64	8/4/39	
Gene "Stick" Michael (as a pitcher)	68	6/2/38	
Peter (Pete) Mikkelsen	64-65	10/25/39	
William "Hooks" Miller	52-54	7/26/26	
George Mogridge (L)	15-20	2/18/89	3/4/62
William (Bill) Monboquette	67	8/11/36	
Edward "Peck" Monroe	17-18	2/22/93	4/29/69
Zachary (Zach) Monroe	58-59	7/8/32	
Earl "Crossfire" Moore	07	7/29/78	11/28/61
Wilcy (Cy) Moore	27-29, 32-33	5/20/97	3/29/63
Thomas "Plowboy" Morgan	51-52, 54-56	5/20/30	
Robert (Bob) Muncrief	51	1/28/16	
John "Grandma" Murphy	32, 34-43, 46	1/14/08	1/14/70
George "Smiler" Murray	22	9/23/98	10/18/55
Francis "Bots" Nekola (L)	29	12/10/07	
Luther (Luke) Nelson	19	12/4/93	
John "Tacks" Neuer	07	1880	unknown

Name	Years	Born	Died
Ernest (Ernie) Nevel	50-51	8/17/19	
Floyd Newkirk	34	7/16/08	
Norman "Bobo" Newsom	47	8/11/07	12/7/62
Eustace "Doc" Newton (L)	05-09	10/26/77	5/14/31
Donald (Don) Nottebart	60	1/23/36	
Andrew (Andy) O'Connor	08	9/14/84	unknown
Francis "Lefty" O'Doul (L)	19-20, 22	3/4/97	12/7/69
Albert (Al) Orth	04-09	9/5/72	10/8/48
Joseph "Professor" Ostrowski (L)	50-52	11/15/16	
Frank "Stubby" Overmire (L)	51	5/16/19	3/3/77
David (Dave) Pagan	73-76	9/15/50	
Joseph (Joe) Page (L)	44-50	10/28/17	
Gilbert (Gil) Patterson	77	9/5/55	
Monte Pearson	36-40	9/2/09	1/27/78
Stephen (Steve) Peek	41	7/30/14	
Herbert "The Knight of Kennett Square" Pennock (L)	23-33	2/10/94	1/30/48
Cecil Perkins	67	12/1/40	
Frederick (Fritz) Peterson (L)	66-74	2/8/42	
Edwin "Cy" Pieh	13-15	9/29/86	9/12/45
William "Wild Bill" Piercy	17, 21	5/2/96	8/28/51
Duane "Dee" Pillette	49-50	7/24/22	
George Pipgras	23-24, 27-33	12/20/99	
Erwin "Bob" Porterfield	48-51	8/10/23	
John (Jack) Powell	04-05	7/9/74	10/17/44
Ambrose Puttman (L)	03-05	9/9/80	6/21/36
Melvin (Mel) Queen	42, 44, 46-47	3/4/18	
Edwin (Ed) Quick (L)	03	unknown	unknown
John (Jack) Quinn	09-12, 19-21	7/5/84	4/17/46
David (Dave) Rajsich (L)	78	9/28/51	
Pedro (Pete) Ramos	64-66	4/28/35	
Victor "The Springfield Rifle" Raschi	46-53	3/28/19	
Harold (Hal) Reniff	61-67	7/2/38	
Allie "Superchief" Reynolds	47-54	2/10/15	

THE ALL—TIME YANKEE ROSTER (Continued)
PITCHERS

Name	Years	Born	Died
John "Dusty" Rhodes	29-32	8/11/07	3/25/60
Edward (Ed) Ricks	77	1/5/51	
Dale "Mountain Man" Roberts (L)	67	4/12/42	
Henry (Hank) Robinson (L)	18	8/16/89	7/2/65
Oscar Roettger	23-24	2/19/00	
Thomas "Shotgun" Rogers	21	2/12/95	3/7/36
James (Jim) Roland (L)	72	12/14/42	
Emerson (Steve) Roser	44-46	1/25/19	
Walter "Dutch" Ruether (L)	26-27	9/13/93	5/16/70
Charles "Red" Ruffing	30-42, 45-46	5/3/04	
Allan Russell	15-19	7/31/93	
Marius "Lefty" Russo (L)	39-43, 46	7/19/14	
George "Babe" Ruth (L) (as a pitcher)	20-21, 30, 33	2/6/95	8/16/48
Wilfred "Rosy" Ryan	28	3/15/98	
John (Johnny) Sain	51-55	9/25/17	
Roy "Simon" Sanders	18	1894	unknown
John (Fred) Sanford	49-51	8/9/19	
Richard (Rick) Sawyer	74-75	4/7/48	
Raymond (Ray) Scarborough	52-53	7/23/17	
Harry "Lefty" Schaeffer (L)	52	6/23/24	
Arthur (Art) Schallock (L)	51-55	4/25/24	
Charles (Butch) Schmidt (L)	09	7/19/87	9/4/52
John "Bear Tracks" Schmitz (L)	52-53	11/27/20	6/1/57
Peter Schneider	19	8/20/95	
Paul "Von" Schreiber	45	10/8/02	
Albert "Lefty" Schulz (L)	12-14	5/12/89	12/13/31
Robert (Bobby) Shantz (L)	57-60	9/26/25	
Robert "Sailor Bob" Shawkey	16-27	12/4/90	
Frank "Spec" Shea	47-49, 51	10/2/20	
Albert (Al) Shealy	28	5/24/00	3/7/67
George Shears (L)	12	4/13/90	

Name	Years	Born	Died
Thomas (Tom) Sheehan	21	3/31/94	
Roland (Rollie) Sheldon	61-62, 64-65	12/17/36	
Roydan (Roy) Sherid	29-31	1/25/08	
Benjamin "Big Ben" Shields (L)	24-25	6/17/03	
Urban Shocker	16-17, 25-28	8/22/90	9/9/28
Ernest (Ernie) Shore	19-20	3/24/91	
William (Billy) Short (L)	60	11/27/37	
Walter (Walt) Smallwood	17, 19	3/24/93	
William (Harry) Smythe (L)	34	10/24/04	
William (Bill) Stafford	60-65	8/13/39	
Gerald (Gerry) Staley	55-56	8/21/20	
Charles (Charley) Stanceu	41, 46	1/9/16	4/3/69
Richard (Dick) Starr	47-48	3/2/21	
Lee Stine	38	11/17/13	
Melvin (Mel) Stottlemyre	64-74	11/13/41	
Marlin Stuart	54	8/8/18	
Thomas (Tom) Sturdivant	55-59	4/28/30	
Stephen "Smokey" Sundra	36, 38-40	3/27/10	3/23/52
Fred (Bubby) Talbot	66-69	6/28/41	
Vitautis (Vito) Tamulis (L)	34-35	7/11/11	
Jesse Tannehill (L)	03	7/14/74	9/22/56
Ralph Terry	56-57, 59-64	1/9/36	
Myles Thomas	26-29	10/22/97	12/12/63
Stanley (Stan) Thomas	76	7/11/49	
Thomas (Tommy) Thompson	12	11/7/89	1/16/63
Herbert Thormahlen (L)	17-20	7/5/96	2/6/55
Richard (Dick) Tidrow	74-current	5/14/47	
Robert (Bobby) Tiefenauer	65	10/10/29	
Raymond (Ray) Tift	07	6/21/84	3/29/45
Thaddeus (Thad) Tillotson	67-68	10/20/40	
Daniel "Big Dan" Tipple	15	2/13/90	3/26/60
Michael (Mike) Torrez	77	8/28/46	
Virgil "Fire" Trucks	58	4/26/19	
Robert "Bullet Bob" Turley	55-62	9/19/30	

THE ALL—TIME YANKEE ROSTER (Continued)
PITCHERS

Name	Years	Born	Died
James "Milkman Jim" Turner	42-45	8/6/03	
George "The Bull" Uhle	33-34	9/18/98	
Cecil Upshaw	84	10/22/42	
Russell "Sheriff" Van Atta (L)	33-35	6/21/06	
Clarence "Dazzy" Vance	15-16	3/4/91	2/16/61
Joseph "Sandy" Vance	37-38	9/16/05	7/4/78
James "Hippo" Vaughn (L)	08, 10-12	4/9/88	5/29/66
Joseph (Joe) Verbanic	67-68, 70	4/24/43	
Jacob "Whistlin' Jake" Wade (L)	46	4/1/12	
Michael (Mike) Wallace (L)	74-75	2/3/51	
John (Jack) Warhop	08-15	7/4/84	10/4/60
George Wasburn	41	10/6/14	1/5/79
Gary Waslewski	70-71	7/21/41	
James "Big Jim" Weaver	31	11/25/03	
Phillip "Lefty" Weinert (L)	31	4/21/01	4/17/73
Edwin (Ed) Wells (L)	29-32	6/7/00	
Charles "Butch" Wensloff	43, 47	12/3/15	
Kemp Wicker (L)	36-38	8/13/06	6/11/73
Robert (Bob) Wiesler (L)	51, 54-55	8/13/30	
William (Bill) Wight (L)	46-47	8/12/22	
Stanley (Stan) Williams	63-64	9/14/36	
Peter (Pete) Wilson (L)	08-09	unknown	unknown
Lewis "Snake" Wiltse (L)	03	12/5/71	8/25/28
William (Bill) Wolfe	03-04	1/7/76	2/27/53
Harry Wolter (L)	07	7/11/84	7/7/70
Horace "Dooley" Womack	66-68	8/25/39	
Richard (Dick) Woodson	74	3/30/45	
Kenneth (Ken) Wright	74	9/4/46	
John Wyatt	68	4/19/35	
James (Jim) York	76	8/27/47	
Jonathan (Tom) Zachary (L)	28-30	5/7/96	1/24/69
William (Bill) Zuber	43-46	3/26/13	

BUILDING A NEW FRANCHISE: 1903

Even the Yankees had to start somewhere, and that somewhere was in 1903, when Bill Devery and Frank Farrell purchased the American League franchise which played in Baltimore as the Orioles in 1902. (Historians generally do not consider the A.L. an official major league until the 1901 season.) The Baltimore franchise had been managed by Hall-of-Famer John McGraw, who jumped to the New York Giants for the 1903 season, and brought many members of the 1902 Orioles with him to the National League.

This left Devery and Farrell with the problem of building what was really a whole new team. Their first step was to hire an established baseball man, Clark Griffith, as the team's new manager. Griffith did double duty as a pitcher, and went on to post a 14-10 record on the mound that year.

Fortunately, for the Yankees, (or Highlanders, as they were originally known because their ballpark was located at one of the highest spots in Manhattan), the rival major leagues were still at war, with each league permitting its teams to sign players from the other league. Griffith had first hand knowledge of the importance of a solid pitching staff, so he and the Yankee owners "raided" the Pittsburgh Pirates for Jack Chesbro and Jesse Tannenhill, both of whom would enjoy success in New York.

The other key acquisition was Hall-of-Famer Willie Keeler, the outfielder credited with coining the phrase "Hit 'em where they ain't." Keeler batted .318 in his first year in New York, and enjoyed four more .300-plus seasons. He came from the Brooklyn N.L. team.

Below is a list of the members of the 1903 Highlanders. Each player's position and batting/pitching record (average for hitters, won-loss mark for pitchers) follows in parenthesis. The column to the right indicates the team each player played for during the 1902 season.

Merle Adkins	(P 0-1)	Red Sox
Henry Beville	(C .194)	rookie
Elmer Bliss	(P 1-0)	rookie
Jack Chesbro	(P 21-15)	Pirates
Wid Conroy	(3B .277)	Pirates
Ernie Courtney	(SS .241)	Baltimore
Al Davis	(OF .245)	Pirates
John Deering	(OF .245)	Tigers*
Kid Elberfeld	(SS .290)	Tigers*
Dave Fultz	(OF .240)	Athletics
John Ganzel	(1B .285)	Giants**
Pat Greene	(3B .308)	Phillies*
Clark Griffith	(P 14-10)	White Sox
Fred Holmes	(1B .000)	rookie
Harry Howell	(P 10-7)	Baltimore
Tim Jordan	(1B .125)	Baltimore
Willie Keeler	(OF .318)	Brooklyn
Herman Long	(SS .225)	Braves
Pat McCauley	(C .096)	Washington ***
Herm McFarland	(OF .223)	Baltimore
Jack O'Connor	(C .197)	Pirates
Ambrose Puttman	(P 2-0)	rookie
Ed Quick	(P 0-1)	rookie
Jesse Tannehill	(P 15-15)	Pirates
James Williams	(2B .281)	Baltimore
Lewis Wiltse	(P 0-3)	Baltimore
Bill Wolfe	(P 6-9)	rookie
John Zalusky	(C .267)	rookie

(* Indicates the player was acquired during the season.

169

The first trade in Highlander history:
Highlanders acquire pitcher John Derring and shortstop Kid Elberfeld from the Tigers for shortstops Ernie Courtney and Herm Long, and third baseman Pat Greene.

The other players acquired during the season were through the outright purchase or waiver methods.

(** Ganzel played for the 1901 New York Giants, but was not in the major leagues in 1902.)

(*** McCauley was with the N.L. Washington team in 1896, his last prior major league club.)

Here is the Highlanders, lineup for the first game ever played by the New York franchise of the American League, April 22, 1903:

Lefty Davis	left field
Willie Keeler	right field
Dave Fultz	centerfield
Jim Williams	second base
John Ganzel	first base
Wid Conroy	third base
Herman Long	shortstop
Jack O'Connor	catcher
Jack Chesbro	pitcher

TRADES

(Or, how the Yankees built those champions)

Baseball fans love to talk about trades, be they ones which have been made, or ones which the fan would like to see in the future. Discussions range from realistic player exchanges to outrageously one-sided deals tinted by home bias, but tune in any sports talk show, and you'll immediately discover the emphasis on this topic.

Traditionally, certain teams have been successful in the trading market, while others repeatedly come up on the short end of the deal. For example, the Red Sox, Philadelphia Athletics, St. Louis Browns, and Washington Senators have earned the eternal ire of their fans by trading away star after star for financial or other reasons. All too often, those same fans are the ones who've refused to go to the team's home games for one reason or another, and their absence can start a never-ending cycle of losing money.

Fortunately, the Yankees have been among the most successful teams in the trade market, especially between the years 1915-1965 and 1973-current. The success began in 1915, when New York purchased pitcher Bob Shawkey from the Athletics for $85,000. He went on to post a 168-131 mark in New York over the next 12 seasons, was a 20-game winner on four occasions, and later managed the Yankees. This deal also established a traditional Yankee policy of spending whatever it would take to strengthen the team, a policy which has angered fans of rival teams across the nation since 1920. Of course those fans fail to realize that the Yankees never had a hand in making the rules, consistently abide by the limits set out therein, and operate by the same rules that their own teams could very well make use of. The Yankees have simply been more successful than other teams in selecting the right players to purchase or trade.

The 1920's featured an era known to baseball fans, and particularly Red Sox fans, as the "Great Rape of Boston." Simply put, the Sox owner, Harry Frazee, was not interested in baseball as much as he was interested in staging theatrical productions. Those productions frequently lost money. As his assets decreased, he needed more cash to pay his debts and begin new productions. Eventually, his most valuable assets were his Red Sox players, whom he began selling to the Yankees. The most notable sale was Babe Ruth, in 1920.

A look at the Yankee rosters of the 1920's shows that Babe Ruth, Waite Hoyt, George Pipgras, Herb Pennock, Joe Dugan, Carl Mays, Wally Schang, Everett Scott, Sam Jones, Joe Bush . . . all came from Boston for either outright cash purchases or one-sided trades for mediocre players and money.

Thirty years later, the Yankees repeatedly took advantage of the Kansas City Athletics, as they acquired stars such as Roger Maris, Clete Boyer, Enos Slaughter, Bobby Shantz, Art Ditmar, Ryne Duren, Ralph Terry, Hector Lopez . . . in many one-sided deals and an occasional cash purchase.

More recently, Yankee fans have benefited from trades with Boston (Sparky Lyle to New York for Danny Cater and Mario Guerrero), Cleveland (the source for Graig Nettles, Chris Chambliss, Oscar Gamble, and Dick Tidrow), Pittsburgh (Willie Randolph), and the White Sox (Bucky Dent) which have all worked overwhelmingly in New York's favor.

To top off the willingness to spend money, along came the free agents Reggie Jackson, Don Gullett, Catfish Hunter, Rich Gossage and Rawley Eastwick. (And lest Yankee haters out there forget, Yankee owner George Steinbrenner opposed the free agent policy from "day one", but said he'd have to be crazy to sit back and let other teams reap its benefits without getting his share. Once again, an example of how the Yankees did not make the rule, but have been more successful than most in its application.)

* * *

Here is the list of the 10 best trades in Yankee history:

1. Purchasing Babe Ruth from the Red Sox for $125,000 plus a loan against the Fenway Park mortgage. (That's right, the Yankees once "owned" Fenway Park!)

2. Yankees purchase outfielder Joe DiMaggio from the San Francisco Seals for $50,000. (1934)

3. Yankees obtain third baseman Graig Nettles and catcher Gerry Moses from the Cleveland Indians for outfielders Charlie Spikes and Rusty Torres, infielder Jerry Kenney, and catcher-first baseman John Ellis. (1972)

4. Yankees obtain pitcher George Pipgras and outfielder Harvey Hendrick from the Red Sox for catcher Al DeVormer. (1923)

5. Yankees obtain pitcher Herb Pennock from the Red Sox for outfielders Norm McMillan and Camp Skinner. (1923)

6. Yankees obtain pitcher Red Ruffing from the Red Sox for outfielder Cedric Durst and $50,000. (1930)

7. Yankees obtain pitcher Eddie Lopat from the White Sox for catcher Aaron Robinson, and pitchers Fred Bradley and Bill Wight. (1948)

8. Yankees obtain second baseman Willie Randolph and pitchers Ken Brett and Dock Ellis from the Pirates for pitcher Doc Medich. (1975)

9. Yankees obtain outfielder Lou Piniella and pitcher Ken Wright from the Royals for pitcher Lindy McDaniel. (1973)

9A. Yankees obtain pitcher Sparky Lyle from the Red Sox for first baseman Danny Cater and shortstop Mario Guerrero. (1972)

10. (TIE) Obtaining first baseman Chris Chambliss and pitchers Dick Tidrow and Cecil Upshaw from the Indians for pitchers Fritz Peterson, Tom Buskey, Fred Beene, and Steve Kline; (1974) and, obtaining shortstop Bucky Dent from the White Sox for outfielder Oscar Gamble and pitchers Bob Polinsky and Dewey Hoyt. (1977)

Honorable mention: The Maris deal of 1959, purchasing John Mize for $40,000 from the Giants in 1949, purchasing Enos Slaughter back from the Athletics in 1956, the Clete Boyer deal in 1957, and the Ed Figueroa and Mickey Rivers trade of 1975, the McDaniel deal of 1968, and the Carl Mays deal of 1919.

(NOTE: Trades selected were based on statistical performances and not personal preferences.)

... AND ...

Here are the 10 worst trades in Yankees history:

1. Trading away pitcher Urban Shocker. (1918)
2. Trading away pitcher Stan Bahnsen for infielder Rich McKinney. (1971)
3. Trading catcher Wally Schang for pitcher George Mogridge. (1926)
4. Selling pitcher Carl Mays. (1923)
5. Trading away first baseman Vic Power and others for mediocre players. (1953)
6. Trading Roger Maris for Charlie Smith. (1966)
7. Trading Joe Pepitone for Curt Blefary. (1969)
8. Trading Clete Boyer for Bill Robinson. (1966)
9. Releasing pitcher Robin Roberts as "over-the-hill" in spring training. (1962)
10. Trading away Hal Chase. (1913)

******

What follows is a chronological, year-by-year, listing of the trades and other roster changes made by the Yankees. The first several years merely list roster changes without dates because the dates are virtually impossible to ascertain. After that, those changes which did not involve acquiring players from within the Yankees' own minor league farm system, and for which dates are confirmed, are listed chronologically.

(An analysis of each dated transaction is included immediately after each trade/acquisition/change.)

I have also included this short explanation of the types of player roster changes. The most frequent roster changes are those involving so-called waivers deals. Waivers is a formal process covered by the major league baseball operating agreement. A player may be placed on waivers at his team's option. The stated purpose of the waiver list is to offer players whom the current club has no use for to the other teams in the leagues. If a player is claimed, the current club may either sell the player to the claiming team for the established waivers price (currently $25,000) or withdraw the player from the waivers list.

Claiming teams get priority based on the inverse of their standings in the current team's division. (The last place team gets first chance.) If none of the teams in the division claim the player, he is similarly offered to the teams in the other division, and then the other league.

The real value of the waivers system today is as a forum for discovering which, if any, teams are interested in particular players a team is thinking about trading. It is also used to shift players between leagues after the inter-league trading deadline has expired, with the receiving team later sending the "shipper" some form of future consideration.

Future considerations are often exchanged for players, and may be anything from an undisclosed amount of cash to a guarantee of a trade at a later date. Another type of consideration could be a promise not to claim a player destined for another team on the waivers market.

172

1904

NEWCOMERS:

John Anderson	OF	St. Louis Browns (waivers)
Pat Doughterty	OF	Red Sox (for Bob Unglaub)
Virgil Garvin	P	Brooklyn (purchase)
Tom Hughes	P	Red Sox (purchase)
James McGuire	C	Tigers (purchase)
Fran McManus	C	Tigers (for Henry Beville)
Al Orth	P	Senators ** (trade)
Champ Osteen	3B	Senators (purchase)
John Powell	P	St. Louis Browns (purchase)
John Thoney	3B	Senators ** (trade)

OUTGOING:

Henry Beville	C	Tigers (for McManus)
Tom Hughes	P	Senators ** (trade)
Bob Unglaub	3B	Red Sox (for Dougherty)
Bill Wolfe	P	Senators ** (trade)
		** indicates multi-player deal)

1905

NEWCOMERS:

Jack Doyle	1B	Phillies (waivers)
Fred Jacklitsch	C	Brooklyn (waivers)
Mike Powers	C	Athletics (loaned to NY for 11 games)
Joe Yeager	3B	Tigers (1903) *

OUTGOING:

John Anderson	OF	Senators (waivers)
John Powell	P	Browns (sale)
Mike Powers	C	Athletics (loan expires)

1906

NEWCOMERS:

Noodles Hahn	P	Reds (purchase)
Dan Hoffman	OF	Athletics (purchase)
George Moriarty	3B	Cubs (1904)*

OUTGOING:

Pat Dougherty	OF	White Sox (sale)
Ed Hahn	OF	White Sox (sale)

1907

NEWCOMERS:

Frank Kitson	P	Senators (waivers)
Earl Moore	P	Indians (for Clarkson)
Branch Rickey	OF	Browns (waivers)

OUTGOING:

Walt Clarkson	P	Indians (for Moore)
James McGuire	PH	Red Sox (waivers)

(* indicates the year in parenthesis was that player's last previous major league team and year)

1908

NEWCOMERS:

Frank Delahanty	OF	Indians (waivers)
Michael Donovan	3B	Indians (1904)
Fred Glade	P	Browns (waivers)
Charles Hemphill	OF	Browns (purchase)
Frank LaPorte	2B	Red Sox (for Niles & Stahl)
Henry McIlveen	OF	Pirates (1906)
Harry Niles	2B	Browns (purchase)
Garland Stahl	OF	Senators (1906)

OUTGOING:

Harry Niles	2B	Red Sox (for LaPorte)
Garland Stahl	OF	Red Sox (for LaPorte)

1909

NEWCOMERS:

John Knight	SS	Red Sox (waivers)
Ed Tiemeyer	1B	Reds (1907)
Joe Ward	2B	Phillies (conditional purchase)

OUTGOING:

Cornelius Ball	SS	Indians (waivers)
Jack Chesbro	1B	Red Sox (purchase)
Joe Ward	2B	Phillies (returned)

1910

NEWCOMERS:

Lou Criger	C	Browns (waivers)
Tom Madden	OF	Braves (1906)
Fred Mitchell	C	Brooklyn (1905)
Harry Wolter	OF	Red Sox (for Kleinow & Engle)

OUTGOING:

Judd Doyle	P	Reds (waivers)
Art Engle	3B	Red Sox (for Wolter)
John Kleinow	C	Red Sox (for Wolter)

1911

NEWCOMERS:

Harry Ables	P	Indians (1909)
Andy Coakley	P	Cubs (1909)
Jim Curry	2B	Phillies (1909)
Cozy Dolan	3B	Reds (1909)
Roy Hartzell	3B	Browns (purchase)

OUTGOING:
None

1912

NEWCOMERS:

August Fisher	C	Indians (waivers)
Jack Lelivelt	OF	Senators (purchase)
Ezra Midkiff	3B	Reds (1909)
Tom McMillan	SS	Reds (1910)
George Simmons	2B	Tigers (1910)
Gabby Street	C	Senators (purchase)
Harry Wolverton (mgr.)	OF	Braves (1905)

OUTGOING:

Cozy Dolan	3B	Phillies (waivers)
Hippo Vaughn	P	Senators (waivers)

1913

January 8 Yankees sign free agent first baseman Frank Chance as a player manager. (He was at the end of a great playing career. His managing was like the end of his career — the less said about it, the better.)

April 15 Yankees purchase infielder Bill McKechnie from the Braves for an undisclosed amount of cash. (He had a dismal year in NY, jumped to the Federal League, and later returned as a mediocre infielder in the N.L.)

April 26 Yankees purchase catcher John Gossett from Columbus for an undisclosed amount of cash. (He hit .159 over two seasons and was released.)

May 1 Yankees release pitcher Chester Hoff. (He was through.)

May 7 Yankees release first baseman Bob Williams. (He returned for 59 games in 1914 and batted .163. That was the end for him.)

May 20 Yankees obtain shortstop Roger Peckinpaugh from the Indians for shortstop Bill Stumpf and outfielder Jack Lelivelt. (Peckinpaugh had eight good seasons in NY and played on the 1921 pennant-winners. He was traded after the '21 season. Lelivelt hit .328 as a part-timer in Cleveland for two seasons, and joined the armed forces in World War I. Stumpf never returned to the major leagues.)

May 31 Yankees obtain infielder Rollie Zeider and first baseman Bill Borton from the White Sox for first baseman Hal Chase. (Zeider proved a weak-hitting infielder. Borton was at the end of a fair career. Chase had several good years, including some .300 seasons.)

June 19 Yankees sell pitcher Ed Klepfer to the Giants on waivers. (He never pitched for the Giants, but later resurfaced with the Indians and went 13-4 in 1917.)

July 7	Yankees obtain first baseman Jack Knight from the Senators on waivers. (He hit .236 and was released.)
August 8	Yankees obtain third baseman Fritz Maisel from Baltimore for third baseman Ezra Midkiff and outfielder Bert Daniels. (Maisel lasted five years and was the only great base stealer in Yankee history until Mickey Rivers came along. In fact, Maisel led the league with 74 steals in 1914. He was sent to the Browns prior to the 1918 season.) (Midkiff and Daniels never returned to the major leagues.)
August 25	Yankees obtain outfielder Frank Gilhooley from the Cardinals for an undisclosed amount of cash. (He hit .341 in 24 games that year, but dropped into the .270's for the rest of his career.)
October 13	Yankees release outfielder George Whiteman. (No loss.)

1914

January 5	Yankees purchase pitcher Boardwalk Brown from the Athletics for an undisclosed amount of cash. (He went 3-6 and was released.)
May 13	Yankeess purchase catcher Les Nunamaker from the Red Sox for an undisclosed amount of cash. This may have been a waiver deal. (He lasted three respectable years in NY and was sent to St. Louis in 1918.)
May 27	Yankees sell pitcher Guy Cooper to the Red Sox for an undisclosed amount of cash. This may have been a waiver deal, or it may have been in lieu of payment for Nunamaker. (He went 1-1 and was released.)
June 1	Yankees purchase outfielder Fritz Meara from Reading for an undisclosed amount. (He went 2-for-7 and was released.)

1915

April 18	Yankees purchase pitcher Ensign Cottrell from the Braves for an undisclosed amount of cash. (He went 0-1 and was released.)
June 28	Yankees purchase pitcher Bob Shawkey from the Athletics for $85,000. (This trade is important for two reasons. First, it established the "new" era of Yankee ownership brought into NY by Colonels Ruppert and Huston; that is, that they would spend whatever it would take to make the Yankees winners. Second, Shawkey was their first important acquisition from a success point of view; that is, he went 168-131 in NY, was a 20-game winner four times, and later managed the Yankees.)
July 1	Yankees purchase pitcher Dan Tipple from Indianapolis for an undisclosed amount of cash. (He went 1-1 and was released.)

July 13	Yankees release pitchers Ensign Cottrell and Marty McHale. (They were both finished.)
July 20	Yankees purchase outfielder Gene Layden from Indianapolis for an undisclosed amount of cash. (He went 2-for-7 and was released.)
July 23	Yankees purchase outfielder Elmer Miller from the St. Louis Browns for an undisclosed amount of cash. (He was a fair outfielder who finished with a .243 career average.)
July 23	Yankees purchase catcher Al Walters from Indianapolis. (He was a weak catcher.)
July 29	Yankees purchase pitcher Cornelius Brady from Hartford for an undisclosed amount. (He went 0-0, sat out the 1917 season, and was released.)
July 30	Yankees release first baseman Harry Kingman. (No loss.)
July 30	Yankees purchase catcher Walt Alexander from the Browns for an undisclosed amount of cash. (He lasted two very mediocre years.)
August 9	Yankees purchase pitcher Cliff Markle from Newark for an undisclosed amount. (Not much.)
August 19	Yankees release outfielder Ed Barney to the Pirates. (He lasted one season.)
August 26	Yankees purchase pitcher Al Russell from Jersey City for an undisclosed amount of cash. (He was mediocre with NY, had a good year with Boston in 1919, and then faded.)

1916

January 14	Yankees purchase outfielder Lee Magee from the Brooklyn Federal League franchise for an undisclosed amount of cash. (He hit .257 and was traded to the Browns in 1917.)
January 21	Yankees purchase pitcher Nick Cullop, infielder Elmer Gedeon and outfielder Germany Schaeffer from Newark of the Federal League for an undisclosed amount of cash. (Nothing significant.)
February 4	Yankees release outfielder Birdie Cree. (He retired.)
February 15	Yankees purchase third baseman Frank Baker from the Athletics for $35,000. (He had six solid seasons in NY and was a key reserve on the 1921-22 champions.)
July 11	Yankees sign outfielder Rube Oldring after his release by the Athletics. (He lasted less than one season and was released back to the Athletics.)
July 28	Yankees release outfielder Roy Hartzell to Baltimore. (He never played in the major leagues again.)

1917

June 23   Yankees purchase shortstop Aaron Ward and outfielder Howie Camp from the Southern League. (Ward lasted 10 years in NY and played well. Camp hit .286 and was released.)

July 6   Yankees purchase outfielder Sam Vick from the Southern League for an undisclosed amount of cash. (He was a mediocre outfielder.)

July 15   Yankees obtain outfielder Armando Marsans from the Browns for outfielder Lee Magee. (Magee was the better outfielder, but neither was particularly good.)

August 21   Yankees purchase catcher Muddy Ruel from the Browns for an undisclosed amount of cash. (He spent three mediocre years in NY and was sent to Boston in 1920.)

1918

January 22   Yankees obtain second baseman Del Pratt and pitcher Eddie Plank from the Browns for catcher Les Nunamaker, pitchers Urban Shocker and Nick Cullop, and second basemen Fritz Maisel and Elmer Gedeon.

(Pratt had three good years in NY, the best of which was 1920, when he hit .314. Plank refused to report to NY and retired.

Nunamaker was traded to Cleveland after hitting .259. Shocker went 126-80 in seven fine years in St. Louis, and his absence certainly cost NY the pennant in 1920 and 1924. Fortunately, the Yankees were smart enough to realize their error, and they reobtained Shocker in 1925. Cullop went 0-2 and was released. Maisel hit .232 and was released. Gedeon played three years, excelled in 1920 with a .292 average, and then retired.)

March 7   Yankees purchase first baseman George Burns from the Tigers for an undisclosed amount of cash and immediately trade him to the Athletics for outfielder Ping Bodie. (The Yankees should have kept Burns, who compiled a .307 career average over a 16-year career. Instead, they got Bodie, who had three respectable years.)

June 19   Yankees purchase outfielder Ham Hyatt from the Browns for an undisclosed amount. (He hit .229 and was released.)

June 20   Yankees purchase pitcher John Robinson from the Browns for an undisclosed amount of cash. (He went 2-4 and was released.)

December 9   Yankees purchase pitcher Pete Schneider from the Reds for an undisclosed amount. (He went 0-1 and was released.)

December 18 Yankees obtain pitchers Ernie Shore and Dutch Leonard, and outfielder Duffy Lewis from the Red Sox for pitchers Ray Caldwell and Elmer Love, catcher Al Walters, and outfielder Frank Gilhooley.

178

(Shore went 7-10 over two seasons and was released. Leonard refused to report to NY and was sent to Washington, instead. Lewis was at the tail end of his career, hit .272 over his two seasons in NY, and was sent to Washington in 1921.

Caldwell went 7-4 in Boston, was traded to Cleveland mid-way through the season, and went on to win 20 games on the 1920 champions.

Love was forwarded to the Tigers, where he did little. Walters never did much. Gilhooley lasted one year and was released.)

1919

February 21   Yankees obtain pitcher John Quinn from the Vernon minor league team for pitcher Joe Finneran, first baseman Zinn Beck, and other considerations. (Quinn went 41-31 in three seasons during his second stand in the pinstripes. Finneran never returned to the major leagues, nor did Beck.)

March 6   Yankees sell pitcher Ray Keating to the Braves for an undisclosed amount of cash. (He went 6-11 and was released.)

March 15   Yankees sell pitcher Ray Fisher to the Reds for an undisclosed amount of cash. (He sat out 1918, went 14-5 in 1919, 10-11 in 1920 and was released.)

April 13   Yankees release outfielders Ham Hyatt and Hugh High, and pitcher Ed Monroe. (No loss.)

July 30   Yankees obtain pitcher Carl Mays from the Red Sox for shortstop Al Russell, pitcher Bob McGraw and $40,000. (Mays went 80-39 in four-and-a-half seasons in NY, including 26-11 in 1920 and 27-9 in 1921. Unfortunately, he and manager Miller Huggins never got along too well, and he was banished to Cincinnati in late 1923.

Actually, there is more to this trade than initially meets the eye because Mays had demanded to be traded to NY, and had even walked out on the Red Sox to force a deal. Originally, the trade was disallowed by the American League, but the Yankees brought suit and got an injunction allowing Mays to make the move.

The other players involved did little.)

December 26   Yankees reach a written agreement with Red Sox owner Harry Frazee for the transfer of Babe Ruth to the Yankees for $125,000 and a $350,000 loan against a mortgage on Fenway Park.

(Frazee never really cared that much about the Sox. His primary interest was in the production of Broadway plays. His recent productions had not done well, so he needed cash to pay his debts, and a loan to begin the production of what would become a great hit, "No, No Nanette." Red Sox fans never forgave him, and how can you blame them!)

1920

February 8   Yankees obtain outfielder Elmer Smith on waivers from the Braves. (He was sent on to Boston Red Sox.)

February 25   Yankees release outfielders George Halas and Al Wickland. (No loss.)

March 26   Yankees release outfielder Ping Bodie. (He retired.)

June 15   Yankees purchase outfielder Tom Connelly from Hartford for an undisclosed amount of cash. (He went 1-for-6 in two years and was released.)

June 25   Yankees purchase shortstop Ray French from Des Moines for $7000. (He went 0-for-2 and was released.)

August 4   Yankees obtain outfielder-third baseman Norman "Bub" McMillan from Greenville of the South Atlantic League for an undisclosed amount of cash. (He hit .256 in 33 games.)

December 15   Yankees obtain pitchers Waite Hoyt and Harry Harper, infielder Mike McNally, and catcher Wally Schang from the Red Sox for second baseman Del Pratt, outfielder Sam Vick, catcher Muddy Ruel, and pitcher Herb Thormahlen.

(Hoyt became the star pitcher of the great teams of the 1920's. He won 20 games in 1927 and '28, and finished his nine-and-a-half-year career in NY with 157 wins. Harper went 4-3 and was released. McNally was a fair utility infielder. Schang became a fine catcher and batted .284 for his 19-year career, including .316 and .319 in two of his five years in NY.

Pratt batted over .300 for two years as the Red Sox second baseman and was traded to Detroit. Vick hit .260 in 1921 and was released. Ruel had two solid seasons in Boston, but the Red Sox foolishly traded him to Washington in 1923 where he became a .300-hitter and lasted eight good years. Thormahlen went 1-7 and was released.)

1921

January 20   Yankees obtain outfielder Bob Roth from the Senators for outfielder Duffy Lewis and pitcher George Mogridge.

(Roth hit .283 with NY in 1921 and was released. Lewis was in the final year of a good career and hit .186. Mogridge had four solid years in Washington before fading.)

January 27   Yankees obtain shortstop John Mitchell from the Vernon minor league team for pitchers Ernie Shore and Bob McGraw, catcher Truck Hannah, and a minor leaguer.

(Mitchell hit .262 as a utility infielder and was sent to Boston in 1922. Shore never returned to the major leagues and McGraw should have followed his example. Hannah retired.)

September 18   Yankees purchase pitcher Oscar Roettger from Joplin. (He did nothing, and left the major with no decisions and a 8.49 earned run average.)

December 12   Yankees obtain outfielder Elmer Miller from St. Paul for pitcher Tom Rogers. (Miller became a solid backup outfielder with NY but was traded in 1922. Rogers retired.)

December 20   Yankees obtain shortstop Everett Scott and pitchers Sam Jones and Joe Bush from the Red Sox for shortstop Roger Peckinpaugh, pitchers Harry Collins and John Quinn, and a minor leaguer of no significance.

(Scott became the Yankee shortstop for three solid seasons. Bush went 62-38 in three seasons in NY, including 26-7 in 1922. Jones went 67-56 over five season, the best of which was a 21-8 mark in 1923.

Peckinpaugh never played for Boston, but had four more solid years as a Senator. Collins went 14-11 in 1922, but was foolishly exiled to Detroit. Quinn never exceeded .500 in Boston, but was later successful with the Athletics.)

1922

January 6   Yankees release outfielder Chicken Hawks, shortstop Ray French and a minor leaguer to the minor league team in Vernon, CT. (This completed the acquisition of catcher Al DeVormer who had hit .346 in 17 games in 1921, but then faded. All three give-aways were marginal players.)

February 24   Yankees release pitcher Alex Ferguson to the Red Sox on waivers. (He did not help Boston, and returned to NY in 1925.)

July 23   Yankees obtain third baseman Joe Dugan and outfielder Elmer Smith from the Red Sox for outfielders Chick Fewster and Elmer Miller, shortstop John Mitchell, and a player to be named later. The player to be named later was pitcher Lefty O'Doul.

(Dugan became the third baseman NY needed to replace the aging Frank Baker. He had six fine years in NY and batted more than .280 in five of them. Smith proved a valuable backup outfielder. He hit .306 in 40 games in 1923 before being released.

Fewster proved a mediocre utility player. Miller hit .190 and was released. Mitchell was a weak shortstop. O'Doul went 1-1 as a pitcher, was released to the N.L., and became a lifetime .346 hitter as an outfielder.)

August 1   Yankees purchase catcher Benny Bengough from Buffalo for an undisclosed amount. (He lasted eight seasons in NY, and if not for an arm injury, might have developed into a fine catcher.)

October 2   Yankees transfer pitcher Lefty O'Doul to the Red Sox. (see July 23, 1922.)

1923

January 3 — Yankees obtain pitcher George Pipgras and outfielder Harvey Hendrick from the Red Sox for catcher Al DeVormer. (Another steal from the hapless Bostons. Pipgras had many fine years in NY. Hendrick proved a capable backup outfielder. DeVormer was weak.)

January 30 — Yankees obtain pitcher Herb Pennock from the Red Sox for outfielders Norm McMillan and Camp Skinner, and pitcher George Murray.

(Pennock, never a winner in Boston, became one of the finest pitchers in Yankee history and starred on the great teams of the late 1920's.

McMillan proved to be a mediocre outfielder. Skinner hit .231 in 7 games and was dropped. Murray went 9-20 in two years with Boston, but was successful for a couple of years with the Senators later on in his career.)

November 27 — Yankees obtain pitcher Milt Gaston.

(He went 5-3 in NY, was traded to the Browns, and lasted 10 more seasons without a .500 record.)

December 23 — Yankees sell pitcher Carl Mays to the Reds for $85,000. (He went 56-36, including 20-9 in 1924, and proved that personality conflicts should not overcome talent — he and manager Huggins never saw eye-to-eye in NY.)

1924

January 7 — Yankees purchase outfielder Earle Combs from Louisville.

(He became one of the finest outfielders of his day, which spanned 12 years and included a .325 lifetime batting average.)

January 10 — Yankees release third baseman Frank Baker. (He retired.)

February 1 — Yankees purchase outfielder Nick Cullop from Omaha. (He went 1-for-2 and was traded to the Senators, where he faded fast.)

July 13 — Yankees purchase pitcher Al Mamaux and outfielder Shags Horan from Reading, PA. (Neither had any kind of a major league career really worth noting.)

July 23 — Yankees release pitcher Cliff Markle to St. Paul. (He was finished — he'd never done much, either.)

August 14 — Yankees purchase outfielder Ben Paschal and pitcher Ray Francis from Atlanta for an undisclosed amount.

(Paschal had several fine years as a utility outfielder and hit more than .300 four times. Francis went 0-0 and was dispatched to Boston in 1925.)

182

| August 28 | Yankees purchase pitcher Walter Beall from Rochester for $50,000. (He went 4-5 before being sent to Washington.) |

| December 11 | Yankees obtain infielder Howard Shanks from the Red Sox for infielder Mike McNally. (Shanks played his final year in NY and hit .258. McNally was sent on to Washington, where he played his final year, hit .143, and quit.) |

| December 12 | Yankees obtain catcher Steve O'Neill on waivers from the Red Sox. (He hit .286 in 35 games and was released in 1925.) |

| December 17 | Yankees obtain pitcher Urban Shocker from the Browns for pitchers Joe Bush, Milt Gaston, and Joe Giard. |

(Shocker went 49-29 in three-plus seasons with NY in his second visit to the pinstripes.

Bush went 14-14 in 1925, then faded. Gaston never had a winning record with St. Louis, but lasted several years. Giard went 10-5 in 1925 and was back in NY in 1927.)

1925

| January 9 | Yankees release pitcher Al Mamaux. (He retired.) |

| May 5 | Yankees obtain outfielder Bobby Veach and re-obtain pitcher Alex Ferguson from the Red Sox for pitcher Ray Francis and at least $8,000. |

(Veach hit .353 in 56 games with NY and became the only Yankee to ever pinch hit for Babe Ruth. He retired after the '25 season. Ferguson went 4-2 and was traded to Washington before the season ended.

Francis went 0-2 in Boston and retired.)

| May 15 | Yankees sell catcher Fred Hoffman to Minneapolis for an undisclosed amount of cash. (He later resurfaced in Boston, where he had one good year, and then faded.) |

| June 16 | Yankees sign free agent first baseman Fred Merkle after his release by the Cubs. (He was over the hill.) |

| July 3 | Yankees release outfielder Whitey Witt. (He signed with Brooklyn, hit .259 in 1926, and then retired.) |

| July 21 | Yankees purchase catcher Roy Luebbe from Iowa for $2,000. (His major league career spanned eight games.) |

| July 22 | Yankees purchase infielder Leo Durocher from Hartford for an undisclosed amount. (He was a utility infielder in NY, but later enjoyed many successful years in the N.L.) |

| July 31 | Yankees release catcher Steve O'Neill. (He was finished.) |

August 10	Yankees release pitcher Charlie Caldwell. (His whole career was three games.)
August 17	Yankees waive outfielder Bobby Veach and pitcher Alex Ferguson to the Senators. (See May 5, 1925.)
September 14	Yankees purchase pitcher Herb McQuaid from St. Paul of the American Association. He had previously been property of the Reds. The price went undisclosed. (He pitched in 17 games, went 1-0, and was returned.)

1926

January 20	Yankees obtain first baseman Spencer Adams from the Senators for an undisclosed amount of cash. (The Yankees used him at second and third in a utility capacity and he hit .120.)
February 6	Yankees obtain pitcher George Mogridge and an undisclosed amount of cash from the Browns for catcher Wally Schang. (Modridge never pitched for NY this time around. Schang starred with the Browns, batted .330 in 1926, and was a rare Ed Barrow trade mistake.)
June 15	Yankees obtain outfielder Roy Carlyle from the Red Sox on waivers. (He hit .377 in 47 games with NY and then retired.)
July 22	Yankees obtain catcher Hank Severeid from the Senators on waivers. (He hit .268 in 41 games and then retired.)
August 18	Yankees obtain pitcher Wilcy Moore from Greenville of the Carolina League for an undisclosed amount of cash. (He became the great relief pitcher of the 1927 Yankees.)
August 27	Yankees obtain pitcher Dutch Ruether on waivers from the Senators. (He went 13-6 on the 1927 team and then retired.)
October 19	Yankees send pitchers Garland Braxton and Nick Cullop to the Senators to complete the Ruether deal. (Braxton had three good seasons. Cullop did nothing.)

1927

January 13	Yankees obtain catcher John Grabowski and infielder Ray Morehart from the White Sox for infielder Aaron Ward. (Although neither of the players starred on the 1927 team, both were valuable backups. Ward hit .270 and then faded in 1928.)
January 22	Yankees release catcher Hank Severeid.
February 8	Yankees obtain outfielder Cedric Durst and pitcher Joe Giard from the Browns for pitcher Sam Jones. (Durst was a mediocre outfielder for three-and-a-half years. Giard had no decisions with NY and retired. Jones pitched eight more seasons including three good years therein.)

November 28   Yankees release pitchers Bob Shawkey and Dutch Reuther. (They retired.)

December 21   Yankees sign pitcher Stan Coveleski after his release by the Senators. (He went 5-1 and then retired.)

December 30   Yankees release infielder Ray Morehart and pitcher Joe Giard. (They retired.)

1928

January 4   Yankees purchase infielders Lyn Lary and Jimmy Reese from Oakland of the Pacific Coast League for $150,000. (Lary had three strong seasons in NY, sputtered in 1932, and was eventually sent to Boston in '34. Reese hit .346 with NY in 1930. He dropped to .241 in '31, was sent to the Cardinals, and retired after the '32 season.)

February 4   Yankees release infielder Julie Wera. (He retired.)

July 6   Yankees release pitcher Urban Shocker. (He also retired.)

August 4   Yankees purchase pitcher Fred Heimach from St. Paul for an undisclosed amount of cash and a player to be named later. (He compiled a 13-9 mark over two seasons and was sent to the Dodgers.)

August 23   Yankees purchase pitcher Tom Zachary from the Senators for an undisclosed amount of cash. (Zachary compiled a 16-4 mark over slightly less than two seasons in NY, including 12-0 in 1929. He was sent to the Braves in 1930.)

December 20   Yankees sell infielder Mike Gazella to the Newark Bears. (End of major league career.)

December 22   Yankees release pitcher Rosy Ryan. (He was never effective after 1928.)

December 28   Yankees waive third baseman Joe Dugan to the Braves. (He hit .304 in 1929, but then faded.)

1929

March 25   Yankees release pitcher Fred Heimach to Toledo of the International League. (He later made the Dodgers and had one good season in four years.)

May 30   Yankees obtain outfielder Harry Rice, pitcher Ownie Carroll, and infielder Yats Wuestling from the Tigers for pitcher Waite Hoyt and infielder Mark Koenig.

               (Rice hit .298 as a regular outfielder in 100 games. Carroll was never effective. Wuestling was a weak utility infielder.

185

Hoyt enjoyed successful seasons in Detroit, Philadelphia (A.L.) and Pittsburgh for the next nine years. His best mark was 15-6 for the 1934 Pirates. Koenig did not do well in Detroit, but subsequently led the Cubs to a pennant in 1932 and followed that with two more good years in the N.L.)

August 25   Yankees purchase infielder Frank Crosetti from the San Francisco Seals of the Pacific Coast League. (He was a regular for 13 years and a part-timer for another 4. He hit more than 20 doubles seven times and scored more than 70 runs in seven seasons.)

October 16   Yankees sell outfielder Bob Meusel to the Reds for an undisclosed amount of cash. (He hit .289 in 113 games and then retired.)

1930

February 2   Yankees waive infielder Leo Durocher to the Reds. (He lasted 14 years in the N.L. as a solid fielder-mediocre hitter.)

May 6   Yankees obtain pitcher Red Ruffing from the Red Sox for outfielder Cedric Durst and $50,000.

(Ruffing starred with the great Yankee teams of the 1930's. Durst hit .245 and retired.)

May 12   Yankees sell pitcher Tom Zachary to the Braves for an undisclosed amount. (He had four respectable years up there, and probably would have been an even better pitcher had he remained in NY.)

October 24   Yankees release catcher Bubbles Hargrave. (He retired.)

October 24   Yankees sign free agent Joe Sewell after his release from Cleveland. (He anchored third base for NY for three years, batted more than .270 every year, including .302 in 1931.)

December 10   Yankees purchase catcher Cy Perkins from the Athletics for an undisclosed amount of cash. (He did little.)

1931

November 4   Yankees purchase outfielder George Selkirk from Jersey City. (He joined NY in 1934, spent nine years with the Yankees, and hit .290.)

1932

May 31   Yankees obtain pitcher Dan MacFayden from the Red Sox for an undisclosed amount of cash and other considerations. (He went 14-10 over less than three seasons in NY and was sent to the N.L., where he enjoyed success.)

June 29   Yankees sign pitcher Charles Devens straight out of Harvard University. (He was not very effective during his three-year career.)

April 15   Yankees release pitcher Charles Devens. (NY re-acquired him from the minor league team later on, but he remained ineffective.)

May 12   Yankees sell pitcher George Pipgras and infielder Billy Werber to the Red Sox for $100,000. (Pipgras was at the end of a fine career. He went 9-8 in 1933, and was ineffective thereafter. Werber had many fine seasons in his nine big league years after leaving NY.)

May 31   Yankees sign free agent minor league pitcher John Broaca for an undisclosed amount of cash. (He went 40-27 in four seasons in NY.)

June 24   Yankees sign free agent pitcher George Uhle after his release by the Giants. (He went 6-1 in 1933, but was ineffective thereafter.)

August 22   Yankees purchase first baseman Don Heffner from Baltimore of the Atlantic Coast League. (He spent four years in NY and was an adequate substitute first baseman.)

December 7   Yankees release pitcher Wilcy Moore and second baseman Roy Schalk. (Neither ever had a good year after leaving NY.)

1934

January 5   Yankees release pitcher Herb Pennock and third baseman Joe Sewell. (Both were at the end of Hall of Fame careers.)

January 9   Yankees send pitcher Don Brennan and outfielder Jesse Hill down to what would subsequently become their Newark farm club. (Brennan wound up in the N.L., where he had four mildly successful seasons. Hill would be back in 1935 and hit .293 in 107 games before being dealt to the Senators.)

January 11   Yankees release infielder Doc Farrell. (No loss.)

May 15   Yankees obtain infielder Fred Muller and $20,000 from the Red Sox for infielder Lyn Lary. (Muller never made NY. Lary did nothing in Boston but later had good years in St. Louis (A.L.) and Cleveland.)

June 1   Yankees release pitcher George Uhle. (He was finished.)

July 28   Yankees grant Earle Combs request for voluntary retirement. (He never recovered from a collision with the outfield wall in 1934.)

November 13   Yankees sell pitcher Dan MacFayden to the Reds on a conditional basis, the purchase price to be finalized if the Reds decided to keep him. (They did not.)

November 11   Yankees purchase the contract of Joe DiMaggio from the San Francisco Seals of the Pacific Coast League for an amount believed to be roughly $50,000. (They allowed DiMaggio to remain in San Francisco until 1936. He became the greatest center fielder in Yankee history, and was voted the Greatest Living Player in Baseball's Centennial Year. For more information, see the Hall of Fame section.)

December 21 Yankees sell outfielder Sammy Byrd to the Reds for an undisclosed amount of cash. (He had two mediocre years in Cincinnati and then retired.)

1935

May 15 Yankees sell pitcher Dan MacFayden to the Braves for an undisclosed amount of cash. (He had three respectable seasons and then faded.)

December 11 Yankees obtain pitchers Monte Pearson and Steve Sundra from Cleveland for pitcher Johnny Allen.

(Pearson went 63-27 over five years in NY, including a 19-7 mark in 1936, and a 4-0 world series record. Sundra went 21-11 over three seasons in NY.

Johnny Allen went 67-36 in five seasons with Cleveland, including a 20-10 mark in 1936 and a league-leading 15-1 in '37.)

1936

January 24 Yankees obtain pitcher Bump Hadley and outfielder Roy Johnson from the Senators for outfielder Jesse Hill and pitcher Jimmy DeShong.

(Hadley went 49-31 over five seasons in NY. Johnson hit .265 as a part-time outfielder, and was traded to the Braves during the following season.

Hill hit .305 as a part-timer in Washington in 1936 and was traded to the Athletics the following year. He hit .293 and then retired. DeShong went 37-36 over four seasons in Washington, including an 18-10 mark in 1936.)

May 4 Yankees waive outfielder Dixie Walker to the White Sox. (He never did anything with NY, but had many good years, particularly with Brooklyn, after leaving the pinstripes.)

June 14 Yankees obtain outfielder Jake Powell from the Senators for outfielder Ben Chapman.

(Powell was a mediocre outfielder with NY. Chapman lasted seven more years and batted more than .290 in five of them.)

August 22 Yankees purchase outfielder-third baseman Babe Seeds from Montreal of the International League for an undisclosed amount of cash and a player to be named later. (He was a respectable player with several teams, and hit .262 in 13 games for NY.)

1937

February 17   Yankees purchase first baseman Babe Dahlgren from the Red Sox for an undisclosed amount of cash. (He lasted four years in NY, and is best remembered for taking Lou Gehrig's place at first base on the day Gehrig ended his own 2,130 game streak. Dahlgren's best year was in 1940, when he hit 24 doubles and batted .262, although he later enjoyed success in the N.L.)

August 14   Yankees obtain pitcher Ivy Andrews from the Indians for $7,500. (He was nothing special.)

October 15   Yankees release infielder Tony Lazzeri upon his request to retire.

1938

February 15   Yankees obtain infielder Billy Knickerbocker from the Browns for first baseman Don Heffner and an undisclosed amount of cash. (Knickerbocker was a utility infielder. Heffner was a slightly better utility infielder.)

August 14   Yankees sign pitcher Wes Ferrell after his release by the Browns. (He went 3-4 with NY over two seasons and was released to the Dodgers.)

October 10   Yankees release outfielder French Bordagary. (He signed with the Dodgers and would return to NY in 1941.)

October 26   Yankees obtain outfielder Buster Mills and pitcher Oral Hildebrand from the Browns for outfielder Myril Hoag and catcher Joe Glenn.

(Mills hit .397 in 14 games with NY in 1940, his only year with the "varsity." Hildebrand went 10-4 in 1939, slipped to 1-1 in '40, and then retired.

Hoag hit .295 in 1939 before slipping into mediocrity for the remainder of his career — five more seasons. Glenn hit .273 and then faded fast.)

1939

June 13   Yankees obtain infielder Roy Hughes from the Browns for outfielder Joe Gallagher. (Hughes never made it to the "varsity." Gallagher's major league career lasted less than two seasons.)

June 14   Yankees recall pitcher Spud Chandler from a minor league affiliate. (He starred on the championship teams of the early '40s.)

June 20   Yankees re-obtain pitcher Jimmy DeShong from the Senators for an undisclosed amount of cash. (He never pitched in the major leagues again.) This was subsequently revealed to have been a waiver deal.

1940

January 4   Yankees obtain pitcher Lee Grissom from the Reds for pitcher Joe Beggs. (He went 0-0 in five games and was sent to Brooklyn.)

May 15   Yankees waive pitcher Lee Grissom to the Dodgers. (He went 2-5 in 1940, was traded to the Phillies where he went 2-13, and was released.)

December 30   Yankees sell pitcher Monte Pearson to the Reds for $20,000 and infielder Don Lang. (Pearson went 1-3 and was released. Lang never played for the Yankees.)

December 30   Yankees obtain catcher Ken Silvestri from the White Sox for infielder Bill Knickerbocker. (Silvestri played 33 games in three years with NY as an adequate backup to Bill Dickey. Knickerbocker remained a utility infielder.)

1941

February 25   Yankees sell first baseman Babe Dahlgren to the Braves for an undisclosed amount.

1942

February 5   Yankees obtain first baseman Buddy Hassett and outfielder Gene Moore, plus an undisclosed amount of cash from the Braves for outfielder Tommy Holmes. (This trade worked out nicely for both teams. It freed Holmes from the impossible task of cracking the Di-Maggio-Keller-Henrich outfield in New York, and Holmes enjoyed may successful seasons in Boston. Hassett helped New York win the pennant in 1942.)

February 25   Yankees sign free agent Tuck Stainback for an undisclosed amount of cash. (He turned out to be over-the-hill.)

June 8   Yankees obtain outfielder Roy Cullenbine and pitcher Bill Trotter from the Browns for pitcher Steve Sundra and outfielder Mike Chartak. (Cullenbine hit .364 as a part-time outfielder and pinch hitter. Trotter never made the Yankees. Sundra did a fair job with the Browns, including a 15-11 mark in 1943. Chartak was a marginal outfielder.)

July 16   Yankees obtain pitcher Jim Turner from the Reds for outfielder Frank Kelleher. (Turner saw limited action as a relief pitcher in New York, and led the league in saves in 1945 with 10. Kelleher never amounted to anything.

July 17   Yankees sign free agent Rollie Hemsley after his release by the Reds. (Hemsley hit .294 in 31 games as a catcher-pinch hitter, and then faded into oblivion.)

August 31   Yankees re-obtain Roy Cullenbine on waivers from the Senators.

September 25   Yankees obtain third baseman Hank Majeski from the Braves on waivers. (He saw no action with New York that year, and was in the armed forces until '46, when the Yankees unloaded his .083 batting average on the Athletics.)

December 17   Yankees obtain outfielder Roy Weatherly and infielder Oscar Grimes from the Indians for catcher Buddy Rosar and outfielder Roy Cullenbine. (Weatherly hit .264 for NY in 1943 as a part-time outfielder. Grimes filled in as a utility infielder in '43, but when he was handed a more regular job in '44 and '45, he responded by hitting .279 and .265.

Rosar caught 114 games for Cleveland in 1943 and batted .283. He later had several good seasons with the Athletics and Red Sox. Cullenbine had consecutive .289 and .284 seasons with Cleveland, and was subsequently traded to the Tigers, with whom he hit .335 in 1946.)

1943

January 22   Yankees obtain first baseman Nick Etten from the Phillies for catcher Tom Padden, pitcher Al Gerheauser and $10,000. (Etten was the Yankee first baseman for three years, and led the league in homeruns with 22 in 1944. Padden, never a member of the Yankees major league squad, hit .293 in 17 games with the Phillies. Gerhaeuser went 10-19 for Phila. in '43, and never had a winning record in the major leagues.)

January 25   Yankees sell pitcher Lefty Gomez to the Braves for an undisclosed amount of cash. (He never pitched for Boston, and went 0-1 with the Senators before retiring.)

January 29   Yankees obtain pitcher Bill Zuber from the Senators for infielder Gerry Priddy and pitcher Milo Candini. (Zuber went 8-4 with NY in 1943, before dropping into mediocrity for the remainder of his career. Priddy had several respectable seasons with Washington, St. Louis and Detroit. Candini went 11-7 in '43, but was ineffective thereafter.)

1944

July 6   Yankees sell outfielder Larry Rosenthal to the Athletics for an undisclosed amount. This may have been a waivers deal. (He was over-the-hill and never batted more than .204 again.)

September 1   Yankees obtain outfielder Paul Waner on waivers from the Dodgers. (There are several reports regarding exactly when this trade was made.)

1945

May 3   Yankees release outfielder Paul Waner. (He retired.)

July 27   Yankees sell pitcher Hank Borowy to the Cubs for $97,000. (Borowy went 11-2 with Chicago and helped the Cubs win the pennant in 1945. In '46, he was 12-10, but never had another winning season.)

1946

June 14   Yankees sell third baseman Hank Majeski to the Athletics for an undisclosed amount. It was probably at the waivers price. (He was washed up.)

June 18   Yankees waive pitcher Bill Zuber to the Red Sox. (He was washed up.)

June 20   Yankees purchase outfielder Hal Peck from the Athletics for an undisclosed amount believed to be in excess of the waivers price. (There is no record of Peck playing for NY in 1946. He did enjoy three good years with the Indians, commencing in '47 — see trade of December 6.)

October 19   Yankees obtain pitcher Allie Reynolds from the Indians for infielders Joe Gordon and Ed Bockman. (Reynolds spent eight highly successful years in NY, including a 20-8 mark in 1952, and was 7-2 in world series play. Gordon had three good years in Cleveland, before fading in 1950. Bockman never amounted to much.)

December 6   Yankees obtain second baseman Ray Mack and catcher Sherm Lollar from the Indians for pitchers Al Gettel and Gene Beardon, and outfielder Hal Peck. (Mack played one game for NY in 1947 and was dealt to Chicago where he batted .218. Lollar played in 19 games over two years with NY before being traded to the Browns. He had many successful seasons in St. Louis and with the White Sox, and proved himself to be a very capable backstop. Beardon went 20-7 for Cleveland in '48, but never did much else, while Gettel proved mediocre at best.)

December 10 Yankees sign free agent George McQuinn after his release by the Athletics. (McQuinn had a tremendous year in 1947, batting .304 and driving in 80 runs as the Yankee first baseman. In '48, he batted only .248, but recorded a .421 slugging percentage. He retired after the '48 season.

1947

April 23   Yankees release relief ace Johnny Murphy. (He signed with the Red Sox and pitched in 32 games in 1947, with an 0-0 mark and a 2.80 earned run average. He had three saves.)

July 11   Yankees sell pitcher Mel Queen to the Pirates for an undisclosed amount of cash. (He never did much.)

July 11   Yankees obtain pitcher Bobo Newsom from the Senators on waivers. (Newsom went 7-5 with New York and was released to the Giants in 1948.)

December 10 Yankees obtain pitcher Red Embree from the Indians for outfielder Al Clark. (Embree went 5-3 with NY and was traded to the Browns in 1948. Clark hit .310 in 1948, his best season after a .373 mark in 16 games with NY in '47.

1948

February 24   Yankees obtain pitcher Eddie Lopat from the White Sox for catcher Aaron Robinson, and pitchers Fred Bradley and Bill Wight. (Lopat starred with NY for seven straight years before being released to Baltimore in 1955. He won 21 games in 1951, led the league in percentage with a 16-4 mark in '53, and was 4-1 in the world series. Robinson proved to be a .260-270 hitter. Bradley never won a game in the major leagues, but did record a 13.50 earned run average in 1949. Wight enjoyed a moderately successful career after losing 20 games in 1948. His best year proved to be '49, when he was 15-13.)

April 12   After a fine 11-year career, the Yankees release pitcher Spud Chandler. (He retired.)

May 13   Yankees obtain outfielder Leon Culberson and $15,000 from the Senators for outfielder Eddie Stewart. (Culberson was returned to the Senators later that month. Stewart never made it.)

July 26   Yankees waive pitcher Randy Gumpert to the Cubs. (Gumpert's only effective season was in 1943, when he was 11-3 as a Yankee.)

August 9   Yankees waive pitcher Karl Drews to the Browns. (He was later traded to the Phillies, where he had his best year, 14-15 with a 2.72 earned run average, in 1952.)

December 13   Yankees obtain pitcher Fred Sanford and catcher Roy Partee from the Browns for catcher Sherm Lollar, pitcher Rich Starr and $100,000. (Sanford went 7-3 and 5-4 in 1949 and '50 before being traded to Washington. Partee never played for NY and retired. Lollar had many good years, (see 12/6/46), while Starr lasted three mediocre years.)

December 14   Yankees obtain outfielder Jim Delsing from the White Sox for outfielder Stephen Souchock. (Delsing saw very little action with NY, but did hit .381 in 17 games over parts of two seasons. He later hit .288 with Detroit in 1953. Souchock hit .234 with the Sox before joining Delsing in Detroit, where Souchock batted .302 in '53.)

1949

May 3   Yankees obtain pitcher Ed Klieman on waivers from the Senators. (He was traded 12 days later.)

May 15   Yankees sell pitcher Ed Klieman to the White Sox for an undisclosed amount of cash. (He went 2-0 with 3 saves, and was never really effective.)

August 6   Yankees sell infielder Jack Phillips to the Pirates for an undisclosed amount. (He was batting .302 at the time of the trade, and hit .293 for the Pirates in 1950 as a utility infielder.)

August 22	Yankees purchase first baseman Johnny Mize from the Giants for $40,000. (A bargain if there ever was one. Mize served five solid years with New York, and became famous for his clutch extra-base hits, and pinch hit homeruns.)
December 7	Yankees release outfielder Charlie Keller. (Keller signed with Detroit and hit .316 as a part-time player and pinch hitter in 1950.)
December 17	Yankees obtain first baseman Dick Wakefield from the Tigers for first baseman Dick Kryhoski. (Wakefield went one-for-two as a pinch hitter, and then became involved in the infamous Wakefield Battle of 1950. Kryhoski had several respectable seasons with Detroit and the Browns, including a .287 mark in 1951.)

1950

April 28	Yankees obtain (albeit, temporarily) pitcher Joe Ostrowski from the White Sox for first baseman Dick Wakefield. (Wakefield refused to report to Chicago unless the Sox gave him a $5,000 raise as compensation for the world series share he believed he would receive as a Yankee. He also claimed that he had signed as a Yankee for less than he wanted because of the expectation of that series money. The issue was brought to Commissioner Chandler, who ruled in favor of the White Sox, nullified the trade, and ordered Wakefield returned to NY, and Ostrowski to Chicago.)
May 15	Yankees waive outfielder Johnny Lindell to the Cardinals. (Lindell had a terrible season during which he suffered emotionally from the trade. After a two season absence from the big leagues, he returned with the Pirates and Phillies in 1953, and combined for a .303 batting average, before calling it a career after the '54 season.)
May 15	Yankees sell pitcher Clarence Marshall to the Browns for an undisclosed amount of cash. (He went 1-3 and retired.)
June 15	Yankees finally obtain pitcher Joe Ostrowski (for keeps) along with pitchers Tom Ferrick and Sid Schacht, and third baseman Leo Thomas from the Browns for infielder Snuffy Stirnweiss, outfielder Jim Delsing, pitchers Don Johnson and Duane Pillette, and $50,000. (Ostrowski proved to be a valuable long relief man, and notched a 6-4 record with 5 saves in 1951. Ferrick went 8-4 in 1950, and was sent to Washington in '51. Schacht never played for NY and was returned to the Browns, as was Thomas, and neither did much.
	Stirnweiss was washed up, Delsing was mediocre, Johnson failed to help the Browns, and Pillette would have been effective on a better team. Of course, the $50,000 came in handy for the near-bankrupt Browns.)
June 16	Yankees waive catcher Gus Niarhos to the White Sox, although the actual purchase-transfer does not occur for several days. (He hit .324 with Chicago that year, and then lapsed into obscurity.)

September 5   Yankees purchase infielder Johnny Hopp from the Pirates for an amount said to be greater than the waiver price. (Hopp hit .333 down the stretch and helped NY win its second consecutive pennant. His bat failed him in 1951, and he was unloaded on the Tigers, where he hit .217 and then retired.)

December 18   Tommy Henrich is released (retires) as an active player and is signed on as a coach for the 1951 season.

1951

May 14   Yankees obtain first baseman Don Bollweg and $15,000 from the Cardinals for third baseman Billy Johnson. (Bollweg reached a career high .297 with NY, and after being dealt away in 1952, never reached the .220 mark again. Johnson hit .262 with the Cards in '51, with 24 doubles, but that proved to be the last good year of his career.)

June 15   Yankees obtain pitchers Bob Kuzava and Bob Ross from the Senators for pitchers Fred Sanford, Bob Porterfield, and Tom Ferrick. (Kuzava went 8-4 with NY in 1951, and recorded two saves during his three world series appearances as a Yankee. Ross never made the Yankees, and his lowest single-season major league earned run average of 6.54 explained why. Sanford went 2-3 with Washington and was forwarded to St. Louis, where he went 2-4 and then retired. Porterfield had a 22-10 mark in 1953, and might have been a 20-game-winner in '52, '54, and '55 if he had remained in NY. Ferrick saw little action with Washington, compiled a 6-3 mark over two seasons, and then retired.)

June 15   Yankees acquire pitcher Frank Overmire from the Browns for pitcher Tom Byrne and $25,000. (Overmire saw limited action with NY and went 1-1 in 1951. He was traded to the Browns in '52, where he finished his career. Byrne was not successful in St. Louis, but he would return to the pinstripes in 1954, and would enjoy four more good seasons in NY.)

July 31   Yankees obtain pitchers Bob Hogue and Lou Sleater, third baseman Kermit Wahl, and shortstop Tom Upton from the Browns for outfielder Cliff Mapes. (Hogue was largely ineffective, and was returned to the Browns the following season. Sleater never made it to the Yankees major league roster and was returned to St. Louis. Upton and Wahl suffered similar fates and also went back to St. Louis. Mapes lasted one season).

August 29   Yankees purchase pitcher Johnny Sain from the Braves for $50,000 and pitcher Lew Burdette. (Sain helped the Yankees win the pennant and world series during three of the next four seasons, and recorded a league-leading 22 saves in 1954.

Burdette came back to haunt the Yankees in the 1957 world series, when he beat them three times. He enjoyed several very fine seasons with the Braves, and was a 20 game winner in 1958 and '59.

195

November 23 Yankees obtain pitcher Jim McDonald from the Browns for Clint Courtney. (McDonald went 16-12 over three seasons in NY, and batted a surprising .316 in 1952. Courtney proved to be a competent catcher and .300 hitter, but never would have beaten out Berra and Howard.)

December 1   Yankees release Tommy Henrich as a coach.

1952

March 26   Yankees waive infielder Gene Mauch to the Cardinals. (Mauch proved to be little more than a utility infielder, although he did hit over .300 on two occasions, albeit in very few at-bats.)

April 7   Yankees waive pitcher Dave Madison to the Browns. (His three-year career stats are 8-7 with five saves. Nothing more need be said.)

May 3   Yankees obtain outfielder Irv Noren from the Senators for outfielders Jackie Jensen and Archie Wilson, infielder Jerry Snyder, and pitcher Spec Shea. (Noren had three solid seasons out of four in NY, including a .319 batting average in 1954.

             Jensen proved to be a fine outfielder and hitter with the Senators and Red Sox. He hit .315 in 1956, and ended his career at .279 lifetime. Wilson hit .228 with the Senators and disappeared from the major leagues. Snyder filled the utility infielder role in Washington, and hit .339 in 31 games in 1953, but was no loss. Shea was mistakenly written off as over-the-hill and came back to notch 11-7 and 12-7 marks with Washington in '52 and '53.)

May 13   Yankees waive pitcher Frank Overmire to the Browns. (He went 0-3 and retired.)

May 26   Yankees release infielder Johnny Hopp to the Tigers for minimal considerations. This meant less than the waiver price. (He hit .217 and retired.)

August 1   Yankees purchase pitcher Johnny Schmitz from the Dodgers for an undisclosed amount. (He went 1-1, was sent to the Reds on a conditional basis in September, was returned to NY at the start of the '53 season, went 0-0, and was then sent on to Washington where he went 11-8 in 1954.)

August 4   Yankees sell pitcher Bob Hogue to the Browns for an undisclosed amount. This was probably a waiver deal. (He went 0-1 and retired.)

August 22   Yankees purchase pitcher Ray Scarborough from the Red Sox on waivers. (He went 5-1 with NY in 1952 and helped the Yankees win their fourth straight pennant and world championship. Midway through the '53 season he was forwarded to Detroit where he went 0-2 and retired.)

August 28   Yankees purchase pitcher Ewell Blackwell from the Reds as part of a deal which sent pitchers Johnny Schmitz and Ernie Nevel, and outfielders Bob Marquis and Jim Greengrass to Cincinnati. (Blackwell went 3-0 with two saves over the month of September and the '53 season.

The Reds returned Schmitz to the Yankees after he went 1-0 in September. Nevel went 0-0 with a 6.10 earned run average in '53, and disappeared from the major leagues. Greengrass hit .309 in 17 games with the Reds in '52, and notched .285 and .280 marks in '53 and '54. Marquis never did much after hitting .273 in '53.)

1953

February 16   The Reds return pitcher Johnny Schmitz to the Yankees.

April 26   Yankees sell third baseman Loren Babe to the Athletics for approximately $30,000. (He never did well in the major leagues.)

May 13   Yankees waive pitcher Johnny Schmitz to the Senators. (He went 2-7 in '53, but turned it around for an 11-8 mark in '54. He should have quit after the '54 season.)

June 12   Yankees purchase infielder Willie Miranda from the Browns for an undisclosed amount believed to be greater than the waivers price.

Miranda did not amount to much and was sent to Baltimore after the 1954 season.)

December 16   Yankees obtain third baseman Loren Babe, first baseman Eddie Robinson, pitcher Harry Byrd, and outfielders Tom Hamilton and Carmen Mauro from the Athletics for first basemen Vic Power and Don Bollweg, outfielder Bill Renna, catcher Jim Robertson, third baseman Jim Finigan and pitcher John Gray.

(Loren Babe was buried in the minor leagues upon his return to NY. Robinson proved a solid pinch hitter, leading the league with 15 pinch hits in 49 attempts in 1954. Byrd went 9-7 with a 2.99 earned run average and was then exiled to Baltimore. Hamilton and Mauro never made the Yankees.

Vic Power became a fine hitter, thrice topping the .300 mark in a solid 12-year career. Bollweg faded fast. Renna was mediocre for five years. Robertson played 54 games in his two-year career. Finigan became a utility infielder and Gray a futility pitcher with a 6.18 lifetime earned run average.)

1954

February 23   Yankees sell pitcher Vic Raschi to the Cardinals for $85,000. (He lasted two years, but was unable to pitch .500 ball.)

April 11   Yankees obtain outfielder Enos Slaughter from the Cardinals for pitcher Mel Wright, outfielders Bill Virdon and Emil Tellinger, and catcher Hal Smith. (Slaughter saw two tours of action with NY, the first being the less successful, largely because Slaughter was upset about the trade. He was dealt to Kansas City in 1955 and returned to NY in '56, and enjoyed nearly three solid seasons over a four-year span.

Wright spent four years in the majors, compiling a 2-4 mark, and a career 7.61 earned run average. Virdon established himself as a fine outfielder and came back to haunt the Yankees in the 1960 world series. Tellinger never made it. Smith had three good years in St. Louis, and also came back to haunt NY in the 1960 world series.)

May 11   Yankees sell infielder Jim Brideweser to the Orioles for an undisclosed amount. This may have been a waiver deal. (Brideweser proved himself to be an adequate utility infielder.)

July 4   Yankees obtain pitcher Marlin Stewart on waivers from the Orioles. (He never played for the Yankees.)

August 8   Yankees waive pitcher Bob Kuzava to the Orioles. (He went 1-3 with Baltimore in 1954, bounced around with the Phillies, Pirates and Cardinals over the next two years, and then disappeared from the major leagues.)

August 22   Yankees obtain pitcher Jim Konstanty from the Phillies on waivers. (He proved a valuable acquisition for a couple of years, including a 7-2 mark in 1955.)

September 3   Yankees purchase pitcher Tommy Byrne from Seattle of the Pacific Coast League. It is generally believed that the Yankees paid more than $50,000, but the amount remained undisclosed. (Byrne went 16-5 with NY in 1955 and totaled four solid seasons in the pinstripes.)

November 18   Yankees obtain pitchers Don Larsen and Bob Turley, and shortstop Billy Hunter from the Orioles for outfielder Gene Woodling, pitchers Jim McDonald and Harry Byrd, catchers Hal Smith (not the same one who was traded to St. Louis) and Gus Triandos, and shortstop Willie Miranda. (Larsen went 45-24 during his five seasons in NY, and pitched a perfect game in the 1956 world series. Turley also enjoyed great success as a Yankee, including a league-leading 21-7 mark in 1958. Hunter was a respectable utility infielder.

Woodling lasted eight more years, batted more than .300 three times, and proved he was far from over-the-hill. McDonald went 3-5 with Baltimore and was traded to the White Sox, where he did nothing. Byrd went 3-2 with the Orioles, was sent on to the White Sox, and faded fast. Smith became a 10-year man and batted .303 in 1957, but never would have replaced Berra or Howard in NY. Triandos proved himself an adequate backstop and lasted 13 years. Miranda was a light-hitting infielder.)

December 1   Yankees obtain first baseman Dick Kryhoski, catcher Darrell Johnson, pitcher Mike Blyzka, and outfielders Jim Fridley and Ted del Guercio from the Orioles for pitcher Bill Miller, third baseman Kal Segrist, second baseman Don Leppert and a minor leaguer to be named later. (Kryhoski was sold to KC in March, 1955. Johnson proved a marginal part-time catcher for two years with NY. Blyzka never played on the Yankees; nor did Fridley and del Guercio.

Miller pitched in five games in 1955 and was dropped by the Orioles. Segrist went 3-for-9 as a utility infielder and was released. Leppert hit .114 in 40 games and was also released.)

1955

March 30   Yankees sell pitchers Ewell Blackwell and Tom Gorman, and first baseman Dick Kryhoski to the Athletics for $50,000. (No loss.)

May 11   Yankees obtain pitcher Sonny Dixon from the Athletics for outfielder Enos Slaughter and pitcher Johnny Sain. (Dixon pitched in three games and went 0-1 before disappearing from the major leagues. Slaughter would be back. Sain was over-the-hill.)

May 11   Yankees sell pitcher Art Schallock to the Orioles for an undisclosed amount of cash. (He went 3-5 with the Orioles and was released.)

September 11 Yankees obtain pitcher Gerry Staley on waivers from the Reds. (Staley went 0-0 in three Yankee appearances, and was waived to the White Sox.)

1956

February 8   Yankees obtain pitcher Maury McDermott and shortstop Bob Kline from the Senators for pitchers Bob Wiesler and Lou Berberet, outfielders Dick Tettelbach and Whitey Herzog, and second baseman Herb Plews. (McDermott went 2-6 and was sent to KC in 1957. Kline never made the Yankees.

Wiesler went 4-13 over three seasons in Washington. Berberet never made the Senators. Tettelbach hit .150 over two seasons. Herzog later had a few good years in KC and Baltimore. Plews had a respectable three-year stint in Washington.)

May 28   Yankees waive pitcher Gerry Staley to the White Sox. (Staley went 8-3 in 1956, and compiled a 38-25 mark over five seasons.)

June 14   Yankees obtain outfielder Bill Renna, pitcher Ed Burtschy, and an undisclosed amount of cash from the Athletics for outfielder Lou Skizas and first baseman Eddie Robinson. (Renna hit .314 in 40 games with NY back in 1953, but never made it back to NY the second time around. Burtschy also labored in the minors.)

(Skizas hit .316 with K.C. that year, but faded fast after that. Robinson never batted more than .204 after leaving NY.)

August 25   Yankees purchase Enos Slaughter from the Athletics for an amount believed to exceed $50,000, despite reports of a mere waiver price. (Slaughter was outstanding in a Yankee uniform for the next three seasons as a part-time outfielder and pinch hitter.)

199

October 16	Yankees sell outfielder Bob Cerv to the Athletics for an undisclosed amount. (Cerv had three solid years in KC before being returned to the Yankees in 1960.)
December 11	Yankees obtain catcher Harry Chiti and two minor leaguers from the Cubs for catcher Charlie Silvera. (Chiti never played for the Yankees. Silvera hit .208 and retired.)

1957

February 19	Yankees obtain pitchers Art Ditmar and Bobby Shantz, and infielders Clete Boyer, Jack McMahon and Wayne Belardi from the Athletics for pitchers Rip Coleman, Tom Morgan and Maury McDermott, shortstop Billy Hunter, and outfielders Irv Noren and Milt Graff.

(Ditmar went 47-32 over slightly more than four full seasons before being unloaded back to KC at the end of his career. Shantz went 30-18 over four seasons before being traded to the Pirates in 1960. Boyer was not allowed to report to the Yankees right away because of a clause in his bonus contract, but he subsequently anchored third base for the championship teams of the late '50's and early '60's. Belardi and McMahon never made it to the varsity in NY.

Coleman went 2-19 in his remaining three major league seasons. Morgan went 29-25 during roughly six seasons with several clubs. McDermott went 2-4 over three seasons. Hunter never bettered the .191 mark in his two remaining years. Noren had one more good season left in him; 1959, .311. Graff's best year was '57, when he hit .181.)

June 15	Yankees obtain pitcher Ryne Duren, outfielders Jim Pisoni and Harry Simpson from the Athletics for pitcher Ralph Terry, infielder Billy Martin, and outfielders Woodie Held and Bob Martyn.

(Duren became the legendary bespectacled reliever whose overpowering fastball made him a favorite with Yankee fans. Frequently, his entry into a game came complete with wild warm-up pitches into the screen and seats. Unfortunately, he ran into a serious alcohol problem, and that combined with an arm injury to prematurely end his Yankee career. He lead the league in saves with 20 in 1958.

Pisoni was returned to KC and proved a weak outfielder. Simpson proved a fair outfielder over the next season-and-a-half before being returned to KC.

Terry went 17-28 with KC over roughly two seasons, but returned to NY and had several good years. Martin was never the same after leaving NY. He never hit more than .267, but lasted 13 more years in the majors. Martyn hit .263 over three seasons.)

September 1	Yankees obtain pitcher Sal Maglie from the Dodgers for $25,000 plus two minor leaguers to be named later. (He went 2-0 with 4

saves for NY that year, but dropped to 3-7 in 1958, a year he split with NY and the Cardinals. He retired after the '58 season.)

September 10   Yankees obtain outfielder Bobby Del Greco for an undisclosed amount of cash from the Cubs. This may have been a waiver deal. (Del Greco responded with a .429 average for the remainder of the season, but never did much after that one hot month.)

1958

May 14   Yankees sell pitcher Al Cicotte to the Senators on waivers. (He went 8-11 over his remaining four seasons.)

June 15   Yankees obtain pitchers Virgil Trucks and Duke Maas from Kansas City for pitcher Bob Grim and outfielder Harry Simpson.

(Trucks went 2-1 in 25 games with NY and retired. Maas went 7-3 that year, 14-8 in '59, and 5-1 in '60 before fading.

Grim went 16-19 over three seasons. Simpson was mediocre for a season-and-a-half before leaving the major leagues.)

August 21   Yankees obtain pitcher Murry Dickson from the Athletics for a player to be named later. It was outfielder John Bella. (Dickson proved ineffective and lasted less than a year. Bella hit .207 in 1959, his only remaining major league season.)

1959

April 12   Yankees obtain outfielder Bob Martyn and infielder Mike Baxes from the Athletics for outfielder Russ Snyder and shortstop Tom Carroll. (Martyn and Baxes did nothing and never made the Yankees. Snyder was a rare Yankee mistake. He went on to enjoy 12 solid seasons in the big leagues and batted over .300 three times. Carroll hit .143 in '59 and was released.)

May 8   Yankees obtain pitcher Mark Freeman from the Athletics for pitcher Murry Dickson. (Freeman played in one game for NY, spent the next season in Chicago, and retired from the major leagues with a 5.56 earned run average.

Dickson went 2-1 and then retired.)

May 26   Yankees re-obtain pitcher Ralph Terry, and outfielder Hector Lopez from the Athletics for pitchers Johnny Kucks and Tom Sturdivant, and infielder Jerry Lumpe.

(Terry went 76-56 over five-and-one-half seasons in NY, including a 23-12 season in 1962. Lopez proved a valuable hitter for roughly seven seasons, although his fielding was rather erratic. He is well-known for his clutch extra-base hits.

Kucks went 12-21 over the '59-60 seasons and never pitched in the big leagues again. Sturdivant had one more good year, 9-5 in'62. Lumpe proved himself a fine second baseman with a good stick, including a .300 season in '62.)

December 15   Yankees sign free agent Elmer Valo after his release by the
               Indians. (He was at the tail end of his career and lasted one more
               season — split between Minnesota and Philadelphia — after
               splitting the '60 season between NY and Washington.)

December 17   Yankees obtain outfielder Roger Maris, infielder Joe DeMaestri
               and first baseman Kent Hadley from the Athletics for outfielders
               Hank Bauer and Norm Siebern, pitcher Don Larsen and first
               baseman Marv Throneberry.

               (Maris had three tremendous years in NY, and played in the
               pinstripes until 1966. DeMaestri proved an adequate utility man,
               and Hadley a fair substitute first baseman for one year.

               Bauer saw limited action with KC over two seasons, batting
               roughly .270, and then retired. Siebern eventually moved over to
               first base and became a .280-.310 hitter for several years. Larsen
               went 26-34 over the next seven years, including a 1-10 mark in
               1960. However, he rebounded with an 8-2 mark in '61.
               Throneberry became a legend with the early NY Mets . . . nothing
               more need be said.)

1960

May 19   Yankees re-obtain outfielder Bob Cerv from Kansas City for
               infielder Andy Carey.

               (Cerv hit .250 over 87 games and was lost to the Angels in the
               expansion draft. He was re-obtained a third time in 1961.

               Carey was never very effective after leaving NY.)

May 23   Yankees release outfielder Elmer Valo. (He may have been waived
               to the Senators. In any case, he was at the end of a fine career.)

August 22   Yankees obtain first baseman Dale Long from the Giants on
               waivers. (This was the first of three stints in a Yankee uniform for
               Long. He hit .366 in 26 games before being lost to Washington in
               the expansion draft.)

December 14   Yankees lose outfielders Bob Cerv and Ken Hunt, and pitcher Elia
               Grba to the Angels in the first expansion draft. (Cerv would be
               re-obtained in a May trade. Hunt and Grba never amounted to
               much.)

December 14   Yankees lose first baseman Dale Long and pitcher John Gabler to
               the expansion Senators.

               (Long returned to NY in 1962. Gabler went 3-8 and was
               released.)

December 16   Yankees obtain infielder Harry Bright, pitcher Bennie Daniels,
               and first baseman R.C. Stevens from the Pirates for pitcher
               Bobby Shantz.

(Bright subsequently went to the Reds before being re-obtained by NY in 1963. Daniels was forwarded to the Senators, as was Stevens.

Shantz went 20-16 over four seasons, but never recovered his fine form of the early '50's.)

December 16   Yankees purchase pitcher Dan McDevitt from the Dodgers for an undisclosed amount. (He went 1-2 and was traded to Minnesota.)

1961

April 3   Yankees obtain pitcher Duke Maas from the Angels for shortstop Fritz rickell. (Maas never pitched in the major leagues again. Brickell hit .122 with L.A.)

May 10   Yankees re-obtain outfielder Bob Cerv, and obtain pitcher Truman Clevenger from the Angels for pitcher Ryne Duren and John James, outfielder Leroy Thomas, and a player to be named later.

(Cerv hit .271 in 1961, but faltered in '62, when he was unloaded to Houston. Clevenger compiled a 3-1 record over two seasons in NY and then retired.

Duren was battling alcoholism and was never the same pitcher he had been in NY. James went 0-2 and disappeared from the major leagues. Thomas had two .280-plus years with L.A.)

June 14   Yankees obtain pitcher Bud Daley from the Athletics for pitcher and first baseman Deron Johnson.

(Daley went 18-16 in three mediocre seasons in NY, but did win a game in the world series. Johnson bounced around quite a bit, but did have several strong years, particularly 1965 when he led the N.L. with 130 runs batted in.)

June 14   Yankees obtain infielder Billy Gardner from the Twins for pitcher Dan McDevitt.

(Gardner remained the good defense, weak bat, player he always was. McDevitt went 1-3 over a season-and-a-half after leaving NY.)

October 16   Yankees purchase pitcher Robin Roberts from the Phillies for an undisclosed amount of cash. (The Yankees made a big mistake cutting Roberts in spring training because he signed with the Orioles and had three good years. In fact, he almost cost NY the pennant in '63 and '64.)

December 14   Yankees obtain pitcher Marshall Bridges from the Reds for catcher Jesse Gonder. (Bridges went 8-4 with 18 saves in 1962 before fading. Gonder hit .304 as a part-time player with the Reds and Mets in '63, but was never much after that.)

June 12	Yankees obtain outfielder Tom Umphlett and an undisclosed amount of cash from the Red Sox for infielder Billy Gardner. (Another swap of weak players.)
November 26	Yankees obtain pitcher Stan Williams from the Dodgers for first baseman Moose Skowron.

(Williams went 9-8 with two saves in 1963, but was later traded to Cleveland, where he enjoyed a pair of good years.

Skowron had a pair of strong seasons in '64-'65 after an off year in '63, but was never the same player he had been in NY.)

1963

April 21	Yankees obtain pitcher Steve Hamilton from the Senators for pitcher Jim Coates.

(Hamilton spent close to seven seasons in New York, and is best remembered for his hesitation blooper pitch called the "Folly Floater" and a wicked side-armed curve.

Coates went 6-8 over four seasons.)

April 21	Yankees re-purchase infielder Harry Bright from the Reds for an undisclosed amount. (Bright never did very much in NY.)

1964

September 5	Yankees purchase pitcher Pedro Ramos from the Indians for an undisclosed amount. (Ramos was super in '65, with 19 saves, but the Yankees were on their way down by that time.)

1965

March 30	Yankees sell pitcher Stan Williams to the Indians for an undisclosed amount. He had a few good years left in him, including a 10-1 mark with 15 saves in 1970.)
May 3	Yankees obtain catcher Doc Edwards from the Athletics for catcher John Blanchard and pitcher Rollie Sheldon.

(Blanchard and Edwards were washed up. Sheldon had one more good year, 10-8, and then failed.)

May 10	Yankees obtain first baseman Buddy Barker from the Indians for infielder Pedro Gonzalez. (Both were mediocre at best . . . very mediocre.)
May 6	Yankees obtain shortstop Bill Bethea from the Twins on waivers. (He never made it.)
November 12	Yankees obtain infielder Ruben Amaro from the Phillies for infielder Phil Linz.

204

(Amaro never hit more than .223 in a Yankee uniform, although his infamous collision with Tom Tresh while chasing a pop fly may have accounted for his failure to live up to the Yankees' expectations.

Linz wound up with the '68 Mets.)

December 10   Yankees obtain pitcher Bob Friend from the Pirates for pitcher Pete Mikkelsen.

(Friend was in the final season of what had been a fine career. Mikkelsen had five good years as a reliever in the N.L.)

1966

January 4   Yankees obtain outfielder Lu Clinton from the Indians for catcher Doc Edwards. (Neither did much. In fact, Edwards never played for Cleveland, and Clinton hit .220 in NY.)

May 11   Yankees purchase shortstop Dick Schofield from the Giants for an undisclosed amount. This may have been a waivers deal. (Schofield was not the answer to the Yankees' infield problems.)

June 10   Yankees obtain pitcher Fred Talbot from the Athletics for outfielder Roger Repoz, and pitchers Gil Blanco and Bill Stafford.

Talbot went 7-7 in NY that year, slipped to 6-8 in '67, and then plunged to 1-9 in '68 before being unloaded on the hapless Pilots.

(Repoz was a fair outfielder who showed occasional power, but never hit more than .240 for any extended period of time. Stafford went 0-5 over his final two major league seasons. Blanco went 2-4 in his final major league season.)

June 15   Yankees sell pitcher Bob Friend to the Mets for an undisclosed amount of cash. (He was finished.)

September 10 Yankees obtain pitcher Thad Tillotson and an undisclosed amount of cash from the Dodgers for shortstop Dick Schofield. (Tillotson went 4-9 over two seasons. Schofield remained a mediocre utility infielder.)

October 19   Yankees release pitcher Whitey Ford and outfielder Hector Lopez.

November 20 Yankees obtain outfielder Bill Robinson from the Braves for infielder Clete Boyer.

(Robinson was billed as the next Mickey Mantle, but never lived up to that billing in a Yankee uniform. In fact, he was very weak. He later did well in the N.L.

Boyer played five solid seasons with Atlanta before retiring.)

| December 8 | Yankees obtain third baseman Charlie Smith from the Cardinals for outfielder Roger Maris. (Maris helped the Cards win the pennant, while Smith helped NY finish in ninth place.) |

December 8 — Yankees obtain third baseman Charlie Smith from the Cardinals for outfielder Roger Maris. (Maris helped the Cards win the pennant, while Smith helped NY finish in ninth place.)

December 20 — Yankees obtain infielder Dick Howser from the Indians for pitcher Gil Downs and an undisclosed amount of cash. (Howser hit .268 in '67, but collapsed in '68. Fortunately, he was retained as a coach after that, and became one of the best third base coaches in the game.)

Downs was appropriately named because he was sent to the minors and never heard from again.)

1967

February 7 — Yankees obtain pitcher Joe Verbanic from the Phillies for pitcher Pedro Ramos.

(Verbanic went 11-10 in three years. Ramos went 4-4 in three.)

April 3 — Yankees obtain infielder John Kennedy from the Dodgers for outfielder John Miller, pitcher Jack Cullen, and the temporary transfer of outfielder Roy White to the Dodgers' Tacoma farm club.

(If the only player you've heard of involved in this deal is White, there's a good reason.)

June 2 — Yankees sign free agent pitcher Bill Monbouquette after his release by the Tigers. (He pitched .500 ball for NY over one season.)

July 4 — Yankees obtain pitcher Steve Barber from the Orioles for first baseman Buddy Barker, two minor leaguers, and an undisclosed amount of cash. (Unfortunately, the Yankees got Barber after his sore arm woes of '66. Then again, the Orioles were unfortunate to get Barker.)

August 3 — Yankees obtain pitchers Ron Klimkowski and Pete Magrini from the Red Sox for catcher Elston Howard. (Klim was a mediocre pitcher. Magrini was less than that. Howard was at the end of the line, but did help Boston win the pennant that year.)

August 8 — Yankees purchase catcher Bob Tillman from the Red Sox for an undisclosed amount. (He hit .254 that year, but never came close to that mark again.)

September 18 — Yankees purchase outfielder Len Boehmer from the Reds for an undisclosed amount. (His best showing in NY was .176 in 1969.)

September 18 — Yankees sell pitcher Bill Henry to the Reds for an undisclosed amount. (He never reached the major leagues again.)

November 20 — Yankees obtain third baseman Bobby Cox from the Braves for catcher Bob Tillman and pitcher Dale Roberts. (Cox lasted two years, never hit more than .229, and wisely became a minor league manager and coach with the Yankee organization. Tillman lasted a few seasons with the Braves, but never hit more than .238. Roberts never made the Braves.)

November 30   Yankees purchase shortstop Gene Michael from the Dodgers for an undisclosed amount. (Michael actually hit .272 in 1969, and remained the Yankee shortstop through the '73 season. In '74 he platooned with Jim Mason, and was sent to Detroit for '75. He subsequently returned to NY as a coach and minor league manager.)

December 2   Yankees purchase catcher John Boccabella from the Cubs for an undisclosed amount. (He never played for the Yankees, was sent to the Expos, and proved a fair utility catcher-first baseman.)

1968

May 16   Yankees purchase pitcher John Wyatt from the Red Sox for an undisclosed amount. This may have been a waiver deal. (He was washed up.)

June 15   Yankees sign free agent Rocky Colavito after his release by the Dodgers. (He was at the end of a fine career, hit .220 for NY, but earned eternal fame by pitching and winning a late-season game.)

June 15   Yankees sell pitcher John Wyatt to the Tigers for $30,000. (See May 16.)

July 12   Yankees obtain pitcher Lindy McDaniel from the Giants for pitcher Bill Monbouquette.

(This was a great trade for the Yankees. McDaniel had three good years out of five in NY, including a 9-5, 25-save season in 1970. To top matters off, he was the bait for Lou Piniella's acquisition in late 1973.

Monbouquette was washed up.)

September 30   Yankees purchase pitcher Jim Rooker from the Tigers on waivers. (He never played in NY, but subsequently had three fine years in the N.L.)

October 7   Yankees release Rocky Colavito. (He retired.)

October 29   Yankees release Dick Howser (as a player) and immediately sign him as a coach.

November 6   Yankees sell infielder Ruben Amaro to the Angels for an undisclosed amount believed to be greater than the waiver price. (He hit .222 and retired.)

November 13   Yankees sell infielder John Kennedy to the Pilots for an undisclosed amount. (He hit .234, was traded to Boston, had a couple of good years, and then faded.)

207

December 4	Yankees obtain outfielder Dick Simpson from the Astros for pitcher Dooley Womack. (Simpson hit .273 in six games and was banished to Seattle. Womack was a mediocre reliever after leaving NY.)
December 4	Yankees obtain pitcher Mike Kekich from the Dodgers for outfielder Andy Kosco. (Kekich had a couple of fair seasons in NY, dropped below .500 after 1971, and then became involved in the infamous "wife-swap" affair with pitcher Fritz Peterson. This guaranteed an early exit, in his case, to Cleveland.

Kosco never lived up to the power-hitter expectations the Yankees had, although he did hit 19 homeruns with the Dodgers in '69. He was a fair outfielder and hitter.) |
| December 6 | Yankees obtain infielder Nate Oliver from the Giants for infielder Charlie Smith. (Nothing for nothing leaves nothing.) |

1969

April 14	Yankees purchase outfielder Jimmie Hall from the Indians for an undisclosed amount. (He hit .236 in 80 games in NY and was sent to the Cubs.)
May 19	Yankees obtain outfielder Jose Vidal from the Pilots for outfielder Dick Simpson. (Vidal never made the Yankees and Simpson hit .176 in Seattle.)
May 20	Yankees obtain pitcher Jack Aker from the Pilots for pitcher Fred Talbot. (Aker had notched two solid seasons as a reliever in NY. Talbot was never successful in Seattle.)
June 9	Yankees purchase pitcher Ken Johnson from the Braves for an undisclosed amount. (He was washed up.)
June 12	Yankees obtain pitcher Rob Gardner from the A's for catcher John Orsino. (Gardner would soon be sent back to Oakland, be re-acquired by NY, and have one good season. Orsino is listed as an outfielder in most rosters . . . the last of which was that of Washington in 1967!)
June 14	Yankees obtain outfielder Ron Woods from the Tigers for outfielder-infielder Tom Tresh. (Woods was a fair outfielder who lasted roughly two years in NY. Tresh was at the end of a fine career which had been hampered by injuries.)
July 26	Yankees sell outfielder Billy Cowan to the Angels for an undisclosed amount of cash. (Cowan hit .276 the next two years in California before fading.)
August 11	Yankees sell pitcher Ken Johnson to the Cubs for an undisclosed amount. This may have been a waiver deal. (He was finished.)

September 11   Yankees obtain pitcher Terry Bongiovanni from the Cubs for outfielder Jimmie Hall. (Bongio never made it. Hall was at the end of the line.)

December 4   Yankees obtain first baseman Curt Blefary from the Astros for first baseman-outfielder Joe Pepitone.

(Blefary murdered Yankee pitching while with the Orioles in the mid-60's. Unfortunately, he continued to contribute to the Yankee pitchers' woes while wearing the pinstripes because he just never lived up to the expectations of a left hand power hitter the Yankees had for him.

Pepitone had four good years left in him, including a .307 mark in '71 with the Cubs.)

December 5   Yankees obtain first baseman-third baseman Danny Cater from the A's for pitcher Al Downing and catcher Frank Fernandez.

(Cater hit .301 with NY in '70, dropped to '276 in '71, and was dispatched to Boston in the GREAT Sparky Lyle deal.

Downing still had arm problems, so the A's sent him to Los Angeles in '71, where he went 20-9. Fernandez was a weak catcher.)

December 18   Yankees obtain infielder Pete Ward from the White Sox for pitcher Mickey Scott and an undisclosed amount of cash. (Another nothing trade because Ward was at the end of a good career.)

1970

January 6   Yankees purchase outfielder Rick Bladt from the Cubs for an undisclosed amount of cash. (He is best remembered for being traded to Baltimore in the 1977 Paul Blair deal.)

February 28   Yankees purchase infielder Ron Hansen from the White Sox for an undisclosed amount. (Unfortunately, he was also at the end of his career.)

May 15   Yankees obtain pitcher Gary Waslewski from the Expos for the first baseman Dave McDonald. (They both did nothing.)

July 20   Yankees obtain pitcher Mike McCormick from the Giants for pitcher John Cumberland. (McCormick went 2-0 in eight games and was sent back to the Giants. Cumberland went 9-6 in '71, his only good season.)

September 9   Yankees sell pitcher Steve Hamilton to the Cubs for an undisclosed amount of cash. (He had a couple of mediocre years and retired.)

209

1971

April 9   Yankees obtain first baseman-outfielder Felipe Alou from the A's for pitchers Rob Gardner and Ron Klimkowski.

(Alou hit .289 in 131 games in 1971, .278 in 120 games in '72, but faded in '73 and was sold to Montreal. Gardner did nothing for Oakland and returned to NY a month later. Klimkowski also did little, and returned to NY in '72.)

May 26   Yankees obtain pitcher Rob Gardner from the A's for first baseman Curt Blefary. (Gardner went 8-5 in '72 with NY, his only good year. Blefary never lived up to his potential.)

May 28   Yankees obtain pitcher Jim Hardin from the Orioles for pitcher Bill Burbach. (Neither did much.)

June 7   Yankees obtain outfielder Danny Walton from the Brewers for outfielder-first baseman Frank Tepedino and outfielder Bobby Mitchell. (Walton never lived up to the right handed power hitter the Yankees were expecting. Tepedino and Mitchell never did much, either.)

June 25   Yankees obtain outfielder Ron Swoboda from the Expos for outfielder Ron Woods. (Both proved to be mediocre outfielders.)

October 13   Yankees obtain pitcher Rich Hinton from the Indians for outfielder Jim Lyttle. (Hinton went 1-0 with NY and was sent to Texas midway through the season. Lyttle was an adequate substitute outfielder who never approached his .310 season in NY in '70.)

December 1   Yankees obtain infielder Bernie Allen from Texas for pitchers Terry Ley and Gary Jones. (Allen was a successful pinch hitter with NY in 1972. Ley and Jones never did much.)

December 2   Yankees obtain infielder Rich McKinney from the White Sox for pitcher Stan Bahnsen. A DISASTROUS DEAL!

(McKinney, an adequate second baseman with a .280-type bat, was unable to make the adjustment to third base in NY. His fielding was atrocious, his hitting died, and he was relieved to be traded to Oakland after the season.

Bahnsen had been a fine young right handed pitcher in NY, and won 21 games for the White Sox in 1973. He had three more respectable years for weak teams, and then faded.)

1972

January 17   Yankees purchase outfielder John Callison from the Cubs for an undisclosed amount of cash. (He hit .258 as a part-time outfielder and pinch hitter in 1972, and proved a valuable acquisition for that season.)

January 19	Yankees purchase pitcher Fred Beene from the Orioles. (Beene had a great assortment of curves which helped him to a 6-0 start in '73 before an injury ruined his career.)
February 2	Yankees purchase utility infielder Hal Lanier from the Giants. (He remained a utility infielder with a weak bat.)
March 22	Yankees obtain pitcher Sparky Lyle from the Red Sox for first baseman Danny Cater and shortstop Mario Guerrero.
	(Lyle became the greatest relief pitcher in baseball history. He led the league in saves with 35 in 1972, notched 27 in '73, won the Cy Young Award in '77, and has repeatedly been selected to All Star teams.
	Cater and Guerrero simply never did a comparable job, although each had respectable seasons.)
March 31	Yankees purchase outfielder Frank Tepedino from the Brewers for $40,000. (He did nothing for NY in his second stay in the pinstripes.)
April 3	Yankees release pitcher Jim Hardin and Gary Waslewski. (They were both finished.)
April 4	Yankees release infielder Ron Hansen. (He retired.)
April 28	Yankees purchase pitcher Jim Roland from the A's on waivers. (Roland's most notable outing came in an extra-inning game in Milwaukee, where he came in and walked four consecutive batters on 16 pitches to lose the game by a run.)
May 6	Yankees obtain pitcher Wade Blasingame from the Astros on a conditional player-to-be-named-later basis. (Blasingame's claim to pinstripe fame came in a start in Detroit where he walked the leadoff hitter and then surrendered three consecutive homeruns, the last of which was a prodigious shot over the roof in left center.)
July 28	Yankees re-purchase pitcher Ron Klimkowski from the A's for an undisclosed amount. (He went 0-3 in his final year of major league play.)
August 30	Yankees purchase pitcher Casey Cox from the Rangers for an undisclosed amount and pitcher Jim Roland. (They did nothing.)
September 16	Yankees obtain pitcher Steve Blateric on waivers from the Reds. (He was never a success.)
October 24	Yankees obtain infielder Fred Stanley from the Padres for pitcher George Pena.
	(Stanley proved to be a valuable acquisition who was the regular shortstop on the 1976 A.L. Championship team, and a valuable backup on the '77 and '78 teams. Pena did nothing.)

October 26	Yankees obtain catcher Rick Dempsey from the Twins for outfielder Danny Walton. (Dempsey proved a fine defensive backup for Thurman Munson. Walton never developed into the power hitter everyone expected.)
November 25	Yankees obtain first baseman-outfielder Matty Alou from the A's for pitcher Rob Gardner and infielder Rich McKinney.

(Alou proved to be the biggest disappointment in the pinstripes since McKinney. McKinney and Gardner did nothing notable.)

November 27	Yankees obtain third baseman Graig Nettles, and catcher Gerry Moses from the Indians for outfielders Charlie Spikes and Rusty Torres, infielder Jerry Kenney, and catcher-first baseman John Ellis. A GREAT trade.

(Nettles was recently voted the greatest third baseman in Yankee history, and with good reason. He rivals Brooks Robinson defensively. He led the league in homeruns with 32 in 1976. His defensive heroics won the '78 world series.

Moses was an adequate backup for Munson.

Spikes, Torres, and Ellis were some of the Yankee "youth movement" of the early '70s who never lived up to expectations. Kenney was a mediocre infielder.)

1973

April 5	Yankees obtain infielder Tom Matchick from the Orioles for shortstop Frank Baker. (Nothing.)
April 16	Yankees purchase Jim Ray Hart from the Giants for an undisclosed amount of cash. He was used as a designated hitter (DH). (Hart had two red hot weeks when he first came to NY, but cooled off and hit .254 for the year.)
April 17	Yankees release pitcher Casey Cox. (No loss.)
June 7	Yankees purchase pitcher Sam McDowell from the Giants for $100,000. (He proved to be a big disappointment.)
June 7	Yankees obtain pitcher Pat Dobson from the Braves for first baseman Frank Tepedino, outfielder Wayne Nordhagen, and pitchers Alan Closter and Dave Cheadle. (Dobson went 9-8 in 1973, but had a good year in '74 when he showed a 19-15 mark. He faded in '75 and was traded in November of that year.

The players given up never really did much.)

June 12	Yankees obtain pitcher Lowell Palmer from the Indians for pitcher Mike Kekich. (Kekich's days were numbered because of the wife swap and was given away for nothing.)

August 7	Yankees obtain pitcher Wayne Granger from the Cardinals for future considerations. The future considerations proved to be a minor league pitcher, Ken Crosby, and cash. (Neither did much.)
August 13	Yankees sell infielder Bernie Allen to the Expos for roughly 25,000. This may have been a waiver deal. (No loss.)
August 18	Yankees purchase first baseman Mike Hegan from the A's for an undisclosed amount of cash. (He had a great glove and showed occasional power, but was soon sent on to Milwaukee.)
August 18	Yankees release outfielder John Callison. (He was finished.)
September 6	Yankees sell outfielder-first baseman Matty Alou to the Cardinals. (No loss.)
September 6	Yankees sell outfielder-designated hitter Felipe Alou to the Expos for an undisclosed amount. (No loss.)
September 24	Yankees obtain catcher Duke Sims on waivers from the Tigers. (At least he hit the last Yankee homerun in the Old Stadium.)
December 6	Yankees purchase shortstop Jim Mason from the Texas Rangers for close to $100,000. (He had a fine 1974 season, but faded in '75.)
December 7	Yankees obtain outfielder-designated hitter Lou Piniella and pitcher Ken Wright from the Royals for pitcher Lindy McDaniel.
	Piniella became a great hitter and was a key to the Yankee winners of 1976-78. Wright and McDaniel were at the end of their careers.)
December 7	Yankees purchase catcher Bill Sudakis from the Rangers for $40,000. (He proved to be a fairly valuable utility player in 1974.)
December 10	Yankees release utility infielder Hal Lanier. (He was finished.)
December 11	Yankees release outfielder Ron Swoboda. (He retired.)

1974

March 23	Yankees purchase outfielder Elliott Maddox from the Rangers for more than $60,000. The price may have been more than $100,000.
	(This proved a tremendous acquisition because Maddox proved to be the great defensive outfielder the Yankees wanted AND a shockingly fine hitter. He hit .303 for NY in 1974, and was batting just under .310 when a knee injury hobbled him for most of the '75 season.

213

Unfortunately, Maddox and manager Billy Martin never got along. Martin traded him away from Texas, and after Maddox had a second knee operation (without permission of the club this time), he was unloaded to Baltimore for Paul Blair.)

April 19 — Yankees obtain outfielder Walt Williams, and pitchers Rick Sawyer and Ed Farmer from the Indians for catcher Gerry Moses. (Neither team really gained or lost much, although Williams did hit .281 for NY in 1975.)

April 26 — Yankees obtain first baseman Chris Chambliss, and pitchers Dick Tidrow and Cecil Upshaw from the Indians for pitchers Fred Beene, Fritz Peterson, Steve Kline and Tom Buskey.

(Chambliss has starred as the regular first baseman through the 1978 season, and has become as fine a fielder as any. His swing is in the classic hitters' mold.

Tidrow has also helped NY tremendously, both as a relief pitcher and occasional starter. Upshaw never did much.

The pitchers given up did little, with the exception of Buskey, who had two solid seasons as a short relief man.)

May 25 — Yankees obtain pitcher Larry Gura from the Rangers for catcher Duke Sims. (Gura went 5-1 that year with NY, but was traded in 1976 because of alleged conflicts with Billy Martin. He enjoyed tremendous success with KC in '78, and was the only KC pitcher to defeat the Yanks in the playoffs that year.)

June 15 — Yankees purchase pitcher Rudy May from the Angels for an amount believed to lie between $75-100,000. (He had two good seasons in NY before being traded to Baltimore in '76.)

July 8 — Yankees purchase infielder Sandy Alomar from the Angels for $50,000. (He proved a valuable utility infielder with the 1974-76 teams.)

September 10 — Yankees purchase outfielder Alex Johnson from the Rangers for an undisclosed amount of cash. (He was a mediocre extra for two seasons, but did come up with a game-winning homerun in his first at-bat as a Yankee.)

October 22 — Yankees obtain outfielder Bobby Bonds from the Giants for outfielder Bobby Murcer.

(Bonds hit 32 homeruns, stole 32 bases, and showed a .270 average in his one season in NY. Unfortunately, he suffered injuries to his knees and legs while playing in NY, so we never got to see how good he could have been in the pinstripes. He was traded to the Angels in the off-season.

Murcer never forgave the Yankees for trading him away, largely because of an alleged promise by owner George Steinbrenner that Murcer, the heir-apparent to Mickey Mantle in centerfield, would remain a Yankee for as long as he owned the Yankees.)

214

December 2	Yankees purchase outfielder Bob Oliver from the Orioles for an undisclosed amount of cash. (He never played for NY.)
December 3	Yankees obtain pitcher Skip Lockwood from the Angels for catcher Bill Sudakis. (Lockwood was released in spring training, signed with the Mets, and has had a couple of good years there. Sudakis was always a utility player.)
December 5	Yankees obtain infielder Eddie Leon from the White Sox for pitcher Cecil Upshaw. (Both of them were washed up.)
December 31	Yankees sign free agent pitcher Catfish Hunter for an estimated $3 million dollars.

(Charlie Finley's failure to honor his contractural obligations regarding a promised loan released this all-time great pitcher. The loan centered on tax issues, with Finley having to pay taxes on the $50,000 in question, something he refused to do. Finley cashed in the loan, and thereby breached the contract.

The acquisition of Hunter was a great story in itself, with Hunter's closeness to Yankee minor league director Clyde Klutz a key to his signing with NY.

He won 23 games in 1975, slumped to 17 wins in '76, suffered arm trouble in '77 and the first half of '78, but rebounded after a shoulder manipulation to win eight straight games in August and September, and won Game VI of the world series against the Dodgers.

1975

February 10	Yankees sign infielder Damaso Garcia as a free agent. (He had a few rough games in 1978, but is considered a potential star second baseman.)
June 13	Yankees purchase infielder Ed Brinkman from the Tigers for an undisclosed amount of cash. (He was at the end of a fine career.)
June 19	Yankees purchase outfielder Rich Coggins from the Expos for an undisclosed amount of cash. (He never realized the potential he showed with the Orioles in 1973.)
November 22	Yankees obtain outfielder Oscar Gamble from the Indians for pitcher Pat Dobson. (Gamble had a super year as the lefty designated hitter and part-time outfielder in 1976. The Yankees traded him to the White Sox in 1978.
December 11	Yankees obtain outfielder Mickey Rivers and pitcher Ed Figueroa from the Angels for outfielder Bobby Bonds.

(This proved to be another fine trade for NY. Rivers hit more than .300 in 1976-77 and became the flashy leadoff hitter the Yankees needed. Figueroa has been a successful pitcher, to say the least, and has 20 and 19 win seasons under his belt in NY.

Bonds continues to hit his 30 homeruns and steal 30 bases, but just doesn't seem to get the hits with men on base.)

December 11 Yankees obtain second baseman Willie Randolph, and pitchers Dock Ellis and Ken Brett from the Pirates for pitcher Doc Medich.

(This was a GREAT trade. Randolph became the regular second baseman, and has been selected to the all-star team three times. Ellis had a good year in NY and was traded for Mike Torrez in 1977. Brett was traded to the White Sox for Carlos May early in the 1976 season.

Medich failed to become the big winner the Priates gambled on, and has bounced around for the last few seasons.)

1976

May 16 Yankees obtain catcher Fran Healy from the Royals for pitcher Larry Gura.

(Healy proved a valuable backup for Munson, and became invaluable in 1977-78 when his close friend Reggie Jackson had trouble adjusting to NY, Thurman Munson, and Billy Martin.

Gura came through BIG in 1978 with a 16-4 season and the only KC win in the playoffs.)

May 18 Yankees obtain outfielder-designated hitter Carlos May from the White Sox for pitcher Ken Brett and outfielder Rich Coggins.

(May was a valuable addition in 1976, but was a big disappointment in the world series. Brett had a fair season in Chicago, then faded. Coggins never realized the potential he showed with the 1973 Orioles.)

June 15 Yankees obtain pitchers Ken Holtzman, Doyle Alexander and Grant Jackson, catcher Elrod Hendricks, and outfielder Jim Freeman from the Orioles for pitchers Rudy May, Tippy Martinez, Dave Pagan, and Scott MacGregor, and catcher Rick Dempsey.

(This deal proved a great one in the short run. The three pitchers each had a good year for NY and helped the Yankees win the pennant. Hendricks chipped in with some valuable pinch hits.

The Orioles gained youth, with MacGregor gaining an opportunity to pitch regularly, one he has made the most of to date. Dempsey was freed from the shadow of Thurman Munson, and is now the Orioles' light-hitting, but fine defensive catcher. May had a good year in 1976-77 and was traded to Montreal. Pagan never lived up to the potential both clubs believed he had.)

November 18 Yankees sign free agent pitcher Don Gullett for close to $2 million. (In spite of injuries, which are part of the Gullett legacy, he went 14-4 in 1977 and helped NY to its first championship since 1962. He sat out most of the '78 season, injured, of course.)

November 29   Yankees sign free agent outfielder Reggie Jackson for $3.5 million, or more. (Whatever the real cost, Jackson has proven his value as one of the great clutch hitters of the decade. Yankee fans would probably be unanimous in their support of Jackson were it not for his legendary conflicts with manager Billy Martin and Yankee captain Thurman Munson. Fortunately, Munson and Jackson smoothed over their differences after Martin's resignation in 1978.)

November 30   Yankees purchase outfielder Jim Wynn from the Braves for $100,000. (Unfortunately, Wynn was at the tail end of his career, and after hitting a game-winning homerun on opening day at Yankee Stadium, never really did much.)

1977

January 20   Yankees obtain outfielder Paul Blair from the Orioles for outfielders Elliot Maddox and Rick Bladt.

(Blair proved his value time and again, with fine late-inning defensive work and several game-winning hits in 1977 and 78. He triggered the pennant-clinching rally in KC in 1977 with a lead-off single in the ninth inning.

Maddox has never fully recovered from the leg injuries he suffered in NY in 1975. Bladt has never really made the major leagues.)

April 5   Yankees obtain shortstop Bucky Dent from the White Sox for outfielder Oscar Gamble, minor league pitchers Bob Polinsky and Dewey Hoyt, and a large amount of cash which may have exceeded the $500,000 mark.

(Dent had a good year in 1977. In 1978 he returned from a series of early season leg injuries to help lead the Yankees to their Eastern Division Championship. Yankee fans will long relish his three-run homerun in Boston during the 1978 Eastern Division Playoff Game. He topped that off with a super world series and was named the series Most Valuable Player.

Gamble helped convert the White Sox into a contender in 1977, but left Chicago in favor of San Diego after the free agent draft of '77. The two pitchers never did much.)

April 27   Yankees obtain pitcher Mike Torrez from the A's for pitcher Dock Ellis, infielder Marty Perez, and outfielder Larry Murray.

(Torrez had a strong season in NY, came through with many clutch wins down the stretch, nailed down Game V in the Playoffs in relief of Ron Guidry on two day's rest, and won two world series games. To top that off, he declared his free agency and signed with the Red Sox, where he was the losing pitcher in the 1978 Eastern Division Playoff Game.

Ellis, Murray, and Perez never did much after the trade to Oakland.)

June 15   Yankees obtain catcher-first baseman-designated hitter Cliff Johnson from the Astros for three minor leaguers and cash.

(Johnson became the righty designated hitter and got many clutch hits for NY in 1977. His 1978 season was less successful.

The minor leaguers (pitchers Randy Neimann, and Mike Fischlin, and first baseman Dave Bergman, have not done much for Houston.)

November 22 Yankees sign relief pitcher Rich Gossage for more than $1 million. (He led the league with 27 saves and had a tremendous regular-and post-season, including saves in the Playoff at Boston in 1978, the Playoffs against the Royals, and wins in the Playoffs and world series.)

December 9   Yankees sign free agent pitcher Rawley Eastwick for more than $1 million.

(Eastwick and Yankee manager Billy Martin never really got along. This culminated in a trade to the Phillies in June, 1978.)

December 12 Yankees obtain first baseman Jim Spencer from the White Sox for minor league pitchers Ed Ricks and Stan Thomas, and an undisclosed amount of cash believed to exceed $100,000.

(Spencer was a bit of a disappointment because he never found the right field stands with the regularity the Yankees hoped his powerful lefty bat would, but he did not get all that much playing time, either.)

December 12 Yankees purchase right-handed pitcher Andy Messersmith from the Braves for at least $100,000. (He appeared ready for a fine season, but suffered a separated shoulder towards the end of spring training and eventually sat out most of the season after undergoing surgery.)

1978

June 14   Yankees obtain outfielder John "Jay" Johnstone from the Phillies for pitcher Rawly Eastwick. (The Yankees also received

218

minor leaguer Bobby Brown as part of this transaction.) Johnstone batted .262 as a pinch hitter — outfielder for New York. Eastwick had a mediocre season in Philadelphia.

June 15 Yankees obtain outfielder Gary Thomasson from the Oakland A's for minor league outfielder Del Alston and infielder Mickey Klutts.

Thomasson proved a valuable addition to the 1978 squad. He hit .276 in 51 games, including three game-winning hits, and filled in for Rivers during the regular centerfielder's inuries in July.

Alston and Klutts saw limited action with Oakland, but are highly regarded prospects.

August 1 Yankees purchase lefthanded pitcher Paul Lindblad from the Texas Rangers for an undisclosed amount.

Lindblad appeared in 7 games with New York without a decision. His Yankee ERA was 4.42. He was released to Seattle after the season.

THE PLAYOFFS

In 1969, the American and National Leagues each split into two divisions. This new format provided for intra-divisional races during the regular season, with the first place team in each division advancing into the league's playoffs.

In 1974, the Yankees came close to reaching the coveted playoffs, only to lose to the Malwaukee Brewers in the next-to-last day of the season and finish two games behind the Orioles. After another year of disappointment in 1975 (largely because of injuries to such stars as Mel Stottlemyre, Bobby Bonds and Elliott Maddox), the Yankees finally won the Eastern Division Championship in 1976 and advanced to the American League Championship Series (ALCS) against the Kansas City Royals. The Yankees and Royals would square off again in 1977 and 1978, with each series providing tremendously exciting baseball, and producing three straight Yankee pennants.

ALCS 1976   (YANKEES 3 v. Royals 2)

GAME I: The Yankees take advantage of a first inning throwing error by Royals third baseman George Brett to score a pair of unearned runs, and go on to win the opener, 4-1. New York loaded the bases with one out, but appeared to have blown a great scoring opportunity when Chris Chambliss slammed a ground ball to Brett. The Royals' third baseman stepped on third for the force out, but then threw wildly to first base on the doubleplay attempt, allowing two runs to score.

K.C. narrowed the gap to 2-1 in the eighth inning, (Al Cowens tripled and scored on a ground out) but New York came right back with a pair of insurance runs in the top of the ninth on a two-run double by Roy White.

The Royals lost more than the game in the first inning. All-Star centerfielder Amos Otis sprained his ankle stepping on first base while running out a ground ball, and was sidelined for the rest of the series.

Linescore:

New York	200	000	002	4	12	0
K.C.	000	000	010	1	5	2

P — Hunter (W) v. Gura (L), Littell (9). Att: 41,077.

GAME II: The Royals come-from-behind with five runs in the final three innings to notch a 7-3 win and even the ALCS at one game each. The Yankees took a 3-2 lead into the bottom of the sixth inning, but watched it disappear when Tom Poquette delivered a two-run double to put the Royals ahead to stay. Yankee nemesis Paul Splittorff pitched 5-and-two-thirds innings of near-perfect relief to notch the win.

Linescore:

New York	012	000	000	3	12	5
K.C.	200	002	03x	7	9	0

P — Leonard, Splittorff (W) (3), Mingori (9) v. Figueroa (L), Tidrow (6). Att: 41,091.

GAME III: After surrendering three Royals runs in the first inning, veteran righthander Dock Ellis settles down and holds the Royals in check to post a 5-3 win, with relief help from Sparky Lyle in the ninth inning.

Chris Chambliss got the Yankees on the scoreboard with a two-run homerun in the fourth inning. New York took the lead in the sixth inning on two walks, two doubles, and a single, with Graig Nettles and Elliott Maddox driving in the runs.

Linescore:

K.C.	300	000	000	3	6	0
New York	000	203	00x	5	9	0

P — Ellis (W), Lyle (9) v. Hassler (L), Pattin (6), Hall (6), Mingori (6), Littell (6). HR: Chambliss. Att: 56,808.

GAME IV: The Royals got even with Catfish Hunter, rocking him for five runs on five hits in the first three innings, and take a series-evening 7-4 decision behind reliever Doug Bird. Shortstop Fred Patek supplied most of the Royals' offense with three hits in four at-bats, good for three RBI's. Jamie Quirk also drove in a pair of runs.

Nettles hit two homeruns, good for three RBI's, but the Yankees came up short.

Linescore:

K.C.	030	201	010	7	9	1
New York	020	000	101	4	11	0

P — Gura, Bird (W) (3), Mingori (7) v. Hunter (L), Tidrow (4), Jackson (7). HR: Nettles 2. Att: 56,355.

GAME V: In one of the most dramatic finishes in baseball history, Chambliss leads off the bottom of the ninth inning by hitting a pennant-winning homerun off reliever Mark Littell, propelling the Yankees into their first world series in 12 years. The historic blow came on the heels of Brett's game-tying three-run homerun in the eighth inning, and a "skin-of-your-teeth" close out on a force play which ended the top of the ninth inning (as the potential go-ahead run was heading home).

Kansas City opened a 2-0 lead in the first inning when John Mayberry hit a two-run homerun off Ed Figueroa. New York came right back when Mickey Rivers led off the bottom of the inning with a triple and scored on a single by Roy White. White later scored on a sacrifice fly by Chambliss, and the score was 2-2 after one inning.

Kansas City moved ahead, 3-2, in the second, on a run-scoring single by Buck Martinez, but the Yankees paired runs in the third and sixth inning to take a 6-3 lead into the eighth.

220

Linescore:

K.C.	210	000	030	6	11	1
New York	202	002	001	7	11	1

P — Figueroa, Jackson (8), Tidrow (W) (9) v. Leonard, Splittorff (1), Pattin (4), Hassler (5), Littell (L) (7). HR: Chambliss; Mayberry, Brett. Att: 56,821.

ALCS 1977   (Yankees 3 v. Royals 2)

For those fans who thought the 1976 ALCS was as fine a championship series as anyone would see for many years, the 1977 ALCS proved to be a pleasant surprise, because (for Yankee fans, at least) it was even more exciting. After dropping the first two-out-of-three games, the Yankees came back to win two straight in Kansas City, including an unbelievable come-from-behind victory in the ninth inning of Game V.

GAME I: The Royals blitzed the Yankees with three homeruns in the early innings, kayoed starter Don Gullett with a sore shoulder, and went on to win the opener, 7-2, at Yankee Stadium. Southpaw Yankee-killer Paul Splittorff was the winner, yielding both Yankee runs on a two-run homerun by Thurman Munson in the third inning.

Linescore:

K.C.	222	000	010	7	9	0
New York	002	000	000	2	9	0

P — Splittorff (W), Bird (9) v. Gullett (L), Tidrow (3), Lyle (9). HR: McRae, Mayberry, Cowens; Munson. Att: 54,930.

GAME II: Remarkable Ron Guidry rallies the Yankees behind his three-hit pitching to notch a seven-strikeout 6-2 win. Cliff Johnson supplied most of the Yankee offense with a fifth inning homerun and a sixth inning run-scoring double.

Linescore:

K.C.	001	001	000	2	3	1
New York	000	023	01x	6	10	1

P — Guidry (W) v. Hassler (L), Littell (6), Mingori (8). HR: Johnson. Att: 56,230.

GAME III: Kansas City's Brooklyn-born 20-game winner Dennis Leonard pushed the Yankees to the brink of disaster by twirling a 4-hitter and winning, 6-2. The key hit was Amos Otis' sixth inning, pinch-hit double, good for two runs and a lot of insurance, as Mike Torrez and Sparky Lyle were ineffective.

Linescore:

New York	000	010	001	2	4	0
K.C.	011	012	10x	6	12	2

P — Leonard (W) v. Torrez (L), Lyle (6). Att: 41,285.

GAME IV: With their backs to the wall, the Yankees ripped Royals starter Larry Gura for four runs and six hits in the opening innings, and Sparky Lyle choked off several Royal rallies after entering the game in the fourth inning, as New York evens the series with a 6-4 win.

Mickey Rivers led the Yankees 13-hit attack with four hits in five at-bats, good for two runs scored and an RBI. Lyle, ineffective the day before, pitched 5-and-one-thirds innings of scoreless relief to gain the victory.

Linescore:

New York	121	100	001	6	13	0
K.C.	002	200	000	4	8	2

P — Figueroa, Tidrow (4), Lyle (W) (4) v. Gura (L), Pattin (3), Mingori (9), Bird (9). Att: 41,135.

GAME V: With the champagne on ice in the Royals' clubhouse, and K.C. leading 3-2 as they entered the ninth inning, the jubilant Royals fans were planning their night-long celebration, when Paul Blair led off the ninth inning with a single to center field. Roy White followed with a walk, and Mickey Rivers quieted the crowd with a run-scoring single to tie the score. A sacrifice fly by Willie Randolph put New York ahead, 4-3, and Rivers came around to score when George Brett threw a ground ball into right field, chilling the hometown fans. K.C. went down easily in the ninth, and the Yankees had their second consecutive pennant.

The game opened with the Royals predicting victory, and with good reason. New York was out of pitchers, and had to start Guidry on just two days rest, while the Royals had a rested Splittorff, the resident Yankee-killer, ready for their starter's role. As predicted, the Royals dispatched Guidry with six hits and three runs in three innings, only to run into a surprise reliever, Mike Torrez. The veteran righthander, pitching with just one day's rest, was equal to the task, and checked the Royals for 5-and-one-third innings before giving way to Lyle in the eighth.

New York entered the eighth trailing, 3-1, but recouped a run on a pinch-hit single by Reggie Jackson. The Yankees appeared ready to take command when Chambliss lined a sure base hit to right field, only to watch in horror as second baseman Frank White made a diving grab of the hit to notch the inning ending out.

The Royals brought out Leonard to start the ninth inning . . . and the rest is history!

Linescore:

New York	001	000	013	5	10	0
K.C.	201	000	000	3	10	1

P — Guidry, Torrez (3), Lyle (W) (8) v. Splittorff, Bird (8), Mingori (8), Leonard (L) (9), Gura (9), Littell (9). Att: 41,133.

(NOTE: The 1978 playoffs are covered in the separate section dealing with that miraculous season.)

THE YANKEES AND THE WORLD SERIES

Yankee fans have been blessed with 32 American League Championship teams, 22 of which have gone on to win the World Series. The Yankees show a team career record of 107-73, the best in baseball. New York's most frequent opponents have been the Dodgers (ten series, 8-2), the Giants (seven, 5-2) and the Cardinals (five, 2-3). Rounding out the opposition: the Reds (three, 2-1), Cubs (two, 2-0), Braves (two, 1-1), Pirates (two, 1-1) and Phillies (one, 1-0).

The Yankees have swept their opponents on six occasions: 1927-Pirates; 1928-Cardinals; 1932-Cubs; 1938-Cubs; 1939-Reds; and, 1950-Phillies. Conversely, New York has gone down to defeat in consecutive games just three times: 1922-Giants (including a controversial 2-2 tie in Game II); 1963-Dodgers; and 1976-Reds. From 1927 through the first game of the 1942 series, the Yankees ran off a 32-4 string, including a 12-0 streak.

Surprisingly enough, the Yankees have not fared well in seventh games, winning five and dropping four. Nor has the home advantage of Yankee Stadium had a positive effect based on New York's 1-3 record in seventh games decided there.

Below is a composite list of the Yankee championship teams, complete with regular season records and percentage, managers, and series record (CAPITALIZED TEAM had home advantage):

222

CHAMPIONSHIP YANKEE CLUBS
32 American League Pennant Winners — 22 World Championship Teams

Year	Won	Lost	Pct.	Games Won by	Manager	World Series Opp.	Games Record W.	L.
1921	98	55	.641	4½	Miller Huggins	GIANTS	3	5
1922	94	60	.610	1	Miller Huggins	Giants	0**	4
*1923	98	54	.645	16	Miller Huggins	GIANTS	4	2
1926	91	63	.591	3	Miller Huggins	Cardinals	3	4
*1927	110	44	.714	19	Miller Huggins	PIRATES	4	0
*1928	101	53	.656	2½	Miller Huggins	Cardinals	4	0
*1932	107	47	.695	13	Joe McCarthy	CUBS	4	0
*1936	102	51	.667	19½	Joe McCarthy	GIANTS	4	2
*1937	102	52	.662	13	Joe McCarthy	Giants	4	1
*1938	99	53	.651	9½	Joe McCarthy	CUBS	4	0
*1939	106	45	.702	17	Joe McCarthy	Reds	4	0
*1941	101	53	.656	17	Joe McCarthy	Dodgers	4	1
1942	103	51	.669	9	Joe McCarthy	CARDINALS	1	4
*1943	98	56	.636	13½	Joe McCarthy	Cardinals	4	1
*1947	97	57	.630	12	Bucky Harris	Dodgers	4	3
*1949	97	57	.630	1	Casey Stengel	Dodgers	4	1
*1950	98	56	.636	3	Casey Stengel	PHILLIES	4	0
*1951	98	56	.636	5	Casey Stengel	Giants	4	2
*1952	95	59	.617	2	Casey Stengel	DODGERS	4	3
*1953	99	52	.656	8½	Casey Stengel	Dodgers	4	2
1955	96	58	.623	3	Casey Stengel	Dodgers	3	4
*1956	97	57	.630	9	Casey Stengel	DODGERS	4	3
1957	98	56	.636	8	Casey Stengel	Braves	3	4
*1958	92	62	.597	10	Casey Stengel	BRAVES	4	3
1960	97	57	.630	8	Casey Stengel	PIRATES	3	4
*1961	109	53	.673	8	Ralph Houk	Reds	4	1
1962	96	66	.593	5	Ralph Houk	GIANTS	4	3
1963	104	57	.646	10½	Ralph Houk	Dodgers	0	4
1964	99	63	.611	1	Yogi Berra	CARDINALS	3	4
1976	97	62	.610	10½	Billy Martin	REDS	0	4
*1977	100	62	.617	2½	Billy Martin	Dodgers	4	2
*1978	100	63			Billy Martin / Bob Lemon	Dodgers	4	2

*World Champions

	Wins	Losses
Totals:	107	73
home:	52	35
away:	55	38

(includes 1-5 at Polo Grounds)

**Tie game in 1922

SERIES BY SERIES, GAME BY GAME

To refresh the memories of veteran Yankee fans, and provide some much sought after information for the younger members of the baseball world, a series by series, game by game, description follows. Linescores are included for easy reference, with the winning team's pitchers and homeruns always listed first. Pitchers who received decisions are underlined, with saves (SV) so indicated.

1921   NEW YORK GIANTS (5), Yankees (3)

This was the Yankees first post-season appearnce, and the last of the best-five-out-of-nine world series preferred by Giants manager John McGraw. It was the first world series played under the reign of baseball commissioner Judge Kennesaw Landis, the first played entirely in one stadium (the Polo Grounds), and it featured Babe Ruth's first world series homerun (Game IV).

Yankee pitcher Waite Hoyt emerged as a hero in a losing cause, hurling 27 consecutive innings without yielding an earned run, but losing the final game when a runner scored from second base on an error by shortstop Roger Peckinpaugh.

Game I: Submarine-throwing Carl Mays baffles all of the Giants, except Frankie Frisch (four hits), and wins 3-0 on a five-hitter.

Game II: Hoyt proves even more baffling, allowing only singles by Frisch and John Rawlings, and giving the Yankees a two-games-to-none lead. This was the first of several pitching duels between Hoyt and Giants pitcher Art Nehf, who would prove to be a Yankee killer of sorts.

Game III: A 5-4 Yankee lead is swamped during the Giants eight-run seventh inning when reliever Jack Quinn runs out of gas (he came on for starter Bob Shawkey in the third).

George Burns and Frank Snyder had four hits apiece for the Giants, including run-scoring doubles in the seventh.

Game IV: With the Yankees leading 1-0, courtesy of Ruth's first world series homerun, the Giants finally solve Mays' submarine style to the tune of a three-run eighth inning highlighted by Burns' two-run double. Phil Douglas scattered seven hits to even the series at 2-2.

Game V: After yielding an unearned run in the first inning, Hoyt settles down and beats Nehf again, 3-1. Ruth shocked the fans and players alike when he beat out a bunt to start the game-winning rally.

Game VI: Giants reliever Jesse Barnes pitches eight-and-one-third innings of 10 strike-out ball and goes home a winner when Shawkey is shelled in the fourth. George Kelly had three run-scoring hits, and Snyder and Irish Meusel, homered. Chick Fewster hit a Yankee homerun.

Game VII: Mays and Douglas hook up in another duel, with the Giants breaking a 1-1 tie in the bottom of the eighth inning on Snyder's run-scoring double.

Game VIII: Facing elimination, Yankee manager Miller Huggins went with Hoyt on two days rest, and might have come out a winner but for an error and some stupid baserunning. The Giants lone run scored on an error by Peckinpaugh, and Nehf held the Yankees well in check until the ninth. With one out, Aaron Ward walked. Frank "Homerun" Baker followed with a hard ground ball which appeared to be heading through the right side of the infield for a hit, but Giants second baseman Rawlings smothered the ball and threw Baker out at first base. What followed was a classic mistake: in an unforgiveable display of foolhardiness (or bad coaching at third base) Ward continued on around second and headed for third, where he was an easy out to hand the Giants the championship.

GAME I (at the Polo Grounds, Oct. 5)
| Yankees | 100 | 011 | 000 | 3 | 7 | 0 |
| Giants | 000 | 000 | 000 | 0 | 5 | 0 |

Pitchers: Mays v. Douglas, Barnes (9). Att: 30,202.

GAME II (at the Polo Grounds, Oct. 6)
| Giants | 000 | 000 | 000 | 0 | 2 | 3 |
| Yankees | 000 | 100 | 02x | 3 | 3 | 0 |

Pitchers: Hoyt v. Nehf. Att: 34,939.

GAME III (at the Polo Grounds, Oct. 7)
| Yankees | 004 | 000 | 010 | 5 | 8 | 0 |
| Giants | 004 | 000 | 81x | 13 | 20 | 0 |

Pitchers: Toney, Barnes (3) v. Shawkey, Quinn (3), Collins (7), Rogers (8).
Att: 36,509.

GAME IV (at the Polo Grounds, Oct. 9)
| Giants | 000 | 000 | 031 | 4 | 9 | 1 |
| Yankees | 000 | 010 | 001 | 2 | 7 | 1 |

Pitchers: Douglas vs. Mays. Homerun: Ruth. Att: 36,372.

GAME V (at the Polo Grounds, Oct. 10)
| Yankees | 001 | 200 | 000 | 3 | 6 | 1 |
| Giants | 100 | 000 | 000 | 1 | 10 | 1 |

Pitchers: Hoyt v. Nehf. Att: 35,758.

GAME VI (at the Polo Grounds, Oct. 11)
| Giants | 030 | 401 | 000 | 8 | 13 | 0 |
| Yankees | 320 | 000 | 000 | 5 | 7 | 2 |

Pitchers: Toney, Barnes (1) v. Harper, Shawkey (2),
Piercy (9). Homeruns: E. Meusel, Snyder; Fewster.
Att: 34,283.

GAME VII (at the Polo Grounds, Oct. 12)
| Yankees | 010 | 000 | 000 | 1 | 8 | 1 |
| Giants | 000 | 100 | 10x | 2 | 6 | 0 |

Pitchers: Douglas v. Mays. Att: 36,503.

GAME VIII (at the Polo Grounds, Oct. 13)
| Giants | 100 | 000 | 000 | 1 | 6 | 0 |
| Yankees | 000 | 000 | 000 | 0 | 4 | 1 |

Pitchers: Nehf v. Hoyt. Att: 25,410.

1922   YANKEES (0) v. New York Giants (4)

This world series is famous for two reasons: the controversial tie in Game II, and the miserable performance of Ruth (.118 batting average on two hits, a single and a double). Game II was called "because of darkness" at 4:45 p.m. after ten innings. The fans were outraged, and swarmed by the hundreds towards Commissioner Landis' box under the mistaken belief that he had ordered the game suspended. Landis refused to over-rule the umpires' decision, but placated the hostile crowd by ordering the game's gate receipts (about $120,000) turned over to charity.

Game I: With the Yankees leading 2-0, the Giants scored three runs in the bottom of the eighth, two of them on Irish Meusel's double, to make Nehf a come-from-behind winner.

225

Game II: Irish Meusel's three run homerun is erased by the umpires' decision to call the game because of darkness. The Giants opened a 3-0 lead in the first inning, but the Yankees battled back with single runs in the first, fourth, and seventh (including a homerun by Ward).

Game III: Meusel continues his assault on Yankee pitching with a run-scoring single to aid Jack Scott's four hit pitching. The Reds discarded Scott as an over-the-hill, sore-armed pitcher mid-way through the season, but McGraw took a chance on him and Scott responded with an 8-2 stretch record and a series victory.

Game IV: The Giants take advantage of a bad hop single by Dave Bancroft to build a four-run fifth inning, and hang on to edge the Yankees, 4-3. Ward hit his second homerun of the series in the seventh inning, but Hugh McQuillan retired the final seven Yankees in order.

Game V: The Giants went to Nehf again, and he responded by pitching his third straight win over the Yankees. Once again, the Giants overcame a Yankee lead, this time on a run-scoring single by George Kelly to cap a three-run eighth inning. Nehf held Ruth hitless for the third straight game in this world series.

GAME I (at the Polo Grounds, Oct. 4)

Yankees	000	001	100	2	7	3
Giants	000	000	03x	3	11	3

Pitchers: Nehf, Ryan (8) v. Bush, Hoyt (8). Att: 36,514.

GAME II (at the Polo Grounds, Oct. 5)

Giants	300	000	000	0	3	8	1
Yankees	100	100	010	0	3	8	0

Pitchers: Barnes v. Shawkey. Homeruns: E. Meusel; Ward. Att: 37,020.

GAME III (at the Polo Grounds, Oct. 6)

Yankees	000	000	000	0	4	1
Giants	002	000	10x	3	12	1

Pitchers: Scott v. Hoyt, Jones (8). Att: 37,620.

GAME IV (at the Polo Grounds, Oct. 7)

Giants	000	040	000	4	9	1
Yankees	200	000	100	3	8	0

Pitchers: McQuillan v. Mays, Jones (9). Homerun: Ward. Att: 36,242.

GAME V (at the Polo Grounds, Oct. 8)

Yankees	100	010	100	3	5	0
Giants	020	000	03x	5	10	0

Pitchers: Nehf v. Bush. Att: 38,551.

1923   YANKEES (4) v. New York Giants (2)

This was another world series of "firsts." It was the first one played at Yankee Stadium, and the first "subway series." (An elevated shuttle train ran between Yankee Stadium and the Polo Grounds; thus, the "subway" aspect, albeit a misnomer because the train ran above ground.) It also featured the Yankees first world championship, the first million dollar gate ($1,063,815 were paid by a record 301,430 fans), and consecutive homeruns by Ruth in Game II.

On the minus side, there were the antics of future Yankee manager Casey Stengel, then a 33-year-old outfielder finishing his playing career with the Giants. Stengel spoiled Yankee Stadium's opening world series appearance with a ninth inning inside-the-park homerun off reliever Joe Bush to break a 4-4 tie and make reliever Rosy Ryan a winner.

226

Stengel continued to annoy Yankee fans when he speared a tremendous drive to center field off the bat of Ruth, after Ruth had hit two consecutive homeruns in Game II.

In Game III, Stengel did it again, this time lining a Same Jones offering into the right field stands to give the Giants a 1-0 win. And guess who was on the mound? Yankee nemisis Nehf, who won his fourth straight series game against the Yankees.

The Yankee bats came alive for six runs in the second inning of Game IV, three of them coming on Everett Scott's bases loaded triple and two more scoring on a three-bagger by Bob Meusel. Shawkey finally won a series game, but needed relief help from Herb Pennock in the eighth inning.

The series returned to Yankee Stadium for Game V, and after two losses in their new home, the Yankees finally found success home. Joe Dugan's three-run homerun highlighted a 14-hit attack to make Bush a three-hitter winner!

Game VI featured what would soon become a Yankee trademark: a late inning rally to come from behind and win. With the Giants leading 4-1, the Yankees scored five runs in the eighth, largely thanks to the wildness of their former nemisis, Nehf, who walked five. Ruth added a homerun, his third of the series, and the Yankees had their first championship.

GAME I (at Yankee Stadium, Oct 10)

Giants	004	000	001	5	8	0
Yankees	120	000	100	4	12	1

Pitchers: Watson, Ryan (3) v. Hoyt, Bush (3).
Homerun: Stengel. Att: 55,307.

GAME II (at the Polo Grounds, Oct. 11)

Yankees	010	210	000	4	10	0
Giants	010	001	000	2	9	2

Pitchers: Pennock v. McQuillan, Bentley (4).
Homeruns: Ruth 2, Ward; E. Meusel. Att: 40,402.

GAME III (at the Yankee Stadium, Oct. 12)

Giants	000	000	100	1	4	0
Yankees	000	000	000	0	6	1

Pitchers: Nehf v. Jones, Bush (8). Homerun: Stengel.
Att: 62,430.

GAME IV (at the Polo Grounds, Oct. 13)

Yankees	061	100	000	8	13	1
Giants	000	000	031	4	13	1

Pitchers: Shawkey, Pennock (8) v. Scott, Ryan (2),
McQuillan (3), Jonnard (8), Barnes (9). Homeruns: Youngs.
Att: 46,302.

GAME V (at Yankee Stadium, Oct. 14)

Giants	010	000	000	1	3	2
Yankees	340	100	00x	8	14	0

Pitchers: Bush v. Bentley, Scott (2), Barnes (4), Jonnard (8).
Homerun: Dugan. Att: 62,817.

GAME VI (at the Polo Grounds, Oct. 15)

Yankees	100	000	050	6	5	0
Giants	100	111	000	4	10	1

Pitchers: Pennock, Jones (8) v. Nehf, Ryan (8).
Homeruns: Ruth; Snyder. Att: 34,172.

1926   St. Louis Cardinals (4) v. YANKEES (3)

The bottom of the seventh inning of Game VII of the 1926 world series is considered among the most dramatic moments in series history, and with good reason. St. Louis led, 3-2, when the Yankees loaded the bases with two outs. Up to the plate stepped Tony Lazzeri, always a dangerous clutch hitter. Out to the mound went Cardinals manager Rogers Hornsby to check on his pitcher, Jesse Haines. Haines had raised a blister on his pitching hand, and coul;not continue. Hornsby looked to the bullpen, seemed to hesitate for a moment, and then signaled for 39-year-old Grover Cleveland Alexander, one of the greatest pitchers in baseball history.

Alexander started and won Games II and VI, and was known to tip the bottle in celebration of every win. What really transpired on the mound that day will never be known, but Alexander warmed up and faced Lazzeri in the most important moment of his career. After throwing a ball and a strike, Alexander served up an inside fastball which Lazzeri lined deep into the seats down the left field line, just foul. On the next pitch, Lazzeri swung and missed on an outside curve, ending the inning.

The Yankees went down quietly in the eighth inning, and with two outs in the ninth, Alexander faced Ruth. Pitching carefully, Alexander walked him. On the first pitch to the next batter (Bob Meusel, a lifetime .300 hitter) Ruth tried to steal second and was an easy series-ending out. It was a rare baserunning mistake for Ruth, and it tended to overshadow his amazing feat of three consecutive homeruns in Game IV, as well as his .300 average.

Game I: Pennock hurls a three-hitter and Gehrig follows Ruth's sixth inning double with a run-scoring single to break a 1-1 tie and put New York ahead to stay.

Game II: Billy Southworth's seventh inning three-run homerun off Urban Shcoker makes a winner out of Alexander, who allowed just four hits, struck out 10, and retired the last 21 men in a row.

Game IV: Ruth explodes for three consecutive homeruns, and Waite Hoyt scatters 14 Cardinal hits, to even the series.

Game V: Herb Pennock outduels Bill Sherdel, 3-2, in ten innings, with Sherdel's wild pitch the key miscue in the tenth inning. Mark Koenig opened the inning with a hit, was sacrificed to second base, and went to third on the wild pitch, enabling him to score on Lazzeri's fly ball.

Game VI: Alexander does it again, benefiting from a five-run seventh inning and four runs batted in by Les Bell. Shawkey, rarely effective in series play, went down again.

Game VII: Alexander v. Lazzeri in one of the great moments in series history, as explained in the introduction to this world series.

GAME I (at Yankee Stadium, Oct 2)

Cardinals	100	000	000	1	3	1
Yankees	100	001	00x	2	6	0

Pitchers: <u>Pennock</u> v. <u>Sherdel</u>, Haines (8). Att: 61,658.

GAME II (at Yankee Stadium, Oct. 3)

Cardinals	002	000	301	6	12	1
Yankees	020	000	000	2	4	0

Pitchers: <u>Alexander</u> v. <u>Shocker</u>, Shawkey (8), Jones (9).
Homeruns: Southworth, Thevenow. Att: 63,600.

GAME III (at Sportsman's Park, Oct. 5)

Yankees	000	000	000	0	5	1
Cardinals	000	310	00x	4	8	0

Pitchers: <u>Haines</u> v. <u>Ruether</u>, Shawkey (5), Thomas (8).
Homerun: Haines. Att: 37,708.

GAME IV (at Sportsman's Park, Oct. 6)

Yankees	101	142	100	10	14	1
Cardinals	100	300	001	5	14	0

Pitchers: <u>Hoyt</u> v. <u>Rhem</u>, Reinhart (5), Bell (5),
Hallahan (7), Keen (9). Homeruns: Ruth 3. Att: 38,825.

GAME V (at Sportsman's Park, Oct. 7)

Yankees	000	001	001	1	3	9	1
Cardinals	000	100	100	0	2	7	1

Pitchers: <u>Pennock</u> v. <u>Sherdel.</u> Att: 39,552.

GAME VI (at Yankee Stadium, Oct. 9)

Cardinals	300	010	501	10	13	2
Yankees	000	100	100	2	8	1

Pitchers: <u>Alexander</u> v. <u>Shawkey</u>, Shocker (7),
Thomas (8). Homerun: Bell. Att: 48,615.

GAME VII (at Yankee Stadium, Oct. 10)

Cardinals	000	300	000	3	8	0
Yankees	001	001	000	2	8	3

Pitchers: <u>Haines</u>, Alexander (SV) (7) v. Hoyt,
Homerun: Ruth. Att: 38,093.

1927   Yankees (4) v. PITTSBURGH PIRATES (0)

It was the year of "Murderers' Row", Ruth's record 60 homeruns, and a Yankee team which won the pennant by 19 games. Strangely enough, the team had only one 20-game winner (Hoyt) but was well-balanced with 19-game winner Herb Pennock, rookie (for all intents and purposes) George Pipgras (10—3) and the first in a line of superior relief pitchers, Wilcy Moore (19-7 with 13 saves).

The Pirates were not to be taken lightly, led by Lloyd and Paul Waner, and Kiki Cuyler, but Cuyler sat out the series for reasons which he and manager Donie Bush took to their graves. The Waners hit .400 and .333 respectively, but the Yankee pitching proved tough in the clutch, limiting Pittsburgh to 10 runs in the series.

More than 20 million people benefited from the first world series radio broadcasts, heard coast to coast, with NBC's Graham McNamee and CBS' Andrew White bringing fans all the action. The series also featured a near perfect game (Game III, Pennock pitching) and included the first of many "unlikely heroes" in the pinstripes: light-hitting Yankee shortstop Mark Koenig, who went nine-for-18.

Game I: Gehrig gets the Yankees off and running with a run-scoring triple in the first inning, and drives in another run in the third, as Hoyt beats the Pirates with relief help from Moore.

Game II: A three-run third inning provides the margin of victory, with Gehrig's run-scoring double highlighting the inning. Pipgras went the distance, allowing seven hits.

Game III: Pennock retires the first 22 men he faces before Pie Traynor singles with one out in the eighth inning. Gehrig's two-run triple in the first inning gave Pennock all the support he needed, and Ruth added a three-run homerun for "insurance" in the eighth.

Game IV: This most exciting game of the series ends in the bottom of the ninth inning. The Yankees loaded the bases with no outs off reliever John Miljus. Miljus regained his composure and struck out Gehrig and Meusel. Lazzeri followed, and with the count no balls, two strikes, Miljus uncorks a wild pitch, allowing Earle Combs to score the series-clinching run.

229

GAME I (at Forbes Field, Oct. 5)
Yankees   103   010   000   5   6   1
Pirates   101   010   010   4   9   2
Pitchers: Hoyt, Moore (8) v. Kremer, Miljus (6).
Att: 41,567.

GAME II (at Forbes Field, Oct. 6)
Yankees   003   000   030   6   11   0
Pirates   100   000   010   2   7   2
Pitchers: Pipgras v. Aldridge, Cvengros (8),
Dawson (9). Att: 41,634.

GAME III (at Yankee Stadium, Oct. 7)
Pirates   000   000   010   1   3   1
Yankees   200   000   60x   8   9   0
Pitchers: Pennock v. Meadows, Cvengros (7).
Homerun: Ruth. Att: 60,695.

GAME IV (at Yankee Stadium, Oct. 8)
Pirates   100   000   200   3   10   1
Yankees   100   020   001   4   12   2
Pitchers: Moore v. Hill, Miljus (7). Homerun:
Ruth. Att: 57,909.

1928   YANKEES (4) v. St. Louis Cardinals (0)
Babe Ruth batted .625 (10 hits in 16 at-bats, still the world series record) and Gehrig hit .545 to lead the Yankees to a surprisingly easy sweep of the Cards. Grover Alexander, the hero of the '26 series, was ineffective in two appearances. Yankee mainstay Hoyt won the first and fourth games.

Perhaps the key to the series was Cardinal manager Bill McKechnie's decision to pitch to, rather than around, Ruth, under the mistaken belief that the Babe's well-publicized sore legs would hamper his swing. The .625 average, and three homeruns in Game IV, speak for themselves. Cards owner Sam Breaden blamed McKechnie for his team's listless performance, and fired the manager after the fourth game. Breaden later said it was the biggest mistake of his baseball life, although his Gashouse Gang of the 30's enjoyed considerable success under Rogers Hornsby's guidance.

Game I: Bob Meusel's two-run homerun provides Hoyt with all the offense he needs, as the Yankee ace three-hit St. Louis. Jim Bottomley's homerun in the seventh inning spoils Hoyt's shutout bid.

Game II: Seeking to even the series, McKechnie went with the hero of the '26 series, Alexander, but the 41-year-old pitcher surrendered a first inning three-run homerun to Gehrig, and was kayoed in the third. Pipgras survives a three-run Cardinal second inning, allowing just one hit after the second.

Game III: Tom Zachary (the man who tossed Ruth's 60th homerun while with the Senators in '27) was a surprise starter, and scattered nine hits to give New York a commanding three-games-to-none lead. Gehrig hit a pair of homeruns, good for three runs, as the Yankees knocked Haines for a loop.

Game IV: Ruth hits three homeruns, Gehrig and Cedric Durst also homer, and Hoyt wins again to clinch the series. A bit of controversy arose in the fourth inning when Sherdel fired a "quick-pitch" past Ruth for what Sherdel thought was strike three, but the two leagues had previously agreed not to allow "quick pitches" in the series, so Ruth remained at bat and hit a homerun!

One final note: the Yankees added insult to injury by holding the Cards to a team batting average of .206!

GAME I (at Yankee Stadium, Oct. 4)

Cardinals	000	000	100	1	3	1
Yankees	100	200	01x	4	7	0

Pitchers: Hoyt v. Sherdel, Johnson (8). Homeruns:
Meusel; Bottomley. Att: 61,425.

GAME II (at Yankee Stadium, Oct. 5)

Cardinals	030	000	000	3	4	1
Yankees	314	000	10x	9	8	2

Pitchers: Pipgras v. Alexander, Mitchell (3).
Homerun: Gehrig. Att: 60,714.

GAME III (at Sportsman's Park, Oct. 7)

Yankees	010	203	100	7	7	2
Cardinals	200	010	000	3	9	3

Pitchers: Zachary v. Haines, Johnson (7), Rhem (8).
Homeruns: Gehrig 2. Att: 39,602.

GAME IV (at Sportsman's Park, Oct 9)

Yankees	000	100	420	7	15	2
cardinals	001	100	001	3	11	0

Pitchers: Hoyt v. Sherdel, Alexander (7). Homeruns:
Ruth 3, Durst, Gehrig. Att: 37,331.

1932   YANKEES (4) v. Chicago Cubs (0)

This was a world series of "lasts." It was Ruth's final post-season appearance, and he closed it out by hitting .333 and his famous "called" (?) homerun. It was also the last hurrah for Pennock, Hoyt (he did not pitch because of a sore arm), Moore, and many other members of the '27 Champions.

On the other hand, this series foreshadowed a new era of Yankee greatness, that of the so-called Bronx Bombers of the '30's. The new faces on the mound included Red Ruffing and Lefty Gomez, winners in Games I and II. Catcher Bill Dickey batted .438, and the old guard pitchers (Moore and Pipgras) each won once. And, as was all too often the case during his tremendous career, Lou Gehrig's .529 average, nine runs scored, eight runs batted in, and three homeruns, was lost somewhere in the changeover.

The series opened in New York, where the Yankees had an easy time, 12-6 and 5-2. Gehrig's homerun highlighted an 8-hit attack, and Ruffing notched 10 strikeouts while going the distance, in Game I. Newcomer Ben Chapman's third inning, two-run single proved the gamewinner in Game II, with Gomez spinning a not-so-nifty nine-hitter.

By the time the teams reached Chicago for Game III, a great deal of antagonism had built up, largely because of the treatment former Yankee Mark Koenig received at the hands of his new Cub teammates. Koenig joined the Cubs midway through the season, played flawlessly at shortstop, and led the team to the pennant. The Cubs responded by voting him a mere half-share of the world series money, causing the Yankees to loudly denounce the Chicagos as cheapskates. Bad feelings increased with every pitch, as the bench jockeying degenerated into every conceivable racial and ethnic remark.

The Yankees' arrival in Chicago produced a crowd reaction rarely seen in the United States. Vocal taunts, spitting, hurling of garbage and bottles, and threats of physical harm greeted the New York contingent. The abuse reached a fever pitch with the start of Game III, with the fans throwing fruit at Ruth, and the Babe responding by throwing it ("playfully", according to contemporary accounts) right back.

231

Ruth began an assault of his own in the first inning, slamming a three-run homerun. Gehrig homered in the second, to put New York ahead, 4-1, but the Cubs tied matters in the fourth inning before Ruth batted again in the fifth. With one out and no one on base, Cubs pitcher Charlie Root threw a perfect strike. Ruth responded by thrusting his right arm out, extending his index finger, and pointing out towards the pitcher, or the bleachers, depending upon whom one believes. The gesture further incited the hostile crowd, and Root brought them to near hysteria by throwing a called strike two. Ruth repeated the gesture, the fans leapt to their collective feet in anticipation of an embarassing strikeout, and Ruth silenced them by blasting a homerun into the centerfield bleachers, the 15th and final four-bagger of his world series career. By the time Ruth reached home plate, the crowd was back on its feet, this time acknowledging the Babe's greatness with a thundering ovation. The fans were still standing when Gehrig hit the next pitch into the same seats, and at least one sportswriter present failed to even mention the homerun (Gehrig's second of the game) in his story, another perfect example of Gehrig's being overshadowed by Ruth.

Did Ruth really call his shot? Ruth alternately "admitted" (in public) and denied it (in private). Contemporary newspaper reports do not specifically mention a gesture, but do state that Ruth made clear his intentions of hitting one out. Zach Taylor, a journeyman catcher sitting on the Cubs' bench, told reporters he was positive the Babe had pointed to the bleachers and told the Cub's bench that he was going to hit the next pitch into the seats. On the other hand, Cubs catcher Gabby Hartnett, the man on the receiving end of the pitch, says Ruth merely gestured towards the Cubs bench and said "it only takes one pitch to hit a homerun." And during the summer of 1978, Cubs manager Charlie Grimm reversed his earlier statements which supported the called homerun, and now says Ruth was merely pointing at the pitcher. Let it suffice to say that the truth will never be known, that its veracity is irrelevant as a part of the Ruth legend, and that if the reader happens to meet someone who says he was there on October 1, 1932, why not get another "expert" opinion!

For the record, Ruth's final series hit was a single in Game IV, and as he left the field for a pinch runner, the Chicago crowd gave him a final, thundering ovation. Lazzeri supplied most of the fireworks with a pair of two-run homeruns, as the Yankees overcame a 4-1 deficit to make Moore a winner in relief (his final series game) and nail down a save for Pennock (his final series appearance).

One final note: the Cubs set a series record with a 9.26 earned run average!

GAME I (at Yankee Stadium, Sept. 28)

Cubs	200	000	220	6	10	1
Yankees	000	305	31x	12	8	2

Pitchers: Ruffing v. Bush, Grimes (6), Smith (8).
Homerun: Gehrig. Att: 41,459.

GAME II (at Yankee Stadium, Sept 29)

Cubs	101	000	000	2	9	0
Yankees	202	010	00x	5	10	1

Pitchers: Gomez v. Warneke. Att: 50,709.

GAME III (at Wrigley Field, Oct. 1)

Yankees	301	020	001	7	8	1
Cubs	102	100	001	5	9	4

Pitchers: Pipgras, Pennock (9) (SV) v. Root, Malone (5),
May (7), Tinning (9). Homeruns: Ruth 2, Gehrig 2; Cuyler,
hartnett. Att: 49,986.

GAME IV (at Wrigley Field, Oct. 2)

Yankees	102	002	404	13	19	4
Cubs	400	001	001	6	9	1

Pitchers: Allen, Moore (1), Pennock (7) (SV) v.
Bush, Warneke (1), May (4), Tinning (7), Grimes (9).
Homeruns: Lazzeri 2, Combs; Demaree. Att: 49,844.

1936   Yankees (4) v. NEW YORK GIANTS (2)

The Bronx Bombers and the New York Giants renewed their rivalry of the early 20's with a cast of completely new faces. Huggins and McGraw no longer mastermined the action, Nehf and Hoyt had long since departed the pitching mounds, and most conspicuously, Ruth was no longer a major league baseball player, let along a Yankee.

Fortunately, a new cast of heroes emerged in Yankee uniforms, led by centerfielder Joe DiMaggio, who batted .346 in his first world series. Another new face, that of Jake Powell, led all hitters with a .455 mark (10-for-22), and Gomez went 2-0. Of course, the Yankees of the 20's made their presence felt, led by Gehrig, who homered twice and drove in seven runs.

Game I: Giants ace Carl Hubbell ends a 12-game world series winning streak by beating the Yankees, 6-1, on a seven-hitter. Hubbell did not allow an outfield putout! In fact, the only ball to reach the "outfield" was George Selkirk's shutout-spoiling homerun which gave the Yankees a short-lived 1-0 lead.

Game II: Lazzeri's grand slam, a three-run homerun by Dickey, and 17 Yankee hits enabled the Yankees to set a world series record by scoring 18 runs to make Gomez' task an easy one. Every Yankee starter had at least one hit.

Game III: Bump Hadley and Fat Freddy Fitzsimmons hooked up in a classic pitching duel, won by the Yankees when Crosetti's eighth inning bouncer back to the mound glanced off Fitzsimmons' glove to score Powell from third. It was a typical Fitzsimmons world series misfortune (see the 1941 series), and was all the tougher to swallow because Jim Ripple had tied the game 1-1 on a rare homerun in the fifth, and because Fitzsimmons pitched a four-hitter.

Game IV: A three-run third inning highlighted by Gehrig's two-run homerun off Hubbell proved decisive as Monte Pearson made a successful world series debut.

Game V: The Giants blow a 4-2 lead on errors in the sixth inning, but pitcher Hal Schumacher hangs tough and wins in the tenth when Bill Terry's sacrifice fly scores Moore from third. Selkirk hits another homerun in a losing cause.

Game VI: A seven-run ninth inning breaks open a 6-5 duel and makes Gomez a winner, with relief from Johnny Murphy. The Yankees blew Fitzsimmons out early, were stifled by Slick Castleman for four innings, and then made shambles of Dick Coffman and Harry Gumbert as they amassed 17 hits.

Two final notes: the Yankees batted .302 as a team; and the Giants pitching staff recorded an earned run average of 6.79!

GAME I (at the Polo Grounds, Sept. 30)

Yankees	001	000	000	1	7	2
Giants	000	011	04x	6	9	1

Pitchers: Hubbell v. Ruffing. Homeruns: Bartell;
Selkirk. Att: 39,419.

GAME II (at the Polo Grounds, Oct. 2)

Yankees	207	001	206	18	17	0
Giants	010	300	000	4	6	1

Pitchers: Gomez v. Schumacher, Smith (3), Coffman (3),
Gabler (5), Gumbert (9). Homeruns: Dickey, Lazzeri.
Att: 43,543.

GAME III (at Yankee Stadium, Oct. 3)

Giants	000	010	000	1	11	0
Yankees	010	000	01x	2	4	0

Pitchers: Hadley, Malone (8) (SV) v. Fitzsimmons.
Homeruns: Gehrig; Ripple. Att: 64,842.

GAME IV (at Yankee Stadium, Oct. 4)

Giants	000	100	010	2	7	1
Yankees	013	000	01x	5	10	1

Pitchers: Pearson v. Hubbell, Gabler (8). Homerun:
Gehrig. Att: 66,669.

GAME V (at Yankee Stadium, Oct. 5)

Giants	300	001	000	1	5	8	3
Yankees	011	002	000	0	4	10	1

Pitchers: Schumacher v. Ruffing, Malone (7).
Homerun: Selkirk. Att: 50,024.

GAME VI (at the Polo Grounds, Oct. 6)

Yankees	021	200	017	13	17	2
Giants	200	010	110	5	9	1

Pitchers: Gomez, Murphy (7) (SV) v. Fitzsimmons,
Castleman (4), Coffman (9), Gumbert (9). Homeruns:
Powell; Moore, Ott. Att: 38,427.

1937   YANKEES (4) v. New York Giants (1)

Two more "old guard" Yankees had their lash hurrahs in the 1937 series: Lazzeri and Gehrig. In Lazzeri's case it was his final appearance as a Yankee, and he made the most of it by batting .400 and hitting a homerun. Gehrig would go on to play in the '38 series, but the '37 classic was his final good one, climaxed by his last world series homerun (his 10th, albeit it meaningless, in Game IV).

For a Yankee of the future, DiMaggio, it was the first of several outstanding post-season performances. DiMaggio belted his first world series homerun, a prodigious shot that struck a flagpole above the roof of the left field stands in the Polo Grounds.

And on a semi-humorous note, pitcher Lefty Gomez, a lifetime .147 hitter, drove in a winning run with a single in Game V.

Game I: With the Giants leading 1-0, the Yankees score seven runs in the sixth inning. DiMaggio and Selkirk each singled home a pair of runs, and Lazzeri hit a homerun. Gomez went the distance, allowing six hits.

Game II: Red Ruffing scatters seven hits, and the Yankees again overcome a 1-0 deficit, to go up two games to none. Ruffing, a lifetime .269 hitter, singled twice and drove in three runs.

Game III: A two-run triple by Dickey is the big hit as the Yankees open a 5-0 lead. Pearson and Murphy combine for a five-hitter.

Game IV: Hubbell stops the Yankees momentarily with a six-hit, 7-3 win. Hank Lieber gets two hits in the Giants six-run second inning. Gehrig homers for the Yankees.

Game V: Lazzeri leads off the Yankees fifth inning with a triple and scores on Gomez's single off second baseman Burgess Whitehead's glove to break a 2-2 tie. DiMaggio and Myril Hoag added solo homeruns in support of Gomez's 10-hit "masterpiece."

234

GAME I: (at Yankee Stadium, Oct. 6)

Giants	000	010	000	1	6	2
Yankees	000	007	01x	8	7	0

Pitchers: <u>Gomez</u> v. <u>Hubbell,</u> Gumbert (6), Coffman (6), Smith (8). Homerun: Lazzeri. Att: 60,573.

GAME II: (at Yankee Stadium, Oct. 7)

Giants	100	000	000	1	7	0
Yankees	000	024	20x	8	12	0

Pitchers: <u>Ruffing</u> v. <u>Melton,</u> Gumbert (5), Coffman (6). Att: 57,675.

GAME III: (at the Polo Grounds, Oct. 8)

Yankees	012	110	000	5	9	0
Giants	000	000	100	1	5	4

Pitchers: <u>Pearson</u>, Murphy (9) (SV) v. <u>Schumacher,</u> Melton (7), Brennan (9). Att: 37,395.

GAME IV: (at the Polo Grounds, Oct. 9)

Yankees	101	000	001	3	6	0
Giants	060	000	10x	7	12	3

Pitchers: <u>Hubbell</u> v. <u>Hadley,</u> Andrews (2), Wicker (8). Homerun: Gehrig. Att: 44293.

GAME V (at the Polo Grounds, Oct. 10)

Yankees	011	020	000	4	8	0
Giants	002	000	000	2	10	0

Pitchers: <u>Gomez</u> v. <u>Melton,</u> Smith (6), Brennan (8). Homeruns: DiMaggio, Hoag; Ott. Att: 38,216.

1938   Yankees (4) v. CHICAGO CUBS (0)

Manager Joe McCarthy hailed the 1938 Yankees as his best team, and it easily disposed of the Cubs. As the trivia expert may recall, Chicago made it to the series on the strength of Gabby Hartnett's famous homerun "in the dark" on the final day of the season, after a long, tough four-way pennant race with Pittsburgh, New York, and Cincinnati.

DiMaggio had a great series, including a pair of homeruns, and Ruffing won two complete ballgames, but the Yankees were generally overshadowed by the heroic efforts of former St. Louis fastball pitcher Dizzy Dean.

An all-star game injury had forced Dean to change his throwing motion, which in turn resulted in permanent damage to his arm in 1937. Winless mid-way through the 38' season, the Cubs obtained him on waivers in July, and Dean responded by winning seven of eight decisions during the stretch drive, mixing curves, changeups, and slip pitches.

Dean drew the starting assignment in GAME II, and might have gone home a winner but for some bad luck and a bad call. In the second inning, with two Yankees on base, Joe Gordon hit what should have been an inning-ending ground ball to the left side of the infield. Third baseman Stan Hack and shortstop Billy Jurges both raced over to make the play, cracked heads together and fell to the ground stunned, while the ball rolled into left field, scoring two runs.

Dean entered the eighth inning leading 3-2. Selkirk singled and Hoag bounced into a force play. On a two-two pitch to Crosetti, Dean threw what appeared to be strike three (an inside corner curve), but the plate umpire ruled ball three. On the next pitch, Crosetti hit a game-winning homerun.

It was Dean's last series appearance ... and Gehrig's final showing (.286, no extra-base-hits), too. No one knew it at the time, but when Gomez won Game II he had his sixth and final series victory, without a loss. The 6-0 career mark still stands as the best undefeated series career record.

Game I: Dickey gets four singles and Ruffing survives nine Cubs hits to win 3-1.

Game II: Dean performs his near-miracle, spoiled by Crosetti's two-run homerun. DiMaggio also homered.

Game III: Gordon and Dickey each homer in support of Pearson's five-hitter.

Game IV: The Yankees open a 4-1 lead, watch the Cubs crawl within one on a two-run homerun by Ken O'Dea, and then explode for four runs in the eighth to win. Crosetti's two-run triple highlighted the Yankees three-run second inning. Henrich's homerun added some insurance.

GAME I (at Wrigley Field, Oct. 5)

Yankees	020	000	100	3	12	1
Cubs	001	000	000	1	9	1

Pitchers: <u>Ruffing</u> v. <u>Lee</u>, Russell (9). Att: 43,642.

GAME II (at Wrigley Field, Oct. 6)

Yankees	020	000	022	6	7	2
Cubs	102	000	000	3	11	0

Pitchers: <u>Gomez</u>, Murphy (8) (SV) v. <u>Dean</u>, French (9). Homeruns: Crosetti, DiMaggio. Att: 42,108.

GAME III (at Yankee Stadium, Oct. 8)

Cubs	000	010	010	2	5	1
Yankees	000	022	01x	5	7	2

Pitchers: <u>Pearson</u> v. <u>Bryant</u>, Russell (6), French (7). Homeruns: Dickey, Gordon; Marty. Att: 55,236.

GAME IV (at Yankee Stadium, Oct. 9)

Cubs	000	100	020	3	8	1
Yankees	030	001	04x	8	11	1

Pitchers: <u>Ruffing</u> v. <u>Lee</u>, Root (4), Page (7), French (8), Carleton (8), Dean (8). Homeruns: Henrich; O'Dea. Att: 59,847.

1939 YANKEES (4) v. Cincinnati Reds (0)

The Yankees made it nine consecutive series games won by sweeping the Reds. Pearson emulated Pennock's near perfect game of 1927 by retiring the first 22 batters he faced in Game II before Ernie Lombardi singled with one out in the eighth inning.

Lombardi was also awarded the "goat's" role (albeit somewhat unfairly) for his infamous "snooze" in the tenth inning of the final game. The Yankees led, 5-4, when DiMaggio singled to left field and Charlie Keller tried to score from first base. The throw to the plate bounced in front of Lombardi and skidded into his groin, leaving him writhing in pain. Pitcher Bucky Walters (the real "goat") failed to back up the throw, enabling DiMaggio to circle the bases while the whole team watched Lombardi.

There was a final, sad note for Yankee fans: Gehrig, still the Yankee captain (in a non-playing role), watched the games in uniform from the Yankee dugout. When Game IV ended, he removed the pinstripes for the final time.

GAME I (at Yankee Stadium, Oct. 4)

Reds	000	100	000	1	4	0
Yankees	000	010	001	2	6	0

Pitchers: <u>Ruffing</u> v. <u>Derringer.</u> Att: 58,541.

GAME II (at Yankee Stadium, Oct. 5)

Reds	000	000	000	0	2	0
Yankees	003	100	00x	4	9	0

Pitchers: <u>Pearson</u> v. <u>Walters.</u> Homerun: Dahlgren.
At t: 59,791.

GAME III (at Crosley Field, Oct. 7)

Yankees	202	030	000	7	5	1
Reds	120	000	000	3	10	0

Pitchers: Gomez, <u>Hadley</u> (2) v. <u>Thompson,</u> Grissom (5),
Moore (7). Homeruns: Keller 2, DiMaggio, Dickey.
Att: 32,723.

GAME IV (at Crosley Field, Oct. 8)

Yankees	000	000	202	3	7	7	1
Reds	000	000	310	0	4	11	4

Pitchers: Hildebrand, Sundra (5), <u>Murphy</u> (7) v.
Derringer, Walters (8). Homeruns: Keller, Dickey.
Att: 32,794.

1941   YANKEES (4) v. Brooklyn Dodgers (1)

This was the first of seven "subway series" between these two teams, and it set the pattern for the future. It featured a crucial error in the field, a tragic loss by a pitcher who deserved a better fate, five close games, and a Yankee world champion in the end.

The tragedy was a career-ending injury to Dodgers ace Freddy Fitzsimmons in the crucial third game of the series, tied one game apiece at the time. Fitzsimmons and Yankee phenom Marius Russo were locked in a scoreless duel, when Russo's seventh inning line drive struck Fitzsimmons' knee cap, chipping a bone. Fitzsimmons had to leave the game, and was never again an effective pitcher. The Yankees scored twice off reliever Hugh Casey, and won, 2-1.

The key fielding play, or lack thereof, came in Game IV. Brooklyn led 4-3 in the top of the ninth inning, when Tommy Henrich came to bat with no one on base and two outs. On a three-two pitch, reliever Casey threw an outside curve which Henrich lunged at and missed. The crowd began pouring onto the field in celebration of what appeared to be a series-tying Dodger win, only to watch in horror as catcher Mickey Owens failed to catch the ball and went racing back towards the screen to fetch it. Henrich was safe at first base, and the Yankees went on to score four unearned runs on hits by DiMaggio, Keller, Dickey, and Gordon, for a come-from-behind 7-4 win.

Was it really a passed ball? Not according to most of the players present, including shortstop Phil Rizzuto and Keller, both of whom say the pitch was a hard breaking spitball that Owens had no chance of holding. Certainly the Ebbet's Field faithful echoed their agreement the next day when they gave Owens a sincere standing ovation prior to his first at bat, a gesture Owens never forgot.

The world championship was manager McCarthy's sixth, breaking Connie Mack's record of five.

Game I: A homerun by Gordon helps the Yankees build a 3-1 lead, and a Dodger rally in the seventh is cut short when Pee Wee Reese is out trying to tag up from second base on a pop foul near the Yankee dugout. Ruffing allowed six hits in route to his fifth consecutive world series win, raising his record to 6-1 in post season play.

Game II: The Yankees' ten-game consecutive world series winning streak ends in the sixth inning when Dolph Camilli's single scores Dixie Walker with the winning run.

Game III: Russo's line drive knocks Fitzsimmons out of the series, and the Yankees score a pair off reliever Casey to give Russo a win in his first series appearance.

Game IV: Dodger catcher Owens fails to catch what would have been the game-winning strike three on Henrich, opening the floodgates for four unearned runs and a Yankee win.

Game V: Henrich homers, and Gordon's second inning run-scoring single drives in the winning run as Tiny Bonham makes a successful series debut. After allowing three hits and one run in the first three innings, Bonham pitches one-hit ball.

GAME I (at Yankee Stadium, Oct. 1)

Dodgers	000	010	100	2	6	0
Yankees	010	101	00x	3	6	1

Pitchers: Ruffing v. Davis, Casey (6), Allen (7).
Homerun: Gordon. Att: 68,540.

GAME II (at Yankee Stadium, Oct. 2)

Dodgers	000	021	000	3	6	2
Yankees	011	000	000	2	9	1

Pitchers: Wyatt v. Chandler, Murphy (6). Att: 66,248.

GAME III (at Ebbet's Field, Oct 4)

Yankees	000	000	020	2	8	0
Dodgers	000	000	010	1	4	0

Pitchers: Russo v. Fitzsimmons, Casey (8), French (8), Allen (9). Att: 33,100.

GAME IV (at Ebbet's Field, Oct. 5)

Yankees	100	200	004	7	12	0
Dodgers	000	220	000	4	9	1

Pitchers: Donald, Breuer (5), Murphy (8) v. Higbe, French (4), Allen (5), Casey (5). Homerun: Reiser.
Att: 33,813.

GAME V (at Ebbet's Field, Oct. 6)

Yankees	020	010	000	3	6	0
Dodgers	001	000	000	1	4	1

Pitchers: Bonham v. Wyatt. Homerun: Henrich. Att: 34,072.

1942 ST. LOUIS CARDINALS (4) v. Yankees (1)

In one of the great upsets in series history, the young and hungry Cards, many of whom stood to double their yearly salaries by winning, shocked the Yankees in five games. The defeat was doubly embarassing because New York lost all three home games, including the finale. And to add insult to injury, Ernie White shut them out for the first time since 1926, when Jesse Haines won 4-0. (Haines' team? The Cardinals, of course!) The less said about this series, the better.

Game I: Ruffing hurls no-hit baseball for seven-and-two-thirds innings. It was before Terry Moore singled. It was his final series victory, raising his record to 7-0, and temporarily breaking Gomez's undefeated career mark. In a bit of foreshadowing, Ruffing surrendered four runs in the ninth inning, and had to be bailed out by Spud Chandler.

Game II: Trailing 3-1 in the eighth inning, the Yankees tie the score on Keller's two-run homerun, but the Cards edge ahead in the bottom of the inning on Enos Slaughter's double and Stan Musial's single. A Yankee threat in the ninth goes by the boards when Slaughter guns down Tuck Stainback trying to go from first to third on a single to right field by Buddy Hassett.

Game III: Ernie White spins a 2-0, six-hit shutout.

Game IV: With the score tied 6-6 in the seventh inning, the Cards score twice in the eighth on a run-scoring single by Walker Cooper and a sacrifice fly by Musial. Keller homered with two on in the sixth inning, during a five-run outburst which tied the score 6-6.

Game V: The Cardinals break a 2-2 tie on Whitey Kurowski's two-run homerun in the ninth inning, and win when catcher Walker Cooper picks Gordon off second base to kill a bottom half of the inning rally.

GAME I: (at Sportsman's Park, Sept. 30)

Yankees	000	110	032	7	11	0
Cardinals	000	000	004	4	7	4

Pitchers: Ruffing, Chandler (9) (SV) v. M. Cooper, Gumbert (8), Lanier (9). Att: 34,385.

GAME II: (at Sportsman's Park, Oct. 1)

Yankees	000	000	030	3	10	2
Cardinals	200	000	11x	4	6	0

Pitchers: Beazley v. Bonham. Homerun: Keller. Att: 34,255.

GAMES III (at Yankee Stadium, Oct. 3)

Cardinals	001	000	001	2	5	1
Yankees	000	000	000	0	6	1

Pitchers: White v. Chandler, Breuer (9), Turner (9) Att: 69,123.

GAME IV: (at Yankee Stadium, Oct. 4)

Cardinals	000	600	201	9	12	1
Yankees	100	005	000	6	10	1

Pitchers: M. Cooper, Gumbert (6), Plllet (6), Lanier (7), v. Borowy, Donald (4), Bonham (7). Homerun: Keller. Att: 69,902.

GAME V: (at Yankee Stadium, Oct. 5)

Cardinals	000	101	002	4	9	4
Yankees	100	100	000	2	7	1

Pitchers: Beazley v. Ruffing. Homeruns: Slaughter, Kurowski; Rizzuto. Att: 69,052

1943   YANKEES (4) v. St. Louis Cardinals (11)

For many members of the 1943 Yankees, this world series was the sweetest because they revenged the embarrassment of '42 in a powerful manner. It also seems sweeter in hindsight because this was manager McCarthy's final world champion, and the Yankees' tenth.

239

Both teams had lost several starting players to the armed forces, and the series' format was changed to hold the first three games in New York to comply with wartime travel restrictions. St. Louis still had Musial and the Cooper Brothers, but the Yankees were without DiMaggio, Henrich, Rizzuto and Red Rolfe. The shortage of veterans was reflected in the offensive stats, with only Billy Johnson batting .300 (exactly .300).

Game I: Crosetti, Johnson and Dickey single to break a five inning 2-2 tie and make Chandler a winner. Gordon added a homerun.

Game II: Ray Sanders' three-run homerun in the fourth inning proves the game-winner as Mort Cooper wins on a six-hitter.

Game III: A five-run Yankee eighth inning erases a 2-1 Cardinal lead, with Johnson's bases loaded triple the key blow. Johnny Murphy relieved starter Hank Borowy in the ninth inning to pick up a save (his fourth) in his final world series appearance.

Game IV: Russo scatters seven hits, allows one unearned run, and scores the game-winner after an eighth inning double to give the Yankees a commanding three-games-to-none lead.

Game V: Chandler adds insult to injury by surviving ten Cardinal hits and stranding 11 men on base. Dickey's sixth inning, two-run homerun is the only score.

GAME I: (at Yankee Stadium, Oct. 5)

Cardinals	010	010	000	2	7	2
Yankees	000	202	000	4	8	2

Pitchers: Chandler v. Lanier. Homerun: Gordon. Att: 68,676.

GAME II (at Yankee Stadium, Oct. 6)

Cardinals	001	300	000	4	7	2
Yankees	000	100	002	3	6	0

Pitchers: Cooper v. Bonham, Murphy (9). Homeruns: Marion, Sanders. Att: 68,578.

GAME III: (at Yankee Stadium, Oct. 7)

Cardinals	000	200	000	2	6	4
Yankees	000	001	05x	6	8	0

Pitchers: Borowy, Murphy (9) (SV) v. Brazle, Krist (8), Brecheen (8). Att: 69,990.

GAME IV: (at Sportsman's Park, Oct. 10)

Yankees	000	100	010	2	6	2
Cardinals	000	000	100	1	7	1

Pitchers: Russo v. Lanier, Brecheen (8). Att: 36,196.

GAME V: (at Sportsman's Park, Oct. 11)

Yankees	000	002	000	2	7	1
Cardinals	000	000	000	0	10	1

Pitchers: Chandler v. M. Cooper, Lanier (8), Dickson (9). Homerun: Dickey. Att: 33,872.

1947   YANKEES (4) v. Brooklyn Dodgers (3)

This is considered by many to have been the classic Yankee-Dodger confrontation, complete with unlikely heroes, clutch hitting, six close games, spectacular fielding, etc. It also marked the series debuts of Jackie Robinson and Yogi Berra, with Berra going on to play in a record 14 series. Another first:

240

television for all seven games, including a near no-hitter by Bill Bevens; one of the greatest catches in series history, by Al Gionfriddo; a 12-strikeout performance by Allie Reynolds; and the first pinch hit homerun in series history, by Berra.

(Note: I have departed from the game-by-game scheme to make this section more readable.)

After a pair of easy victories at Yankee Stadium, (see linescores below), including Reynolds' 12 strikeout outing in Game II, the Yankees entered the unfriendly confines of Ebbet's Field. Bobo Newsom and Vic Raschi received their world series baptisms as Yankees, and in a most rude fashion, as the Dodgers routed the pair in route to a 9-8 win in Game III, despite DiMaggio's two-run homerun, and Berra's pinch hit shot.

Game IV was a classic. Yankee starter Bill Bevens, 7-13 during the regular season, held the Dodgers hitless going into the ninth inning. The inconsistent right hander had walked nine, and allowed a run in the fifth inning on a pair of walks, a sacrifice, and an infield out, but somehow entered the ninth inning leading, 2-1. After retiring the leadoff hitter, Bevens walked Carl Furillo. One out later, pinch runner Al Gionfriddo (don't forget his name) stole second base. This put Yankee manager Bucky Harris on the spot: do you walk the next batter (pinch-hitter Pete Reiser) and set up a force out while risking that to do so would put the winning run on base, thereby violating a basic baseball tenet? Harris elected to walk Reiser, ignoring the fact that Reiser had suffered a leg injury which should have cut down on his swing and power, and would undoubtedly be pinch run for (by Eddie Miksis).

Dodger manager Leo Durocher called on another pinch hitter, 34-year-old Cookie Lavagetto, in place of the scheduled batter, Eddie Stanky. Lavagetto looked at the first pitch, and swung at the second, lifting a high fly ball to right field which sailed up and off the concrete wall, scoring both runners, and sending Bevens and the Yankees down to a heart-breaking defeat.

Game V was the DiMaggio Show, as the Yankee Clipper came through with a game-winning homerun in the fifth inning off Rex Barney and made two fine running catches in centerfield to stop Dodger rallies. Yankee starter Spec Shea went the distance, allowing just four hits, and making two of his own, one a run-scoring single in the fourth inning.

Some 74,065 fans jammed Yankee Stadium for Game VI, and the largest crowd in series history up to that time saw one of the greatest catches in baseball history. The Dodgers led, 8-5, when the Yankees came to bat in the sixth inning and put runners on first and second with two outs. DiMaggio stepped up and belted reliever Joe Hatten's inside fastball towards the 415-foot sign in left centerfield for an apparent game-tying homerun. But Gionfriddo, a lefty, raced back to the fence and made the spectacular, rally-killing catch. A righthander might not have caught the ball! In a rare display of emotion, DiMaggio kicked second base in disgust, perhaps realizing that the Dodgers were destined to win that battle, but not the war. (One final note: the teams used a record 38 players in this game)

The seventh game proved a bit anti-climactic. After spotting the Dodgers two runs in the second inning, the Yankees got on the scoreboard with a run in the bottom of the inning, and used Tommy Henrich's two-run single in the fourth to go ahead permanently. It was Henrich's third game-winner of the series.

GAME I: (at Yankee Stadium, Sept. 30)

Dodgers	100	001	100	3	6	0
Yankees	000	050	00x	5	4	0

Pitchers: <u>Shea,</u> Page (6) (SV) v. <u>Branca,</u> Behrman (5), Casey (7). Att: 73,365.

GAME II: (at Yankee Stadium, Oct. 1)
```
Dodgers        001   100   001    3    9    2
Yankees        101   121   40x   10   15    1
```
Pitchers: Reynolds v. Lombardi, Gregg (5), Behrman (7),
Barney (7). Homeruns: Henrich; Walker. Att: 69,865.

GAME III: (at Ebbet's Field, Oct. 2)
```
Yankees        002   221   100    8   13    0
Dodgers        061   200   00x    9   13    1
```
Pitchers: Hatten, Branca (5), Casey (7) v. Newsom,
Raschi (2), Drews (3), Chandler (4), Page (6).
Homeruns: DiMaggio, Berra. Att: 33,098.

GAME IV: (at Ebbet's Field, Oct. 3)
```
Yankees        100   100   000    2    8    1
Dodgers        000   010   002    3    1    3
```
Pitchers: Taylor, Gregg (1), Behrman (8) v. Bevens,
Att: 33,443.

GAME V: (at Ebbet's Field, Oct 4)
```
Yankees        000   110   000    2    5    0
Dodgers        000   001   000    1    4    1
```
Pitchers: Shea v. Barney, Hatten (5), Behrman (7),
Casey (8). Homerun: DiMaggio. Att: 34,379.

GAME VI (at Yankee Stadium, Oct. 5)
```
Dodgers        202   004   000    8   12    1
Yankees        004   100   001    6   15    2
```
Pitchers: Lombardi, Branca (3), Hatten (6), Casey (9) v.
Reynolds, Drews (3), Page (5), Newsom (6), Raschi (7),
Wensloff (8). Att: 74,065.

GAME VII (at Yankee Stadium, Oct. 6)
```
Dodgers        020   000   000    2    7    0
Yankees        010   201   10x    5    7    0
```
Pitchers: Shea, Bevens (2), Page (5) v. Gregg,
Behrman (4), Hatten (6), Barney (6), Casey (7).
Att: 71,548.

1949   YANKEES (4) v. Brooklyn Dodgers (1)

This was the first in a streak of five consecutive world championships under the helm of Hall-of-Famer Casey Stengel. It was also a surprisingly close series, despite the Yankees four games to one victory, with the first three games all decided by one run.

Game I: Allie Reynolds and Don Newcombe hook up in a scoreless duel until the bottom of the ninth inning, when Henrich lines a Newcombe fastball into the right field stands to give the Yankees a 1-0 win. Coincidentally, the last time a series game was won 1-0 on a homerun was in 1923, when a 34-year-old outfielder with the New York Giants did it against the Yankees. The culprit: Stengel!

Game II: Another pitcher's duel, this time matching the Dodger's Preacher Roe against Raschi. The lone run came in the second inning when Robinson doubled and scored on a single by Gil Hodges.

Game III: Back to Ebbet's Field they went for Game III, and in an instant replay of the third game of the '41 series, the Yankees edged the Dodgers by one

242

run, this time 4-3. But it wasn't all that simple. The teams entered the ninth inning tied 1-1. The Yankees scored three runs, two of them on the first of many clutch pinch hits by Johnny Mize. In the bottom of the inning, the Dodgers gave New York a good scare when Roy Campanella and Luis Olmo homered off reliever Joe Page before Page finally ended the game.

Game IV: The Yankees use a pair of three-run innings to take a 6-0 lead, but require outstanding relief pitching by Reynolds after Lopat surrendered four runs in the sixth. Once again, Newcombe came out on the short end.

Game V: The Yankees open a 10-1 lead, largely thanks to the wildness of Dodger starter Rex Barney, and the ineffective relief work of Jack Banta. The Dodgers battle back with a run in the sixth, and Page comes in to nail it down after Brooklyn scores four more in the seventh. DiMaggio homered for the Yankees, Hodges (with two men on base) for Brooklyn.

One final note: with all those runs scoring, the teams hit only .226 (NY) and .210 (Bkn), while the Yankees earned run average of 2.80 seemed miniscule to Brooklyn's 4.30.

GAME I: (at Yankee Stadium, Oct. 5)

Dodgers	000	000	000	0	2	0
Yankees	000	000	001	1	5	1

Pitchers: Reynolds v. Newcombe. Homerun: Henrich.
Att: 66,224.

GAME II: (at Yankee Stadium, Oct. 6)

Dodgers	010	000	000	1	7	2
Yankees	000	000	000	0	6	1

Pitchers: Roe v. Raschi. Att: 70,053.

GAME III: (at Ebbet's Field, Oct. 7)

Yankees	001	000	003	4	5	0
Dodgers	000	100	002	3	5	0

Pitchers: Byrne, Page (4) v. Branca, Banta (9).
Homeruns: Reese, Olmo, Campanella. Att: 32,788.

GAME IV: (at Ebbet's Field, Oct. 8)

Yankees	000	330	000	6	10	0
Dodgers	000	004	000	4	9	1

Pitchers: Lopat, Reynolds (6) (SV) v. Newcombe,
Hatten (4), Erskin (6), Banta (7). Att: 33,934.

GAME V: (at Ebbet's Field, Oct. 9)

Yankees	203	113	000	10	11	1
Dodgers	001	001	400	6	11	2

Pitchers: Raschi, Page (7) (SV) v. Barney, Banta (3),
Erskine (6), Hatten (6), Palica (7), Minner (9).
Homeruns: DiMaggio; Hodges. Att: 33,711.

1950   Yankees (4) v. PHILADELPHIA PHILLIES (0)

Until 1950, only two teams had ever swept a world series: the Yankees (five times) and Braves (1914). (I suppose we could include the Giants, whose 1922 champions played a 3-3 tie with the Yankees.) In 1950, the Yankees added sweep number six to their record in a world series decided on, of all things, pitching (as usual!).

Game I: Raschi allows just two singles, and edges surprise starter Jim Konstanty, 1-0, on a fourth inning double by Bobby Brown and sacrifice flies by Hank Bauer and Jerry Coleman.

Game II: Reynolds and Robin Roberts hook up in the second consecutive pitcher's duel, with this one ending 2-1 on DiMaggio's tenth inning homerun.

Game III: With the Phillies leading 2-1 in the eighth inning, the Yankees load the bases and tie the score when shortstop Granny Hamner boots a ground ball. The Yankees score the game-winner in the ninth on a run-scoring single by Coleman.

Game IV: Whitey Ford makes his series debut successfully, pitching shutout ball for eight-and-two-thirds innings. The Phillies scored twice in the ninth when Gene Woodling dropped a fly ball, but Reynolds came in to nail it down. The Yankees scored all the runs they needed during their three-run fifth inning, highlighted by Berra's homerun and Brown's triple.

GAME I: (at Shibe Park, Oct. 4)

Yankees	000	100	000	1	5	0
Phillies	000	000	000	0	2	1

Pitchers: Raschi v. Konstanty, Meyer (9). Att: 30,746.

GAME II: (at Shibe Park, Oct. 5)

Yankees	010	000	000	1	2	10	0
Phillies	000	010	000	0	1	7	0

Pitchers: Reynolds v. Roberts Homerun: DiMaggio. Att: 32,660.

GAME III: (at Yankee Stadium, Oct. 6)

Phillies	000	001	100	2	10	2
Yankees	001	000	011	3	7	0

Pitchers: Lopat, Ferrick (9) v. Heintzelman, Konstanty (8), Meyer (9). Att: 64,505.

GAME IV (at Yankee Stadium, Oct. 7)

Phillies	000	000	002	2	7	1
Yankees	200	003	00x	5	8	2

Pitchers: Ford, Reynolds (9) v. Miller, Konstanty (1), Roberts (8). Homerun: Berra. Att: 68,098.

1951   YANKEES (4) v. New York Giants (2)

If momentum ever meant a thing, the 1951 World Series proved an exception to the rule. The Giants entered the Series after their "Miracle of Coogan's Bluff" season climaxed with Bobby Thomson's "shot heard round the world." The Giants won Game I at Yankee Stadium, 5-1, thereby breaking the home advantage. The Giants won Game III at the Polo Grounds, to go up 2-1 in games, and had their aces, Sal Maglie and Larry Jansen rested and ready for the next two games. Yet somehow, the Yankees rebounded to win Games IV and V easily, and then came from behind to win Game VI and the Series.

This was another Series of firsts and lasts. It was the rookie year for Mickey Mantle and Willie Mays, both of whom had shone for their clubs during the year, and both of whom had dismal series (Mantle was injured while chasing a fly ball in Game II. Mays batted .182.). More significantly, it marked the end of an era: the final World Series for DiMaggio.

Game I: Giants surprise starter Dave Koslo went the distance, yielding one run while scattering seven hits. Monte Irvin starred for the Giants on offense with four hits and a steal of home. Alvin Dark added a three-run homerun to cap the Giants' scoring.

Game II: A clutch homerun by Joe Collins, and the five-hit pitching of Ed Lopat, tied the series at one game each. Irvin continued his assault on Yankee pitching with three more hits.

Game III: Ask Phil Rizzuto about this game and you'll get an answer which includes some good-natured moans and groans about a play involving Eddie Stanky. With Stanky trying to steal second and Rizzuto covering the bag, Berra's throw had Stanky dead, but the Giants' pesky second baseman kicked the ball out of Rizzuto's glove and went on to score the first of five runs that inning. Rizzuto still swears Stanky never touched second base, and is frequently the subject of good-natured kidding about his "buddy."

Game IV: After going hitless in the first three games, DiMaggio explodes for a run-scoring single and a two-run homerun to pace the Yankees' 12 hit attack.

Game V: Gil McDougald hit a grand slam, and Phil Rizzuto surprised the baseball world with a homerun of his own, as the Yankees battered five Giant pitcher for 12 hits and 13 runs.

Game VI: Hank Bauer's bases loaded triple in the sixth inning enabled DiMaggio to finish with a world champion. The finale was given the usual touch of class by the time-honored veteran After DiMaggio doubled in the eighth inning and was subsequently forced at third base, he trotted off the field, slowly, amid a rising outpouring of adulation from the 61,711 fans present who doubtlessly sensed it was his final game.

GAME I: (at Yankee Stadium, Oct. 4)

Giants	200	003	000	5	10	1
Yankees	010	000	000	1	7	1

Pitchers: Koslo v. Reynolds, Hogue (7), Morgan (8).
Homerun: Dark. Att: 65,673.

GAME II: (at Yankee Stadium, Oct. 5)

Giants	000	000	100	1	5	1
Yankees	110	000	01x	3	6	0

Pitchers: Lopat v. Jansen, Spencer (7). Homerun: Collins.
Att: 66,018.

GAME III: (at the Polo Grounds, Oct. 6)

Yankees	000	000	011	2	5	2
Giants	010	050	00x	6	7	2

Pitchers: Hearn, Jones (8) (SV) v. Raschi, Hogue (5), Ostrowski (7).
Homeruns: Lockman; Woodling. Att: 52,035.

GAME IV: (at the Polo Grounds, Oct. 8)

Yankees	010	120	200	6	12	0
Giants	100	000	001	2	8	2

Pitchers: Reynolds v. Maglie, Jones (6), Kennedy (9).
Homerun: DiMaggio. Att: 49,010.

GAME V: (at the Polo Grounds, Oct. 9)

Yankees	005	202	400	13	12	1
Giants	100	000	000	1	5	3

Pitchers: Lopat v. Jansen, Kennedy (4), Spencer (6), Corwin (7).
Konikowski (9). Homeruns: McDougald, Rizzuto. Att: 47,530.

GAME VI: (at Yankee Stadium, Oct. 10)

Giants	000	010	002	3	11	1
Yankees	100	003	00x	4	7	0

Pitchers: Raschi, Sain (7), Kuzava (9) (SV) v.
Koslo, Hearn (7), Jansen (8). Att: 61,711.

1952   Yankees (4) v. BROOKLYN DODGERS (3)

A pair of Billys (Martin of the Yankees, Loes of Brooklyn) figured prominently in the '52 series. So did 39-year-old Mize, and 28-year-old Hodges. Fortunately for Yankee fans, the Yankees mentioned made positive contributions, while Hodges' and Loes' made errors of ommission.

Game I: Homeruns by Jackie Robinson, Duke Snider, and Reese provided all the offense, and Joe Black, the first black man to win a world series game, went the distance, allowing just six hits. Gil McDougald homered for the Yankees.

Game II: Martin figured prominently. With the Yankees ahead 2-1, he hit a three-run homerun to highlight a five-run sixth inning in support of Raschi's three-hit pitching.

Game III: A ninth inning passed ball by Berra allowed two unearned runs to score and enabled the Dodgers to survive Mize's pinch hit homerun in the bottom of the inning.

Game IV: Reynolds and Black met again. Both pitched well enough to win, but this time Reynolds came out on top, 2-0. Mize supplied the only run necessary on a fourth inning homerun, and Reese kicked in an insurance run on a rare (for him) error in the eighth.

Game V: In this wildest game of the '52 series, Brooklyn jumped out to a 4-0 lead, largely thanks to a Snider two-run homerun, only to have the Yankees score five runs in the fifth inning, three on a homerun by Mize. But Dodger starter Carl Erskine settled down and retired the next 19 men in a row, and went home a winner on Snider's run-scoring single in the eleventh inning.

The Yankees appeared headed for their first series loss since 1942, and only the fifth in their history. The Dodgers led in games, 3-2, and were returning to the friendly confines of Ebbet's Field for the remaining games. All of Brooklyn waited in eager anticipation of their first championship since the two leagues started meeting in post-season competition.

Game VI: After hurling six innings of scoreless baseball, Loes entered the seventh inning with a one-run lead. The lead disappeared on a Berra homerun. Gene Woodling followed with a single, and Loes obligingly balked him to second base. Raschi was the next batter, and he smacked a ground ball right back to Loes, who somehow failed to catch it and allowed it to bounce off his glove for a run-scoring single. (And to add to the zaniness, Loes later said he "lost the ball in the sun.") Mantle followed with a homerun in the eighth, and the Yankees hung on for a 3-2 win.

Game VII: Lopat and Black started, and neither was around for the finish, but Black hung around long enough to surrender a tie-breaking homerun to Mantle. Roe relieved, and gave up an insurance run in the seventh inning.

It wasn't quite over. The Dodgers loaded the bases with one out in the bottom of the seventh, bringing Stengel out to the mount, and reliever Bob Kuzava into the game. Kuzava induced Snider to pop out on a three-two pitch, and faced Robinson. Again the count went to three-and-two, and again the batter lofted a pop up on the right side of the pitcher's mound. This time, first baseman Collins, and Kuzava, merely stared at the ball, forcing Martin to come flying in from second base to make a game-saving catch off his shoe tops.

(A final note: Hodges had a disastrous series, going 0-for-21 with a walk.)

GAME I: (at Ebbet's Field, Oct. 1)

Yankees	010	000	010	2	6	2
Dodgers	010	002	01x	4	6	0

Pitchers: <u>Black</u> v. <u>Reynolds,</u> Scarborough (8).

Homeruns: Robinson, Snider, Reese; McDougald.
Att: 34,861.

GAME II: (at Ebbet's Field, Oct. 2)

Yankees	000	115	000	7	10	0
Dodgers	001	000	000	1	3	1

Pitchers: Raschi V. Erskine, Loes (6), Lehman (8).
Homerun: Martin. Att: 33,792.

GAME III: (at Yankee Stadium, Oct. 3)

Dodgers	001	010	012	5	11	0
Yankees	010	000	011	3	6	2

Pitchers: Roe v. Lopat, Gorman (9). Homeruns.
Berra, Mize. Att: 66,698.

GAME IV: (at Yankee Stadium, Oct. 4)

Dodgers	000	000	000	0	4	1
Yankees	000	100	01x	2	4	1

Pitchers: Reynolds v. Black, Rutherford (8).
Homerun: Mize. Att: 71,787.

GAME V: (at Yankee Stadium, Oct. 5)

Dodgers	010	030	100	01	6	10	0
Yankees	000	050	000	00	5	5	1

Pitchers: Erskine v. Blackwell, Sain (6). Homeruns:
Snider; Mize. Att: 70,536.

GAME VI: (at Ebbet's Field, Oct. 6)

Yankees	000	000	210	3	9	0
Dodgers	000	001	010	2	8	1

Pitchers: Raschi, Reynolds (8) (SV) v. Loes, Roe (9).
Homeruns: Berra, Mantle; Snider 2. Att: 30,037.

GAME VII: (at Ebbet's Field, Oct. 7)

Yankees	000	111	100	4	10	4
Dodgers	000	110	000	2	8	1

Pitchers: Lopat, Reynolds (4), Raschi (7), Kuzava (7) (SV)
v. Black, Roe (6), Erskine (8). Homeruns: Woodling,
Mantle. Att: 33,195.

1953   YANKEES (4) v. Brooklyn Dodgers (2)
With baseball celebrating the 50th anniversary of the first world series, the
Yankees and Dodgers met again, and some familiar names added another chapter
to the series record book.
Billy Martin, the fielding hero of '52, became the batting star of '53. He made
12 hits, the most ever in a six game series (including a double, two triples, and
two homeruns) and batted .500.
When Martin wasn't tormenting Brooklyn, Mantle was exploding for key
homeruns, and whenever the Dodgers silenced the first edition of "M & M
Boys", McDougald, Collins or Berra chipped in with homeruns.
This series was also a personal triumph for Stengel. By winning, he became the
first manager in baseball history to record five consecutive pennants and world
championships. Stengel had come a long way since managing the Dodgers of the
30's and Braves of the early 40's, both among the weaker teams of their eras.

247

And lest we forget the Dodgers, Carl Erskine made a little history of his own, striking out a record 14 Yankees in Game III (subsequently broken by Sandy Koufax in '63).

Game I: Martin got the Yankees off and running with a first inning bases loaded triple. The Dodgers battled back to tie the score, 5-5, on homeruns by Jim Gilliam, George Shuba, and Hodges, but reliever Clem Labine was ineffective surrendering game-winning homeruns to Berra and Collins. Sain was the winner in relief.

Game II: Martin continued his assault on the record book by hitting a two-run homerun in the first inning. The Dodgers battled back to tie, but Mantle's two-run homerun in the eighth inning made Lopat a winner and Roe a loser.

Game III: The series returned to Ebbet's Field, where Erskine gave the Brooklyn fans a lot to cheer about. He struck out every starter at least once, and "k'd" Mantle four times, in what was not an easy game. The score was tied 2-2 until Campanella hit an eighth inning homerun.

Game IV: Duke Snider's double and homerun score four runs to aid Loes' effort over Ford. McDougald homered for the Yankees.

Game V: Mantle unlimbered his bat again, stroking a tie-breaking grand slam off Johnny Podres in the third inning. Martin chipped in with a two-run shot of his own, while Woodling and McDougald also homered. The two teams combined for a record 47 total bases.

Game VI: Another Yankee-Dodger classic, with the usual result. New York led, 3-1, entering the ninth inning, when Carl Furillo hit a two-run homerun off Reynolds to tie the score. In the bottom of the inning, Bauer led off with a walk, Mantle singled, and Martin stroked his twelfth hit of the series to center field to score the game-winning run.

GAME I: (at Yankee Stadium, Sept. 30)

| Dodgers | 000 | 013 | 100 | 5 | 12 | 2 |
| Yankees | 400 | 010 | 13x | 9 | 12 | 0 |

Pitchers: Reynolds, Sain (6) v. Erskine, Hughes (2), Labine (6), Wade (8). Homeruns: Berra, Collins; Gilliam, Hodges, Shuba. Att: 69,374.

GAME II: (at Yankee Stadium, Oct. 1)

| Dodgers | 000 | 200 | 000 | 2 | 9 | 1 |
| Yankees | 100 | 000 | 12x | 4 | 5 | 0 |

Pitchers: Lopat v. Roe. Homeruns: Martin, Mantle. Att: 66,786.

GAME III: (at Ebbet's Field, Oct. 2)

| Yankees | 000 | 010 | 010 | 2 | 6 | 0 |
| Dodgers | 000 | 011 | 01x | 3 | 9 | 0 |

Pitchers: Erskine v. Raschi. Homerun: Campanella. Att: 35,270.

GAME IV: (at Ebbet's Field, Oct. 3)

| Yankees | 000 | 020 | 001 | 3 | 9 | 0 |
| Dodgers | 300 | 102 | 10x | 7 | 12 | 0 |

Pitchers: Loes, Labine (9) (SV) v. Ford, Gorman (2), Sain (5), Shallock (7) Homeruns: Snider; McDougald. Att: 36,775.

GAME V (at Ebbet's Field, Oct. 4)

| Yankees | 105 | 000 | 311 | 11 | 11 | 1 |
| Dodgers | 010 | 010 | 041 | 7 | 14 | 1 |

Pitchers: McDonald, Kuzava (8), Reynolds (9) (SV) v. Podres,

Meyer (3), Wade (8), Black (9). Homeruns: Woodling, Mantle, Martin, McDougald; Cox, Gilliam. Att: 36,665.

GAME VI (at Yankee Stadium, Oct. 5)

Dodgers	000	001	002	3	8	3
Yankees	210	000	001	4	13	0

Pitchers: Ford, Reynolds (8) v. Erskine, Milliken (5), Labine (7). Homerun: Furillo. Att: 62,370.

1955 Brooklyn Dodgers (4) v. YANKEES (3)

After a one-year absence from post-season play, the Yankees and Dodgers found themselves staring at each other again. As usual, the fans were in for a real treat, and for a rare occasion, the Dodgers won the series. It was Brooklyn's only world championship, coming after six misses, and the Dodgers would miss again in '56 before deserting the borough in '58.

The teams combined for a record 17 homeruns (nine by Brooklyn), all of which were hit in five of the seven games. Snider led the homerun parade with four, including two game-winners. Collins hit a pair for New York.

With all that hitting going on, its hard to believe that the series was decided on a great fielding play and gutsy pitching, but that's the way it was.

Game I: Collins' fourth inning two-run homerun broke a 3-3 tie, and his two-run shot in the sixth gave the Yankees what proved to be badly needed insurance runs. The Dodgers rebounded with a pair of runs in the top of the eighth, the second scoring on Robinson's steal of home, and Brooklyn left the tying run on base in the ninth inning.

Game II: Tommy Byrne pitched and batted his way to victory. His two-run single highlighted the Yankees' four-run fourth inning, and his five-hit pitching made him the first lefthander to pitch a complete game victory against Brooklyn in 1955.

Game III: The Dodgers bats came alive in Ebbet's Field. Campanella sparked an 11-hit attack with three of his own, including a two-run homerun. Mantle supplied a somewhat reduced punch for New York with a homerun.

Game V: Don Larsen makes his first series appearance, and pitches a mere four innings. Homeruns by Campanella and Hodges chase Larsen in the fourth, and Snider's three-run shot off Johnny Kucks in the fifth ices it.

Game V: The Dodgers make it a clean sweep in Ebbet's Field on homeruns by Sandy Amoros (keep that name in mind) and Snider (he hit two). The Yankees countered with solo shots by Berra and Bob Cerv, but came up short.

Game VI: Moose Skowron's first inning three-run homerun highlights a five-run outburst as the Yankees rally behind Ford to send the series into a seventh game.

Game VII: Brooklyn went with Podres, winner of Game III, while the Yankees gave the nod to Byrne, master of Game II, as the teams met in a seventh game for the second time in three world series. Podres came out on top, 2-0, with a big assist from that fellow named Amoros.

The Dodgers led 2-0 when the Yankees came to bat in the sixth inning. Manager Walter Alston had inserted Amoros in left field after pinch hitting for second baseman Don Zimmer, which forced Gilliam to come in from left field to play second base. Martin led off with a walk, McDougald beat out a bunt, aud Berra stepped up to the plate. Always a notorious non-strike hitter, Berra whacked an outside fastball down the left field line for what appeared to be a game-tying double. BUT, Amoros came from nowhere to one-hand the ball at the last second, wheeled, and threw to Reese, who fired over to first base for the rally-killing double play. Had Amoros been righthanded, he never would have caught the ball.

Next year had finally come to Flatbush.

GAME I: (at Yankee Stadium, Sept. 28)
Dodgers   021   000   020   5   10   0
Yankees   021   102   00x   6   9   1
Pitchers: Ford, Grim (9), (SV) v. Newcombe, Bessent (6),
Labine (8). Homeruns: E. Howard, Collins, 2; Furillo,
Snider. Att: 63,869.

GAME II: (at Yankee Stadium, Sept. 29)
Dodgers   000   110   000   2   5   2
Yankees   000   400   00x   4   8   0
Pitchers: Byrne v. Loes, Bessent (4), Spooner (5),
Labine (8). Att: 64,707.

GAME III: (at Ebbet's Field, Sept. 30)
Yankees   020   000   100   3   7   0
Dodgers   220   200   20x   8   11   1
Pitchers: Podres v. Turley, Morgan (2), Kucks (5),
Sturdivaut (7). Homeruns: Campanella; Mantle. Att: 34,209.

GAME IV: (at Ebbet's Field, Oct. 1)
Yankees   110   102   000   5   9   0
Dodgers   001   330   10x   8   14   0
Pitchers: Erskine, Bessent (4), Labine (5) vs
Larsen, Kucks (5), Coleman (6), Morgan (7),
Sturdivant (8). Homeruns: Campanella, Hodges,
Snider; McDougald. Att: 36,796.

GAME V: (at Ebbet's Field, Oct. 2)
Yankees   000   100   110   3   6   0
Dodgers   021   010   01x   5   9   2
Pitchers: Craig, Labine (7) (SV) v. Grim, Turley (7),
Homeruns: Snider 2, Amoros; Cerv, Berra. Att: 36,796.

GAME VI: (at Yankee Stadium, Oct. 3)
Dodgers   000   100   000   1   4   1
Yankees   500   000   00x   5   8   0
Pitchers: Ford v. Spooner, Meyer (1), Roebuck (7).
Homerun: Skowron. Att: 64,022.

GAME VII: (at Yankee Stadium, Oct. 4)
Dodgers   000   101   000   2   5   0
Yankees   000   000   000   0   8   1
Pitchers: Podres v. Byrne, Grim (6), Turley (8).
Att: 62,465.

1956   Yankees (4) v. BROOKLYN DODGERS (3)
   This was the last Brooklyn-New York confrontation, and as if to sum up the
previous six great contests, this one not only went seven games, but also featured
the greatest world series pitching performance ever: a perfect game. The hurler
was the Yankees' Don Larsen, 11-5 during the regular season (with a rather
imperfect 3.26 earned run average). He was the same Larsen the Dodgers shelled
in Game IV in '55, and in Game II in '56.
   But there he was, standing on the mound in the bottom of the ninth inning,
leading 2-0, with 64,519 fans cheering him on, and eight perfect innings behind
him. Sure, the Dodgers had come close to a hit on three occasions: Robinson's
second-inning line drive off the glove of third baseman Audy Carey, which

richocheted to shortstop McDougald, who threw the speedy Robinson out by half a step; a fifth inning line drive by Hodges, speared by Mantle after a long run into left center field; and a near homerun by that pesky Amoros on a shot that hooked foul at the last second, according to Bauer.

The dangerous Furillo led off the ninth and flew out. Campanella followed with a ground out to second. Up to the plate stepped pinch hitter Dale Mitchell, in what proved to be his final major league bat. The count went to one ball, two strikes, and Berra ("I was worried about just winning the game.") called for a fastball, up and away. Larsen threw to the target, the umpire called strike three, and it was all history.

Game I: Gil Hodges' three-run homerun breaks a third inning, 2-2 tie, and leads the Dodgers past Ford.

Game II: Another series record-breaker, as the Yankees and Dodgers play the longest nine-inning game in series history (3 hours, 26 minutes), and the. Yankees used a record seven pitchers. New York opened a 6-0 lead, four of the runs scoring on Berra's second inning grand slam off the luckless Newcombe. Brooklyn came back with six runs of their own in the second, three of them on Snider's homerun off Larsen, and went on to a 13-8 win.

Game III: The series returned to Yankee Stadium, where Enos Slaughter's sixth inning three-run homerun led New York to a come-from-behind 5-3 win.

Game IV: Martin's fourth inning single drives in the go ahead run off Erskine, and Mantle and Bauer add homeruns, to even the series

Game V: Larsen's day in the sun, aided by Mantle's homerun (his third of the series).

Game VI: Reliever Clem Labine is a surprise starter, and responded with a seven-hit, 10-inning, 1-0 win over Turley. The winning run scored when when Slaughter misjudged a fly ball hit by Robinson, allowing Jim Gilliam to score from second base.

Game VII: For the third time in their last four meetings, these same two teams faced a seventh game, and this time the Yankees won easily. Newcombe, a 27-game winner during the regular season, started for Brooklyn, and surrendered a pair of two-run homeruns to his arch nemesis, Berra. Kucks got the nod from Stengel, and pitched a three-hit masterpiece. Skowron hit a grand slam, and Howard added a solo shot. The loss was Newcombe's fourth without a victory in his series career, and he never won (or lost) another series game. Despite his career mark of 149-90, he remained ineffective in the post-season affairs. One final note: Newcombe's series earned run average: 8.59.

There is an interesting sidelight: this was one series in which statistics really told the story (see the 1960 series for a perfect example of how they can be false indicators). The Yankees batted .253 to the Dodgers' .195. New York hit 12 of the 15 homeruns and outhit the Dodgers 58-42. The pitching stats showed the Yankees with a sparkling earned run average (2.48) to a rather dismal (4.72) mark for Brooklyn. One consolation remained for Dodger fans: they only struck out 43 times to New York's 47!

GAME I: (AT Ebbet's Field, Oct. 3)

Yankees	200	100	000	3	9	1
Dodgers	023	100	00x	6	9	0

Pitchers: <u>Maglie</u> v. <u>Ford</u>, Kucks (4), Morgan (6).
Homeruns: Robinson, Hodges; Mantle, Martin.
Att: 34,479.

GAME II: (at Ebbet's Field, Oct. 5)

Yankees	150	100	001	8	12	2
Dodgers	061	220	02x	13	12	0

Pitchers: Newcombe, Roebuck (2), <u>Bessent</u> (3) v.
Larsen, Kucks (2), Byrne (2), Sturdivant (3),

251

Morgan (3), Turley (5), McDermott (6), Homeruns:
Snider; Berrav Att: 36,217.

GAME III (at Yankee Stadium, Oct. 6)

Dodgers	010	001	100	3	8	1
Yankees	010	003	01x	5	8	1

Pitchers: Ford v. Craig, Labine (7). Homeruns:
Martin, Slaughter. Att: 73,977.

GAME IV: (at Yankee Stadium, Oct. 7)

Dodgers	000	100	001	2	6	0
Yankees	100	201	20x	6	7	2

Pitchers: Sturdivant v. Erskine, Roebuck (5),
Drysdale (7). Homeruns: Mantle, Bauer. Att: 69,705.

GAME V: (at Yankee Stadium, Oct. 8)

Dodgers	000	000	000	0	0	0
Yankees	000	101	00x	2	5	0

Pitchers: Larsen v. Maglie. Homerun: Mantle.
Att: 64,519.

GAME VI: (at Ebbet's Field, Oct. 9)

Yankees	000	000	000	0	0	7	0
Dodgers	000	000	000	1	1	4	0

Pitchers: Labine v. Turley. Att: 33,224.

GAME VII: (at Ebbet's Field, Oct. 10)

Yankees	202	100	400	9	10	0
Dodgers	000	000	000	0	3	1

Pitchers: Kucks v. Newcombe, Bessent (4), Craig (7),
Roebuck (7), Erskine (9). Homeruns: Berra 2, Howard,
Skowron. Att: 33,782.

1957   Milwaukee Braves (4) v. YANKEES (3)

Historically speaking, young players who came to the Yankees often played over their heads, while veterans were frequently rejuvenated. On the other side of the coin, players who were traded away usually did very little to hurt their former team. This appeared to be the case, at least in the short run, in a 1951 deal which sent rookie pitcher Lew Burdette to Milwaukee for veteran Johnny Sain. Sain compiled a 33-20 mark in three-plus seasons in New York, including a win in the '53 series, and was released to Kansas City in 1955.

Meanwhile, Burdette had several .500 or better seasons with the Braves, but attracted very little attention until the '57 series, when he came back to haunt his former team. Burdette won three complete games, two of them shutouts, and led Milwaukee to a surprise championship.

Game I: Warren Spahn and Ford hooked up in a five-inning duel before Andy Carey's run-scoring single and Jerry Coleman's suicide squeeze bunt in the sixth inning drove Spahn out and made Ford a winner.

Game II: Burdette tied the series by scattering seven hits after surrendering single runs in the second and third innings. The Braves broke a 2-2 tie in the fourth on three singles and an error by shortstop Tony Kubek.

Game III: The Yankee bats exploded for 12 runs, taking advantage of 11 walks issued by the Braves' pitchers. Kubek balanced his second-game miscue by hitting two homeruns, and Mantle hit a two-run shot of his own. For Milwaukee, a fellow named Henry Aaron hit a two run homerun.

252

Game IV: Elston Howard's two-out ninth inning three-run homerun ties the score at 4-4, and Bauer triples home Kubek in the tenth to put New York ahead.

All that remained was for reliever Bob Grim to retire the Braves, and New York would have a commanding three-games-to-one lead. BUT, it was not to be.

Utility infielder Nippy Jones lead off the inning by pinch hitting for Spahn. Earlier that day, Jones had elected to polish his well-worn spikes, and when a curve in the dirt was called a ball, Jones argued vehemently that he had been hit by the pitch. He retrieved the ball and showed umpire Augie Donatelli the tell-tale shoe polish scuff, forcing the embarassed umpire to award Jones first base. Stengel emerged from the dugout in a rare rage, but the call would not change again. Johnny Logan followed with a double, and Eddie Matthews hit a three-run homerun to give Milwaukee a 7-5 win.

Game V: Burdette shuts the Yankees out again, this time 1-0. Wes Covington saves the game by robbing McDougald of a homerun with a great catch. Joe Adcock singled home the lone run scored off Ford.

Game VI: The Yankees take a 2-0 lead on Berra's two-run homerun in the third inning, but homeruns by Joe Torre and Aaron tie it up. The teams go to the bottom of the seventh inning tied, 2-2, when Bauer hits a game-winning homerun for Turley.

Game VII: This time there was no Newcombe for the Yankees to bounce around. Instead, Burdette was back on just two days rest, and he somehow found the strength to hurl a seven-hit shutout. It was the Braves first championship since 1914, and the only one they won in Milwaukee.

GAME I: (at Yankee Stadium, Oct. 2)

Braves	000	000	100	1	5	0
Yankees	000	012	00x	3	9	1

Pitchers: Ford v. Spahn, Johnson (6), McMahon (7).
att: 69,476.

GAME II: (at Yankee Stadium, Oct. 3)

Braves	011	200	000	4	8	0
Yankees	011	000	000	2	7	2

Pitchers: Burdette v. Shantz, Ditmar (4), Grim (8),
Homeruns: Logan; Bauer. Att: 65,202.

GAME III: (at County Stadium, Oct. 5)

Yankees	302	200	500	12	9	0
Braves	010	020	000	3	8	1

Pitchers: Turley, Larsen (2) v. Buhl, Pizarro (1),
Conley (3), Johnson (5), Trowbridge (7), McMahon (8).
Homeruns: Kubek 2, Mantle; Aaron. Att: 45,804.

GAME IV: (at County Stadium, Oct. 6)

Yankees	100	000	003	1	5	11	0
Braves	000	400	000	3	7	7	0

Pitchers: Spahn v. Sturdivant, Shantz (5), Kucks (8),
Byrne (8), Grim (10). Homeruns: Aaron, Torre,
Matthews; Howard. Att: 45,804.

GAME V: (at County Stadium, Oct. 7)

Yankees	000	000	000	0	7	0
Braves	000	001	00x	1	6	1

Pitchers: Burdette v. Ford, Turley (8). Att: 45,811.

GAME VI: (at Yankee Stadium, Oct. 9)

Braves	000	010	100	2	4	0
Yankees	002	000	10x	3	7	0

Pitchers: Turley v. Buhl, Johnson (3), McMahon (8),
Homeruns: Berra, Bauer; Torre. Att: 61,408.

GAME VII: (at Yankee Stadium, Oct. 10)

Braves	004	000	010	5	9	1
Yankees	000	000	000	0	7	3

Pitchers: Burdette v. Larsen, Shantz (3), Ditmar (4),
Sturdivant (6), Byrne (8), Homerun: Crandall.
Att: 61,207.

1958 Yankees (4) v. MILWAUKEE BRAVES (3)

Repeating the pattern established in 1943 and 1956, the Yankees faced the same opponent who defeated them the year before and took revenge in a record-tying manner. Trailing Milwaukee three-games-to-one, the Yankees came back to win Game V in New York, and then embarassed the Braves in Milwaukee in Games VI and VII, to become the first team since the 1925 Pirates to come back from a three-one deficit and win the series.

The key difference between '58 and '57 was Burdette, who went 1-2 this time around, losing Games V and VII by lopsided scores. Also of importance: the four homeruns hit by the pesky Bauer, who had a great series at the plate (.323, ten hits, eight runs batted in).

Game I: Milwaukee wins in ten innings, 4-3, on singles by Joe Adcock, Del Crandall, and Bill Bruton. Spahn went the distance, despite homeruns by Bauer and Skowron.

Game II: The Braves pounded Turley for seven runs in the first inning, including a three-run homerun by Burdette, and survived homeruns by Mantle (a pair) and Bauer to take a two-games-to-none lead.

Game III: Larsen gained a measure of revenge for the beating he took in Game VII of the '57 series by combining with Ryne Duren to shut out the Braves, 4-0. Bauer had the key hit: a two-run homerun.

Game IV: Spahn hurls a two-hitter and stops Bauer's 17-game world series hitting streak which dated back to 1955.

Game V: Stengel goes with Turley in hopes of avoiding a home field clinching loss, and Turley responded with a five-hit shutout. McDougald hit a third inning homerun, and the Yankees exploded in a six-run seventh to win easily.

Game VI: New York breaks a tenth-inning 2-2 tie on a homerun by McDougald and a run-scoring hit by Skowron. When reliever Duren got in trouble in the bottom of the inning, Stengel called on Turley, who stopped the Braves, leaving the tying and winning runs on base.

Game VII: The momentum was all New York's way, and the Yankees broke a 2-2 tie with a four-run eighth inning, highlighted by Skowron's three-run homerun, to beat Burdette, 6-2. It was Stengel's seventh and final championship, still a record.

GAME I: (at County Stadium, Oct. 1)

Yankees	000	120	000	0	3	8	1
Braves	000	200	010	1	4	10	0

Pitchers: Spahn v. Ford, Duren (8). Homeruns: Skowron,
Bauer. Att: 46,367.

GAME II: (at County Stadium, Oct. 2)

Yankees	100	100	003	5	7	0
Braves	710	000	23x	13	15	1

Pitchers: Burdette v. Turley, Maas (1), Kucks (1), Dickson (5), Monroe (8). Homeruns: Bruton, Burdette; Mantle 2, Bauer. Att: 46,367.

GAME III: (at Yankee Stadium, Oct. 4)

Braves	000	000	000	0	6	0
Yankees	000	020	20x	4	4	0

Pitchers: Larsen, Duren (8) v. Rush, McMahon (7). Homerun: Bauer. Att: 71,599.

GAME IV: (at Yankee Stadium, Oct. 5)

Braves	000	001	110	3	9	0
Yankees	000	000	000	0	2	0

Pitchers: Spahn v. Ford, Kucks (8), Dickson (9). Att: 71,563.

GAME V: (at Yankee Stadium, Oct. 6)

Braves	000	000	000	0	5	0
Yankees	001	006	00x	7	10	0

Pitchers: Turley v. Burdette, Pizarro (6), Willey (8). Homerun: McDougald. Att: 65,279.

GAME VI: (at County Stadium, Oct. 8)

Yankees	100	001	000	2	4	10	1
Braves	110	000	000	1	3	10	4

Pitchers: Ford, Ditmar (2), Duren (6), Turley (10) v. Spahn, McMahon (10). Homeruns: Bauer, McDougald. Att: 46,367.

GAME VII: (at County Stadium, Oct. 9)

Yankees	020	000	040	6	8	0
Braves	100	001	000	2	5	2

Pitchers: Larsen, Turley (3) v. Burdette, McMahon (8). Homeruns: Skowron; Crandall. Att: 46,367.

1960   PITTSBURGH PIRATES (4) v. Yankees (3)

Seldom has a world series been so dominated statistically by the losing team as was the 1960 Series. The Yankees hit .338 to Pittsburgh's .256 on 91 hits to Pittsburgh's 60. The Pirates managed only three homeruns, to the Yankees 10, but two of those three were game-winners hit by Bill Mazeroski, including his tenth inning shot in Game VII which made the Pirates the World Champions. As for pitching, the Yankees combined for a 3.54 earned run average to Pittsburgh's monstrous 7.11.

So how did the Pirates do it? For starters, take relief pitcher Elroy Face, who had 24 saves during the regular season, and added three in the Series. Consider pitcher Vernon Law, 20-9, but suffering from a leg injury during the series, who still managed to win Games I and IV. Defensively, former Yankee player (and future manager) Bill Virdon made two game-saving catches and hit the famous ground ball which took a bad hop and hit Tony Kubek in the neck and helped build a key rally in Game VII. And at the plate, Mazeroski (.320), Roberto Clemente (.310), Hal Smith (a game-tying three-run homerun in Game VII), and Law (a game-tying double) did most of the damage.

Game I: Art Ditmar faced Law and the Pirates kayoed Ditmar in the first inning by scoring three runs. Mazeroski added a fourth inning two-run homerun off reliever Jim Coates, enabling the Pirates to hold off homeruns by Roger Maris and Howard.

Game II: This was the first of three Yankee onslaughts against some rather beleaguered Pirate pitchers. New York made 19 hits to Pittsburgh's 13 and the teams combined to set a new record for most hits in a nine-inning series game. Mantle hit two homeruns and drove in five runs.

Game III: The Yankees exploded again, with Richardson's record six runs driven in leading the way. Mantle also homered as the Yankees pounded six Pirate pitchers for 16 hits.

Game IV: A three-run fifth inning, plus two-and-two-thirds innings of perfect relief from Face, evened the series at two games each. Pirates starter Law doubled home the tying run, and Virdon singled in the game-winner.

Game V: Pittsburgh won again at Yankee Stadium, this time on the strength of Harvey Haddix's five hitter and another two-and-two-thirds innings of perfect relief by Face.

Game VI: Ford notched his second shutout of the series as the Yankees blew out Bob Friend, 12-0. Richardson hit two triples in route to his record 12 runs batted in one series.

Game VII: Once again, the world series came down to a seventh game, and what a classic. Pittsburgh jumped in front, 4-0, on a first inning two-run homer by Rocky Nelson, and a second inning two-run single by Virdon. Skowron got New York on the board with a fifth inning homer. Mantle's run-scoring single, followed by Berra's three-run, sixth inning, homerun put New York ahead, 5-4. The Yankees added two insurance runs in the eighth, and with Shantz cruising along since the third inning, it looked like another championship effort.

Gino Cimoli opened the Pirates' eighth inning with a single to center field. Virdon followed with a ground ball to Kubek which struck a pebble and took a wicked hop into the shortstop's throat, turning the double play ball into an infield hit. (The injury forced Kubek's premature retirement.) Dick Groat singled home Cimoli.

Stengel responded with a pitching change which was the subject of great controversy after the game. The next batter was Bob Skinner, a lefty who would undoubtedly be bunting, followed by another lefty, Nelson. Despite Southpaw Shantz's reputation as the best fielding pitcher in the American League, Stengel opted for righthanded reliever Coates. Skinner bunted the runners over, but Coates got Nelson to pop up for the second out. Clemente followed with an infield hit, scoring Virdon, and then Smith hit a tremendous homerun over the left field wall to put Pittsburgh ahead, 9-7.

The game was far from over. Friend was on the mound in the top of the ninth. Richardson led off with a single. Pinch hitter Dale Long singled, and Friend was replaced by Haddix. Mantle singled in Richardson, with Long moving to third base. The next batter was Berra, and he hit into one of the strangest plays in series history when his ground ball to first baseman Nelson (a perfect first-second-first double play ball) became a mere out at first because Nelson elected to step on first base before throwing to second (losing the force out at second) and Mantle dove back into first base. It was a heady base-running move by baseball's greatest switch-hitter, and allowed the tying run to score.

It all went for naught when Mazeroski led off the bottom of the ninth with a one ball, no strikes homerun, sending the Yankees and Ralph Terry down to defeat.

Prior to the series, there were rumors that Stengel was finished as manager of New York, and an October press conference made it official, ending an era.

GAME I: (at Forbes Field, Oct. 5)

Yankees	100	100	002	4	13	2
Pirates	300	201	00x	6	8	0

Pitchers: Law, Face (8) v. Ditmar, Coates (1), Maas (5), Duren (7),
Homeruns: Mazeroski; Maris, Howard. Att: 36,676.

GAME II: (at Forbes Field, Oct. 6)

Yankees	002	127	301	16	19	1
Pirates	000	100	002	3	13	1

Pitchers: Turley, Shantz (9) v. Friend, Green (5), Labine (6),
Witt (6), Gibbons (7), Cheney (9). Homeruns: Mantle 2.
Att: 37,308.

GAME III: (at Yankee Stadium, Oct. 8)

Pirates	000	000	000	0	4	0
Yankees	600	400	00x	10	16	1

Pitchers: Ford v. Mizell, Labine (1), Green (1), Witt (4),
Cheney (6), Gibbon (8). Homeruns: Richardson, Mantle.
Att: 70,001.

GAME IV: (at Yankee Stadium, Oct. 9)

Pirates	000	030	000	3	7	0
Yankees	000	100	100	2	8	0

Pitchers: Law, Face (7) v. Terry, Shantz (5), Coates (8).
Homerun: Skowron. Att: 67,812.

GAME V: (at Yankee Stadium, Oct. 10)

Pirates	031	000	001	5	10	2
Yankees	011	000	000	2	5	2

Pitchers: Haddix, Face (7) v. Ditmar, Arroyo (2), Stafford (3),
Duren (8). Homerun: Maris. Att: 62,753.

GAME VI: (at Forbes Field, Oct. 12)

Yankees	015	002	220	12	17	1
Pirates	000	000	000	0	7	1

Pitchers: Ford v. Friend, Cheney (3), Mizell (4), Green (6),
Labine (6), Witt (9). Att: 38,580.

GAME VII: (at Forbes Field, Oct. 13)

Yankees	000	014	022	9	13	0
Pirates	220	000	051	10	11	0

Pitchers: Law, Face (6), Friend (9), Haddix (9) v. Turley,
Stafford (2), Shantz (3), Coates (8), Terry (8). Homeruns:
Nelson, Smith, Mazeroski; Skowron, Berra. Att: 36,683.

1961   YANKEES (4) v. Cincinnati Reds (1)

The '61 series was one of the more lackluster ones. The Yankees outscored the
Reds, 27-13, and won in five games. Fortunately, some outstanding pitching by
Ford, and a pair of unexpected homeruns by Johnny Blanchard, kept the fans
interested.

Game I: Ford hurled a two-hit, 2-0 win to extend his series shutout innings
streak to 27 straight. Homeruns by Howard and Skowron accounted for New
York's runs.

Game II: Joey Jay hurled a four-hitter, and Elio Chacon scored from second
base on a passed ball, to lead the Reds to their only win. Terry was the loser,
despite a homerun by Berra.

257

GAME III: Roger Maris' ninth inning homerun gave the Yankees a 3-2 win in the most exciting game of the series. The Reds led 1-0 in the seventh inning when, with Kubek on second base, Berra lofted a bloop to short right field which fell for a hit when Chacon and Frank Robinson collided. The Reds moved ahead 2-1 in the bottom of the inning, but Blanchard's pinch hit homerun in the eighth tied matters, setting the stage for Maris.

Game IV: Ford pitched five more shutout innings before leaving the game with an ankle injury. The streak had reached 32, and eclipsed Ruth's favorite record of 29-and-two-thirds scoreless series innings accomplished while Ruth was a Red Sox.

GAME I: (at Yankee Stadium, Oct. 4)

Cincinnati	000	000	000	0	2	0
New York	000	101	00x	2	6	0

P — Ford v. O'Toole, Brosnan (8). HR: Howard, Skowron. Att: 62,397.

GAME II: (at Yankee Stadium, Oct. 5)

Cincinnati	000	211	020	6	9	0
New York	000	200	000	2	4	3

P — Jay v. Terry, Arroyo (8). HR: Coleman; Berra. Att: 63,085.

GAME III: (at Crosley Field, Oct. 7)

New York	000	000	111	3	6	1
Cincinnati	001	000	100	2	8	0

P — Stafford, Daley (7), Arroyo (8) v. Purkey. HR: Maris, Blanchard. Att: 32,589.

GAME IV: (at Crosley Field, Oct. 8)

New York	000	112	300	7	11	0
Cincinnati	000	000	000	0	5	1

P — Ford, Coates (6) (SV) v. O'Toole, Brosnan (6), Henry (9). Att: 32,589.

GAME V: (at Crosley Field, Oct. 9)

New York	510	502	000	13	15	1
Cincinnati	003	020	000	5	11	3

P — Terry, Daley (3) v. Jay, Maloney (1), Johnson (2), Henry (3), Jones (4), Purkey (5), Brosnan (7), Hunt (9). HR: Blanchard, Lopez; Robinson, Post. Att: 32,589.

1962 Yankees (4) v. GIANTS (3)

Odds are that if someone had told John McGraw and Miller Huggins that someday their teams would meet in a coast to coast world series, neither would have believed it. After all, the Giants were as much a part of New York as Broadway. Why, you couldn't beat that old elevated shuttle train between Yankee Stadium and the Polo Grounds, just a five-cent ride. The Giants would never leave New York . . .

Yet, there they were, 41 years after the two teams met in the Yankees first world series, and 3,000 miles apart, ready to compete in a world series which would be remembered for: a three-day rain delay which gave the Yankees pitching staff some badly needed rest; a ninth-inning, two out line drive hit right to Bobby Richardson in game VII, with the winning run on second base; and, two of the lowest team batting averages in world series history (NY .199, SF .226).

It was also the Yankees final world championship of the era, featured Ford's final series victory, the end of Ford's scoreless inning streak, and Mantle's last championship team.

Game I: Ford's consecutive scoreless inning streak ends at 33 when Willie Mays scores from third on an infield out in the second inning, but Ford rebounded and won his 10th and final world series victory, 6-2. The key blow: light-hitting third baseman Clete Boyer's seventh inning, tie-breaking homerun.

GAME II: In the first of three matchups between the Yankees Ralph Terry and the Giants Jack Sanford, the San Francisco hurler comes out on top, 2-0, on a three-hitter. Willie McCovey hit a homerun in the seventh inning.

GAME III: The series shifted to New York, where surprise starter Bill Stafford hurled a four-hitter and beat the Giants, 3-2. Roger Maris' two-run single highlighted the Yankees three-run seventh inning, and enabled the Yankees to survive Ed Bailey's two run homerun in the ninth.

GAME IV: Chuck Hiller's seventh inning, tie-breaking grand slam homerun, the first ever hit by a National Leaguer in world series play, leads the Giants to a 7-3 win. A familiar face was the winner: Don Larsen, of perfect game fame, but now a Giant reliever.

GAME V: Tom Tresh slams an eighth inning, tie-breaking three-run homerun to lead the Yankees to a 5-3 win in the second Terry-Sanford matchup. The Giants' starter struck out 10 Yankees in seven-and-one third innings.

GAME IV: After three days of downpour gave Ford a good rest, the Yankees had high hopes of ending the series in six games. It was not to be, largely because of Orlando Cepeda's three run-producing hits, and Billy Pierce's three-hitter. Maris hit a homerun, but it was far from enough, as the Yankees lost, 5-2.

GAME VII: So, once again, a seventh game would decide the championship of the world, and it proved to be another classic in the annals of world series history. Terry and Sanford took the mound, and matched goose egg for goose egg, until Bill Skowron scored on a ground ball doubleplay off the bat of Tony Kubek in the fifth inning.

The score remained 1-0 until the ninth. Matty Alou had reached first base with two outs, when Willie Mays lined a shot down the right field line. Maris fielded it flawlessly, holding Mays at second and preventing Alou from scoring. Up came McCovey, and Terry elected to pitch to the powerful lefty-swinging first baseman. Visions of Bill Mazeroski danced in Giants fans heads, and for a second their hopes appeared to have born fruit. McCovey slammed a line drive, right at second baseman Richardson, to end the series, and the fans' dreams.

GAME I: (at Candlestick Park, Oct. 4)

New York	200	000	121	6	11	0
San Francisco	011	000	000	2	10	0

P — Ford v. O'Dell, Larsen (8), Miller (9).
HR: Boyer. Att: 43,852.

GAME II: (at Candlestick Park, Oct. 5)

New York	000	000	000	0	3	1
San Francisco	100	000	10x	2	6	0

P — Sanford v. Terry, Daley (8). HR: McCovey.
Att: 43,910.

GAME III: (at Yankee Stadium, Oct. 7)

San Francisco	000	000	002	2	4	3
New York	000	000	30x	3	5	1

P — Stafford v. Pierce, Larsen (7), Bolin (8). HR:
Bailey. Att: 71,434.

GAME IV: (at Yankee Stadium, Oct. 8)

San Francisco	020	000	401	7	9	1
New York	000	002	001	3	9	1

P — Marichal, Bolin (5), Larsen (6), O'Dell (7) (SV) v.
Ford, Coates (7), Bridges (7). HR: Haller, Hiller. Att: 66,067.

GAME V: (at Yankee Stadium, Oct. 10)

San Francisco	001	010	001	3	8	2
New York	000	101	03x	5	6	0

P — Terry v. Sanford, Miller (8). HR: Tresh; Pagan.
Att: 63,165.

GAME VI: (at Candlestick Park, Oct. 15)

New York	000	010	010	2	3	2
San Francisco	000	320	00x	5	10	1

P — Pierce v. Ford, Coates (5), Bridges (8). HR: Maris.
Att: 43,948.

GAME VII: (at Candlestick Park, Oct. 16)

New York	000	010	000	1	7	0
San Francisco	000	000	000	0	4	1

P — Terry v. Sanford, O'Dell (8)
Att: 43,948.

1963   Dodgers (4) v. YANKEES (0)

For Yankee fans, the proper word was humiliation, because that's what the 1963 series would always mean to the members of that Yankee team. It wasn't just the four straight losses. The Yankees batted .171 (the record low for a four-game series), scored only four runs, made just 22 hits, and lost the fourth game on a pitiful error. Adding insult to injury, Los Angeles only batted .214 . . . but their pitchers recorded a sparkling 1.00 ERA.

Game I: Dodger ace southpaw Sandy Koufax strikes out the first five Yankees he faces and goes on to strike out a record 15, as the Dodgers win, 5-2. The Yankee pitchers also joined the strike out parade, K'ing 10 Dodgers, and enabling the teams to combine for a record 25 strikeouts in one world series game.

Among those who did hit the ball were John Roseboro (the game-winning three run homerun in the second inning) and New York's Tom Tresh (a two-run blow of his own in the eighth).

Game II: Johnny Podres (of 1955 Brooklyn fame) scatters 7 hits and draws the full benefits of the wet turf when Maris slips in pursuit of a fly ball off the bat of Willie Davis (it went for a two-run double) en route to a 4-1 win. The lone Yankee run came on a Bill Skowron homerun.

Game III: A classic pitcher's duel, with Drysdale out-dueling Jim Bouton, 1-0. The Dodger run came in the first inning, when Jim Gilliam scored on a single by Tommy Davis. Drysdale struck out nine while walking one and scattering three hits. Bouton allowed three Dodgers safeties.

Game IV: Koufax and Ford meet again, with Koufax conquering the Yankee southpaw, 2-1. Mickey Mantle and Frank Howard matched homeruns, but the Yankees lost the series in the seventh inning, when Jim Gilliam was safe on an error by Joe Pepitone ("I lost the ball in the white shirts of the crowd") and eventually scored on Davis' fly out.

260

GAME I: (at Yankee Stadium, Oct. 2)

Los Angeles	041	000	000	5	9	0
New York	000	000	020	2	6	0

P — Koufax v. Ford, Williams (6), Hamilton (9).
HR: Roseboro; Tresh. Att: 69,000.

GAME II: (at Yankee Stadium, Oct. 3)

Los Angeles	200	100	010	4	10	1
New York	000	000	001	1	7	0

P — Podres, Perranoski (9) (SV) v. Downing, Terry (6), Reniff (9).
HR: Skowron. Att: 66,455.

GAME III: (at Dodgers Stadium, Oct. 5)

New York	000	000	000	0	3	0
Los Angeles	100	000	00x	1	4	1

P — Drysdale v. Bouton, Reniff (8). Att: 55,912.

GAME IV: (at Dodgers Stadium, Oct. 6)

New York	000	000	100	1	6	1
Los Angeles	000	010	10x	2	2	1

P — Koufax v. Ford, Reniff (8). HR: F. Howard; Mantle.
Att: 55,912.

1964   CARDINALS (4) v. Yankees (3)

The 1964 series marked the last hurrah of the great Yankee teams of the early 60's. Two men whose names had become household words, Mickey Mantle and Whitey Ford, would make their final post-season appearances. In fact, no member of this team would ever play for another Yankee pennant winner, with only manager Yogi Berra and catcher Elston Howard getting a taste of a Yankee championship in coaching roles in the middle 70's.

At least Mantle's farewell to the world series was as a losing hero. He batted .333 and hit three homeruns, to pass Ruth's career series mark of 15, and set a new mark of 18. His ninth inning, game-winning homerun in game III is considered one of the greatest moments in series history.

Unfortunately, Ford was not to enjoy even a last hurrah. He started Game I, took a 4-2 lead into the sixth inning, and was blown off the mound when St. Louis exploded for 4 runs. Little did anyone realize that Ford's aching arm would never really heal, and that this was to be his final showing in the autumn classic.

Game I: The Yankees open a 4-2 lead, only to have Mike Shannon's two-run sixth inning homerun tie the score. Hits by Carl Warwick and Curt Flood drove in two more runs that inning, and the Yankees and Ford were finished for the day. The 9-5 loss was the Yankees' fifth straight in series play, still the team's record.

Game II: Rookie Mel Stottlemyre scatters seven hits, and light-hitting utility infielder Phil Linz provides a pleasant surprise with a homerun, as the Yankees even matters with an 8-3 win. New York forged a 4-3 lead through 8 innings, and when Bob Gibson was removed for a pinch hitter in the 8th, the Yankees jump all over three relievers to blow the game open.

Game III: Mantle's last hurrah, a ninth inning, lead-off homerun off knuckleballer Barney Schultz to give the Yankees a 2-1 win. The homerun was his 16th in series play, snapping Ruth's record, and came with Ruthian-like flair: Mantle had called his shot by telling Elston Howard that he would hit the first pitch out of the park!

261

Game IV: A sixth inning grand slam homerun wipes out New York's 3-0 lead, and proves to be the game-winning blow, as relievers Roger Craig and Ron Taylor hold the Yankees to one hit in 8-and-two-thirds innings!

Game V: Tim McCarver's tenth inning three-run homerun off Pete Mikkelsen gives the Cardinals a 5-2 win. The Yankees used similar tactics to send the game into the extra innings, relying on Tom Tresh's two out, two-run homerun in the bottom of the ninth to tie the game. Bob Gibson went the distance, striking out 13 Yankees.

Game VI: Roger Maris and Mantle, the heroes of the early 60's championship teams, combine for one last explosion when they slug back-to-back homeruns in the sixth inning to give the Yankees a 3-1 lead. Joe Pepitone adds an eighth inning grand slam homerun to ice it.

Game VII: The Cardinals preserved their perfect (5-0 to that date; it ended at 6-0 in 1968, when the Tigers stopped them) seventh game streak, largely thanks to Gibson's pitching and homeruns by Ken Boyer and Lou Brock. The Cardinal hurler battled Stottlemyre, both on two days rest, and was better able to handle the short notice. The Cards chased Stott in the fourth with a three-run outburst, and eventually opened a 6-0 lead before Mantle's final series homerun, a three-run shot in the sixth, closed the gap. The Cards added an insurance run in the seventh, and survived solo homeruns by Clete Boyer and Linz in the Yankee ninth to win the game, 7-5, and the series.

GAME I: (at Sportsman's Park, Oct. 7)

New York	030	010	010	5	12	2
St. Louis	110	004	03x	9	12	0

P — Sadecki, Schultz (7) (SV) v. Ford, Downing (6), Sheldon (8), Mikkelsen (8). HR: Shannon; Tresh. Att: 30,805.

GAME II: (at Sportsman's Park, Oct. 8)

New York	000	101	204	8	12	0
St. Louis	001	000	011	3	7	0

P — Stottlemyre v. Gibson, Schultz (9), G. Richardson (9), Craig (9). HR: Linz. Att: 30,805.

GAME III: (at Yankee Stadium, Oct. 10)

St. Louis	000	010	000	1	6	0
New York	010	000	001	2	5	2

P — Bouton v. Simmons, Schultz (9). HR: Mantle. Att: 67,101.

GAME IV: (at Yankee Stadium, Oct. 11)

St. Louis	000	004	000	4	6	1
New York	300	000	000	3	6	1

P — Sadecki, Craig (1), Taylor (6) (SV) v. Downing, Mikkelsen (7), Terry (8). HR: K. Boyer. Att: 66,312.

GAME V: (at Yankee Stadium, Oct. 12)

St. Louis	000	020	000	3	5	10	1
New York	000	000	002	0	2	6	2

P — Gibson v. Stottlemyre, Reniff (8), Mikkelsen (8). HR: McCarver; Tresh. Att: 65,633.

GAME VI: (at Sportsman's Park, Oct. 14)

New York	000	012	050	8	10	0
St. Louis	100	000	011	3	10	1

P — Bouton, Hamilton (9) (SV) v. Simmons, Taylor (7), Schultz (8), G. Richardson (8), Humphreys (9). HR: Maris, Mantle, Pepitone. Att: 30,805.

GAME VII: (at Sportsman's Park, Oct. 15)
New York   000   003   002   5   9   2
St. Louis   000   330   10x   10   1   7
P — Gibson v. Stottlemyre, Downing (5), Sheldon (5), Hamilton
(7), Mikkelsen (8). HR: Brock, K. Boyer; Mantle, C. Boyer,
Linz. Att: 30,364.

1976   REDS (4) v. Yankees (0)

This was one of those world series everyone would just as soon forget about, largely because it was so one-sided, and because it came on the heels of the 1975 Reds-Red Sox series (considered among the best ever). Simply put, the Yankees were devastated by a better club, better in several ways. First, and most significantly, the Reds were an experienced group of veterans looking for thier second consecutive world championship. Secondly, they had eliminated their Eastern Division opponents (the Phillies) in three games, while the Yankees struggled through a tough five-game series with Kansas City. The Yankees also admitted that they had over-celebrated after the fifth game, and were not mentally prepared — "we were just so happy to be in the world series that we forgot what we had to do until it was too late," according to one member of the '76 team.

There were also three major disappointments: the Yankee pitching staff's inability to hold down the highscoring "Big Red Machine", Mickey Rivers inability to get on base (.167, no extra-base hits, one stolen base), and a general collapse in the clutch hitting department (the Yankees were outscored 22-8).

Game I: The series opened with a bang in Cinncinati, when Joe Morgan slammed one of Yankee starter Doyle Alexander's first-inning pitches into the seats for a homerun. Earlier that inning, the Reds had unveiled their new "Mickey Rivers defense," which featured third baseman Pete Rose playing incredibly close to home plate in what proved to be a series-long strategy which successfully intimidated the Yankees leadoff hitter.

The Yankees evened the score, briefly, in the second, when Lou Piniella doubled and eventually scored on a sacrifice fly by Graig Nettles.

The Reds edged ahead in the third, when Dave Concepcion tripled, and came home on a Rose fly out. The lead went to 3-1 in the sixth, on Perez's run-scoring hit, and reached the 5-1 final in the seventh on a single by George Foster, Johnny Bench's triple, and a wild pitch.

Game II: The Yankees went with Catfish Hunter, and psychologically placed all their eggs in one basket, when several players admitted that if they didn't win with Hunter they might not win at all. The Reds got to Hunter for three runs in the third inning, including a double by Dan Driessen (the first hit by a National League designated hitter in world series history), and run-scoring hits by Foster and Concepcion.

Hunter slammed the door for the next five innings, while his teammates battled back. New York got on the board in the fourth on a run-scoring single by Graig Nettles, and tied matters in the seventh when Willie Randolph singled, Fred Stanley doubled him home, Roy White's single advanced Stanley to third, and Stanley came home on Munson's force out.

The game remained knotted until the ninth inning, when with two outs, Tom Griffey was safe at second on an error by Stanley and scored on a single by Perez.

Game III: The Reds pounded Yankee starter Dock Ellis for three runs in the third inning and were never headed in route to a 6-2 win. Dan Driessen led off the inning with an infield hit, stole second, and scored on Foster's double. Bench singled Foster to third, and Foster scored when Geronimo grounded into a force play. Geronimo stole second and scored on Concepcion's hit.

Driessen made it 4-0 with a homerun in the fourth inning, the first homerun ever hit by a DH in the world series. A run-scoring single by Oscar Gamble, and a solo homerun by Jim Mason (the only Yankee homerun of the series) brought New York within striking distance, but the Reds came up with two runs in the eighth inning to ice it.

Game IV: For the first time in the series, the Yankees take the lead, when Munson singles with two outs in the first inning, and scores on Chambliss' double. The Reds reply with a three-run fourth inning, highlighted by Bench's two-run homerun.

Again, the Yankees edged close, when Rivers singled in the fifth, stole second, and scored on another hit by Munson, but the Reds broke the game and series open with a four-run ninth inning, highlighted by Bench's second three-run homerun.

POSTSCRIPT: Munson hit .435, to set a record for the highest batting average for a player on a team which lost the world series (10 hits in 23 at-bats). After the series, Reds manager Sparky Anderson infuriated the Yankee catcher by saying that as good a hitter as Munson is, he simply could not be compared to Bench as a catcher.

GAME I: (at Riverfront Stadium, Oct.   )

New York	010	000	000	1	5	1
Cinn.	101	001	20x	5	10	1

P — Gullett (W), Borbon (8) v. Alexander (L), Lyle (7).
HR: Morgan. Att: 54,826.

GAME II: (at Riverfront Stadium, Oct.   )

New York	000	100	200	3	9	1
Cinn.	030	000	001	4	10	0

P — Norman, Billingham (W) (7) v. Hunter (L). Att: 54,816.

Game III: (at Yankee Stadium, Oct.   )

Cinn.	030	100	020	6	13	2
New York	000	100	100	2	8	0

P — Zachry (W), McEnaney (7) v. Ellis (L), Jackson (4),
Tidrow (8). HR: Driessen; Mason. Att: 56,667.

GAME IV: (at Yankee Stadium)

Cinn.	000	300	004	7	9	2
New York	100	010	000	2	8	0

P — Nolan (W), McEnaney (8) v. Figueroa (L), Tidrow (9),
Lyle (9). HR: Bench 2. Att: 56,700.

1977   YANKEES (4) v. Dodgers (2)

For the ninth time in world series history, the Yankees and Dodgers clash in the Fall Classic, and for the seventh time, the Yankees emerged victorious. The Yankee heroes ranged from substitute outfielder Paul Blair to reliever Sparky Lyle, but when all things are considered, this was Reggie Jackson's world series.

The controversial Yankee slugger set new world series records by hitting three consecutive homeruns in one game (the sixth), hitting five homeruns in one series, scoring 10 runs in one series, and collecting 25 total bases. Jackson tied several world series marks, including the most runs scored in one game (4), most total bases in one game (12), and most homeruns in one game (3).

Lost somewhere in the shuffle were two complete game victories by Mike Torrez (the pivotal third game, and the clinching sixth) and another fine series by Yankee captain and catcher, Thurman Munson (.320, eight hits, two doubles, one homerun, three RBI's).

Game I: A 12-inning thriller ends when Blair singles home Willie Randolph to give the Yankees a 4-3 win. The strange part of this episode was that Blair, who came to bat after a leadoff double by Randolph and an intentional walk to Munson, had been sent up there to bunt. After bunting the first two offerings from reliever Rick Rhoden into foul territory, Blair was told to swing away, and bounced a single through the left side of the infield to win the game.

The Dodgers had taken a 2-0 lead in the first inning, and led, 2-1, going into the sixth, when Randolph hit a homerun to tie the score. The Yankees edged ahead, 3-2, in the eighth, when Munson drove in the go-ahead run with a double, but the Dodgers tied it in the ninth.

Game II: To many Yankee fans, this will always be known as the "giveaway game." Faced with an exhausted pitching staff, manager Billy Martin elected to go with his injury-plagued veteran righthander, Catfish Hunter, who had not pitched an inning in more than a month. The goal was to buy time, because the next day was an off day for travel, and would give Torrez enough rest to be ready for Game III in Los Angeles.

Unfortunately, Hunter was ineffective, and the Dodgers buried him with early homeruns by Ron Cey and Reggie Smith to win, 6-1.

Game III: A well-rested Torrez scattered seven Dodgers hits, and centerfielder Mickey Rivers led the 10-hit Yankee attack with two doubles and a single, as the Yankees took a two-games-to-one lead with a 5-3 win. The Yankees opened an early 3-0 lead, only to watch Dusty Baker maul a Torrez fastball into the seats in the third inning for a game-tying three-run homerun. The Yankees rebounded by scoring the go ahead run in the fourth inning and added an insurance run in the fifth.

Game IV: Remarkable Ron Guidry tossed a neat four-hitter, and Jackson's double triggered a three-run second inning, as the Yankees downed L.A., 4-2. The key play of the game came in left field, when Lou Piniella (who had singled home a run in the third) leaped high above the wall in left field to rob Cey of a homerun which would have tied the score. Jackson sent one into orbit in the sixth inning for insurance, and New York had a three-games-to-one bulge.

Game V: Faced with the potential embarassment of losing the world series in

five games, and at home, to boot, the Dodgers rebounded with a 10-4 win. The Yankees went with Don Gullett, but his sore shoulder gave way in the fourth inning, when L.A. scored four runs. Eventually, the Dodgers built up an insurmountable 9-0 lead, before Jackson and Munson hit late-inning homeruns to save some face.

Game VI: With a jubilant Yankee Stadium crowd of 56,407 fans rocking the House That Ruth Built (and Lindsay rebuilt) with every pitch, Jackson and Torrez combined to get the Yankees their first world championship since 1962. For the record, the final score was 8-4, but the real story was Jackson.

The game opened with the Dodgers scoring twice in the first inning. After two outs, Smith was safe on an error and went to second base on a passed ball. Cey walked, Garvey tripled, and two runs scored.

Chambliss' homerun on the heels of Jackson's walk tied the score in the second inning, but the Dodgers added a run in their half of the third when Reggie Smith hit his third homerun of the series.

Munson led off the fourth inning by singling, and Jackson followed with the first of three straight homeruns, to put New York ahead to stay. Jackson added a two-run homerun in the fourth inning, and hit his third homerun (a 440-foot blast into the center field bleachers) off reliever Charlie Hough on the first pitch of the eighth inning.

Linescores:
GAME I

Los Angeles	200	000	001	000	3	6	0
New York	100	000	010	001	4	11	0

P — Gullett, Lyle (W) (9) v. Sutton, Rautzhan (8), Sosa (9), Rhoden (L) (12). HR: Randolph. Att: 56,668.

GAME II: (at Yankee Stadium, Oct. 12)

Los Angeles	212	000	001	6	9	0
New York	000	100	000	1	5	0

P — Hooton (W) v. Hunter (L), Tidrow (3), Clay (6), Lyle (9). HR: Cey, Yeager, Smith, Garvey. Att: 56,691.

GAME III: (at Los Angeles, Oct. 14)

New York	300	110	000	5	10	0
Los Angeles	003	000	000	3	7	1

P — Torrez (W) v. John (L), Hough (7). HR: Baker. Att: 55,992.

GAME IV: (at Los Angeles, Oct. 15)

New York	030	001	000	4	7	0
Los Angeles	002	000	000	2	4	0

P — Guidry (W) v. Rau (L), Rhoden (2), Garman (9). HR: Jackson; Lopes. Att: 55,995.

GAME V: (at Los Angeles, Oct. 16)

New York	000	000	220	4	9	2
Los Angeles	100	431	00x	10	13	0

P — Sutton (W) v. Gullett (L), Clay (5), Tidrow (6), Hunter (7). HR: Yeager, Smith; Munson, Jackson. Att: 55,955.

GAME VI: (at Yankee Stadium, Oct. 18)

Los Angeles	201	000	001	4	9	0
New York	020	320	01x	8	8	1

P — Torrez (W) v. Hooton (L), Sosa (4), Rau (5), Hough (7). HR: Jackson 3, Chambliss; Smith. Att: 56,407.

The 1978 World Series is covered in the special section on the miracle year.

THE PARKS THEY PLAYED IN

Hilltop Park: 1903-12

Hilltop Park was a hastily-constructed, all-wood stadium seating 15,000 fans. Standing room, and on-the-field extra seating space (crowds were allowed to spill over to the foul lines), allowed for increased capacity, but the Highlanders rearely drew large crowds because they were not very competitive (except in 1904 and 1906).

The Park was named because it was located at one of the highest spots in Manhattan, 168th Street and Broadway (now the site of the Columbia Presbyterian Medical Center). A favorite distraction of the fans was to walk back to the rear rows of the grandstand and observe the ships in the Hudson River, clearly visible from the Park.

A covered grandstand extended from an area beyond third base down the left field line, around behind home plate, and as far up the first base line as the base itself. Wooden bleachers extended to the foul poles. There were no outfield seats between the foul poles, although there was a large exit in right field for draining the bleacher crowds.

Box seats cost 35-cents, grandstand admission was a quarter, and the bleachers cost a dime when the place opened in 1903. Ticket prices eventually reached 50-cents for boxes, 35-cents for the grandstand, and 20-cents for bleacherites.

The Highlanders drew their largest crowds against the Athletics and Red Sox, occasionally breaking the 20,000 mark, according to contemporary reports, but their average attendance never exceeded 4500 for a season at Hilltop. Frequently, it dipped below the 2000 mark, including a low of 1400 in 1912.

An interesting challenge to the reader: see if you can find a picture of the interior of Hilltop Park. The Yankees don't have one. Neither does UPI, the Baseball Hall of Fame, the New York Historical Society . . . only two are known to exist.

The Polo Grounds: 1913-22

The Yankees became tenants of the Giants after generously allowing their rivals to use Hilltop Park after a fire had ravaged the Polo Grounds in 1912. Pinstripes were welcome as paying tenants until the early 20's, when a fellow named Ruth became a drawing card, and the Yankees established themselves as real rivals.

In 1913, the Polo Grounds were a part-concrete, part-wood structure, seating 34,000. Two decks extended from foul pole to foul pole. The facades were decorated with a unique frieze which made the old ballpark easily identifiable, and something of a work of art. The bleachers extended across the outfield and were wood, but sat 10,000. As tenants of the Giants, the Yankees frequently crowded more than 40,000 fans into the building — there were no fire laws in those days.

For the curious, the Polo Grounds were always located between 155th and 158th Streets and 8th Avenue during the Yankees' tenure. For the picture-conscious fan, once again, try finding a shot of the Yankees playing in the Polo Grounds before 1922. There are a few.

Yankee Stadium 1923-73

In 1921, the Yankees outdrew their Polo Grounds hosts, the New York Giants, and were politely told that they would no longer be welcome after the 1922 season. Manager John McGraw longed for the day when the Yankees would move to Queens, or some other faraway place, to wither away. A new ballpark had to be built, and quickly.

The result was the construction of the first three-tiered stadium in the United States, a massive concrete-and-steel structure which sat close to 80,000 people when it first opened its doors in 1923. When the park opened that year, it looked somewhat different than the pre-renovation Stadium last seen in 1973. The famous three decks, with the roof top facade, did not extend beyond the foul poles. Instead, the bleachers stretched across that vast space, from the 281 marker in left field (the original distance), to the 295 marker (original) in right field. Along that stretch one also discovered a 490-foot sign in dead center field, making the Stadium the largest of its time, and giving its vast outfield expanses the sobroquette of "death valley."

In 1928, the first of two major expansions extended the three-tiers beyond the foul pole in left field, and pushed the distance to the foul pole to 301 feet. The distance to straightaway left field was set at 385 feet, and the center field fence was brought in to 475. In 1937, the second expansion similarly extended the three-tiers beyond the right field foul pole, changing the distance to that pole to 296 feet, and reducing the center field distance to 463. These reductions in bleacher seats sharply reduced the building's seating capacity to 67,000. A minor renovation in 1966 further chopped the number to 65,010.

The Stadium earned the nickname "The House That Ruth Built" largely because his popularity was the key to bringing in the huge crowds the Giants were jealous of. It only followed that the crowds made the Yankee owners wealthy, and that the new Stadium should be tailored to Ruth's lefty swing. Thus, the short right field porch (295 down the line, 355 to straight away right) became a permanent fixture.

A word or two about its construction and location:

Yankee Stadium, located in the Bronx, at 161st Street and River Ave. was designed by the Osborne Engineering Company of Cleveland, Ohio and built by the White Construction Company of New York at the request of then Yankee owner Colonel Jacob Ruppert. Construction began on May 5, 1922, and it was completed the following April at a cost of $2,305,000. The job took only 284 days, and as a construction company employee pointed out later, "There was no penalty or bonus attached to the contract, but there was a definite moral obligation to finish the Stadium by the beginning of the 1923 season." The contractor met the deadline nearly a month in advance.

The Stadium opened on April 18, 1923, with the Yankees defeating Boston 4-1. Babe Ruth hit the first Stadium home run and the winning pitcher was Bob Shawkey, who threw out the first ball on Golden Anniversary Day in 1973.

The playing field covers 3.5 acres and the Stadium plus surrounding grounds covers 11.6 acres.

Lights were installed in 1946 (2,400,000 watts) and a new scoreboard (cost — $120,000) was installed in 1950. By 1959, the Yankees were ready to add a new board — with the first changeable message area at a major league park in America. The cost of the new board was $300,000, and the message area has carried on and has been expanded upon by every park since constructed. (Now, the new Yankee Stadium has the new scoreboard which is 560 feet long and 24 feet high, except for the dramatic "Telscreen" which reaches a height of 40 feet at its center, and features "instand replay capabilities". Designed by the Conrac Corporation, the board is the most modern, up-to-date facility in any baseball stadium in the country. And while capturing the new, the board — like Yankee Stadium itself — holds onto the proud Yankee history, with the famous Stadium facade gracing the top of the board. It is operated by a team working out of the press box.)

The first night game played at the Stadium was on May 28, 1946, when the Yankees were defeated by the Washington Senators 2-1.

In 1953, Yankee Stadium and the grounds were sold to Earl and Arnold Johnson of Kansas City. Two years later, the Johnsons sold the Stadium and grounds to John William Cox, a Chicago banker. The purchase price was $6.5 million, which also included the Stadium of the Kansas City Blues, a Yankee minor league club. The Yankee grounds were then sold to the Knights of Columbus for $2.5 million. In 1962, Mr. Cox donated as a gift a "substantial amount" of stock in the corporation he headed (which owned Yankee Stadium) to Rice University in Houston, Texas.

Other sports history has been made at Yankee Stadium as well. The New York Football Giants enjoyed their greatest years as Stadium tenants, moving in for the 1956 season. Many outstanding collegiate football games have been played there, including Army-Notre Dame matches. Thirty boxing championships have been decided at the Stadium, and professional soccer has been played on Stadium turf.

The ballpark has also been the scene of outstanding non-sports events. Political assemblies have been scheduled as well as famous circuses. Jehovah Witnesses have frequently held huge gatherings there, as well as the Billy Graham Crusade. Cardinal Spellman said Mass there in 1957 and on October 4, 1965, Pope Paul VI delivered the only Papal Mass ever delivered in America. Over 80,000 people attended.

The stadium has also been the scene of many concerts, and in 1972 served as host to the Newport Jazz Festival. Several motion pictures and many advertisements have been shot on Stadium grounds.

In 1938, the Yankees and the Red Sox, THE baseball rivalry, drew 81,841 fans for a Memorial Day doubleheader, a Stadium record. (Since that time the Yankees have cut down on the number of seats). The largest crowd to see the football Giants in Yankee Stadium was 71,163 on November 9, 1958, vs the Baltimore Colts; and the 79,222 people at the Max Schmeling-Jack Sharkey heavyweight title fight on June 12, 1930, was the top boxing crowd.

In centerfield at Yankee Stadium — 430 feet from home plate — are three monuments erected in memory of Babe Ruth, former manager Miller Huggins, and Lou Gehrig. Behind them are wall plaques honoring General Manager Edward G. Barrow and owner Colonel Jacob Ruppert. To their left is a plaque commemorating the Pope's 1965 visit, and further down the wall are plaques honoring Joe DiMaggio and Mickey Mantle, which the two greats presented to each other at Mickey Mantle's uniform retirement ceremony in 1969. There are also plaques honoring Casey Stengel and Joe McCarthy.

In addition to Mantle's retirement, which produced a 9-minute standing ovation for the superstar, other nostalgic events in Stadium history include the tearful farewell appearances of a dying Lou Gehrig (July 4, 1939) and Babe Ruth (June 13, 1948).

The annual Old-Timers Day, held each summer, has become a highlight for fans seeing old heroes one more time. Since 1965, the Yankees have given away thousands of baseball bats, caps, jackets, mugs, and T-shirts in highly popular promotional dates for youngsters. Thousands of seats are additionally provided for underpriviledged children.

During the winter of 1966-67, Yankee Stadium was given a new look as 90 tons of paint turned the Stadium white on the outside and royal blue on the inside. All of the bleacher seats were converted to fiberglass at that time. Inside, fans were treated to a "Telephonic Hall of Fame", which allowed them to hear the recorded voices. of great names from the past and receive playing tips from the current players. The modernization and refurbishing program gave the Stadium its most complete facelifting since 1923, and cost $1,350,000.

The main complaints about Yankee Stadium were the many obstructed view seats, a serious shortage of parking space, and a decaying neighborhood. The obstructed views were largely caused by the many supporting poles which held up the mezzanine and upper deck, and by the "depth" from the playing field of the rear rows of the lower grandstands, resulting in the loss of all fly balls until caught. Also, many of the field box seats had actually sunk below the level of the playing field, forcing viewers to strain and stretch in an effort to see the game from the front row seats.

As for the parking, the problem was that the Stadium was built in an era in which the subway and bus was the main mode of transportation. No one foresaw the age of the automobile.

Similarly, no one thought the Bronx would ever decay the way it has. In 1923, there were farms in the northern areas of that borough. The Grand Concourse was becoming one of the choice places to live. By 1940, if you dated a boy or girl from the Grand Concourse, you were really living. Now, the Grand Concourse south of Fordham Road is one of the less desireable places to live in the United States in many people's minds. The whole South Bronx has become an urban wasteland.

In 1972, the Football Giants announced plans to move to a new complex in the Meadowlands of New Jersey. The State of New Jersey approached Michael Burke, former president of the Yankees, with a similar proposal but Mr. Burke maintained that the Yankees' first desire was to remain in their home, providing the City of New York would undertake a program to modernize the surrounding environment, and create better parking and roadway conditions.

Mayor John V. Lindsay for the City, and the Yankees agreed on a plan whereby the Stadium would be completely modernized during 1974-75, while the Yankees shared Shea Stadium with the New York Mets. The Yankees would then return to the full-remodeled Yankee Stadium in time for the 1976 baseball season. After the City of New York took over the ownership of the structure in 1972, the Yankees signed a 30-year lease to remain in Yankee Stadium.

Shea Stadium: 1974-75

For two agonizing years, the Yankees were forced to play their home games at Shea Stadium, the home of the Mets while the Yankee Stadium was being rebuilt. The effect was a 162-game road schedule. The players never felt comfortable in Flushing.

Shea is a four-tiered stadium which also features a luxury box — press box level. It has no outfield bleachers, and is best described as a cold, dull structure, typical of an attempt to build a stadium for football and baseball. The upper level seats are at helicopter height, and a great horizontal distance from the field as well. It seats 55,101 . . . although you wouldn't know it the way the Mets are drawing these days.

Its dimensions are 341 down the left and right field lines, and 410 to center. Dull and symmetrical, just like the Mets.

The NEW Yankee Stadium 1976-current

The fully-remodeled Yankee Stadium re-opened on April 15, 1976, with the Yankees defeating the Twins, 11-4. Rudy May started the game, while reliever Dick Tidrow picked up the win. Minnesota's Dan Ford hit the first homerun in the new park. Two days later, Thurman Munson hit the first Yankee homerun.

The new Stadium was the subject of a great deal of controversy during 1976-77, largely because its original expected cost, $24 million, had been exceeded by anywhere from $16-80 million. Some claimed the Yankees and the City had conspired to commit a public fraud. More pressure was brought to bear when many expected improvements in the neighborhood, particularly those not directly related to the ballpark, were never completed. All of this criticism became particularly volatile when the City reached the verge of bankruptcy in 1975-76, and when newspapers revealed that the total rent paid by the Yankees was only $150,000/year, give or take a percentage on attendance.

270

An examination of the facts is essential. Like it or not, the Yankee Stadium is the only major business attracting money into the South Bronx. Try visiting the area during the winter months, and compare it to a Yankee home stand.

Furthermore, the City gets four percent of the gross admission, at an average ticket price of $5 and a home attendance of 2.3 million. That yields almost $500,000. Factor in the sales tax on the concession stands. The average fan spends $3 at a game, so you generate another $280,000 for the city. Add in the city-owned parking lots, leased to Kinney Corporation for a healthy fee. Throw in the local businesses which survive only because the Stadium operates from April through September.

Add all that up, and then consider another factor: the psychological value of the Yankees to New York. In 1972, the football Giants told the City they were leaving for the Meadowlands in New Jersey. A similar lucrative proposal was offered to the Yankees, but Yankee President Mike Burke preferred to stay in New York if the city would remodel the Stadium and improve its environs. With other businesses fleeing New York in droves, and with all the bad publicity the city was getting, could the City have afforded to let the Yankees get away? Similarly, could the Yankees, as a business, not shoot for a reasonable deal, especially in light of their CBS ownership at that time? (An ownership which treated the Yankees as a separate business.)

At any rate, the new stadium was constructed on the site of the old one (between 157th-161st Streets and River Avenue). Two new, triple-decked lots, and several smaller ones, were built to handle roughly 10,000 cars. Two new exits/entrances to the Major Deegan were created. Lou Gehrig Plaza, a pedestrian mall to the south side of the stadium, was installed. A pollution-free smokestack, in the form of a baseball bat serves as a landmark of the exterior.

Inside the stadium there are three new escalator towers, in addition to the numerous pre-renovation ramps. Many new concession stands have been added. Several new rest rooms dot the walkways. The seats in the arena are ultra-modern plastic, painted Yankee Blue, and larger and more comfortable than the wood variety which filled the Old Stadium. The bleachers are no longer benches, but have been filled with slightly smaller seats than those in the main structure.

Overall, the old three-decked face of the Stadium remains the same, with the addition of a new luxury box level beneath the loge (formerly known as the mezzanine) and a modern press box, behind home plate. An electronic cartoon and message board was erected in centerfield, and is supported by two auxiliary boards behind first and third bases. A special scoreboard in left field gives the out-of-town scores on a revolving basis.

The monuments and plaques, once located on the playing field in center field, have been placed in a small memorial park in left center field, between the bullpens. (The Yankee bullpen was moved to left center field as part of the renovation.) A replica of the old facade, long a highlight of the stadium's character, stands atop the outfield bleachers' rear retaining wall.

There are no longer any obstructed view seats because all of the poles were removed as part of the renovation. Seating capacity is officially listed at 57,545, including large areas set aside for the handicapped. The seats are broken down as follows:

Field level boxes	7521
Main Level boxes	8098
Main level reserved	5780
Loge boxes	6302
Upper boxes	7955
Upper reserved	15652 — (Some of these are usually
Bleachers	5523 sold as general admission
	on the day of the game)

Yankee Stadium's playing field covers 3.5 acres of land. The Stadium's structure and pedestrian walkways cover a total of 11.6 acres. A combination of 800 multivapor and incandescent lights with powers of up to 1500 watts light the field. The new dimensions are 312-feet to the left field foul pole, 430-feet to left center, 417 to dead center, and 310 to the right field foul pole. (The Stadium is not symmetrical). The interior outfield fences range from seven to 10 feet in height, and are padded with the same Yankee Blue that covers the seats. The exterior of the Stadium is an off-color white, which remains graffiti-free, in sharp contrast to the elevated trains cars which rumble past the outfield walls. The playing surface is natural grass.

Only Cleveland's Municipal Stadium (capacity — 76,713), Seattle's Kingdome (capacity — 59,059), Philadelphia's Veterans Stadium (capacity — 58,651), San Francisco's Candlestick Park (capacity — 58,000), and Montreal's Olympic Stadium (capacity — 59,511) contain more seats than Yankee Stadium.

The Yankees apparently find the New Stadium much to their liking, because they've responded with a pennant in 1976, and consecutive world championships in 1977-78.

Most importantly, the New Yankee Stadium is a comfortable, clean and safe place to watch a game from . . . but even with the increased parking, get there early when the Red Sox come to town!

YANKEE ATTENDANCE RECORDS

Largest Season Home Attendance (1948) 2,373,901
Largest Single Game Home Attendance (Vs.Boston, May 16,
   1947 — Night) 74,747
Largest Single Game Home Attendance — Day (Vs. Boston, Sept.
   26, 1948) 69,755
Largest Doubleheader Home Attendance (Vs. Boston, May 30,
   1938) 81,841
Largest Twi-Night Home Doubleheader Attendance —
   (Vs. Boston, Aug. 29, 1967) 40,314
Largest Opening Day Home Attendance (Vs. Washington,
   April 19, 1946) 54,826
Largest Home Series Attendance (Cleve. at N.Y., June 11, 12, 13,
   1948) 186,151
Largest Crowd in Baseball History (Yanks at Los Angeles —
   Exhibition Game, May 7, 1959) 93,103
Largest Yankee Old Timers' Day Attendance (s. Boston, Aug. 9,
   1958) 67,916
Largest Season Road Attendance (1962) 2,216,159
*Major League Record

YANKEE   ATTENDANCE   RECORDS

(New Yankee Stadium)

Largest Night Game Attendance (vs. Boston, Tuesday, September 13, 1977)
. . . . 55,239

Largest Single Day Game Attendance (vs. Boston, Saturday, Sept. 16 1978) 55,091
Largest Doubleheader Attendance (vs. Detroit, Sunday, September 12, 1976) 52,707
Largest Weekday, Day Game Attendance (vs. Baltimore, July 28, 1977) . 40,918
Largest Home Series Attendance (4 game series) Yankees vs. Boston, May 20-23, 1976 167,267
Largest Home Series Attendance (3 game series) Yankees vs. Boston, September 15-17, 1978 165,080

The Largest crowd in the "New" Yankee Stadium (opened in April, 1976) was 56,821 for the final game of the 1976 ALCS vs. Kansas City, October 14, 1976.

TOP CROWDS AT NEW YANKEE STADIUM

56,821 (vs. KC, 5th Game of 1976 ALCS)
56,808 (vs. KC, 3rd Game of 1976 ALCS)
56,700 (vs. Cinncinnati, 4th Game of 1976 W.S.)
56,691 (vs. L.A. 2nd Game of 1977 W.S.)
56,683 (All Star Game, July 19, 1977)
56,668 (vs. L.A. 1st Game of 1977 W.S.)
56,667 (vs. Cinncinnati, 3rd Game of 1976 W.S.)
56,448 (vs. L.A. 5th Game)
56,447 (vs. L.A. 3rd Game)
56,445 (vs. L.A. 4th Game)
56,407 (vs. L.A. 6th Game of 1977 W.S.)
56,356 (vs. KC, 4th Game)
55,535 (vs. KC, 3rd Game of '78 ALCS)
56,355 (vs. KC, 4th Game of 1976 ALCS)
56,230 (vs. KC 2nd Game of 1977 ALCS)
55,239 (vs. Boston, September 13, 1977)
55,039 (vs. Boston, June 26, 1977)
54,940 (vs. Boston, June 24, 1977)

YANKEE ATTENDANCE MARKS

The Yankees for the 3rd straight year drew over 2 million fans at Yankee Stadium and for the 2d straight year also played before 2 million fans on the road. In accomplishing that feat the Yankees remain one of only 3 teams in baseball history, and the first in the American League ever to play before 2 million fans both at home and on the road. The 1966 Dodgers and the 1977 Reds also accomplished it. By drawing 2 million on the road they join the Dodgers, Giants and Reds as the only other teams ever to accomplish that. The Yankees 3 Game series with the Red Sox, September 15, 16 and 17th, (1978), drew 165,080 into Yankee Stadium, making it the largest 3 game series in the major leagues since 1958, and the largest in the American League since 1950.

ROAD ATTENDANCE: The Yankees have drawn over one million on the road for 33 consecutive years, including a record 2,216,159 in 1962.

NEW YORK YANKEES — Year-by-Year

Year	Position	Won	Lost	Pct.	Manager	Attendance
1903	Fourth	72	62	.537	Clark Griffith	211,808
1904	Second	92	59	.609	Clark Gfiffith	438,919
1905	Sixth	71	78	.477	Clark Griffith	309,100
1906	Second	90	61	.596	Clark Griffith	434,700
1907	Fifth	70	78	.473	Clark Griffith	350,020
1908	Eighth	51	103	.331	Griffith-N. Elberfeld	305,500
1909	Fifth	74	77	.490	George T. Stallings	501,000
1910	Second	88	63	.583	Stallings-Hal Chase	355,857
1911	Sixth	76	76	.500	Hal Chase	302,444
1912	Eighth	50	102	.329	Harry Wolverton	242,194
1913	Seventh	57	94	.377	Frank Chance	357,551
1914	†Sixth	70	84	.455	Chance-R. Peckinpaugh	359,477
1915	Fifth	69	83	.454	William E. Donovan	256,035
1916	Fourth	80	74	.519	William E. Donovan	469,211
1917	Sixth	71	82	.464	William E. Donovan	330,294
1918	Fourth	60	63	.488	Miller J. Huggins	282,047
1919	Third	80	59	.576	Miller J. Huggins	619,164
1920	Third	95	59	.617	Miller J. Huggins	1,289,422
1921	First	98	55	.641	Miller J. Huggins	1,230,696
1922	First	94	60	.610	Miller J. Huggins	1,026,134
1923	†First	98	54	.645	Miller J. Huggins	1,007,066
1924	Second	89	63	.586	Miller J. Huggins	1,053,533
1925	Seventh	69	85	.448	Miller J. Huggins	697,267
1926	First	91	63	.586	Miller J. Huggins	1,027,095
1927	†First	110	44	.714	Miller J. Huggins	1,154,015
1928	†First	101	53	.656	Miller J. Huggins	1,072,132
1929	Second	88	66	.571	Huggins-Fletcher	960,148
1930	Third	86	68	.558	Robert Shawkey	1,169,230
1931	Second	94	59	.614	Joe McCarthy	912,437
1932	†First	107	47	.695	Joe McCarthy	962,320
1933	Second	91	59	.607	Joe McCarthy	728,014
1934	Second	94	60	.610	Joe McCarthy	854,682
1935	Second	89	60	.597	Joe McCarthy	657,508
1936	†First	102	51	.667	Joe McCarthy	976,913
1937	†First	102	52	.662	Joe McCarthy	998,148
1938	†First	99	53	.651	Joe McCarthy	970,916
1939	†First	106	45	.702	Joe McCarthy	859,785
1940	Third	88	66	.571	Joe McCarthy	988,975
1941	†First	101	53	.656	Joe McCarthy	964,722
1942	First	103	51	.669	Joe McCarthy	988,251
1943	†First	98	56	.636	Joe McCarthy	645,006
1944	Third	83	71	.539	Joe McCarthy	822,864
1945	Fourth	81	71	.553	Joe McCarthy	881,846
1946	Third	87	67	.565	McCarthy-W. Dickey-Neun	2,265,512
1947	†First	97	57	.630	Bucky Harris	2,178,937
1948	Third	94	60	.610	Bucky Harris	2,373,901
1949	†First	97	57	.630	Casey Stengel	2,281,676
1950	†First	98	56	.636	Casey Stengel	2,081,380
1951	†First	98	56	.636	Casey Stengel	1,950,107
1952	†First	95	59	.617	Casey Stengel	1,629,665
1953	†First	99	52	.656	Casey Stengel	1,537,811
1954	Second	103	51	.669	Casey Stengel	1,475,171
1955	First	96	58	.623	Casey Stengel	1,490,138

NEW YORK YANKEES — Year-by-Year

Year	Position	Won	Lost	Pct.	Manager	Attendance
1956	†First	97	57	.680	Casey Stengel	1,491,784
1957	First	98	56	.636	Casey Stengel	1,497,134
1958	†First	92	62	.597	Casey Stengel	1,428,438
1959	Third	79	75	.513	Casey Stengel	1,552,030
1960	First	97	57	.630	Casey Stengel	1,627,349
1961	†First	109	53	.673	Ralph Houk	1,747,736
1962	†First	96	66	.593	Ralph Houk	1,493,574
1963	First	104	57	.646	Ralph Houk	1,308,920
1964	First	99	63	.611	Yogi Berra	1,305,638
1965	Sixth	77	85	.475	Johnny Keane	1,213,552
1966	Tenth	70	89	.440	Keane-Houk	1,124,648
1967	Ninth	72	90	.444	Ralph Houk	1,141,714
1968	Fifth	83	79	.512	Ralph Houk	1,125,124
1969	Fifth	80	81	.497	Ralph Houk	1,067,996
1970	Second	93	96	.574	Ralph Houk	1,136,879
1971	Fourth	82	80	.506	Ralph Houk	1,070,771
1972	Fourth	79	76	.510	Ralph Houk	966,328
1973	Fourth	80	82	.494	Ralph Houk	1,262,077
1974	Second	89	73	.549	Bill Virdon	1,273,075
1975	Third	83	77	.519	Virdon-Martin	1,288,048
1976	First	97	62	.610	Billy Martin	2,012,434
1977	†First	100	62	.617	Billy Martin	2,103,092
	Totals	6598	4946	.571		

Finished First — 31, Second — 12, Third — 9, Fourth — 7, Fifth — 5,
Sixth — 5, Seventh — 2, Eighth — 2, Ninth — 1 Tenth — 1.
Highest Percentage — .714 in 1927; Lowest — .329 in 1912.

†World Championship
††Tied with Chicago

Total Attendances —

Hilltop Park (1903-12)	3,451,542
Polo Grounds (1913-22)	6,220,031
Yankee Stadium (1923-73)	64,788,405
Shea Stadium (1974-75)	2,561,123
Yankee Stadium (1976-)	4,115,526
	81,136,627

THE MANAGERS AND THEIR RECORDS

	Years	W — L	Pct.	Pnts.	Chmps.
Clark Griffith	1903-08	419 — 370	.531	0	0
Kid Elberfeld	1908	27 — 71	.276	0	0
George Stallings	1909-10	153 — 138	.524	0	0
Hal Chase	1910-11	85 — 78	.521	0	0
Harry Wolverton	1912	50 — 102	.328	0	0
Frank Chance	1913-14	118 — 170	.410	0	0
Roger Peckinpaugh	1914	9 — 8	.529	0	0
William Donovan	1915-17	220 — 239	.480	0	0
Miller Huggins	1918-29	1067 — 719	.597	6	3
Art Fletcher	1929	6 — 5	.545	0	0
Bob Shawkey	1930	86 — 68	.558	0	0
Joe McCarthy	1931-46	1460 — 867	.627	8	7
Bill Dickey	1946	57 — 48	.543	0	0
Johnny Neun	1946	8 — 6	.571	0	0
Bucky Harris	1947-48	191 — 117	.620	1	1
Casey Stengel	1949-60	1149 — 696	.619	10	7
Ralph Houk	1961-63	309 — 176	.637	3	2
Yogi Berra	1964	99 — 63	.611	1	0
Johnny Keane	1965-66	81 — 101	.445	0	0
Ralph Houk	1966-73	635 — 630	.501	0	0
		(Houk overall: .539)			
Bill Virdon	1974-75	142 — 123	.536	0	0
Billy Martin	1975-78	279 — 192	.571	2	1
Dick Howser	1978	0 — 1	.000		
Bob Lemon	1978	48 — 30	.726	1*	1

*Martin was replaced by Dick Howser (interim) and then by Bob Lemon (permanent) midway through the 1978 season. On that date (7-25-78) the Yankees were 52-43, 10-and-one-half-games out of first place, and mired in fourth place. In fairness to Martin, the team had embarked upon a five game winning streak just prior to his resignation, and more baseball people agree that that streak had started the club's remarkable pennant drive.

YANKEE TEAM OWNERS

1903-1914: Frank Farrell and Bill Devery
1915-1922: Jacob Ruppert and Colonel Tillinghast L'Hommedieu Huston
1922-1939: Jacob Ruppert
1939-1945: The Ruppert Estate through Edward Barrow
1945-1947: Larry MacPhail, Dan Topping, and Del Webb
1947-1964: Dan Topping and Del Webb
1964-1973: Columbia Broadcasting System
1973-   : A group headed by George M. Steinbrenner

YANKEE TEAM PRESIDENTS

1903-06: Joseph Gordon
1907-14: Frank Farrell
1915-39: Jacob Ruppert
1939-45: Edward Barrow
1945-47: Leland MacPhail
1947-53: Daniel Topping
1954-64: Daniel Topping and Del Webb shared the duties
1964-66: Daniel Topping, Sr.
1966-73: Michael Burke
1973-77: Gabriel Paul
1978-   : Albert Rosen

Yankees Who Lost Years In World War II

(members of the NY roster who served in the armed forces)

Bill Dickey	Phil Rizzuto
Joe DiMaggio	George Selkirk
Joe Gordon	Roy Weatherly
Buddy Hassett	Spud Chandler
Rollie Hensley	John Murphy
Tommy Henrich	Mel Queen
Billy Johnson	Red Ruffing
Charlie Keller	Marius Russo
Johnny Lindell	Aaron Robinson
Henry Majeski	Charles Wensloff

RUNS BATTED IN

(Yankees who drove in 100 or more runs in one season)

1920 —	Ruth	137*			Gehrig	126
1921 —	Ruth	170*			Lazzeri	106
	Meusel	135		1930 —	Gehrig	174*
1923 —	Ruth	131*			Ruth	153
	Pipp	108			Lazzeri	121
1924 —	Ruth	121		1931 —	Gehrig	184*
	Meusel	120			Ruth	163
	Pipp	113			Chapman	122
1926 —	Ruth	145*			Lary	107
	Lazzeri	114		1932 —	Gehrig	151
	Gehrig	107			Ruth	137
1927 —	Gehrig	175*			Lazzeri	113
	Ruth	164			Chapman	107
	Meusel	103		1933 —	Gehrig	139
	Lazzeri	102			Lazzeri	104
1928 —	Gehrig	142*			Ruth	103
	Ruth	142*		1934 —	Gehrig	165*
	Meusel	113		1935	Gehrig	119
1929 —	Ruth	154		1936 —	Gehrig	152

277

	DiMaggio	125		Henrich	100
	Dickey	107	1949 —	NONE	
	Selkirk	107	1950 —	Berra	124
1937 —	DiMaggio	167		DiMaggio	122
	Gehrig	159	1951 —	NONE	
	Dickey	133	1952 —	NONE	
1938 —	DiMaggio	140	1953 —	Berra	108
	Dickey	115	1954 —	Berra	125
	Gehrig	114		Mantle	102
1939 —	DiMaggio	126	1955	Berra	108
	Gordon	111	1956 —	Mantle	130*
	Dickey	105		Berra	105
	Selkirk	101	1957-59 —	NONE	
1940 —	DiMaggio	133	1960 —	Maris	112
	Gordon	103	1961 —	Maris	142*
1941 —	DiMaggio	125*		Mantle	128
	Keller	122	1962 —	Maris	100
1942 —	DiMaggio	114	1963	NONE	
	Keller	108	1964 —	Mantle	111
	Gordon	103		Pepitone	100
1943 —	Etten	107	1975 —	Munson	102
1944 —	Lindell	103	1976 —	Munson	105
1945 —	Etten	111*	1977 —	Jackson	110
1946 —	Keller	101		Nettles	107
1947	NONE			Munson	100
1948 —	DiMaggio	155*			

(*Indicates league leader)

RUNS SCORED

(Yankees who scored 100 or more
runs in one season)

1920 —	Ruth	158*		Combs	137
	Pipp	109	1928 —	Ruth	163*
	Peckinpaugh	109		Gehrig	139
1921 —	Ruth	177*		Combs	118
	Peckinpaugh	128	1929 —	Gehrig	127
	Meusel	104		Ruth	121
1923 —	Ruth	151*		Combs	119
	Witt	113		Lazzeri	101
	Dugan	111	1930 —	Ruth	150
1924 —	Ruth	143*		Gehrig	143
	Dugan	105		Combs	129
1925 —	Combs	117		Lazzeri	109
	Meusel	101	1931 —	Gehrig	163*
1926 —	Ruth	139*		Ruth	149
	Gehrig	135		Combs	120
	Combs	113		Chapman	120
1927 —	Ruth	158*		Sewell	102
	Gehrig	149		Lary	100

1932 —	Combs	143	
	Gehrig	138	
	Ruth	120	
	Chapman	101	
1933 —	Gehrig	138*	
	Chapman	112	
1934 —	Gehrig	128	
1935 —	Gehrig	125*	
	Chapman	118	
	Rolfe	108	
1936 —	Gehrig	167*	
	Crosetti	137	
	DiMaggio	132	
	Rolfe	116	
1937 —	DiMaggio	151*	
	Rolfe	143	
	Gehrig	138	
	Crosetti	127	
1938	Rolfe	132	
	DiMaggio	129	
	Gehrig	115	
	Crosetti	113	
	Henrich	109	
1939 —	Rolfe	139*	
	Crosetti	109	
	DiMaggio	108	
	Selkirk	103	
1940 —	Gordon	112	
	Keller	102	
	Rolfe	102	

1941 —	DiMaggio	122
	Henrich	106
	Rolfe	106
	Gordon	104
	Keller	102
1942 —	DiMaggio	123
	Keller	106
1944 —	Stirnweiss	125*
1945 —	Stirnweiss	107*
1947 —	Henrich	109
1948 —	Henrich	138*
	DiMaggio	110
1949 —	Rizzuto	110
1950 —	Rizzuto	125
	Berra	116
	DiMaggio	114
1953 —	Mantle	105
1954 —	Mantle	129
1955 —	Mantle	121
1956 —	Mantle	132*
1957 —	Mantle	121*
1958 —	Mantle	127*
1959 —	Mantle	104
1960 —	Mantle	119*
1961 —	Mantle	132*
	Kubek	132*
1970 —	White	109
1972 —	Murcer	102*
1976 —	White	104

(* Indicates league leader)

DOUBLES
(20 or more in one season)

1903 —	Jim Williams	28
	Wid Conroy	23
	Kid Elberfeld	22
1905 —	Jim Williams	20
1906	Jim Williams	25
	Hal Chase	23
	Frank LaPorte	23
1907 —	Hal Chase	23
	Frank LaPorte	20
1908 —	Jake Stahl	22
	Wid Conroy	22
1909 —	John Knight	25
	Hal Chase	20
1910 —	John Knight	25
	Hal Chase	20
1911 —	Hal Chase	32
	Birdie Cree	30
1912 —	Bert Daniels	25
	Hal Chase	21

1913 —	Birdie Cree	25
1914 —	Fritz Maisel	23
1915 —	Wally Pipp	20
1916 —	Frank Baker	23
	Roger Peckinpaugh	22
	Wally Pipp	20
1917 —	Frank Baker	24
	Roger Peckinpaugh	24
1918 —	Frank Baker	24
1919 —	Del Pratt	27
	Ping Bodie	27
	Wally Pipp	23
	Duffy Lewis	23
	Frank Baker	22
	Roger Peckinpaugh	20
1920 —	Bob Meusel	40
	Del Pratt	37
	Babe Ruth	36
	Wally Pipp	30
	Ping Bodie	26

Roger Peckinpaugh	26
1921 — Babe Ruth	44
Bob Meusel	40
Wally Pipp	35
Wally Schang	30
Aaron Ward	30
Roger Peckinpaugh	25
1922 — Wally Pipp	32
Joe Dugan	31
Bob Meusel	26
Babe Ruth	24
Everett Scott	23
Wally Schang	21
1923 — Babe Ruth	45
Joe Dugan	30
Bob Meusel	29
Aaron Ward	26
1924 — Bob Meusel	40
Babe Ruth	39
Joe Dugan	31
Wally Pipp	30
Whitey Witt	26
1925 — Earle Combs	36
Bob Meusel	34
Lou Gehrig	23
Aaron Ward	22
1926 — Lou Gehrig	47
Earle Combs	31
Babe Ruth	30
Tony Lazzeri	28
Mark Koenig	26
Bob Meusel	22
1927 — Lou Gehrig	52
Bob Meusel	47
Earle Combs	36
Tony Lazzeri	29
Babe Ruth	29
Joe Dugan	24
Mark Koenig	20
1928 — Lou Gehrig	47
Bob Meusel	45
Earle Combs	33
Tony Lazzeri	30
Babe Ruth	29
1929 — Tony Lazzeri	37
Earle Combs	33
Lou Gehrig	33
Bill Dickey	30
Mark Koenig	27
Babe Ruth	26
1930 — Lou Gehrig	42
Tony Lazzeri	34
Ben Chapman	31
Earle Combs	30
Babe Ruth	28

Bill Dickey	25
Harry Rice	23
Lyn Lary	20
1931— Lyn Lary	35
Lou Gehrig	31
Babe Ruth	31
Earle Combs	31
Ben Chapman	28
Tony Lazzeri	27
Joe Sewell	22
1932 — Lou Gehrig	42
Ben Chapman	41
Earle Combs	32
Tony Lazzeri	28
Joe Sewell	21
Frank Crosetti	20
Bill Dickey	20
1933 — Lou Gehrig	41
Ben Chapman	36
Bill Dickey	24
Earle Combs	22
Tony Lazzeri	22
Babe Ruth	21
Frank Crosetti	20
1934 — Lou Gehrig	40
Bill Dickey	24
Tony Lazzeri	24
Frank Crosetti	22
Ben Chapman	21
1935— Ben Chapman	38
Red Rolfe	33
George Selkirk	29
Lou Gehrig	26
Bill Dickey	26
Jesse Hill	20
1936 — Joe DiMaggio	44
Red Rolfe	39
Lou Gehrig	37
Frank Crosetti	35
Tony Lazzeri	29
George Selkirk	28
Bill Dickey	26
1937 — Lou Gehrig	37
Bill Dickey	35
Joe DiMaggio	35
Red Rolfe	34
Frank Crosetti	29
Jake Powell	22
Tony Lazzeri	21
1938 — Red Rolfe	36
Frank Crosetti	35
Joe DiMaggio	32
Lou Gehrig	32
Bill Dickey	27
Joe Gordon	24

	Tommy Henrich	24		1953—	Gil McDougald	27
1939—	Red Rolfe	46			Gene Woodling	26
	Joe Gordon	32			Mickey Mantle	24
	Frank Crosetti	25			Billy Martin	24
	Bill Dickey	23			Yogi Berra	23
	Charlie Keller	21			Phil Rizzuto	21
1940 —	Joe Gordon	32			Hank Bauer	20
	Joe DiMaggio	28		1954 —	Yogi Berra	28
	Tommy Henrich	28			Gil McDougald	22
	Red Rolfe	26			Irv Noren	21
	Babe Dahlgren	24			Joe Collins	20
	Frank Crosetti	23		1955 —	Mickey Mantle	25
1941 —	Joe DiMaggio	43			Hank Bauer	20
	Tommy Henrich	27			Yogi Berra	20
	Joe Gordon	26		1956 —	Yogi Berra	29
	Charlie Keller	24			Billy Martin	24
	Red Rolfe	22			Mickey Mantle	22
	Phil Rizzuto	20			Bill Skowron	21
1942 —	Tommy Henrich	30		1957 —	Mickey Mantle	28
	Joe DiMaggio	29			Gil McDougald	25
	Joe Gordon	29			Hank Bauer	22
	Charlie Keller	24			Tony Kubek	21
	Phil Rizzuto	24		1958 —	Hank Bauer	22
1943 —	Nick Etten	35			Bill Skowron	22
	Joe Gordon	28			Tony Kubek	21
	Billy Johnson	24			Mickey Mantle	21
1944 —	Snuffy Stirnweiss	35		1959 —	Hector Lopez	25
	Johnny Lindell	33			Yogi Berra	25
	Nick Etten	25			Tony Kubek	25
1945 —	Snuffy Stirnweiss	32			Elston Howard	23
	Nick Etten	24			Mickey Mantle	23
1946 —	Charlie Keller	29		1960 —	Bill Skowron	34
	Tommy Henrich	25			Tony Kubek	25
	Joe DiMaggio	20			Clete Boyer	20
1947 —	Tommy Henrich	35		1961 —	Tony Kubek	38
	Joe DiMaggio	31			Bill Skowron	23
	Phil Rizzuto	26		1962 —	Bobby Richardson	38
	George McQuinn	24			Roger Maris	34
1948	Tommy Henrich	42			Tommy Tresh	26
	Joe DiMaggio	26			Clete Boyer	24
	Yogi Berra	24			Elston Howard	23
	Billy Johnson	20		1963 —	Tommy Tresh	28
	Snuffy Stirnweiss	20			Elston Howard	21
1949 —	Phil Rizzuto	22			Tony Kubek	21
	Jerry Coleman	21			Clete Boyer	20
	Yogi Berra	20			Bobby Richardson	20
	Tommy Henrich	20		1964 —	Elston Howard	27
1950 —	Phil Rizzuto	36			Mickey Mantle	25
	Joe DiMaggio	33			Bobby Richardson	25
	Yogi Berra	30			Tommy Tresh	25
	Gene Woodling	20			Phil Linz	21
1951 —	Gil McDougald	23		1965 —	Tommy Tresh	29
	Joe DiMaggio	22			Bobby Richardson	28
	Phil Rizzuto	21			Clete Boyer	23
1952 —	Phil Rizzuto	24		1966 —	Clete Boyer	22
	Hank Bauer	22			Joe Pepitone	21

	Bobby Richardson	21	1974 —	Elliott Maddox	26
1967 —	Tommy Tresh	23		Lou Piniella	26
1968 —	NONE			Bobby Murcer	25
1969 —	Roy White	30		Graig Nettles	21
	Horace Clarke	26	1975 —	Chris Chambliss	38
	Gene Michael	24		Roy White	32
	Bobby Murcer	24		Thurman Munson	24
1970 —	Roy White	31		Graig Nettles	24
	Danny Cater	26	1976 —	Chris Chambliss	32
	Thurman Munson	25		Mickey Rivers	31
	Horace Clarke	24		Graig Nettles	29
	Bobby Murcer	23		Roy White	29
1971 —	Bobby Murcer	25		Thurman Munson	27
	Horace Clarke	23	1977 —	Reggie Jackson	39
	Roy White	22		Chris Chambliss	32
	Felipe Alou	20		Thurman Munson	28
1972 —	Bobby Murcer	30		Willie Randolph	28
	Roy White	29		Roy White	25
	Ron Blomberg	22		Graig Nettles	23
	Horace Clarke	20	1978 —	Lou Piniella	34
1973 —	Thurman Munson	29		Thurman Munson	27
	Bobby Murcer	29		Chris Chambliss	26
	Matty Alou	22		Mickey Rivers	25
	Roy White	22		Graig Nettles	23
	Horace Clarke	21			

TRIPLES

**(Yankees who hit more than 10 triples
in one season)**

1903 —	Wid Conroy	13		Wally Pipp	10
	Jim Williams	12	1923 —	Babe Ruth	13
1904 —	John Ganzel	10		Aaron Ward	11
1906 —	Hal Chase	10		Bob Meusel	10
	Wid Conroy	10		Whitey Witt	10
1907 —	Jim Williams	13	1924 —	Wally Pipp	19
	Frank LaPorte	11		Bob Meusel	11
	Wid Conroy	11		Aaron Ward	10
1908 —	Jake Stahl	10	1925 —	Earle Combs	13
1909 —	Birdie Cree	16		Bob Meusel	12
1910 —	Birdie Cree	16	1926 —	Lou Gehrig	20
1911 —	Birdie Cree	22		Tony Lazzeri	14
	Harry Wolter	15		Earle Combs	12
1912 —	Bert Daniels	11	1927 —	Earle Combs	23
	Roy Hartzell	11		Lou Gehrig	18
	Guy Zinn	10	1928 —	Earle Combs	21
1915 —	Wally Pipp	13		Lou Gehrig	13
1916 —	Wallp Pipp	14		Tony Lazzeri	11
1919 —	Wally Pipp	10	1929 —	Earle Combs	15
1920 —	Wally Pipp	14		Tony Lazzeri	11
	Ping Bodie	12	1930 —	Earle Combs	22
1921 —	Babe Ruth	16		Lou Gehrig	17
	Bob Meusel	16		Tony Lazzeri	15
1922 —	Bob Meusel	11		Ben Chapman	10

Year	Player		Year	Player	
1931	Lou Gehrig	15	1940 —	Charlie Keller	15
	Earle Combs	13		Joe Gordon	10
	Ben Chapman	11	1941 —	Joe DiMaggio	11
	Bill Dickey	10		Charlie Keller	10
1932 —	Tony Lazzeri	16	1942 —	Joe DiMaggio	13
	Ben Chapman	15	1943 —	John Lindell	12
	Bill Dickey	10	1944 —	Snuffy Stirnweiss	16
1933 —	Earle Combs	16		John Lindell	16
	Lou Gehrig	12	1945 —	Snuffy Stirnweiss	22
	Tony Lazzeri	12	1946	Charlie Keller	10
1934 —	Ben Chapman	13	1947 —	Tommy Henrich	13
	Frank Crosetti	10		Joe DiMaggio	10
1935 —	George Selkirk	12	1948	Tommy Henrich	14
	Lou Gehrig	10		Joe DiMaggio	11
1936 —	Joe DiMaggio	15		Yogi Berra	10
	Red Rolfe	15	1950 —	Joe DiMaggio	10
1937 —	Joe DiMaggio	15		Gene Woodling	10
	Red Rolfe	10	1952 —	Phil Rizzuto	10
1938 —	Joe DiMaggio	13	1955 —	Mickey Mantle	11
1939 —	Red Rolfe	10	1977 —	Willie Randolph	11

THE 20 HOMERUN CLUB

(Yankees Who've Hit 20 or More Homeruns In One Season)

Year	Player		Year	Player	
1920 —	Babe Ruth	54*	1933 —	Babe Ruth	34
1921 —	Babe Ruth	59*		Lou Gehrig	32
	Bob Meusel	24	1934 —	Lou Gehrig	49*
1922 —	Babe Ruth	35		Babe Ruth	22
1923 —	Babe Ruth	41*	1935 —	Lou Gehrig	30
1924 —	Babe Ruth	46*	1936 —	Lou Gehrig	49*
1925 —	Bob Meusel	33*	1937 —	Joe DiMaggio	46*
	Babe Ruth	25		Lou Gehrig	37
	Lou Gehrig	20		Bill Dickey	29
1926 —	Babe Ruth	47*	1938 —	Joe DiMaggio	32*
1927 —	Babe Ruth	60*		Lou Gehrig	29
	Lou Gehrig	47		Bill Dickey	27
1928 —	Babe Ruth	54*		Joe Gordon	25
	Lou Gehrig	27		Tommy Henrich	22
1929 —	Babe Ruth	46*	1939 —	Joe DiMaggio	30
	Lou Gehrig	35		Joe Gordon	28
1930 —	Babe Ruth	49*		Bill Dickey	24
	Lou Gehrig	41		George Selkirk	21
1931 —	Babe Ruth	46*	1940 —	Joe DiMaggio	31
	Lou Gehrig	46*		Joe Gordon	30
1932 —	Babe Ruth	41		Charlie Keller	21
	Lou Gehrig	34	1941 —	Charlie Keller	33

(On a technicality, one might say Gehrig "really" won the homerun crown in 1931 because he lost a homerun when baserunner Lyn Lary thought the right fielder had caught one of Gehrig's fence jobs. Lary left the basepath after reaching second base, causing Gehrig to be called out for passing a preceding runner!)

	Tommy Henrich	31	
	Joe DiMaggio	30	
	Joe Gordon	24	
1942 —	Charlie Keller	26	
	Joe DiMaggio	21	
1943 —	Charlie Keller	31	
1944	Nick Etten	22*	
1946 —	Charlie Keller	30	
	Joe DiMaggio	25	
1947 —	Joe DiMaggio	20	
1948 —	Joe DiMaggio	39	
	Tommy Henrich	25	
1949 —	Tommy Henrich	24	
	Yogi Berra	20	
1950 —	Joe DiMaggio	32	
	Yogi Berra	28	
	Johnny Mize	25	
1951 —	Yogi Berra	27	
1952 —	Mickey Mantle	23	
1953 —	Yogi Berra	27	
	Mickey Mantle	21	
1954 —	Mickey Mantle	27	
	Yogi Berra	22	
1955 —	Mickey Mantle	37*	
	Yogi Berra	27	
	Hank Bauer	20	
1956 —	Mickey Mantle	52*	
	Yogi Berra	30	
	Hank Bauer	26	
	Moose Skowron	23	
1957 —	Mickey Mantle	34	
	Yogi Berra	24	
1958 —	Mickey Mantle	42*	
	Yogi Berra	22	
1959 —	Mickey Mantle	31	
1960 —	Mickey Mantle	40*	
	Roger Maris	39	
	Moose Skowron	26	

1961 —	Roger Maris	61*
	Mickey Mantle	54
	Moose Skowron	28
	Yogi Berra	22
	Elston Howard	21
	Johnny Blanchard	21
1962 —	Roger Maris	33
	Mickey Mantle	30
	Moose Skowron	23
	Tom Tresh	20
1963 —	Elston Howard	28
	Joe Pepitone	27
	Tom Tresh	25
	Roger Maris	23
1964 —	Mickey Mantle	35
	Joe Pepitone	28
	Roger Maris	26
1965 —	Tom Tresh	26
1966	Joe Pepitone	31
	Tom Tresh	27
	Mickey Mantle	23
1967 —	Mickey Mantle	22
1969 —	Joe Pepitone	27
	Bobby Murcer	26
1970 —	Bobby Murcer	23
	Roy White	22
1971 —	Bobby Murcer	25
1972 —	Bobby Murcer	33
1973 —	Graig Nettles	22
	Bobby Murcer	22
	Thurman Munson	20
1974 —	Graig Nettles	22
1975 —	Graig Nettles	21
1976 —	Graig Nettles	32*
1977 —	Graig Nettles	37
	Reggie Jackson	32
1978 —	Reggie Jackson	27
	Graig Nettles	27

*Led league

THE .300 CLUB

(Yankees who batted .300 or better in one season)

1903 —	Willie Keeler	.318
1904 —	Willie Keeler	.343
1905 —	Willie Keeler	.302
1906 —	Hal Chase	.323
	Kid Elberfeld	.306
	Willie Keeler	.304
1910 —	John Knight	.312
1911 —	Birdie Cree	.348
	Hal Chase	.315

	Harry Wolter	.304
1914 —	Birdie Cree	.309
1918 —	Frank Baker	.306
	Wally Pipp	.304
1919 —	Roger Peckinpaugh	.305
1920	Babe Ruth	.376
	Bob Meusel	.328
	Del Pratt	.314
1921 —	Babe Ruth	.378

284

	Bob Meusel	.318
	Wally Schang	.316
	Aaron Ward	.306
1922 —	Wally Pipp	.329
	Bob Meusel	.319
	Wally Schang	.319
	Babe Ruth	.315
1923 —	Babe Ruth	.393
	Whitey Witt	.314
	Bob Meusel	.313
	Wally Pipp	.304
1924 —	Babe Ruth	.378
	Bob Meusel	.325
	Joe Dugan	.302
1925	Earle Combs	.342
1926 —	Babe Ruth	.372
	Bob Meusel	.315
	Lou Gehrig	.313
1927 —	Lou Gehrig	.373
	Babe Ruth	.356
	Earle Combs	.356
	Bob Meusel	.337
	Tony Lazzeri	.309
1928 —	Lou Gehrig	.374
	Babe Ruth	.323
	Mark Koenig	.323
	Earle Combs	.310
1929 —	Tony Lazzeri	.354
	Babe Ruth	.345
	Earle Combs	.345
	Bill Dickey	.324
	Lou Gehrig	.300
1930 —	Lou Gehrig	.379
	Babe Ruth	.359
	Earle Combs	.344
	Bill Dickey	.339
	Ben Chapman	.316
	Tony Lazzeri	.303
1931 —	Babe Ruth	.373
	Lou Gehrig	.341
	Bill Dickey	.327
	Earle Combs	.318
	Ben Chapman	.315
	Joe Sewell	.302
1932 —	Lou Gehrig	.349
	Babe Ruth	.341
	Earle Combs	.310
	Tony Lazzeri	.300
1933 —	Lou Gehrig	.334
	Bill Dickey	.318
	Ben Chapman	.312
	babe Ruth	.301
1934 —	Lou Gehrig	.363
	Bill Dickey	.322
	Ben Chapman	.308
1935 —	Lou Gehrig	.329

	George Selkirk	.312
	Red Rolfe	.300
1936 —	Bill Dickey	.362
	Lou Gehrig	.354
	Joe DiMaggio	.323
	Red Rolfe	.319
	George Selkirk	.308
	Jake Powell	.306
1937 —	Lou Gehrig	.351
	Joe DiMaggio	.346
	Bill Dickey	.332
1938 —	Joe DiMaggio	.324
	Bill Dickey	.313
	Red Rolfe	.311
1939 —	Joe DiMaggio	.381
	Charlie Keller	.334
	Red Rolfe	.329
	George Selkirk	.306
	Bill Dickey	.302
1940 —	Joe DiMaggio	.352
1941 —	Joe DiMaggio	.357
	Phil Rizzuto	.307
1942 —	Joe Gordon	.322
	Joe DiMaggio	.305
1944 —	Snuffy Stirnweiss	.319
	Johnny Lindell	.300
1945 —	Snuffy Stirnweiss	.309
1947 —	Joe DiMaggio	.315
	George McQuinn	.304
1948 —	Joe DiMaggio	.320
	Tommy Henrich	.308
	Yogi Berra	.305
	Bobby Brown	.300
1950 —	Phil Rizzuto	.324
	Yogi Berra	.322
	Hank Bauer	.320
	Joe DiMaggio	.301
1951 —	Gil McDougald	.306
1952	Mickey Mantle	.311
	Gene Woodling	.309
1953 —	Hank Bauer	.304
1954 —	Irv Noren	.319
	Yogi Berra	.307
	Andy Carey	.302
	Mickey Mantle	.300
1955 —	Moose Skowron	.319
	Mickey Mantle	.306
1956 —	Mickey Mantle	.353
	Gil McDougald	.311
	Moose Skowron	.304
1957 —	Mickey Mantle	.365
	Moose Skowron	.304
1958 —	Elston Howard	.314
	Mickey Mantle	.304
	Norm Siebern	.300
1959 —	Bobby Richardson	.301

1960 —	Moose Skowron	.309		1973 —	Bobby Murcer	.304
1961 —	Elston Howard	.348			Thurman Munson	.301
	Mickey Mantle	.317		1974 —	Lou Piniella	.305
	Johnny Blanchard	.305			Elliott Maddox	.303
1962 —	Mickey Mantle	.321		1975 —	Thurman Munson	.318
	Bobby Richardson	.302			Chris Chambliss	.304
1963	Mickey Mantle	.314		1976 —	Mickey Rivers	.312
1964 —	Elston Howard	.313			Thurman Munson	.302
	Mickey Mantle	.303		1977 —	Mickey Rivers	.326
1970 —	Thurman Munson	.302			Thurman Munson	.308
	Danny Cater	.301		1978 —	Lou Piniella	.312
1971 —	Bobby Murcer	.331		*Led league		

STRIKEOUTS

(Yankees who struck out 75 or more times in one season)

1915 —	Pipp	81	1958 —	Mantle	120*
1920 —	Ruth	80		Siebern	87
1921 —	Meusel	88*		McDougald	75
	Ruth	81	1959 —	Mantle	126*
1922	Ruth	80	1960 —	Mantle	125*
1923 —	Ruth	93*		Skowron	95
1924 —	Ruth	81		Boyer	85
1926 —	Lazzeri	96*	1961	Mantle	112
	Ruth	76		Skowron	108
1927 —	Ruth	89*	1962 —	Boyer	106
	Gehrig	84		Skowron	99
	Lazzeri	82		Mantle	78
1928 —	Ruth	87*		Maris	78
1931 —	Lazzeri	80		Howard	76
	Chapman	77	1963 —	Tresh	79
1933 —	Ruth	90	1964 —	Tresh	110
1935 —	Lazzeri	75		Mantle	102
1936 —	Crosetti	83		Boyer	93
1937 —	Crosetti	105*		Maris	78
	Lazzeri	76	1965 —	Tresh	92
1938 —	Crosetti	99*		Boyer	79
	Lazzeri	75		Mantle	76
1939 —	Crosetti	81	1966 —	Tresh	89
1940 —	Crosetti	77		Mantle	76
1941	Grodon	80	1967 —	Mantle	113
1942 —	Gordon	95*		Smith	110
1943	Gordon	75		Whittaker	89
1955 —	Stirnweiss	87		Tresh	86
1946 —	Keller	101*	1968 —	Mantle	97
1952 —	Mantle	111*		Tresh	97
1953 —	Mantle	90		Cox	85
1954 —	Mantle	107*	1969 —	Murcer	103
1955 —	Mantle	97	1970 —	Murcer	100
	McDougald	77		Michael	93
1956 —	Mantle	99	1973 —	White	81
1957 —	Mantle	75		Nettles	76

286

1974 —	Mason	87
	Nettles	75
1975 —	Bonds	137
	Nettles	88
1976 —	Nettles	94

1977 —	Jac...	
	Nettles	
1978 —	Jackson	1ɔɔ

(* Indicates league leader)

BASES ON BALLS

(Yankees who drew 50 or more
walks in one season)

Note: this statistic was not kept prior to the 1913 season.

1913 —	Wolter	83	1928 —	Ruth	135*
1914 —	Maisel	76		Gehrig	95
	Hartzell	68		Combs	77
	Peckinpaugh	51	1929 —	Gehrig	122
1915 —	Pipp	66		Ruth	72
	Cook	62		Lazzeri	69
	High	62		Combs	69
	Hartzell	57	1930 —	Ruth	136*
1916 —	Peckinpaugh	61		Gehrig	101
	Pipp	54		Combs	74
	Magee	50		Lazzeri	60
1917 —	Peckinpaugh	64	1931 —	Ruth	128*
	Hendryx	62		Gehrig	117
	Pipp	60		Lary	88
1918 —	Gilhooley	53		Lazzeri	79
1919 —	Peckinpaugh	59		Chapman	75
1920 —	Ru	148*		Combs	68
	Peckinpaugh	72		Sewell	62
	Pratt	50	1932 —	Ruth	130*
1921 —	Ruth	144*		Gehrig	108
	Peckinpaugh	84		Lazzeri	82
	Schang	78		Combs	81
1922 —	Witt	89*		Chapman	71
	Ruth	84		Sewell	56
	Pipp	56	1932 —	Ruth	130*
	Schang	53		Gehrig	108
1923 —	Ruth	170*		Lazzeri	82
	Witt	67		Combs	81
	Ward	56		Chapman	71
1924 —	Ruth	142*		Sewell	56
	Pipp	51		Crosetti	51
1925 —	NONE			Lary	52
1926 —	Ruth	144*	1933 —	Ruth	114*
	Gehrig	105		Gehrig	92
	Collins	73		Lazzeri	73
	Lazzeri	54		Chapman	72
1927 —	Ruth	138*		Sewell	71
	Gehrig	109		Crosetti	55
	Combs	62	1934 —	Gehrig	109
	Collins	54		Ruth	103

287

	Lazzeri	71		Stirnweiss	73
	Chapman	67		Metheny	56
	Crosetti	61	1945 —	Etten	90
1935 —	Gehrig	132*		Grimes	97
	Lazzeri	63		Stirnweiss	78
	Chapman	61		H. Martin	65
	Rolfe	57		Crosetti	59
1936 —	Gehrig	130*		Metheny	54
	Selkirk	94	1946 —	Keller	113
	Crosetti	90		Henrich	87
	Rolfe	68		Stirnweiss	66
1937 —	Gehrig	127*		DiMaggio	59
	Rolfe	90	1947 —	Stirnweiss	89
	Crosetti	86		McQuinn	78
	Dickey	73		Henrich	71
	Lazzeri	71		DiMaggio	64
	DiMaggio	64		Rizzuto	57
1938 —	Gehrig	107	1948 —	Stirnweiss	86
	Crosetti	106		Henrich	76
	Henrich	92		DiMaggio	67
	Rolfe	74		Rizzuto	60
	Dickey	75		Niarhos	52
	Selkirk	68	1949 —	Henrich	86
	DiMaggio	59		Rizzuto	72
	Gordon	56		Coleman	63
1939 —	Selkirk	103		Mapes	58
	Keller	81		DiMaggio	55
	Rolfe	81		Woodling	52
	Dickey	77	1950 —	Rizzuto	91
	Gordon	75		DiMaggio	80
	Crosetti	65		Woodling	69
	Dahlgren	57		Coleman	67
	DiMaggio	52		Berra	55
	Henrich	51	1951	Woodling	62
1940 —	Keller	106		DiMaggio	61
	Selkirk	84		Rizzuto	58
	Crosetti	72		McDougald	56
	DiMaggio	61	1952 —	Mantle	75
	Rolfe	57		Rizzuto	67
	Gordon	52		Berra	66
1941 —	Keller	102		Woodling	59
	Henrich	81		McDougald	57
	DiMaggio	76		Collins	55
	Gordon	72		Bauer	50
	Rolfe	57	1953 —	Woodling	82
1942 —	Keller	114*		Mantle	79
	Gordon	79		Rizzuto	71
	DiMaggio	68		McDougald	60
	Henrich	58		Bauer	59
1943 —	Keller	106*		Collins	59
	Gordon	98		Berra	50
	Etten	76	1954 —	Collins	59
	Johnson	53		Berra	50
	Lindell	51	1954 —	Mantle	102
1944 —	Etten	97*		McDougald	62

	Berra	56			Tresh	84
	Woodling	53			White	79
	Collins	53	1969 —	White	85
1955 —	Mantle	113*			Clarke	54
	McDougald	67			Murcer	52
	Berra	66			Kenney	50
	Bauer	57	1970 —	White	95
	Carey	50			Murcer	87
1956 —	Mantle	112			Munson	63
	Berra	72			Michael	55
	McDougald	69			Kenney	54
	Skowron	50	1971 —	Murcer	91
1957 —	Mantle	146*			White	86
	Berra	67			Clarke	66
	McDougald	60			Kenney	59
1958 —	Mantle	129*			Michael	56
	Siebern	69			Munson	52
	McDougald	60	1972 —	White	99*
1959 —	Mantle	94			Murcer	63
1960 —	Mantle	111			Munson	52
	Maris	74	1973 —	Nettles	78
1961 —	Mantle	126*			White	78
	Maris	94			Murcer	50
1962 —	Mantle	122	1974 —	Maddox	69
	Maris	98			White	67
	Tresh	70			Nettles	59
	Boyer	59			Murcer	57
1963 —	Tresh	88	1975 —	Bonds	89
1964 —	Mantle	99			White	72
	Maris	63			Nettles	51
	Howard	60	1976 —	White	84
1965 —	Mantle	73			Nettles	68
	Tresh	63			Randolph	58
	Pepitone	54	1977 —	Jackson	75
1966 —	Tresh	91			White	74
	Mantle	57			Nettles	68
	Boyer	50			Randolph	64
1967 —	Mantle	107	1978 —	Randolph	82
1968 —	Mantle	106			Nettles	59
					Jackson	58

THE 200-HIT CLUB
(Yankees who made 200 or more hits in one season)

1921 —	Ruth	204	1934 —	Gehrig	210
1923 —	Ruth	205	1936 —	DiMaggio	206
1924 —	Ruth	200		Gehrig	205
1925 —	Combs	203	1937 —	DiMaggio	215
1927 —	Combs	231*		Gehrig	200
	Gehrig	218	1939 —	Rolfe	213*
1928 —	Gehrig	210	1944 —	Stirnweiss	205*
1929 —	Combs	202	1950 —	Rizzuto	200
1930 —	Gehrig	220	1962 —	Richardson	209
1931 —	Gehrig	211*			
1932 —	Gehrig	208	(*Indicates league leader)

289

STOLEN BASES

(Yankees who stole 30 or more bases in one season)

1903 —	Conroy	33	1913 —	NONE	
1904 —	Conroy	30	1914 —	Maisel	74
1905 —	Fultz	44		Peckinpaugh	38
1906 —	Hoffman	33	1915 —	Maisel	51
	Conroy	32	1916-30	NONE	
1907 —	Conroy	41	1931 —	Chapman	61*
	Chase	32	1932 —	Chapman	38*
	Hoffman	30	1933-43	NONE	
1908 —	Hemphill	42	1944 —	Stirnweiss	55
	Ball	32	1945 —	Stirnweiss	33
1909 —	Austin	30	1946-68	NONE	
1910 —	Daniels	41	1969 —	Clarke	33
	Chase	40	1970-74	NONE	
	Wolter	39	1975 —	Bonds	30
1911 —	Cree	48	1976 —	Rivers	43
	Daniels	40		Randolph	37
	Chase	36		White	31
1912 —	Daniels	37	1977 —	NONE	
	Chase	33	1978 —	Randolph	36

(*Indicates league leader)

YANKEES WHO HIT MORE THAN 40 HOMERUNS IN ONE SEASON

61 —	Roger Maris	1961	Henry Gehrig	1927
60 —	George Ruth	1927	46 — George Ruth	1924, 1929, 1931
59 —	George Ruth	1921	Henry Gehrig	1931
54 —	George Ruth	1920, 1928	Joseph DiMaggio	1937
	Mickey Mantle	1961	42 — Mickey Mantle	1958
52 —	Mickey Mantle	1956	41 — George Ruth	1923, 1932
49 —	George Ruth	1930	Henry Gehrig	1930
	Henry Gehrig	1934, 1936	40 — Mickey Mantle	1960
47 —	George Ruth	1926		

Only one Yankee has hit 30 homeruns and stolen 30 bases in one season: Bobby Bonds, 1975, 32 homeruns, 30 stolen bases. Bonds is the all-time leader in this category, having done it twice with the San Francisco Giants (1969, 32 homeruns, 45 stolen bases; and 1973, 39 homeruns, 43 stolen bases) and once with the California Angels (1977, 37 homeruns, 41 stolen bases).

The only other major leaguer to accomplish this twice in his career was Willie Mays (New York Giants: 1956, 36 homeruns, 40 stolen bases; and 1957, 35 homeruns, 38 stolen bases). Three others have hit similar single season plateaus: Ken Williams (St. Louis Browns, 1922, 39 homeruns, 37 stolen bases); Henry Aaron (Milwaukee Braves, 1963, 44 homeruns, 31 stolen bases); and Tommy Harper (Milwaukee Brewers, 1970, 31 homeruns, 38 stolen bases).

YANKEES WHO HIT SEVEN OR MORE GRAND SLAMS
IN THEIR CAREERS

Henry Gehrig	23	(all-time leader)
George Ruth	16	
Joseph DiMaggio	13	
Lawrence Berra	9	
Mickey Mantle	9	
William Dickey	8	
Anthony Lazzeri	8	
Charles Keller	7	
Joseph Pepitone	7	

Jack Jensen (8) and Rocco Colavito (7) each made the list, but never hit a grand slam homerun in a Yankee uniform.

Reggie Jackson leads active Yankees in grand slams with five, but hit only one of them in a Yankee uniform. Roy White, with three as a Yankee, is the "in-pinstripes" leader.

Four Yankee pitchers have hit grand slams: Charles Ruffing, Spurgeon Chandler, Don Larsen, and Mel Stottlemyre.

YANKEES WHO HIT THREE OR MORE HOMERUNS
IN ONE GAME

(This is an alphabetical listing. An asterisk indicates consecutive at bats, an H indicates the homeruns were hit at Yankee Stadium, and an R indicates they were hit on the road.)

William Chapman	July 9, 1932 (H) (2d game)
William Dickey	July 26, 1939* (H)
Joseph DiMaggio	July 13, 1937 (2d game) (H), May 23, 1948* (H), May 10, 1950 (H)
Henry Gehrig	June 23, 1927 (A), May 4, 1927 (A), May 22, 1930 (A) (2d game)
Clifford Johnson	June 30, 1977* (H)
Charlie Keller	July 28, 1940 (A) (1st game)
Anthony Lazzeri	June 8, 1927 (H), May 24, 1936 (A)
Mickey Mantle	May 13, 1955 (H)
John Mize	September 15, 1950* (A)
Robert Murcer	June 24, 1970* (H) (2d game), July 13, 1973 (H)
George Ruth	May 21, 1930 (A) (1st game)
Thomas Tresh	June 6, 1965* (H)

Henry Gehrig hit four consecutive homeruns in one game on June 3, 1932 at Philadelphia, tying the major league record set by Robert Lowe (Boston Nationals) in 1894. Mike Schmidt and Rocco Colavito have tied Gehrig's mark. Six other players have hit four non-consecutive homeruns in one game: Ed Delahanty, Charles Klein, Gil Hodges, Joe Adcock, Willie Mays, and J. Patrick Seerey.)

THE MEN WHO WON TWENTY

1903 — Jack Chesbro	21-15	.583
1904 — Jack Chesbro	41-12*	.774*
John Powell	23-19	.548
1906 — Al Orth	27-17*	.614
Jack Chesbro	24-16	.600

1910 — Russ Ford	26-6	.813
1911 — Russ Ford	22-11	.656
1916 — Bob Shawkey	24-14	.622
1919 — Bob Shawkey	20-13	.645
1920 — Carl Mays	26-11	.703
Bob Shawkey	20-13	.606
1921 — Carl Mays	27-9*	.750
1922 — Leslie Bush	26-7	.788*
Bob Shawkey	20-12	.625
1923 — Sam Jones	21-8	.724
1924 — Herb Pennock	21-9	.700
1926 — Herb Pennock	23-11	.676
1927 — Waite Hoyt	22-7*	.759
1928 — George Pipgras	24-13*	.649
Waite Hoyt	23-7	.767
1931 — Vernon Gomez	21-9	.700
1932 — Vernon Gomez	24-7	.774
1934 — Vernon Gomez	26-5*	.839*
1936 — Charles Ruffing	20-12	.625
1937 — Vernon Gomez	21-11*	.656
Charles Ruffing	20-7	.741

(Note: Gomez and Ruffing were the league's only twenty game winners in 1937!)

1938 — Charles Ruffing	21-7*	.750*
1939 — Charles Ruffing	21-7	.750
1942 — Ernest Bonham	21-5	.808*
1943 — Spurgeon Chandler	20-4*	.833*
1946 — Spurgeon Chandler	20-8	.714
1949 — Vic Raschi	21-10	.677
1950 — Vic Raschi	21-8	.724*
1951 — Ed Lopat	21-9	.700
Vic Raschi	21-10	.677
1952 — Allie Reynolds	20-8	.714
1954 — Robert Grim	20-6	.769
1958 — Robert Turley	21-7*	.750
1961 — Edward Ford	25-4*	.862*
1962 — Ralph Terry	23-12*	.657
1963 — Edward Ford	24-7*	.774*
James Bouton	21-7	.750
1965 — Melvin Stottlemyre	20-9	.690
1968 — Melvin Stottlemyre	2112	.636
1969 — Melvin Stottlemyre	20-14	.588
1970 — Frederick Peterson	20-11	.645
1975 — James Hunter	23-14*	.622
1978 — Ronald Guidry **	25-3*	.893*
Ed Figueroa	20-9	.690

(* Indicates league leader in wins or percentage, depending on location of the asterisk.)
(** In 1978, Ron Guidry set all sorts of records, including the highest winning percentage for a starting pitcher who won more than 20 games in one season. He also became the first lefthanded American League pitcher to strike out 18 batters in one game (v. California Angels, June 17, 1978, at Yankee Stadium), and the first Yankee pitcher to strike out more than 15 batters in a game.

(Another interesting note: in 1945, the Yankees traded pitcher Hank Borowy to the Cubs mid-way through the season. Borowy left New York with a 10-5 mark, and went on to win 11 games while losing two for Chicago. He finished that season 21-7, and thereby became one of three pitchers in baseball history to win 20 games during a "split" season. (The other two: Joe McGinty, 1902, Baltimore, A.L. 13-10, and New York N.L., 8-8; and, Patrick Flaherty, 1904, Chicago, A.L., 2-2, and Pittsburgh, N.L., 19-9.)

THE 200-STRIKEOUT CLUB

(Yankee pitchers who struck out 200 or more
batters in one season)

1904 —	Chesbro	239
1910 —	Ford	209
1955 —	Turley	210
1961 —	Ford	209
1964 —	Downing	217*
1978 —	Guidry	248

(OTHER YANKEE PITCHERS WHO LED THE LEAGUE IN STRIKEOUTS)

1932 —	Ruffing	190
1933 —	Gomez	163
1934 —	Gomez	158
1937 —	Ruffing	194
1951 —	Raschi	164
1952 —	Reynolds	160

(NOTE: As is quite obvious, the strikeout pitcher has always been something of a rarity in a Yankee uniform.)

APPEARANCES

(Yankee pitchers who appeared in 30 or
game in more games in one season)

1903 —	Chesbro	40	1908 —	Chesbro	45
	Tannehill	32		Manning	41
1904 —	Chesbro	55*		Lake	38
	Powell	47	1909 —	Warhop	26
1905 —	Chesbro	41		Lake	31
	Orth	40	1910 —	Warhop	37
	Hogg	39		Ford	36
	Powell	36		Quinn	35
1906 —	Chesbro	49*		Vaughn	30
	Orth	45	1911 —	Caldwell	41
	Clarkson	32		Quinn	40
1907 —	Orth	36		Ford	37
	Chesbro	30		Warhop	31

1912 — Warhop	39		Jones	39
Ford	36		Thomas	33
Caldwell	30	1927 —	Moore	50
1913 — Fisher	43		Hoyt	36
Schulz	38		Pennock	34
McConnell	35		Shocker	31
Ford	33	1928 —	Pipgras	46
1914 — Warhop	37		Hoyt	42
Keating	34		Moore	35
Cole	33		Johnson	31
Caldwell	31	1929 —	Moore	41
McHale	31		Pipgras	39
1915 — Caldwell	36		Hiemach	35
Fisher	30		Sherid	33
1916 — Shawkey	53		Wells	31
Fisher	31		Hoyt	30
Mogridge	30	1930 —	Pipgras	44
1917 — Love	33		Johnson	44
Caldwell	32		Sherid	37
Shawkey	32		Ruffing	34
Cullop	30	1931 —	Gomez	40
1918 — Mogridge	45		Johnson	40
Love	38		Ruffing	37
1919 Shawkey	41		Pipgras	36
Quinn	38	1932 —	Gomez	37
Mogridge	35		Ruffing	35
Thormahlen	30		Allen	33
1920 — Mays	45		Pipgras	32
Quinn	41	1933 —	Ruffing	35
Shawkey	38		Gomez	35
Collins	36		Moore	35
1921 — Mays	49*	1934 —	Murphy	40
Hoyt	43		Gomez	38
Shawkey	38		Ruffing	36
1922 — Jones	45		DeShong	31
Shawkey	39	1935 —	Murphy	40
Hoyt	37		Gomez	34
1923 — Jones	39		Ruffing	30
Bush	37		Tamulis	30
Hoyt	37	1936 —	Broaca	37
Shawkey	36		Malone	35
Pennock	35		Ruffing	33
1924 — Hoyt	46		Pearson	33
Pennock	40		Gomez	31
Bush	39		Hadley	31
Shawkey	38	1937 —	Murphy	39
Jones	36		Gomez	34
1925 — Pennock	47		Ruffing	31
Hoyt	46	1938 —	Murphy	32
Jones	43		Gomez	32
Shocker	41		Ruffing	31
Shawkey	33	1939 —	Murphy	38
1926 — Shocker	41	1940 —	Murphy	35
Pennock	40		Ruffing	30
Hoyt	40		Russo	30

1941 — Murphy	35	Kucks	34
1942 — Murphy	31	Ford	31
1943 — Murphy	37	1957 — Ditmar	46
Chandler	30	Grim	46
1944 — Borowy	35	Kucks	37
Turner	35	Turley	32
Dubiel	30	Shantz	30
Donald	30	1958 — Duren	44
1945 — Turner	30	Ditmar	38
1946 — Chandler	34	Kucks	34
Gumpert	33	Turley	33
Bevens	31	Ford	30
Page	31	1959 — Duren	41
1947 — Page	56	Maas	38
Reynolds	34	Ditmar	38
Drews	30	Coates	37
1948 — Page	55*	Shantz	33
Reynolds	39	Turley	33
Raschi	36	Ford	35
Lopat	33	1960 — Shantz	42
Byrne	31	Duren	42
1949 — Page	60*	Coates	35
Raschi	38	Terry	35
Reynolds	35	Maas	35
Byrne	32	Turley	34
Lopat	31	Ditmar	34
1950 — Page	37	Ford	33
Reynolds	35	1961 — Arroyo	65
Rascht	35	Coates	43
Byrne	31	Ford	39
Ferrick	30	Stafford	36
1951 — Reynolds	40	Sheldon	35
Raschi	35	Terry	31
Ostrowski	34	1962 Bridges	52
Lopat	31	Coates	50
1952 — Reynolds	35	Terry	43
Sain	35	Daley	43
Raschi	31	Ford	38
1953 — Reynolds	41	Bouton	36
Sain	40	Stafford	35
Gorman	40	Sheldon	34
Kuzava	33	1963 — Reniff	48
Ford	32	Bouton	40
1954 — Sain	45	Terry	40
Grim	37	Ford	38
Reynolds	36	Hamilton	34
Ford	34	1964 — Mikkelsen	50
Morgan	32	Reniff	41
1955 — Konstanty	45	Ford	39
Morgan	40	Bouton	38
Ford	39	Downing	37
Turley	36	1965 — Ramos	65
1956 — Morgan	41	Reniff	51
Larsen	38	Mikkelsen	41
Byrne	37	Stottlemyre	37

	Ford	37	Peterson	37
	Downing	35	Kekich	37
	Bouton	30	Bahnsen	36
1966 —	Reniff	56	Stottlemyre	35
	Ramos	52	Kline	31
	Hamilton	44	1972 — Lyle	59
	Womack	42	Stottlemyre	36
	Stottlemyre	37	Peterson	35
	Peterson	34	Kline	32
	Downing	30	1973 — Lyle	51
1967 —	Womack	65	McDaniel	47
	Hamilton	44	Stottlemyre	38
	Tillotson	43	Medich	34
	Peterson	36	Peterson	31
	Stottlemyre	36	1974 — Lyle	66
	Downing	31	Dobson	39
1968 —	Womack	45	Medich	38
	Hamilton	40	Upshaw	36
	Verbanic	40	Tidrow	33
	Bahnsen	37	1975 — Lyle	49
	Stottlemyre	36	Hunter	39
	Peterson	36	Medich	38
1969 —	McDaniel	51	Tidrow	37
	Bahnsen	40	Dobson	33
	Stottlemyre	39	May	32
	Aker	38	1976 — Lyle	64
	Peterson	37	Tidrow	47
	Burbach	31	Hunter	36
	Downing	30	Figueroa	34
1970 —	McDaniel	62	1977 — Lyle	72*
	Klimkowski	45	Tidrow	49
	Aker	41	Figueroa	32
	Peterson	39	Guidry	31
	Stottlemyre	37	1978 — Gossage	63
	Bahnsen	36	Lyle	59
	Hamilton	35	Figueroa	35
1971 —	McDaniel	44	Guidry	35
	Aker	41	Tidrow	31

THE 250-INNING CLUB

(Yankee pitchers who pitched 250 or
more innings in one season)

1903 — Chesbro	325	1909 —	NONE	
1904 — Chesbro	455*	1910 —	Ford	300
Powell	390		Warhop	254
1905 — Orth	305	1911 —	Ford	281
Chesbro	303		Caldwell	255
1906 — Orth	339	1912 —	Ford	292
Chesbro	325		Warhop	258
1907 — NONE		1913-14 —	NONE	
1908 — Chesbro	289	1915 —	Caldwell	305
Lake	269	1916 —	Shawkey	277

Year	Pitcher		Year	Pitcher	
1917-17 —	NONE		1947-48 —	NONE	
1919 —	Quinn	264	1949 —	Raschi	275
	Shawkey	261	1950 —	Raschi	257
1920 —	Mays	312	1951 —	Raschi	258
	Shawkey	268	1952-54 —	NONE	
	Quinn	253	1955 —	Ford	254
1921 —	Mays	337*	1956-60 —	NONE	
	Hoyt	282	1961 —	Ford	283*
1922 —	Shawkey	300	1962 —	Terry	299*
	Hoyt	265		Ford	258
	Jones	260	1963 —	Ford	269*
1923	Bush	276		Terry	268
	Shawkey	259	1964 —	Bouton	271
1924 —	Pennock	286	1965 —	Stottlemyre	291*
	Bush	252	1966 —	Stottlemyre	251
1925 —	Pennock	277*	1967 —	Stottlemyre	255
1926 —	Pennock	266	1968 —	Stottlemyre	279
	Shocker	258		Bahnsen	267
1927 —	Hoyt	256	1969 —	Stottlemyre	303
1928 —	Pipgras	301*		Peterson	272
	Hoyt	273	1970 —	Stottlemyre	271
1929-31 —	NONE			Peterson	260
1932 —	Gomez	265	1971 —	Peterson	274
	Ruffing	259		Stottlemyre	270
1933 —	NONE		1972 —	Stottlemyre	260
1934 —	Gomez	282*		Peterson	250
	Ruffing	256	1973 —	Stottlemyre	273
1935 —	NONE		1974 —	Dobson	281
1936 —	Ruffing	271		Medich	280
1937 —	Gomez	278	1975 —	Hunter	328*
	Ruffing	256		Medich	272
1938-42 —	NONE		1976 —	Hunter	299
1943 —	Chandler	253		Figueroa	257
1944 —	Borowy	253	1977 —	NONE	
1945 —	NONE		1978 —	Guidry	273
1946 —	Chandler	257		Figueroa	253
	Bevens	250			

(*Indicates league leader)

EARNED RUN AVERAGE (ERA)
(Yankees pitchers who allowed less than 3.00
earned runs/9-innings pitched in one season)

Based on a minimum of 200 innings pitched

Year	Pitcher		Year	Pitcher	
1903 —	Griffith	2.70		Manning	2.94
	Chesbro	2.77	1909 —	Lake	1.88
1904 —	Chesbro	1.82*		Warhop	2.40
	Powell	2.44	1910 —	Ford	1.65
1905 —	Chesbro	2.20		Vaughn	1.83
	Orth	2.86		Quinn	2.36
1906 —	Hogg	2.93		Warhop	2.87
	Chesbro	2.96	1911 —	Ford	2.27
1907 —	Chesbro	2.53	1912 —	Warhop	2.85
	Orth	2.61	1913 —	Caldwell	2.41
1908 —	Chesbro	2.93		Ford	2.66

Year	Pitcher	ERA		Year	Pitcher	ERA
1914 —	Caldwell	1.94		1946 —	Chandler	2.10
	Fisher	2.28			Bevens	2.23
	Warhop	2.37		1947 —	Chandler	2.46*(b)
	Keating	2.96		1948 —	NONE	
1915 —	Fisher	2.11		1949-50 —	NONE	
	Caldwell	2.89		1951 —	Lopag	2.91
1916 —	Shawkey	2.21		1952 —	Reynolds	2.06*
1917 —	Shawkey	2.44			Raschi	2.78
	Caldwell	2.86		1953 —	NONE	
1918 —	Mogridge	2.27		1954 —	Ford	2.82
1919 —	Quinn	2.63		1955 —	Ford	2.63
	Shawkey	2.72		1956 —	Ford	2.47
1920 —	Shawkey	2.45*		1957 —	Shantz	2.45*(c)
1921 —	NONE				Sturdivant	2.54
1922 —	Shawkey	2.91		1958 —	Ford	2.01*
1923 —	NONE				Turley	2.97
1924 —	Pennock	2.83		1959 —	Ditmar	2.90
1925 —	Pennock	2.96		1960-61 —	NONE	
1926 —	NONE			1962 —	Ford	2.90
1927 —	Moore	2.28(a)		1963 —	Bouton	2.53
	Hoyt	2.63*			Ford	2.74
	Shocker	2.84		1964 —	Ford	2.13
1928 —	Pennock	2.56		1965 —	Stottlemyre	2.63
1929-30	NONE			1966 —	NONE	
1931 —	Gomez	2.63		1967 —	Downing	2.63
1932-33	NONE				Stottlemyre	2.96
1934 —	Gomez	2.33*		1968 —	Bahnsen	2.05
1935-36	NONE				Stottlemyre	2.45
1937 —	Gomez	2.33*			Peterson	2.63
	Ruffing	2.98		1969 —	Peterson	2.55
1938 —	NONE				Stottlemyre	2.82
1939 —	Ruffing	2.93		1970 —	Peterson	2.91
1940-41	NONE			1972 —	Stottlemure	2.87
1942 —	Bonham	2.27		1972 —	Kline	2.40
	Chandler	2.38		1973 —	Medich	2.91
1943 —	Chandler	1.64*		1974 —	NONE	
	Bonham	2.27		1975 —	Hunter	2.58
	Wensloff	2.54		1976 —	NONE	
	Borowy	2.82		197 —	Guidry	2.82
1944 —	Borowy	2.64		1978 —	Guidry	1.74*
	Bonham	2.99			Figueroa	2.99
1945 —	NONE					

(* Indicates league leader)

(a) — In 1927, the official league statistics show Waite Hoyt as the ERA champion, despite Wilcy Moore's superior mark. Moore pitched 213 innings to Hoyt's 256.)

(b) — In 1947, Spud Chandler was the A.L. ERA champion, even though he pitched only 128 innings, so I have included him in the list.)

(c) — In 1957, Bobby Shantz was declared the league's ERA champion. He pitched 173 innings and went 11-5, so he is included herein.)

It is important to realize that many other Yankee pitchers broke the 3.00 mark. To list all of them would serve no purpose. Similarly, any minimum cutoff based on innings pitched is somewhat artificial.

ALL-TIME YANKEES — TOP 20
PITCHING CATEGORIES

	Games		Innings		Wins		Pct. (100 decls.)
1.	Ford, W.	498	Ford, W.	3171	Ford, W.	236	Chandler .717
2.	Ruffing	426	Ruffing	3169	Ruffing	231	Raschi .706
3.	Shawkey	415	Stottlemyre	2662	Gomez	189	Ford, W. 6.90
4.	Murphy	383	Gomez	2498	Shawkey	168	Reynolds .686
5.	Gomez	367	Shawkey	2489	Stottlemyre	164	Mays .670
6.	Hoyt	365	Hoyt	2273	Pennock	162	Lopat .657
7.	LYLE	361	Pennock	2189	Hoyt	157	Ruffing .651
8.	Stottlemyre	360	Chesbro	1953	Reynolds	131	Gomez .649
9.	Pennock	346	Peterson	1856	Chesbro	126	Pennock .643
10.	Hamilton	311	Caldwell	1718	Raschi	120	Byrne .643
11.	Reynolds	295	Reynolds	1700	Lopat	113	Murphy .637
12.	Peterson	288	Raschi	1537	Peterson	109	Hoyt .616
13.	Page	278	Lopat	1497	Chandler	109	Bonham .612
14.	Chesbro	269	Chandler	1485	Caldwell	96	Turley .612
15.	Caldwell	248	Warhop	1423	Murphy	93	Pipgras .595
16.	Pipgras	247	Pipgras	1352	Pipgras	93	Chesbro .577
17.	Reniff	247	Quinn	1279	Turley	82	Terry .569
18.	Turley	234	Turley	1268	Mays	79	Shawkey .562
19.	Quinn	228	Downing	1236	Bonham	79	Downing .559
20.	Byrne	221	Terry	1198	Terry	78	Ford, R. .545
	Warhop	221					Jones .545

	Strikeouts		Shutouts		Complete Games		ERA (Over 800 Inn.)	
1.	Ford, .	1956	Ford, .	45	Ruffing	261	Ford, R.	2.54
2.	Ruffing	1526	Stottlemyre	40	Gomez	173	Chesbro	2.58
3.	Gomez	1468	Ruffing	37	Chesbro	169	Orth	2.72
4.	Stottlemyre	1257	Reynolds	27	Pennock	165	Bonham	2.73
5.	Shawkey	1163	Chandler	26	Shawkey	161	Ford, W.	2.74
6.	Downing	1028	Gomez	26	Ford, W.	156	Chandler	2.84
7.	Reynolds	967	Shawkey	26	Hoyt	156	Stottlemyre	2.97
8.	Chesbro	913	Raschi	24	Stottlemyre	152	Caldwell	2.99
9.	Turley	909	Turley	21	Caldwell	151	Warhop	3.09
10.	Peterson	893	Lopat	20	Chandler	109	Peterson	3.10
11.	Raschi	832	Pennock	19	Warhop	105	Shawkey	3.10
12.	Caldwell	803	Peterson	18	Ford, R.	103	Bahnsen	3.10
13.	Hoyt	713	Bonham	17	Orth	102	Quinn	3.12
14.	Pennock	700	Chesbro	16	Raschi	99	Lopat	3.21
15.	Pipgras	656	Terry	16	Reynolds	96	Downing	3.25
16.	Terry	615	Hoyt	15	Bonham	91	Mays	3.25
17.	Chandler	614	Pipgras	13	Lopat	91	Reynolds	3.30
18.	Byrne	592	Caldwell	13	Pipgras	84	Gomez	3.34
19.	Bouton	561	Downing	12	Quinn	82	Bouton	3.36
20.	Ford, R.	553	Bouton	11	Peterson	81	Terry	3.44
			Orth	11				
			Borowy	11				

CAPS — Active Yankee Player

LEADING YANKEE RELIEF PITCHERS

Year	Pitcher	W	S	Pts.	Year	Pitcher	W	S	Pts.
1977	Lyle	13	26	39	1960	Shantz	5	11	16
1976	Lyle	7	23	30	1959	Duren	3	14	17
1975	Lyle	5	6	11	1958	Duren	6	20*	26
	Tidrow	6	5	11	1957	Grim	12	19*	31*
1974	Lyle	9	15	24	1956	Morgan	6	11	17
1973	Lyle	5	27	32	1955	Konstanty	7	11	18
1972	Lyle	9	35*	44*	1954	Sain	6	22*	28
1971	McDaniel	5	4	9	1953	Reynolds	7	13	20
1970	McDaniel	9	29	38	1952	Sain	3	7	10
1969	Aker	8	11	19	1951	Kuzova	5	5	10
1968	McDaniel	4	10	14	1950	Ferrick	8	9	17
1967	Womack	5	17	22	1949	Page	13	27*	40*
1966	Ramos	3	12	15	1948	Page	7	16	23
1965	Ramos	5	14	19	1947	Page	14	17*	31
1964	Mikkelson	7	9	16	1946	Murphy	4	7	11
1963	Reniff	4	13	17	1945	Turner	3	10	13
1963	Bridges	8	18	26	1944	Turner	4	7	11
1961	Arroyo	15	29*	44*	1943	Murphy	12	8	20

*Denotes League Leader

SEASON LEADERS PITCHING

	Innings	Wins	ERA	Strikeouts (Pitchers)
1903	Chesbro 325	Chesbro 21-15	Chesbro 2.77	Chesbro 147
1904	Chesbro* 455	Chesbro* 41-12	Chesbro 1.82	Chesbro 239
1905	Orth 305	Chesbro 20-15	Chesbro 2.20	Chesbro 156
1906	Orth* 339	Orth 27-17	Clarkson 2.32	Chesbro 152
1907	Orth 249	Orth 14-21	Chesbro 2.53	Doyle 94
1908	Chesbro 289	Chesbro 14-20	Chesbro 2.93	Chesbro 124
1909	Warhop 243	Lake 14-11	Lake 1.88	Lake 117
1910	Ford 300	Ford 26-6	Ford 1.65	Ford 209
1911	Ford ..... .281	Ford 22-11	Ford 2.28	Ford 158
1912	Ford 292	Ford 13-21	McConnell ... 2.75	Ford 112
1913	Fisher 246	Fisher 11-17	Caldwell 2.43	Fisher 92
		Ford 11-18		
1914	Warhop 217	Caldwell 17-9	Caldwell 1.94	Keating 109
1915	Caldwell 305	Caldwell 19-16	Fisher 2.11	Caldwell 130
1916	Shawkey 277	Shawkey 23-14	Cullop 2.05	Shawkey 122
1917	Shawkey 236	Shawkey 13-15	Fisher 2.19	Caldwell 102
1918	Mogridge 230	Mogridge 16-13	Mogridge 2.27	Love 95
1919	Quinn 264	Shawkey 20-11	Thormahlen .. 2.62	Shawkey 122
1920	Mays 312	Mays 26-11	Shawkey* ... 2.46	Shawkey 126
1921	Mays* 337	Mays* 27-9	Mays 3.08	Shawkey 126
1922	Shawkey 300	Bush 26-7	Shawkey 2.91	Shawkey 130
1923	Bush 276	Jones 21-6	Hoyt 3.01	Bush, Shawkey..125
1924	Pennock 286	Pennock 21-9	Pennock 2.83	Shawkey 114
1925	Pennock* 277	Pennock 15-17	Pennock 2.85	Jones 92
1926	Pennock 266	Pennock 23-11	Shocker..... 3.38	Hoyt 79
1927	Hoyt 256	Hoyt* 22-7	W. Moore* .. 2.28	Hoyt 86
1928	Pipgras 301	Pipgras* 24-13	Pennock 2.56	Pipgras 139
1929	Pipgras 225	Pipgras 18-12	Zachary 2.47	Pipgras 125
1930	Ruffind 222	Pipgras 15-15	Pipgras 4.11	Ruffing 117
		Ruffing 15-8		
1931	Gomez 243	Gomez 21-9	Gomez 2.63	Gomez 150
1932	Gomez 265	Gomez 24-7	Ruffing 3.10	Ruffing 117
1933	Gomez, Ruffing .235	Gomez 16-10	Gomez 3.16	Gomez* 163

Year	Innings	Wins	ERA	Strikeouts (Pitchers)
1934	Gomez* 282	Gomez* 26-5	Gomez* 2.33	Gomez* 158
1935	Gomez 246	Ruffing 16-11	Ruffing 3.12	Gomez 138
1936	Ruffing 271	Ruffing 20-12	Pearson 3.71	Pearson 118
1937	Gomez 278	Gomez* 21-11	Gomez* 2.33	Ruffing* 194
1938	Ruffing 247	Ruffing* 21-7	Ruffing 3.12	Gomez 129
1939	Ruffing 233	Ruffing 21-7	Ruffing 2.94	Gomez 102
1940	Ruffing 226	Ruffing 15-12	Russo 3.29	Ruffing 97
1941	Russo 210	Ruffing 15-6	Russo 3.09	Russo 105
		Gomez 15-5		
1942	Chandler 201	Bonham 21-5	Chandler 2.37	Borowy 85
1943	Chandler 253	Chandler* 20-4	Chandler* ... 1.64	Chandler 134
1944	Borowy 253	Borowy 17-12	Borowy 2.63	Borowy 107
1945	Bevens 184	Bevens 13-9	Bonham 3.28	Bevens 76
1946	Chandler 257	Chandler 20-8	Chandler 2.10	Chandler 138
1947	Reynolds 242	Reynolds 19-8	Chandler* ... 2.46	Reynolds 129
1948	Reynolds 236	Raschi 19-8	Lopat 3.65	Raschi 124
1949	Raschi 275	Raschi 21-11	Lopat 3.27	Byrne 129
1950	Raschi 257	Raschi 21-8	Lopat 3.47	Reynolds 160
1951	Raschi 258	Raschi 21-10	Lopat 2.91	Raschi* 164
		Lopat 21-9		
1952	Reynolds 244	Reynolds 20-8	Reynolds* ... 2.07	Reynolds* 160
1953	Ford 207	Ford 18-6	Lopat 2.43	Ford 110
1954	Ford 211	Grim 20-6	Ford 2.82	Ford 125
1955	Ford 254	Ford 18-7	Ford 2.62	Turley 210
1956	Ford 226	Ford 19-6	Ford* 2.47	Ford 141
1957	Sturdivant 202	Sturdivant 16-6	Shantz* 2.45	Turley 152
1958	Turley 245	Turley* 21-7	Ford* 2.01	Turley 168
1959	Ford 204	Ford 16-10	Ditmar 2.90	Ford 114
1960	Ditmar 200	Ditmar 15-9	Ditmar 3.06	Terry 92
1961	Ford* 283	Ford* 25-4	Stafford 2.68	Ford 209
1962	Terry* 299	Terry* 23-12	Ford 2.90	Terry 176
1963	Ford 269	Ford 24-7	Bouton 2.53	Ford 189
1964	Bouton 271	Bouton 18-13	Ford ······· 2.13	Downing* 217
1965	Stottlemyre ...291	Stottlemyre ... 20-9	Stottlemyre .. 2.63	Downing 179
1966	Stottlemyre ...251	Stottlemyre .. 12-20	Peterson 3.31	Downing 152
		Peterson 12-11		
1967	Stottlemyre ...255	Stottlemyre .. 15-15	Downing 2.63	Downing 171
1968	Stottlemyre ...279	Stottlemyre .. 21-12	Bahnsen ... 2.06	Bahnsen 162
1969	Stottlemyre ...303	Stottlemyre .. 20-14	Peterson 2.55	Peterson 150
1970	Stottlemyre ...271	Peterson .. 20-11	Peterson 2.91	Peterson 127
1971	Peterson 274	Stottlemyre . 16-12	Stottlemyre .. 2.87	Peterson 139
1972	Stottlemyre ...200	Peterson 17-15	Kline 2.40	Stottlemyre 110
1973	Stottlemyre ...273	Stottlemyre . 16-16	Medich 2.95	Medich 145
1974	Dobson 281	Dobson 19-15	Dobson 3.07	Dobson 157
		Medich 19-15		
1975	Hunter 328	Hunter 23-14	Hunter 2.58	Hunteer 177
1976	Hunter 299	Figueroa .. 19-10	Figueroa ... 3.02	Hunter 173
1977	Figueroa 239	Guidry 16-7	Guidry 2.82	Guidry 176
		Figueroa 16-11		

ALL-TIME YANKEE PITCHING RECORDS
INDIVIDUAL

Most years with Yankees	Whitey Ford	16
Most games, righthander, season	Pedro Ramos	64 (1965)
	Dooley Womack	65 (1967)
Most games, lefthander, season	Sparky Lyle	72 (1977)
Most games started, season	Jack Chesbro	51 (1904)
Most complete games, season	Jack Chesbro	48 (1904)
Most games finished, RHP, season	Dooley Womack	48 (1967)
Most games finished, LHP, season	Sparky Lyle	60 (1977)
Most innings pitched, season	Jack Chesbro	454 (1904)
Most victories, season	Jack Chesbro	41 (1904)

Most 20-victory seasons	Bob Shawkey	4
	Lefty Gomez	4
	Red Ruffing	4
Most losses, season	Al Orth	21 (1907)
	Sam Jones	21 (1925)
	Joe Lake	21 (1908)
	Russ Ford	21 (1912)
Highest winning percentage, season	Whitey Ford (25-4)	.862 (1961)
Most consecutive victories, season	Jack Chesbro	14 (1904)
	Whitey Ford	14 (1961)
Most consecutive losses, season	Fritz Peterson	8 (1967)
	Fred Talbot	8 (1968)
Most saves, season	Sparky Lyle	35 (1972)
Most walks, lefthander, season	Tommy Byrne	179 (1949)
Most walks, righthander, season	Bob Turley	177 (1955)
Most strikeouts, season	Jack Chesbro	240 (1904)
Most strikeouts, 9-inning games	Bob Shawkey	15 (9/27/19)
Most strikeouts, extra-inning game	Whitey Ford	15 (4/22/59)
Most shutouts, season	Whitey Ford	8 (1964)
Most 1-0 shutouts won, career	Bob Shawkey	7
Most shutouts lost, season	Bill Zuber	7 (1945)
Most runs allowed, season	Russ Ford	165 (1912)
Most earned runs allowed, season	Sam Jones	127 (1925)
Most hits allowed, season	Jack Chesbro	337 (1904)
Most hit batsmen, season	Jack Warhop	26 (1909)
Most wild pitches, season	Al Downing	14 (1964)
Most home runs allowed, season	Ralph Terry	40 (1962)
Lowest earned run average, season	Spud Chandler	1.64 (1943)

*Major League Record   †American League Record

Games Pitched

Lyle	72	1977
Lyle	66	1974
Arroyo	65	1961
Ramos	65	1965
Womack	65	1967
Lyle	64	1976
McDaniel	62	1970
Page	60	1949
Lyle	59	1972
Page	56	1947
Reniff	56	1966

Complete Games

Chesbro	48	1904
Powell	38	1904
Orth	36	1906
Chesbro	33	1903
R. Ford	32	1912
Mays	30	1921
Hunter	30	1975
R. Ford	29	1910
Orth	26	1905
Mays	26	1920

Wins

Chesbro	41	1904
Orth	27	1906
Mays	27	1921
R. Ford	26	1910
Mays	26	1920
Bush	26	1922
Gomez	26	1934
W. Ford	25	1961
Chesbro	24	1906
Shawkey	24	1916
Pipgras	24	1928
W. Ford	24	1963

Shutouts

1. R. Ford	8	1910
2. W. Ford	8	1964
3. Reynolds	7	1951
4. W. Ford	7	1958
5. Stottlemyre	7	1951
6. Stottlemyre	7	1971
7. Hunter	7	1975
8. 12 tied with 6		
9.		
10.		

Strikeouts (Pitcher)

Chesbro	239	1904
Downing	217	1964
Turley	210	1955
R. Ford	209	1910
W. Ford	209	1961
Powell	202	1904
Ruffing	194	1937
Ruffing	190	1932
W. Ford	189	1963
Downing	179	1965

Earned Run Average

Chandler	1.64	1943
R. Ford	1.65	1910
Chesbro	1.82	1904
Vaughn	1.83	1910
Lake	1.88	1909
Caldwell	1.94	1914
W. Ford	2.01	1958
Cullop	2.05	1916
Bahnsen	2.06	1968
Reynolds	2.07	1952

NEW YORK YANKEE TWENTY-GAME WINNERS

Year	Pitcher	W	L	Year	Pitcher	W	L
1903 —	Jack Chesbro	21	15	1937 —	Lefty Gomez	21	11
1904 —	Jack Chesbro	41	12		Red Ruffing	20	7
	John Powell	23	19	1938	Red Ruffing	21	7
1906 —	Albert Orth	27	17	1939 —	Red Ruffing	21	7
	Jack Chesbro	24	16	1942 —	Ernie Bonham	21	5
1910 —	Russell Ford	26	6	1943	Spud Chandler	20	4
1911 —	Russell Ford	22	11	1946 —	Spud Chandler	20	8
1916 —	Bob Shawkey	24	14	1949 —	Vic Raschi	21	10
1919 —	Bob Shawkey	20	13	1950 —	Vic Raschi	21	8
1920 —	Carl Mays	26	11	1951 —	Eddie Lopat	21	9
	Bob Shawkey	20	13		Vic Raschi	21	10
1921 —	Carl Mays	27	9	1952 —	Allie Reynolds	20	8
1922 —	Joe Bush	26	7	1954 —	Bob Grim	20	6
	Bob Shawkey	20	13	1958 —	Bob Turley	21	7
1923 —	Sam Jones	21	8	1961 —	Whitey Ford	25	4
1924 —	Herb Pennock	21	9	1962 —	Ralph Terry	23	12
1926 —	Herb Pennock	23	11	1963 —	Whitey Ford	24	7
1927 —	Waite Hoyt	22	7		Jim Bouton	21	7
1928 —	George Pipgras	24	13	1965 —	Mel Stottlemyre	20	9
	Waite Hoyt	23	7	1968 —	Mel Stottlemyre	21	12
1931 —	Lefty Gomez	21	9	1969 —	Mel Stottlemyre	20	14
1932 —	Lefty Gomez	24	7	1970 —	Fritz Peterson	20	11
1934 —	Lefty Gomez	26	5	1975 —	Catfish Hunter	23	14
1936 —	Red Ruffing	20	12				

NO-HIT GAMES BY YANKEE PITCHERS

1910 — Thomas L. Hughes, vs. Cleveland, August 30 (9 innings lost in 11th) 0-5
1917 — *George A. Mogridge, at Boston, April 24 2-1
1923 — Samuel P. Jones, at Philadelphia September 4 2-0
1938 — M. Monte Pearson, vs. Cleveland, August 27 (2nd game) 13-0
1951 — Allie P. Reynolds, at Cleveland, July 12 (night) 1-0
Allie P. Reynolds, vs. Boston, September 28 (1st game) 8-0
1956 — Don J. Larsen, vs. Brooklyn, October 8 (Fifth Game of World
Series — only PERFECT GAME in Series history) 2-0

*Left-handed pitcher

ABOUT ONE-HITTERS

Yankee pitchers have hurled 46 one-hitters over the years, the most recent being by Catfish Hunter at Texas on May 31, 1975, in which Cesar Tovar got a 6th inning single. Bob Turley and Whitey Ford each hurled 3 for the Yankees and both men participated in a fourth. Bob Shawkey, Rip Collins. Lefty Gomez, Vic Raschi and Floyd Bevens each threw two one-hitters, with one of Bevens' coming in a World Series. The Yankees have been one-hit 40 times, most recently on August 29, 1973 in California by Nolan Ryan with Thurman Munson collecting a first inning single. The Yankees have been one-hit 12 times since they were last no-hit in 1958. Joe Wood and Earl Hamilton are the only men with a pair of one-hitters against New York, both of Hamilton's coming in 1913. No-hit pitcher Hoyt Wilhelm also one-hit the Yanks in 1959. Horace Clarke is the only Yankee to twice serve as a spoiler breaking up no hitters by Jim Palmer and Joe Niekro. In 1970, Clarke broke up three no hitters in the 9th inning in one month, two of which wound up being more than one-hitters.

20-GAME LOSERS

Only six Yankee hurlers ever suffered the ignonimity of losing 20 or more games in one season, and each of them enjoyed many successful seasons which eased the pain.

1907 —	Al Orth	13-21
1908 —	Jack Chesbro	12-20
1908 —	Joe Lake	10-21
1912 —	Russ Ford	13-21
1925 —	Sam Jones	14-21
1966 —	Mel Stottlemyre	12-20

The poorest winning percentage by a Yankee pitcher who reached 20 or more decisions in one season came in 1908, when Bill Hogg went 4-16. More recently, Fred Talbot reached the modern lowlight with a 1-9 mark in 1967.

MISCELLANEOUS AWARDS, RECORDS, AND SEASONAL LEADERS

BABE RUTH AWARD
(Top World Series Player)

Joe Page	1949
Jerry Coleman	1950
Phil Rizzuto	1951
Johnny Mize	1952
Billy Martin	1953
Don Larsen	1956
Elston Howard	1958
Whitey Ford	1961
Ralph Terry	1962
Reggie Jackson	1977
Bucky Dent	1978

DID YOU KNOW . . . After Babe Ruth, uniform number 3 was worn by George Selkirk, Allie Clark, Joe Medwick (in spring training), Bud Metheny, and Cliff Mapes, until it was retired.

DID YOU KNOW . . . Lou Gehrig was pinch-hit for eight times in his career, but only twice after 1925 — by Earle Combs in 1932 and by Myril Hoag in 1935. Babe Ruth was pinch-hit for by Bobby Veach on Aug. 9, 1925.

DID YOU KNOW . . . Tom Zachary, the man who gave up Babe Ruth's 60th homerun in 1927, was 12-0 for the Yankees two years later — the best 1,000 pitching record ever recorded.

YANKEE ALL-TIME PACE-SETTERS

Batting Champions
Babe Ruth 1924
Lou Gehrig 1934
Joe DiMaggio 1939, 1940
Geo. Stirnweiss 1945
Mickey Mantle 1956

Homer Champions
Wally Pipp 1916, 1917
Babe Ruth 1920, 1921, 1923,
1924, 1926, 1927,
1928, 1929, 1930, 1931
Bob Meusel 1925
Lou Gehrig 1931, 1934, 1936
Joe DiMaggio 1937, 1948
Nick Etten 1944
Mickey Mantle 1955, 1956
1958, 1960
Roger Maris 1961
Graig Nettles 1976

A.L. Rookie of Year Awards
Gil McDougald 3b 1951
Bob Grim, p 1954
Tony Kubek, inf-of 1957
Tom Tresh, ss-of 1962
Stan Bahnsen, p 1968
Thurman Munson, c 1970

R.B.I. Leaders
Babe Ruth 1920, 1921, 1923,
1926, 1928
Bob Meusel 1925
Lou Gehrig 1927, 1928, 1930
1931, 1934
Joe DiMaggio 1941, 1948
Nick Etten 1945
Mickey Mantle 1956
Roger Maris 1960, 1961

Most Valuable Player
Babe Ruth 1923
Lou Gehrig 1927, 1936
Joe DiMaggio 1939, 1941, 1947
Joe Gordon 1942
Spud Chandler 1943
Phil Rizzuto 1950
Yogi Berra 1951, 1954, 1955
Mickey Mantle 1956, 1957, 1962
Roger Maris 1960, 1961
Elston Howard 1963
Thurman Munson 1976

Cy Young Award
Bob Turley 1958
Whitey Ford 1961
Sparky Lyle 1977

LONGEST YANKEE WINNING STREAKS

19 1947
15 1960
18 1953
14 1941
16 1926
13 1954
15 1906
13 1954

LONGEST YANKEE LOSING STREAKS

12 1913
9 . . . . .1912 (twice)
9 1945
9 1953
8 1973

ALL-TIME YANKEE TEAM RECORDS

Most players .... 46 in 1946
Fewest players .... 25 in 1923, 1927
Most games .... 164 in 1964, 1968
Most at-bats .... 5705 in 1964
Most runs .... 1067 in 1931
Fewest runs .... 459 in 1908
Most opponents runs .... 898 in 1930
Most hits .... 1683 in 1930
Fewest hits .... 1137 in 1968
Most singles .... 1157 in 1931
Most doubles .... 315 in 1936
Most triples .... 110 in 1930
Most homers .... 240 in 1961
Most home runs by pinch-hitters, season .... 10 in 1961
Most home runs with bases filled .... 7 in 1948
Most total bases .... 2703 in 1936
Most sacrifices, (S.H. and S.F.) .... 218 in 1922, 1926
Most sacrifice hits .... 178 in 1906
Most sacrifice flies .... 72 in 1974
Most stolen bases .... 289 in 1910
Most caught stealing .... 82 in 1920
Most bases on balls .... 766 in 1932
Most strikeouts .... 1043 in 1967
Fewest strikeouts .... 420 in 1924
Most hit by pitch .... 46 in 1955
Highest batting average .... 309 in 1930
Lowest batting average .... 214 in 1968
Highest slugging average .... 489 in 1927
Lowest slugging average .... 287 in 1914
Most grounded into double play .... 142 in 1973
Fewest grounded into double play .... 91 in 1963
Most left on bases .... 1239 in 1934
Fewest left on bases .... 1010 in 1920
Most .300 hitters .... 9 in 1930
Most putouts .... 4520 in 1964
Fewest putouts .... 3993 in 1935
Most assists .... 2086 in 1904
Fewest assists .... 1493 in 1948
Most chances accepted .... 6377 in 1968
Fewest chances accepted .... 5551 in 1935
Most errors .... 386 in 1912
Fewest errors .... 109 in 1947, 1964
Most errorless games .... 91 in 1964
Most consecutive errorless games .... 10 in 1977
Most double plays .... 214 in 1956
Fewest double plays .... 81 in 1912
Most consecutive games, one or more double plays .. 18 (23 double plays) 1941
Most passed balls .... 32 in 1913
Fewest passed balls .... 0 in 1931
Highest fielding average .... 983 in 1964
Lowest fielding average .... 939 in 1912
Most games won .... 110 in 1927
Most games lost .... 103 in 1908

Highest percentage games won .... 714 in 1927
Lowest percentage games won .... 329 in 1912
Most shutouts won season .... 24 in 1951
Most shutouts lost season .... 27 in 1914
Most 1-0 games won .... 6 in 1908, 1968
Most 1-0 games lost .... 9 in 1914
Most consecutive games won, season .... 19 in 1947
Most consecutive games lost, season .... 13 in 1913
Most times league champions 31
Most runs, game .... New York 25, Philadelphia 2, May 24, 1936
Most runs, game by opponent on road Cleveland 24, New York 6, July 29, 1928
Most runs, game by opponent on road Cleveland 24, New York 1, June 17, 1925
Most runs, game by opponent at home . . Detroit 19, New York 1, June 17, 1925
                      Toronto 19, New York 3, September 10, 1977
Most runs, shutout game .... New York 21, Philadelphia 0
                      Aug. 13, 1939, 2nd game, 8 innings
Most runs shutout game, by opponent ...... Chicago 15, N.Y., July 15, 1907
                      Chicago 15, N.Y. O, May 4, 1950
Most runs, inning .... 14, N.Y. vs. Washington, July 6, 1920, fifth inning
Most hits, game .... 30, New York vs. Boston, September 28, 1923
Most home runs, game . . 8 New York vs. Philadelphia, June 28, 1939, first game
Most consecutive games, one or more home runs .... 25 (40 homers). 1941
Most home runs in consecutive games in which home runs were made
                      40 (25 games) 1941
Most total bases, game 53, New York vs. Philadelphia, June 28, 1939, first game

ALL-TIME YANKEE BATTING RECORDS
INDIVIDUAL

Most years with Yankees	Yogi Berra,	18
	Mickey Mantle	
Most games, season	Bobby Richardson	162 (1961)
	Roy White	162 (1970)
Most at bats, season	Bobby Richardson	692 (1952)†
Most runs, season	Babe Ruth	177 (1921)*
Most hits, season	Earle Combs	231 (1927)
Most singles, season	Willie Keeler	166 (1906)
	Earle Combs	166 (1927)
Most doubles, season	Lou Gehrig	52 (1927)
Most triples, season	Earle Combs	23 (1927)
Most home runs, right hander, season	Joe DiMaggio	46 (1937)
Most home runs, left hander, season	Roger Maris	61 (1961)*
	Babe Ruth	60 (1927)*
Most home runs, rookie, season	Joe DiMaggio	29 (1936)
Most grand slam home runs, season	Lou Gehrig	4 (1934)
	Tommy Henrich	4 (1948)
Most Grand slam home runs, career	Lou Gehrig	23*
Most home runs, season, at home	Babe Ruth	32 (1921) (PG)*
	Lou Gehrig	30 (1934) (YS)
	Roger Maris	30 (1961) (YS)
Most home runs, season, on the road	Babe Ruth	32 (1927)*
Most home runs, one month, right hander	Joe DiMaggio	15 (7/37)
Most home runs, one month, left hander	Babe Ruth	17 (9/27)
Most total bases, season	Babe Ruth	457 (1921)*

307

Most sacrifice hits, season	Willie Keeler	42 (1905)
Most sacrifice flies, season	Roy White	17 (1971)†
Most stolen bases, season	Fritz Maisel	74 (1914)
Most caught stealing, season	Ben Chapman	23 (1931)
Most walks, season	Babe Ruth	170 (1923)
Most strikeouts, season	Bobby Bonds	137 (1975)
Fewest strikeouts, season	Joe Sewell	3 (1932)
Most hit by pitch, season	Frank Crosetti	15 (1938)
Most runs batted in, season	Lou Gehrig	184 (1931)†
Most consecutive games with an RBI	Babe Ruth	11 (1931)*
Highest batting average, season	Babe Ruth	.393 (1923)
Highest slugging average, season	Babe Ruth	847 (1920)*
Longest hitting streak	Joe DiMaggio	56 (1941)*
Most grounded into double plays, season	Billy Johnson	27 (1943)
Fewest grounded into double plays, season	Mickey Mantle	2 (1961)
	Mickey Rivers	2 (1977)

ALL TIME HOME RUN LIST THROUGH 1977

1. Aaron	.755	11. Ott	.511
2. Ruth	.714	12. Gehring	.493
3. Mays	.660	13. McCovey	.493
4. Robinson	.586	14. Musial	.475
5. Killebrew	.573	15. Williams, B.	.426
6. Mantle	.536	16. Snider	.407
7. Foxx	.534	17. Stargen	.401
8. Williams, T.	.521	18. Howard, F.	.382
9. Banks	.512	19. Cepeda	.379
10. Mathews	.512	20. Cash, N.	.377

YANKEE GRAND SLAMS, CAREER
CURRENT PLAYERS

JACKSON —5 (1 with Oakland, 3 with Baltimore) . . . WHITE 3 . . . BLAIR-3 (with Baltimore) . . . NETTLES 2 . . CHAMBLISS—2 (with Cleveland) . . . JOHNSON-2 (1 with Houston) . . . STANLEY-1 . . . PINIELLA-1 (with K.C) DENT-1.

OUTSTANDING YANKEE BATTING FEATS

Three Home Runs One Game		TRIPLE CROWN WINNERS	
Tony Lazzeri	1927, 1936	Lou Gehrig	1934
Lou Gehrig	1927, 1929, 1930	Mickey Mantle	1956
Babe Ruth	1930		
Ben Chapman	1932	**Two Home Runs One Inning**	
Joe DiMaggio	1937, 1948, 1950	Joe DiMaggio	1936
Bill Dickey	1939	Joe Pepitone	1962
Charlie Keller	1940	Cliff Johnson	1977
Johnny Mize	1950	**Four Consecutive Home Runs**	
Mickey Mantle	1955	Lou Gehrig	1932
Tom Tresh	1965	John Blanchard	1961
Bobby Murcer	1970, 1973	Mickey Mantle	1962
Cliff Johnson	1977	Bobby Murcer	1970

Two Consecutive Pinch HRs

Ray Caldwell 1915
Charlie Keller 1948
John Blanchard 1961
Ray Barker 1965

200 Hits Rookie Season

Earle Combs . . . .(203) 1925
Joe DiMaggio . . . .(206) 1936

Six Hits One Game

Myril Hoag 1934

Home Runs Into Visiting Bullpen, New Yankee Stadium

Ford, Minnesota 1976
Munson, New York 1976

Centerfield Bleacher Home Runs New Yankee Stadium

Singleton, Baltimore 1977
Jackson New York (World Series) 1977

HOME RUNS, ONE MONTH . . . Babe Ruth hit 17 homers in September, 1927. Mickey Mantle hit 16 in May, 1956. Ruth had 15 in a month three times. DiMaggio once, and Maris once.

GREAT GAMES . . . Myril Hoag had six singles in a game, June 6, 1934. Johnny Lindell (8/17/44) and Jim Mason (7/8&74) had four doubles in a game. Hal Chase (8/30/06), Earle Combs (9/22/27) and Joe DiMaggio (8/27/38) had three triples in a game. Lou Gehrig had 16 total bases on June 3, 1932. Tony Lazzeri drove in 11 runs on 5/24/36, ten Yankees have had eight RBIs in a game, most recently Elston Howard (8/19/62). Nine Yankees have had five walks in a game, most recently Maris 5/22/62. Eleven Yankees have scored five runs in a game, most recently Bobby Murcer (6/3/72).

JOE DIMAGGIO'S HITTING STREAK

Starting on Thursday, May 15, 1941 in Yankee Stadium and continuing until Thursday night, July 17 in Cleveland's Municipal Stadium, where he was finally stopped by pitchers Al Smith and Jim Bagby, DiMaggio piled up this amazing mark:

Consecutive games hit safely 56		Home Runs 15	
At bats 223		Triples 4	
Hits 91		Doubles 16	
Average for streak 408		Singles 56	
Total bases for streak 160		Strikeouts 7	
Runs scored 56		Bases on Balls 21	
RBIs 55		Hit by pitcher 2	

DID YOU KNOW . . . The 1927 Yankees, Murderer's Row, considered by many the greatest team in baseball history went through the entire 154 game schedule that year using only 25 men.

PINCH-HIT, GRAND SLAM HOMERS AND TRIPLE PLAYS ... The Yankees have hit 140 pitch-hit home runs since 1903, and last by Dave Kingman on September 19, 1977 (Chambliss and Johnson also hit pinch-hit RH's last year) ... they have hit 204 Grand Slam HR's, the most recent by Reggie Jackson on September 28, 1977 (Johnson and Dent also hit grand slam HR's last year). The Yankees have performed 21 triple plays in their history, the last on June 3, 1968 (Womack-Cox-Mantle) They haven't hit into a triple play since May 22, 1953 when Irv Noren did it in Washington.

BATTING STREAKS ... The longest Yankee consecutive game hitting streak in recent years was the 20 straight Mickey Rivers hit in safely in 1976 ... it was the longest since Joe Gordon hit in 29 straight in 1942.

TOP TEN YANKEES, SINGLE SEASON

At Bats			Runs Scored			Hits		
1. Richardson	692	1962	Ruth	177	1921	Combs	231	1927
2. Clarke	686	1970	Gehrig	167	1936	Gehrig	220	1930
3. Richardson	679	1964	Ruth	163	1928	Gehrig	218	1927
4. Richardson	664	1965	Gehrig	163	1931	DiMaggio	215	1937
5. Richardson	662	1961	Ruth	158	1920	Rolfe	213	1939
6. Crosetti	656	1939	Ruth	158	1927	Gehrig	211	1931
7. Combs	648	1927	Ruth	151	1953	Gehrig	210	1928
8. Rolfe	648	1927	DiMaggio	151	1937	Gehrig	210	1934
9. Dugan	644	1923	Ruth	150	1930	Richardson	209	1962
10. Stirnweiss	643	1944	Gehrig	149	1927	Gehrig	208	1932
			Ruth	149	1931			

Doubles			Triples			Home Runs		
1. Gehrig	52	1927	Combs	23	1927	Maris	61	1961
2. Gehrig	47	1926	Combs	22	1930	Ruth	60	1927
3. Gehrig	47	1928	Stirnweiss	22	1945	Ruth	59	1921
4. Meusel	47	1927	Cree	22	1911	Ruth	54	1928
5. Rolfe	46	1939	Combs	21	1928	Ruth	54	1920
6. Ruth	45	1923	Gehrig	20	1926	Mantle	54	1961
7. Meusel	45	1928	Pipp	19	1924	Ruth	49	1930
8. Ruth	44	1921	Gehrig	18	1927	Gehrig	49	1934
9. DiMaggio	44	1936	Gehrig	17	1930	Gehrig	49	1936
10. DiMaggio	43	1941	4 tied 16			Ruth	47	1926
						Gehrig	47	1927

Runs Batted In			Total Bases			Stolen Bases		
1. Gehrig	184	1931	Ruth	457	1921	Maisel	74	1914
2. Gehrig	175	1927	Gehrig	447	1927	Chapman	61	1931
3. Gehrig	174	1930	Gehrig	419	1931	Stirnweiss	55	1944
4. Ruth	170	1921	DiMaggio	418	1937	Maisel	51	1915
5. DiMaggio	167	1937	Ruth	417	1927	Cree	48	1911
6. Gehrig	165	1934	Gehrig	410	1931	Fultz	44	1905
7. Ruth	164	1927	Gehrig	409	1934	Rivers	43	1976
8. Gehrig	159	1937	Gehrig	403	1936	Hemphill	42	1908
9. Ruth	155	1926	Ruth	399	1923	Conroy	41	1907
10. DiMaggio	155	1948	Ruth	391	1924	Daniels	41	1910

Walks			Strikeouts (Batter)			Batting Average		
1. Ruth	170	1923	Bonds	137	1925	Ruth	.393	1923
2. Ruth	148	1920	R. Jackson	129	1977	DiMaggio	.381	1939
3. Mantle	146	1957	Mantle	126	1959	Gehrig	.379	1930
4. Ruth	144	1921	Mantle	125	1960	Ruth	.378	1921
5. Ruth	144	1926	Mantle	120	1958	Ruth	.378	1924
6. Ruth	142	1924	Mantle	111	1952	Ruth	.376	1920
7. Ruth	138	1927	Mantle	107	1954	Gehrig	.374	1928
8. Ruth	136	1930	Crosetti	105	1937	Gehrig	.373	1927
9. Ruth	135	1928	Keller	101	1946	Ruth	.373	1931
10. Gehrig	132	1935	Crosetti	97	1938	Ruth	.372	1925

Hitting Streaks

DiMaggio	56	1941	DiMaggio	23	1940
Peckinpaugh	29	1919	DiMaggio	22	1937
Combs	29	1931	DiMaggio	20	1937
Gordon	29	1942	Hassett	20	1942
Chase	27	1907	Rivers	20	1976
Ruth	26	1921			

ALL-TIME YANKEES -- TOP 20
HITTING CATEGORIES

Games		At Bats		Runs		Hits	
1. Mantle	2401	Mantle	8102	Ruth	1959	Gehrig	2721
2. Gehrig	2164	Gehrig	8001	Gehrig	1888	Ruth	2518
3. Berra	2116	Berra	7546	Mantle	1677	Mantle	2415
4. Ruth	2084	Ruth	7217	DiMaggio	1390	DiMaggio	2214
5. Dackey	1789	DiMaggio	6821	Combs	1186	Berra	2148
6. DiMaggio	1736	Dickey	6300	Berra	1174	Dickey	1969
7. WHITE	1697	Crosetti	6277	Crosetti	1006	Combs	1866
8. Crosetti	1682	WHITE	6099	Lazzeri	952	Lazzeri	1784
9. Rizzuto	1661	Lazzeri	6094	Rolfe	942	WHITE	1666
10. Lazzeri	1659	Rizzuto	5816	Dickey	930	Rizzuto	1588
11. Howard	1492	Combs	5748	Henrich	901	Pipp	1577
12. Pipp	1488	Pipp	5594	WHITE	896	Meusel	1565
13. Combs	1455	Richardson	5386	Rizzuto	877	Crosetti	1541
14. Richardson	1412	Howard	5044	Pipp	820	Richardson	1432
15. Bauer	1406	Meusel	5032	Bauer	792	Howard	1405
16. McDougald	1336	Rolfe	4827	Meusel	764	Rolfe	1394
17. Meusel	1294	Bauer	4784	Keller	714	Bauer	1326
18. Henrich	1284	Clarke	4723	McDougald	697	Henrich	1297
19. Clarke	1230	McDougald	4676	Peckinpaugh	670	McDougald	1291
20. Peckinpaugh	1220	Henrich	4603	Richardson	643	MUNSON	1265

Doubles		Triples		Home Runs		RBIs	
1. Gehrig	535	Gehrig	162	Ruth	659	Gehrig	1991
2. Ruth	424	Combs	154	Mantle	536	Ruth	1970
3. DiMaggio	389	DiMaggio	131	Gehrig	493	DiMaggio	1537
4. Mantle	344	Pipp	121	DiMaggio	361	Mantle	1509
5. Dickey	343	Lazzeri	115	Berra	358	Berra	1430
6. Meusel	338	Ruth	106	Maris	203	Dickey	1209
7. Lazzeri	327	Meusel	87	Dickey	202	Lazzeri	1154

ALL-TIME YANKEES — TOP 20
HITTING CATEGORIES

Doubles		Triples		Home Runs		RBIs	
8. Berra	321	Henrich	73	Keller	184	Meusel	1005
9. Combs	309	Mantle	72	Henrich	183	Pipp	825
10. WHITE	294	Dickey	72	Lazzeri	169	Henrich	795
11. Henrich	269	Keller	69	Pepitone	166	Howard	732
12. Crosetti	260	Rolfe	67	Skowron	165	Keller	723
13. Pipp	259	Stirnweiss	66	Howard	161	WHITE	730
14. Rolfe	257	Crosetti	65	Bauer	158	Skowron	672
15. Rizzuto	239	Chapman	64	Gordon	153	Bauer	654
16. Howard	211	Rizzuto	62	WHITE	157	Crosetti	649
17. Bauer	211	Cree	62	Meusel	146	Combs	629
18. Chapman	209	Conroy	59	Murcer	140	Gordon	617
19. Richardson	196	Bauer	56	Tresh	140	MUNSON	662
20. McDougald	187	Peckinpaugh	53	NETTLES	161	Chapman	589

BATTING AVERAGE
(800 or more games)

1. Ruth	.349	11. Skowron	.294
2. Gehrig	.340	12. Lazzeri	.293
3. DiMaggio	.325	13. MUNSON	.292
4. Combs	.325	14. Selkirk	.290
5. Dickey	.313	15. Rolfe	.289
6. Meusel	.311	16. Dugan	.286
7. Chapman	.305	17. Keller	.285
8. Mantle	.298	18. Koenig	.285
9. Schang	.297	19. Berra	.285
10. Keeler	.295	20. Chase	.284

CAPS — Active Yankee Player

YANKEE SINGLE SEASON LEADERS
BY POSITION

	HOME RUNS			RBIs			Avg.	
Pitchers	5	Ruffing 1936	22	Ruffing 1936, 1941		.339	Ruffing	1935
Catcher	30	Berra 1952, 1956	133	Dickey 1937		.362	Dickey	1936
First Base	49	Gehrig 1934	184	Gehrig 1931		.379	Gehrig	1930
Second Base	30	Gordon 1940	115	Lazzeri 1926		.354	Lazzeri	1929
Third Base	37	Nettles 1977	107	Nettles 1977		.329	Rolfe	1939
Shortstop	15	Tresh 1962	107	Lary 1931		.324	Rizzuto	1950
Outfield	61	Maris 1961	170	Ruth 1921		.393	Ruth	1923
	60	Ruth 1927						

SEASONAL LEADERS — OFFENSE

NEW YORK YANKEE LEADERS
1903-1977
*Led League

Year	Batting Average	Runs	Hits
1903	Keeler 313	Keeler 98	Keeler 164
1904	Keeler 343	Dougherty* 80	Keeler 185
1905	Keeler 302	Keeler 81	Keeler 169
1906	Chase 323	Keeler 96	Chase 193
1907	Chase 287	Hoffman 81	Chase 143
1908	Hemphill . . .297	Hemphill 62	Hemphill 150
1909	LaPorte 298	Demmitt 68	Engle 137
1910	Knight 312	Daniels 68	Cree 134
1911	Cree 348	Cree 90	Cree 181
1912	Paddock 288	Daniels 72	Chase 143
1913	Cree 272	Hartzell 60	Cree 145
1914	Cree 309	Maisel 78	Cook 133
1915	Maisel 281	Maisel 77	Maisel 149
1916	Pipp 262	Pipp 70	Pipp 143
1917	Baker 282	Pipp 82	Baker 156
1918	Baker 306	Baker, Pratt 65	Baker 154
1919	Peckinpaugh .305	Peckinpaugh 89	Baker 166
1920	Ruth 376	Ruth* 158	Pratt 180
1921	Ruth 378	Ruth* 177	Ruth 204
1922	Pipp 329	Witt 98	Pipp 190
1923	Ruth 393	Ruth* 151	Ruth 205
1924	Ruth* 378	Ruth* 143	Ruth 200
1925	Combs 343	Combs 117	Combs 203
1926	Ruth 372	Ruth* 139	Ruth 184
1927	Gehrig 373	Ruth* 158	Combs* 231
1928	Gehrig 374	Ruth* 163	Gehrig 210
1929	Lazzeri 354	Gehrig 127	Combs 202
1930	Gehrig 379	Ruth 150	Gehrig 220
1931	Ruth 373	Gehrig* 163	Gehrig* 211
1932	Gehrig 349	Combs 143	Gehrig 208
1933	Gehrig 334	Gehrig* 138	Gehrig 198
1934	Gehrig 363	Gehrig 128	Gehrig 210
1935	Gehrig 329	Gehrig 125	Rolfe 192
1936	Dickey 362	Gehrig* 167	DiMaggio 206
1937	Gehrig 351	DiMaggio* 151	DiMaggio 215
1938	DiMaggio . .324	Rolfe 132	DiMaggio 194
1939	DiMaggio* . .381	Rolfe* 139	Rolfe* 213
1940	DiMaggio* . .352	Gordon 112	DiMaggio 179
1941	DiMaggio . . .357	DiMaggio 122	DiMaggio 193
1942	Gordon 322	DiMaggio 123	DiMaggio 186
1943	Johnson 280	Keller 97	Johnson* 166
1944	Stirnweiss . . .319	Stirnweiss* 125	Stirnweiss* 205
1945	Stirnweiss* . .309	Stirnweiss* 107	Stirnweiss* 195
1946	DiMaggio . . .290	Keller 98	Keller 148
1947	DiMaggio . .315	Henrich 109	DiMaggio 168
1948	DiMaggio . .320	Henrich* 138	DiMaggio 190
1949	Henrich 287	Rizzuto 110	Rizzuto 169
1950	Rizzuto 324	Rizzuto 125	Rizzuto 200
1951	McDougald . .306	Berra 92	Berra 161

313

Year	Batting Average	Runs	Hits
1952	Mantle 311	Berra 97	Mantle 171
1953	Bauer 304	Mantle 105	McDougald 154
1954	Noren 319	Mantle* 129	Berra 179
1955	Mantle 306	Mantle 121	Mantle 158
1956	Mantle* . . .353	Mantle* 132	Mantle 188
1957	Mantle 365	Mantle* 121	Mantle 173
1958	Mantle 304	Mantle* 127	Mantle 158
1959	Richardson .301	Mantle 104	Mantle 154
1960	Skowron . . .309	Mantle* 119	Skowron 166
1961	Howard . . .348	Mantle, Maris* . .132	Richardson 173
1962	Mantle 321	Richardson 99	Richardson* 209
1963	Howard . . .287	Tresh 91	Richardson 167
1964	Howard . . .318	Mantle 92	Richardson 181
1965	Tresh 279	Tresh 94	Tresh 168
1966	Mantle 288	Pepitone 85	Richardson 153
1967	Clarke 272	Clarke 74	Clarke 160
1968	White 267	White 89	White 154
1969	White 290	Clarke, Murcer . .82	Clarke 183
1970	Munson . . .302	White 109	White 180
1971	Murcer 331	Murcer 94	Murcer 175
1972	Murcer 292	Murcer* 102	Murcer 171
1973	Murcer 304	White 88	Murcer 187
1974	Piniella 305	Maddox 75	Murcer 166
1975	Munson . . .318	Bonds 93	Munson 190
1976	Rivers 312	White* 104	Chambliss 188
1977	Rivers 326	Nettles 99	Rivers 184

SEASONAL   LEADERS — OFFENSE

	Doubles	Triples	Home Runs
1903	Williams 30	Williams, Conroy . .12	McFarland 5
1904	Williams 31	Anderson, Conroy .12	Ganzel 6
1905	Williams 20	Williams 8	Williams, Keller 4
1906	Williams 25	Chase, Conroy 10	Conroy 4
1907	Chase 23	Conroy, LaPorte Williams 11	Hoffman 4
1908	Conroy 22	Hemphill 9	Niles 4
1909	Engle 20	Demmitt 12	Chase, Demmitt . . .4
1910	Knight 25	Cree 16	Wolter, Cree 4
1911	Chase 32	Cree 22	Wolter,Cree 2
1912	Daniels 25	Hartzell, Daniels . .11	Zinn 6
1913	Cree 25	Peckinpaugh 7	Wolter, Sweeney . . .2
1914	Maisel 23	Maisel, Hartzell 9	Peckinpaugh 3
1915	Peckinpaugh . .18	High, Peckinpaugh . .7	Peckinpaugh 5
1916	Baker 23	Pipp 14	Pipp* 12
1917	Pipp 29	Pipp 12	Pipp* 9
1918	Baker 23	Pipp 2	Baker 8
1919	Pratt, Bodie . . .27	Pipp 10	Baker 10
1920	Ward 40	Peckinpaugh 14	Ruth* 54
1921	Ruth 44	Ruth 16	Ruth* 59
1922	Pipp 32	Meusel 11	Ruth 35
1923	Ruth 45	Ruth 13	Ruth* 41
1924	Meusel 40	Pipp* 19	Ruth 46
1925	Combs 36	Combs 13	Meusel* 33

Year	Doubles	Triples	Home Runs
1926	Gehrig 47	Gehrig* 20	Ruth* 47
1927	Gehrig* 52	Combs* 23	Ruth* 60
1928	Gehrig* 47	Combs 21	Ruth* 54
1929	Lazzeri 37	Combs 15	Ruth* 46
1930	Gehrig 42	Gehrig 17	Ruth* 49
1931	Lary 35	Combs* 22	Ruth 41
1932	Gehrig 42	Chapman 15	Ruth*, Gehrig* ...46
1933	Gehrig 41	Combs 15	Ruth 34
1934	Gehrig 40	Chapman* 13	Gehrig* 49
1935	Chapman 46	Selkirk 12	Gehrig 30
1936	DiMaggio 44	DiMaggio* 15	Gehrig* 49
1937	Gehrig 37	DiMaggio 15	DiMaggio* 45
1938	Rolfe* 36	DiMaggio 13	DiMaggio 32
1939	Rolfe* 46	Rolfe 10	DiMaggio 30
1940	Gordon 32	Keller 15	DiMaggio 31
1941	DiMaggio 43	DiMaggio 11	Keller 33
1942	Henrich 30	DiMaggio 13	Keller 26
1943	Etten 35	Lindell* 12	Keller 31
1944	Stirnweiss 35	Stirnweiss* 22	Etten* 22
1945	Stirnweiss 32	Stirnweiss* Lindell*.16	Etten 18
1946	Keller 29	Keller 10	Keller 30
1947	Henrich 35	Henrich* 13	DiMaggio 20
1948	Henrich 42	Henrich* 14	DiMaggio* 39
1949	Rizzuto 22	Rizzuto, Woodling ..7	Henrich 24
1950	Rizzuto 36	Woodling, DiMaggio .10	DiMaggio 32
1951	McDougald ...23	Woodling ....8.	Berra 27
1952	Mantle 37	Rizzuto 10	Berra 30
1953	McDougald ...27	McDougald 7	Berra 27
1954	Berra 28	Mantle 12	Mantle 27
1955	Mantle 25	Mantle* 11	Mantle* 37
1956	Berra 26	Bauer 7	Mantle* 52
1957	Mantle 28	Bauer* Simpson* McDougald* 9	Mantle 34
1958	Bauer, Skowron .22	Bauer 6	Mantle* 42
1959	Lopez 27	McDougald 8	Mantle 31
1960	Skowron 34	Maris 7	Mantle* 40
1961	Kubek 38	Mantle, Kubek 6	Maris* 61
1962	Richardson ...38	Skowron 6	Maris 33
1963	Tresh 28	Howard, Richardson. .6	Howard 28
1964	Howard 27	Tresh, Boyer 5	Mantle 35
1965	Tresh 29	Tresh, Boyer 6	Tresh 26
1966	Boyer 22	Boyer, Clarke, Tresh, Pepitone 4	Pepitone 31
1967	Tresh 23	Pepitone, Smith, Tresh, Whitaker 3	Mantle 22
1968	White 20	White, Robinson 7	Mantle 18
1969	White 30	Clarke 7	Pepitone 27
1970	White 31	Kenney 7	Murcer 23
1971	Murcer 25	Clarke, White 7	Murcer 25
1972	Murcer 30	Murcer 7	Murcer 33
1973	Murcer, Munson .29	Munson 4	Murcer, Nettles ...22
1974	Maddox, Piniella.26	White 8	Nettles 22
1975	Chambliss 38	White 5	Bonds 32
1976	Chambliss 32	Rivers 8	Nettles 32
1977	Jackson 39	Randolph 11	Nettles 37

315

SEASON LEADERS OFFENSE

	RBI's		Stolen Bases	
1903	Williams	82	Conroy	33
1904	Anderson	82	Conroy	30
1905	Williams	60	Fultz	44
1906	Williams	77	Hoffman	33
1907	Chase	68	Conroy	41
1908	Hemphill	44	Hemphill	42
1909	Engle	71	Austin	30
1910	Chase	73	Daniels	41
1911	Hartzell	91	Cree	48
1912	Chase	58	Daniels	37
1913	Cree	63	Daniels	27
1914	Peckinpaugh	51	Maisel	74
1915	Pipp	58	Maisel	51
1916	Pipp*	99	Magee	29
1917	Pipp	72	Maisel	29
1918	Baker	68	Bodie	16
1919	Baker	78	Pratt	22
1920	Ruth*	137	Ruth	14
1921	Ruth*	170	Meusel, Pipp, Ruth	17
1922	Ruth	96	Meusel	13
1923	Ruth*	130	Ruth	17
1924	Ruth*	121	Meusel	26
1925	Meusel*	138	Paschal	14
1926	Ruth*	155	Meusel	16
1927	Gehrig*	175	Meusel	24
1928	Gehrig*, Ruth*	142	Lazzeri	15
1929	Ruth	154	Combs, Lazzeri	11
1930	Gehrig*	174	Combs	16
1931	Gehrig*	184	Chapman*	61
1932	Gehrig	151	Chapman*	38
1933	Gehrig	139	Chapman*	27
1934	Gehrig*	165	Chapman	26
1935	Gehrig	119	Chapman	17
1936	Gehrig	152	Crosetti	18
1937	DiMaggio	167	Crosetti	13
1938	DiMaggio	140	Crosetti	27
1939	DiMaggio	126	Selkirk	12
1940	DiMaggio	133	Gordon	18
1941	DiMaggio*	125	Rizzuto	14
1942	DiMaggio	114	Rizzuto	22
1943	Etten	107	Rizzuto	14
1944	Lindell	103	Stirnweiss*	55
1945	Etten*	111	Stirnweiss*	33
1946	Keller	101	Stirnweiss	18
1947	Henrich	98	Rizzuto	11
1948	DiMaggio*	155	Rizzuto	6
1949	Berra	91	Rizzuto	18
1950	Berra	124	Rizzuto	12
1951	Berra	88	Rizzuto	18
1952	Berra	98	Rizzuto	17
1953	Berra	108	Mantle	8
1954	Berra	125	Mantle, Carey	5

RBIs		Stolen Bases	
1955	Berra 108	Hunter 9	
1956	Mantle* 130	Mantle................10	
1957	Mantle 94	Mantle................16	
1958	Mantle 97	Mantle................18	
1959	Lopez 93	Mantle................21	
1960	Maris* 112	Mantle................14	
1961	Maris* 142	Mantle................12	
1962	Maris 100	Richardson 11	
1963	Pepitone 89	Richardson 15	
1964	Mantle 111	Tresh 13	
1965	Tresh 74	Richardson 7	
1966	Pepitone 83	White 14	
1967	Pepitone 64	Clarke 21	
1968	White 62	Clarke, White 20	
1969	Murcer 82	Clarke 33	
1970	White 94	White 24	
1971	Murcer 94	Clarke 17	
1972	Murcer 96	White 23	
1973	Murcer 95	White 16	
1974	Murcer 88	White 15	
1975	Munson 102	Bonds 30	
1976	Munson 105	Rivers 43	
1977	Jackson 110	Rivers 22	

STOLEN BASES
NEVER REALLY A RUNNING TEAM

DID YOU KNOW ... The top 1-2 punch the Yankees ever had in stolen bases was in 1914, when Fritz Maisel set the club record of 74 steals, and Roger Peckinpaugh added 38 for 112. The Yanks stole 252 bases that year.

ALL-TIME YANKEE TOP 20 IN STOLEN BASES

1. Chase	248	11. Peckinpaugh	143
2. WHITE	231	12. Cree	132
3. Chapman	184	13. Meusel	131
4. Conroy	184	14. Stirnweiss	130
5. Maisel	183	15. RIVERS	121
6. Mantle	153	16. Ruth	117
7. Clarke	151	17. Pipp	114
8. Rizzuto	149	18. Crosetti	113
9. Lazzeri	147	19. Gehrig	102
10. Daniels	145	20. Hartzell	98
		21. Combs	96

FIELDING   RECORDS

YANKEES WHO LED LEAGUE IN FIELDING

1B —Ganzel (1903), Pipp (1915, 1924), Skowron (1958), Pepitone (1965-66, 1969)
2B — Ward (1923), Stirnweiss (1944, 1948), Coleman (1949), McDougald (1955), Clarke (1967), Alomar (1975).
SS — Scott (1922-23), Crosetti (1939), Rizzuto (1949-50)
3B — Dugan (1923), Rolfe (1935-36)
OF — Cree (1913), Witt (1923), Byrd (1934), Selkirk (1939), DiMaggio (1947), Woodling (1952-53), Mantle (1959), Tresh (1964), White (1971).
C — Sweeney (1912), Dickey (1931, 1935, 1937, 1939, 1941), Berra (1957, 1959), Howard (1962-64), Munson (1971)
P — Howell (1903), Griffith (1906), Pennock (1924), Chandler (1938), Terry (1961), Ford (1965), Stottlemyre (1968)

YANKEE GOLD GLOVE WINNERS

1957	Bobby Shantz, p		1964	Elston Howard, c
1958	Bobby Shantz, p			Bobby Richardson, 2b
	Norm Siebern, of		1965	Joe Pepitone, 1b
1959	Bobby Shantz, p			Bobby Richardson, 2b
1960	Bobby Shantz, p			Tom Tresh, of
	Roger Maris, of		1966	Joe Pepitone, 1b
1961	Bobby Richardson, 2b		1969	Joe Pepitone, 1b
1962	Bobby Richardson, 2b		1972	Bobby Murcer, of
	Mickey Mantle, of		1973	Thurman Munson, c
1963	Elston Howard, c		1974	Thurman Munson, c
	Bobby Richardson, 2b		1975	Thurman Munson, c
			1977	Graig Nettles, 3b

YANKEES' HIGHEST FIELDING PERCENTAGE
(by position)

1b —	Joe Pepitone	.997	(1965)
2b —	Geo. Stirnweiss	.993	(1948)
3b —	Joe Dugan	.974	(1923)
	Joe Sewell	.974	(1932)
	Graig Nettles	.974	(1977)
ss —	Phil Rizzuto	.982	(1950)
of —	Roy White	1.000	(1971)
c —	Elston Howard	.998	(1964)
	Thurman Munson	.998	(1971)
p —	Harry Howell	1.000	(1903)

(110 chances)

YANKEE KILLERS

TOP CAREER WINNING PERCENTAGE
VS YANKEES
(Based on 10 Victories)

	W-L	PCT		W-L	PCT
Kerr	14-4	.778	Hall	12-7	.632
Ruth	17-5	.773	Rowe	20-12	.625
LEE	12-5	.706	HILLER	10-6	.625
Boland	16-7	.696	McLain	15-9	.625
Lary	28-13	.683	Cuellar	18-11	.621
Marberry	21-11	.667	TIANT	22-14	.611
BLUE	14-7	.667	Kinder	14-9	.609
Boswell	10-5	.667	Barber	17-11	.607
PALMER	22-11	.667	Chance	15-10	.600
SPLITTORFF	12-7	.632	McDowell	14-10	.583

CAPS denotes active pitcher

Luis Tiant is the only pitcher to defeat the Yankees five times in one season since expansion in 1961. In fact, when he was 5-1 against the Yankees in 1974, he was the first to do it since 1959, when Frank Lary, Don Mossi and Cal McLish all accomplished it.

THIRTY CAREER WINS VS. YANKEES

Johnson	60
Grove	35
Cicotte	35
Wynn	33
Newhouser	33
Faber	32
S. Coveleski	32
Feller	30
Bender	30
Mullin	30
Dauss	30

NO-HIT GAMES PITCHED AGAINST YANKEES

1908 — Cy Young, Boston at New York, June 30 8-0
1916 — George Foster, Boston vs. New York at Boston, June 21 2-0
1919 — Raymond B. Caldwell, Cleveland at New York,
September 10 (1st game) 3-0
1946 — Robert W. A. Feller, Cleveland at New York, April 30 1-0
1952 — Virgil O. Trucks, Detroit at New York, August 25 1-0
1958 — James Hoyt Wilheim, Baltimore vs. New York at Baltimore
September 20 1-0

319

YANKEE ALL-STAR GAME SELECTIONS

1933 — Chapman, of; Dickey, c; Gehrig, 1b; Gomez, p; Lazzeri, 2b;
Ruth, of.

1934 — Chapman, of; Dickey, c; Gehrig, 1b; Gomez, p; Ruffing, p;
Ruth, of.

1935 — Chapman, of; Gehrig, 1b; Gomez, p.

1936 — Crosetti, ss; Dickey, c; DiMaggio, of; Gehrig, 1b; Gomez, p; Pearson,
p; Selkirk, of.

1937 — Dickey, c; DiMaggio, of; Gehrig, 1b; Gomez, p; Murphy, p;
Rolfe, 3b.

1938 — Dickey, c; DiMaggio, of; Gehrig, 1b; Gomez, p; Rolfe, 3b;
Ruffing, p.

1939 — Crosetti, ss; Dickey, c; DiMaggio, of; Gomez, p; Gordon, 2b; Murphy,
p; Rolfe, 3b; Ruffing, p; Selkirk, of.

1940 — Dickey, c; DiMaggio, of; Gordon, 2b; Keller, of; Pearson, p;
Rolfe, 3b; Ruffing, p.

1941 — Dickey, c; DiMaggio, of; Gordon, 2b; Keller, of; Ruffing, p;
Russo, p.

1942 — Bonham, p; Chandler, p; Dickey, c; DiMaggio, of; Gordon, 2b;
Henrich, of; Rizzuto, ss; Rosar, c; Ruffing, p.

1943 — Bonham, p; Chandler, p; Dickey, c; Gordon, 2b; Keller, of; Lindell,
of.

1944 — Borowy, p; Hemsley, c; Page, p.

1945 — NO GAME.

1946 — Chandler, p; Dickey, c; DiMaggio, of; Gordon, 2b; Keller, of;
Stirnweiss, 3b.

1947 — Chandler, p; DiMaggio, of; Henrich, of; Johnson, 3b; McQuinn, 1b;
Page, p; Robinson, c; Shea, p; Keller, of.

1948 — Berra, c; DiMaggio, of; Henrich, of; McQuinn, 1b; Page, p;
Raschi, p.

1949 — Berra, c; DiMaggio, of; Henrich, of; Raschi, p; Reynolds, p.

1950 — Berra, c; Byrne, p; Coleman, 2b; DiMaggio, of; Henrich, 1b; Raschi,
p; Reynolds, p; Rizzuto, ss.

1951 — Berra, c; DiMaggio, of; Lopat, p; Rizzuto, ss.

1952 — Bauer, of; Berra, c; Mantle, of; Raschi, p; Reynolds, p; Rizzuto,
ss; McDougald, 2b.

1953 — Bauer, of; Berra, c; Mantle, of; Mize, 1b; Reynolds, p; Rizzuto,
ss; Sain, p.

1954 — Bauer, of; Berra, c; Ford, p; Mantle, of; Noren, of; Reynolds, p.

1955 — Berra, c; Ford, p; Mantle, of; Turley, p.

1956 — Berra, c; Ford, p; Kucks, p; Mantle, of; Martin, 2b; McDougald, ss.

1957 — Berra, c; Grim, p; Howard, c; Mantle, of; McDougald, ss; Richardson,
2b; Shantz, p; Skowron, 1b.

1958 — Berra, c; Duren, p; Ford, p; Howard, c; Kubek, inf; Mantle, of;
McDougald, 2b; Skowron, 1b; Turley, p.

1959 — Berra, c; Duren, p; Ford, p; Mantle, of; McDougald, ss; Richardson,
2b; Skowron, 1b; Howard, c; Kubek, ss.

1960 — Berra, c; Coates, p; Ford, p; Howard, c; Mantle, of; Maris, of;
Skowron, 1b.

1961 — Arroyo, p; Berra, of; Ford, p; Howard, c; Kubek, ss; Mantle, of;
Maris, of; Skowron, 1b.

1962 — Berra, c; Howard, c; Mantle, of; Maris, of; Richardson, 2b; Terry, p;
Tresh, ss.

1963 — Bouton, p; Howard, c; Mantle, of; Pepitone, 1b; Richardson, 2b; Tresh, of.

1964 — Ford, p; Howard, c; Mantle, of; Pepitone, 1b; Richardson, 2b.
1965 — Stottlemyre, p; Richardson, 2b; Pepitone, 1b; Howard, c; Mantle, of.
1966 — Stottlemyre, p; Richardson, 2b.
1967 — Downing, p; Mantle, 1b.
1968 — Stottlemyre, p; Mantle, 1b.
1969 — Stottlemyre, p; White, of.
1970 — Stottlemyre, p; Peterson, p; White, of.
1971 — Murcer, of; Munson, c.
1972 — Murcer, of.
1973 — Murcer, of; Munson, c; Lyle, p.
1974 — Murcer, of; Munson, c.
1975 — Bonds, of; Munson, c; Nettles, 3b; Hunter, p.
1976 — Rivers, of; Munson, c; Nettles, 3b; Hunter, p; Lyle, p; Chambliss, 1b; Randolph, 2b.
1977 — Munson, c; Nettles, 3b; Randolph, 2b; Jackson, of; Lyle, p.
1978 — Gossage, p.; Guidry, p.; Nettles, 3b.

ALL-STAR GAMES

IN YANKEE STADIUM

July 11, 1939
NL
NL 001 000   000 — 1 7 1
AL 000 210   00x — 3 6 1
Derringer, Lee (4), Fette (7) & Lombardi
Ruffing, Bridges (4), Feller (6) & Dickey.

WP-Bridges; LP-Lee
HR-DiMaggio, Att.-62,892

July 13, 1960 (2nd game)
NL 021 000   102 — 6 10 0
AL 000 000   000 — 0 8 0
Law, Podres (3), Williams (5), Jackson (7), Henry (8), McDaniel (9) & Crandall, Bailey, Burgess
Ford, Wynn (4), Staley (6), Lary (8), Bell (9) & Berra, Lollar.

WP-Law; LP-Ford
HR-Mathews, Mays, Musial, Boyer
Att-38,362

July 19, 1977
NL 401 000   020 — 7 9 1
AL 000 002   102 — 5 8 0
Sutton, LaVelle (4), Seaver (6), R. Reuschel (8), Gossage (9) & Bench, Simmons, Stearns
Palmer, Kern (3), Eckersley (4), LaRoche (6), Campbell (7), Lyle (8) & Fisk, Wynegar.
WP-Sutton; LP-Palmer
HR-Morgan, Luzinski, Garver, Scott.
Att.-56,683

YANKEES ON SPORTING NEWS ALL-STAR TEAMS
Selected at Conclusion of Season

1926 — Ruth, Pennock
1927 — Ruth, Gehrig
1928 — Ruth, Gehrig, Hoyt
1929 — Ruth
1930 — Ruth
1931 — Gehrig, Ruth
1932 — Lazzeri, Dickey
1933 — Dickey
1934 — Gehrig, Gomez
1936 — Gehrig, Dickey
1937 — Gehrig, DiMaggio, Rolfe, Ruffing
1938 — Rolfe, DiMaggio, Dickey, Ruffing, Gomez
1939 — Gordon, DiMaggio, Rolfe, Dickey, Ruffing
1940 — Gordon, DiMaggio
1941 — Gordon, DiMaggio, Dickey
1942 — Gordon, DiMaggio, Bonham
1943 — Johnson, Chandler
1945 — Stirnweiss
1946 — A. Robinson
1947 — DiMaggio
1948 — DiMaggio
1949 — Rizzuto, Henrich, Page
1951 — Rizzuto, Berra, Raschi

1952 — Rizzuto, Reynolds
Rizzuto, Mantle, Berra,
1954 — Reynolds
1955 — Berra
1956 — Ford
1957 — Mantle, Berra, Ford
1958 — Mantle, McDougald, Berra
1960 — Turley
1961 — Skowron, Maris
Richardson, Kubek, Mantle,
1962 — Maris, Howard, Ford
Richardson, Tresh, Mantle,
1963 — Terry
Richardson, Pepitone, Howard,
1964 — Ford
1965 — Richardson, Mantle, Howard
1966 — Richardson, Stottlemyre
1971 — Richardson
1972 — Murcer
1973 — Murcer
1974 — Munson, Murcer
1975 — Munson
1976 — Munson, Nettles
1977 — Munson, Chambliss, Rivers
1978 — Nettles, Randolph

ROGER MARIS' 61 HOME RUNS — 1961

HR No.	N.Y. Game	Date	Opposing Pitcher and Club
1	11	April 26	Foytack (R), Detroit
2	17	May 3	Ramos (R), Minnesota
3	20	May 6	Grba (R), Los Angeles
4	29	May 17	Burnside (L), Washington
5	30	May 19	Perry (R), Cleveland
6	31	May 20	Bell (R), Cleveland
7	32 H	May 21	Estrada (R), Baltimore
8	35 H	May 24	Conley (R), Boston
9	38 H	May 28	McLish (R), Chicago
10	40	May 30	Conley (R), Boston
11	40	May 30	Fornieles (R), Boston
12	41	May 31	Muffett (R), Boston
13	43	June 2	McLish (R), Chicago
14	44	June 3	Shaw (R), Chicago
15	45	June 4	Kemmerer (R), Chicago
16	48 H	June 6	Palmquist (R), Minnesota

ROGER MARIS' 61 HOME RUNS — 1961 (Continued)

HR No.	N.Y. Game	Date	Opposing Pitcher and Club
17	49 H	June 7	Ramos (R), Minnesota
18	52 H	June 9	Herbert (R), Kansas City
19	55 H	June 11	Grba (R), Los Angeles
20	55 H	June 11	James (R), Los Angeles
21	57	June 13	Perry (R), Cleveland
22	58	June 14	Bell (R), Cleveland
23	61	June 17	Mossi (L), Detroit
24	62	June 18	Casale (R), Detroit
25	63	June 19	Archer (L), Kansas City
26	64	June 20	Nuxhall (L), Kansas City
27	66	June 22	Bass (R), Kansas Caty
28	74 H	July 1	Sisler (R), Washington
29	75 H	July 2	Burnside (L), Washington
30	75 H	July 2	Klippstein (R), Washington
31	77 H	July 4	Lary (R), Detroit
32	78 H	July 5	Fund (R), Cleveland
33	82	July 9	Monbouquette (R), Boston
34	84	July 13	Wynn (R), Chicago
35	86	July 15	Herbert (R), Chicago
36	92	July 21	Monbouquette (R), Boston
37	95 H	July 25	Baumann (L), Chicago
38	95 H	July 25	Larsen (R), Chicago
39	96 H	July 25	Kemmerer (R), Chicago
40	97 H	July 25	Hacker (R), Chicago
41	106 H	August 4	Pascual (R), Minnesota
42	114	August 11	Burnside (L), Washington
43	115	August 12	Donovan (R), Washington
44	116	August 13	Daniels (R), Washington
45	117	August3	Kutyna (R), Washington
46	118 H	August 15	Pizarro (L), Chicago
47	119 H	August 16	Pierce (L), Chicago
48	119 H	August 16	Pierce (L), Chicago
49	124 H	August 20	Perry (R), Cleveland
50	125	August 22	McBride (R), Los Angeles
51	129	August 26	Walker (R), Kansas City
52	135 H	September 2	Lary (R), Detroit
53	135 H	September 2	Aguirre (R), Detroit
54	140 H	September 6	Cheney (R), Washington
55	141 H	September 7	Stigman (L), Cleveland
56	143 H	September 9	Grant (R), Cleveland
57	151	September 16	Lary (R), Detroit
58	152	September 17	Fox (R), Detroit
59	155	September 20	Pappas (R), Baltimore
60	159 H	September 26	Fisher (R), Baltimore
61	163 H	October 1	Stallard (R), Boston

Note: Yankees played tie game, April 22, second game, thus No. 59 was hit in 154th completed game.

BABE RUTH'S 60 HOME RUNS — 1927
HR   N.Y.

No.	Game	Date	Opp. Pitcher and Club
1	4 H	April 15	Ehmke (R), Philadelphia
2	11	April 23	Walberg (L), Philadelphia
3	12	April 24	Thurston (R), Washington
4	14	April 29	Harris (R), Boston
5	16 H	May 1	Quinn (R), Philadelphia
6	16 H	May 1	Walberg (L), Philadelphia
7	24	May 10	Gaston (R), St. Louis
8	25	May 11	Nevers (R), St. Louis
9	29	May 17	Collins (R), Detroit
10	33	May 22	Karr (R), Cleveland
11	34	May 23	Thurston (R), Washington
12	37 H	May 28	Thurston (R), Washington
13	39 H	May 29	MacFayden (R), Boston
14	41	May 30	Walberg (L), Philadelphia
15	42	May 31	Quinn (R), Philadelphia
16	43	May 31	Ehmke (R), Philadelphia
17	47 H	June 5	Whitehill (L), Detroit
18	48 H	June 7	Thomas (R), Chicago
19	52 H	June 11	Buckeye (L), Cleveland
20	52 H	June 11	Buckeye (L), Cleveland
21	53 H	June 12	Uhle (R), Cleveland
22	55 H	June 16	Zachary (L), St. Louis
23	60	June 22	Wiltse (L), Boston
24	60	June 22	Wiltse (L), Boston
25	70 H	June 30	Harris (R), Boston
26	73	July 3	Lisenbee (R), Washington
27	78	July 8	Hankins (R), Detroit
28	79	July 9	Holloway (R), Detroit
29	79	July 9	Holloway (R), Detroit
30	83	July 12	Shaute (L), Cleveland
31	94	July 24	Thomas (R), Chicago
32	95 H	July 26	Gaston (R), St. Louis
33	95 H	July 26	Gaston (R), St. Louis
34	98 H	July 28	Stewart (L), St. Louis
35	106 H	August 5	Smith (R), Detroit
36	110	August 10	Zachary (L), Washington
37	114	August 16	Thomas (R), Chicago
38	115	August 17	Connally (R), Chicago
39	118	August 20	Miller (L), Cleveland
40	120	August 22	Shaute (L), Cleveland
41	124	August 27	Nevers (R), St. Louis
42	125	August 28	Wingard (L), St. Louis
43	127 H	August 31	Welzer (R), Boston
44	128	September 2	Walberg (L), Philadelphia
45	132	September 6	Welzer (R), Boston
46	132	September 6	Welzer (R), Boston

BABE RUTH'S 60 HOME RUNS — 1927 (Continued)

HR   N.Y.

No.	Game	Date	Opp. Pitcher and Club
47	133	September 6	Russell (R), Boston
48	134	September 7	MacFayden (R), Boston
49	134	September 7	Harriss (R), Boston
50	138 H	September 11	Gaston (R), St. Louis
51	139 H	September 13	Hudlin (R), Cleveland
52	140 H	September 13	Shaute (L), Cleveland
53	143 H	September 16	Blankenship (R), Chicago
54	147 H	September 18	Lyons (R), Chicago
4	148 H	September 21	Gibson (R), Detroit
56	149 H	September 22	Holloway (R), Detroit
57	152 H	September 27	Grove (L), Philadelphia
58	153 H	September 29	Lisenbee (R), Washington
59	153 H	September 29	Hopkins (R), Washington
60	154 H	September 30	Zachary (L), Washington

Note: New York AL played 155 games in 1927 (one tie on April 14), with Ruth participating in 151 games.

JOE DiMAGGIO'S 56—CONSECUTIVE —GAME HITTING STREAK—1941

Date	Opp. Pitcher and Club	AB	R	H	2B	3B	HR	RBI
May 15 —	Smith, Chicago	4	0	1	0	0	0	1
16 —	Lee, Chicago	4	2	2	0	1	1	1
17	Rigney, Chicago	3	1	1	0	0	0	0
17 —	Harris (2) Niggeling (1), St. Louis	3	3	3	1	0	0	1
19 —	Galehouse, St. Louis	3	0	1	1	0	0	0
20 —	Auker, St. Louis	5	1	1	0	0	0	1
21	Rowe (1), Benton (1), Detroit	5	0	2	0	0	0	1
22 —	McKain, Detroit	4	0	1	0	0	0	1
23	Newsome, Boston	5	0	1	0	0	0	2
24 —	Johnson, Boston	4	2	1	0	0	0	2
25 —	Grove, Boston	4	0	1	0	0	0	0
27 —	Chase (1), Anderson (2), Carrasquel (1), Washington	5	3	4	0	0	1	3
28 —	Hudson, Washington (Night)	4	1	1	0	1	0	0
29 —	Sundra, Washington	3	1	1	0	0	0	0
30 —	Johnson, Boston	2	1	1	0	0	0	0
30 —	Harris, Boston	3	0	1	1	0	0	0
June 1 —	Milnar, Cleveland	4	1	1	0	0	0	0
1 —	Harder, Cleveland	4	0	1	0	0	0	0
2 —	Feller, Cleveland	4	2	2	1	0	0	0
3 —	Trout, Detroit	4	1	1	0	0	1	1
5 —	Newhouser, Detroit	5	1	1	0	1	0	1
7 —	Muncrief (1), Allen (1), Caster (1), St. Louis	5	2	3	0	0	0	1
8 —	Auker, St. Louis	4	3	2	0	0	2	4
8 —	Caster (1), Kramer (1), St. Louis	4	1	2	1	0	1	3

Di MAGGIO'S 56-CONSECUTIVE GAME HITTING STREAK —1941

Date	Opp. Pitcher and Club	AB	R	H	2B	3B	HR	RBI
10 —	Rigney, Chicago	5	1	1	0	0	0	0
12 —	Lee, Chicago (Night)	4	1	2	0	0	1	1
14 —	Feller, Cleveland	2	0	1	1	0	0	1
15 —	Bagby, Cleveland	3	1	1	0	0	1	1
16 —	Milnar, Cleveland	5	0	1	1	0	0	0
17 —	Rigney, Chicago	4	1	1	0	0	0	0
18 —	Lee, Chicago	3	0	1	0	0	0	0
19 —	Smith (1), Ross (2), Chicago	3	2	3	0	0	1	2
20 —	Newsom (2), McKain (2), Detroit	5	3	4	1	0	0	1
21 —	Trout, Detroit.	4	0	1	0	0	0	1
22 —	Newhouser (1), Newsom (1),Detroit	5	1	2	1	0	1	2
24 —	Muncrief, St. Louis	4	1	1	0	0	0	0
25 —	Galehouse, St. Louis	4	1	1	0	0	1	3
26 —	Auker, St. Louis	2	0	1	0	0	0	0
27 —	Dean, Philadelphia	5	1	4	0	0	1	2
28 —	Babich (1), Harris (1), Philadelphia	5	1	2	1	0	0	1
29 —	Leonard, Washington	4	2	3	0	0	0	0
29 —	Anderson, Washington	4	0	1	0	0	0	0
July 1 —	Harris (1), Ryba (1), Boston	4	0	1	1	0	0	1
1 —	Wilson, Boston	3	1	2	0	0	1	2
2 —	Newsome, Boston	5	1	2	1	0	0	0
5 —	Marchildon, Philadelphia	4	1	1	1	0	0	0
6 —	Babich (1), Hadley (3), Philadelphia	5	1	1	0	0	0	1
6 —	Knott, Philadelphia	4	0	2	0	0	0	1
10 —	Niggeling, St. Louis (Night)	3	1	1	0	0	0	1
11 —	Harris (3), Kramer (1), St. Louis	5	1	1	0	0	1	3
12 —	Auker (1), Muncrief (1), St. Louis	4	2	1	0	0	1	2
13 —	Lyons (2), Hallett (1), Chicago	5	2	4	1	0	0	2
13 —	Lee, Chicago	4	0	2	0	1	0	2
14 —	Rigney, Chicago	3	0	1	0	0	0	0
15 —	Smith, Chicago	4	1	2	1	0	0	2
15 —	Milnar (2), Krakauskas (1), Cleveland	4	3	3	1	0	0	0
	Totals for 56 games	223	56	91	16	4	15	55

B.B., 21; SO., 5; HBP., 2; BA, .408.

Ended July 17 at Cleveland, night game; New York won 4-3. First inning, Al Smith pitching, thrown out by 3B Keltner. Fourth inning, Smith pitching, base on balls. Seventh inning, Smith pitching, thrown out by Keltner. Eighth inning, Bagby pitching, grounded into a double play.

YANKEES FOR A DAY

**(Players who played only one
game in a Yankee uniform or only
once in a particular position)**

PITCHERS

Rocco Colavito	1968	WINNING PITCHER (Two-and-two thirds-innings, no runs, one hit, two walks, one strikeout.)

YANKEES FOR A DAY

(Players who played only one
game in a Yankee uniform)

PITCHERS:

Lloyd Colson*	1970	NO DECISION (two innings, no runs, three hits, two strikeouts.)
Art Goodwin *	1905	NO DECISION (One-third inning, three runs, two hits, two walks.)
Ted Gray	1955	NO DECISION (specifics unavailable)
Clem Llewellyn*	1922	NO DECISION (One inning, one hit, no runs.)
Gene Michael	1968	NO DECISION (three innings, five unearned runs, five hits, three strikeouts.)
Floyd Newkirk*	1934	NO DECISION (One inning, no runs, one hit, one walk.)
Andrew O'Connor*	1908	LOSING PITCHER (eight innings, 10 runs, 15 hits, seven walks.)
Ed Quick*	1903	NO DECISION (Four innings, two runs, five hits, one walk, one strikeout.)
Charles Schmidt*	1909	NO DECISION (Five innings, four runs, 10 hits, one walk, two strikeouts.)
George Washburn*	1941	LOSING PITCHER (two innings, seven runs, two hits, five walks.)

*Indicates that player's entire major league career consisted of
that one appearance.

OTHERS

Rugger Anderson*	1947	pinch runner
John Barnes*	1926	catcher (one walk)
Phil Cooney*	1905	third baseman (three at-bats, no hits.)
George Davis	1926	Outfielder (no at-bats)
Jack Doyle	1905	First baseman (three at-bats, no hits)
Ray French	1920	Shortstop (two at-bats, one RBI, one run scored.) (May have appeared in two games.)
Joe Hanson*	1913	catcher (two at-bats, no hits)
Fred Holmes	1903	first base (one walk)
Malcolm Hills	1924	second baseman (one at-bat, no hits, one run scored)

Fred Jacklitsch	1905	catcher (three at-bats, no hits, one RBI, one run scored.)
Felix Jimenez*	1964	outfield (six at-bats, two hits)
Thomas Madden	1910	pinch hitter (one at-bat, no hits)
Joe McCarthy	1905	catcher (two at-bats, no hits.
Larry McClure*	1910	outfielder (one at-bat, no hits.)
Patrick O'Connor	1918	catcher (three at-bats, one hit, one strikeout.)
Charles Sands	1967	Pinch hitter (one at-bat, one strikeout.)
Herman Schaeffer	1916	outfield (did not bat.)
Bill Schwartz*	1914	catcher (one at-bat, one strikeout.)
Thomas Thompson*	1912	catcher (did not bat.)
Frank Verdi*	1953	shortstop (did not bat.)
William Walker	1919	pinch hitter (one at-bat, no hits.)
Nicholas Witek	1949	pinch hitter (one at-bat, one hit

*Indicates that the appearance was that player's entire major league career!

Special mention goes to Arthur "Dutch" Schult because he appeared in seven games as a Yankee, all of them as pinch runner. He never played the field, never batted, but did score three runs in 1953!

THE LONGEST DAYS

22 INNINGS: June 24, 1962 Yankees at Tigers

New York	610	000	000	000	000	000	000	2	9	20	4
Detroit	303	001	000	000	000	000	000	0	7	19	3

Winning Pitcher: Jim Bouton. Losing Pitcher: Phil Regan.
Time: 7 hours. Game-winning runs scored on a two-run
homerun by Jack Reed (the only homerun of his career).

20 INNINGS: August 29, 1967 Red Sox at Yankees (2nd game)

Boston	020	000	000	010	000	000	00	3	12	2
New York	000	100	100	010	000	000	01	4	15	1

Winning Pitcher: Fred Talbot. Losing Pitcher: Darrell Brandon.
Time: 5:15. Game-winning run scored on singles by John Kennedy,
Fred Talbot, and Horace Clarke.

19 INNINGS: May 24, 1918 Indians at Yankees

Cleveland	001	000	100	000	000	000	1	3	14	0
New York	000	000	101	000	000	000	0	2	12	1

Winning Pitcher: Stan Coveleski. Losing Pitcher: George Mogridge.
Time: 3:45. Game-winning run scored on a homerun by Cleveland
starter Joe Wood (his second of the game).

August 23, 1968 Tigers at Yankees

								R	H	E
Detroit	001	010	010	000	000	000	0	3	15	1
New York	000	010	020	000	000	000	0	3	9	1

The game was suspended because of the 1 p.m. curfew regulation.

August 25, 1976 Twins at Yankees

								R	H	E
Minnesota	040	000	000	000	000	000	0	4	12	0
New York	010	030	000	000	000	000	1	5	16	4

Winning Pitcher: Grant Jackson. Losing Pitcher: Tom Burgmeier.
Time: 5:36. Game-winning run scored on a walk to Oscar Gamble,
a sacrifice by Willie Randolph and a single by Mickey Rivers.

18 INNINGS: June 25, 1903 Yankees at White Sox

								R	H	E
Chicago	102	101	010	000	000	000	6	16	5
New York	002	011	002	000	000	000	6	14	6

(Note: The White Sox elected to bat first!)
This game was called because of darkness. In 1903, such games were not made
up or completed at a later date, regardless of their effect on the standings.
Contemporary reports vary as to the length of the game, and range from 3:45 to
5:15.

September 5, 1927 Yankees at Red Sox

								R	H	E
New York	004	200	002	000	000	030	11	21	2
Boston	300	410	000	000	000	031	12	20	5

Winning Pitcher: Snake Wiltse. Losing Pitcher: Waite Hoyt.
Time: 4:20. Winning run scored on a double by Buddy Myer and
a single by Ira Flagstead.

August 21, 1933 Yankees at White Sox

								R	H	E
New York	000	000	001	020	000	000	3	11	0
Chicago	000	000	001	020	000	000	3	11	0

This game was suspended by darkness after approximately
3:40 playing time.

April 16, 1967 Red Sox at Yankees

								R	H	E
Boston	201	002	001	000	000	000	6	20	2
New York	003	003	000	000	000	001	7	15	3

Winning Pitcher: Al Downing. Losing Pitcher: Lee Stange.
Time: 5:50. Winning run scored when Jake Gibbs walked,
stole second base, and came home on Joe Pepitone's two-
out single.

July 26, 1967 Twins at Yankees

								R	H	E
Minnesota	010	001	000	000	000	001	3	9	2
New York	000	020	000	000	000	000	2	9	0

Winning Pitcher: Al Worthington. Losing Pitcher: Thad Tillotson. Time: 4:20.
Winning run scored when Rod Carew walked, stole second and continued on to
third base on the catcher's throwing error, and came around when Rich Rollins
singled.

April 22, 1970 Yankees at Senators

								R	H	E
New York	000	000	001	000	000	000	1	11	1
Washington	000	001	000	000	000	001	2	11	1

Winning Pitcher: Joe Grzenda. Losing Pitcher: Ron Klimkowski. Time: 4:40.
Winning run scored on a walk to Ed Stroud, a single by Hank Allen which
advanced Stroud to third base, and a sacrifice fly by Mike Epstein.

YANKEES IN THE HALL OF FAME

	(year elected)
Babe Ruth	1936
Lou Gehrig	1939
Willie Keeler	1939
Clark Griffith	1945
Frank Chance	1946
Jack Chesbro	1946
Herb Pennock	1948
Paul Waner	1952
Ed Barrow	1953
Bill Dickey	1954
Home Run Baker	1955
Dazzy Vance	1955
Joe DiMaggio	1955
Joe McCarthy	1957
Miller Huggins	1964
Casey Stengel	1966
Bill McKechnie	1966
Red Ruffing	1967
Branch Rickey	1967
Waite Hoyt	1969
Stan Coveleski	1969
Earle Combs	1970
George Weiss	1970
Yogi Berra	1971
Lefty Gomez	1972
Mickey Mantle	1974
Whitey Ford	1974
Bucky Harris	1975
Joe Sewell	1977
Larry MacPhail (owner)	1978
Mel Allen (broadcaster)	1978
Red Barber (broadcaster)	1978

AND NOW, A WORD OR TWO ABOUT EACH OF THEM

BABE RUTH: Its really hard to say anything that hasn't already been said about the greatest baseball player of all time. Historians agree that he probably singlehandedly saved the national pastime after the Black Sox Scandal of 1919. Ruth created the homerun as a serious threat, and the fans not only came to love it, they expected it.

As a pitcher, he recorded a lifetime record of 94-46, plus three wins without a loss in the world series. What most fans don't know, or recall, is that Ruth was 5-0 as a pitcher for the Yankees. His most well-known victory came in the final game of the 1933 season. Ruth staggered through the full nine innings and beat the Red Sox, 6-5. And of course, Ruth hit what proved to be the game-winning homerun!

330

As a hitter, his 714 homeruns stood as the all-time record until Henry Aaron surpassed it a few years ago. Even more impressive was his lifetime .342 batting average, including a .393 season in 1923. He led the league in homeruns 12 times, but never led in doubles or triples. His complete statistics are listed below:

RUTH'S CAREER STATISTICS

With the Yankees:

Year	G	AB	R	H	RBI	2B	3B		HR	BB	SO	SB	BA	SA	Pos.
1920	142	458	158*	172	137*	36	9	54*	148*	80		14	.375	.847*	OF,1B,P
1921	152	540	177*	204	171*	44	16	59*	144*	81		17	.378	.846*	OF,1B,P
1922	110	406	94	128	99	24	8	35	84	80		2	.315	.672*	OF,1B
1923	152	522	151*	205	131*	45	13	41*	170*	93*		17	.393	.764*	OF
1924	153	529	143*	200	121	39	7	46*	142*	81*		9	.378*	.739*	OF
1925	98	359	61	104	66	12	2	25	59	68		2	.290	.543	OF
1926	152	495	139*	184	145*	30	5	47*	144*	76		11	.372	.737	OF,1B
1927	151	540	158*	192	164	29	8	60*	138*	89*		7	.356	.772*	OF
1928	154	536	163*	173	142*	29	8	54*	135*	87*		4	.323	.709*	OF
1929	135	499	121	172	154	26	6	46*	72	60		5	.345	.697*	OF
1930	145	518	150	186	153	28	9	49*	136*	61		10	.359	.732*	OF,P
1931	145	534	149	199	163	31	3	46*	128*	51		5	.373	.700*	OF,1B
1932	133	457	120	156	137	13	5	41	130*	62		2	.341	.661	OF,1B
1933	137	459	97	138	103	21	3	34	114*	90		4	.301	.582	OF,P
1934	125	365	78	105	84	17	4	22	103	63		1	.288	.537	OF

Yankee totals during regular season:

15 yrs. 2081 7117 1959 2518 1970 424 106 659 1845 1906 110 .354 .765

Cumulative career totals (includes five-plus seasons with Red Sox and one with Braves)

22 yrs. 2503 8399 2174 2873 2204 506 136 714 2056 1330 123 .342 .690.

Ruth is second in homeruns, first in walks and slugging average, and second in runs and RBI's, too.

World Series Performance as a Yankee:
7 series 36 118 37 41 30 5 1 15 UA UA UA .347 .746

Career series performance (includes appearances with Red Sox)
10 series 41 129 37 42 33 5 2 15 33 30 4 .326 .744

Ruth is first in career world series slugging average, and second in career walks and homeruns in the series. He ranks third in runs scored and fourth in RBI's and strikeouts.

RUTH'S CAREER PITCHING STATISTICS

With the Yankees:

Year	W	L	Pct.	ERA	IP	R	H	ER	BB	K	SV
1920	1	0	1.000	4.50	4	4	3	4	2	0	0
1921	2	0	1.000	9.00	9	10	14	9	9	2	0
1930	1	0	1.000	3.00	9	3	11	3	2	3	0
1933	1	0	1.000	5.00	9	5	12	5	3	0	0

With Boston Red Sox:

Year	W	L	Pct.	ERA	IP	R	H	ER	BB	K	SV
1914	2	1	.667	3.91	23	12	21	10	7	3	0
1915	18	8	.692	2.44	217.2	80	166	59	85	112	0
1916	23	12	.657	1.75*	323.2	83	230	63	118	170	1
1917	24	13	.649	2.01	326.1	93	244	73	108	128	2
1918	13	7	.650	2.22	166.1	51	125	44	49	49	0
1919	9	5	.643	2.97	133.1	59	148	49	58	30	1

Major league pitching totals:

	W	L	Pct.	ERA	IP	R	H		ER	BB	K	SV
	94	46	.676	2.24	1220	400	974		443		486	4

Ruth was 3-0 in world series competition, all with the Red Sox.

LOU GEHRIG: "The Iron Horse" played in an all-time record 2,130 consecutive games, a record which will probably stand forever. He hit 494 career homeruns, including an all-time record 23 grand slams, and is among a handful of players to hit four homeruns in four consecutive at bats. His lifetime batting average (.340) is second only to Ruth's as a Yankee. Gehrig won the Most Valuable Player Award three times, the Triple Crown (1934 — .363, 49 homeruns, 165 runs batted in), and set the American League record for runs batted in one season (1931 — 184).

His career was cut short by a rare form of paralysis which caused his death in 1941. His career statistics are listed below:

GEHRIG'S CAREER STATISTICS

Year	Games	AB	R	H	RBI	2B	3B	HR	BB	K	SB	BA	SA	Pos.
1923	13	26	6	11	9	4	1	1	2	5	0	.423	.769	1B
1924	10	12	2	6	6	1	0	0	1	3	0	.500	.583	1B,OF
1925	126	437	73	129	68	23	10	20	46	49	6	.295	.531	1B,OF
1926	155	572	135	179	107	47	20*	16	105	72	6	.313	.549	1B
1927	155	584	149	218	175*	52*	18	47	109	84	10	.373	.765	1B
1928	154	562	139	210	142*	47*	13	27	95	69	4	.374	.648	1B
1929	154	553	127	166	126	33	9	35	122	68	4	.300	.582	1B,OF
1930	154	581	143	220	174*	42	17	41	101	63	12	.379	.721	1B,OF
1931	155	619	163*	211*	184*	31	15	46*	117	56	17	.341	.662	1B
1932	156	596	138	208	151	42	9	34	108	38	4	.349	.621	1B
1933	152	593	138*	198	139	41	12	32	92	42	9	.334	.605	1B
1934	154	579	128	210	165*	40	6	49*	109	31	9	.363*	.706*	1B,SS
1935	149	535	125*	176	119	26	10	30	132*	38	8	.329	.583	1B
1936	155	579	167*	205	152	37	7	49*	130*	46	3	.354	.696	
1937	157	569	138	200	159	37	9	37	127*	49	4	.351	.643	1B
1938	157	576	115	170	114	32	6	29	107	75	6	.295	.523	1B
1939	8	28	2	4	1	0	0	0	5	1	0	.143	.143	1B

TOTALS
17 yrs.	2164	8001	1888	2721	1991	535	162	493	1508	789	102	.340	.632	

World Series Totals
7 series	34	119	30	43	35	8	3	10	26	17	0	.361	.731

*Indicates league leader.

Gehrig ranks third among all players in career RBI's and slugging percentage.
He ranks second in slugging percentage for world series and third in RBI's in world series.

His 184 RBI's is also a record (1931).

WILLIE KEELER: Considered by many to have been one of baseball's greatest hitters. Came to the Yankees towards the tail end of his career and batted .318 (1903), .343 (1904), .302 (1905), .304 (1906) before tailing off to .234 (1907). His lifetime batting average (.345) places him first on the all-time list. Coined the phrase "Hit 'em where they ain't."

CLARK C. GRIFFITH: The first manager of the Highlanders. He also pitched for NY after a long and superb career in the National League. Pitching record as a Yankee: 31-23. Managerial record as a Yankee: 419-370. Overall, ranks tenth in wins, losses, and total games managed.

FRANK CHANCE: A lifetime .297 hitter, Chance earned his way into the Hall of Fame largely thanks to his player-manager days with the Chicago Cubs from 1905-1912. His Cubs teams won four pennants in five years (1906-07-08-10) and never finished below third place.

Unfortunately, his playing and managerial career with New York was less successful. Under his direction in 1913, the Yankees went 57-94 and finished in 7th place. The 1914 record improved to 70-84, good for a sixth place tie with the White Sox, after which Chance was dismissed.

Chance appeared in 12 games as a player in a Yankee uniform, and batted .208. Had he chosen to stay off the field, he would have finished with a .300 lifetime average.

JACK CHESBRO: Set the modern American League record for wins with 41 in 1904 (while losing 12). Yankee career mark: 129-85. Pitched an incredible 454.2 innings in 1904 to lead the league. Also hit four career homeruns as a Yankee, a real rarity in those days.

HERB PENNOCK: "The Knight of Kennett Square" pitched 11 years in a Yankee uniform (1923-33), recording a 142-90 mark. Was 5-0 in world series play, including a near-perfect game in Game III of the '27 series.

PAUL WANER: "Big Poison" came to the Yankees at the tail end of a brilliant 20-year career with the Pirates (1925-40), Dodgers (1941, 1943-44) and Braves (1941-42). He batted .300 or more 14 times, and finished with a career .333 average over 2,549 games. He was one of a handful of players to record more than 3,000 career hits (3,152), and he also set a National League record by making 200 or more hits in eight of his major league seasons.

Waner spent part of the 1944 and 1945 seasons with the Yankees. He appeared in 9 games in 1944 and batted .143. His lone appearance in 1945 was as a pinch hitter, and he drew a walk.

EDWARD G. BARROW: The architect behind the Yankee champions of the 1920's and 30's, Barrow jumped from Boston to New York in October 1920, and proceeded to acquire many former Red Sox players (Joe Dugan, Herb Pennock, Waite Hoyt, etc.) to help build the pennant winners of the 20's. He was instrumental in the signing of Joe McCarthy as manager of the Yankees in 1931.

BILL DICKEY: The first in what has become a Yankee tradition of great catchers. Batted over .300 in 10 of his 13 years as the Yankees regular backstop, including a .362 mark in 1936. Topped the 100 RBI mark four years in a row (1936-39). Also managed the Yankees for part of the 1946 season (57-48) after McCarthy resigned, and stayed on as a coach under Bucky Harris and Casey Stengel. Yogi Berra credits Dickey with teaching him the fundamentals of catching, and making him into the Hall-of-Famer Yankee fans know and love.

HOME RUN BAKER: Came to the Yankees at the end of his career and solidified the infield of the 1921 American League Champions, before yielding to Joe Dugan. Baker's sobriquet "home run" came as a result of a pair of four-baggers he hit in the world series of 1911. Twice hit more than 10 homeruns for New York (1916, 1919-10).

ARTHUR "Dazzy" VANCE: Arm trouble spoiled Vance's two trial runs with New York, and when it finally cleared up, he had been exiled to the Dodgers. His career mark was 197-140 (ERA: 3.24 over 16 seasons), but his Yankee stats were 0-3 (ERA: roughly 12.57). A most unfortunate situation, because while Vance was winning 28 games for a weak Brooklyn team in 1924, the Yankees were edged out by the Senators in the American League.

JOE DIMAGGIO: The Yankee Clipper was voted the Greatest Living Player during baseball's centennial in 1976, and with good reason. Historians consider him the finest center field ever to don the pinstripes, and among the best in the game's history. His record of hitting safely in 56 consecutive games (1941) will probably stand forever as baseball's greatest streak. American League Most Valuable Player three times (1939, 1941, 1947). Lifetime batting average of .325. Hit 361 career homeruns.

What few fans realize is that DiMaggio's career lasted less than 13 seasons because of World War II and injuries. In those years he reached the .300 mark 11 times, including a career high .381 in 1939. The rest of his career statistics are shown below:

DiMAGGIO'S CAREER STATISTICS

Year	G	AB	R	H	RBI	2B	3B	HR	BB	K	SB	BA	SA	Pos.
1936	138	637	132	206	125	44	15*	29	24	39	4	.323	.576	OF
1937	151	621	151*	215	167	35	15	46*	64	37	3	.346	.673*	OF
1938	145	599	129	194	140	32	13	32	59	21	6	.324	.581	OF
1939	120	462	108	176	126	32	6	30	52	20	3	.381*	.671	OF
1940	132	508	76	93	179	28	9	31	61	30	1	.352*	.626	OF
1941	139	541	122	193	125*	43	11	30	76	13	4	.357	.643	OF
1942	154	610	123	186	114	29	13	21	68	36	4	.305	.498	OF
1946	132	503	81	146	95	20	8	25	59	24	1	.290	.511	OF
1947	141	534	97	168	97	31	10	20	64	32	3	.315	.522	OF
1948	153	594	110	190	155*	26	11	39*	67	30	1	.320	.598	OF
1949	133	273	58	94	67	14	6	14	55	18	0	.346	.596	OF
1950	139	525	114	158	122	33	10	32	80	33	0	.301	.585*	OF,1B
1951	116	415	72	109	71	22	4	12	61	36	0	.263	.422	OF
13 yrs.	1736	6821	1390	2214	1537	389	131	361	790	369	30	.325	.579	

(An interesting note: Of the 1736 games he played in, DiMaggio started in 1721 in the outfield and one at first base!)

World Series:														
10 yrs.	51	199	27	54	30	6	0	8	19	23	0	.271	.422	OF

JOE McCARTHY: Considered by many to be the greatest manager of all time, and clearly recognized as the manager who contributed the most to the Yankee "mystique." Among other things, he is credited with instituting a dress code, banning card playing and clowning around in the clubhouse before the game, and requiring that each player have three uniforms so no Yankee would ever wear a dirty one.

As a manager, his players held him in awe for his baseball knowledge and powers of recall. His record as the manager of the Yankees from 1931-46 (1460-867, .627 winning percentage) is the highest in Yankee history, and includes four consecutive world championship teams between 1936-39). He also won a pennant while managing the Cubs (1932), lost out to the Yankees on the last day of the 1949 season while leading the Red Sox, and never finished worse than 4th place in his 24-year managerial career. In fact, his career record of 2126-1335 gives him the best winning percentage in baseball history (.614), and his seven world champions in nine tries outshines Stengel's seven of 10.

Unfortunately, McCarthy and the Yankees did not part on the best of terms, at least according to close friends of the family, who claim Marse Joe did not get along well with owner Larry MacPhail. These claims have *never* been substantiated, and may well be largely based upon McCarthy's sudden resignation as Yankee manager in 1946. Other reasons offered for the resignation include: poor health, belief that the team was headed for a less successful era, a desire to take some time off and relax. The truth will never be known. McCarthy died at 90 years of age, January 13, 1978.

MILLER HUGGINS: The Mighty Mite led the Yankees to their first pennant in 1921, first world championship in 1923, and managed the 1927 Yankees, considered by many fans to have been the greatest in history. Came to the Yankees in 1918 over the objections of co-owner Col. Huston, and his selection by Col. Ruppert was the catalyst in Huston's sell-out of his stock. His battles with Babe Ruth are a legend in themselves, and culminated in Ruth's suspension in 1925.

Gehrig always credited Huggins with making him a successful first baseman, and guiding him through bad slumps in his first two seasons. And even the Babe wept openly when Huggins, a victim of exhaustion and blood poisoning, died on September 25, 1929.

CASEY STENGEL: When a player bats .284 over a 14-year career, and then goes on to a long, successful career as a manager, you've got a rarity. And such was Stengel. Statistically, he ranks second to McCarthy as the most successful Yankee manager (1149-696, .619), but his career also included stretches with the second division Braves, Dodgers, and Mets. His 10 pennant winners is a record, as is his 37 world series games won. Of course, Stengel's greatest moment came in October, 1953, when his team won a record fifth consecutive pennant and world championship, a feat unmatched in baseball history.

Stengel shepherded 19-year-old Mickey Mantle through the traumas of a difficult rookie season, and became Mantle's substitute father after the death of Mantel's dad. He also made Billy Martin the great player he was, a fact Martin always remembered, and the basis for the dedication of the 1976 season to Stengel.

If Stengel had a fault, it was in his relationship with Joe DiMaggio. The two never got along well, partially because DiMaggio was close to Stengel's predecessors, Bucky Harris and Joe McCarthy. The straw that broke the camel's back came on July 3, 1950, when Stengel moved DiMaggio to first base. The move was requested by Stengel, but he did not approach the slugger directly. Instead, he asked Yankee owner Dan Topping, a great friend of DiMaggio's, to ask the Yankee Clipper to make the switch in hopes of solving the team's nagging problem at first base.

DiMaggio made the move, and fielded flawlessly, but his discomfort was clear. When Hank Bauer was injured during the game, DiMaggio returned to the more familiar outfield pastures.

The second break occured in 1951, while DiMaggio was undergoing some rather intense personal problems with his former wife, Dorothy Arnold. The off-the-field problems were affecting DiMaggio's play, and after he misplayed a hit during an early July contest, Stengel sent Jackie Jensen out to centerfield to replace DiMaggio, after DiMaggio had already taken his position. Every Yankee player present on that day contacted by this author believes that DiMaggio never forgave Stengel for that action.

Off the diamond, Stengel's unique language ("Stengelese"— see p. 387 for some samples) and great sense of humor combined to make him the most colorful manager in Yankee history. He was one of the game's greatest personalities and his recent death was the world's loss.

BILL McKECHNIE: McKechnie earned his Hall of Fame berth as a manager in the National League, where he led the Cardinals (1928) and Reds (1939) into world series against the Yankees. He also managed the Pirates to a world championship (1925) and won a second pennant with the Reds in 1940.

McKechnie spent 12 seasons as a mediocre infielder, and it was in that capacity that he played 44 games for the Yankees in 1913 and batted .314.

RED RUFFING: Another of Ed Barrow's "steals" from the Red Sox, Ruffing came to the Yankees in 1930 and recorded 231 wins as a Yankee (second only to Whitey Ford's 236) while losing 127, a .651 percentage. He was 7-2 in world series games, and batted over .300 six times, including a game-winning pinch hit homerun!

BRANCH RICKEY: "The Mahatma" is best known for re-shaping the face of the baseball world by instituting team-owned farm systems. In that light, he built the Gashouse Gang Cardinal teams of the 1930's, and laid the foundation for the great Brooklyn teams of the 40's and 50's, while serving as business (general) manager in those cities. Also broke the "color line" by bringing Jackie Robinson into the major leagues.

Prior to embarking upon a successful career as an executive, Rickey spent parts of four seasons in the major leagues as a catcher-outfielder-first baseman. In 1907 Rickey saw action at all three positions in 52 games with the Highlanders, batting .182. His lifetime batting average was .239.

WAITE HOYT: Came to the Yankees in 1921 from Red Sox, and went on to win 157 games while losing 98 (.616 percentage). The only 20-game winner (22-7) with the '27 Yankees, and considered by those living members of that team to be the best Yankee pitcher of that era. Posted a 6-4 record in world series games, and an incredible 1.83 earned run average. Later became a broadcaster with the Cincinnati Reds for many years.

STAN COVELESKI: "The Silent Pole" compiled a 214-141 won-loss mark in 14 major league seasons, the majority of which were spent with the Indians. He was one of 17 pitchers allowed to continue throwing the spitball after it was banned in 1920 (pitchers currently in the major leagues who announce that the spitball was their "bread and butter" were allowed to continue throwing it). Coveleski averaged 23 wins a year, and won 20 or more games five times, with a 2.88 ERA.

Coveleski joined the Yankees after the 1927 season and posted a 5-1 mark with the world champions that year. When the post-season final statistics confirmed that his ERA was 5.74, Coveleski decided to retire, rather than risk finishing his career above the 3.00 mark.

EARLE COMBS: A lifetime .325 hitter who played his entire 12-year career with the Yankees. Recorded 648 at bats in 1927 to lead the major leagues. Led the American League in triples three times (1927-23; 1928-21; 1930-22). His career was cut short by serious injuries suffered while attempting a desperation catch in 1933. Batted .340 in four world series, eighth highest in history.

GEORGE M. WEISS: The hand-picked successor to Ed Barrow. Served as general manager of the Yankees, and in other capacities, for 29 years. Engineered brilliant trade after brilliant trade to keep the Yankee dynasty going. Later returned to baseball in the Mets organization and is credited with putting together the young players who built a world championship in 1969.

YOGI BERRA: Baseball's most beloved figure, and one of the greatest catchers the game has even known. Famous for his extraordinary ability in the clutch, and his success at hitting pitches which were not in the strike zone. Played 18 years as a Yankee, and managed the American League Champion club of 1964. Batted .285, but hit more than .320 with men on base. Holds the record for most world series played in (14), world series hits (71), and world championships (10).

His sense of humor and friendliness have made him one of the most popular players in history. Perhaps his most famous quote, involving a restaurant in

Chicago: "Nobody goes there anymore. It's too crowded." Also coined the phrase "You're never out of it until you're out of it," while managing the Mets National League champion in 1973.

LEFTY GOMEZ: Holds the highest winning percentage among world series pitchers with five or more decisions (6-0). Spent 13 of his 14 years in baseball as a Yankee, recording 189 wins, 101 losses (.649 percentage). Ranks third on the all-time Yankee strikeout list with 1468, and second on the complete games list with 173.

MICKEY MANTLE: The greatest switch-hitter of all time. Hit 536 homeruns, including a record 18 in world series competition. Won the Triple Crown in 1956 (.353, 130 RBI's, 52 homeruns), selected for 20 all star games, and won the American League Most Valuable Player Award three times (1956, 1957, 1962). Played more games as a Yankee (2401) than any other player, despite his injury-plagued career.

His complete statistics are shown below:

MANTLE'S CAREER STATISTICS

Year	Games	AB	R	H	RBI	2B	3B	HR	BB	K	SB	BA	SA	Pos.
1951	96	341	61	91	65	11	5	13	43	74	8	.267	.443	OF
1952	142	549	94	171	87	37	7	23	75	111*	4	.311	.530	OF,3B
1953	127	461	105	136	92	24	3	21	79	90	8	.295	.497	OF,SS
1954	146	543	129*	163	102	17	12	27	102	107*	5	.300	.525	OF,SS,2B
1955	147	517	121	158	99	25	11*	37*	113*	97	8	.306	.611*	OF,SS
1956	150	533	132*	188	130*	22	5	52*	112	99	10	.353*	.705*	OF
1957	144	474	121*	173	94	28	6	34	146*	75	16	.365	.665	OF
1958	150	519	127*	158	97	21	1	42*	129*	120*	18	.304	.592	OF
1959	144	541	104	154	75	23	4	31	94	126*	21	.285	.514	OF
1960	153	527	119*	145	94	17	6	40*	111	125*	14	.275	.558	OF
1961	153	514	132*	163	128	16	6	54	126*	112	12	.317	.687*	OF
1962	123	377	96	121	89	15	1	30	122*	78	9	.321	.605	OF
1963	65	172	40	54	35	8	0	15	40	32	2	.314	.622	OF
1964	143	465	92	141	111	25	2	35	99	102	6	.303	.591	OF
1965	122	361	44	92	46	12	1	19	73	76	4	.255	.452	OF
1966	108	333	40	96	56	12	1	23	57	76	1	.288	.538	OF
1967	144	440	63	108	55	17	0	22	107	113	1	.245	.434	1B
1968	144	435	57	103	54	14	1	18	106	97	6	.237	.398	1B

Regular season totals:

Year	Games	AB	R	H	RBI	2B	3B	HR	BB	K	SB	BA	SA
18 yrs.	2401	8102	1677	2415	1509	344	72	536	1734	1710	153	.298	.557

Mantle ranks sixth in homeruns among career leaders. He is third in career walks, and second in career strikeouts.

World series totals:

12 series	65	230	42	59	40	6	2	18	43	54	3	.257	.535

He is first in world series homeruns, runs scored, RBI's, BB's and strikeouts.
He is second in world series games played, at-bats, and total hits.

WHITEY FORD: Compiled a 236-106 (.690 percentage) career mark in 16 years as a Yankee. Came to New York in the late summer of 1950 and proceeded to go 9-1, giving the Yankees some badly needed pitching help. Holds the Yankee record for career strikeouts (1956), shutouts (45), games (498) and total innings (3171). Holds the world series record for most wins by a pitcher (10) and most losses (8), as well as the all-time world series consecutive scoreless innings streak (33). Posted a career earned run average of 2.74.

Strangely enough, Ford won 20 games only twice (1961: 25-4, .862, the highest winning percentage for a 20-game winner in Yankee history; and 1963: 24-7) before having his career shortened by arm trouble in the mid-60's. His complete statistics are shown below:

FORD'S CAREER STATISTICS

Year	G	IP	H	FR	BB	K	W	L	SV	Pct.	ERA
1950	20	112	87	35	52	59	9	1	1	.900	2.81
1953	32	207	187	69	110	110	18	6	0	.750	3.00
1954	34	210.2	170	66	101	125	16	8	1	.667	2.82
1955	39	253.2	188	74	113	137	18*	7	2	.720	2.63
1956	31	225.2	187	62	84	141	19	6	1	.760	2.47*
1957	24	129.1	114	37	53	84	11	5	0	.688	2.57
1958	30	219.1	174	49	62	145	14	7	1	.667	2.01*
1959	35	204	194	69	89	114	16	10	1	.615	3.04
1960	33	192.2	168	66	65	85	12	9	0	.571	3.08
1961	39	283*	242	101	92	209	25*	4	0	.862*	3.21
1962	38	257.2	243	83	69	160	17	8	0	.680	2.90
1963	38	269.1*	240	82	56	189	24*	7	1	.774*	2.74
1964	39	244.2	212	58	57	172	17	6	1	.739	2.13
1965	37	244.1	241	88	50	162	16	13	1	.552	3.24
1966	22	73	79	20	24	43	2	5	0	.286	2.47
1967	7	44	40	8	9	21	2	4	0	.333	1.64

TOTALS

16 yrs.	498	3170.1	2766	967	1086	1956	236	106	10	.690	2.75

BUCKY HARRIS: Managed the Yankees in 1947-48, including a world championship over the Dodgers in '47. Considered one of the better infielders in the American League during his playing days (1920's and 30's), Harris ranks third in games managed with 4410, third in wins with 2159, and second in losses (2219).

BOB LEMON: Lemon pitched his way into the Hall of Fame during a 15-year career with the Indians. He posted a lifetime 207-128 mark with a 3.23 ERA, before arm trouble forced a premature retirement after the 1957 season. Few fans remembered that Lemon started his career as an outfielder, and batted .327 in 47 games in 1947.

Lemon joined the Yankees midway through the 1978 season, and became the first manager in major league history to win a world championship after taking over for another man midway through the year.

(There are some remarkable similarities between Lemon's playing career and that of Ron Guidry. Aside from the fact that both are lefthanded, and the aces of their respective staffs, both were unsuccessful in the early years of their careers. In fact, they both had their first big pitching year when 27 years old, and Guidry had toyed with a conversion to the outfield after disappointments in 1975-76.)

JOE SEWELL: A lifetime .312 hitter, Sewell came to the Yankees at the end of his 14-year career after starring with the Indians. Sewell batted .302 in 1931, his best mark in a Yankee uniform, and played on the 1932 world champions.

LARRY MACPHAIL: Owner, innovator, and general baseball genius, MacPhail came to the Yankees as co-owner in 1945 with Dan Topping and Del Webb. Brought night baseball with him from Cincinnati (where he staged the first major league night game in 1939). After years of world series frustration with the Reds and Dodgers, MacPhail finally got his world championship in 1947, and promptly sold his interest in the team to his two partners.

MEL ALLEN: "The Longtime Voice of the Yankees" was as much a part of the Pinstripes and their tradition as any man who ever donned a Yankee uniform. His opening greeting before every game, "Hello there, everybody", and his "that ball is going, going, gone" to describe a homerun, are known throughout the country. Allen coined virtually every Yankee nickname from 1939 on, including "The Yankee Clipper" (DiMaggio), "The Springfield Rifle" (Vic Raschi), "Old Reliable" (Henrich), etc.

If Allen had a fault, it was that he was a real Yankee fan, a fact which was never lost or forgotten by the anti-Yankee listeners, who generally disliked him.

Perhaps some day Allen will reveal the real circumstances surrounding his sudden dismissal from the Yankee broadcasting team after the 1964 season. Allegations range from salary disputes and anti-Semitism (Allen's real name was Mel Allen Israel) to poor health and too big an ego. Nothing has ever been verified, and knowing the class reputation Allen has, nothing ever will be.

To Yankee fans, he was the greatest.

RED BARBER: "The Old Redhead" coined the phrase "The House That Ruth Built" and is also recognized as one of the greatest broadcasters ever behind a microphone. His calls of Cookie Lavagetto's game-winning double which spoiled Bill Bevens' no-hitter in the 1947 world series, and his call of Al Gionfriddo's catch off Joe DiMaggio in that same series, are among the best known in baseball history.

A great deal of information about Barber's dismissal after the 1965 season is available. The problem was that Barber was never really a diehard Yankee fan, and was a real newsperson. The event usually cited as the straw that broke the camel's back came on a late September day in '65, when Barber demanded that the television cameras pan the empty Stadium (419 fans were in attendance) to show how the mighty had fallen. The director refused, the dispute went to Yankee President Mike Burke, who said no way, and Barber was assured of an end to his 30-plus years behind the mike.

AND ONE WHO ISN'T . . . BUT SHOULD BE

Every baseball fan has a favorite player whom he or she firmly believes should be in the Hall of Fame, but isn't.

And every fan also has a particular player singled out as undeserving of the honor, but taking up space in Cooperstown, anyway.

In my book, and in the eyes of most of the men who played with him, Johnny Mize has been unfairly denied his rightful spot in baseball's holiest shrine.

The case for Mize is simple:

A .312 lifetime batting average.

356 career homeruns (and he lost four years in the prime of his career to World War II).

The eighth-highest slugging percentage in the history of major league baseball (.562).

A four-time National League homerun champion, including 51 homeruns (the most ever by a lefty in the National League) in 1947.

Nine consecutive .300-plus seasons.

One of the greatest pinch-hitters of all time, including three league-leading years with the Yankees, and a lifetime .283 pinch hitting average.

Casey Stengel cited Mize as "the greatest pinch hitter I've ever seen, and I've been around long enought to have seen everything and some things which was never seen . . ."

So why isn't "The Big Cat" already enshrined in the Hall of Fame?

339

THE YANKEES AND THE METS

Once upon a time, there were three major league baseball teams that played in New York City: the Yankees, Giants, and Brooklyn Dodgers. In 1958, there was only one, the Yankees, because the other pair had left for the riches of the West Coast.

National League fans had been raised on hating the Yankees. They needed something in the way of baseball to appease their appetites. That something came along in 1962, when the original New York Mets opened their first season at the antiquated Polo Grounds. In the beginning, the Mets were clowns to be laughed at, especially by Yankee fans, whose teams were winning championships in the early 60's. The mid-60's were bleak for both teams, but the Mets exploded onto the baseball world in 1969 with an amazing world championship.

The residue of that explosion turned New York's more vocal fans into Met rooters. After all, the Yankees were still a mediocre ball club, and the Mets were young, exciting, had a new stadium, plenty of parking, etc. They also made another world series appearance in 1973, losing to Oakland in seven games.

No one realized it at the time, but the tide was about to turn in the Yankees' direction. In 1974, the Yankees battled Baltimore and Boston down to the wire for the Eastern Division Championship, while the Mets faded from their pennant battles in August. In 1975, both teams had poor years.

Then came 1976. The Mets were dismal, and the Yankees were pennant winners. In 1977, the trend continued, with the Yankees providing the excitement and winning a world championship, while the Mets let Tom Seaver go to the Reds and finished with one of the worst records in baseball.

Yet, the rivalry between the two teams continues, albeit quietly these days, and they do square off in annual mayor's trophy games each year.

Actually, the mayor's trophy game is nothing new. The Yankees used to battle the Giants three times, every year, as mayor's series. Those games were largely unpublicized and their results were often unrecorded in the contemporary media.

The same cannot be said for the Mets-Yankees games, which have remained the subject of great excitement. Here are the annual results:

YANKEES VS. METS
Overall Record — Won 34, Lost 24. Mayor's Trophy Game — 8-7, Spring — 26-17

MAYOR'S TROPHY RESULTS & ATTENDANCES

6/20/63 — Yankee Stadium — Mets 6, Yanks 2 — 52,430
8/24/64 — Shea Stadium — Yanks 6, Mets 4 — 60,167
5/3/65 — Yankee Stadium — Mets 2, Yanks 1 (10) — 23,556
6/27/66 — Shea Stadium — Yanks 5, Mets 2 — 56,367
7/12/67 — Yankee Stadium — Mets 4, Yanks 0 — 32,752
5/27/68 — Shea Stadium — Mets 4, Yanks 3 — 35,198
9/29/69 — Shea Stadium — Mets 7, Yanks 6 — 36,082
8/24/72 — Yankee Stadium — Yanks 2, Mets 1 — 53,949
5/10/73 — Shea Stadium — Mets 8, Yanks 4 — 36,915
5/30/74 — Shea Stadium — Yanks 9, Mets 4 — 35,894
5/15/75 — Shea Stadium — Yanks 9, Mets 4 — 26,427
6/14/76 — Yankee Stadium — Yanks 8, Mets 4 — 36,361
6/23/77 — Shea Stadium — Mets 6, Yanks 4 — 15,012

A total of 590,623 tickets have been sold for the 15 games, raising a total of $1,662,785.20 for the development of the Greater New York Sandlot Baseball Program.

1978 THE MIRACLE YEAR

On July 19, 1978, the New York Yankees were 14 games out of first place.
On October 2, the Yankees defeated the Red Sox, 5-4, in the first American
League Divisional Championship Playoff Game in history. This chapter is the
exciting story of that 1978 season, from the dog days of injuries and frustration
that were June and early July, to the triumph of the Pinstripes in September and
October.

BEGINNINGS

The 1978 season dawned with the Yankees and Red Sox named as
co-favorites to win their division. The teams had finished 2½ games apart in
1977, and both believed they had strengthened themselves.
Boston featured a tremendous offense, led by Jim Rice, Carlton Fisk and Carl
Yastrzemski. Their outfield of Yastrzemski, Lynn and Evans was among the best
in the game. Pitching, a real weakness in '77, had been strenghthened by the
acquisition of former Yankee Mike Torrez via the free agent route, as well as
Tom Burgmeier and Dick Drago. A trade for Dennis Eckersley, and a healthy Bill
Campbell, gave Boston fans good reason to believe that they were the best in the
East.
The 1977 World Champion New York Yankees had not rested on their laurels.
Instead, they'd gone out and signed two free agent relief pitchers (Rich Gossage
and Rawley Eastwick), purchased veteran starting pitcher Andy Messersmith
from the Braves, and obtained first baseman power hitter Jim Spencer from the
White Sox.
The Yankee offense could be compared with any in baseball, thanks to names
like Thurman Munson, Reggie Jackson, Graig Nettles, Mickey Rivers and Willie
Randolph. They sported an under-rated, and amazingly consistent first baseman,
Chris Chambliss, and a superb bench which would prove the ultimate savior
when injuries struck down several starters.
New York's pitching included remarkable Ron Guidry, veterans Ed Figueroa
and Catfish Hunter, super southpaw Don Gullett (an injury-prone pitcher),
Messersmith, steady Dick Tidrow, and the 1977 Cy Young Award winner,
Sparky Lyle.
The Yankees appeared equal to any challenge Boston might offer as the team
left spring training.
The season began somewhat inauspiciously with a 2-1 loss to the Rangers, in
Texas. Newcomer Rich "Goose" Gossage was the loser when he surrendered
a homerun to Richie Zisk in the bottom of the ninth inning. On the bright side —
Ron Guidry showed signs of things to come by pitching seven innings and
allowing one run.
On April 9th, the Yankees pounded out 15 hits and rode Ed Figueroa's
three-hitter to a 7-1 win. It was to be their only victory on a five-game road trip.
On the 11th, the Brewers pounded Catfish Hunter for four homeruns, another
portend of the future (for the first half of the season, anyway). On the 12th,
Brewers hurler Moose Haas struck out 14 Yankees to decision New York, 5-3,
with Gossage losing in relief, again, to drop the team's record to 1-4.

There's nothing like a taste of home cooking to heal what ails you, and when the world champion Yankees returned home, they started a three game winning streak with a 4-2 win over the White Sox. The festivities began with a special introduction. Everyone's attention was directed to the electronic pictureboard in centerfield, where the fans watched a forgotten Red Sox pitcher (Tracy Stallard) deliver a 2-0 pitch to a Yankee wearing number 9. The lefthander swings, and drives the ball into the seats in right field in a ballpark everyone recognized as the pre-renovation Stadium.

Many of those present were too young to recognize that number 9, but for those who remembered the 1961 season, and for those who've learned their Yankee history, it spelled one thing: Roger Maris. Yes, the holder of the record for the most homeruns in one season (61), had finally been pursuaded to return to New York, for the first time since he was traded to the Cardinals in 1966, and for owner George Steinbrenner, it was the culmination of a two-year effort to bring this great Yankee home.

"I had been trying to convince him to come back ever since we re-opened the Stadium in 1976," Steinbrenner said. "But, he was worried that the fans would boo him. Finally, I told him that I'd bet a year's salary that he'd receive a thundering ovation, and he agreed."

The fans went wild, cheering the returning hero like he'd never been cheered during his all too brief Yankee career, and, according to Steinbrenner, sending chills up and down the spines of all those present.

"You know, Mickey Mantle came up to me and told me that the fan reaction to Maris had him tingling with excitement," said Steinbrenner. "And for a man who's been through many similar receptions to say that, well, you know you've really made a hit."

The Maris reception spilled over into the Mickey Mantle introduction, and then the pair made their way out to center field to raise the 1977 World Champions banner to the top of the flagpole.

After continued ceremonies, the game began, with Ron Guidry on the mound, about to notch the first of 13 consecutive wins. In the bottom of the first inning, Reggie Jackson rockets a Wilbur Wood knuckleball into the seats in right, a three-run homerun, and the fans responded by deluging the field with the free sample "Reggie Bars" handed out before the game.

An off day on the 14th was followed by a sweep of the White Sox when Mickey Rivers' inside-the-park homerun gave Figueroa his second straight win (3-2), and Dick Tidrow and Sparky Lyle combined for a 3-0 win. The Yankees were .500, and appeared ready to "take off."

THE REST OF THE MONTH

April 17 — The Orioles pound Hunter and drop the Yankees one game under .500 with a 6-1 decision.

April 18 — Jackson's ninth inning homerun makes Lyle a winner in relief of Guidry, 4-3, against Baltimore.

After the game, the Yankees place pitcher Don Gullett on the disabled list because of shoulder troubles, and recalled Jim Beattie from Tacoma. The Gullett injury was also a portent of things to come, as the Yankees were destined to lose three-fifths of their starting pitchers (add Hunter and Messersmith), and every regular except Chris Chambliss, for at least one week of the season.

A two-day trip to Toronto was cut short by rain, after the Yankees dropped the opener, 4-3, with Gossage again coming out on the short end. Next, a visit to Milwaukee, where the Brewers pounded Figueroa in route to a 9-2 win which dropped the Yankees 4 games behind the first place Tigers.

April 22 — Roy White sparkles as the Yankees edge the Brewers, 4-3, in 12 innings. With the score tied 2-2 in the 7th inning, White makes a leaping catch to rob Charlie Moore of what would have become a game-winning homerun. In the 12th, the veteran Yankee outfielder drives in Fred Stanley with the winning run.

The next stop was Baltimore, where the Yankees shocked the Birds by sweeping the two game set. In the opener, Ron Guidry posts his second consecutive win, riding an 8-run fifth inning to an 8-2 win. Game two matched rookie Beattie against veteran great Jim Palmer, and the Yankee kid edged Palmer, 4-3, with relief help from Lyle. The game-winning hit: Jim Spencer's 100th career homerun.

After splitting the first two games in Minnesota, the Yankees take the rubber match, 3-2, as Gossage gets his first win as a Yankee.

As the month comes to a close, the Yankees are 10-9, in third place, 3½ games behind Detroit.

MAY

The Yankees opened the month at home, and swept a three game series with the Royals. After winning the opener, 8-4, behind newcomer Rawly Eastwick (and beating long-time nemesis Paul Splittorff), the Yankees turned to Hunter for Game II. The righthander responded with a masterful 4-2 win, his first since August 24th, 1977. Lou Piniella struck the key blow, a homerun, and Sparky saved again.

The sweep was completed on May 3rd, when Graig Nettles hit an eighth inning homerun, and Gossage notched his first Yankee save, in a 6-5 victory.

May 5 — Guidry wins his third straight, and the Yankees continue a five game winning streak, with a 5-2 victory over the Rangers. Gossage notched his second save, and Thurman Munson went 3-for-4.

May 7 — Yankees 3, Rangers 2 (12 innings). Chris Chambliss powers a game-winning homerun to send more than 50,000 fans home happy on Helmet Day. Gossage strikes again, gaining the win in relief after hurling four hitless innings. The Yankees are 15-10, three games behind the Tigers.

May 12 — The Yankees take a 3-2 lead into the ninth inning at Kansas City, only to lose, 4-3, when Jackson and Paul Blair collide after Blair caught Amos Otis fly ball, thereby allowing the Royals' outfielder to circle the bases on what was scored an inside-the-park homerun.

May 13 — Yankees 5, Royals 2. The largest regular season crowd in Royals history (40,903) is on hand as Guidry wins his fourth with ninth inning relief from Gossage. Royals righthander Dennis Leonard retires the first 11 Yankees, before Munson singles and Jackson hits his 7th homerun.

May 15 — Yankees 4, White Sox 1. Jim Beattie wins his second game, with relief help from Lyle, and hitting courtesy of Piniella (3-for-4) and Bucky Dent's run-scoring double.

May 18 — Guidry notches his fifth straight, 5-3, over Cleveland, when Rivers triples home the go-ahead run in the seventh inning.

The next stop on the schedule was Toronto, a town the Yankees have had difficulty with ever since the Blue Jays came into the league. New York finally enjoyed some success in Canada's environs, taking three of four from the hosts . . .

May 21 — Yankees 2, Blue Jays 1; Yankees 9, Blue Jays 1. Figueroa wins his fifth game in the opener, and surprise starter Ken Clay takes the nightcap, to raise the Yankees record to 23-14, and pull New York within 1 game of the Tigers and Sox.

May 23 — Guidry wins his sixth straight, a five-hit 10-1 win over Cleveland. The Yankee ace lowered his earned run average (ERA) to 1.71. Nettles and Chambliss each hit a homerun to pace a 14-hit attack.

May 26 — Jim Spencer's pinch hit grand slam homerun in the bottom of the seventh inning makes Lyle a winner, 4-3, against Toronto. Lyle also pitched the 1,000th inning of his career as New York runs up a five game winning streak.

343

May 29 — Andy Messersmith and Eastwick combine for a one-hitter, and Nettles slams a seventh inning two-run homerun to lead the Yankees to a 2-0 win. Cleveland's only hit was a first inning single by their number two batter, Jim Norris. It was Messersmith's only successful outing, but he did not win the game because Eastwick came on in the sixth.

The Yankees closed out the month of May by dropping a 5-1 loss at Cleveland, and losing to Baltimore, 3-2. The Yankees were 29-17, three games behind the Red Sox.

JUNE

June was a disastrous month. The Yankees went 14-15 to fall 9 games behind Boston. Injuries began to decimate the team. and if not for Guidry . . .

June 1 — Palmer outpitches Beattie, 1-0. The Orioles veteran allowed just two hits to Beattie's four.

June 4 — The Yankees lose their fifth game in their last six outings. Don Gullett makes his first start of the year, has control problems, and is kayoed after one-third of an inning, as the Yankees lose, 6-4, in Oakland.

June 7 — Guidry wins his ninth straight game, his seventh following a Yankee loss, and Jackson hits two homeruns, as the Yankees snap a 4-game skid and win, 9-1, at Seattle.

June 10 — During a 12-inning, 4-3 loss to the Angels, shortstop Bucky Dent pulls his hamstring muscle and is placed on the disabled list. This game also featured a minor brawl when rookie catcher Mike Heath is pummeled by consecutive Angels trying to score from third base. After the second "collision", Heath comes up swinging, and is subsequently ejected from the game.

June 11 — Angels 9, Yankees 6. New York drops 6 full games behind the Sox, their lowest point since the 1975 season. The Yankees have now lost 9 of 12.

June 12 — Guidry does it again, notching victory number 10, and his 8th win following a Yankee loss. The 2-0 win against Oakland featured 11 strikeouts, and an ERA which dropped to 1.57.

June 13 — The Yankees win their second straight game, 5-3, but second baseman Willie Randolph suffers a knee injury and is eventually placed on the disabled list.

June 15 — Yankees 5, Mariners 2. Don Gullett wins his first game of the season, and Lyle earns his seventh save, as the Yankees down Seattle, 5-2. Rivers and Nettles each hit homeruns as the Yankees win their fourth straight game.

After the game, the Yankee announce that outfielder Gary Thomasson has been acquired from the A's for infielder Mickey Klutts and outfielder Del Alston. (The original deal included Roy White for catcher Gary Alexander, but White, a 5-and-10-year man, turned down the trade.)

In another deal announced before the game, the Yankees acquired outfielder Jay Johnstone from the Phillies for pitcher Rawley Eastwick.

June 17 — Guidry wins his 11th straight, and sets an American League record for lefthanded pitchers by striking out 18 Angels in route to a 4-0 win. The 18 "K's" are a Yankee record. It was Guidry's ninth win following a Yankee loss.

After the game, Mickey Rivers is placed on the disabled list because of a fractured wrist suffered when he was hit by a pitch during June 16th's 10-7 loss.

SHOWDOWN IN BOSTON

Trailing the Red Sox by 7 games, the Yankees arrived in Boston on June 18th to start a three game series with the first place Sox. The Yankees were without the services of Bucky Dent, Willie Randolph, Mickey Rivers, and Andy Messersmith. The Red Sox were healthy, and sensed an opportunity to open up a big lead at this early date.

344

June 18 — Boston 10, New York 4. The Sox scored 6 runs to break a 4-4 tie in the eighth inning. Tom Burgmeier is the winner in relief, while Gossage is the loser. The loss drops the Yankees 8 games behind the Sox.

June 19 — New York 10, Boston 4. The Yankees rebound with an identical 10-4 win, chasing former teammate Mike Torrez in the process. Fred Stanley highlights the Yankee win with a shocking grand slam homerun, and Jackson put it away with a three-run shot in the eighth.

June 20 — Boston 9, New York 2. With Yankee fans clamoring for Guidry, but getting rookie Beattie instead, the Sox pound the youngster back to Tacoma and leave the Yankees 8 game back. Boston also shelled Hunter in a one inning relief appearance which led to his being placed on the disabled list.

A QUICK TRIP TO DETROIT

Reeling from the two losses in Boston, the Yankees collected their survivors and headed west for the Motor City for four games. The season was clearly on the line. Anything less than a split would leave the Yankees reeling, and heading into another Boston battle, albeit at Yankee Stadium.

June 21 — Yankees 4, Tigers 2. Guidry wins his 12th straight to tie the Yankee record for most consecutive wins at the start of a season, and lowers his ERA to 1.43. The win was Guidry's 10th following a Yankee loss, and was supported by Jackson's 12th homerun.

June 25 — After splitting the middle pair of games, the Yankees take the series with a 4-2 win behind Gullett.

SHOWDOWN IN NEW YORK: I

Less than one week after losing two of three in Fenway Park, the Yankees and Sox collide again, this time in the friendlier confines of Yankee Stadium. The teams enter the series separated by 8½ games . . . and leave with the same margin between them.

June 26 — Boston 4, New York 1. Jim Rice and Carlton Fisk homer to give Dennis Eckersley and the Sox a big win.

June 27 — In one of the most important games of the season, the Yankees rebound with a 14-inning, 6-4 win over Boston. At one point, the Yankees led 4-1, only to watch the Sox struggle back to tie, as Guidry tires after six innings. Lyle comes on in relief, and is effective against the Sox (a rarity in his career against his former teammates), for his sixth win.

The game lasted 4 hours and 8 minutes, finally ending when Nettles launched a space shot off Dick Drago.

DISASTER IN MILWAUKEE

A quirk in the schedule sent the Yankees flying to Milwaukee for a twi-night doubleheader with the Brewers. The Yankees flight left New York at approximately 2 a.m., following the 12:15 a.m. Nettles homerun that ended the marathon with Boston.

The Yankees were exhausted, and dropped a listless doubleheader to the Brewers, 5-0 and 7-2. New York managed only 13 hits off the Brewers dynamic duo of Mike Caldwell and Jerry Augustine, and dropped 9½ games behind Boston.

AN END TO JUNE

New York closed out the month with a 10-2 win versus the Tigers, with Gullett winning his final game of the 1978 season. The month ended with New York 9 games behind the Red Sox, and one game behind the Brewers. For those who thought the worst was over; well, a rude awakening lay in store.

345

JULY

The Yankees opened the month with an 8-4 loss to the Tigers, with Messersmith making his final appearance of the year (and possibly his career, because he was placed on waivers in November). It was an omen of what lay in store for the pinstripe faithful.

Fortunately, the "plague" did not strike too swiftly, with the Yankees taking time out to sweep a double-header from the Tigers, 3-2 and 5-2. Guidry won his 13th straight in the opener, with Gossage recording his 12th save, and Gary Thomasson's ninth inning, two out, three-run homerun won the nightcap.

BACK TO BOSTON

July 3 — Boston 9, New York 5. The Yankees hit three Fenway homeruns, but the Sox pound out 12 hits as Eckersley beats the Yankees for the third time in the last 12 days. The loss dropped New York 9 games behind Boston.

July 4 — I've often heard disgruntled Red Sox fans protest that G-d is a Yankee fan, and one need only look to this date in Yankee history for support. The Yankees were reeling with injuries and losses, and scheduled to meet the Red Sox again. So what was this divine miracle? RAIN. The game would be made up in September!

THESE WERE THE DAYS THAT TRIED FANS' SOULS

On July 5, the Yankees lost to the Texas Rangers, 3-2, and fell 10 games behind the Sox. The loss started a near-fatal 2-8 streak which dropped New York 14 games behind the Sox. The streak featured the nadir of the season when Reggie Jackson was suspended for insubordination (July 17) and Billy Martin resigns as manager (July 24).

Here are the lowlights:

July 9 — The Brewers dump the Yankees, 8-4, to sweep all seven games against the New Yorkers in County Stadium. In fact, up to this date, the Yankees are 1-9 against Milwaukee in 1978.

New York is 46-38, 11½ games out, mired in third place, and already dead and buried in the eyes of most fans, as the schedule pauses for the All-Star Game.

July 14 — The Yankees battle the White Sox for 11 innings before scoring a 7-6 win behind Gossage, and thereby salvage a split of this two-game series.

July 16 — Royals 3, Yankees 1. The Yankees drop into fourth place, 13 games behind Boston. Munson's knees have forced him to "permanently" give up catching. Jackson is the full-time designated hitter. Heath takes over behind the plate.

Several articles are published in the New York papers alleging that the Yankees have "given up" on catching Boston, and will concentrate on giving their young players experience so they will be ready for 1979. This included playing Thomasson as the regular centerfielder, Heath behind the plate, etc.

July 17 — Royals 9, Yankees 7 (11 innings). Kansas City scores two runs in the ninth inning to tie the score, and four in the 11th to win. Only 1 of the 6 late-inning runs is earned, as the Yankee defense collapses.

In the bottom of the 10th, Reggie Jackson ignores manager Martin's orders to bunt the runner on first over to second base, and he is removed from the game. Jackson admitted that he disobeyed the signals, and is suspended indefinitely for insubordination. The loss dropped the Yankees 14 games behind Boston, the low point of the season.

AND ON THE 18TH DAY, THEY RESTED

After 90 games, the Yankees were in fourth place with a 48-42 record, some 14 games behind Boston. Only one regular had played in all 90 games, Chris Chambliss. Nettles and Munson had made 86 and 83 respectively. Dent had missed 27 games. Randolph was out for 23, and Rivers 20. Jackson was hitting .260, and suspended for five games.

The pitching staff was a nightmare. Hunter appeared finished for good, with a 5.97 ERA, and a sore shoulder. Messersmith was out for the year with a dislocated shoulder. Gullett also suffered from a shoulder ailment which would sideline him for the rest of the season. Dick Tidrow was 4-7 with a 3.78 ERA. Ken Clay was 1-3 with an 5.87 ERA. Highly touted rookie Jim Beattie had been battered back into the minor leagues, leaving Fenway Park in tears. Figueroa was 8-7 with a 3.64 ERA.

There were some bright spots. Guidry was 13-1 with a 2.23 ERA. Gossage, although 5-9, showed a 2.23 ERA with 12 saves. Lyle was 6-1 with 7 saves.

Similarly, Piniella was hitting .303. Heath was at .314 and looking like a veteran. Chambliss was his old self, steady, at .289. Thomasson was hitting .344 as a Yankee.

Through it all, Yankee president Al Rosen maintained that the Yankees would somehow catch the Red Sox and win the A.L. Eastern Division. He never lost faith . . . and was to be rewarded for his loyalty.

Below are the pertinent Yankee statistics as they stood on July 29, 1978:

NEW YORK YANKEES STATISTICS
THROUGH GAME NO. 90,
PLAYED JULY 19, 1978

Batter	Pct	G	AB	R	H	2B	3B	HR	RBI	BB	SO	SH-SF	IB	SB-CS	E
Blair	.190	44	84	5	16	5	0	2	10	8	12	2 0	0	1 1	2
Chambliss	.289	90	350	44	101	14	1	6	49	21	28	0 3	2	2 0	2
Dent	.244	63	193	19	47	7	0	3	21	13	10	3 2	0	1 1	4
Doyle	.233	21	30	4	7	0	0	0	0	0	2	1 0	0	0 1	0
Garcia	.195	17	41	5	8	0	0	0	0	2	6	0 1	0	1 0	4
Heath	.314	11	35	4	11	1	0	0	2	1	5	1 0	0	0 0	1
Jackson	.260	77	292	52	76	8	3	14	51	27	65	0 3	6	11 9	3
Johnson	.194	51	124	14	24	7	0	5	14	20	22	0 0	1	0 0	2
Johnstone	.222	15	36	2	8	0	0	1	4	0	5	0 1	1	0 1	0
Munson	.295	83	342	31	101	16	1	5	43	14	37	0 4	0	1 1	7
Nettles	.246	86	317	44	78	10	0	17	43	36	41	1 2	4	1 0	9
Piniella	.303	65	231	31	70	12	3	2	29	18	12	3 0	1	3 1	4
Randolph	.251	67	255	44	64	9	1	3	20	43	28	1 3	1	16 5	9
Rivers	.251	70	279	30	70	9	5	5	24	14	25	4 4	2	11 3	7
Spencer	.218	50	119	11	26	8	1	7	20	13	25	0 0	0	0 1	0
Stanley	.239	46	109	7	26	4	0	1	6	18	23	1 0	0	0 0	6
Thomasson	.344	20	61	13	21	4	1	3	15	6	9	0 0	0	0 1	0
Thoman'n (T)	.242	67	215	30	52	8	2	8	31	21	53	2 0	0	4 2	4
White (L)	.204		108	17	22	3	1	4	9	17	17	0 0	0	6 3	1
White (R)	.293		82	11	24	2	0	2	11	7	5	2 1	1	1 1	0
White	.242	53	190	28	46	5	1	6	20	24	22	2 1	1	7 4	1
DH Hitters	.230		330	42	76	18	2	15	50	32	59	1 0	3	4 2	0
PH Hitters	.317		60	11	19	3	0	3	16	3	12	0 0	0	0 0	0
Others	.167		12	2	2	1	0	0	0	0	3	0 0	1	0 0	12
Totals	.259		3100	390	802	120	17	80	372	278	380	19 24	2055	29	73

Pitchers	ERA	W	L	AP	GS	CG	SV	SHO	IP	H	R	ER	HR	BB	SO	HB	WP
Beattie	4.42	2	4	12	10	0	0	0	53.0	58	29	26	4	32	17	3	3
Clay	5.87	1	3	18	4	0	0	0	38.1	52	28	25	0	15	18	2	2
Figueroa	3.64	8	7	18	18	6	0	1	131.0	141	62	53	9	34	46	2	5
Gossage	2.23	5	9	35	0	0	12	0	80.2	54	29	20	9	31	69	1	2
Guidry	2.23	13	1	19	19	6	0	2	149.0	117	40	37	8	43	137	0	4
Gullett	3.63	4	2	8	8	2	0	0	44.2	46	19	18	3	20	28	1	1
Hunter	5.97	2	3	7	6	0	0	0	31.2	32	21	21	8	12	17	0	0
Kammeyer	3.24	0	0	6	0	0	0	0	16.2	14	6	6	1	3	8	1	0
Lyle	3.33	6	1	34	0	0	7	0	73.0	72	29	27	3	7	18	4	1
Messersmith	5.64	0	3	6	5	0	0	0	22.1	24	21	14	7	15	16	1	0
Tidrow	3.78	4	7	18	14	3	0	0	109.2	111	51	46	5	34	33	3	1
Others	3.97	3	2	17	6	0	0	0	59.0	64	26	26	4	17	25	1	1
Totals	3.55	48	42	198	90	17	19	5	809.0	785	361	319	61	274	432	19	20

AMERICAN LEAGUE EASTERN DIVISION STANDINGS

Boston	62	28	.689	—
Milwaukee	53	37	.589	9
Baltimore	51	42	.548	12½
New York	48	42	.533	14

STRANGER THINGS HAVE HAPPENED . . . I THINK

The Yankees made an All-Star break resolution: to stop the infighting, stop the excuse-making, beat back the injuries, and defend their world championship to the last day.

On July 19, they put their money where their mouths were. The first come back streak featured a five game winning streak, which ended when Billy Martin suddenly resigned as manager on July 23.

July 19 — Yankees 2, Twins 0. Figueroa six-hits the Twins, but the Yankees remain 14 games out.

July 20 — Guidry wins his 14th, a 4-hit 4-0 win over the Twins. No Minnesota runner went beyond second base, as the Yankees close to within 13 games of Boston.

July 23 — New York notches its fifth straight win, a 3-1 Figueroa victory, and pulls to within 10 games of Boston.

After the game, manager Martin allegedly told at least two reporters that Reggie Jackson and George Steinbrenner "were made for each other. One's a convict and the other is a proven liar." These comments were immediately relayed to the Yankee owner, setting off a series of events which led to Martin's resignation on July 24. Strangely enough, Martin first told the reporters that he wanted to be quoted, and then turned around and denied making the statement. (He later admitted he said it during a July 29th press converence.)

July 24 — With third base coach Dick Howser acting as interim manager, the Yankees lose to the Royals, 5-2, and the five game winning streak ends. The loss dropped the Yankees 10½ games behind the Sox.

July 25 — The Yankees introduce their new manager, Hall-of-Famer Bob Lemon. His reputation for being a quiet, behind-the-scenes-type manager, patience, and baseball knowledge were the qualities Al Rosen cited as the criteria for his selection. Rosen also made a point that Lemon and he were close friends in their playing days with Cleveland, and that Lemon had agreed to accept the job based on that friendship.

Lemon announced several changes in the Yankee lineup. Jackson would return to right field. Munson would go back to catching every game possible. Roy White, a forgotten man, would return to left field, and Piniella would play every day. The rationale: "That's the lineup which won the world series last year, and you can't dispute something which worked so well."

The Yankees responded to their new, quiet manager, who "Planned to let the players go out and play", by downing the Royals, 4-0, behind Guidry's 15th win. The deficit was now 9½ games.

July 26 — Superlative relief by Gossage leads New York to a 3-1 win, and brings the Yankees within 8½ games of the Sox.

July 27 — In a wild doubleheader, the Yankees trounce the Indians, 11-0, in the opener, and are trounced in turn, 17-5, in the nightcap. Jackson returns to the lineup and goes 5-for-8 with 4 RBI's, to support Figueroa's three-hitter in the opener.

Hunter started the nightcap, had control problems, and was shelled out of the box in the first inning. But, according to Lemon, there was nothing wrong with the Cat's arm, he'd just lost the plate. How right he proved to be.

July 29 — Its Old Timers Day at Yankee Stadium, honoring the five consecutive championship teams of 1949-53. Yankee manager Bob Lemon is introduced to a chorus of boos, courtesy of the Billy Martin crowd. Yankee public address announcer Bob Sheppard drew the pleasant task of making the next announcement, and after begging for the crowd's attention, received an assist from the scoreboard in announcing that the manager of the Yankees in 1980, and for many seasons thereafter (hopefully) would be Billy Martin.

What followed was an outburst of emotion the likes of which had lain dormant in the breasts of Yankee fans since Mickey Mantle Day in 1969. Martin received a seven-minute ovation. The official Yankee release read as follows:

New York Yankee Principal Owner George Steinbrenner, and President Al Rosen, announced today that Bob Lemon has agreed to a five-year contract to serve as Manager for the balance of the 1978 season, and for 1979, and that he will become the Vice President and General Manager of the New York Yankees beginning in 1980.

As General Manager, Lemon will replace Cedric Tallis who has been requested to stay on for another year before returning to his family and home in Kansas City to resume his duties as Vice President and Director of Scouting for the Yankees.

At the same time, it was announced that Billy Martin has had his contract extended for two years and will return as Manager of the New York Yankees, beginning with the 1980 season. In the interim, Martin will be consulting and working regularly with Al Rosen and Bob Lemon in the evaluation of the existing talent in the Yankee organization, from his home in Arlington, Texas.

A press conference will be held in the Press Room on the basement level, immediately following the 2-inning Old Timers exhibition game.

7/29/78

Oh, yes, there was a baseball game that day, won by Kenny Clay, 7-3. The Yankees scored twice in the bottom of the first inning on run-scoring hits by Thomasson and Chambliss, added a pair in the second on a run-scoring single by Stanley and Rivers' double, and were never headed. The win left New York 8 games out.

The next day, the Yankees split a doubleheader with the Twins, to close the gap to 7½ games, and took a 6-1 decision from Texas on July 31st to finish the month with a 58-46 record. New York had gained 6½ games on the Sox in 11 playing dates.

AUGUST: 30 MEANINGLESS DAYS

The month opened with New York hosting Texas, and winning, 8-1, behind Hunter. The Cat allowed just three hits in eight innings, and with Bucky Dent's return to the familiar shortstop position, the Yankees were almost all healthy. More importantly, the Yankees closed to within 6½ games of the Sox, WITH Boston coming to New York the next day.

THE DOG DAYS OF SUMMER

Some 52,701 fans entered the Yankee Stadium environs on August 2, 1978, confident that their heroes were ready to deal another telling blow to the reeling Red Sox. Boston had been slumping for two weeks, and the Yankees had been hot.

After a scoreless first inning, the Yankees nailed Sox starter Andy Hassler for 4 runs in the second. Piniella singled with one out, Jackson walked, and then Chris Chambliss lofted an opposite field fly ball down the left field line which Jim Rice never quite got to. It fell in front of him, allowing Piniella to score. Nettles followed with a two-run single, and later scored on a double by Randolph.

The Yankees upped the lead to 5-0 in the third, when Piniella doubled and Chambliss singled him home. That was to be the end of the Yankees attack for the night.

The Sox got on the board with two runs in the fourth, thanks to a walk, a single, a wild pitch, a ground out, and a two out single by Carlton Fisk. Boston kayoed Yankee starter Dick Tidrow in the sixth on singles by Rick Burleson and Jerry Remy, and a walk to Rice. Gossage came in and walked Carl Yastrzemski to force in a run, got Fisk on a pop up and struck out Lynn, before walking Jack Brohamer for run number four.

The Yankees stranded runners on first and third in the seventh, and Boston replied by tying the score in the eighth. Rice led off with a double and went to third on a wild pitch. At that point, a 35 minute rain delay kept the fans in suspense. When play resumed, Yastrzemski hit a sacrifice fly to center, and the score was 5-5.

The Yankees left a runner on first base with two outs in the ninth. The Sox stranded Remy at first in the tenth. Hobson walked for Boston in the 12th, but stayed there. In the bottom of the 12th, the Yankees put together a serious threat. Rivers singled and went to second on Randolph's sacrifice. Munson was passed intentionally. Piniella popped up, aud Jackson struck out to end the inning.

Inning number 13 came and went, and suddenly a new factor entered into this insanity: the one o'clock a.m. curfew rule, which prohibited the start of an inning after that hour. Boston threatened in the 14th, but left Lynn stranded at second base with one out.

Then came the bottom of the 14th. Again, Rivers led off with a single. This time he stole second base while Randolph drew a walk. Munson followed with a line drive up the alley in right center, a shot which was hauled down by Lynn, and one on which Rivers should have tagged up at second base and advanced to third. Unfortunately, he did not, and only made it to third when Piniella flied out to the warning track in center.

That brought up Jackson, again with the winning run on base, this time against Dick Drago, and again the slugger struck out.

The evening's activities were suspended.

August 3 — In the continuation of the suspended game, the Sox took the Yankees with two runs in the 17th inning, to end the five-hour marathon. The regularly scheduled contest was shortened to 6½ innings, with Boston taking the rain-curtailed contest, 8-1, to drop New York 8½ games out.

THE SECOND GREAT TURNING POINT

When Ron Guidry lost his second game of the year, 2-1, to Baltimore, Yankee fans thought it was all over. The loss cost the Yankees an opportunity to gain ground on the Sox, who also lost, and seemed to signal the end of what might have been a pennant race.

Few fans really cared when New York came back and downed the Orioles, 3-2 on August 5th, because Boston had won again. A few eyebrows lifted when Hunter outpitched Palmer, 3-0, for his second straight win, first shutout since mid-1977, and the 42nd of his career . . . but Boston won again.

The Yankees made it three straight with a 3-0 win over the Brewers on August 8th, but Boston won again.

And then came the great turning point of August. The Yankees trailed the Brewers, 7-3, in the bottom of the ninth inning. Boston had already lost, so it appeared that the Yankees would miss another opportunity to gain ground. Bucky Dent opened the bottom of the ninth with a single, but Roy White flied out to dampen the fans' faint hopes. Rivers got the crowd excited with a two-run homerun. Randolph was safe on an error, Munson drew a walk, and now the fans had something to scream about. Chambliss doubled down the right field line to score Randolph, closing the gap to 7-6. Nettles was passed intentionally to load the bases.

The batter was Jackson, and the Yankee slugger came through with a clutch "hit" — he took a Bill Castro fastball on the helmet for a run-scoring hit by pitch. With the bases still loaded, the Brewers obviously shaken, and the Yankee fans tasting victory, Piniella laid down a successful suicide squeeze, and New York had a 8-7 win. The gap was 7½ games.

August 10 — New York 9, Milwaukee 0. Guidry hurls his fifth shutout and avenges his first loss of the year. Chambliss drives in four runs with three hits.

August 11 — Hunter wins his third straight, a rain-shortened 5½ inning, 2-1 win in Baltimore. The Yankees have now won six straight, and 13 of 19 since Lemon took over the managerial reigns. The gap is 6½ games.

August 12 — This was the night the lights went out in Baltimore . . . three times! With repeated delays caused by power failures, and a gutsy performance by Orioles starter Mike Flanagan, the Birds stopped the Yankees, 6-4, to drop New York 8 games back of Boston. The Yankees were more than annoyed at the repeated delays, but worse was in store.

August 13 — Last night the lights went out, perhaps costing New York a win. This time, the rains came down, certainly costing the Yanks a win.

New York entered the seventh inning, trailing the Birds, 3-0, and proceeded to score five runs. Along came the rains (or so the umpires said) and out went the game, because the seventh inning was never completed, so Baltimore won, 3-0. The Yankees argued in vain that the field was salvageable, and that the game could have been continued if the Orioles ground crew had attempted to fix it.

There was a bit of irony to the whole thing. Baltimore manager Earl Weaver had registered a similar gripe after the 5½ inning Yankee win two days before.) The loss dropped New York 9 games behind the Sox.

August 14 — Yankees 4, Orioles 1. Gossage outduels Palmer in a relief role, and New York is 8 games out.

August 15 — Guidry hurls shutout number six and win number 17, a 6-0, four-hitter against Oakland. Jackson chipped in with his 17th homerun, and the Yankees were 7 games out.

August 20 — The Yankees drop a 5-4 decision to Seattle, and fall 8½ games behind Boston. This was the last time the Yankees would lose ground to the Sox until after their positions in the standings were reversed! August 26 — New York 6, California 2. Catfish continues his miraculous comeback from an arm "manipulation" which tore open all the adhesions in his shoulder, by winning his fifth straight game. The Yankees pounded 15 hits, including three each by Munson and Chambliss.

August 25 — Guidry wins his 18th, Jackson hits career homerun number 331 and drives in his 1,001 run, to lead the Yankees past the A's, 7-1. The game was worked by four amateur umpires because of the strike by the Major League Baseball Umpires Association. Unfortunately, the Red Sox continue to match the Yankees game for game, and New York remains 7½ out.

August 27 — Hunter wins again, to finish the month with a 6-0 record and 1.64 ERA. Chambliss and Nettles each hit two homeruns to highlight the 6-2 win, but Boston wins again.

August 30 — The Yankees down the Birds, 5-4, and gain ½ game on the idle Sox, as Guidry wins his 19th.

August 31 — Dick Tidrow pitches New York to a 6-2 win in Baltimore, and the Yankees close to within 6½ games of the Sox.

The month of August was over. Despite going 19-8, the Yankees had gained NO ground on the Sox . . . but they hadn't lost any, either.

SEPTEMBER

As the Yankees entered the month of September, they realized that their whole season depended on two things: gaining whatever ground was possible until they played the Sox, and taking at least 5 of the 7 remaining games with Boston. That later task seemed a bit unlikely, with four of the games scheduled to be staged in Fenway Park, a place the Yankees had won two games in during the last season-and-a-half.

"We knew that if we got within, let's say four games or so, that we had a real shot," said Piniella. "The trick was getting there. We had to play some awfully good ball to gain any ground, and we had two difficult teams to beat before we got to Fenway: Seattle and Detroit. Both of them had given us a lot of trouble."

CLIMBING TO WITHIN FOUR GAMES

September 1 — The Yankees open the month with a 3-0 loss to the Mariners, but Boston loses, also, so the gap remains 6½ games.

September 2 — Jackson and Chambliss slam homeruns to lead the Yankees to a 6-2 win against the Mariners. Figueroa is on the mound, and notches his 14th win. Jackson's homerun, his 20th of the season, makes him the 19th player in baseball history to hit 20 or more homeruns for 11 straight years. The Yankees are now 5½ games out.

September 3 — This was the GOOSE game. The Yankees led Seattle, 4-0, in the ninth inning, when the Mariners scored three times and had runners on second and third with no outs. Into the game came Gossage. He strikes out the side on 11 pitches. The Yankees remain 5½ games out.

September 3 — The Yankees split a Labor Day doubleheader with the Tigers, taking the opener, 9-1, for Guidry's 20th victory, but dropping the nightcap, 5-4. The Red Sox lost again, so the Yankees were 5 games behind.

September 5 — A 4-2 win over Detroit brings New York to within 4 games of Boston.

THE TAKING OF BOSTON 1 . . . 2 . . . 3 . . . 4

As the Yankees prepared themselves for their final, and most crucial foray into Fenway, a new spirit had engulfed the team vis-a-vis Boston's home ballpark. The talk on the bench and in the clubhouse was dramatically different from what the media had heard in recent years. Simply put, the Yankees weren't talking about how tough it was to win up there, or how happy they'd be with a split. Instead, there was a unanimous air of confidence, a spirit which filled the air with an exciting attitude of winning.

"Its hard to explain," said Jackson, "but somehow we all seemed to believe we would win up there. Sure, we had our work cut out for us, and we knew it wouldn't be easy, but there was something in the air which made everyone even more confident."

The pitching matchups were set: Hunter versus Torrez in the opener, Beattie versus Jim Wright in Game II, the Game-of-the Week pitcher's duel between the aces of the staffs, Guidry and Eckersley on Saturday, and the finale with Figueroa taking on rookie Bobby Sprowl.

The Yankees were healthy. The Sox were not. Remy was out with a hand injury. Hobson was suffering from bone chips in his elbow which hampered his throwing. Yastrzemski was playing a back brace. Fisk was exhausted. Scott had a bad finger.

It was exactly the reverse of the June series, in which the Sox had won two-of-three in Fenway, and split the pair in New York. In those games, the Yankees bench had kept New York alive. Now the Sox bench was to be tested. They were not equal to the task.

September 7 — Every seat in Fenway Park was filled this Thursday evening as the series opened. Yankee fans bravely talked of taking three-out-of-four games, but secretly admitted that a split would be acceptable. Red Sox fans jubilantly greeted the home team with expectations of a three-out-of-four showing, knowing that the performance would put Boston 6 games ahead.

What followed came as a shock to everyone. The Yankees opened a 2-0 lead on an error by Hobson, a single by Munson, Jackson's run-scoring hit, and Chambliss' sacrifice fly. Burleson gave the Sox fans a momentary thrill when he led off the home half of the first inning with a double, but Hunter left him stranded.

In the second inning, the Yankees struck again, scoring three runs on five hits, all of them singles. Two more runs came home in the third, and five runs crossed the plate in the fourth. It was all over except the screaming, with the Yankees winning, 15-3.

One side note: Hunter pulled a groin muscle in the third inning and had to be replaced by Ken Clay, who went the rest of the way. The Yankees were 3 games out.

September 8 — Sox fans shrugged off the opening game loss, recalling that their heroes had won the opener in June by a similar lopsided margin, and then watched the Yankees rebound the next night. After all, 15-3 losses were made to be laughed at. It could never happen again . . .

First inning: Rivers singles, steals second, goes to third when Fisk's throw sails into center field, and scores when Burleson bobbles Randolph's ground ball. Chambliss' two-out single scores Randolph, and the Yankees lead, 2-0.

Bottom of the first inning: Fred Lynn doubles, and like Burleson the night before, is stranded.

Top of the second: Piniella doubles up the alley in right field, and scores on White's single. White steals second, continues on to third when Fisk's throw again finds a home in center field, and scores on Dent's sacrifice fly. Rivers singles. Munson walks, and up comes the highly unpopular Jackson. Amid the ever-present chant of "Reggie Sucks" (one of the more printable mouthings, I

353

might add), the Yankee slugger drives a Tom Burgmeier screwball into the bleachers in right field for a three run homerun. Chambliss follows with a single, Nettles is safe on an error by the pitcher, Piniella doubles home the sixth run of the inning, and the Yankees finally go down on White's fly ball. SIX big runs on six hits and two errors.

Meanwhile, Beattie was playing the role of the master, holding the Sox to 2 hits until the eighth, and keeping them shut out until the 9th, when two unearned runs came in. A bit of a contrast to his June debacle in Fenway.

Final score: New York 13, Boston 2. The Yankees are two games out.

September 9 — The talk in Boston was that all the Sox had to do was win the next two, and the Yankees would have wasted all those runs and hits for nothing. Besides, today the "Eck" was on the mound, 3-0 against the Yankees in 1978. Sure, Guidry was tough, but he was a lefthander about to get his first start in Fenway, with that nice, close leftfield wall. And, the Sox were due to wake up with the bats, weren't they?

When the Yankees were retired in the first inning without scoring a run, the Sox fans were positive that this was their day in the sun. When Burleson and Rice got singles to put runners on first and second, the fans saw the big explosion on its way. All they got was a puff of smoke, as the Sox smoldered when Yastrzemski grounded out and Fisk was called out on strikes.

Guidry looked a bit shakey. He gave the Yankee fans another scare by walking the leadoff batter in the second and third innings, but left them stranded.

The Yankees struck paydirt in the fourth. Munson led off with a single, but was erased when Yastrzemski made a great catch of Jackson's opposite field line drive and threw to the infield in time to double Munson off first. Chambliss doubled with two outs, and Nettles was walked intentionally. (That made no sense, because the next batter was the Red Sox killer himself, Lou Piniella.)

Piniella lofted a towering pop fly into short right center field, a ball caught only by the wind. It fell to earth between four Red Sox (Lynn should have made the catch, but was not charging with the crack of the bat), allowing Chambliss to score. The Sox walked White intentionally (a good move because White is second to Piniella as a Sox-smasher), but Dent foiled the strategy by lining a single into left center field. A rare error by Yastrzemski allowed a second runner to score.

Rivers added a two-run single, and Munson singled home another run after a walk to Randolph, to give the Yankees a 7-0 lead.

Guidry did not allow another hit, finished with a two-hit, 7-0 shutout, and the Yankees were just one game behind the first place Sox.

September 10 — Suddenly, the Sox fans were hoping to salvage the fourth game. Luis Tiant was demanding the starting assignment, but his demand was denied in favor of rookie Bobby Sprowl. Chalk up another mistake for Red Sox manager Don Zimmer. Chalk up another Yankee win.

First inning: Rivers walks, steals second. Randolph walks, but is erased on a double play by Munson. Jackson singles home a run. Piniella walks. Chambliss walks. Sprowl is replaced by Bob Stanely, and the reliever gives up a two-run single to Nettles.

Second inning: Dent singles and steals second base. After Rivers strikes out, Randolph is safe on an infield hit, and Munson's bunt is allowed to roll too far, so the bases are loaded. Jackson drives in a run with a ground out, and Piniella singles home a run, with Munson thrown out at the plate trying to score from second base.

The lead eventually built to 7-4 with Gossage coming on to replace Figueroa in the seventh and yielding the fourth run.

The Sox almost tied it in the ninth. With two outs, and runners on first and second, Jack Brohamer lofted a high drive towards the wall in left field. The ball appeared headed for the screen, but descended into the glove of White at the last possible second. Another foot, and . . .

The impossible had happened. For the first time since 1949, the Yankees had swept a series comprised of more than three games in Fenway Park.

September 13 — Yankees 7, Tigers 3. After being ½ game out for two days, the Yankees take over sole possession for first place by one-half game. Rivers gets three hits, Beattie wins his third straight.

September 14 — Yankees 4, Tigers 2. Figueroa wins his 17th game, and the Yankees increase their lead to 1½ games over the slumping Sox.

THREE MORE WITH THE RED SOX

The Yankees and Sox squared off for the final time during the regular season, and for the first time, it was the Yankees were healthy, *and* in first place *by 1½ games). Furthermore, the Yankee pitching rotation was geared perfectly for this confrontation, with Guidry ready for the opener, Hunter in game II, and Beattie for game III. Boston countered with Luis Taint, Torrez, and Eckersley.

September 15 — New York 4, Boston 0. Guidry wins his second consecutive two-hitter against the Sox as the Yankees take a 2½ game lead. Chambliss and Nettles each hit homeruns to the delight of the 54,901 fans, who cheered Guidry's 8th shutout (tying him with Whitey Ford for the most shutouts in one season by a Yankee pitcher) and 22nd win.

An unusual play got the Yankees off and running in the fourth inn'ng. After Rivers led off with a single, and Randolph had also singled, Piniella hit into a double play. When Yastrzemski took the throw at first base, he noticed that Rivers was one third of the way down the line towards home plate. His throw bounced past Hobson ("I cocked to throw once, but Hobson wasn't ready. When I went to throw again, I was off balance.").

Tiant walked Jackson, went three-and-one on Chambliss, and surrendered a two-run homerun. Two pitches later, Nettles hit his third homerun in six at-bats.

September 16 — The lead stretches to 3½ games when Munson's sacrifice fly scores Rivers with the winning run in the bottom of the ninth inning, giving Hunter his 10th win.

For the first time since anyone could remember, the Sox drew first blood on Rice's first-inning, two-run homerun. The Yankees answered with three hits and a run in their half of the inning, and tied the game on Jackson's homerun off Torrez in the fifth. In the ninth, Rivers drove a shot over Yastrzemski's head, good for three bases. Randolph bounced out with the infield in, so Rivers held at third. The next batter was Munson, the best clutch hitter in baseball, and the game ended on a line drive caught by a diving Jim Rice while Rivers tagged up and scored.

September 17 — The Sox salvage the final game of the series, 7-3, behind Eckersley. George Scott breaks an 0-for-33 slump with a fly ball double to right center field, good for two big runs to break the game open.

The final regular season confrontation was over. The three-game series drew more than 165,000 people into the House that Ruth Built, the largest total for a three game series in the major leagues since 1958, the largest in the A.L. since 1950. It ended with the Sox holding on for dear life, and the Yankees up 2½ games with 14 to play.

EN ROUTE TO A TIE

September 20 — After the Blue Jays nailed Guidry with his 3rd loss (8-1), sparkling relief by Gossage and a three-run ninth inning rally wins the second game (3-2). That second game was of great importance, because, as Bob Lemon admitted after the game, "we'd started to doubt ourselves." After all, the Yankees had lost two straight games, and watched the lead dwindle down to 1½ games.

The big hits: run-scoring singles by Piniella, Chambliss and Nettles. Even better news came in from Detroit later that night: the Sox were mauled, 12-2. The lead was once again 2 games.

September 23 — Cleveland 10, New York 1. The Yankees drop their second in a row to the Indians, and suffer their fourth loss in six games, thereby enabling the Sox to close the gap to 1 game with seven to play.

September 24 — New York 4, Cleveland 0. Guidry raises his record to 23-3, lowers his ERA to 1.74, and pitches his third two-hitter in his last four starts. The shutout in his ninth of the season, breaking the Yankee record of eight (Ford) and tying the A.L. record for lefthanders set by Babe Ruth in 1916. It was his 14th win after a Yankee loss, and enabled the Yankees to maintain a one game margin over Boston.

September 26 — Figueroa earns his 19th win, and Gossage notches his league-leading 25th save, as the Yankees dump the Blue Jays, 4-1. Rivers' two-out, two-run double in the second inning opens an early lead for New York, enabling Figueroa to coast towards his goal of becoming the first Puerto Rican-born pitcher to win 20 games.

September 27 — Hunter wins his 9th game in his last 10 decisions, a six-hit, 5-1 victory over Toronto, enabling the Yankees to maintain a one-game lead. Nettles (27th) and Jackson (25th) hit homeruns.

September 28 — Guidry wins his 24th, a 4-hit, 3-1 win over Toronto. White has another fine day, driving in the first Yankee run, and robbing Otto Velez of a late-inning homerun which would have tied the score. The lead remains 1 game.

September 29 — Beattie hurls 4-hit ball for eight innings, and the Yankees score three runs in the eighth, to down the Indians, 3-1, and maintain the 1 game lead. Munson, Jackson, and Piniella each drove in a run, and Gossage earns his league-leading 26th save. The lead remains one game.

September 30 — Figueroa reaches his goal, and becomes the first native-born Puerto Rican to win 20 games via a 7-0 shutout over Cleveland. It is his 13th win in his last 15 decisions.

October 1 — Rick Waits throws a five hitter, and the Indians pound Catfish Hunter and four relievers for 13 hits and a 9-2 win, to force a playoff game at Boston to decide the AMERICAN LEAGUE EASTERN DIVISION CHAMPIONSHIP.

(Boston defeated Toronto, 5-0, to force the Boston Tie Party).

THE GREATEST GAME IN BASEBALL HISTORY

The Yankees and Red Sox, tied for first place, battling it out for the right to meet the Royals in the American League Championship Series (ALCS). Who could ask for anything more?

There they were, the arch rivals, a pair of teams whose antagonism dates back to 1904, when the Yankees (Highlanders) lost the pennant on the next-to-last day of the season on a wild pitch. The victors: the Red Sox.

In 1949, they clashed at Yankee Stadium the last two days of the season. The Yankees swept, and won the pennant by one game.

In 1974, a Red Sox sweep of a doubleheader at Shea Stadium cost the Yankees the Eastern Division Championship. In 1975, the Sox had embarassed the Yankees, burying them more than 10 games out of first place. The 1976 season saw the teams reverse their roles, with New York finishing on top.

1977 was a story in itself, with the teams battling until the next-to-last-day of the season, and the Yankees ultimately winning the pennant by one game.

And here it was, 1978, a year which had seen the Yankees fall 14 games behind, rally to a 3½ game lead in mid-September, and then falter just enough to enable Boston to tie. It was the year of the Great Boston Massacre, when New

York swept a four-game series in Fenway Park for the first time since 1949. It was a year of near hysteria every time the teams met, with the fans frequently taking matters into their own hands with violence in the stands. It was a year of baseball at its best, and October 2 would be no different . . .

And, it was also destined to be the year of the Great Comeback, the Year of the Yankees.

The stage was set. Some 32,925 fans had fought their way into Fenway for a Monday afternoon game. They booed the Yankee introductions, and wildly cheered their Red Sox. Mike Torrez was on the mound for Boston. His opponent was Guidry . . . what Yankee fan could ask for anything more?

After a quiet first inning, the Sox jumped on top on a tremendous homerun by their leader, Yastrzemski. They made it 2-0 in the sixth, when Burleson doubled and scored on a single by Rice (RBI 139 for the 1978 MVP). The victory champagne was on ice in the Sox clubhouse. Torrez had handcuffed the Yankees on two hits through six innings. The Boston Evening Globe printed its late edition with a banner scoreboard headline, showing the Sox ahead, 2-0, and predicting victory. Even Paul Blair, normally the most confident of Yankees, had told his teammates that it just didn't seem like the Yankees day.

In the top of the seventh, Blair told his teammates he had a feeling that this was their inning, and that they'd go out and score four runs. Nettles apparently didn't hear him. The third baseman flied out to right . . . but White and Chambliss came through with singles. Pinch hitter Jim Spencer flied out to left. The batter was Bucky Dent.

Dent took the first pitch, then fouled a pitch off his left ankle, hobbled around in pain, and accepted a new bat from the batboy, a bat belonging to Mickey Rivers. When he returned to the batter's box, he drove a long fly ball on to the screen atop the wall in left field . . . a three-run homerun . . . the Yankees led, 3-2. Who'd a thunk it!

Torrez walked Rivers, and was replaced by Bob Stanley. Rivers stole second, and scored on a double by Munson. The Yankees led 4-2, and Gossage came on to pitch the bottom of the seventh.

In the top of the eighth, Jackson deposited a Stanley fastball in the right-center field bleachers, a 420-foot homerun, whose significance became paramount one half inning later.

Boston had the heart of its order ready for the eighth inning, ready for another desperate shot at Gossage. Jerry Remy led off with a double. Rice flied out, but Yastrzemski singled home Remy, went to third on a hit by Fisk, and scored on Lynn's single. The score was now 5-4, and the Goose was in the pressure cooker. He turned down the heat, temporarily, by retiring Hobson on a fly to right, and striking out George Scott.

On to the ninth inning, and a classic finish to a heartstopping game. Evans led off and flew out. Burleson drew a walk. The next play was the game, the season, the everything.

Remy stepped in, and slashed a wicked line drive right at Piniella, a drive the sun-blinded outfielder never saw in the air. The rocket hit about five feet in front of him and bounced to his left. If it got past, it was a sure triple, and a tie game, with Rice the next hitter and only one out. Piniella lunged, and snagged the ball, then fired to third base to hold Burleson at second. (Burleson had to hold at first base until the ball bounced because no one knew whether Piniella would make the catch.)

Still, the Sox had runners on first and second, one out, and Rice was the hitter. The slugger brought the fans to their feet, ever so briefly, by driving a bullet deep to right field, but Piniella grabbed it near the wall for the second out.

The next man was Yastrzemski, the dean of Boston baseball, the time-honored veteran who'd have given a year of his life to play on a world champion. The Sox captain took one, and then took a tremendous cut at a Gossage fastball — and popped up to Nettles. The Yankees were champs, again.

The fans filed out of Fenway, a silent throng, suffering a pain only a Red Sox fan probably knows. The Yankees had arrived, seen and conquered, as only they could. It had been the strangest season anyone had ever seen.

For the statistically minded, the win was Guidry's 25th of the year (divisional playoff games count as part of the regular season) against 3 losses, the best percentage for a 20-game-winner in the history of baseball. (For more on Guidry, flip to the special chapter on Remarkable Ron.) The homerun was Jackson's 27th, enabling him to tie Nettles for the team's regular season championship. It was also his 10th game-winning hit. Shed a tear for Yastrzemski — it was the third time in his career that he made the final out in a post-season decisive game the Sox lost.

The boxscore/linescore is shown below:

AMERICAN LEAGUE EASTERN DIVISION CHAMPIONSHIP GAME

(October 2, 1978 at Boston)

New York		AB	R	H	RBI	Boston		AB	R	H	RBI
Rivers	(cf)	2	1	1	0	Burleson	(ss)	4	1	1	0
Blair	(cf)	1	0	1	0	Remy	(2B)	4	1	2	0
Munson	(c)	5	0	1	1	Rice	(dh)	5	0	1	1
Piniella	(rf)	4	0	1	0	Yastrzemski	(lf)	5	1	2	2
Jackson	(dh)	4	1	1	1	Fisk	(c)	3	1	1	0
Nettles	(3b)	4	0	0	0	Lynn	(cf)	4	0	1	1
Chambliss	(1b)	4	1	1	0	Hobson	(dh)	4	0	1	0
White	(1f)	3	1	1	0	Scott	(b1)	4	0	2	0
Doyle	(2b)	2	0	0	0	Brohamer	(3)	1	0	0	0
Spencer	(ph)	1	0	0	0	Bailey	(ph)	1	0	0	0
Stanley	(2b)	1	0	0	0	Duffy	(3b)	0	0	0	0
Dent	(ss)	4	1	1	3	Evans	(ph)	1	0	0	0
		35	5	8	5			36	4	11	4

									R	H	E
New York	0	0	0	0	0	0	4	1	0	5	8	0
Boston	0	1	0	0	0	1	0	2	0	4	11	0

LOB — New York 6, Boston 9. Doubles — NY: Rivers, Munson; Bos: Scott, Burleson, Remy. Homeruns — NY: Dent (5), Jackson (27); Bos: Yastrzemski (17). Stolen Base — NY: Rivers. Sacrifices — Bos: Brohamer, Remy.

Pitchers			IP	R	H	ER	BB	K
Guidry	W	(25-3)	6.1	2	6	2	1	5
Gossage			2.2	2	5	2	1	2
Torrez	L	(16-13)	6.2	4	5	4	3	4
Stanley			.1	1	2	1	0	0
Hassler			1.2	0	1	0	0	2
Drago			.1	0	0	0	0	0

Save — Gossage (27). Passed Ball — Munson. Time — 2:52. Attendance — 32,925.

358

1978 ALCS   YANKEES (3) v. Royals (1)

For the third straight year, the Yankees and Royals squared off in the best-of-five series which determines the American League Championship. For the third consecutive year, the fans were treated to an exciting series won by New York. There were two changes in the script: the series only lasted four games, and the Yankees did not wait until the ninth inning of the final game to win it.

Kansas City had high hopes as they entered the ALCS, even though they lacked the home advantage. The Yankees traditionally had trouble winning on the Royals' astroturf (forgetting the last two games of the '77 ALCS), the site of the first two games. A sweep, and, well, the Royals believed they could win at least one game in New York. More importantly, the Yankees were a tired baseball team. They had played the afternoon before the first playoff game in Kansas City, and won a tension-filled thriller from the Red Sox. Best of all, New York had been forced to use the best pitcher in baseball, Ron Guidry, during that Boston affair, so he would face the Royals a maximum of one game. (Had the Yankees won their division without the playoff against Boston, Guidry would have been available for Games I and V).

So much for the theoretical advantages. When the money was on the table, the Yankees found a second wind and embarassed the Royals, 7-1, in the opener, thereby gaining the split in Kansas City they so desperately needed. That win turned the Royals' fans against the home team, and even a 10-4 destruction of Dick Tidrow and Ed Figueroa in Game II failed to ease the pain.

For the Yankees, there were heroes galore, ranging from "The October Man" (Reggie Jackson) and the Yankee Captain (Thurman Munson), to "The Forgotten Man" (Roy White) and the "Golden Glove" (Graig Nettles). Guidry continued his magic by winning the clincher, 2-1, with relief help from "the savior", Goose Gossage.

The Royals were not without their heroes. Former Yankee southpaw Larry Gura gained a measure of revenge when he beat New York, 10-4, in Game II. And, of course, George Brett continued his career-long habit of destroying Yankee pitching, including an ALCS record three consecutive homeruns in Game IV.

GAME I: "The October Man" (Jackson) led the exhausted (?) Yankees to an easy 7-1 win in an outright embarassment of the Royals. Yankee starter Jim Beattie combined with reliever Ken Clay to hold the Royals to two hits, as Kansas City's "sluggers" repeatedly swung at curves in the dirt. The Royals also chipped in with six fielding mistakes, only two of which were "dignified" by an official scoring of errors.

New York drew first blood when White doubled and scored on Bucky Dent's single in the second inning. The lead grew to 2-0 in the third, when Jackson doubled, and scored on Graig Nettles' triple off the top of the right field fence. Two more runs corssed the plate in the fifth, and Jackson's three-run-homerun off reliever Al Hrabosky in the 8th inning iced it. (Hrabosky had put his foot in his mouth prior to Game I by repeatedly telling reporters that he couldn't wait to face Jackson, guaranteeing he'd strike the Yankee slugger out every time he batted.)

Linescore: (at K.C., Oct. 3,)

New York	011	020	030	7	16	0
K.C.	000	001	000	1	2	2

P — Beattie (W), Clay (6) (SV) v. Leonard (L), Mingori (4), Hrabosky (8), Bird (9). HR: Jackson. Att: 41,143.

GAME II: The Royals gained a measure of revenge by crowning the Yankees, 10-4, behind Gura. After scoring a run in the first inning off Yankee starter Ed Figueroa, the Royals blew the game open in the second. Clint Hurdle and Al Cowens led off with singles. Fred Patek followed with a chopper to shortstop Bucky Dent, whose only play was to third base. The throw struck the sliding Hurdle, and bounded away, allowing Hurdle to score. The Yankees pulled their infield in on the next batter, and Frank White responded by chopping a ground ball back up the middle for a two-run single. Tidrow came on in relief of Figueroa, but hits by Hal McRae and Darrell Porter scored another run.

Dent's two-run single in the 7th got the Yankees on the board, but Patek's three-run homerun in the bottom of the inning iced it.

```
Linescore
New York          000 000 220      4   12   1
K.C.              140 000 32x     10   16   1
```

P — Gura (W), Pattin (7), Hrabosky (8) v. Figueroa (L), Tidrow (2), Lyle (7). HR: Patek. Att: 41,143.

GAME III: "Neither team gave an inch," said Yankee manager Bob Lemon after the Yankees come-from-behind 6-5 win. The lead changed hands four times, and neither team ever led by more than one run. Brett hit three consecutive homeruns, several strange events occurred on the playing field, and Thurman Munson hit a monstrous two-run homerun in the eighth to rescue the Yankees.

The insanity began when Brett lined Catfish Hunter's second pitch of the game into the seats in right field, gaving K.C. a 1-0 lead. Jackson evened the score with a similar shot in the second. Gutsy pitching by Hunter averted a near disaster in the Royals half of the second inning, when he stranded leadoff batter Pete LaCock at third base.

Amos Otis was involved in the first strange play of the day. It came in the third inning, after Brett had led off with his second homerun off Hunter. With two outs, Otis walked. Porter looped a fly ball into short rightcenter which Mickey Rivers raced for and appeared to have grabbed on a shoestring catch (the replay supported the catch), but the umpire (Rich Garcia, in rightfield because of the six-umpire system used in the playoffs to get close-coverage and a better view!) ruled the ball had been trapped. Instead of speeding around the bases, Otis merely jogged around second base, and wound up on third, when he could easily have scored.

New York took the lead for the first time in the fourth inning. Munson led off with a double, and scored on Jackson's single. Piniella followed with a drive into the left field corner which Clint Hurdle snagged on one hop. Jackson slammed on the brakes at second base, but Piniella, running head down on what he believed was a sure double, went all the way to second. The result was two Yankees on the same base, and the Royals merely needed to tag Piniella to get an out. Hurdle realized the simplicity of the situation, and wisely threw to Patek at shortstop. Unfortunately (for the Royals), Patek threw to first base, and his throw sailed into the seats, allowing Jackson to score and Piniella to reach third. It also set up the second strange play.

With Piniella on third, Nettles lofted a fly to left field. Piniella tagged up, and appeared to have scored on a close play (once again, the replay backed the Yankees), only to have plate umpire Ron Luciano call him out. The "bad" call triggered a "Wild Man from Borneo" reaction by Piniella, who spent the next few minutes rolling on the ground, howling, gesticulating, and otherwise trying to prove that he had been safe. The fans loved it, Luciano didn't, but Piniella was not thrown out of the game, thanks to quick action by Bob Lemon, who got between the player and umpire.

Brett unloaded number three off Hunter in the fifth to tie the score, but the Yankees edged ahead on singles by White and Munson, and a sacrifice fly by Jackson in the sixth.

Gossage replaced Hunter to start the seventh. Brett was the second batter, and he drove a Gossage fastball to the wall in center field — the additional speed of Gossage's fastball (95 mph) to Hunter's (88) being the difference between a fourth homerun and a long out.

The Royals took the lead in the eighth. Otis led off with a double, and scored on Porter's single. After LaCock struck out, Hurdle singled Porter to third, and Porter scored when Cowens bounced into a force out at second. K.C. led, 5-4, entering the bottom of the eighth.

Royals' starter, southpaw Paul Splittorff, retired Rivers to start the inning, but surrendered a single to White with one out. The next hitter was Munson, a superb right-handed clutch hitter, so the Royals opted for righthanded reliever Doug Bird. His fourth pitch was driven some 430 feet into the Yankee bullpen for the game-winning homerun.

Linescore:

K.C.	101	010	020	5	10	1
New York	010	201	02x	6	10	0

P — Hunter, Gossage (7) (W) v. Splittorff, Bird (7) (L), Hrabosky (7). HR: Munson, Jackson; Brett 3. Att: 55,535.

GAME IV: Guidry and Gossage combine for a seven-hitter, as the Yankees edge the Royals, 2-1, to win the ALCS. Once again, the Royals drew first blood, thanks to a leadoff triple by Brett (inches short of a homerun) and a single by McRae. Nettles answered the Royals with a game-tying homerun in the second, and White hit what proved to be a game-winning homerun in the sixth. When Otis led off the ninth with a double, Gossage replaced Guidry, and retired Hurdle (strikeout) and Porter and LaCock (fly outs).

Linescore:

K.C.	100	000	000	1	7	0
New York	010	001	00x	2	4	0

P — Guidry (W), Gossage (9) (SV) v. Leonard (L). HR: Nettles, White. Att: 56,356.

Postscript: For Roy White, the pennant-clinching homerun capped a wonderful second half of the season. Back in June, he had been "traded" to the A's, but he invoked the "no trade" clause in the player's general agreement (players who've been in the major leagues for 10 years, and with the same team for five have the right to reject a trade) and subsequently had a tremendous second half. It couldn't have happened to a classier gentleman.

WHY THE YANKEES WON THE PENNANT

The fact that the Yankees came back and won the 1978 Eastern Division Championship is undisputed. The question to be explored is the methodology, or reasons, why New York won it. What follows is an attempt to make sense out of an insane season.

1. The Yankees depth: New York featured a bench which would have placed starters on any major league team. Time and again, Roy White, Lou Piniella, Gary Thomasson, Fred Stanley, Paul Blair, Mike Heath, Jim Spencer, Cliff Johnson, Jay Johnstone and Brian Doyle came off the bench to win big games. When Mickey Rivers was lost for two weeks with a wrist injury, Thomasson

361

filled in, hit .300, and drove a game-winning, ninth inning, three-run-homerun. (When Dwight Evans was injured, the Sox had to rely on Gary Hancock, a .150 stick.) When aching knees forced Munson out from behind home plate, Mike Heath came forward and hit .314. (Carlton Fisk played virtually every game for Boston, many with a broken rib.) When Dent suffered a pulled hamstring and an ankle injury, Fred Stanley filled in and hit a grand slam to beat Boston. (When Burleson and Hobson were injured at different stages of the season, Frank Duffy and Jack Brohamer simply did not do the job.) The comparison could go on and on.

2. Ron Guidry: When you have the pitcher with the best record in baseball, a man who repeatedly stops your losing streaks with super outings, a man who pitches consecutive two-hitters against Boston, you have a key cog for any team. The simple fact is that Guidry prevented the Yankees from ever losing more than five games in a row. The truth is that he, not Jim Rice, was the most valuable player in the American League.

3. Catfish Hunter: In June, it looked like the Cat had had it. In August, thanks to a shoulder manipulation which is among those miracles of modern medicine, the Cat ran off six straight wins. Psychologically, and on the mound, the Cat's recovery was crucial.

4. Bob Lemon: Billy Martin is a great manager for a certain kind of team. The 1976 Yankees were that kind of team. The '77 Yankees became that kind of team. The '78 Yankees were not, and would not change their ways.

When Lemon took over on July 24, he exerted a calming influence which healed all wounds and relaxed a tense atmosphere. He repeatedly handled touchy situations with a stern, but behind-the-scenes, form of discipline. His ego did not need credit for wins — he gave it all to the players. Without a manager who did his talking behind closed doors, and who let the best team in the world go out and play, there would have been no miracle of 1978.

5. The Yankees themselves: When the going gets tough, the tough get going. An overused cliche, but overused with good reason. The Munsons, Piniellas, Nettles, Jacksons, and White all showed their true professionalism by putting their differences behind them and going out and winning as a team. As Jackson said after the winning of the series, it was a team of professionals, a team you had to respect, regardless of the personalities involved. It was the Pride of the Yankees, that little bit of Lou Gehrig and Joe DiMaggio which will always be there.

6. Al Rosen: The Yankee president deserves a lot of credit. Other club executives would have pushed the panic button, but Rosen sat back, confident that the Yankees would catch Boston when they got healthy. He refused to make any rash trades to "shake things up". Instead, he concentrated on deals to strengthen his ballclub, trades that brought men like Thomasson and Johnstone to New York.

Rosen also served as the peacemaker between some of his warring Yankees, and added an understanding voice to a delicate atmosphere. Most of all, it was Rosen, and his long-term friendship with Lemon, that brought Lemon to New York Without that long-cultivated closeness between the two, dating back to their playing days in Cleveland, there would have been no Bob Lemon and no pennant.

7. The Newspaper strike in New York City: Without newsmen to complain to, the team settled down and played baseball. It's funny how the lack of a listening audience tends to quiet a crying child; even more unique that the analogy carries through to complaining adults.

8. The Boston Media: Take a look at the Boston newspapers for the month of September. All they did was talk about an upcoming, and steadily progressing choke. All they did was criticize everything that every player and coach, except

Carl Yastrzemski and Dennis Eckersley, did. They were like a pack of wolves waiting for the herd of lambs to make one mistake.

9. Yankee Stadium: don't know what it is, but there is a certain magic about the place.

10. The Yankee fans: Unlike their contemporaries in Boston, the Yankee fans stuck with their team through the lean days of June and July. True, the fans turned against Jackson during the Martin battle, but other than that they remained loyal, by and large, to their team. They deserve a lot of credit. They could have booed the Pinstripes into oblivion. They cheered Guidry, instead.

THE 1978 WORLD SERIES

Yankees (4) v. DODGERS (2)

The Yankees entered the 1978 World Series with all of the odds seemingly stacked against them:

*** No major league baseball team which had changed managers during the regular season had ever gone on to win a world series. (Only three such teams ever won the pennant . . . It is left to the reader to discover their identities.)

*** The Yankees were once again a squad of walking and disabled wounded. All-Star second baseman Willie Randolph was out for the duration. Mickey Rivers was suffering from a chronic leg injury which severely reduced his speed. Chris Chambliss was physically exhausted . . . so the list goes on . . . and rumor had it that Ron Guidry's bionic arm was "tired."

*** Randolph's replacements were utility man Fred Stanley and rookie Brian Doyle.

*** The Dodgers were a better club than the team the Yankees defeated in six games in 1977. The significant change was the addition of lefthanded reliever Terry Forster, the player the experts and oddsmakers believed would have made the difference in 1977   . . so they installed the Dodgers as 9-5 favorites.

*** As a team, the Yankees had been through a grueling season, and were tired.

*** The Dodgers were emotionally charged up because of the death of their veteran and beloved coach, Jim Gilliam. In fact, they actually dedicated the series to his memory.

*** Tired arm or not, superpitcher Ron Guidry (25-3 in the regular season, 1-0 in the ALCS) would not be available until the third game of the world series because he had pitched GAME IV of the ALCS.

*** Los Angeles had the home advantage.

Add it up any way you want, and the Dodgers looked like shoe-ins for the world championship.

***

How wrong the experts, gamblers, ghosts and Yankee-haters proved to be. Randolph's replacement, Doyle, proved to be a standout offensively and defensively. Forster turned in a very inconsistent series, and surrendered a crucial hit to Thurman Munson in Game III. The day of rest between Games II and III gave the Yankees the short-term relief they needed, and they proceeded to win four straight games after dropping the opening pair in L.A. IF the Dodger pitching was better, their defense had deteriorated remarkably, with Dodger after Dodger making key errors in clutch situations. As for the Gilliam factor, it proved non-existent in New York (perhaps the ghost got stuck in a midwestern snowstorm) and was exorcised out of Dodger Stadium by the time the teams returned for Game VI.

GAME I: With future Yankee southpaw Tommy John tossing sinker after sinker, and the Yankees pounding those pitches hopelessly into the ground, the Dodger offense exploded for three homeruns and pulled out an easy 11-5 win.

The Yankees went with Ed Figueroa, who remained a post-season enigma (20 wins in the regular season this year, 19 in 1976, but 0-for-4 in post-season decisions). Dave Lopes and Dusty Baker each reached Figgy for homeruns, and chased him in the second inning. Reliever Ken Clay gave up a three-run homerun to Lopes in the fourth, and by the end of the fifth inning, it was 7-0.

Reggie Jackson got the Yankees started with a homerun in the seventh inning (his eighth career four-bagger in world series play, and his sixth series homerun in his last four games), and Bucky Dent added a two-run single to make it 7-3, but the Dodgers came back with three runs of their own in the bottom of the inning, and were never headed.

GAME II: Most of the 55,982 fans who came to Dodger Stadium for Game II were undoubtedly familiar with the Biblical tale of David versus Goliath . . . But few, if any, could have guessed that a modern-day re-enactment was about to unfold before their very eyes.

Yet there they were, rookie Bob Welch on the mound, facing the Goliath of Gotham, Reggie Jackson, in the ninth inning of a one-run ball game. Bucky Dent (a single to lead off the inning) and Paul Blair (a one out walk) were on base. Thurman Munson had just lined out to right field. The count grew to three-and-two. Twice, the rookie fired fastballs towards the plate. Twice, Jackson fouled them off.

The ninth pitch was also a fastball. It crossed the plate six inches inside. Jackson swung and missed. The game was over. Jackson hurled his bat into the dugout, disgusted. Welch was mobbed by his teammates. Another classic chapter, reminiscent of the 1926 Grover Alexander — Tony Lazzeri episode, had been added to the annals of world series history.

(The Yankees took an early 2-0 lead on Jackson's two-run double in the third inning. L.A. replied with a run on a hit by Ron Cey in the third, and moved ahead, 4-2, when Cey took Catfish Hunter downtown with two men on base. Roy White brought the Yankees within one when he singled and eventually scored on Jackson's ground out in the seventh. That made it 4-3 as the teams entered the ninth inning.)

(Postscript: Graig Nettles robbed Steve Garvey of an extra-base-hit in the fourth inning, and later turned a neat tag-'em-out, throw-'em-out double play to end the inning. His acts proved to be an omen of things to come.)

GAME III: If things had looked bad for the Yankees when the series started, they looked bleak by the time Game III rolled around. New York trailed the series, 2-0. No team had ever lost the first two world series games and come back to win four straight games. Only a handful had lost the first two games, and come back to win four of the remaining five.

True, the Yankees had their season-long miracle worker on the mound, Ron Guidry, but he had hinted to members of the media that his arm felt "tired." The hint proved to be reality. Guidry was far from his best. He walked seven, struck out only four, and was hit hard in virtually every inning . . . BUT somehow, he won.

The "somehow" was Graig Nettles. Four times, Nettles was called upon to save the game. Four times, he responded with a variety of outrageous defensive plays which demoralized the Dodgers and kept Guidry in the game. Without him, 1976, dejavu, swept into disgraceful oblivion.

364

New York staked Guidry to a 1-0 lead in the first inning when White lined a homerun off Dodger starter Don Sutton. The lead grew to 2-0 in the second, when Nettles singled, went to second on a walk to Chambliss, advanced to third on a ground ball, and scored on Dent's bouncer.

(Well, there was a little more to it than that. The first ground ball might have been a double play, but Chambliss barreled over Lopes at second base, to prevent it. The second ground ball should have been a double play, but Brian Doyle duplicated Chambliss' cross body block, dumped Lopes, and allowed Nettles to score while Dent reached base safely.)

The Graig Nettles Show began in the third inning. Bill North opened the inning with a single, stole second, and moved to third on Steve Yeager's ground out. Lopes stepped up and smashed a line drive down the third base line . . . right to Nettles. After Bill Russell's run-scoring infield hit, up stepped the dangerous Reggie Smith. The right fielder smashed a one-hopper down the third base line. Nettles dove behind the base, got up, and threw Smith out at first base, thereby saving a run.

Nettles continued his show in the fifth. L.A. loaded the bases with two-outs. Up came Garvey. Result: a wicked ground ball down the line — the crowd moans at an apparent two-run double — but Nettles comes from nowhere, snares the ball, gets up, and forces the runner at second base.

The sixth inning was a near-duplicate of the fifth. L.A. loaded the bases, Lopes stepped up with two outs, and smashed a line drive towards Nettles. Nettles grabbed the ball on one hop and flipped to second for the force out.

It was still 2-1, New York.

Finally, the stalled Yankee offense got the bats rolling again. Dent led off the seventh with a single. Rivers was safe at first base when catcher Jerry Grote held his sacrifice bunt attempt too long. White's potential double play grounder became a mere forceout when pinch runner (for Rivers) Paul Blair dumped Lopes, again. Munson followed with a bouncer to third which Cey bobbled, allowing Dent to score. Lance Rautzhan replaced Sutton, and Jackson greeted him with a single, scoring Blair. Piniella followed with a run-scoring ground out, to make it 5-1

(Postscript: The Dodgers later admitted that they were totally psyched out by Guidry's reputation. "We lost to a mere shadow," said manager Tom Lasorda. "We made changes in our game plan because he was on the mound. We didn't have to. He didn't have his good stuff. We missed the boat."

Jackson's run-scoring ground out gave him 20 career world series RBIs, and ran his consecutive world series game RBI streak to seven, one short of Lou Gehrig's record.)

GAME IV: What would a Yankee-Dodger world series be without a controversial call. And, wouldn't you know it, Mr. Controversy himself (Reggie Jackson), was at the heart of the event in question.

The play came in the Yankees two-run sixth inning. New York trailed, 3-0. With one out, White singled and Munson walked. Jackson singled home White. Piniella was the next batter, and he lined a shot right to shortstop Russell, who dropped the ball. Russell raced towards second for the forceout, and then threw on towards first for what appeared to be an inning-ending doubleplay. . . . BUT, the throw hit Jackson, bounced away, and allowed Munson to score.

The Dodgers screamed interference. Manager Lasorda legitimately argued Rule 709F (a batter or baserunner who has just been put out, and who hinders the completion of the following play, shall cause the succeeding runner to be called out, too.) The umpires ruled Jackson had not intentionally interfered.

But that was not the only crazy play in this weirdest of world series games. In the first inning, Russell bunted for a hit, Smith walked, and Garvey lined to

Piniella on a hit and run. Piniella's throw back to the infield was directed towards first base, in hopes of doubling off Smith. Smith returned to the base safely. Russell, who was running on the play, never bothered to return to second. Instead, he stood and watched Chambliss calmly take the throw and relay it to second, where Russell was called out for a double play.

The Yankees countered with a bit of a miscuing of their own in the bottom of the frame. Blair led off with an infield hit, advanced to second on White's ground out, and tried to score on Munson's hit. He was gunned down, easily, by Smith.

Nettles was at it again in the third inning, robbing Lopes of an extra-base hit with a diving catch, but L.A finally got through to Figueroa on a double by Yeager, a walk, and a three-run homerun by Smith.

A 40-minute rain delay followed, but Dodger ace Tommy John appeared to have weathered the storm . . . until the seventh inning controversy.

The Yankees tied the game in the eighth when Blair singled and eventually scored on Munson's double off reliever Terry Forster.

The teams battled into the tenth inning, when the Yankees finally got even with rookie Welch by scoring the game-winning run at his expense: White walked to lead off the frame, Jackson singled, and Piniella singled.

(Postscript: Jackson's run-scoring single in the seventh gave him an RBI in his eighth straight world series game, thereby tying the record held by Lou Gehrig.)

GAME V: The dormant Yankee bats exploded for 18 hits, and rookie Jim Beattie scattered nine hits, as the Yankees won their third straight game, 12-2. (It was Beattie's first complete game of the year.)

Perhaps it would be fairer to say the Dodgers gave it away. After all, they made three errors, allowed a passed ball, threw two wild pitches, and had their best RBI man, Steve Garvey, struck out twice in succession with runners in scoring position.

Actually, the Dodgers should have known something was afoot when Mickey Rivers suddenly announced that his leg was healthy, and a desire to start in center field. He responded by getting three straight hits, two of which came in run scoring innings.

Then there was Mr. Yankee, Thurman Munson, banging out three hits and driving in five runs. Add in three hits by Doyle and Dent, and three more RBI's by veteran Roy White, and you had a day for Yankee fans to savor.

Interestingly enough, the Dodgers led 2-0 before the Yankee attack began in the third inning. Both runs were largely courtesy of Lopes, who used his speed to slip into home plate just ahead of relay throws in both the first and third innings. The Dodgers also wasted a great scoring opportunity in the second when Beattie retired Garvey and Cey with a runner on second, and missed a chance to open things up when Cey bounced out to strand two runners in the third.

The Yankees scored all the runs they needed in the bottom of the third. Dent walked. Rivers singled. White singled, to score Dent. Munson singled (after Rivers and White pulled a double steal) with two strikes on him, scoring Rivers. When Reggie Smith's throw to the plate sailed into the seats, White also scored, and Munson went to third. Piniella singled him home.

(For those who savor embarassment, read on.)

In the fourth inning, Doyle singled with one out. Dent bounced a ground ball in the hole at short, and Russell could not handle it, so the Yankees wound up with runners on second and third. Rivers bounced a single to left for a run. White bounced a ground ball to Garvey at first — he stepped on the bag for one out, and then fired home to get Dent . . . but the throw was wild, Dent scored and Rivers reached third. Munson greeted reliever Charlie Hough with a single, and the Yankees led, 7-2.

Hough, the erratic knuckleballer, continued to bounce pitches all around home plate, and in the seventh inning, he paid the price of such wildness. Jim Spencer and Doyle singled, and advanced to second and third on a wild pitch. Dent struck out, as did Rivers, BUT the third strike to Rivers found a resting place somewhere near the screen behind home plate, allowing Spencer to score. White singled home Doyle, and Munson drove home White and Rivers with a double.

The teams would return to L.A. that night, with the Yankees leading, three-games-to-two.

GAME VI: If one were to dream up an ending for this insanely miraculous season, he or she probably would have had the Yankees walking miracle, Catfish Hunter, pitch and win the final game . . . and that's exactly the way it happened. After all, Hunter was the flesh and bones embodiment of the miracle of '78. Like the Yankees in July, everyone believed that the Cat was finished before he submitted to a desperation shoulder manipulation, and like the Yankees, he recovered and attained new glory.

Admittedly, there was reason to wonder if the Cat had run out of lives when Lopes reached him for a homerun leading off the first inning, but Hunter settled down and pitched six hit ball into the eighth inning, when Goose Gossage came in to notch the save.

The Yankees scored the series-clinching runs in the second inning. With one out, Graig Nettles (who had been 3-for-21, .143) singled. Jim Spencer walked. The outfield moved in for the light-hitting Brian Doyle, who shocked the baseball world by driving a double to the opposite field, over the left fielder's head, scoring Nettles. Dent followed with a single, and advanced to second when catcher Joe Ferguson inexcusably dropped the throw to the plate (Doyle was a dead duck). Further embarassment was temporarily avoided when starter Don Sutton got Rivers on a ground out and White on a drive to left.

L.A. edged closer in the third, when Ferguson doubled, went to third on a sacrifice, and scored on Lopes' single. When Russell followed with a walk, the Yankee fans once again doubted Hunter, and he responded by enticing Smith to hit into a 4-6-3 double play.

Further embarassment was not avoided in the sixth inning. Piniella led off with a single. After Nettles flied out, Spencer struck out . . . BUT Ferguson did not field the ball cleanly and threw to first base, believing he had to make that play to get the hitter. Unfortunately for Fergy, when first base is occupied with less than two outs, the batter is automatically out on strike three. The throw should have been to second base to get Piniella on an attempted steal.

Of course Doyle added insult to injury by singling home Piniella, and to really rub salt in the Dodgers' wounds, Ferguson dropped centerfielder Rick Monday's perfect throw home, thereby allowing Piniella (who should have been dead out) to score.

In the seventh inning, Jackson drove home New York's final pair of runs via a tremendous two-run homerun to right center field.

The Dodgers staged a last-ditch battle in the eighth. Ferguson led off with a double, and advanced to third on Vic Davalillo's single. Out went the Cat (to a standing ovation from the respectful Dodger denizens) and in came the Goose . . . to strike out the dangerous Lopes, and induce Russell to hit into an inning ending double play (started by Nettles, of course.)

Final score: New York 7, L.A., 2. The Yankees had won their 22nd world championship.

* * *

Its still hard to believe that the 1978 season is over. The thrills that it provided the baseball fans of the world, and particularly the Yankee fans who

367

never gave up on their team, will never be forgotten. Somehow, I just can't help but wonder if somewhere in that great ballpark in the sky, Miller Huggins, Jake Ruppert, Ed Barrow, Joe McCarthy, George Weiss, Casey Stengel . . . Babe Ruth, Lou Gehrig, Earle Combs, Bob Meusel . . . are all sitting there, contentedly, just smiling, knowing that the Yankees are back, on top, where they belong.

Game I: (at Dodgers Stadium, Oct. 10)

New York	000	000	320	5	9	1
Los Angeles	030	310	31x	11	15	2

Pitchers: John (W), Forster v. Figueroa (L), Clay (2), Lindblad (5), Tidrow (7). HR: Lopes (2), Baker; Jackson. Att: 55,992.

Game II: (at Dodgers Stadium, Oct. 11)

New York	002	000	100	3	11	0
Los Angeles	000	103	00x	4	7	0

Pitchers: Hooton (W), Forster (7), Welch (SV) (9) v. Hunter (L), Gossage. HR: Cey. Att: 55,887.

Game III: (at Yankee Stadium, Oct. 13)

Los Angeles	001	000	000	1	8	0
New York	110	000	30x	5	10	1

Pitchers: Guidry (W) v. Sutton (L) (7), Rautzhan, (7), Hough (8). HR: White. Att: 56,447.

Game IV: (at Yankee Stadium, Oct. 14)

Los Angeles	000	030	000	0	3	6	1
New York	000	002	010	1	4	9	0

Pitchers: Figueroa, Tidrow, (6) Gossage (W) (9) v. John, Forster (8), Welch (L) (8). HR: Smith. Att: 56,445.

Game V: (at Yankee Stadium, Oct. 15)

Los Angeles	101	000	000	2	9	3
New York	004	300	41x	12	18	0

Pitchers: Beattie (W) v. Hooton (L), Rautzhan (3), Hough (3). HR: NONE. Att: 56,448.

Game VI: (at Dodgers Stadium, Oct. 17)

New York	030	002	200	7	11	0
Los Angeles	101	000	000	2	7	1

Pitchers: Hunter (W), Gossage (SV) (8) v. Sutton (L), Welch (6), Rau (8). HR: Jackson, Lopes. Att: 55,985.

(For the record, the Yankees broke four world series team batting records, all of which had been held by the 1936 Yankees. The total of 68 hits eclipsed their old 65 mark, their 57 singles surpassed the old record of 49, the team batting average of .306 edged out the '39 record by four percentage points, and their 222 at-bats broke the '36 record of 215.

The Yankees also extended their record for most world series games won, 107, and most world series won, 22.

The teams combined to set two records:

*** by using a total of 47 players, they broke the old mark of 45 set in 1951 (Giants-Yankees) and tied in 1959 (White Sox-Dodgers) and 1977 (Yankees-Dodgers).

*** by totaling 120 hits, the teams tied the record for hits in a six game series, set by the Dodgers-Yankees in 1953.

The Dodgers pitching staff also tied some negative records:

*** Don Sutton allowed 10 runs, tying the series mark shared by Don Gullett of the Yankees (1977), Slim Sallee of the Giants (1917), and Red Ruffing of the Yankees (1936).

*** Sutton's two losses tied the record for losses in one series, shared by more than a dozen, and accomplished most recently by former Dodger Clem Labine in 1953.

*** As a whole, the Dodgers failed to pitch a complete game, tying the record set in 1959 by both the White Sox and Dodgers.

And as for the almighty dollar, the teams set a world series record for the highest winning share ($31,236.99) and losing share ($25,483.21).

REMARKABLE RON GUIDRY

In 1978, Yankee southpaw hurler Ron Guidry had the greatest season any Yankee pitcher ever recorded. The 5'11" native of Lafayette, Louisiana, posted a league-leading 25-3 record, good for an .893 winning percentage, the highest for any 20-game-winner in baseball history. His 1.74 ERA was the second-lowest by a left-hander in American League history, bettered only by Dutch Leonard's 1.01 in 1914. His selection as the A.L. Cy Young Award winner was unanimous.

The list of record-breaking and record-tying performances goes on and on, and is listed below. It is the story behind Ron Guidry which is told here, first.

Born on August 28, 1950, Guidry grew up in the small city of Lafayette. His high school did not play interscholastic baseball, so he was forced to do his pitching in local amateur leagues. Surprisingly enough, he was a Yankee fan as a child, and remains one through this day.

His success as an amateur eventually attracted the attention of the University of Southwestern Louisiana, where Guidry pitched his college baseball. A fine collegiate career, including a no-hitter, attracted the Yankees, who drafted him in the third round of the June 1971 Free Agent Draft (not to be confused with today's Major League Free Agent Re-Entry Draft).

His minor league career was statistically unimpressive. Assigned to the rookie league club in Johnson City in 1971, Guidry posted a 2-2 record in 7 starts, with 2.11 ERA. The ERA boosted him up to Ft. Lauderdale (Class A) in 1972, where he went 2-4 with a 3.82 mark in 15 games. The Yankees saw something they liked, and promoted him to their Kinston club in 1973, where he went 7-6 with a 3.21 ERA.

In 1974, he was converted to a relief pitcher at West Haven, where his ERA ballooned to 5.26, but his progress up the chain of farm clubs continued. A 6-5 record, with a 2.86 ERA at Syracuse earned him a visit to the varsity in 1975, where he went 0-1. A phenomenal 0.68 ERA with Syracuse the following year gained him a late-season shot on the Yankees, where he got no decisions in 7 outings, but again cracked the high ERA barrier at 5.62.

Then came 1977, a surprise start in late April, a series of successful starts in May and June, and stardom by the time August rolled around. The 1978 season is best described in the list below:

RON GUIDRY HIGHLIGHTS — 1978

— Recorded Yankee record 13 straight wins to begin the season (2 short of AL record)

— Posted .893 winning percentage, the highest in baseball history by a 20 game winner.

— On June 17, he struckout 18 California Angels at Yankee Stadium to set a Yankee club record, and A.L. record for most strikeouts in a 9 inning game by a lefthander.

— 248 strikeouts on the season, tied him for 3rd in the Major Leagues with Phil Niekro, behind J.R. Richard and Nolan Ryan; it was 2nd in the A.L. — the 248 strikeouts broke the Yankee single season record previously set by Jack Chesbro in 1904 with 239.

— His 9 shutouts tied Babe Ruth's A.L. record for most shutouts by a lefthander set in 1917.

— Led the major leagues in wins (25), ERA (1.74), winning percentage (.893), and shutouts (9).

— 15 of his 25 wins during the regular season followed a Yankee loss; his World Series win also followed a Yankee loss.

— American League Player of the Month in June and September.

— His 1.74 ERA is the second lowest in history by an A.L. lefthander to Dutch Leonard's 1.01 in 1914.

— His 1.74 ERA is the lowest by a lefthander since Sandy Koufax' 1.73 in 1966.

— Yanks won 30 of the 35 games that Guidry started this year, and in the 5 they lost, they scored only 7 runs.

— Ron has won 33 of his last 37 regular season decisions; if you add his perfect 4-0 post season record, Ron has gone 37-4 since August 10, 1977.

— Ron won 12 of his last 14 regular season decisions in 1978, including 7 shutouts; 3 of his last 5 wins were 2-hit shutouts.

— The American League batted .193 vs Guidry this year, as opposed to .261 overall.

— Struckout 10 or more in a game 8 times.

1978

ERA	W	L	G	GS	CG	SV	SHO	IP	H	R	ER	HR	BB	SO	HB	WP
1.74	25	3	35	35	12	0	9	273.2	187	61	53	13	72	248	1	7

CY YOUNG AWARD VOTING (5 pts for 1st, 3 for 2nd, 1 for 3rd)

	First	Second	Third	Points
GUIDRY	28	0	0	140

GAME BY GAME WITH RON GUIDRY

Date	Opp.	IP	R	H	ER	BB	K	W	L	ERA	score
4-8	Tex	7	1	6	1	2	2	0	0	1.29	1-2
4-13	CHI	9	2	10	2	2	3	1	0	1.69	4-2
4-18	BALT	6.2	3	7	3	2	4	1	0	2.38	4-3
4-24	Balt.	7	1	6	0	2	2	2	0	1.82	8-2
4-30	Minn	6.1	2	3	0	4	7	2	0	1.50	3-2
5-5	TEX	6.1	1	5	1	5	7	3	0	1.49	5-2
5-13	kc	8	2	8	2	2	6	4	0	1.61	5-2
5-18	Clev	8.1	3	6	3	3	5	5	0	1.84	5-3
5-23	CLEV	9	1	5	1	2	11	6	0	1.73	10-1
5-28	TOR	9	3	6	3	0	6	7	0	1.88	5-3
6-2	Oak	8.1	1	6	1	2	11	8	0	1.80	3-1
6-7	Sea	9	1	6	1	2	10	9	0	1.72	9-1
6-12	OAK	9	0	3	0	2	11	10	0	1.57	2-0
6-17	CAL	9	0	4	0	2	18	11	0	1.45	4-0
6-22	Det	8	2	6	2	2	8	12	0	1.50	4-2
6-27	BOS	6	4	8	4	3	6	12	0	1.71	6-4
7-2	DET	8	2	6	2	2	6	13	0	1.75	3-2
7-7	Mil	6	5	8	5	1	3	13	1	1.99	0-6
7-14	CHI	9	6	8	6	3	10	13	1	2.23	7-6
7-20	Minn	9	0	4	0	3	8	14	1	2.11	4-0
725	kc	9	0	6	0	0	8	15	1	1.99	4-0
7-30	MINN	6.2	3	6	2	3	10	15	1	2.02	4-3
8-4	BALT	9	2	5	1	0	10	15	2	1.97	1-2
8-10	MIL	9	0	3	0	1	9	16	2	1.88	9-0
8-15	Oak	9	0	4	0	3	9	17	2	1.79	6-0
8-20	Sea	5	2	3	1	1	3	17	2	1.79	4-5
8-25	OAK	8	1	5	1	4	5	18	2	1.77	7-1
8-30	Balt.	7	4	7	4	1	8	19	2	1.88	5-4
9-4	DET	9	1	5	1	3	8	20	2	1.84	9-1
9-9	Bos	9	0	2	0	4	5	21	2	1.77	7-0
9-15	BOS	9	0	2	0	3	5	22	2	1.71	4-0
9-20	Tor	1.2	5	6	3	0	1	22	3	1.81	1-8
9-24	Cle	9	0	2	0	1	8	23	3	1.74	4-0
9-28	TOR	9	1	4	1	1	9	24	3	1.72	3-1
10-2	Bos	6.1	2	6	2	2	5	25	3	1.74	5-4

ALCS

10-7	KC	8	1	7	1	1	7

WS

10-13	LA	9	1	8	1	7	4

(lower case team indicates road game)

Guidry was 12-1 at Yankee Stadium, 13-2 on the road.

371

HOW CAN I GET GOOD SEATS?
(Or; the ticket department nobody knows)

At least once in every fan's "career", he or she wants to obtain good seats for that special game.

Do you really have to know someone?

"Absolutely not," says Yankee ticket Manager Mike Rendine, a 29-year-veteran of Yankee ticket office. "The key is shopping for your tickets. The wise buyer knows which games to select and why."

"For example, the biggest series of the season are ususally with Boston," he continued. "The wise buyer will come to the Stadium (because it usually has a better selection) and will shoot for the game(s) which is (are) not on the combination ticket plans. The absence of those combo ticket holders opens up hundreds of choice seats in Sections 16-20. That's just one of the tricks of the trade." (For more "tricks" see the section entitled: "Hints for Yankee Ticket-Buyers . . .")

Rendine joined the Yankees in 1950, and was assigned to the old downtown ticket office, long since supplanted by Ticketron. He advanced up the chain (director of group sales . . . director of season tickets . . . assistant ticket manager . . .) and became the ticket manager in 1972.

"The one thing I've learned in those 29 years is that anything can, and usually does, happen in the area of ticket orders," Rendine said. "And, we've become pretty sophisticated around here in the areas of stopping scalpers, screening would be buyers of large ticket orders, and generally protecting the fan's rights to get a ticket for every game and enjoy their visit at Yankee Satdium."

Hindering scalpers has become something of a hobby. First, Rendine limits the number of tickets a customer may purchase for a "big" game to a maximum of four. Groups must apply by mail, on the organization's stationery, and expect at least one phone call checking for authenticity. Frequently, the Yankees require the group purchaser to pick up the tickets in person, with positive proof of identification.

Of course the job is eased somewhat by the staff's knowledge of who the scalpers are.

"We don't sell any tickets to the scalpers we know," he said. "As the sellor. we reserve the right to refuse to sell to undesirable individuals. Of course, this policy occasionally causes problems. A favorite scalper technique is to get a couple of the local kids, and have them do the buying. Fortunately, we have men out on the street, watching for the buyer-scalper exchange. They can fool us once, but not twice. Sometimes, the kids yell racism or other excuses, but that's only when they're caught."

The ticket manager's job is a year-round burden. No sooner does the 1978 season end, than the 1979 planning gets into full gear. Season ticket plans renewals must be sent out, and new combination plans devised for the 1979 year.

"One of the headaches is trying to decide which games to put on our three combination plans Plan C (all Sundays and Opening Day, Old Timers Day, and a Holiday), Plan B (32 night games) and Plan A (more or less a combination of B & C)," according to Rendine. I try to include at least two games with every opponent, although that is sometimes impossible. In 1978, for example, we couldn't work in a second White Sox game. Our policy is to replace those games with a desireable substitute, so we added a Red Sox game. No one complained!"

Once the season ticket and combo plans are taken care of, the real ticket work begins: selling the single games to fans.

"We take all of the remaining tickets and separate them into four groups, with equal distributions of quality, lesser quality, and least preferred seats. One group stays here for mail orders. Another is released to Ticketron. The third goes to our facsimile ticket outlets (banks, restaurants, etc.) and the rest sit out by the Advanced Ticket Window at the Stadium. The tickets in each group are released in sections, with the best seats going on sale first. When a group exhausts its choice seats, we release its second most desireable section, and so on, until that outlet sells out its quota. We usually do not allow a group to use seats which have been "fed" to another outlet."

Another advantage of the Advance Ticket Window is the unique opportunity to bargain for better seats.

"The fan who comes down to the Stadium has an opportunity to talk to the man who fills his or her order," Rendine said. "That way, if you can't get the seats in the number and location you desire, you may be able to find an equally inviting alternative. For example, let's say six fans want to go to a game. If they mail in a letter asking for six seats in section 10 in the field boxes, chances are we won't be able to fill it. But, if they come down to the Stadium, they may learn from the man behind the window that he has six nice main level seats in section 6, or that he has two sets of three fine seats in section 6. I cannot emphasize enough the advantages of coming down here to do your buying."

The Yankees also offer an in-the-Stadium ticket exchange program designed to handle any problems which may occur while you're at the game. Its possibilities range from exchanging two pairs of tickets for four seats which are together, to moving from the upper deck to the main level.

"Our exchange window is designed to provide a service," Rendine said. "Once the customer is inside the stadium, we want him or her to have a good time. Sometimes, problems arise, making a change in seating location desirable. These can range from minor things, like the people in front of you being so tall that you can't see the field, to an escape from fans engaging in socially unacceptable behavior."

"At most games, the Exchange Window does a healthy business," he continued. "But, the fans should be aware that it is usually closed when a sell-out occurs, largely because of the volume of tickets sold, and the dangers of blocking up the lower passageways with people waiting to make exchanges."

Another problem is the lost ticket syndrome. Frequently, Rendine receives a call claiming to have lost tickets.

"Claims of lost tickets are always a touchy situation," Rendine said. "If the order came through the mail, at least we have a record of it, so we can issue a lost ticket voucher. If the party knows the section and seat numbers, we could also issue a lost ticket voucher. Unfortunately, this leads to abuses of the system, but we've become pretty adept at handling them."

"The general policy is to honor the original tickets if they show up until we can determine who really belongs in the disputed seats," he said. "If a party claims their tickets were stolen, we would like to see the police report of the theft before we'll issue a lost ticket voucher. In the end, I guest a few people sneak by, but our success ratio in this area is very strong, largely because we have a few other secret tricks up our sleeves to deal with those individuals who are slightly less than honest in their dealings with us."

What about the fan who suffers a death in the family, or other serious mishap and is thereby unable to attend a game?

"Every so often we receive a letter or phone call detailing a unique situation in which someone who purchased tickets for a game was unable to use them," Rendine said. "If the party indicates that there were exigent circumstances beyond their control, we attempt to work things out to the ultimate satisfaction of all parties. Of course, we evaluate each such claim via an in depth analysis before making a decision, because we know there are a few people out there who would attempt to take advantage of this type of situation. A lot of thought goes into it. We always try to be fair, especially because we want people to come to the Stadium and see the game."

HINTS FOR YANKEE TICKET BUYERS

The following is a "secrets to getting good seats" formula, compiled with the help of Mike Rendine (Yankee ticket manager) and his staff (Marty Roth, Irv Mehlmen, Luis Morales and Betty Rosenblum).

BEFORE you go to purchase tickets for a Yankee game, you should know:

1. There are close to 9,000 season and combination plan ticket holders. Their seats are largely in the field, main level and loge box seats, and occupy virtually all of sections 6-18 on the third base side, and 5-19 on the first base side.

2. The upper deck is by and large devoid of season ticket holders, so there are many superior seats located there, available on a first-come, first-serve basis.

3. You should learn the general locations of all of the sections, by number. (For example, sections 1-5 and 2-6 are by and large completely behind the screen behind home plate.)

4. Select the location you most desire to sit in, and have at least two alternates in mind.

5. There will probably be a better selection of seats at the Yankee Stadium Advance Ticket Window because they sell at a slower rate than Ticketron and the facsimile ticket outlets. Its only a 10 minute ride on the D train or Number 4 IRT line from downtown Manhattan.

Another advantage of the Stadium Window is that you can do more negotiating (see below).

BEARING THAT IN MIND,

1. Try to select games which are not on the Combination Box Plan. This frees hundreds of choice seats in sections 16-18 on the left field side, and 15-19 on the right field side. There is always at least one game in every home series which is not on the Combo Plans.

2. Decide exactly which of the following criteria is most important to you: type of seat (box or reserved — the boxes are closer to the field in all levels, and are slightly larger in leg room), location (field level, main level, loge, upper deck), quantity (not only how many seats but whether your group can split into smaller groups), and sections (do you want to sit by first/third base, etc.).

3. Go to the Advance Ticket Window and ask for seats for a specific game in a specific location. If the vendor has what you've asked for, you'll get it. If not . . .

4. NEGOTIATE! Maybe the vendor has reserve seats in that location, or maybe there are some box seats in the next section. Perhaps if you break your group into two smaller units, the order will fill. Or, if you're willing to go to the Saturday game instead of Friday night or Sunday, you'll have better luck. Maybe there's a good seat in the main level, but not in the loge. The possibilities are endless.

5. BE COURTEOUS. If you aren't, don't expect the vendor to be — they're human, too! Furthermore, the nicer you are, the more likely the vendor will take the time to search through the stacks of tickets for something you will like.

6. BRIBES simply don't work at the advance window, so forget about it. The regular staff doesn't dare take the chance. The part-timers are only around during the biggest games and post-season competition, and they are heavily supervised.

7. BUY WELL IN ADVANCE OF THE GAME, especially for Boston. (Simple law of supply and demand.)

If you have a special problem, contact the ticket manager directly. For example, if a member of your group is confined to a wheelchair, the Yankees have special wheelchair locations in choice areas for them. Usually, you're whole group will be seated there.

Similarly, if you have a complaint, remain calm and contact the ticket manager's office. You'd be surprised at how cooperative Rendine and his staff really are, and if the problem is one they can't solve, you'll generally be referred to the Stadium Manager, Pat Kelly.

The investment of 10 minutes time today can bring you better seats for the June Red Sox series ... and a more enjoyable visit to the House That Ruth Built.

WHO THE HECK RUNS THIS JOINT, ANYWAY?
(Or, the lonely life of the
Stadium Manager

Did you ever wonder how Yankee Stadium "works?" You know, why and how its kept clean, or what to do if you have a complaint. Or why certain exit gates are periodically opened and closed while the crowd is exiting? Or how much crime really goes on in and around the ballpark?

The purpose of this section is to take the fan behind the scenes at America's most famous sports structure, and in the process, supply fans with some valuable tips on how to cope with the occasional problems which arise at the old ballgame. The information was supplied by Pat Kelly, the Yankees veteran Stadium Manager, one of the leading experts on practical crowd behavior and control.

Cleaning Yankee Stadium

"I've often been asked how the Stadium is kept as clean as it is, both inside and out," said Kelly. "Most fans are amazed at the absence of graffiti, which is a sharp contrast to the elevated train cars which pass above the outfield wall every 10 or 15 minutes. Its not that we don't ever get any graffiti; it's our strict policy against letting it remain on our walls.

We firmly believe that graffiti attracts more graffiti. People see something written, and they figure that its okay to write on that wall. That's why at Yankee Stadium any graffiti which is discovered is removed from our walls within one-half hour.

The results have been tremendous. We really haven't had much graffiti around here since the park first opened in 1976. We're also grateful to the people in the neighborhood who always report any they see — they have pride in this ballpark and the team that plays in it.

As for the cleaning of the park's public areas inside the Stadium, we have a very definite system. Within 15-20 minutes of the end of every game, 75-150 sweepers come in. (The exact number depends on the size of the crowd that day.) They clean everything from the toilets to the aisles in the stands. The seating areas are swept and washed from the last row down to the front, where other employees wait with bags to collect the garbage. Once all the debris is picked up, it is taken to our two garbage trucks in the left field loading dock, and hauled away IMMEDIATELY.

It would be a lot less expensive if we waited until the next day to do the cleaning, but then we'd probably develop a rodent problem. Right now we have no rats or other vermin in the Stadium environs, and we consider ourselves very fortunate in that respect. After all, we are near a river in a large city, and that usually means river rats, but we don't have any. We do have four cats, though.

At the end of the season, every morsel of food is removed from the Stadium. Any and every area used by the public is cleaned, as are all pantries, concessions, etc.

Our basic policy is simple: a lot of money was spent creating a bright, new, clean, modern arena for the Yankees, and we have an almost holy obligation to keep it that way."

Crowd Behavior

"When people see Yankee Stadium, they think baseball. They expect to go to the game, have an enjoyable afternoon, and then leave in 10 minutes, after the game ends. The majority of them get exactly that, but occasionally, a problem comes up.

You see, people don't realize that when Yankee Stadium is filled to capacity, what we really have is a city of 55,000 people contained within four city blocks. Keeping all of them safe and satisfied is an amazing feat, and we are proud of our record in that respect.

Crowd behavior is one of the biggest problems in all modern Stadiums in America. Here at Yankee Stadium, we have a supervisory staff of experts trained in crowd control. They can pick out areas of potential trouble, and groups which are likely to cause trouble, before anything happens.

Our security system centers in the press box, where I sit with a couple of my assistants and scan 90-percent of the Stadium through binoculars. If we discover anything unusual or if we get a report of trouble, the information is immediately broadcast over our internal radio system. Every supervisor carries a walkie talkie. The result is instant communication, so our staff can get to a problem within 2-3 minutes, and solve it within 4-5. Obviously, I cannot divulge certain procedures we have for dealing with special situations, such as a large disorderly group, but we have set procedures which have been successfully and safely used for three years."

When the Red Sox come to town

"There's no doubt about it, the Red Sox present a special problem. Our rivalry with them is the oldest in baseball, and the fans on both sides are the most knowledgeable. Our problem is coping with the emotional involvement. Most of the incidents are not vicious, but happen because of that emotional tie to the respective teams. Fans get involved with every pitch.

Our preparation for Boston is to increase our in-house security from our standard contingent of special officers to double that number. Otherwise, there is not much else we do differently.

We even had a plan ready in the event that October 2, 1978 playoff game had been held here. We knew we'd have to sell 55,000 tickets in 4-8 hours of lead time. Just the crowd control of those lines, and then getting people into the Stadium, staggers my mind. We would have had to get the party ready for a full house right after it had been full the afternoon before. It would have been a challenge, but I can tell you something else: it would have been handled in good taste, and we'd have beaten them here, too."

The Fans and The Field

"Fans running on to the field after the clinching of a championship is a recent phenomena which has expanded throughout the country. The reason behind it is no mystery: the fans' enthusiasm simply spills on to the field.

We've come to realize that at the end of a playoff or world series, fans are going to come on to the field. There is no way to prevent it, and, in fact, it may not be such a bad thing anyway.

Our answer is to let the fans have the field after a championship is won. We've got a happy and exuberant crowd, and all they want to do is get out there and celebrate. The actual damage to the field is minimal (less than $1,500 after the American League Playoffs, and less than $3,000 after the fifth game of the 1978 world series), so our concern is simply that no one gets hurt. We also know that a major reason for going on the field is to get on television. That's why we start turning down the lights after about 5 minutes — it becomes too dim for the cameras, and that encourages people to leave. A ten-minute celebration is enough for most fans.

You know, there was a time when the fans were invited onto the field after every home game. Unfortunately, that was in a different era. We had a different type of life style then. People took directions in those days. They were told to stay on the warning track, and they did. They understood that the worst thing for a sod lawn is people with heavy shoes walking all over it. In those days, the fans just walked around the park once, stopped to see the monuments and plaques close up, and then left the park.

Unfortunately, we can't do it anymore, because there are a handful of people who simply will not cooperate, and because the monuments are now located in an area which is fenced in."

Crime at Yankee Stadium

"People should feel safe when they come to a ballpark, especially because baseball is a family spectator sport, and Yankee Stadium is no exception. In fact, our crime rate is very low for a sports stadium, and especially low when you consider that we are located in the South Bronx. To use realistic ballpark figures, we had only 2 or 3 felonies reported in and around the Stadium on game days and nights during the 1978 season. None of the perpetrators escaped apprehension by the police. Similarly, we had less than 100 misdemeanors, and less than 10 escaped.

Those statistics are pretty impressive when you remember that we are dealing with a total of 2½ million fans who came to Yankee Stadium in 1978.

Any fan who suffers any kind of criminal incident should report it to a member of the Stadium staff (i.e. — usher, stadium police, supervisor, etc.) immediately. Within seconds, the crime and a description of the perpetrator are put over our walkie talkie system, and within 5 minutes the Stadium is effectively sealed off and on the look out for the perpetrator.

Fans should also know that we have an official New York City Police Dept. sub-station located in Yankee Stadium. We also have a full-scale anti-crime force outside, including many plain clothesmen walking beats all over the area.

(The author recently had an experience with one of those plain clothesmen. After the fifth game of the 1978 world series, the author returned to his car and discovered a bearded man leaving the car on the passenger side. When challenged, he identified himself as a police officer, and explained that he and his partner had just apprehended the person seated in the squad car to our right trying to steal the author's family car. The point is simple: the police are doing their job effectively in the area.)

It all comes down to the same thing: we want the fans who come here to feel safe. Baseball has to be a family tradition. We want dad and mom and the kids here, and we want them to come again."

Alcoholic Beverages

"Recently, a friend of mine told me that up in Boston he could not buy a beer in the stands. They have returned to their old policy of no vendor sales of alcoholic beverages in the stands, and a maximum of two beers per buyer at the concessions.

Fortunately, we don't have the same problems in our stands as Boston does in their stands. The availability of alcoholic beverages is only a problem when people make it one, and our experience has by and large shown that only a handful of groups in Yankee Stadium ever cause alcohol-related problems. It would make no sense to ban the sale of alcoholic beverages because of a scattered few.

377

Let me point something else out. The only time I really get to watch a game is when I go to Shea Stadium and see the Mets while we're on the road. Its impossible for me to watch the Yankees at home because that's when I'm the busiest. Anyway, when I go out to Shea, I like to have a beer and a hot dog; that's as much a part of baseball as the pitcher's mound.

Besides, people are used to service nowadays. If you paid $7 to go to a game, and had to go to a concession stand from which you can't see the game to get a beer, you would not be too happy. You'd probably miss an inning or two, because the lines would be long. This way, by selling through vendors in the stands, the fan gets to sit and watch the game he paid to see. It only seems fair. Do you penalize 2.49 million people because of less than 1,000 who cannot control themselves? My opinion, and that of the Yankees, is to cater to the best fans in the world, the Yankee fans."

And If A Fight Breaks Out

"If a fight or incident is spotted from our control location, or reported by anyone, we send a supervisor to the area immediately. We have about 15 of them on duty at every game, and each is a specialist in the field of crowd behavior and fan psychology. There are two or three on every level of the stadium. The supervisor arrives on the scene and oversees the special officers who do the dirty work of calming things down. The supervisor makes an evaluation of the situation. More often than not, it is not a serious condition, and the emotions quickly dissipate. If the supervisor believes that the parties involved have to be separated for the remainder of the event, we move one or the other. If the incident is criminal in nature, we bring the parties down to the in-house police sub-station."

If You Have A Problem While You Are At Yankee Stadium

I frequently receive letters about incidents or unpleasant situations that occur during a game. The thing that really irks me is: why in the world do people sit through a game and suffer? Why not report the problem immediately, so it will be rectified in a few short minutes, so you can enjoy yourself for the rest of the game.

If a fan has a problem, he or she should immediately inform a park employee (usher, special policeman, etc.). The fan should not feel obligated to sit still and suffer. The fan has paid good money for a good time, and the stadium personnel are there to insure it. Don't let a socially unacceptable situation continue.

I recently received a letter from a fan who complained that his seat was broken and he had to sit through a doubleheader in great discomfort. On the same day, I received a letter from another fan, thanking me for the rapid repair of his seat during the same doubleheader. The point is obvious: any person who has a broken seat, or any other problem, should report it immediately. If the problem isn't rectified within 5 minutes, go to the Patron Services Room behind first base, and file a complaint there. Your problem will be funneled to the proper department head, and the situation will be resolved within minutes.

LETTERS

If for any reason a fan did not complain during the game, and decides to write a letter describing a problem, it is essential that he or she indicate the section, and preferably the seat, that he or she sat in for the given game. We have section by section assignment sheets for every home event, so I can easily find out who was stationed there.

When we receive a letter, we immediately check out the complaint. If we can confirm that a problem did occur, and in the case of misconduct by a stadium employee, we will invite the people back for another game. We try to put our best foot forward. Fans have to understand that we have 400-800 people on duty at every game. Each employee gets to make one mistake in dealing with the fans. After the second one, he or she is gone, provided we have some formal proof of misconduct.

When I say formal proof, I mean a name or a badge number. Every usher has a name printed on his hat. Every officer wears a badge with a number. WE WANT FEEDBACK ABOUT OUR PERSONNEL, and we invite complimentary and antagonistic letters. The reason we need a name or badge number is that we are dealing with unions, and we have to substantiate our hiring/firing decisions.

On Your Way Out

One of the most common complaints I get is from fans who can't understand why it takes 10 minutes to get into the ballpark, and 20 or 30 minutes to get out. Fans are always asking why all of the gates aren't open.

The answers to these types of questions are simple. Fans begin entering the park two hours before game time. If we have a crowd of 48,000 people, that means an average of 400 fans a minute coming in. The entry is spread over a 120 minute time span, and its really longer than that because many fans arrive after the game has begun.

When the game ends, we are faced with the task of sending those same 48,000 people out of the park and on to the streets. If we let them out in 10 minutes time, that would mean herding them out at a rate of 4800 a minute. There simply isn't enough room on the concourses and streets adjacent to the Stadium to handle that type of crowd at that rate. Dozens would get hurt. Our solution is to control the rate by selectively opening and closing different gates. The goal is a safe, and reasonably quick, exit from the park.

Also, if everyone got out in 10 minutes, they'd get to their car, or to the subway, at virtually the same time. Then, what would they do? They'd wind up sitting in a smoke-filled parking lot, waiting half an hour or more to get out. This way, we try to ease the congestion in the lots as well.

A Final Word

The Yankees have a committment to the baseball fans of the world, and particularly to the Yankee fans, to offer the best in baseball, every year and in every way. The fan pays his or her way into Yankee Stadium, and that's the fact the New York Yankees want their employees to keep in mind all the time. Our fans deserve only the best, and my job is to see that they get it.

ANDY CAREY REMEMBERS:

(A trip down memory lane with a key member of the champions of the world from 1952-60.)

Looking back, I'd have to say I was very fortunate to play for the Yankees during the 1950's. Our manager was Casey Stengel, a man many people consider the greatest manager in baseball history. My teammates were the cream of the crop — their records stand out for all to see. We won the pennant every year, except 1954 and 59, and we did it playing in front of the greatest fans in the world, the Yankee fans of New York City.

I guess that the best place to start this trip is with Don Larsen's perfect game in the 1956 world series. A lot of people may have forgotten that I was the third baseman in that game, and I'm proud to have been able to make a real contribution. Early in the game, Jackie Robinson hit a line shot that I just got my glove on. The ball deflected on two bounces to Gil McDougald (at shortstop). He threw to first base, and we had Robinson by a hair. Interestingly enough, we'd practiced that play several times, never expecting it to come up, but there it was, in a crucial situation.

In the eighth inning, Gil Hodges hit a low line drive that I snagged to help preserve the perfect game. The rest is history, but there is an interesting sidelight that very few people have ever heard about.

My dad and Larsen were good friends. The night before the game, Dad had gone down to Times Square to one of those old newspaper places where you could have any headline printed up that you wanted. He printed two: Larsen Pitches No-Hitter" and "Gooney Bird Wins Fifth Game." (Note: that was Larsen's nickname.) Dad went up to Larsen's room and put them on the doorknob. Later, he went back and took the "No-Hitter" sign down and ripped it up. The rest is history, but I still have the other headline in my scrapbook.

Now, let's go back to the beginning. I began my career at the AAA level. My manager was former Yankee George "Twinkletoes" Selkirk. Midway through the season, I was in a terrible batting slump, and I let it affect my fielding. One day I actually dropped a pop fly with the bases loaded and cost us a ballgame. Selkirk got me in the clubhouse after the game and really bawled me out. He tore me apart, right in front of the whole team. I was actually in tears, and boy was I angry. In fact, I go so angry that I went out and got 18 hits in my next 21 at-bats.

Maybe Selkirk was the one who tipped off Stengel, and maybe Stengel learned it himself, but Casey was an expert at getting the most out of me. He knew I was a feisty player, so he'd yell at me, blame things on me, do anything to make me angry, because I was a better ballplayer when I was enraged. The angrier I got, the better I played, and the better I played, the more I loved him for it. Casey and I got along great.

The first time I met Stengel was in spring training at St. Petersburg. He found me alone, in the locker room, shaving, and he started talking to me. Well, to be respectful, I stopped shaving and listened to him . . . half an hour later, the shaving cream on my face had disappeared, and he was still talking. Funniest thing about it: I never remembered a word he said. Maybe that's why he always called me Max Carey (a fine outfielder for the Pirates and Dodgers from 1910-1929, the years in which Stengel did most of his playing in the National League.).

Casey's clubhouse meetings were something. He never mentioned any names, and he was always comical and relating outside life into the game. Did you ever hear him when he went before Congress during the baseball hearings of the 1950s? He drove them crazy with his "Stengelese", that crazy language he had. It was really a language in itself.

One other Stengel story. We were playing up in Boston one day, losing by a run or two. There were two outs in the ninth inning, and I was the batter. The count was two strikes. All of a sudden, Billy Martin comes out of the dugout, calls time, and comes over to tell me something: "The Old Man (Stengel) wants you to hit a homerun." And, I did. You should have heard their catcher, I think it was Haywood Sullivan, muttering unprintables when I crossed the plate. He just couldn't believe it.

On a personal basis, my greatest thrill came in the 1953 world series, when I was sent up to pinch hit against Johnny Podres. I hit a triple, and was ecstatic. Unfortunately, we lost the game, but not the series.

By 1960, I knew that my days as a Yankee were numbered. I'd missed most of the previous season with a chronic back problem, and then I came down with mononucleosis. Along came Clete Boyer, and in spring training I wasn't playing much. The trade came as no surprise. First I went to Kansas City. They sent me to the White Sox, who sent me to the Phillies. I really didn't want to go to Philadelphia, so I worked out my own deal to go to the Dodgers instead. We almost won the pennant in 1962, but we lost to the Giants in the playoff series. It would have been interesting playing against the Yankees in a world series.

Today, People always ask me about today's ballplayers, and especially about the money they make. All I can say is that I'd like to be making their money, and I think its great for them because their playing careers are limited. I was lucky. I signed with the Yankees for a large bonus, and I took home five world series checks. Also, I was in the broker's business on the side, so I was financially secure.

I guess that I'll close it out by saying that I was fortunate enough to be a part of history in a pleasant way. How many people can look back and say that?

THE LANGUAGE CALLED STENGELESE

No book about the Yankees could ever be complete without at least a touch of the language immortalized by former Yankee skipper Casey Stengel. "The Ol Professor" thrilled the media and fans alike with a combination of nonsense and an incredible sense of humor, mixed in with some surprisingly deep reflections on life. Here are a few samples.

"I always heard it couldn't be done, but sometimes it don't always work." (Stengel's remarks to the press after learning that Indians manager Al Lopez planned to use a three-man rotation — Mike Garcia, Early Wynn and Bob Lemon — for the final 12 games of the 1952 pennant race.)

"They examined all my organs. Some of them are quite remarkable, and others are not so good. A lot of museums are bidding for them." (Stengel's remarks to the media after his release from the hospital in 1974.)

In 1958, the United States Senate held a series of committee hearings regarding legislation which would have ended baseball's special exemption from federal anti-trust laws. The Kefauver committee invited several current and former stars to speak as witnesses, including Stengel.

Given the opportunity to give some inside information to the "powers that be, unless of course, they lose the election, in which case they were but aren't," Stengel responded with a lecture which ranks among the finest of his career. The lecture began after Senator Kefauver asked Stengel why baseball wanted to maintain its exempt status:

"Well, I would have to say at the present time, I think that baseball has advanced in this respect for the player help. That is an amazing statement for me to make because you can retire with an annuity at 50, and what organization in America allows you to retire at 50 and receive money?

I want to further state that I am not a ball player, that is, put into that pension fund committee. At my age, and I have been in baseball, well, I say I am possibly the oldest man who is working in baseball. I would say that when they start an annuity for the ball players to better their conditions, it should have been done, and I think it has been done . . .

The reason they possibly did not take the managers in at that time was because radio and television or the income to the ballclubs was not large enough that you could have put in a pension plan . . .

Now the second thing about baseball that I think is very interesting to the public or to all of us that it is the owner' fault if he does not improve his club, along with the officials in the ball clubs and the players. Now what causes that?

381

If I am going to go on the road and we are a travelling ball club and you know the cost of transportation now — we travel sometimes with three Pullman coaches, the New York Yankees, and remember I am just a salaried man and do not own stock in the New York Yankees. I found out that in travelling with the Yankees on the road and all, that it is the best, and

We have broken records in Washington this year, we have broken them in every city but New York and we have lost two clubs that have gone out of the city of New York.

Of course, we have had some bad weather, I would say that they are mad at us in Chicago, we fill the parks. They have come out to see good material, I will say they are mad at us in Kansas City, but we broke the attendance record.

Now on the road we only get possibly 27 cents. I am not positive of these figures, as I am not an official. If you go back 15 years, or if I owned stock in the club, I would give them to you . . ."

(Stengel continued on for more than 45 minutes, never addressing the legislation before the committee, and never answering any of the material questions put before him.)

(Note: the next witness was Mickey Mantle, a man whose great sense of humor could not pass up the opportunity to answer Senator Kefauver's first question by quipping: "My views are about the same as Casey's.")

CAREER HIGHLIGHTS

HANK BAUER: I had two real highlights with the Yankees. My favorite came in the 1958 world series, when I hit four homeruns. The second was the 1951 series, when I tripled with the bases loaded in the final game, and then caught the final out while lying on my side on a sliding catch.

YOGI BERRA: "I'd have to say my career highlight was (Don) Larsen's perfect game in the 1956 world series. Funny thing about that game — nowadays, everyone talks abou the pressure of keeping the perfect game going in the late innings, but the truth is that we were just worried about winning the game. People forget that we were only leading 2-0. That's a walk and a homerun, and a tie ballgame. As things turned out, we got to bake the cake and eat it."

BILL BEVENS: My major league highlight came on October 3, 1947, during the world series against the Dodgers. I pitched eight-and-two-thirds-innings of hitless baseball, and led 2-1 in the ninth inning. The Dodgers had two men on base on walks, and sent Cookie Lavagetto up to pinch hit. He slashed a double off the right field wall, driving in both runs, and giving the Dodgers a win.

The second highlight came in 1944, when the Yankees recalled me from Newark, and I pitched a one-hitter against the Red Sox.

I also have to mention two other games. In 1946, Bob Feller no-hit us, and I was the losing pitcher. I had a shutout until the ninth inning, when I gave up a homerun, and lost, 1-0. At least I got to win a couple of games, like in 1939, when I pitched two no-hitters in the minor leagues.

JOHNNY BLANCHARD: Just being a small part of the great Yankee tradition is a highlight in itself, but on a personal level, the highlight of my career came in the fifth game of the 1961 world series against the Reds. I batted in the cleanup position in that game, and went three-for-four. The non-hit was an error, and I also drew a walk, so I was on base all five times that I batted. It was also the only time in my career that I batted in the fourth spot in our lineup.

DR. BOBBY BROWN: Go back to the 1947 world series and you'll see that I came in to pinch hit in the fourth inning of the seventh game and I hit a double off Dodger pitcher Hal Gregg, driving in the tying run. I later scored the game-winning run.

SPURGEON "Spud" CHANDLER: I had many great thrills, but I guess the greatest ones came in 1943 when I went 20-4 with a 1.64 earned run average, and was voted the Most Valuable Player in the American League. I went on to pitch two wins in that world series against St. Louis, and gave up just two runs in 18 innings.

That world series performance came on the heels of another memorable event. During my final regular-season start of the '43 season, Hank Greenberg hit a shot out towards the left center field bleachers in the Old Yankee Stadium. Joe DiMaggio turned his back to the ball, raced out towards the wall, and made what most people consider to be the greatest catch of his glorious career. We went on to win, 2-1, in 14 innings, giving me my 20th win. It was a great thrill for me as well as for DiMaggio.

BEN CHAPMAN: I have two. The first came in the 1932 world series, specifically in the second game. I don't remember the inning, but I remember the situation. We had runners on second and third with two outs. The Cubs walked Bill Dickey intentionally to load the bases because they prefered to pitch to me. Anyway, I got a single to win the game.

The other highlight was when I hit three homeruns in the second game of a doubleheader at Yankee Stadium on July 6.

JOE COLLINS: It's funny that you ask because last night former White Sox pitcher Saul Rogovin and I were talking about it. It was back in 1953. We were losing by two runs when I hit a three-run homerun off Rogovin in the ninth inning. It proved to be the game-winning hit, and it was extremely important because the win put us one game ahead of the Red Sox, and we were scheduled to open a series with Boston the next day.

As long as I've got the opportunity, I'd like to say something I've never really had a chance to say before. The one thing I'll never forget about those teams was the whole attitude that each player was just one organ in a 25-organ animal. Everyone was treated alike, and that's one of the reasons I loved Casey (Stengel).

EARLE COMBS: (Courtesy of Mrs. Earle Combs, wife of the late, great Hall-of-Famer). My husband's career highlight came in August 1928, when the bleacher fans at Yankee Stadium presented him with an engraved watch in appreciation of his efforts in the Yankee outfield. He treasured that watch all his life, largely because the fans had contributed their pennies, nickels and dimes to purchase it.

He always gave all he had to the game he loved, and was always honored to have been a Yankee. In fact, for him, it was a tremendous thrill just to have been a baseball player. He got to know the best players in the history of the game, and played on the best teams.

BUCKY DENT: That's a pretty easy answer, because it just happened. On October 2, 1978, we had to play the Red Sox because both teams had finished the season with identical records. We entered the game knowing that we had allowed them to tie us because we lost to Cleveland on the last day of the regular season. The tie-breaker was up in Fenway Park, where we had swept four important games from them in early September. They didn't think we could do it again, and supposedly said a lot of things about how they had a better starting eight than we did, and how the last time we beat them they were all injured.

Anyway, they led 2-0 when I came up with two outs and runners on first and second bases. If I remember right, I hit a two strike pitch down the left field line, up and onto that screen they have there, for a three-run homerun. The homerun put us ahead, and sort of broke a streak of hard luck in the game, because we had hit several hard shots which were caught. We scored another run that inning, and went ahead 5-2 when Reggie Jackson hit a homerun in the next inning. We needed those extra runs, because Boston came back with two runs in the eighth, and left the tying and winning runs on base in the ninth.

All in all, its hard to describe the feeling of even being in that game. Every pitch was crucial.

JOE DiMAGGIO: Just putting on the Yankee uniform.

JOE DUGAN: To be honest, my career highlight did not occur with the Yankees. It came in 1921, right after Connie Mack had traded me away from the Philadelphia Athletics to the Boston Red Sox. Our opening road game was in Philadelphia, and I came to bat in the first inning with two men on base. Ed Rommel, a good one, was pitching for them. The fans halted the game for 10 minutes by throwing debris all over the field. On a 3-2 pitch, I hit that homerun into the bleachers in left field, and we won the game, 5-2. On my way around the bases I was feeling pretty good, and I let the fans know it.

MIKE GAZELLA: My highlight was when I first faced Walter Johnson. He beat us, 10-0. I was sent up to pinch hit, and I was tickled to death that he didn't strike me out.

LEFTY GOMEZ: I have three highlights I'd like to mention. The first came in 1932, when I pitched my first world series game. We defeated the Cubs, 5-2, to take a two-games-to-none lead in the series.

My second highlight came in 1934, when I had a pitching year I still think about. My record was 26-5, and I led the league in wins, percentage, ERA (2.33), complete games (25), innings pitched (281.2), strikeouts (158) and shutouts (6).

The third highlight, and the one that topped them all, was my selection to the Baseball Hall of Fame in 1972.

TOMMY HENRICH: I'm not going to pick out any one highlight because just making the Yankees was my dream. When I was a kid I was a great Yankee fan. I always rooted my heart out for the Yankees. Then there came a day when I got to be one. No words can describe the feeling.

Baseball has been real good to me. I've always loved the game, and its been my whole life. My wife's always asking me when I'll get tired of talking about baseball, but it's never going to happen.

ELSTON HOWARD: The highlight of my career was undoubtedly during the 1955 world series when I hit a homerun off Brooklyn's Don Newcombe. I was just a rookie   back then, scared to death, and then 'boom', a homerun.

REGGIE JACKSON: (Note: This conversation with Reggie occured soon after Jackson's suspension for failing to obey a bunt sign, and after manager Billy Martin had been re-hired for the 1980 season.) I have no highlights in my Yankee career. I'm sorry that that's the way it is, but that's really the way I feel.

JACKIE JENSEN: My highlight was just playing on the same team with so many all-time greats like Joe DiMaggio, Ted Williams, and Mickey Mantle. DiMaggio and Williams were my idols, and I ended up right beside them in the outfield. My thrills were many, and my memory is filled with moments that will last forever.

Playing in the major leagues is a privilege only a few attain, and I was one of the blessed.

CLIFF JOHNSON: Eith the homerun I hit off Andy Hassler in the 1977 Playoffs, which sewed up a win in Game II; or, my three homeruns in one game against the Blue Jays that same year.

CHARLIE KELLER: The well-known fourth game of the 1941 world series, played in Ebbet's Field. That's the one in which Brooklyn catcher Mickey Owens dropped the third strike on Tommy Henrich in the ninth inning. There were two outs, and Henrich wound up safe on first base. DiMaggio followed with a hit, and then I doubled off the right field wall to score the tying and winning runs. When I got to second base, you could have heard a pin drop in Ebbet's Field. If you ask anyone who was ever there to see a game, they'll tell you that there was probably never another day on which those fans were quiet.

You have to realize that 1941 was the year in which the Dodgers had done a lot of talking about how they were going to run us out of New York. To top it off, on the way home we were in a cab driven by a big Brooklyn fan. The cabbie was really angry about the game, so I couldn't resist the opportunity to agitate him and rub it in. He got so hot that my wife practically forced my mouth shut because she was worried that he'd drive us right off the Triborough Bridge.

There's one other thing I'd like to set straight for the record. The blame has been unfairly laid on Owens. As far as I'm concerned, he never had a chance to catch that ball. It should have been scored a wild pitch.

MARK KOENIG: Its impossible for me to select a career highlight. There were too many great moments which I was lucky to share with so many great players and teams. I'd just like to say that it was wonderful being a participant in the finest era of baseball history.

JOHNNY KUCKS: In 1956 I pitched the seventh game of the world series and beat the Dodgers in Ebbet's Field, 9-0, on a three-hitter. It capped a great year. I was 18-9 during the regular season, and was picked for the All-Star Team, so that was my best year.

BOB KUZAVA: The 1952 world series stands out because of my relief role in the seventh game. We were playing the Dodgers at Ebbet's Field. They loaded the bases with one out, and I came in to relieve Vic Raschi. On a three-two pitch, I got Duke Snider to pop out. The next batter was Jackie Robinson, and on a three-two pitch he hit that famous pop up on the first base side of the pitcher's mound. For some reason, no one went for the ball. I thought it would fall, until Billy Martin came racing in to grab it. We won the game and the series.

DON LARSEN: My biggest thrill came when I was the winning pitcher in the pennant-clinching game against the Red Sox in 1955. That win gave me my first opportunity to play in the world series.

Of course the perfect game in the 1956 world series was the most memorable and important game of my life.

EDDIE LOPAT: "One game stands out. I think it was back in '48. We were hosting the Browns at the Stadium. I pitched an 11-hit shutout against them. The most amazing part of it was that I pitched all nine innings and threw just 88 pitches. The game lasted one hour and 48 minutes, and we won, 4-0. If an 11-hit shutout isn't a bit out of the ordinary, I don't know what is!

But, now that you've got me thinking, there was also the year I won 21 games (1951), capped with two wins over the Giants in the series. Then again, 1953 was a great year, too, because I led the league in wins (16-4), percentage (.800), and earned run average (2.62).

I guess the best thing to say is that just becoming a Yankee was my thrill. I was a Yankee fan since I was old enough to understand baseball, and getting to put on the pinstripes was a thrill in and of itself.

HECTOR LOPEZ: The 1961 world series against the Reds. In Game V, I drove in seven runs on a homerun, triple, and a bunt single.

MICKEY MANTLE: My greatest thrill as a player came in the 1964 world series against the Cardinals when I hit a lead-off homerun in the bottom of the ninth inning to give the Yankees a 2-1 win. The pitcher was knuckleballer Barney Schultz. The homerun was important to the team because it put us ahead, two games to one, and was also important on a personal level because it was my 16th in world series play, thereby breaking Babe Ruth's record of 15.

However, my greatest thrill as a member of the Yankee family came on Sunday, June 8, 1969, the day they retired my uniform number 7. The handling of the ceremony, complete with Joe DiMaggio presenting me a plaque they'd hang on the outfield wall, and then my opportunity to present a similar plaque to the greatest centerfielder I ever saw, was the greatest thrill of my life. I will never forget it.

CLIFF MAPES: Most of the guys you'll talk to will tell you about the big hits they made, but my great day came in right field in 1949. As every Yankee fan knows, we came down to the last two games of that season, trailing Boston by one game. We had to win both to win the pennant.

Anyway, there we were, in a key game, and the Sox had the bases loaded with less than two outs. I was out in right field, tense as a guy could get, and someone, I don't recall who, hit a line drive on one hop, right at me. I came charging in, came up throwing home, and I'll be darned if the runner on third base hasn't come across the plate yet. So the ball gets there first, and Yogi (Berra) has his foot on the plate, and we get the force out on what should have been a base hit. The craziest part of it was that the home plate umpire didn't realize that it was a force play, so he originally called the runner, Johnny Pesky, safe at home.

Its funny that Berra was probably the only one in the ballpark who realized it was a force out, and boy did he let the umpire have it. Naturally, the umpire changed his call when he saw the mistake. And to think that I've heard so many people say Berra wasn't all that smart. He was the only smart one that day, that's for sure.

ROGER MARIS: I guess everyone knows that my 61st homerun in 1961, and really that whole season, was the highlight of my career. There's really nothing else to be said about that year that hasn't already been said or written. Instead, I'd rather concentrate on 1978 and say that I'm glad to be back here for my first Old Timers Day, and I really appreciate the way the fans treated me out there today.

GIL MCDOUGALD: I spent 10 years with the Yankees, and in those 10 years, no particular game stands out. Every game was important because we were winning a pennant virtually every year. I'm sorry that I can't be more specific, but at least its an honest answer.

GEORGE McQUINN: Rather than cite one game of the highlight, I'd rather talk about the whole 1947 season as the highlight of my career. In 1946, Connie Mack released me from the Philadelphia Athletics because I was 'washed up.' Yankee manager Bucky Harris had enough confidence in me to get the Yankees to sign me that spring, and I went on to lead the league in hitting until the end of June. The fans recognized the good year I was having by voting me the starting first baseman on the American League All-Star Team. I also made a contribution to our 19-game winning streak that year by batting around .350 over that span. Winning the world series topped it all off nicely.

JOHNNY MIZE: I have three highlights I'd like to mention. The first came in 1947 when I hit 51 homeruns, the most ever hit by a left-handed hitter in National League history. Number two is a combination of the seven times I hit three homeruns in one game. Unfortunately, the one time that I did that with the Yankees we lost the game, to the Tigers, I believe. My third highlight is being one of the few major leaguers in history to hit a homerun in every ballpark I ever played in in the major leagues, including the long since demolished Baker Bowl.

There are a couple of Yankee world series highlights which also come to mind. The first was in 1949, when I pinch hit a two-run single in the ninth inning of the third game, to give us a 4-1 lead. It proved important because the Dodgers came back with a pair of homeruns in their half of the inning, so the single was a game-winning hit.

The other world series highlight came in 1952 when I hit a homerun in the fourth inning off Dodger pitcher Joe Black. We wound up winning the game, 2-0, so it was another game-winning hit, and it tied up the series at two games each. In fact, that '52 series was a pretty good one for me. I batted .400 and hit three homeruns, but the other two were in losing efforts.

JOE OSTROWSKI: In August, 1952, we had a big game against the Indians, and we were out of starting pitchers. Casey (Stengel) turned to Stubby Overmire and me and said, 'well fellas, its all yours'. We combined to shut them out, and we went on to win the pennant. I always felt that in a small way, by pitching well in that game, I helped contribute something to the three pennant-winners I played on. It was a thrill to be a Yankee.

HERB PENNOCK (courtesy of his surviving spouse, Esther): Two games stand out in my husband's career. The first came in the 1927 world series, when he pitched the third game. We were up against the Pirates that year, and they had a lineup which was supposed to be "death" to lefthanded pitchers. Herb pitched 7-and-one-third innings of no hit ball, and the Yankees won, 8-1.

The other game came in 1925. He pitched the first game of the doubleheader against the Philadelphia Athletics on July 5, and defeated Lefty Grove, 1-0, in 15 innings. Herb pitched to exactly 18 batters in the first six innings, and faced only 21 in the final seven. In between, they got four hits, one of which was a misjudged fly, and three walks.

FRITZ PETERSON: There are a few that come to mind, mostly in that 1970 season when I went 20-11. I got selected to the All-Star Game, and was thrilled.

Of course my first major league game, a nine-inning, 3-2 win, also stands out in my mind.

'THE' highlight was undoubtedly playing on those 'great' Yankee teams of the 60's, especially when I broke in as a rookie on the 1966 team.

LOU PINIELLA: The last two games against Kansas City in the 1976 and 1977 playoffs. Just think about the situation. In '76, Chambliss hit that ninth inning homerun to win it all after they scored three runs to tie us in the eighth inning. And in '77, we trailed them, two games to one, and had to sweep the last two in Kansas City. We've always had trouble winning out there, and we did it, including a come-from-behind 5-3 win in the final game. The excitement, pressure, and sweet taste of victory, added to the fact that those were the only two pennant-winners in my career, made those years my highlights.

BOB PORTERFIELD: As you know, I suffered an injury which had a bad effect on my Yankee career. There's no way I can pick a highlight other than just being a Yankee for a short while, just being a part of the tradition of the pinstripes.

VIC RASCHI: Back in 1946, towards the end of the season, the Yankees brought me up from Newark along with Frank Coleman, Dr. Bobby Brown, and Yogi Berra. We had just lost the International League World Series to Montreal, and I'd just gotten home in Canisius, NY, when the sheriff comes up to my door and tells me to report to Yankee Stadium, immediately. I hadn't even unpacked, or said hello to my family when I was off and running again.

I went to the Stadium the next day, and reported to interim manager Johnny Neun (he had replaced Bill Dickey) and learned that I was going to be the starting pitcher that day! Yogi was the catcher, Brown was the shortstop, and Coleman was at first base when we took the field against the Athletics.

Let me tell you, that was some walk out from the clubhouse to the field. My hands started sweating like crazy. The old heavy flannel uniform and sweatshirt felt like lead weights. I was so scared that I'd forgotten to ask for a rubdown or loosen up. I seriously doubted whether I'd make it out to the field without collapsing, let alone take batting practice. Eventually, I made it out to the batting cage, and after a minute or two, got into a conversation with Joe DiMaggio and the other guys. Somehow, that relaxed me a little.

When the time came to return to the diamond for the start of the game, well, I can't even remember going out to the mound. There I was, out there in the Old Stadium, in a sort of death agony. Fortunately, I pitched okay, and we won the game, 7-4.

Its probably hard to believe today, but every time I come back here for an Old Timers' Day, I still get that same tingling sensation. And, you know something, I wouldn't take any ballplayer on my team who didn't get that same anxious feeling, those same sweaty palms.

But, looking back, I guess I was pretty lucky. I was the winning pitcher in the 1948 All-Star Game, and in 1949 I pitched a complete game in the season finale against Boston to clinch the pennant. That was some game. We had tied them for first place the day before by beating them, and the pennant was on the line that day.

Anyway, the score was 1-0 in our favor until the eighth inning, when we scored four runs. Talk about pitching under pressure, a 1-0 lead against a team with Ted Williams, with the pennant at stake. It was a good thing we scored those extra runs, because I gave up three in the ninth before retiring the side. The best part of that win was that it was only the beginning. We went on to win five straight world series.

There is one other thing I have to say, but I wouldn't call it a highlight in the common sense of the words. It was really a turning point. In 1947, the Yankees sent me back down to the minor leagues. I told them I wouldn't go, that I'd quit instead. They threatened to blackball me from baseball. I went home to talk it over with my family, because they wanted me to go out to Oregon, and we'd just gotten settled in New York. I was terribly upset.

My wife sat me down and talked me into going. Looking back, it was the best move she, and I, ever made. I met pitching coach Jim Turner out there, and he really helped me.

When I returned to New York later that season, I started a streak of my own. No one probably knows this, but after I came back from the minors I never missed a game I was scheduled to pitch in, injured or not.

JIMMIE REESE: My first thrill came in 1927 when I was sold to the Yankees with Lyn Lary for $125,000. That was a fortune in those days, and the Yankees had won the pennant in 1926. That was quickly overshadowed by my long associations with Babe Ruth, a friendship which exceeded all my dreams and hopes.

One thing stands out, and it involves the Babe. During a game against Cleveland in 1930, I hit a grand slam homerun into the right field bleachers. It was a most unusual feat for me (Reese hit eight homeruns in his three years in the major leagues.), and we won the game, 7-6. When I crossed the plate, Ruth walked up to me and casually said 'now you are only 59 behind me.'

ALLIE REYNOLDS: Picking one game is awfully tough, but I guess I'd rate the first game of the 1949 world series ahead of all the others (including a pair of no-hitters in 1951). I pitched a two-hitter, and we beat the Dodgers, 1-0, when Tommy Henrich led off the bottom of the ninth inning by hitting a homerun into the right field stands at Yankee Stadium.

MARIUS RUSSO: Go back to October, 1941, the third game of the world series against the Dodgers. We were playing them in Ebbet's Field, after splitting the first two games in Yankee Stadium. I was pitching against Fred Fitzsimmons, and we were locked in a scoreless duel. In the top of the seventh, with Joe Gordon on second base and two outs, I hit a line drive off Fitzsimmons' knee. The ball deflected to shortstop Pee Wee Reese for a "pop out", but Fred had to leave the game. We scored two runs off his reliever, Hugh Casey, in the eighth inning. Brooklyn scored once in the 8th. We won, 2-1.

GEORGE SELKIRK: I joined the Yankees in Boston in August, 1934. Babe Ruth had announced his retirement, and this would be his last appearance in Boston in a Yankee uniform. The park was filled to capacity for this occasion. Ruth played five or so innings, and was replaced by Sammy Byrd. As Ruth crossed from our dugout on the third base side to the Red Sox dugout (the clubhouses were both behind the Sox dugout in those days) a thundering ovation began. It grew louder when Ruth stopped at home plate to shake hands with the umpires, several players, and even a few fans. Everyone seemed to realize that this was the final act in the greatest show on earth.

The lasting applause and emotions shown by everyone gave me the biggest thrill I have ever experienced. Just being present on that day, and living through such a heartwarming and emotional experience, provided a highlight which exceeded anything I accomplished as a player on, or off, the field.

JOE SEWELL: I singled to right field off Cubs pitcher Jackie May in the sixth inning* of the fourth game of the 1932 world series and drove in the tie-breaking runs. There were two outs, and runners on second and third. It was a great thrill.

BOBBY SHANTZ: My career highlight came in 1952 when I was picked as the Most Valuable Player in the American League.

BOB SHAWKEY: My favorite highlight was in 1915 when I was sold from Connie Mack's Athletics to the Yankees. I went on to win 204 games and played on five world series teams, including the 1927 Yankees. I also had the honor of pitching the first game ever played at Yankee Stadium in 1923, and after Ruth hit a homerun, I hit one in the eighth inning. More recently, the Yankees were kind enough to give me another great thrill, that of throwing out the first ball at the opening of the New Yankee Stadium.

CHARLIE SILVERA: Winning the first of five consecutive pennants and world series in 1949 by defeating the Red Sox on the last day of the season and then beating Brooklyn in the series were great thrills. That '49 series had a special significance to me because I got to play in Game II. I was in seven world series, and that was the only game I ever played in, and although I didn't get a hit, it was my greatest thrill.

BILL "Moose" SKOWRON: The 1958 world series seventh game in Milwaukee when I hit a three-run homerun off Lew Burdette to clinch the championship was my career highlight. It was a very personal thing for me because in 1957 I'd been hurt and everyone kept on kidding me that we lost to the Braves in '57 because of my injury. They also got on me for making the last out in '57, when I hit a shot right at Eddie Matthews, to end the game. But we got even with them in '58 by coming back from a three-games-to-one deficit to win the whole thing.

I'd also like to mention the grand slam I hit off Roger Craig in Ebbet's Field in 1956. It was the third grand slam hit in world series history, and provided me with another great thrill.

ENOS SLAUGHTER: In the 1956 World Series against the Dodgers I hit a three-run homerun off Roger Craig to win the first game. We went on to win the world series, four-games-to-three, and that homerun, coming with two outs, has always meant a lot to me.

TOM TRESH: The 1962 world series provided my greatest thrill. In Game V, with the score tied, 2-2, I hit a three-run homerun in the bottom of the eighth inning to give us the victory, and a three-two advantage. It meant all the more to me because I was just a rookie, and because my father, Mike Tresh, was in the stands. He played 12 years with the White Sox and never played in a world series.

BOB TURLEY: I'd have to list three games: a 10-inning, 1-0 loss to the Dodgers in the sixth game of the 1956 world series; my 20th victory of the 1958 season, versus the Senators; and the seventh game of the 1958 world series which we won and thereby defeated the Braves.

ROY WHITE: I guess the answer is that homerun I hit off Bill Campbell in 1977 to tie up the game, 5-5, and help turn our season around. We had been up in Boston the week before, and the Red Sox had clobbered us in three straight games in Fenway. They came to New York hoping to finish us off, and things looked rather bleak when we came to bat in the ninth inning. With two outs, Willie Randolph tripled to left center, and I followed with a homerun into the right field seats.

Reggie Jackson singled with the bases loaded in the tenth inning, and we won, 6-5. We went on to sweep them three straight, and most people tell me that that homerun was the key to our championship season.

I'd also like to say that winning the pennant in 1976, and the series in 1977, were personal thrills because there was a time when I never thought a Yankee team I played on would ever come close.

GENE WOODLING: Fans will probably find this hard to understand, but I really don't have a single career highlight. I can't even begin to pick one because all too often you are the hero one day, and the goat the next. I had too many bad days to pick out one good one. If I have to say something, let's just leave it at the world series in general.

A CHAT WITH GEORGE M. STEINBRENNER, III

When George M. Steinbrenner and his 13 limited partners purchased the New York Yankees for $10,200,000 in 1973, he promised the baseball fans of the world that the Yankees would be a championship team again, "within three years."

And on October 16, 1976, there he was, sitting in the owner's box in Cincinnati, waiting for the Yankees and Reds to start Game I of the 73rd Annual World Series.

The man had delivered.

"People thought I was foolish to go out on the limb like that," recalled the 47-year-old sportsman, "but I wanted every fan to know from Day One that we had one goal in mind: to give the greatest fans in the world the championship team they so rightly deserve."

"And as I sat there, waiting for the first pitch by Don Gullett (he was with the Reds in those days), I got this tingling sensation up and down my spine as I suddenly realized that we had delivered. Yes, losing in four straight games hurt, but everyone knew that the Yankees were back on top of the American League. There is no other place for a Yankee team to be except a contender ever."

Steinbrenner's fascination with, and admiration for, the Yankees dates back to his earliest childhood baseball memories. When he was a boy of seven or eight years old, he was always among the first on line to greet the Yankee players when they arrived in Cleveland.

"In those days, the arrival time and location was always announced in the newspapers," he said. "We used to race down to the Hotel Cleveland to see the Yankees come in. It was a thrill just seeing the luggage of Tony Lazzeri, Lou Gehrig, and Bill Dickey being wheeled into the lobby, let alone to see those great players."

"Understand one thing," he continued. "I was an Indians fan. I hated the Yankees, but I deeply respected them for what they were, and are: the greatest baseball team in the world. If someone had told me back then that I'd one day be in a position to be their principal owner, I'd have been overwhelmed. It still is the greatest thrill of my life.

In 1972, the Yankees finished in fourth place in the American League Eastern Division with a 79-76 record. The franchise was a shambles. Its farm system, once a robust source of quality players, had shriveled up into a bone-dry skelton. An organization which once employed two dozen full-time scouts, and countless part-time "bird-dogs", listed six scouts on its books. Worst of all, the fans were not being fooled — in 1972, the Yankees failed to break the one million mark in home paid attendance for the first time since 1945. Baseball in New York could be summed up in two words: the Mets.

"When we purchased the team in 1973, it was, well, mediocre," Steinbrenner said. "But in its mediocrity, it also presented a challenge and an opportunity to restore it. Fortunately, I had one of the greatest baseball minds in the history of the game with me, Gabe Paul, just as I am fortunate to have Al Rosen with me today."

"We knew we had our work cut out for us," he continued. "We went out and made the trades, we spent the money, to build what New York deserved: a contender. We have continued to do so, and we will continue to do so."

Although the Yankees have used the new free agent system to acquire the likes of Reggie Jackson, Don Gullett, Rich Gossage, and Luis Tiant, the management opposes it to the hilt.

"I've gone on record again and again in opposition to the free agent system," Steinbrenner said. "Its a perfect example of what was wrong with baseball for the last 20 or more years — we had great baseball minds owning and running the teams, but few, if any, business minds. Today, we are fortunate that a new group of owners with a real business sense is emerging, and that is a credit to Commissioner Bowie Kuhn. He has encouraged these much-needed changes, as have some of the more veteran owners."

But, as long as free agents are the name of the game, Steinbrenner will play it.

"Look, we could take the same attitude as another team and put ads in the newspapers saying 'come see our young exciting team because we didn't raise ticket prices' (an obvious reference to the Mets). And, we could also finish in last place like they did. We didn't make the rules, but we're going to live by them."

The issue of ticket prices is not unfamiliar to Steinbrenner; in fact, after the Yankees won their second straight world championship in 1978, and drew more than 2,300,000 fans to Yankee Stadium, a 50-cent increase in box and reserved seats prices was announced. It was met with the usual reaction to such increases, especially when they come on the heels of such a financially successful season.

"We knew that people would complain about the increases, but the public has to understand that the costs of running a baseball team, and especially a winning one, are constantly increasing," said Steinbrenner. "Look around you and you can't miss the inflation. It costs $4 to go to a movie. Our bleacher tickets are $1.50, and our general admissions are $2.50, and we are committed to maintaining them at that level, so that the public will always be able to see the Yankees. It's the season ticket holder, and the person who can afford the better seat, who will be affected."

"Another factor to consider is that we have never issued a dividend to our partners," he said. "Every penny we've earned has been re-invested in the organization. That's why we've been able to be innovators as well as winners. That's why we're adding another minor league franchise for 1979. That's why the Yankees are the first team to have a manager and two coaches with every minor league team we own, from the rookie league to AAA ball. We want the fans to know that we are committed to keeping the Yankees on top."

With all that dollar-talk, what are the Yankees worth? Close to $25,000,000, according to Steinbrenner, who said that more than $20,000,000 has already been offered by two different parties.

"A selling price is hard to figure, because we just aren't interested in selling," he said. "The Yankees are too important to me, to the partners, and to New York to sell them."

In fact, money does not particularly impress the Yankees owner in a truly materialistic sense. Instead, he views it as an outlet for "living (his) religion."

"I am a Protestant, and I consider myself to be a religious man, although that doesn't mean going to church every Sunday," Steinbrenner said. "church attendance does not make you religious. The key is to live your religion, and in my book, that means helping those people who are less fortunate than I am,"

If that's the standard, then Steinbrenner might best be described as the most pious of men. His contributions range from putting 72 underprivileged kids through college, to agreeing to do a television commercial only if the sponsor would turn over $25,000 to the Bronx Mission Society, an organization which sponsors countless summer programs for the borough's youth.

"I kept turning the Miller beer people down for more than a year," Steinbrenner said, "until I got that letter from the Society, informing me that they were out of funds and might have to suspend operations. That's when I went to Miller and said I'd do the commercial, but only if they turned over $25,000 to the Society. I didn't want a penny, and never accepted any money from Miller. They agreed to my price, and we did the commercial."

As one delves into Steinbrenner's past, one obstacle always comes to the fore: the illegal campaign contributions he admitted making in 1972,which led to his one-year suspension from all operations of the Yankees.

"Its something I have to live with," said Steinbrenner on July 29, 1978, at a press conference called to announce the agreement between the Yankee owner and Billy Martin, which would turn the team's managerial reigns back over to Martin in 1980, provided certain criteria are met. "I've regretted it time and again, but what's done is done. Hopefully, there are other ways I can make up for it."

Recently, a child needed a $13,000 operation to remove a spike from her skull. No one would come forward with the money . . . until the Yankee owner (himself a father of four) heard about her plight, and paid the bill.

"Can you imagine that," said Steinbrenner, with a dazed expression covering his face. "Here we had a little girl who needed an operation which cost thousands of dollars, and couldn't have it because she didn't have the money. That's exactly the kind of thing I'm talking about when I say people have to live their religion. Money for those kinds of things has to be raised."

"I guess I'm something of an isolationist," he continued, "but I want everything that's wrong with this country solved before we go looking overseas. Children should not go hungry in the United States, nor should they be denied adequate medical care and a quality education. Kids are my bag. I try to do my share for them."

Steinbrenner also has the reputation for being a demanding boss. Many of his former employees speak in rather uncomplimentary fashion about his demands and unpredictability. They spoke of sudden phone calls demanding vast amounts of information, or an incident where the Yankee owner allegedly fired a secretary one minute, and then re-hired her and gave her a $1,000 bonus the next.

"I know I'm not an easy many to work for," said Steinbrenner, "but that's largely because I insist upon holding everyone of my employees to the same high standards I set for myself and for the Yankees."

"Outsiders and insiders can say anything they want, but you have to be the best to win for three straight years. Getting to the top requires hard work. Staying there is even tougher. The Yankees intend to stay there."

A ROOKIE (?) IN THE FRONT OFFICE
(Or, a word or two with New York's reigning baseball genius, Albert "Flip" Rosen)

June 1978, was a good month for panickers.

July, 1978, was a great month for quitters.

After all, the Yankees were 14 games out of first place. Their pitching staff was decimated by injuries, and the team was riddled with dissension. The Red Sox were pounding out win after win, and were planning to sell their ALCS tickets in August.

Experts throughout the baseball world wrote the Yankees off as victims of the new contagion from New England: Red Sox Fever.

"Why, only a madman would pick this club to win," wrote one veteran baseball scribe.

In the midst of all the carnage stood one such "madman", one who did not panic in June or hide in July, one who dared to deny the Red Sox invincibility and offered a guaranteed cure to Red Sox Fever.

393

"I got the feeling we'd win the pennant back in the spring," said former Cleveland Indians third baseman, Al Rosen, the 55-year-old rookie president of the New York Yankees. "I never gave up. You can ask the people in our offices, and they'll confirm the fact that I stuck by my convictions that this ballclub had too much talent not to make a run at the Red Sox."

"Simple baseball common sense went into it," he continued. "Something was bound to happen to the Red Sox — teams rarely go through a season without injuries to key personnel — and we were bound to get healthy. I felt that when something happened to the Red Sox front line players, or when their pitching failed enough to force them to use their bullpen, they would be confronted by some real holes they would not be able to fill."

June really was a tough month in New York. One by one, the pitchers began dropping like flies. Then, in rapid succession, Willie Randolph, Bucky Dent, Mickey Rivers, and Thurman Munson suffered chronic injuries which forced the Yankees to dip deep into the farm system that George Steinbrenner and Gabe Paul (Rosen's predecessor) had rebuilt.

The pressure to trade, and above all, to win, was on Rosen.

"You have to remember that I had nothing to do with building this team," Rosen said. "It was built by George Steinbrenner and Gabe Paul, so I had nothing personal to gain by winning ... BUT, I knew that I'd bear the responsibility for losing. People would say I'd blown it by not making any trades, or that I was a rookie executive who had no front office experience in the major leagues."

"But, I knew all along that this club didn't need anything except to get healthy. Just making a trade for the sake of pleasing the writers is ridiculous."

Not that Rosen sat back and did nothing. He engineered a deal which stole outfielder Gary Thomasson from Oakland for a pair of minor leaguers. Thomasson responded to this grant of freedom from Charlie Finley by batting .350 for the first three weeks with New York, the weeks when the Yankee outfield was devastated by injuries, the weeks in which the team needed him most.

Rosen also dealt an unhappy (and unused) reliever (Rawly Eastwick) to the Phillies for outfielder Jay Johnstone, who proved invaluable as a team man, and a popular item with the fans. ("People will never realize how important it was to have Jay around here," said Yankee skipper Bob Lemon. "He made many of the behind-the-scenes contributions that helped keep the club's mind on one thing: catching the Red Sox.")

"Sure, those deals helped us, but there were two other things I did which were more important," according to Rosen. "First, I was a good sounding board for the players, and that was important. They respected me because I'd been one of them, and many of them had known me for a long time. I was able to listen, and to resolve some differences."

"The other key was getting Bob Lemon," he continued. "That was very important. We had gained five games on Boston, but I don't know if we'd have sustained that drive under anyone else. The man's accomplishments speak for themselves. He was able to resolve the Reggie Jackson situation. He was able to cope with the Mickey Rivers incident which migh have exploded into a very sticky situation. When Ed Figueroa threw the ball at Lemon after being removed from a game, Lemon handled it and got things going again. He did not make a tactical mistake on the field, not one."

* * *

(In late October, Rosen and the author sat down for a chat about the overall operation of the Yankees. The "chat" developed into a two-hour, in-depth discussion about everything from selecting a manager to scaling ticket prices. His frankness ("I'm straightforward, and everything I say is on the record, or I wouldn't say it," he said.) and tremendous ability as a speaker led to the single most interesting discussion held during the compilation of this book.

A transcript of the questions and answers follows below:)

AUTHOR: We might as well start with something controversial.   Everywhere I go, all anyone ever says to me when they hear about the subject of my book is: "are they going to buy another pennant next year?" How do you silence the critics?

ROSEN: Well, its really very simple. You can't 'buy' a pennant. Tom Yawkey learned that a long time ago. You can't simply spend money to build a championship. There has to be something else that transcends money. You have to have a strong organization, filled with knowledgeable people from top to bottom. A lot of teams have a lot of talent on the field, but they don't win.

Specifically, what I tell my friends to use as an answer to that type of criticism is that we don't like the re-entry draft, but that's the game they're playing, and we're going to play it. We have a debt of gratitude to the New York Yankee fans. We owe them our best. We could horde our dollars and pay them out as dividends to our partners, and let the franchise go down the drain, but that's not our style.

Instead, we spend our money on our farm system and on enlarging what has become an extensive scounting system. We've already developed Jim Beattie, Ron Guidry and Ken Clay in our farm system, and we have a dozen youngsters down there who are ready to burst onto the scene.

Everyone else is always criticizing what we do here. I don't tell anyone else how to run their business, but they always seem ready to tell me how to run mine. They forget that one man's cup of tea   may be another man's poison.

Besides, we're the King of the Hill, so to speak. No franchise in sports history can show the championship trophies we can. This club had 12 long, lean, hard hungry years. No one said "let's help the Yankees." Those years are not going to happen again, not with this ownership. Our destiny is to win.

AUTHOR: In the Yankee organization, how is the decision to trade, purchase, sell, or sign a player arrived at?

ROSEN: Most people in front offices who take credit for trades are not being fair in delineating their role. If you stop and recognize the fact that all of us see 162 games/season, because if I'm not travelling with the team, I'm watching the games on television, you also realize that we don't see other clubs too often. In fact, just about the only time we see them is when they play us.

In evaluating a player, I can only look at him against the Yankees. If I did that with certain men, and an outstanding example is Jim Rice, they might not be as impressive. (Rice has never hit well against the Yankees.) Conversely, an average player might tear through our pitching staff, and will look super.

The point I'm leading up to is that no one man can make a trade. I need to know what a player does against the other teams, and the only way I can get that information is through our network of scouts and trained personnel.

A trade begins to form in a general manager's or president's mind when he decides what he believes his ballclub needs. You send out your people to watch players you think are available, and could help you. They send in reports. Eventually, you sit down with the general manager and owner and evaluate the reports. When you finally make a decision, it's made with the knowledge of a great many people around you.

AUTHOR: To what extent, if any, are the manager and coaches of the team consulted?

ROSEN: Frankly, the manager and coaches are not brought into it too much, largely because as a rule they become emotionally involved and attached to a player. They form likes and dislikes. We try to stay away from that kind of subjectivity.

AUTHOR: What are the factors you look at when examining a potential trade?

ROSEN: Longevity, age, baseball ability, family and community ties, value to the ballclub, and the player's options. Remember, the player has some options as to where and when he's traded (the 5-and-10 year rule), and as a former player, I'm glad to see it.

Let me address some of those issues this way. Earlier this year, I made the difficult decision to trade Roy White. We had the opportunity to obtain a young catcher named Gary Alexander, a kid who is going to be a great catcher. The only reason he was available was because Charlie Finley was angry at him.

White had been with the Yankees since 1964. He deserves every consideration, and I'm almost glad he said no. That man is a credit to the Yankees, the city of New York, and the human race. He's given his whole career here. His family and kids are entrenched here. I want that man to stay in our organization after his playing days are over. A man like that deserves the right to say no.

Now, let's turn to the other side of the trading coin. How do you make a trade for a Gary Thomasson, a man who's hitting .230 with Oakland, who comes to New York and bats .350 for the first three weeks, when we needed it most, and finishes the season around the .270 mark?

Or, did you know that the Mets once released Ed Figueroa because they thought he'd never make it? That man just won 20 games, and has had three fine years with us.

I'll tell you how you get a Thomasson or a Figueroa. You get lucky. Very lucky.

AUTHOR: We've gone through the playing end of it. How did you select a manager?

ROSEN: I look for patience, understanding, and knowledge. That's enough. The answer is Bob Lemon.

You have to go back to July. Things had gotten out of hand because of emotions, and the resignation of Billy Martin forcd us to make a move. Bob Lemon was available. He was my dear friend. He could've collected all the money the White Sox owed him, and relaxed on a beach in California, but he knew I was in trouble. He came into trouble, into a pressure cooker. The lure of managing the Yankees was great one, but a great deal of personal friendship went into it. He knew he was going to have problems, and he knew he'd be following a very popular man.

But he came here, and he worked for two weeks without even signing a contract.

AUTHOR: Let's return to the controversial end of things again. One of the most frequent complaints I hear about the Yankees is that they made so much money last year, and that Mr. Steinbrenner is worth a lot of money, yet they've raised their ticket prices again. What are the justifications for a 50-cent increase on the box and reserve seats?

ROSEN: Well, first of all, Mr. Steinbrenner's net worth and his other business interests are irrelevant in terms of how the Yankees operate. They are his personal affairs, and whatever money he has is kept totally separate from the Yankees. Furthermore, whatever he's worth is because he's a prudent businessman, and a prudent businessman does not operate at a loss. Just as he'd raise the price of building a large ship for someone — the costs of steel, labor, transit, etc. have all gone up — the Yankees have been forced to a price increase because the cost of operating a major league franchise has gone up. It's funny how we can all talk about how the cost of bread has gone up. The wheat itself may only cost 20-cents for a loaf, but then you've got all of the other costs: transportation, advertising, packaging, supermarket labor, etc. You also have to deal with greater demand.

We have an obligation to the fans of New York to field the best possible team, and to keep the prices of our tickets reasonable. We have committed ourselves to hold the line on the bleacher and general admission seats. We are always comparing our prices to those the other teams charge, and we feel that we're very much in line. The Mets just raised their ticket prices $1.50, so there's only a 50-cent difference, and the difference is there only because of the law of supply and demand, and our philosophy of spending to build a better club and future.

You also have to realize that this is a partnership, and I have to answer to Mr. Steinbrenner and all our limited partners. Those people all invested money at a time when the situation here was not a happy one, and we feel that our partners are entitled to an efficiently managed, successful product.

AUTHOR: Suppose a wealthy reader wanted to purchase a few "points" in the Yankees. How could he or she do so?

ROSEN: If and when a current partner decides to sell his or her "points" in the club, notice is given to the other existing partners of that intent to sell. The partnership agreement includes a right of first refusal for the other members on any part of the partnership that becomes available.

In as much as we are really one big happy family, the chances of a new partner coming into the picture are virtually nil.

AUTHOR: What would it take in the way of a buyer's offer to purchase the entire club?

ROSEN: Well, as you know, the partners acquired the team in 1973 at a price of $10 million. Clearly, the franchise's net worth has increased dramatically. I don't have a dollar figure value, and even if I fabricated one, it would be false, because I have no price, and neither does Steinbrenner — we just aren't interested in selling.

You only sell when you need money or when thyoffer is so overwhelming that only a fool wouldn't sell. We don't need the money. As for being overwhelmed, we're having too much of an enjoyable and exciting time running things here to be overwhelmed by any offer.

You don't always get involved in a business venture strictly for the money you expect to make. The New York Yankees are the number 1 name in professional sports. They always have been. Where else do you have a ballpark known throughout the world as "the House that Ruth Built?" What other players have songs written about them, like "Joe, Joe DiMaggio?"

Candy bars are named after their players. You can take all the glamor of Hollywood and Los Angeles, and it doesn't compare to what we have here. Hollywood and LA haven't been major league baseball cities all that long, while the Yankees got back to 1903. The Yankees have always meant pride, confidence, winning, and the legendary mystique of the pinstripes.

AUTHOR: You mentioned the New York Mets before. What is the official attitude of the Yankees to their crosstown rivals?

ROSEN: Our main objective is to continue winning. We've captured the hearts of New York, just like the Mets once did, and we intend to keep it that way. I harbor no animosity towards the Mets; I just don't want them to ever do anything which would take one Yankee fan away from us.

AUTHOR: If you had to pinpoint a reason, or the reasons, why the Yankees have been so successful these last three years, what would you say?

ROSEN: Its clearly the strength of our organization, led by George M. Steinbrenner III. The entire franchise has been rebuilt from top to bottom, and we've got good people filling all the key, and minor, positions.

Another key is the year-round nature of our business. If I called around the major leagues right now (November), I bet I could find at least 10 teams whose executives are out playing golf. After all, from their point of view, the season's over. To the Yankees, the season has just begun. We are a year-round operation.

We expect a great deal from our people because the people at the top give so much of their time and energy.

AUTHOR: This has become the age of re-negotiation of contracts. A man's word no longer seems worth more than the scrap of paper its written on. How do you feel about that?

ROSEN: Well, there are two things you should know. The first is that I never discuss salaries during the season. The second is that I've never re-negotiated a contract. I am willing to extend a contract on merit, especially if its for a player I want to see out there for the next five years. In this day and age, a player is entitled to that kind of long-term security and money.

When it comes to the actual negotiation end of it, I always want the player to be there for the finality of the negotiations. I'm willing to sit down with his agent as many times as it takes to reach a reasonable and fair agreement, and during the course of those negotiations, I prefer to listen rather than talk. Also, I don't believe in taking a "hard line" or hardening my position — all that does is burn bridges.

AUTHOR: What is the overall status of the Yankees today?

ROSEN: The franchise has never been healthier from a business and on-the-field perspective. We've been incredibly lucky to have enjoyed so much success so quickly. People have almost forgotten that when we bought this club six years ago, it was a mess.

In fact, people don't realize how bad the situation was. All of the team's contractural obligations were in a shambles. The radio and television contracts were expiring, as was the concession deal. Our farm system was a shell, and our scouting system had been drastically reduced. We were a third or fourth place team in a six-team division.

Today we can sit back and look at three pennants and two world championships in the last three years. We've made the Yankees what they should always be: the best baseball team in the world. Our destiny is to win.

WAS THERE EVER A GUY LIKE RUTH?

From "One Old Cat" to the last "At Bat", was
    there ever a guy like Ruth?
He can start and go, he can catch and throw, he
    can field with the very best.
He's the Prince of Ash and the King of Crash,
    and that's not an idle jest.
He can hit the ball o'er the garden wall, high up
    and far away.
Beyond the aftermost picket lines where the fleet-
    footed fielders stray.
He's the Bogey Man of the pitching clan and he
    clubs 'em soon and late;
He has manned his guns and hit homeruns from
    here to the Golden Gate;
With vim and verve he has walloped the curve
    from Texas to Duluth,
Which is no small task, and I beg to ask: Was
    there ever a guy like Ruth?

John Kieran

BABE RUTH'S FORMULA FOR HITTERS

You step up to the platter
And you gaze with flaming hate
At the poor benighted pitcher
As you dig in at the plate

You watch him cut his fast ball loose,
Then you swing your trusty bat
And you park one in the bleachers —
Nothing's simpler than that.

I WONDER WHERE MY BABE RUTH IS TONIGHT

I wonder where my Babe Ruth is tonight
He grabbed his hat and coat and ducked from sight
I wonder where he'll be
At half past two or three —
He may be at a dance or in a fight
He may be in some cozy roadside inn
He may be drinking beer or maybe gin
I know he's with a dame
I wonder what's her name —
I wonder where my Babe Ruth is tonight.

(The above ditty was written by William J. Slocum, Dean of Baseball Writers of America, for their annual meeting following the 1924 season. The "ghost poet" is Yankee manager Miller Huggins, long an opponent of Ruth's nightly escapades.)

THE YANKEES AND THE CURVE BALL

Little curve ball, the Yankees all miss you
They miss you in springtime and fall;
With swings debonair
They shatter the air,
They hit everything but the ball!
Bob Meusel, and Wardie, and Shangie and Pipp
How great is their pride and their fall.
They miss you, only you
Yet they miss quite a few
But I miss you most of all.

William J. Slocum

(This time Slocum took a turn as "Babe Ruth" commenting on Ruth's and the Yankees' inability to hit the curveball. Written in 1925 as a reflection upon that dismal season — the Yankees plummeted to seventh place in what was then an eight team league — it was typical Slocum tongue-in-cheek poetry. Contemporary accounts indicate that Ruth and the rest of the Yankees were present when the poem was first read to the Baseball Writer's Association, and that Ruth led all others in hysterical laughter. The poem had its positive side: the Yankees won the pennant during the next three seasons!)

TO BABE RUTH — 1934

Sultan of Swat and Czar of Clout,
High Mandarin of Maul,
Assaulter of the well-known snout
Of each fast-moving ball.
For twenty years your mighty mace
Has drummed its battle cry,
Beyond the azure fields of space,
In wavelengths to the sky.

Now time, that ancient cockeyed yap,
Is pointing to the gate,
Where Cobb and Speaker took the rap,
And Wagner met his fate;
Where one by one they passed from sight,
To hear above the roar,
'Game called.' along the rim of night,
That knew their final score.

But not yet Babe. Your blasting bulk
Has one more year of smoke.
Let time the snatcher sit and sulk,
Grab some other bloke.
We need the songs your big mace sings,
The old heart-lifting crash.
We need the melody that rings
Its music from your ash.

Grantland Rice

Go to it, Babe,
Go to it, Lou,
Hit the ball
To Kalamazoo!

A chant popular among fans of the Yankees in 1927-28.

THE DISGRACE TO THE PINSTRIPES:
(The Yankees of 1959 through the eyes of a fan)

Although you were defeated, Yanks,
You shouldn't feel too blue;
Just think of all your bars and banks,
And bowling alleys too.
As businessmen you guys are tops,
It really seems a shame
That you should leave your shops
For just a lousy game.

AN AUTOGRAPH FOR EVERY FAN

Every baseball fan should have at least one autograph of a favorite player . . . and here's your opportunity to get one!

Below is a list of former Yankee personnel who've agreed to have their current addresses listed in this book for the express purpose of soliciting fan mail, or to at least enable interested fans to write and request autographs. Each player listed has agreed to give autographs, provided the instructions listed below are complied with.

Here is the required procedure:

1. Send a courteous letter, requesting an autograph, to the player at the address listed below.

2. Be sure to send something upon which you want the autograph signed, preferably a picture, but a 3 x 5 card is acceptable in most cases. Certain players will only sign pictures, so check the special instructions (if any) next to your player(s) name.

3. Limit your request to a maximum of two (2) per player. (Most of the players do keep track of autograph requests, and have indicated they will not cooperate with people requesting large numbers.)

4. Include a stamped, self-addressed envelope for return mailing. If the "thing" to be autographed requires additional postage, be sure to enclose a money order large enough to cover it. (Many of these players have been retired for many years, and like your grandparents, are living off fixed incomes in an era of inflation. NONE of the players listed below will pay the return postage.)

5. Be PATIENT. Some of the better known players receive more than 1,000 autograph requests a month. Yours will eventually reach the top of the pile.

6. Many of the more veteran players enjoy hearing about YOU, the fan, so feel free to write a few brief paragraphs about your life, and anything in particular you remember about them. This is especially true when the letter is written by a child.

7. REMEMBER: this opportunity is a privilege, NOT a right. It may be withdrawn at any time if fans abuse it. Please make a personal commitment to comply with the regulations set out herein.

8. Thank you.

Hank Bauer
Regent's Walk, Apt. 6B
6600 West 93rd Street
Overland Park, KS 66212

Yogi Berra
c/o The New York Yankees
Yankee Stadium
Bronx, NY 10451

Floyd (Bill) Bevens
5067 8th Avenue, NE
Salem, Oregon 97303

John Blanchard
13541 Larkin Drive
Minnetoka, Minn. 55343

Dr. Robert Brown
1324 Thomas Place
Fort Worth, TX 76107

Ben Chapman
401 Shadeswood Circle
Birmingham, Alabama 35226

Joe Collins
731 Suburban Road
Union, NJ 07083

Joe Dugan
38 High Street
Walpole, MA

Tommy Henrich
104 Piebald Lane
Prescott C.C. Dewey Rt.
Prescott, AZ 86301

Elston Howard
c/o The New York Yankees
Yankee Stadium
Bronx, NY 10451

Charles Keller
Yankeeland Farm
Route No. 7
Box 250
Frederick, MD

John Kucks
15 Oakland Street
Hillsdale, NJ 07642

Bob Kuzava
1118 Vinewood
Wyandotte, MI

Hector Lopez
666 Janos Lane
West Hempstead, NY 11552

Mickey Mantle*
c/o Mr. Roy True
Reserve Life Insurance
Dallas Federal Savings Tower
Dallas, TX 75225

Roger Maris
Maris Distributing Co.
3820 NE 49th Road
Gainesville, FL 32601

Billy Martin
c/o The New York Yankees
Yankee Stadium
Bronx, NY 10451

Gil McDougald
10 Warran Avenue
Spring Lake, NJ 07762

Gene Michael
c/o The New York Yankees
Yankee Stadium
Bronx, NY 10451

Johnny Mize
P.O. Box 112
Demorest, GA 30535

Joe Ostrowski
441 Tripp Street
West Wyoming, PA 18644

Bob Porterfield
7041 Quail Hill Road
Charlotte, NC 28210

Vic Raschi
1255 West Lake Road
Conesus, NY 14435

Allie Reynolds
2709 Cashion Place
Oklahoma City, OK

Bobby Richardson
Ben Lippen School
10 Lippen School Rd.
Asheville, NC 28806

Phil Rizzuto
c/o The New York Yankees
Yankee Stadium
Bronx, NY 10451

Marius Russo
27 Norfolk Drive
Elmont, NY 11003

George Selkirk
405 N. Ocean Blvd.
Apt. 1903
Pompano Beach, FL 33062

Bobby Shantz
152 Mt. Pleasant Avenue
Ambler, PA 19002

Bob Shawkey
1207 Almond Street
Suite 2003
Syracuse, NY 13210

Charles Silvera
1240 Manzanita Drive
Millbrae, CA 94030

Bill Skowron
1812 Kingston Lane
Schaumburg, IL 60172

Enos Slaughter
Route 2
Box 179
Roxboro, NC 27573

Tom Tresh
North Hall
Central Michigan University
Mt. Pleasant, MI 48858

Bob Turley
5629 Ball Mill Road
Dunwoody, GA 30338

Whitey Witt
R.D. No. 1
Woodstown, NJ 08098

Gene Woodling
926 Remsen Road
Medina, OH 44256